Armand Priedītis

Language as a Cognitive Process

Volume 1: Syntax

Language as a Cognitive Process

Volume I: Syntax

Terry Winograd

Stanford University

Addison-Wesley Publishing Company

Reading, Massachusetts · Menlo Park, California · London

Amsterdam · Don Mills, Ontario · Sydney

Library of Congress Cataloging in Publication Data

Winograd, Terry.
   Language as a cognitive process.

   Includes bibliographies and index.
   Contents: v. 1. Syntax.
   1. Linguistics—Data processing. 2. Psycholinguistics.
I. Title.
P98.W55   410$'$.72   81-14855
ISBN 0-201-08571-2 (v. 1)   AACR2

Reproduced by Addison-Wesley from camera-ready copy supplied by the author.

ISBN 0-201-08571-2
  BCDEFGHIJ-MA-89876543

For Carol

Preface

In writing this book, I had several different purposes in mind. First, it is a textbook for students beginning graduate work in computer science or linguistics. It includes detailed technical material and exercises designed to help the student master a body of concepts and techniques. Second, it is a practical guide for people who are building computer systems that deal with natural language. It is not structured as a 'how-to' book, but it describes the relevant techniques in detail and includes an extensive outline of English grammar, which should be useful in both the design and testing of systems. Third, it is a reference source with many pointers into the literature of both linguistics and computer science. Although it is not an encyclopedic survey, I have attempted to introduce a wide variety of material in order to provide newcomers with broad access to the field. Each chapter includes suggestions for further reading, and there is an extensive bibliography. In both linguistics and computer science there is an 'underground literature' of unpublished dissertations, mimeographed papers, and local technical reports. Many papers find their way into more solid print many years later or not at all. However, I have tried whenever possible to limit the references to easily available material—books, journals, and published conference proceedings. Finally, one of my most deeply felt purposes was to convey my own wonderment at the intricacy of human language and at the kind of creature we are that we may master it.

Organization of the volumes

This book started out nearly ten years ago as the notes for a one-term course on 'Computer models of natural language.' Over the years I have rarely resisted the temptation to include additional material that seemed interesting and relevant, and the resulting content has become enough for a full three-term sequence.

The present volume deals with the syntactic structure of natural language, adopting the classical linguistic methodology of studying syntax independently. This does not reflect a theoretical commitment to an 'autonomous syntax' and several of the later chapters discuss some of the problems that arise in trying to separate syntax from meaning. However, from a pedagogical standpoint there exists a broad self-contained literature on syntactic theory and technique that needs to be mastered before the interaction between syntax and meaning can be understood. This volume brings together a variety of syntactic theories within the general framework of cognitive processing.

The second volume, dealing with meaning, will be based more on work in artificial intelligence and the philosophy of language. It will go into areas that have been called both 'semantics' and 'pragmatics,' showing how the issues raised within these perspectives can be dealt with in the cognitive processing framework. In addition to discussions of linguistically motivated topics (such as speech acts, quantification, and reference), there will be a presentation of basic representational issues, including discussions of representations based on formal logic, procedural languages, semantic networks, and frames. I have attempted to make the material in each volume independent enough that a student with the appropriate background can understand one without the other.

Teaching from the text

My original intent was to make the entire book understandable to a student with no prior background in either linguistics or computer science. This was in some sense a necessity, since the number of potential enrollees with background in both was very small and I did not want to eliminate one group in favor of the other. From my observations of students taking the course over the years, I feel pleased with getting as close to this goal as I have, but it is clear that there are two basic prerequisites:

Experience with the manipulation of formal symbols. In this book there are three kinds of formal symbol manipulation: syntactic rules and structures; formal logic and deduction; and computational algorithms. All three are introduced at a fairly elementary level, but a student who has had no experience with any of them will be at a disadvantage. A good undergraduate course in one of the three areas should suffice.

Minimal acquaintance with programming. One strong consideration in the writing of these books was the desire to introduce the computational paradigm to people who were not already skilled programmers. Instead of requiring familiarity with any standard programming language, I devised a pedagogical language (DL) for describing objects and processes. This language has a number of features designed to make it understandable to people with little previous programming exposure. However, it is impossible to include a genuine introduction to programming as an appendix. Students who have had no experience with the idea of the precise specification of programs will need to be helped through the first few contacts. This has been done successfully by some of the fine teaching assistants I have worked with, but it does require some care.

Given these basics, I have found the volumes suitable for teaching beginning graduate students in both computer science and linguistics, and many upper-level undergraduates have done quite well. The exercises range from simple recipe-following to open-ended, thought-provoking questions. In assigning them, I have generally asked students to individually select those that were challenging, since the great variations in background made it impossible to give uniform assignments that were both worthwhile and feasible for everyone.

In a course more oriented to linguistics, some of the detailed material on parsing in Chapter 3 and on systems (Chapter 7) might well be omitted, and Appendix C (Current Directions in Transformational Grammar) could be included. In a more programming-oriented course, the material in Chapters 3 and 5 is suitable as a basis for programming projects, and correspondingly less emphasis could be given to Chapters 4 and 6.

Due to large enrollments and the concomitant large organizational effort that would be needed to get sufficient computer access to high level languages, I have never taught this material with either a programming project or mandatory programming assignments. The exercises involving programming call for paper algorithms in DL. Many students have had access to computer systems on their own, and have substituted programs written in whatever languages were available. For them, the experience of actually getting the programs running has been both exciting and edifying. I hope in the future to introduce programming experience as a regular feature, especially of the course on syntax.

A last note

During the course of working on this book, my own views on the nature of language and the cognitive processing approach have undergone considerable evolution. I have been tempted to incorporate some of these changes into the text, but have resisted, since a serious attempt to do so would have added years to an already overextended project. I have described the evolving course of my own understanding in the paper 'What does it mean to understand language?' (1981), and the broader context in which it arose is presented in *Understanding Computers and Cognition* (Flores and Winograd, forthcoming).

At the moment there is a gap—what I say in these newer writings does not mesh smoothly with what is presented here. I believe that in the long run the technical material presented in these volumes will retain its usefulness, but that it will fit in new ways into our interpretation of language as a human phenomenon. Perhaps then will be the time for a new volume, or for a revision of the present volumes. For the time being we all share the enterprise of creating a new understanding.

Palo Alto
March 1982

Acknowledgments

In a project of this duration, it is both sobering and heartening to realize how many people have given freely of their help and support. My greatest debt is to the students who have worked with me as teaching assistants and helped in every aspect of the preparation of the book. Those who helped with the material in this volume include Doug Appelt, Anne Gardner, Annette Herskovits, Elaine Kant, David Levy, David Lowe, Mitch Model, and Andee Rubin. The material in the second volume has been developed in courses assisted by Jim Bennett, Jim Davidson, David Evans, Jonathan King, Mike Lowry, Paul Martin, Larry Masinter, and Chris Tong.

In addition, a number of people have read drafts and taken the time and effort to provide detailed written critiques. These include Bill Bregar, Joan Bresnan, Danny Bobrow, Rusty Bobrow, Dave Gifford, Ron Kaplan, Martin Kay, Walter Savitch, Brian Smith, Henry Thompson, and Tom Wasow.

The technical skill and individual help of innumerable people at Stanford and at Xerox PARC have made it possible for me to produce this book in a unique and satisfying way. Using a large repertoire of text-editing, graphics, and formatting programs, I was able to go from initial sketchy outlines all the way to camera-ready copy of the laid-out pages, dealing with every aspect of editing, book-design, and typography. Everything was done 'on-line,' from the taking of notes as I read through the hundreds of books and articles to the generation of photographic images from which printing plates could be made. As this work evolved from course notes into a book, then into multiple volumes, it made several moves, from one computer system to another and from one format to another. The final version uses the TEX typesetting program created by Donald Knuth, making possible a level of quality substantially higher than that of earlier computer systems. Leo Guibas, Lyle Ramshaw, and Doug Wyatt were especially helpful in getting TEX to handle the demands of this text and David Fuchs was very generous in giving the crucial assistance needed in printing the finished pages on the Alphatype printer.

In addition to their help in teaching, David Levy and David Lowe did a good deal of work on the text. Anne Gardner has continually put in effort above and beyond the call of duty, making a major contribution to the quality of the book. John Strawn and Haychan Sargent were instrumental in the final preparation of this volume, and having them to work with has helped me through the last-mile doldrums. I especially appreciate the work and enthusiasm of Marikka Rypa, who put in a tremendous amount of effort in editing the text and steering it through the arduous weeks of final preparation.

Finally, I cannot begin to express my appreciation to my wife Carol for the support and love she has given me. She exhibited uncommon patience in seeing me through the fifth consecutive year in which 'I'm going to finish the book this summer,' and when it finally underwent fission into volumes, she gave me needed encouragment with her faith that it would indeed some day be done.

Contents

Chapter 1

Viewing Language as a
Knowledge-Based Process

This is a book about human language. Its goal is to present a framework for the study of language as a process of communication. Its approach is motivated by two intertwined questions:

What knowledge must a person have to speak and understand language?

How is the mind organized to make use of this knowledge in communicating?

In looking at language as a cognitive process, we deal with issues that have been the focus of linguistic study for many years, and this book includes results and insights gained from these studies. But we look at language from a different perspective. The emphasis is less on the structure of the sounds or sentences, and more on the structure of the processes by which they are produced and understood. Our study of these processes leads in turn to study of the structure of the knowledge an individual language user must acquire and employ.

Our study of the mental processes involved in language draws heavily on concepts that have been developed in computer science, particularly in the area called *artificial intelligence (AI)*. In the forty years since digital computers were first developed, people have programmed them to perform many activities that we think of as requiring some form of intelligence. In doing this, they have developed new ways of talking about knowledge—what it is, and how it can be stored, modified, and used. They have also developed tools for describing complex processes in the form of programs and for building devices that run these programs to carry out information processing operations.

Much of the work in computer science has been pragmatic, based on a desire to produce computer programs that can perform useful tasks. But the design of computational systems also has a theoretical side, which is often called *cognitive science*. The same concepts of program and data that serve as a framework for building and understanding computer programs can be applied to the understanding of any system carrying out processes that can be understood as the rule-governed manipulation of symbols. Computational theories are the basis for current studies in many areas of psychology related to language.

This chapter sets the computational approach into the context of other approaches to language by giving a brief history of the major directions in linguistics over the past century. In order to give some feeling for the complexity of the task of language understanding and the range of issues that must be explored, we begin in Section 1.1 by asking some intuitive questions about language, as exemplified by a short dialog taken from a children's play. Section 1.2 describes the evolution of different paradigms for the study of language and Section 1.3 outlines the computational paradigm, on which this book is based. Section 1.4 discusses some of the practical consequences and uses of the theories developed here.

1.1 What every language user knows

In performing a mental task like calculating a sum or deciding on a chess move, we are aware of going through a sequence of thought processes. To a large extent, we can discuss what we have done, decide what to do next, and even teach our methods to another person. The ordinary acts of speaking

---

SCENE: *Living room in a country home. Shirley is seated at a desk. Enter Anne carrying an egg.*

Anne: Look, Shirley, Elspeth has laid another egg.

Shirley: It's awfully big! What does it taste like?

Anne: Duck eggs are very good. Just like a chicken's, only more to eat. Here... (*places egg on table*) You can have it for breakfast tomorrow. After all, I had the first, you know.

Shirley: But Elspeth is your duck. Are you sure you don't mind?

Anne: Oh, no. (*Enter John*)

John: Well, everything is finally settled. We're leaving for the city right away.

. . .

Figure 1–1. Dialog from a children's play (MacLellan and Schroll, 1949).

Anne: Look, Shirley Elspeth had laid another egg.

> *Look, Shirley, Elspeth has laid another egg.*

Shirley: She's badly big! What taste does it like?

> *It's awfully big! What does it taste like?*

Anne: Mozart sonatas are very good. Just like a burdick's, only more to eat.

> *Duck eggs are very good. Just like a chicken's, only more to eat.*

There... (*placed egg on table*) You can have it for mother tomorrow. After all, I had the last, you think.

> *Here... (places egg on table) You can have it for breakfast tomorrow. After all, I had the first, you know.*

Shirley: And Elspeth is your duck. Are you sure you don't mind?

> *But Elspeth is your duck. Are you sure you don't mind?*

Anne: Well, no. (*John just came in*)

> *Oh, no. (Enter John)*

John: Oh, everything was finally settled. We're leaving for a city wrong away.

> *Well, everything is finally settled. We're leaving for the city right away.*

Figure 1-2. A garbled version of the same dialog.

and understanding language are not open to the same kind of scrutiny. Like breathing or walking, we do them all the time without conscious effort. We think explicitly about understanding only when the communication process breaks down in some way.

The unconsciousness with which we use language gives the illusion that language communication is basically a simple process, not involving much knowledge. When we try to learn a new language, we are aware of needing to 'know' some new information, including the meanings of words and the grammatical structure of sentences, but we are still unaware of the degree to which our underlying knowledge of language and communication is simply being carried over from our native abilities. Figure 1-1 is a fragment of a play written for children, and Figure 1-2 gives a garbled version with the same basic structure. The original dialog can be understood by an average adult reader without any particular effort. The modified version is 'wrong' in a number of ways. Some of the changes violate obvious rules, but most of them are strange in more subtle ways for which we have no simple descriptions. By comparing the two, we can bring to light some of the knowledge needed by a reader to detect the anomalies. The informal categories listed below are only a beginning, and there are many other issues raised by the same dialogs.

Word order rules. When we learn a foreign language, much of our effort goes into the *syntax,* or grammar. The same set of words with two slightly different orderings can mean completely different things, and the rules for ordering are different in every language. *What does it taste like?* and *What taste does it like?* are both meaningful, but not the same. Much of modern linguistics has been devoted to analyzing the knowledge that underlies this ordering. This is not the same as knowing officially 'correct' grammar, since every native speaker understands phrases such as *Just like a chicken's, only more to eat,* which do not fit into the constraints of school grammar.

Vocabulary and word structure. Any speaker of a language must obviously know the form and meaning of its words. In addition, there are ways of understanding properties of new words that appear in context. In Figure 1–2 it is clear that *burdick* is a noun, due to its place in the structure and our knowledge of how the ending - *'s* is used. Along with general rules, a person must know a large number of special cases and exceptions. For example, a simple suffixing rule takes the closely related adjectives *bad* and *awful* to produce the adverbs *badly* and *awfully.* But the phrases *It's awfully big* and *It's badly big* are not at all the same. An idiom such as *right away* is another example. Its meaning has little to do with either word in isolation, and the parallel phrases *wrong away* and *left away* are meaningless.

Semantic features. The meanings of words can be classified in many ways. A simple form of *semantic* classification depends on distinctions like those between animate and inanimate objects or between male and female animals. A language user must know the classification in order to understand the use of pronouns. Following the sentence *Elspeth has laid another egg* the word *it* would refer to the egg, while *she* refers to Elspeth. As with many features of language, even a simple distinction like animacy defies straightforward analysis. A duck might well be referred to as *it* in some contexts, and *she* in others. A ship is *she* and an infant is often *it.*

Reference. Every language has mechanisms for indicating whether objects being referred to are known by the speaker and hearer. Words such as *a* and *the* (called *articles*) play a large role in determining this aspect of meaning in English, while many languages use other mechanisms such as word endings or dependence on the context. The phrase *We're leaving for the city* implies that the speaker expects the hearer to know of a particular city. The parallel *We're leaving for a city* implies that the speaker does not believe the hearer already knows which city, and therefore sounds funny in the context of this play.

Time. Every user of a language knows about simple past, present, and future, and can describe their relationships. Every speaker also knows about combined tenses and uses them in subtle ways, but few people can describe the rules that govern their use. If Anne comes into the room and says *Elspeth had laid another egg,* we find it strange, but not wrong. If she had said this in response to the question *Why were you so happy yesterday?*, it would be completely appropriate. The problem is that in choosing *had laid* instead of *has laid* or simply *laid* we convey an impression of 'past in past.' One event is described as having happened previous to some other (specified or implicit) event that was also in the past. In other cases, verbs seem to be used in ways that violate the simple ideas of past, present, and future. *We're leaving for the city* could be an answer to the question *What are you doing right now?* or the question *What will happen tomorrow?*

Discourse structure. In understanding a discourse, we make many assumptions about how the statements in it will be connected. When asked the question *What does it taste like?* a person can answer with a statement of fact about a general class of objects (*Duck eggs are very good*). The hearer assumes that the speaker is answering in good faith, and therefore connects the two by assuming that the object in question must be a duck egg and that by *good* the speaker means *good tasting*. The answer *Mozart sonatas are very good* in the garbled dialog is of exactly the same form but it makes no sense, since its relationship to the question cannot be inferred. Without trying to make this kind of connection, it is impossible to interpret the intended meaning of many sentences.

Attitude messages. Words like *well* and *oh* cannot be assigned a meaning in the same way as words like *duck* or *settle*. However, they convey crucially important messages having to do with the attitudes of the speaker. In response to *Are you sure you don't mind?* the phrase *Oh, no* indicates an assurance that the speaker doesn't mind, while *Well, no* indicates quite the opposite—that the speaker isn't sure at all. When John enters the room, a phrase beginning with *well* indicates that he wants to interrupt the conversation with a statement of a fact he has learned, while *oh* would imply that he learned the fact from something he saw just as he came into the room or had just remembered.

Prosodic conventions. Much of the meaning of spoken language is conveyed by the presence of intonation and stress patterns. These are not reflected directly in writing, although punctuation provides related information. The first sentence of the dialog (*Look, Shirley, Elspeth has laid another egg*) uses commas to indicate that *Shirley* is a direct address to the hearer. With the comma after *Shirley* omitted in the garbled version, we can read the sentence with an entirely different rhythm and intonation pattern, taking *Shirley Elspeth* as a person's full name. Whenever we read, we fill in information that would be in the spoken form according to our knowledge and understanding of the utterance.

Style conventions. A language like English is not described by a unified single set of rules. A native speaker knows several *registers,* or styles, which are appropriate for different forms of communication. Forms like stories, newspapers, broadcasts, books, and plays have their own specialized registers. The parenthetical remark *John just entered* is perfectly good English, but it is wrong when it appears as a stage instruction in place of the special form *Enter John* (or *John enters*).

World knowledge. Underlying all of the areas of knowledge described above is a person's knowledge of the world, the objects in it, and the relationships between them. If a person does not know that eggs can be laid by ducks, and that they can be eaten, the original dialog makes as little sense as the modified one. Of course, it is not the domain of linguistic theory to include all the knowledge a person has. However, it is necessary to understand how world knowledge and language understanding are interrelated. In order to describe the process of producing or comprehending language, we must know when world knowledge is being brought to bear and how its use is integrated into the more superficial linguistic processes involving words and structures. Much of the value in a cognitive processing approach to language comes from its attempts to integrate these different aspects of knowledge.

1.2 The evolution of linguistic science

The study of linguistics may be as old as language itself, and current linguistic science can trace its origins back at least as far as the Sanskrit grammarians of two thousand years ago. In looking over this history, we find a number of major turning points at which the focus of the study changed and linguists felt that they had finally arrived at the 'real' issues of language. There are many good histories of linguistics available for the interested reader, and this book does not try to provide yet another. Instead, by presenting some basic ideas from the philosophy of science, it attempts to give some perspective on this history. In looking at how science progresses in general, we can arrive at some useful insights into how language has been studied.

Kuhn's notion of scientific paradigm

There is a popular view of science in which its evolution is seen as linear progress. Nature presents us with a set of observable phenomena and scientists build theories that explain the regularities and predict what will happen. Over time these theories get better and better, explaining more phenomena, making more accurate predictions, and becoming more elegant.

Thomas Kuhn, in his book *The Structure of Scientific Revolutions,* presented an alternative view based on a notion of recurrent *revolutions* that shift the entire foundation on which a science stands. Nature does not present simple packages of data with a message 'Explain me.' The scientist is faced with a complex interconnected world, and a major part of defining any science involves selecting the questions to be asked about the phenomena and determining what kinds of answers will be considered acceptable.

Kuhn describes a cycle that includes periods of *normal science* separated by revolutions. During a period of normal science, there is widespread agreement about the questions to be dealt with and the kinds of answers being sought. The foundations of the science are taken for granted, and very little questioning is done of the basic assumptions. During this period, there are many specific details of the theories to be worked out, and the scientist is making progress as assumed in the popular viewpoint. Science in this state is said to be operating within a particular *paradigm*. This term has been used to describe both the social structure of a science and the conceptual framework that the scientists within that structure apply. There is disagreement about how it is best used, but for the purposes of this brief introduction we will allow it to stand for both.

After a period of time, problems arise on the fringes of the area staked out by the science—problems that cannot be explained within the current paradigm. At first, such problems are ignored or excuses found, but gradually, as the central phenomena of the paradigm become overstudied, more scientists move toward the difficult areas and the shortcomings of the whole framework become increasingly apparent. Finally, one or more of the dissatisfied researchers comes up with a radically different paradigm—one that views the subject in a different enough way so that it cannot be seen as an extension of the old theories. The new paradigm calls into question the basic assumptions of the current standard approach and there is usually heated debate between the established scientists and the revolutionaries.

Most attempts to establish new paradigms are not successful, so they are rejected as they fail to demonstrate their potential for new discoveries. A few, however, create enough interest to become part of the discourse in the field. As people begin exploring a successful new paradigm, they discover that many of the greatest difficulties of the old theories are eliminated and that there are many areas previously unexplored in which it appears that the new theories are promising. They may also note that some of the phenomena covered by the old paradigm do not seem to be as well explained by the new one, and in adopting the revolution they must give up some of the apparent progress made before. Often this goes along with a shift of attention in which the old issues appear to be less relevant to the 'real science' and are simply dropped from consideration.

If the revolution is successful, the new paradigm becomes normal science. Its advocates take over the positions of academic power, its ideas get formalized into textbooks, and scientists explore the range and power of its perspective until they reach its limits and the cycle is repeated. It is rare for practitioners of the old paradigm to be converted. In general, the time it takes to go through the cycle includes enough time for new younger scientists to replace the old establishment.

Kuhn uses the so-called 'hard sciences' as his examples, pointing to revolutions in astronomy, chemistry, and physics. He emphasizes the social aspect of this process. The evolution of a science is not predetermined by the nature of the phenomena, but is the outcome of a process involving the goals and attitudes of the societies in which the scientists live and the interplay of personal and political factors in the academic establishment. His examples are convincing even in those sciences where the image of progress is well established and backed up by obviously expanding technological power. The concept of scientific revolution applies even more convincingly in the 'human sciences,' such as psychology, linguistics, and sociology, where the revolutions are more frequent and more radical in throwing away all that came before, and where there are few technological applications to use as an effective measure of progress.

The changes in linguistic theory over the past hundred years clearly reflect a series of major paradigm shifts, and it is important for any student of language to be aware of the fact that these represent not a simple progress but changes in assumptions about what theories should look like and which phenomena are important. By viewing current normal science not as an ultimate answer, but as a step in a succession of radically different approaches, we are less prone to the error of blinding ourselves to ideas and approaches that do not fit within the constraints of our assumptions.

Metaphors for the study of language

Another way to view the changes in a science is to look at the sequence of metaphors on which it is built. At first glance, *science* and *metaphor* seem to come from different worlds. Science is based on mathematics, formal reasoning, and precision, while metaphor emphasizes poetry, imprecise analogy, and suggestion. This may be true for the detailed theories of normal science, but it is certainly not the case for the way in which new paradigms are developed and the basic assumptions of a field determined.

A scientist looking for a new paradigm is strongly affected by the other sciences currently enjoying successful development. Either consciously or unconsciously, the successful sister science is viewed as a model, and there is a metaphorical imposition of its ideas of what kinds of questions should be asked and what kinds of answers should be accepted. Linguistics and the other human sciences have been especially open to this kind of redefinition, using the hard sciences as bases for analogy.

The survey of linguistic history presented below is structured as a series of metaphors. These are not precisely the same as paradigms in Kuhn's sense, since he deals with the social organization of science rather than the conceptual forms. The connection, however, can be useful in understanding why paradigms have such compelling force for the people who work within them. The first metaphor is not part of a simple time sequence, but represents a regulative approach that has been with us for centuries and continues to dominate much of the popular understanding of language, although it has long been rejected by scientists studying actual language use. The rest of the metaphors fit into a sequence spanning the last century, covering the major directions of linguistic thought during that time. Of course, any such list does not do justice to the realities of how ideas were actually developed but can only give an idea of how paradigms arose.

Prescriptive grammar—linguistics as law

Language is a form of human social behavior, and like all behavior, has been the subject of legislation and control throughout history. Unfortunately, the metaphor of law is the predominant view of language structure in our society. Schools teach grammar not as an analysis of language as it is really used, but as a set of rules that must be followed by students who wish to take their appropriate place in the social structure. The main concern of prescriptive grammar is with *correctness* or *purity* of the language. As with any legal structure, those who live within it agree that there is a right way and a wrong way to do things, and the job of the linguist (as judge and policeman) is to make sure that things get done the right way.

All of the current theories of linguistics reject this metaphor. A language is a naturally occurring phenomenon that changes over time and is defined by what people actually say, not what teachers or academies think they should say. The job of the linguist is to understand how language is structured and how it came to be that way, not to fight the losing battle of preventing its evolution or forcing the conventions of one social class onto the rest of society. Of course, there may be practical reasons why one wants to teach 'correct' grammar to people, such as to enable them to function within the social structure. A practical theory of linguistics can provide a basis for language teaching.

Comparative linguistics—linguistics as biology

In the nineteenth century, a paradigm for linguistics emerged under the title *comparative philology*. Its main concern was with the relationships between different languages and the ways in which languages changed. Darwin's theory of evolution was causing major upheavals in people's world view and was being applied to many areas of science and social science. Linguists began to pay more attention to the similarities between languages, particularly the vocabulary and sound patterns. They noted that through comparisons of structures they could build a family tree of languages just as biologists developed taxonomies of organisms and that they could explain the features they saw by postulating common ancestral structures in languages that no longer existed.

Most of the success of this paradigm was in the style of natural history. As with early studies of biological evolution, only vague general principles could be developed to explain why things evolved in the way they did, but there was a great task of classifying and structuring the existing data into a complete phylogenetic tree. Languages like 'Proto-indo-european' were postulated as long vanished common ancestors. As the study progressed, a linguist could be challenged by a language (or specific word or sound pattern) that had not yet been located in the taxonomy, and gratified when its structure turned out to be derivable from ancestral languages that had already been postulated, or when the ancestors needed to explain it turned out to have power in explaining other missing links.

This kind of puzzle-solving activity is common to all periods of normal science, and its success provides the motivation for scientists to continue working within the paradigm. The feeling that pieces are naturally fitting together gives assurance that the science must be on the right track and that progress is being made. As philologists began to exhaust the body of well-known languages, some of the study turned to more remote languages reported by anthropologists, but excitement waned as the task became simply a repetition of tedious cataloging and few satisfying general principles were discovered.

Structural linguistics—linguistics as chemistry

The revolution that overthrew comparative philology as the center of linguistics was based on a shift of focus from the family of languages to the structure of a single language. Questions of language change were set aside and linguists looked for ways to describe the regularities they found in the utterances of an individual language. A Swiss linguist named Ferdinand deSaussure was one of the early advocates of a structural approach, but the greatest development was in the United States, beginning with the publication of Leonard Bloomfield's *Language* in 1933. This paradigm maintained its predominance through the 1950's, and is still actively pursued in many departments of linguistics.

Structural linguistics was strongly influenced by the tenets of *behaviorism,* a paradigm that dominated American psychology during approximately the same period. Behaviorists felt that most of the previous work in psychology was unscientific because it described human behavior in terms of mental processes that could not be observed by objective scientific experiment. They asserted that a true science of psychology must be based strictly on observations of behavior. In linguistics, this implied that the correct objects of study were observable bodies of language behavior. The appropriate raw material for the linguist was a collected *corpus* of naturally occurring utterances.

The analysis of language data was modeled after a positivist view of the empirical sciences that emphasize the use of experimental techniques to rigorously determine underlying structure. A chemist performs experiments to determine the set of molecules of which a complex substance is composed, and in turn analyzes those molecules in terms of their basic *elements.* The great success of chemistry was in finding a small set of primitive elements whose combinations could account for the vast number of different substances found in nature. Language, with its sentences, made up of words, made up of sounds, was subject to the same kind of analysis.

The analogy to chemistry is closest in the way sounds are organized into words. Even though an infinite variety of sounds can be produced by the human speech apparatus, every language has a small set (between 20 and 50) of distinct sound categories called *phonemes*. Slight variations in the pronunciation of a phoneme (such as 'b' in English) do not affect the identity of a word in which it appears unless the variation is enough to make it sound like a different phoneme (such as 'p'). The set of phonemes is different for each language, and structural linguists concentrated on developing *discovery procedures* that laid out an objective and systematic approach to determining the phonemes of a language not known to the scientist doing the analysis.

In the study of *syntax*—the way that words combine into grammatical utterances—the same methods were used but were less satisfying. The set of meaning elements (or *morphemes*) in a language is much larger and less well structured than the set of phonemes. Linguists could catalog the different kinds of syntactic structures that occurred in a language, just as early chemists could do little more than catalog the multitude of compounds with large molecular structure. Many different languages were described in terms of the structures that appear in them and there was an emphasis on trying to analyze as wide a range as possible of the different languages in the world. Much of the work was done by anthropologists engaged in the study of peoples and cultures outside of modern Western society. As a result of the emphasis on describing the structures for each of a large number of different languages, the entire paradigm is often referred to as *descriptive linguistics*.

Generative linguistics—linguistics as mathematics

In the past twenty-five years, a new paradigm has gained predominance, largely due to the work of Noam Chomsky and his students, beginning with Chomsky's *Syntactic Structures,* published in 1957. It rejects the empirical methodology of structural linguistics and shifts the focus of analysis from observable behavior to the intuitions of native speakers about their language.

Chomsky argued that the structural analysis of texts or recorded collections of utterances could not capture the essential *creativity* of human language. Utterances do not simply appear in nature, but rather are the result of mental capacities of the speaker. The proper domain of study, according to the generative paradigm, is not the sentences themselves but the underlying faculty that enables us to create and understand them. The central problem is to characterize the *grammar* of a language—the tacit knowledge whereby a speaker or hearer uses it. This calls for an explanation of people's intuitions about whether a particular sequence of words (or sounds) is or is not a valid sentence of the language, and about the structural relationships (such as paraphrase) among different sentences. The theory must explicitly postulate mental structures and processes, since there are no techniques available for directly observing what goes on in the mind of a language user. Rather than follow rigorous procedures for analyzing a language, the linguist makes use of intuitions based on his or her native language abilities.

The empiricist arguments against trusting intuition in doing formal science formed the basis for much heated debate between behaviorists and generativists, most notably between Chomsky and the psychologist B.F. Skinner. Chomsky argued that linguists could study the abstract mental structures that form a basis for linguistic ability without indulging in unprovable speculations about actual mental processes. He distinguished between *performance,* the processes that actually determine what a speaker will say or how an utterance will be understood in a particular context, and *competence,* an abstract characterization of a speaker's knowledge of the language.

The concept of abstract competence is closely related to notion of proof in mathematics. We can think of mathematics as a 'language' of formulas, and the job of the mathematician as explaining which combinations of symbols represent true propositions, given a set axioms and rules of inference. The expression '$(x+1)^2 = x^2 + 2x + 1$' is a true sentence of ordinary algebra, while another sequence made up of the same symbols, such as '$(x+2)^2 = x^2 + 4x + 2$,' is not. Mathematics is not the study of how people invent such expressions or what goes on in their minds when they read or try to prove them. Its goal is to produce a set of rules and formal mechanisms that precisely determine which ones are true. The measure of success for an *axiomatization* (the laying down of the rules and operations) for a field of mathematics lies in its elegance and economy.

Generative linguistics views language as a mathematical object and builds theories that are very much like sets of axioms and inference rules in mathematics. A sentence is grammatical if there is some *derivation* that demonstrates that its structure is in accord with the set of rules, much as a proof demonstrates the truth of a mathematical sentence. Much confusion has come from the use of the word *generative,* since to many people it falsely implies that the theory is a description of how people generate sentences. A helpful analogy is to recognize that although formal mathematics provides a precise way of recognizing whether a particular proof is valid, it has no way whatever of describing how a mathematician sets out to generate it.

The major successes of generative linguistics have been in the area of syntax—the specification of how sequences of morphemes or words are structured into sentences, but there has also been work in *generative phonology,* and current theories of semantics have been strongly influenced by the generative paradigm.

1.3 The computational paradigm

This book presents a view of language as *a communicative process based on knowledge*. In any situation of language use, the producer and comprehender are processing information, making use of their knowledge of the language and of the topics of conversation. Our task as linguists is to understand the organization of these processes and the structure of the knowledge. Our metaphor is that of computation, as we understand it from our experience with *stored program digital computers*.

The computer shares with the human mind the ability to manipulate symbols and carry out complex processes that include making decisions on the basis of stored knowledge. Unlike the human mind, the computer's workings are completely open to inspection and study, and we can experiment by building programs and knowledge bases to our specifications. Theoretical concepts of *program* and *data* can form the basis for building precise computational models of mental processing. We can try to explain the regularities among linguistic structures as a consequence of the computations underlying them.

Much of the material in this book is an explanation of techniques for structuring data and programs in computers. The details of these techniques are not intended to be precise theories of human language use, but rather building blocks from which theories can be constructed as we explore the metaphor further. The motivation for presenting detailed computational descriptions is to develop the student's mastery of the concepts of computational processing. In order to set a general stage on which the theories can stand, we begin by presenting an abstract model of the processes of producing and comprehending language.

A basic model of communicative processing

Language is a process of communication between intelligent active processors, in which both the producer and the comprehender perform complex cognitive operations. The producer begins with communicative goals, including effects to be achieved, information to be conveyed, and attitudes to be expressed. These include such things as: causing an action, either verbal or non-verbal, on the part of the comprehender; causing the comprehender to make inferences or have reactions, either about the subject matter or about the interaction between producer and comprehender; conveying information about some thing assumed to be known to the comprehender; getting the comprehender to be aware of some new thing known to the producer; and directing the comprehender's attention to some thing or some of its properties, to establish context for a

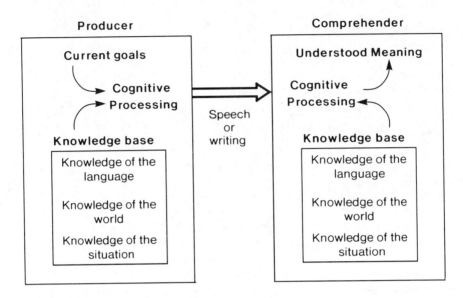

Figure 1–3. Basic model of cooperative communication.

subsequent utterance. Some of these goals are subgoals of others. For example, an utterance might have to establish a reference to an object in order to state a fact about it. Some goals are at least partially independent. For example, one might draw the comprehender's attention to some entity while conveying an overall posture. At times, a producer's goals can be conflicting and/or unconscious.

In order to communicate, the producer must map this multi-dimensional collection of goals onto a sequence of sounds that can be uttered or marks that can be drawn on a page. The details of language structure and the nature of the processes involved in its use are greatly affected by the need to transmit meaning through these media. Except for a small amount of information conveyed in tone and vocal gesture, the message is forced into a linear form. There are a variety of mechanisms that make it possible to merge multiple messages into a single structure that enables the comprehender to perform the reverse process, inferring the original goals and messages from the information received.

A language provides a variety of *information resources* that can be manipulated by the producer. The choice of words, the structure of phrases, and the patterns of emphasis and intonation all play a part in providing the necessary cues for the comprehender to infer the producer's communicative goals. In order to make appropriate selections from this set of resources, the producer must combine the intended goals of the utterance with knowledge of what is being discussed and what the comprehender already knows. The design of an utterance depends critically on the producer's expectations that the comprehender will make use of knowledge and intelligent reasoning to find interpretations and fill in information that is not explicit. This reflexiveness is one of the key features of natural language, and must be taken into account explicitly in order to deal with any but the most trivialized notion of communication.

Figure 1–3 illustrates the overall structure of the model. It indicates that the relevant knowledge includes general knowledge of the language and of the world being talked about and specific knowledge about the situation in which a text appears or an utterance is performed.

A model of the processing done by a language user

The communication process involves simultaneous related activities by producer and comprehender. Rather than study these in isolation, we will take the approach of first outlining the processing they share in common and then detailing the differences between the two processes. Figure 1–4 is a more detailed model of the cognitive processing that goes on for producer and comprehender. This figure indicates the structure for spoken language. For written language, the 'sound patterns' would be replaced by corresponding 'writing patterns.' Most work in linguistics has concentrated on spoken language, since it is more fundamental than written language, and even though most computational models deal only with typewritten character sequences, this orientation is preserved in the theoretical discussions.

The language user is tied to the world in two ways: through linguistic interactions and through action and perception. The basic assumption of the model, which is shared by most work in artificial intelligence, is that there are *representations* that operate in mental processes and that can be formally described as *data structures* like those of a computer. These structures are the basis for the processes described in the previous section.

Figure 1–4 indicates three separate kinds of structure, representing sound patterns, syntactic structures, and beliefs about the world. Although there has been much debate about the nature of these components and the appropriateness of dividing them in this way, most computational models and computer

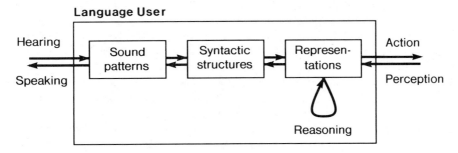

Figure 1–4. Model of processing done by the language user.

programs make some sort of division along these lines, and the model is a useful first approximation for understanding them. Later in the section we will look at *stratified* systems in which the different levels of processing are intermixed.

The arrows between the structures indicate processes that relate them. When an utterance is heard, sound pattern structures are created, which are then analyzed to produce syntactic structures, which in turn are used to form appropriate representations. These representations then become part of the material (along with what was previously stored) for doing reasoning, which can lead to the construction of further representations. This may then result in action, or in the production of an utterance by going in the opposite direction—from representation to syntax to sound.

This general model corresponds quite closely to the model of language and meaning developed by the analytic philosophers of language, drawing on ideas dating back to Aristotle and beyond. The element in this model that distinguishes it from non-computational approaches is its focus on the description of processes that explicitly manipulate formal structures. The general idea of a process operating with a knowledge base and acting to generate structures and interact with an environment is central to all areas of computer science, and it is the framework for linguistic description used in the computational paradigm.

The stratification of linguistic structure

Traditionally, linguistic structures have been represented using a variety of formalisms corresponding to different levels of structure, such as sounds, words and phrases. There appears to be a natural series of levels common to all human languages, and much of the effort in structural linguistics went into defining these levels. The organization at each level is to some extent independent of how it relates to the levels around it. For example, the regularities in how sounds are organized to form words are largely independent of how words are organized to form phrases. This *stratification* is a natural organization for any complex mapping process, since it allows the mapping to be organized into stages, each of which is simple relative to the overall result.

Computational models are also based on the idea that a complex process can be decomposed into a collection of simpler processes, each operating to some extent independently of the others. The language user's knowledge can be analyzed as comprising a number of separate components, with different processes using the different components. By operating in levels, the system has the advantage of *modularity*. Modularity is extremely important for a system to be flexible and expandable, since it ensures that the effects of detailed changes to the rules can be localized. What is needed for effective integration of the levels is a uniform definition for the structures that the components accept as inputs and produce as outputs.

Figure 1–5 illustrates a simple stratified model of language comprehension. As pointed out above, comprehension and production can be thought of as

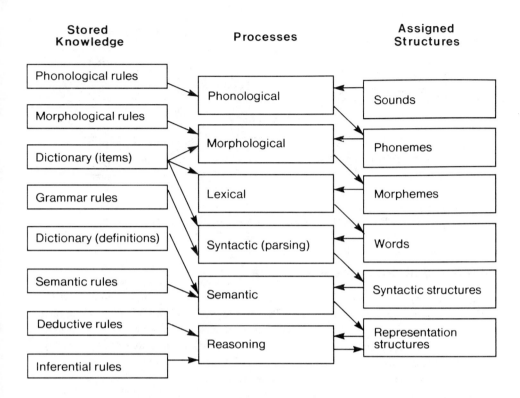

Figure 1–5. A stratified model of language comprehension.

inverse processes operating in opposite directions. According to this model, the knowledge of a language is made up of rules for manipulating the different levels of structure. When a person hears a sentence, the sequence of sounds form an initial level of structure. The phonological process applies rules to analyze these into a sequence of phonemes. The morphological process applies other rules to analyze the phoneme sequence into a sequence of morphemes, the dictionary is used to relate these to words, the syntactic rules are used to analyze these into phrases, and so on down through the levels. A producer would proceed in a similar way, working from bottom to top.

There are ways in which this model is wrong in its suggestion that the levels and processes can be separated. For example, a person makes use of *stock phrases* or *idioms,* in which patterns of words or morphemes are related directly to meaning rather than analyzed in terms of their syntactic structure. However, like the other figures in this section, it represents a simplification that has served as the basis both for the design of computer systems and for the organization of psychological models.

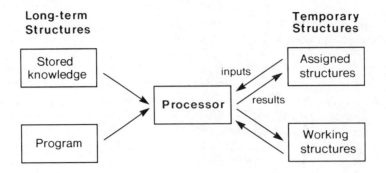

Figure 1–6. Structure of an individual process.

Structure of a process and its data

Figure 1–6 gives a more detailed picture of the processing that is indicated by the arrows in Figures 1–4 and 1–5. There is a *processor,* which makes use of a body of stored knowledge (such as a grammar, a dictionary, or a collection of structures representing facts about the world) to operate on temporary structures according to a stored *program.* The processor operates on structures that it is given (produced by other processes) and generates structures that other processes can use. These are the structures appearing in the right-hand column of Figure 1–5, which we have called the *assigned structures.* In the course of processing, other structures are created and used (called the *working structures*) that are not preserved as part of the structure resulting from the process. This distinction is important when we analyze the overall process as being made up of components. The assigned structures are those that cross between components, while the working structures are internal to a single component.

The division of the long-term structures into program and stored knowledge (or *data*) is more problematic than it might seem at first. One of the key issues of computer science is understanding how a program (which is itself a body of stored data) and a process (what happens when a program is run) are interrelated. Within artificial intelligence there has been much discussion of the contrast between *procedural representations,* which embody knowledge in the program and *declarative representations,* which emphasize the structure of the stored knowledge. In describing syntax, this distinction is not as critical as it is when we come to meaning, and in most of this volume we will adopt the conventional distinction between program and data.

The distinction between processor and program is also problematic. The same process can be carried out by a specialized processor designed specifically for it, or by a more general processor that uses a program describing the specific process. In designing computer systems, there are many tradeoffs between specialized and general processors. In creating computational models for the human mind, we need to be careful to distinguish those cases in which we are hypothesizing that a particular process is going on (without having a hypothesis as to the nature of the processor/program combination that does it) and those in which we are making a stronger hypothesis about the design of the processor and its program. The models described in this book (and in most of artificial intelligence) are of the first kind—they characterize a process without any model of the 'hardware' structures of the brain that might perform such a process. The overall activity described in Figure 1–5 could be carried out by a single processor with programs corresponding to the different processes indicated in the middle column, or by a collection of specialized processors, each designed for one process.

Going one step further, we can develop models in which both the processor and the program are identical for all components, and the only differences are in the stored knowledge (the collections of rules they make use of). However, in most detailed models the stages of processing are different enough that it is more revealing to describe them as using separate programs.

Finally, it should be noted that the distinction between temporary and long-term structures is also a simplification. Most computational models of language deal with the processing of sentences with a given body of language knowledge, rather than with the acquisition of new knowledge. Any comprehensive theory of human language must account for the fact that we do not begin with a body of stored knowledge about the language but acquire it as part of the process of using language. This *language acquisition* process is one of the central problems of linguistics that has not been dealt with in a comprehensive way in the computational paradigm.

In computer systems, information is often stored in very different ways, depending on whether it is to remain permanently or is to be available only for the time span of the current process. In most of this volume we will assume a fairly sharp division in which all of the general knowledge of the language is permanent and all of the knowledge of the particular conversation or text (including the structures of the individual sentences) is temporary.

Non-stratified process structure within a stratified system

Figure 1–5 depicts the understanding process as a sequence of stages, beginning with sounds and progressing toward meanings. A strict sequence is observed in the processing of information through the levels—each component operates with the results of the one above it, producing structures for the one below it. If we look at human language understanding, it is clear that a simple sequential model is wrong. People often make use of meanings to understand structures that would otherwise be incomprehensible, and many experiments have demonstrated that in listening to speech we often use knowledge of the expected meaning as an aid in analyzing the sounds in order to decipher the words of the message.

A system organized in sequential stages is 'brittle.' If there is a problem at a beginning stage of the analysis, the whole process breaks down. It is possible to maintain the advantages of stratification while increasing the flexibility of a system if we separate the processing sequence from the structural levels. Figure 1–5 can serve as a model of the structures produced, without determining the order in which the information is processed. We can think of the assigned structures as all being written on a *blackboard* and the component processes (often called *knowledge sources*) as reading information from that blackboard and writing new information onto it. The order in which things are added to the blackboard can be determined by the availability of information to any one of the processes, and a process need not be limited to reading only what was written by its upper neighbor.

Since the simpler stratified processing model has been the most developed, much of the material presented in this book will be based on it. In particular, most of the material on syntax will assume that there is a separate component called the *parser* which operates on words that have already been recognized and found in a dictionary and which produces syntactic structures for use in a separate phase of semantic analysis. In presenting the current research problems in each part of the book, we will discuss the advantages and problems of the increased intercommunication between the different knowledge sources in a non-stratified processing model.

The generative and computational paradigms

Some philosophers of science have decried the abandon with which Kuhn's notion of paradigms is bandied about. At times, it seems that anyone who wants to gain attention for an idea that is dismissed by the currently powerful scientists in a field declares it to be a 'new paradigm.' Indeed this is a danger, and our presentation of recent linguistic history in terms of paradigms can be seen as an oversimplification. In particular, there is a distinction made between the 'generative' paradigm and the 'computational' paradigm, which may obscure a high degree of commonality. From a greater distance, they may be seen as two variants of a single 'cognitive' paradigm, which is based on the following principles:

The proper domain of study is the structure of the knowledge possessed by an individual who uses a language. In adopting this mentalist individual-oriented stance, the cognitive paradigm sets itself off both from approaches that deal with the text itself as the central focus and those that consider social interaction to be primary.

This knowledge can be understood as formal rules concerning structures of symbols. In hypothesizing that the relevant aspects of language knowledge can be characterized in formal structures, the cognitive paradigm is in disagreement with views such as *phenomenology,* which argue that there is an ultimate limitation in the power of formalization and that the most important aspects of language lie outside its limits. Much of the debate about the possibility of artificial intelligence centers around this question.

Within this overall area of agreement there are differences of both theoretical orientation and methodology that distinguish the generative and computational approaches:

Attention to process organization. The most important difference lies in whether the organization of the processes of comprehension and production is assumed to play a central or peripheral role. In the computational paradigm, the structure of language is derived from the structure of the processes. Computational models deal with the organization of knowledge in a way that can serve as data for an effective procedure. In the generative paradigm, knowledge of language is divided into two aspects—those dealing with *competence* and those dealing with *performance.* The structure of a person's linguistic competence is characterized independently of any processes by which it is manifested, as we saw in applying the metaphor of mathematics above. The performance component is recognized as relevant to the description of actual linguistic behavior but is seen as theoretically secondary to the independent specification of competence.

The relevance of non-linguistic knowledge. Most researchers in the computational paradigm give a good deal of attention to the interaction between linguistic and non-linguistic knowledge. It is assumed that the knowledge structures and processes for dealing with language are to a large degree shared with other aspects of intelligence. In developing computational models, researchers emphasize the commonalities between language and other faculties. In the generative paradigm, in contrast, it is generally assumed that there is a distinct *language faculty,* possessed by humans but not by other animals, which determines the structure of language. Much of the research adopts the *autonomy of syntax hypothesis*—that there is a relatively independent body of phenomena that can be characterized by syntactic rules without considering other aspects of language or thought. Although a comprehensive generative theory of language must integrate language with thought in general, this ultimate goal does not directly impact the theories and methodologies used in characterizing syntactic competence.

Some other differences in orientation tend to follow the generative/computational distinction, such as the generativist's tendency to view language in terms of independent objects (sentences or utterances) versus the computational researcher's interest in how linguistic acts fit into a larger context of action and knowledge. These are more important in dealing with meaning, and will be discussed further in the volume on meaning.

In light of these similarities and differences we will continue to speak of both the 'generative' and 'computational' paradigms, and will use the term 'cognitive' for the areas that they cover in common. The phrases 'computational' and 'cognitive processing' will be used interchangeably, depending on whether the particular context emphasizes the computational details or the general approach to modeling human language.

1.4 Practical relevance

If we ask a scientist in any area why he or she studies a particular phenomenon or takes a particular approach, we may get a very personal answer. There are reasons of individual history, of external rewards, and of personal satisfaction gained from solving the puzzles posed by nature, possibly without regard to any practical results. However, from a social viewpoint, any pursuit that uses resources of labor and equipment must be weighed against other ways of using the same resources, and in most modern societies science has been valued for its applications more than for its aesthetic pleasures. The current level of support for linguistics is not due to increased appreciation of the beauty of language. It arose because there are potential uses for the theories and techniques that the research produces. In particular, the computer has opened many new possibilities for applications of linguistics, and much of current linguistics (including work that is not explicitly computational) has as its major goal the description of language with the formality and precision needed for computer implementations.

This is not to say that computers *per se* were the origin of the linguistic theories. Much relevant work on structural linguistics and formal semantics dates to the early part of this century and beyond. However, the selection of particular lines of research for support has been strongly influenced by intended computer applications. For example, the United States Air Force funded much of the early development of transformational grammar at the same time that it was one of the primary supporters of research on machine translation. For the most part, this book does not deal with specific applications or with the problems that arise in making practical use of linguistic theories. It is structured around the basic concepts that underlie a range of possible applications. Nevertheless, it is useful to have an understanding of practical relevance as an orientation towards what problems have been pursued and what kinds of solutions have been accepted. At the end of each volume there is a chapter on specific systems that have been built using the principles described in the text. The selection of the systems presented was influenced by their success and/or notoriety; it is not possible to cover all of the interesting work that has been done. One of the main goals of the book is to give students sufficient technical background to read independently and understand a wide range of systems, both those existing now and those to be built in the future.

Computer applications for natural language

Before the invention of the digital computer, language was seen as the exclusive province of human beings. The signaling systems of other animals were too rigid and simple to deserve the designation 'language,' and all that mechanical and electrical devices could do was to store and transmit sequences of codes to be interpreted by people. With the computer, new possibilities appeared. The essential quality of the digital computer is its ability to manipulate symbols—not just numbers, but symbols of any kind. It was recognized from the very earliest days of computing that, in addition to their obvious applications in scientific calculation and bookkeeping, computers could work with language.

Since computer technology also included the development of specialized artificial languages such as programming languages, computer scientists adopted the practice of logicians and mathematicians (who develop their own formal languages) in using the term *'natural language'* for languages like English, Russian, and Swahili. In this book 'natural language' is used when there might be confusion as to whether artificial languages are being included, but most of the time the simpler term 'language' is used in referring to natural languages.

A broad range of potential applications of computers to language has been proposed over the years, and the following paragraphs describe those that have been most extensively explored:

Machine translation. The first application area to receive significant attention (see Weaver, 1949) was the translation of texts (specifically, scientific and technical papers) from one language to another. It was widely believed that there would be a tremendous problem caused by the expansion of the international scientific community during the post-war years, and that without machine translation it would be impossible to handle the massive number of documents to be translated. The main focus of research in this country was Russian-to-English translation (and in the Soviet Union, English-to-Russian), although there was also work on a variety of other languages. The work focused on the syntactic structure of language and on the development of appropriate computer forms for storing and using bilingual dictionaries.

Although the attempt to develop *fully automatic high quality translation* was not successful (for reasons mentioned in Chapter 7), there has been a continuing interest in machine translation and today there are a large number of systems performing limited translation or translation-related tasks. Recently the European Economic Community has created a multi-national project to develop machine translation systems for use in commercial communications.

Information retrieval. Another early vision of computer possibilities was the 'library of the future.' If the amount of information to be translated was growing rapidly, the amount to be stored and retrieved was growing even faster. With computers it is possible to do much more than simply catalog books and papers. One can store representations of their contents and use computer programs to get back information on the basis of what a document says, not just its title, author, and appearance in a publication. Systems of two different types were developed: those for *text retrieval* and those for *question answering*. In text retrieval, the goals are to interpret what information the user of the system wants and to respond by identifying the relevant documents. In question answering, the system attempts to generate answers to specific questions based on stored information.

The techniques applied to text retrieval have often not been based on a cognitive processing approach to language. Their theoretical foundations lie in *information theory* with its measures of information based on statistics and probabilities. Question answering, on the other hand, has been a central project in the development of computational models of language. Much of the research dealing with syntactic structure, representation, and meaning has been done by people engaged in constructing computer programs to carry on question-answer dialogs in natural language. In some cases, the information on which the answers are based is presented to the system in the form of natural language, while in others it is stored in a pre-defined data base. Much of the current work on *front ends* (the interface seen by a user of a computer system) for data base systems includes modules that accept some form of natural language.

Human-machine interaction. A question-answering system carries on a dialog with a person in order to provide information from some stored body of knowledge. However, the same kind of interaction can be used in situations where the computer is being used in an activity and natural language is a means of specifying what is to be done and monitoring what is going on. A person using an interactive computer system of any kind gives commands, asks questions, and enters information. A number of researchers have developed systems in which this interaction is in natural language. Such systems can also include a generation component, producing natural language descriptions of what is going on to be read by the user of the system. These can be used in *explanation systems* that enable a program to explain why certain actions were taken, or what state it is in at a given time. A related research area is the development of systems that allow programmers to specify computer programs in natural language or in natural-language-like programming languages.

The desire for more effective human-machine interaction has been one of the major motivations for extensive government support of research on natural language. One prominent area was the work on *speech understanding systems* in the early 1970s. Communicating with a computer using written language (typed at a keyboard) is slow and clumsy compared with the spoken language we use so effectively in communicating with other people. Although that particular research effort did not lead to practical systems, there are simple (individual-word-based) systems currently in use, and it is generally agreed that more flexible spoken communication with computers will be practical in many contexts in the coming years.

Text analysis. The statistical methods used for text retrieval have other applications in the analysis of texts. Tone, style, and other global properties of text can often be related to measurable differences in its structure—the average length of words and sentences, the frequency of occurrence of different words and structures, etc. For many purposes (such as the attribution of authorship), the kinds of measures that can be made from the information-theoretic point of view can be directly useful. As with text retrieval, the bulk of the work in this area is not directly relevant to the view of language being described in this book. However, there are also some more recent efforts to do text analysis based on programs that analyze the text using cognitive models (for example, in skimming newspaper stories in order to keep track of the travels of a political figure). Such systems have applications in intelligence gathering of the kind that might be done by a government or business organization. They make use of many of the models and theories developed in artificial intelligence and will be described in the volume on meaning.

Knowledge acquisition. In describing systems for human-machine communication, we assumed the existence of a functioning computer system operating in a domain that is complex enough to warrant interacting with a person in natural language. Some such systems (often referred to as *expert systems*) are based on a large body of stored knowledge about a particular problem area, such as medical diagnosis or oil well exploration. In the building of such systems, it is necessary for the programmer (or *knowledge engineer*) to incorporate bodies of material that are known to experts in the field. This requires interactions with those experts and can be both tedious and costly.

Much of the current work on expert systems includes efforts to provide some form of natural language interaction between the program and an expert, through which the program's body of knowledge is built up. Some longer-term research is based on the hope that after reaching a certain level such systems could be given material in the form of text (such as journal articles and textbooks) and incorporate the contents without human intervention.

Computer aided instruction (CAI). Computers have been used for education in many different ways, often involving some kind of question-answer interaction between student and computer. For many domains (such as arithmetic drill) this interaction can be in a coded symbolic form. However, for most areas it is natural for the questions, answers, and other discussion to be in natural language. Most existing systems make use of 'canned' language in the form of questions, answers, and explanations that are pre-planned and entered by the person preparing the lesson. In this case the computer system does not deal with the structure of language, but simply types out appropriate text strings at the programmed times.

It has long been recognized that much more effective teaching programs could be built if the computer could deal with the content of both the pre-stored material and the student's queries and responses. Several systems have been built that integrate natural language interaction with other uses of the computer (such as graphics and simulation) in teaching specific subject domains.

Aids to text preparation. One of the most widespead applications of computers today is as *word processors,* which are used in the preparation and editing of texts. Word processing systems have not generally involved the use of linguistic theory, but there are several areas in which they will depend on theory as they are further developed. An advanced word processor can include *spelling checkers* and *text critiquing* facilities. By looking up words in a stored dictionary and performing a syntactic analysis of sentences, such systems can point out (and at times correct) possible errors. In a much longer time range, researchers hope to develop computer *dictation* systems which use techniques of speech understanding. The user of such a system could dictate material which the computer would convert into text.

Other applications

In addition to practical applications using computers, the computational approach to language can lead to theories and frameworks that can be applied to other practical aspects of language. In this it shares much of its potential with other approaches, such as structural and generative linguistics. As mentioned above, it is not the goal of this book to deal with applications in detail, but the following paragraphs suggest some of the possibilities:

Effective communication. Language is for human communication, and one obvious goal for a theory of language would be the improvement of the effectiveness of that communication. In fact, in ancient Greece the study of language was directed towards *rhetoric,* the art of effective argument. In modern times there have been a number of popular writers whose topic is 'semantics.' Their work grew out of the approach, called *general semantics,* developed by Alfred Korzybski. This work has not been held in high regard by academic linguists, largely because it emphasizes common sense exhortations in place of detailed analysis. In principle, a cognitive linguistic theory should form a solid basis from which principles of effective communication could be generated and analysis could be done. An experienced linguist can often see the theoretical reason for a particular awkward sentence, ambiguity, or misunderstanding. However, as with many skills, the naive wisdom of the coach is often more useful in practice than the theoretical constructs of the scientists, and there has been little formal application of the theories.

A related area, also spurned by academic linguists, is the attempt by teachers and writers to preserve the 'purity' of language. Current views of language (including most of the paradigms described in Section 1.2) treat each language as undergoing continuing natural evolution. Linguists see their role as studying and understanding that evolution, not trying to control or prevent it. The attempt to fight the adoption of specific grammatical constructions (such as the use of *hopefully*) seems futile, although the general advice given by the same authors (such as the importance of using simple terms in place of technical jargon) is often sound in the same way as are the principles of general semantics.

Language design. From time to time throughout the centuries, there have been attempts to design new languages that are superior to natural languages for human communication. The best known of these is Esperanto, which is spoken by over a million people. As with effective communication, it seems clear that such efforts would be helped by a solid theory of just how people use language—how their knowledge of the language is organized and how it is used in processing. One could imagine using the principles of cognitive processing to design languages that were easier to understand and to learn. In practice this has not been the case, partly because the development of such theories is still at an early stage, and partly because the general enterprise of creating a new human language is seen as questionable. A language embodies a culture and a tradition and is the result of thousands of years of evolution and use. It is doubtful that a newly created language could have the kind of subtlety and richness that provide for full human communication.

A related area is the design of artificial languages, such as computer programming languages. Here many of the formalisms of linguistic theory have been applied, and in fact much of the material in this volume was developed concurrently in linguistics and for the engineering of computer systems.

Translation. Aside from the direct use of computers in machine translation, there is also the possibility that computational theories could be of use in the teaching or work of human translators. Much of the support for work in structural linguistics came from religious groups with an interest in translating the Bible into the thousands of languages of primitive tribes all over the world. The emphasis in that work was on the *discovery procedures* that could be used by a missionary to analyze the structure of a new language in order to be able to translate. Current work in cognitive linguistics is less immediately relevant to translation, but it can provide a theoretical framework for dealing with grammatical complexities.

Language teaching. Of all the areas to which linguistic theory might be applied, the most widespread is the teaching of language. This includes both second language instruction and the teaching of *language skills* in elementary and secondary schools. There is a tremendous literature on linguistics for language teachers, and some of the major linguistic theorists, such as Halliday, have aimed much of their writing at this audience. There have been some attempts to make use of transformational grammar in language teaching, and the National Institute of Education is currently sponsoring a number of projects related to language teaching that make use of a cognitive processing approach like the one described in this book.

Language therapy. Some of the most fascinating phenomena of language are the *language deficits* exhibited by people suffering from brain injuries and other organic and mental disorders. Work on *neurolinguistics* has revealed that the neural mechanisms underlying language are complex and diverse. For example, some kinds of *aphasia* (loss of language) seem to involve syntactic abilities without affecting vocabulary, while others interfere with the ability to produce words even though understanding is unimpaired. The eventual goal is to integrate cognitive processing models with neural models, describing both the 'hardware' and the 'software' of the brain. These models in turn could be used to develop techniques for curing or ameliorating specific deficits. At the moment, the gap between the computational models and the physiological description is very large, and it is likely to be quite a while before there are practical connections.

Psychology. It has often been remarked that language is a 'mirror of the mind.' If we understood how language worked, we would be a long way towards understanding how the rest of the mind works in reasoning, learning, and remembering. Much of the research on *psycholinguistics* has a double aim— to understand language, and to understand the mind through its linguistic abilities. This is not a direct application like language teaching or translation, but an indirect one. The development of cognitive theories of language plays a role in the development of more general theories of cognition, and these in turn have many practical applications. Just as this section describes the relevance of linguistic theory, a similar one at least as long could be written for the relevance of psychology.

Limitations of the approach

As with all paradigms, the computational paradigm is successful at dealing with some aspects of language at the cost of ignoring others. There are aspects that were considered highly important in earlier approaches but have been downplayed, and others that are important to many people who work with language but are not central to the cognitive processing approach. To a large degree, these limitations are common to the computational and generative paradigms, following from their basic cognitive orientation.

Social aspects of language. In looking at language as a process going on in the mind of an individual, we lose sight of the social dynamics of language use. When people talk to each other, they are doing much more than conveying ideas. They are participating in a social interaction of which language is only one part, and from which it takes its meaning. In the field of *sociolinguistics* the focus is on social phenomena and social meanings. The cognitive processing approach has little to offer when, for example, we want to understand why a particular dialect is adopted by some members of society but not others, or how dialect differences play a role in establishing and maintaining group identity and cohesiveness. At the individual level, we may want to understand how linguistic devices serve to establish personal power relationships or to reinforce social distinctions of rank and status. All of these issues have important practical consequences in addition to being a fascinating area of study. Although work in the cognitive paradigm need not be contradictory to them, it is not in the mainstream.

Evocative aspects of language. When a person hears a poem or reads a novel, much more goes on than a transfer of information or knowledge. A thorough analysis of the lexical, syntactic, and semantic structure may be of use to the scholar, but it doesn't begin to touch upon the issues that are of interest when we look at language as literature. In some ways the issues are again social. Literature is what it is because it plays a part in an ongoing tradition of a culture. In other ways it is individual, affecting the emotions of the reader or hearer. But the cognitive approach has not had any significant insights to offer along the emotive dimension, and despite some feeble attempts at 'computer poetry,' it seems ill suited to the task.

Historical aspects of language. As described in Section 1.2, some of the earlier paradigms for language study emphasized the historical side of language— the ways that languages evolve, divide, and merge. These phenomena are again outside the domain of an approach that focuses on the knowledge of an individual at a particular moment. Although all change takes place as the result of language acts by individuals, the relevant patterns are not visible at that level.

In addition to having limitations imposed by its focus on the structure of knowledge in the individual language user, the cognitive paradigm has other potential limitations due to its premise that this knowledge can be modeled as a set of formal structures. Many critics of artificial intelligence argue that much of our skill at using language is not in the nature of formal rules, but is more akin to physical skills like walking or playing tennis. They do not believe that the individual's ability to use language can be explained by any formal characterization analogous to the data structures of computers or the rules of formal logic. They see the success of computer programs that deal with natural language in specialized domains as due to the constrained nature of those domains.

For many of the applications mentioned above, it may be possible to have effective communication based on the computational model. However, for fuller language use (including things like adequate translation of general text) they see ultimate limitations that will prevent the computer from performing successfully. In looking at potential applications, it is also important to consider the social effects that would surround their use. It has been pointed out that attempts to create computer therapists or computer judges can have effects far beyond the particular cases in which they are applied. The very notion of what it means to judge is a social construct, and the attempt to give computers this role is a highly political act reflecting a particular view of justice and social organization.

It would take us far beyond the scope of this book to treat these issues with the seriousness they deserve. The reading list suggests some directions for further reading, and it is vital for any serious student to understand the larger context in which the technical work is carried out.

Further Reading for Chapter 1

Scientific paradigms. Kuhn's *The Structure of Scientific Revolutions* was originally published in 1962, and a second edition is available that includes some of the debate that followed the original publication. An extended discussion of this book and related topics appears in Lakatos and Musgrave (eds.), *Criticism and the Growth of Knowledge.* The applicability of Kuhn's notion of paradigms to linguistics is controversial, and Percival (1976) argues that it is misleading in important ways.

History of linguistics. There are many histories of linguistics, each taking a point of view shaped by the paradigms that were current at the time it was written. Some useful modern histories are included in Bierwisch's *Modern Linguistics, Its Development, Methods and Problems,* Crystal's paperback *Linguistics,* Lyons's *Language and Linguistics,* and Newmeyer's *Linguistic Theory in America.*

Computational paradigm for language. There have been no comprehensive texts on the computational paradigm for the study of language. *Computational Semantics,* edited by Charniak and Wilks, introduces some of the basic ideas, and Tennant's *Natural Language Processing* gives several case studies of implemented natural language processors. The best way to get a current overview of the field is to look through the proceedings of conferences such as *Theoretical Issues in Natural Language Processing* and the annual meetings of the Association for Computational Linguistics, as well as the more general artificial intelligence and cognitive science meetings mentioned below. Relevant papers appear in the journals *Artificial Intelligence* and *Cognitive Science* and in the *Journal of the Association for Computational Linguistics.* A number of papers have been published in collections such as Schank and Colby (eds.), *Computer Models of Thought and Language,* Norman and Rumelhart (eds.), *Explorations in Cognition,* Rustin (ed.), *Natural Language Processing,* Bobrow and Collins (eds.), *Representation and Understanding,* Zampolli (ed.), *Linguistic Structures Processing,* Joshi, Webber, and Sag (eds.), *Elements of*

Discourse Understanding, Lehnert and Ringle (eds.), *Strategies for Natural Language Processing,* and Brady (ed.), *Computational Theories of Discourse.* Some of the early work (before 1970) appears in Feigenbaum and Feldman (eds.), *Computers and Thought* and Minsky (ed.), *Semantic Information Processing.*

Artificial intelligence. Several of the introductory texts in artificial intelligence discuss natural language, including *Artificial Intelligence* by Winston and *Artificial Intelligence and Natural Man* by Boden. The style of programming that has evolved in the LISP language for artificial intelligence is explained in *Artificial Intelligence Programming* by Charniak, Riesbeck, and McDermott. Papers on AI appear in the journal *Artificial Intelligence* and in the proceedings of the alternating biennial meetings of the International Joint Conference on Artificial Intelligence and the American Association for Artificial Intelligence. There are also volumes of collected papers, such as Winston and Brown (eds.), *Artificial Intelligence: An MIT Perspective,* Webber and Nilsson (eds.), *Readings in Artificial Intelligence,* and a series of volumes entitled *Machine Intelligence,* edited by Michie and others. *The Handbook of Artificial Intelligence,* edited by Barr and Feigenbaum, gives a comprehensive overview of AI research and techniques.

Cognitive paradigm in psychology. Lindsay and Norman's *Human Information Processing* is an introductory psychology text that takes a cognitive processing viewpoint. Newell and Simon's *Human Problem Solving* deals with a more specialized set of topics taking an explicitly computational approach. The journals *Cognition, Cognitive Psychology,* and *Cognitive Science* publish many relevant papers, and there is an annual meeting of the Cognitive Science Society as well as other psychological meetings with a cognitive orientation.

Differences between the generative and computational paradigms. An extensive debate on this issue appears in a series of papers in *Cognition* in 1976-77 by Dresher and Hornstein, Schank and Wilensky, and Winograd.

Computer applications of natural language. The technical literature on computer applications is much larger than that on theory, but there are few books that deal in a general way with the applications of natural language processing. *The Computer Age: A Twenty Year View,* edited by Dertouzos and Moses, includes a number of essays on computer applications, including those involving natural language. Speech understanding systems are described in Newell et al., *Speech Understanding Systems;* Reddy (ed.), *Speech Recognition;* and Walker (ed.), *Understanding Spoken Language.* Some papers and reports dealing with specific applications are mentioned in Chapter 7.

Text retrieval. The basic issues and techniques are described in Sparck-Jones and Kay, *Linguistics and Information Science.* For theoretical background in information theory, the original key work by Shannon and Weaver, *The Mathematical Theory of Communication,* is fairly readable, and a good introduction is provided by Pierce in *Symbols, Signals and Noise.*

Psycholinguistics. There are several introductions to psycholinguistics, including Clark and Clark's *Psychology and Language* and Fodor, Bever, and Garrett's *The Psychology of Language.* Some recent work is described in Halle, Bresnan, and Miller (eds.), *Linguistic Theory and Psychological Reality.*

General semantics and language purity. There is a large popular literature on semantics and language. Much of the original inspiration was in Korzybski's work, such as *Science and Sanity,* and among the best known is Hayakawa's *Language in Thought and Action.* Current popular works include Newman's *Strictly Speaking: Will America be the Death of English?*

Language teaching. *Linguistics, a Revolution in Teaching,* by Postman and Weingartner, is an introduction designed for high school teachers that provides an excellent perspective on what linguistics is all about. Much of the literature in systemic grammar (see Chapter 6) has been oriented towards teachers of English. Some current work oriented towards the use of computational models in the teaching of reading is described in Spiro, Bruce, and Brewer (eds.), *Theoretical Issues in Reading Comprehension.*

Limitations of the cognitive approach. The most prominent critic of artificial intelligence and the cognitive approach in general is Dreyfus. His book *What Computers Can't Do* sets out the basic arguments, and the second edition includes a lengthy new introduction that deals explicitly with work in natural language. *Mind Design,* edited by Haugeland, contains a number of important papers relevant to understanding the cognitive/computational paradigm. The social consequences of artificial intelligence and of seeing computation as a model for human thought are discussed by Weizenbaum in *Computer Power and Human Reason.* Flores and Winograd, in *Understanding Computers and Cognition,* give a theoretical framework in which the cognitive approach can be evaluated and explain why the current work on artificial intelligence cannot provide a basis for understanding and modeling the full range of human language understanding.

Exercises for Chapter 1

Note: The exercises for this introduction are more in the style of questions for discussion, in contrast to the more technical exercises of the subsequent chapters.

Exercises for Section 1.1

1.1 Some of the modifications in the dialog of Figure 1–2 were not mentioned in the discussion. For each of them, describe the kind of knowledge that is needed to recognize the anomaly.

1.2 Try to write a set of rules for the use of the pronouns *he, she,* and *it,* taking into account the kinds of complexities mentioned in the text (e.g., what about babies and hurricanes?). How have the conventions changed over the past few years?

1.3 Consider two different circumstances in which you are trying to help someone understand the dialog of Figure 1–1. In one case, it is a person who doesn't know English but who is an ordinary native speaker of some other language. The other is a Martian who has a complete dictionary and grammar of English and can apply them with great facility, but knows nothing about earthly ways. What would you have to tell each of them?

Exercises for Section 1.2

1.4 Describe the sequence of paradigms that have dominated some other human science (such as psychology or sociology) over the last century. Which of them can be associated with an obvious metaphor from the hard sciences?

1.5 In the text it was mentioned that the structural paradigm was useful in the practical work of Bible translation. For each of the different paradigms, describe some practical problems or activities for which the approach is best suited.

Exercises for Section 1.3

1.6 Give some examples of language acts in which the stratified structure of Figure 1–5 does not apply. For example, the word *Oh* spoken with an appropriate rising and falling intonation can convey many different messages even though there may be no relevant analysis at the level of words or syntax.

1.7 (*For students familiar with computing*) How do the concepts of stratification and stratified processing apply to the design of compilers and interpreters?

1.8 Give a stratified description of the game of baseball. At the top level there are individual movements (like swinging an arm or moving legs rapidly), while at the bottom there is an analysis of the game in terms of things like winning and losing. Are there recognizable layers that lie in between?

Exercises for Section 1.4

1.9 As we will see in later chapters, it is much more difficult for computers to process ordinary colloquial language than to deal with carefully written text. For what applications is it important to go beyond the limitations of fully grammatical, well organized text?

1.10 What are some potentially undesirable effects of developing and using computer systems for natural language?

1.11 What kinds of problems would a computer 'text critiquing' system be able to detect most easily? What kinds would present more difficulty?

Chapter 2

Word Patterns and Word Classes

Syntax is the part of linguistics that deals with how the words of a language are arranged into phrases and sentences and how components (like prefixes and suffixes) are combined to make words. In theory, it would not be necessary for languages to have a systematic syntax. We could imagine, for example, a language that was simply a list of all the things that could be said. The linguist's work would consist of compiling giant dictionaries of all the possible phrases with the meaning of each. In fact, there are *finite languages* for which such a dictionary exists, such as those of military and diplomatic code books. Even in ordinary conversation, many of our utterances are copied whole from a stock of phrases and cliches, including social formulas, such as *How do you do?,* and expressions, such as *The more the merrier* and *It takes one to know one.*

Human language taken as a whole, though, is infinite. We can produce sentences that we have never heard or spoken before, and they can be understood by others for whom they are totally new. At the other extreme from a finite language we could imagine a completely free language in which any sequence of words that had a possible interpretation was in the language. The sentence *Language interesting is* would be just as reasonable as *Language is interesting,* since it would have a clear interpretation. But no human language is syntax-free. Our freedom to create novel utterances operates within a framework of *grammar,* which puts strong constraints on the *patterns* that are used in the language.

Chapters 2 through 6 present a view of the knowledge needed by a language user to interpret and produce syntactic structures, and some mechanisms are given by which the processing can be accomplished. In this chapter, we will look at some simple kinds of linguistic patterns and introduce some of the computational mechanisms that will be used throughout the book. Section 2.1 describes the idea of patterns and pattern matching in an elementary form and introduces the notation for describing objects and procedures. Section 2.2 describes the classification of words and its use in matching. Section 2.3 describes a more complex kind of pattern represented in a *transition network*, and Section 2.4 gives some procedures for recognizing sentences of a language using such networks.

2.1 Patterns and matching

The notion of *pattern* at its simplest is that of a physical object whose form is identical to the form of a piece of material to be cut. It can be used to determine the shape of an infinite variety of garments, differing in material, color, and texture. A comparable idea of linguistic patterns can be used to describe the possible forms of a language. Individual sentences such as *Traveling is a pleasure* can be viewed as being 'cut out' on the basis of more general forms that have blanks in place of specific words, such as '␣ *is a* ␣.'

Some of the early computer programs that interacted with people in English used these simple patterns. Figure 2–1 lists the entire set of patterns used by SIR (Raphael, 1967). Of course, it was clear that this was an extremely limited part of English, and the importance of the program lay not in its handling of

␣ is ␣.	Is ␣ ␣?
␣ has ␣.	How many ␣ does ␣ have?
␣ owns ␣.	How many ␣ does ␣ own?
Where is ␣?	What is the ␣ of ␣?
Is ␣ part of ␣?	How many ␣ are parts of ␣?
Does ␣ own ␣?	How many ␣ are there on ␣?
␣ is ␣ part of ␣.	␣ has as a part one ␣.
There are ␣ on ␣.	There is one ␣ on ␣.
␣ is to the left of ␣.	␣ is just to the left of ␣.
Is ␣ to the left of ␣?	Is ␣ just to the left of ␣?
␣ is to the right of ␣.	␣ is just to the right of ␣.
Is ␣ to the right of ␣?	Is ␣ just to the right of ␣?

Figure 2–1. Patterns recognized by SIR.

```
┌─────────────────────────────────────────────────────────────┐
│ Search for a match in a set of patterns                     │
├─────────────────────────────────────────────────────────────┤
│ Purpose: Test whether a sequence of words matches any pattern│
│ Inputs: a sequence of words and a set of patterns       2–3 │
│ Basic Method: For each pattern in the set:                   │
│   If the pattern matches the sequence of words, succeed. 2–3 │
│ Conditions:                                                  │
│   If every element of the set is tested without a match, fail.│
└─────────────────────────────────────────────────────────────┘
```

Figure 2–2. Search for a match in a set of patterns.

syntax, but in the reasoning mechanisms it used to answer questions (which will be described in the volume on meaning).

The knowledge of syntax represented in such a program consists of a set of alternative sentence patterns, each specifying a particular sequence of words and places for words. A sequence of words is a sentence of the language if there is some pattern in the set which matches it. The patterns are used independently—a single pattern matches a whole sentence. In later chapters we will see more complex uses of patterns in which a sentence is described in terms of several patterns applying jointly. For the simple mechanisms of this chapter, we will deal only with sentences that can be matched by a single pattern.

A pattern matching procedure

As an introduction to the notation used for describing procedures and knowledge structures in this book, we will explain the definition of a simple pattern matcher in detail. The mechanism used here may seem overly complex for the structures being described, since it is being introduced in a very simple case to make clear just what the notations mean and how they are used.

Figure 2–2 describes how a set of patterns like those in Figure 2–1 could be used in a recognition procedure. The procedure goes through the patterns one at a time, stopping as soon as it finds one that fits. The input to the procedure is a word sequence, and successful recognition of the sequence means that it is a sentence of the language characterized by the set of patterns. We have not described here just what a 'word' is, but the definition will be discussed later in the chapter. In a full language understander, the input would be a sequence of sounds or written characters, and some other part of the language analysis process would divide it into words.

The definition is written in DL, a notation developed for this book and explained in Appendix A. Each definition describes a *procedure* (as this one does), a *class* of objects (as in the definition of 'pattern' in Figure 2–3), or a *predicate* used in logical expressions. The numbers to the right of the box are the figure numbers of definitions for classes of objects, procedures, and predicates that are used in this definition. In each case, the term being cross-referenced appears in italics somewhere in the line next to which the number appears. A cross-reference is given only for the first appearance of a term in a particular figure, and will not be given for terms related to standard entities (such as words, characters, and sequences), which are used throughout the book and defined in Section A.4.

Several features of the definition deserve note:

Undefined objects, steps, and expressions. In describing this basic matching procedure, we have not said just what a pattern is or what it means for a pattern to match a word sequence. Any one of a number of different definitions for pattern could be 'plugged in' and the procedure would work in the same way. A general feature of descriptions in DL (and programming languages in general) is that we can write definitions that make use of objects, predicates, or procedures that are defined independently. If we look at this definition alone, it gives us an outline of what is to be done, but it is not detailed enough to actually carry it out.

The ultimate goal in designing a procedure is to make it complete and precise enough to be carried out by an *interpreter,* either a person or a program, which has the basic ability to carry out a collection of primitive steps. Appendix A describes the primitives of the DL interpreter. They include primitive objects such as sets and characters, primitive procedures such as stepping through a sequence, and primitive predicates such as equality. A procedure definition is a *fully defined algorithm* if each step, object, or expression is either a primitive of the language or refers to a definition that in turn is fully defined. We will discuss later what it takes for an object or predicate to be fully defined. Careful readers will note that this description of what it means for a procedure to be fully defined does not deal with *recursive definitions*—those that include a step making use of the definition in which it appears. For the moment, no such problems arise. See Section A.3 for a more comprehensive discussion.

Unspecified order. In saying 'For each pattern in the set...' we have not specified in what order to take them. For our purposes in this definition it does not make any difference, as long as they are taken one by one until a match succeeds or they have all been tried. One of the features of DL is that we can avoid being specific about ordering when it is irrelevant. A definition that includes a series of steps with an unspecified order is considered a fully defined algorithm, since any interpreter that actually carried out these instructions could choose some order arbitrarily. Of course, there are times when we want to be more specific. For example, the pattern set might contain two patterns that could apply to the same sequence of words, such as 'X ⌣' and '⌣ Y', which both apply to 'X Y'. The procedure as we have described it would find one or the other but does not determine which. If the procedure used an ordered *sequence* of patterns instead of a set, we could determine which one would be found by the order in which they appeared.

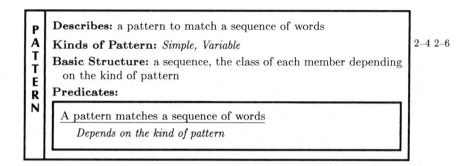

Figure 2–3. Pattern.

Success and failure. The description of what to do for each pattern indicates that if it matches, the search will succeed. Once a successful pattern is found, no more are tried, even though the instruction says 'For each pattern....' Similarly, at the end, if nothing has been found the procedure fails. A procedure can include any number of steps that call for it to 'Succeed' or 'Fail.' Whenever such a step is reached in following the procedure, it has two consequences—the immediate stopping of the procedure and the determination of its outcome as success or failure.

Results. In many procedure descriptions, we want to describe some *results* that are produced. In Figure 2–2 we have not—the only result is that the search procedure succeeds or fails. It is an example of a program for *recognition* rather than for *parsing* or *understanding*. In most real applications, we are not interested in simply recognizing the fact that a sequence of words is a sentence of a language. We want to determine its structure and use it in some other procedure, such as question answering. A parsing procedure has as its result a structure describing the organization of the sequence of words as a sentence, while an understanding procedure produces an interpretation based on some notion of meaning. In most of this volume, we will be dealing with parsing—producing structures that are not interpreted for meaning, but which show the internal organization of the sentence. However, it is often useful to explain parsing procedures by first explaining the corresponding recognition procedures and then adding the additional detail needed to produce a structure.

A formal definition of patterns

Figure 2–3 gives a formal definition of patterns that begins to fill in some of the detail missing from Figure 2–2. It is still quite general, describing what is common to all patterns and indicating two specific kinds—*simple patterns,* in which the elements are matched independently, and *variable patterns,* in which variables are used to keep track of what was matched for each element (explained below).

This definition illustrates three additional features of the notation:

Classes and kinds. The definition describes objects of the class 'Pattern.' Class definitions are indicated by a label running down the left side. Figure 2–3 indicates that there are two specific kinds (or *subclasses*) of patterns, each having its own definition (as indicated by the cross-reference numbers on the right). Those properties common to all kinds of patterns are included in this definition, while those specific to one kind appear in its definition.

Basic structure. Each pattern is in turn made up of a sequence of pattern elements. Not every kind of object has such a simple structure. For example, in Chapter 3 we will define a 'phrase structure node' as having 'roles' consisting of a 'label,' a 'parent,' and a set of 'children.' In the case of simple structures like the one defined in Figure 2–3, it is sufficient to indicate that it is a set or sequence and to say what class the elements belong to.

Predicates. A definition of a predicate such as 'A pattern matches a word sequence' is different from a procedure definition in that it describes the logical conditions for something to be true rather than a procedure to be carried out. There are primitive predicates in the language, such as equality of two objects and membership of an object in a set. These can be combined using logical operators such as 'not,' 'and,' and 'or.' It is also possible to define a predicate by giving the definition of a procedure that tests whether it is true or not, as is done in Figure 2–4. A predicate is *fully defined* if: it is primitive; or there is a fully defined algorithm for testing it; or it is defined as a combination of logical operators and fully defined predicates. Predicate definitions are indicated by underlining the phrase for the predicate. In Figure 2–4 we do not actually give the definition, leaving it to be defined for each kind of pattern. However, it is included here inside the definition of pattern to indicate that for every kind of pattern such a predicate must be provided.

Figure 2–4 gives yet more detail, providing a procedure by which we can test whether a pattern matches a sequence of words. This procedure is the obvious one of running through the pattern and sequence in parallel (a primitive procedure of the DL interpreter), checking to see if the elements match. However, the question of what it means for an element to match is once again left open to allow for different kinds of elements in patterns. Other things to note are:

Class hierarchy. A simple pattern is a kind of pattern, and in turn there are three kinds of simple patterns. We can describe a *hierarchy* of this sort to any depth. Anything appearing in a definition applies to all of the subclasses to any depth. A literal simple pattern is a kind of simple pattern and is therefore also a kind of pattern. Everything appearing in the definition of pattern (Figure 2–3) applies to it as well.

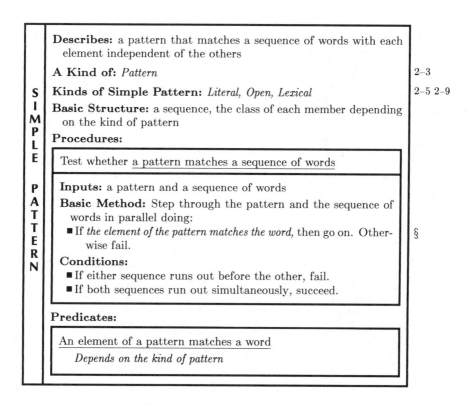

Figure 2–4. Simple pattern.

Nested definitions. The box containing the definition of simple pattern has within it a box defining the procedure 'Test whether a pattern matches a sequence of words.' This could have appeared in a separate figure, since it is a full definition. However, by including it inside the definition of this kind of pattern, we indicate that it constitutes a basic part of our understanding of what a simple pattern is. Without some notion of what it means to match a pattern, its definition as a sequence of elements would be uninteresting. In carrying out the procedure defined in Figure 2–2, the interpreter needs to use the appropriate definition of matching for the particular kind of pattern. In general, we will include definitions inside other definitions to indicate this kind of relevance. The character '§' is used in place of a cross-reference number when the definition being referred to appears in the same figure.

Procedures for testing predicates. The procedure defined within Figure 2–4 is the means of testing whether a pattern matches. It corresponds to the predicate that was mentioned in Figure 2–3. If the procedure succeeds for a given pattern and sequence, then it is true that the pattern matches the sequence. If it fails, the corresponding expression is false.

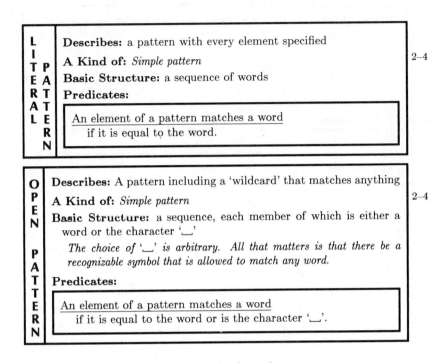

Figure 2–5. Two kinds of simple patterns.

Conditions. The procedure for matching a pattern includes conditions indicating what is to happen when the sequences run out. One feature of DL that is different from many programming languages is the ability to separate out special conditions like these from the description of the basic method. Whenever a condition is true of the current state of things, whatever it says to do is done, which may involve the success or failure of the procedure as a whole. The details of what can be included in such conditions are given in Section A.4.

Figure 2–5 defines two kinds of patterns, a literal pattern (a sequence to be matched exactly) and an open pattern of the kind shown for SIR in Figure 2–1. It fills in more details that were left open by the definition of simple patterns in Figure 2–4, specifying what the pattern elements are and what it means for an element to match a word. Comments appearing in italics are not part of the formal definition but are included as explanation. With this definition, we have a fully defined algorithm for searching for a match in a set of literal or open patterns, since all of the objects, steps, and expressions for which we have not given definitions are primitive. Note that the predicate 'An element of a pattern matches a word' is defined not by giving a test procedure, but by a logical expression built up out of primitive tests for equality and the logical 'or.'

V A R I A B L E   P A T T E R N

Describes: a pattern whose elements are words and variables

A Kind of: *Pattern*   2–3

Basic Structure: a sequence, each member of which is either a word or an integer

Integers indicate the variables. If the same integer appears more than once, it must match the same word in all occurrences.

Procedures:

Match a variable pattern against a sequence of words

Purpose: Produce a table associating variables with words in the sequence

Inputs: a pattern and a sequence of words

Working Structures:
   Bindings: a table whose keys are integers and whose entries are words; initially empty

Results: The table of bindings when the match is done

Basic Method: Step through the pattern and the sequence of words in parallel doing:
   If the pattern element is:
   ■ a word, then:
      ▪If it is the same as the corresponding word in the sequence go on. Otherwise the match fails.
   ■ an integer, then:
      ▪If there is an entry for that integer in the bindings, then:
         ▪If the word in the sequence is equal to the entry, go on. Otherwise the match fails.
      ▪If there is no entry, add the word as an entry in the table with the integer as the key and go on.

Conditions:
   If either sequence runs out before the other, the match fails.
   If both sequences run out simultaneously then return the bindings.

Figure 2–6. Variable pattern.

Patterns with variables

The matching procedure of Figure 2–2 applied to simple patterns as defined in Figure 2–4 would not be very useful for a real language analyzer. Once it has finished its work, all we know is whether it succeeded or failed. There is no trace left of what words were matched against the pattern elements, or even of which pattern the whole sequence matched.

In order to perform a task like question answering, the input analyzer must not only see that the input is a real sentence, but it must also gather information

Pattern	Word	Bindings	Word	Bindings
1	*row*	1=*row*	*please*	1=*please*
2	*row*	1=*row*, 2=*row*	*turn*	1=*please*, 2=*turn*
2	*row*	1=*row*, 2=*row*	*in*	FAIL
your	*your*	1=*row*, 2=*row*	*your*	
3	*boat*	1=*row*, 2=*row*, 3=*boat*	*exam*	

Figure 2–7. Matching a pattern with variables.

on what was in it. The simplest mechanism for gathering information is to let the blanks be associated with *variables,* and to keep a pairing of these variables with the words that they matched. SIR in fact used variables of this kind.

Figure 2–6 defines a pattern with variables and its use in a more complex matching procedure. To distinguish variables from English words in patterns, we use integers. Figure 2–7 illustrates the sequence of steps in matching the pattern '1 2 2 your 3' against the sequences *row row row your boat* and *please turn in your exam.*

The definition of Figure 2–6 introduces a number of other features of DL:

Results. The table produced in the process of matching is returned as a result of the procedure. A procedure can have any number of results, which can be any kinds of objects. Part of the definition is a statement of what kind of things the results will be. If the procedure fails, no results are returned. A step calling for a 'Return' causes an immediate stopping of the procedure, just like a 'Succeed' or 'Fail.'

Working structures. During the process of matching, the procedure makes use of a table (one of the primitive objects of DL) to keep track of what word has matched what variable. This is an example of a *working structure.* In this case, it is returned as a result, but a procedure can define and make use of any number of additional structures that are not returned.

Complex conditionals. The nesting of 'If...then...' statements illustrates how one logical expression can be used as part of another. The alignment of the lines in an outline form, along with the little boxes, is DL's way of indicating just how they are structured. Appendix A gives more details both on logical expressions and on the use of outline form.

Generate a sentence from a pattern and bindings

Purpose: Produce a sentence using the result of a match to fill in the blanks of an output pattern

Inputs: a *variable pattern* and a table whose keys are integers and entries are words

Working Structures:
  Response: a sequence of words, initially empty

Results: the completed response

Basic Method:
■ Step through elements of the pattern, doing:
  If the pattern element is:
    ■ a word, then add it to the end of the response.
    ■ an integer, then:
      If there is an entry for it in the table, add the entry to the end of the response. Otherwise fail.
■ Return the response.

2–6

Figure 2–8. Generate a sentence.

Patterns and generation

In addition to the procedure for recognizing sentences, we can also use patterns and bindings to generate sentences. An early computer program called ELIZA carried on a dialog in which the program simulated a nondirective psychiatrist talking to a patient. To produce the dialog, the program repeatedly read an input sequence, matched it, and then generated and printed a reply using pairs of patterns such as:

My 1 is 2 → How long has your 1 been 2 ?
1 thinks I am 2 → Do you think you are 2 ?

If the person typed *My luck is down,* the program would respond *How long has your luck been down?* Given *Everyone thinks I am crazy,* it would reply *Do you think you are crazy?* The program produced quite convincing dialogs using this simple mechanism, as illustrated by the following dialog (from Weizenbaum, 1966). The computer's responses are in italics:

Men are all alike.
  In what way?
They're always bugging me about something or other.
  Can you think of a specific example?
Well, my boyfriend made me come here.
  Your boyfriend made you come here?
He says I'm depressed much of the time.
  I am sorry to hear you are depressed.

Of course, ELIZA also produced blunders, since it had no analysis of meaning beyond the recognition of simple patterns, and for many inputs it had no matching patterns and responded with phrases like *Tell me more* and *Please go on.* We could obtain a simplified version of the program by changing our overall search procedure (Figure 2–2) to use a set of pairs, each consisting of a recognition pattern and a generation pattern. Responses would be generated using the procedure of Figure 2–8 on the preceding page. In the actual ELIZA program, variables could be matched against sequences of words, rather than just against single words. This further complexity is given as an exercise.

2.2 Word classes

The first thing to do in building a better pattern recognizer is to make it more selective. The pattern $I \_ to \_$ matches many real sentences such as *I want to go,* but it also matches *I elephant to the,* which is not a sentence. A person's knowledge of a language includes a more precise notion of what words can fill in the blanks.

Much of what is taught in elementary school grammar is the identification of *lexical categories,* often called *word classes* or *parts of speech.* Students learn to assign words to categories like *noun, verb,* and *adjective,* based on their intuitions about language structure. With these classes the sentences *Fat giraffes munch leaves* and *Brainy rabbits nibble carrots* can both be described by the single pattern 'ADJECTIVE NOUN VERB NOUN.'

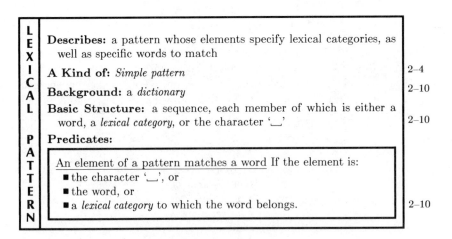

Figure 2–9. Lexical pattern.

Figure 2–9 defines a lexical pattern as one whose elements can specify lexical categories, and gives a definition of matching that assumes the language user has a simple *dictionary* (defined in Figure 2–10) listing the classes to which each word belongs. This is indicated as part of the 'background' rather than as an input to the matching procedure, since structures like dictionaries and grammars tend to serve as a fairly permanent common body of knowledge used by many procedures. This is not a firm distinction—the choice of whether to consider something as an input or a background depends on how we are thinking of the structure of the overall system of definitions.

The dictionary

By putting the definition of lexical category inside a definition of dictionary, we indicate that it makes sense for a word to be in a category only with respect to some dictionary—different dictionaries may have different sets of categories that do not correspond to each other in a simple way. A number of problems are ignored in this simplified notion of a dictionary. For example, we do not deal with the relationships between words like *gopher* and *gophers* or *go* and *going*. However, for many computer applications a dictionary not much more complex than this one is sufficient.

One extension to this simple dictionary would be to use word endings to identify the class to which a word belongs. For example, a word ending with *-ly* is likely to be an adverb, while one ending with *-ing* is probably going to be

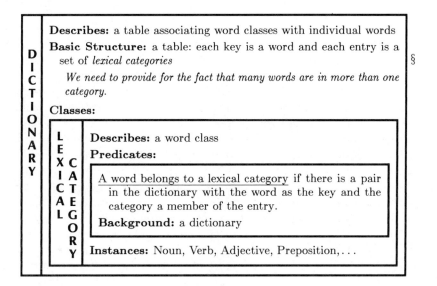

Figure 2–10. Dictionary.

a verb. If there is an analysis program that can use knowledge about standard suffixes, then the dictionary does not need to contain *thinking* in addition to the verb *think.*

Some programs reduce the dictionary even further, including in it only the stems of a few hundred very common words. They derive the rest of the categories by guessing, with a high degree of accuracy. Since these programs do not expect to find a stem for every word, they make mistakes with words like *anomaly* and *thing,* whose endings belie their real class. The practicality of such an approach depends on whether occasional mislabeling of a word prevents the rest of the system from handling a sentence. If a system can make flexible use of multiple knowledge sources, it is even possible to guess the class of an unknown word on the basis of analyzing the rest of the sentence. Human language users gain much of their vocabulary this way, as illustrated by our ability to understand (in some sense) sentences like *Twas brillig and the slithy tove...*

In most of our discussion of syntax, we will assume that there is a procedure that operates on the initial input (a typed sequence of characters), using some kind of simple dictionary and pre-processor to determine a sequence of words and assign each word to a set of word classes. However, before going on we will describe some of the problems presented by the facts of natural language.

What is a word?

The first impression of a literate language user is that the notion of *word* is basic and simple. A word is whatever appears between blanks and punctuation marks on a page. Even in spoken language, it seems quite reasonable to attempt to say something 'one word at a time.' As with many features of language, though, a simple definition works for a great majority of the items in the language but also leaves many unsolved problems.

Structural linguists emphasized the need to provide clear formal definitions of the components of linguistic utterances, and in doing this found the need to talk about a unit called a *morpheme,* which corresponded in some but not all ways to our common sense notion of a word. The morpheme is defined to be the basic unit of meaning, and several morphemes can be combined in a single word. New problems come up in trying to formalize the idea of 'unit of meaning,' but to a large extent we can get agreement on the presence of morphemes. The word *computerization* is made up of *compute, -er, -ize,* and *-ation.* In German, the phrase *life insurance company employee* is expressed as the single multi-morpheme word *Lebensversicherungsgesellschaftsangestellter.* Some languages (called *agglutinating languages*) build up complex words to convey some of the same information that we express with syntactic structures in English. In Turkish, for example, much of the verb and preposition structure is 'glued together.' *Kullanilamiyacak* means *it will not be able to be used,* and *cocuklarinizdan* means *from your children.*

In view of phenomena like these, it is clear that our notion of what constitutes a single word cannot depend on our intuitions about how much separate meaning each word should convey. It is also not reliable to depend on the way things are spelled or pronounced. Even in English, which compared to many languages has a clear separation of words, there are examples that cause problems for analysis. The phrases *can not, cannot,* and *can't* share a common meaning. *Can not* is clearly two words, but the others are less certain. The term *contraction* is used for a class of problematic structures such as *we've, wouldn't,* and *she'll,* which behave very much like single words although they are derived from pairs of words.

The native speaker's intuition of what constitutes a word seems to be most closely captured by some scale that combines *external mobility* with *internal stability.* If a combination of morphemes can be shifted together to different places in a sentence, it is more wordlike than one with a fixed position. If it is possible to insert an item between two morphemes, they are not parts of a single word. *Haven't* is more wordlike than *have not,* since we can say things like *have usually not,* but not *have usually n't.*

Within the paradigm of structural linguistics, many scholarly papers dealt with these problems and pointed out the failings of all the simple criteria that had been proposed for separating words. This was one of the dissatisfactions that led to moving away from the structural paradigm. In this book, we give rather little attention to the problems of *morphology,* as the study of morphemes is called. This does not imply that these problems are irrelevant to theories of how people understand and produce language. It is rather an indication that little exploration has been done of how the computational paradigm can add new insights to the large body of knowledge accumulated by the structuralists.

The classification of words

Anyone with a traditional grammar education from high school comes to linguistics with a seriously limited view of word classes. The impression conveyed in most English courses is that there is a well-defined set of *parts of speech* and that every English word can be straightforwardly assigned to one or more of them. This is true in an artificial language (for example, a computer language), where we can invent arbitrary categories, but in natural languages the grouping of words into classes is highly dependent on the purposes of classification.

Common sense ways of classifying words operate along several dimensions that are partially independent. One set of classes is based on meaning, as in the traditional definition, 'a noun names a person, place, thing, or concept.' A second set of criteria is based on the kinds of endings words will take. We can expect, for example, that any word that will accept *-ing* as a suffix is a verb. Another method of classification is based on the set of patterns in which a word can appear. A word that will fit into *It was a very ___ year* is an adjective.

Category	Frame
Noun	*I saw a ⌣ .*
Verb	*The sun will ⌣ .*
Article	*⌣ sun will explode.*
Auxiliary	*The sun ⌣ explode.*

Figure 2–11. Distributional frames.

The problem is that these dimensions do not necessarily go together. In any classification system, it is critical to separate distinctions being made on the basis of *function* from those being made on the basis of *form*. For example, how should we classify the word *laughing? Laugh* is a verb, which fits into frames such as *They will ⌣. Laughing* is its *progressive* form which fits into verb frames such as *They had been ⌣.* However, *laughing* also fits into the frame *I saw a ⌣ cow,* which is associated with adjectives like *purple,* and the frame *The ⌣ lasted for days and days,* which fits nouns like *merriment.*

Looking at the form of *laughing* and the way it is derived, we should classify it as a verb. Looking at the way it functions in sentences, we would sometimes call it a verb, sometimes a noun, and sometimes an adjective. A word like *flash* is both a verb and a noun and represents the same event in both cases. Many classes (particularly in languages like English, with weak inflectional systems) do not take suffixes and prefixes that can be systematically used to classify them. Informally, we can say that the same word is used in different classes, depending on its specific form and context. We run into problems when we try to characterize this formally in a way that could be used to provide detailed rules for syntax.

Categories based on distribution. Structural linguists felt that the best criteria for classifying linguistic entities (including words) were *distributional* tests, since these could be objectively applied to samples of a language. Figure 2–11 illustrates a distributional definition for noun, verb, article, and auxiliary, based on finding distinct *frames* in which they can appear.

There are many problems with the simple idea of distribution. In a real language sample, we are very unlikely to see the word string *I saw a recognition* or *Colorless green ideas sleep furiously.* Does this mean that the words are of the wrong classes, or simply that they do not have appropriate meanings? In fact, as we try to make more precise distinctions, we find that very few words have really identical distribution patterns (see the exercises). It is possible to come up with distributional criteria if we are dealing with a computer program that accepts a carefully limited subset of English, but if we attempt to apply the technique to the language as a whole, we bog down in the details.

Categories based on meaning. It is possible instead to adopt a categorization based on meaning. This approach has been proposed primarily for use in computer systems that do not try to analyze the structure of sentences fully. In Chapter 7 we will describe some of these systems, including a program for machine translation designed by Wilks, in which the word classes include categories such as: SUBSTANTIVE-ELEMENT, ENTITY, POTENT-ELEMENT (those that can designate actors), and MARK-ELEMENT (those that can designate items that themselves designate, like thoughts and writings). Some practically oriented computer systems carry this to an extreme, letting the classes of objects they discuss (such as AIRLINE-NAME, AIRPORT-NAME, and PERSON-NAME) serve directly as the word classes. Such systems are said to use a *semantic grammar.*

In many classification systems, it is convenient to introduce a notion of *subcategorization* in order to account for the fact that all members of one class can automatically be members of another. Every human is also animate. Every animate object is a physical object, and so on. This kind of categorization has been applied both in computer models and in more traditional approaches within the structural and generative paradigms. In Section 6.3 we will discuss the issues of subcategorization further as it applies to both words and structures.

The problem with a meaning-based approach is that semantic word classes are not sufficient for analyzing syntactic structures, since meaning categories correspond so poorly to the determination of which words appear in which structures. A person can *go to town* or *return to town,* and it is clear that the verbs *go* and *return* are in the same overall meaning class. It is normal English to say *We were waiting for your return,* but not *We were waiting for your go.* The fact that *return* but not *go* is also a noun cannot be determined from meaning criteria.

Whatever criteria we use for classification, we will find that some word classes are *closed*—they contain a fixed set of members, and additions are extremely rare—while other classes are *open,* and there are mechanisms for generating new members as new concepts need to be expressed. In English, the class containing the words *and, or,* and *nor* is a closed class with fewer than a dozen members while nouns, verbs, adjectives, and adverbs are open classes. We can invent new names for objects, actions, and properties either by producing totally new words or by adding endings to words from other classes. The noun *computer* came from the verb *compute,* and in turn is the basis for the verb *computerize,* which can be further adapted to form an adjective *computerizable.* This process is discussed further in Section B.4.

Traditional word class definitions

As pointed out earlier, there is an established set of classes for English, used in the traditional teaching of grammar, which is not adequate for developing comprehensive formal accounts of syntax. It nevertheless serves as a basic vocabulary that most linguists use as a starting point, and it is important to be familiar with these classes.

Most of the categories had their origins in studies of Latin grammar in the Middle Ages. In fact, for many years preceding the segment of linguistic history presented in Chapter 1, the study of language in Europe was dominated by analogies with Latin. It is now accepted as obvious by linguists that the categories applying to one language cannot be applied directly to a different language, even one that is related or is a derivative. However, there appear to be some fundamental similarities among the structures of all languages, for instance the presence of categories corresponding roughly to our notions of noun and verb.

There are a number of fascinating questions about the form of a *universal grammar* that would capture these similarities and shed light on the underlying mental structures on which words and categories are based. It must take into account the possibility emphasized by Whorf (in *Language, Thought, and Reality*) that although our language is shaped by our thinking, our thinking is also shaped by our language. He pointed out that the basic conceptual structure of a society may be based on the mechanisms offered by its language for describing objects and events. Unfortunately, such issues are far beyond the scope of what has been explored within the computational paradigm for language, and they will not be pursued in this book.

The following description of English categories makes use of phrases that might appear in a high school grammar book. These phrases are enclosed in quotes to indicate that they are to be taken as rough guides, not formal definitions. This brief summary is intended to provide terminology for the discussions of syntax in this chapter and in Chapter 3. These chapters do not deal with the complexities of full English but present some basic mechanisms using simplified grammars. Section B.4 of Appendix B presents a more systematic set of categories based on the formalisms described in the rest of the book.

Noun. A noun represents a 'person, place, thing, or concept.' Nouns can take endings to represent plural (*bug* → *bugs*) and possessive (*bug* → *bug's*). There is a subclass of nouns called *proper nouns,* which are names for people, places, etc. There is another subclass called *pronouns,* which 'substitute for a noun.' These include *personal pronouns* (*she, he, they, it, we, I, you,...*), *demonstrative* pronouns (*this, that, these, those*), *possessive* pronouns (*my, your, her, his, hers,...*), and *relative* pronouns (*who, which, that,...*), which connect subordinate clauses, as in *The man <u>who</u> sold Gustav the goldfish.*

Verb. A verb 'signals the performance of an action, the occurrence of an event, or the presence of a condition.' Verbs take the largest variety of endings of any English class, including *present participle* (*-ing*), *past tense* (*-ed*) and *past participle* (*-en*). Many verbs have irregular forms instead of the standard endings, for example, *ring, rang, rung; break, broke, broken.* There is a subclass of *auxiliary verbs* (*will, can, has, is,...*) which precede a main verb in a phrase like *He must have been planning it all along.* A subclass of the auxiliaries is the *modals* (*can, may, must, should,...*). There are a number of *verbal* forms that function as nouns and adjectives. These include the *past participle* (*broken, finished,...*) and the *present participle* (*running, laughing*). When a verb in present participle form is used as a noun (as in '*Laughing makes you live longer*), it is called a *gerund*.

Adjective. Adjectives 'modify nouns or noun equivalents,' as in *a contented child* or *the slow running.* They can also appear as a *complement* following certain verbs, as in *She seems sad.*

Article (Determiner). There is a small closed class of words (*the, a, some, an, this,...*) which precede nouns in standard noun group structures. We will divide this class into a number of important subclasses later (as described in Appendix B).

Preposition. Prepositions 'relate a noun or noun equivalent to the rest of the sentence.' They are a fairly small closed class (*in, on, until, by, at,...*).

Adverb. Adverbs 'modify other parts of a sentence or the sentence as a whole.' This is the leftover category—anything that doesn't have another class gets called an adverb. It includes words that modify adjectives (*very, somewhat,...*), words that specify time (*usually, now,...*), place (*here, there, somewhere,...*), manner (*quickly, easily,...*), reasoning (*thus, so,...*), and a variety of other stray but useful things (*only, not, even,...*). They are almost always treated as a set of special cases, except for the adverbs generated from adjectives by adding *-ly*, which specify manner.

Conjunctive adverb. One of the adverb classes is used to connect major parts of sentences. Although some such adverbs (*therefore, so,...*) may also introduce a clause that stands alone, there are others (*while, because, unless,...*) that are limited to introducing an embedded clause. These are often called *subordinate conjunctions*.

Coordinate conjunction. Conjunctions, as their name implies, join things. They are one of the hardest things in the grammar to handle well, and their treatment is a major issue of syntax. They form a small closed class (*and, or, but,...*). The conjunctive adverbs can be thought of as a kind of conjunction as well as a kind of adverb.

Interjection. When all is said and done, there are a few stray things like *oh, hey, ouch,* (and many others unprintable) that are interjected into utterances as a way of conveying reactions. This class is rarely handled in computer systems, since people tend not to use them in written language, and current computer programs are not able to make use of the kinds of meanings they convey.

2.3 Transition networks

This section generalizes the idea of a pattern in a way that brings it much closer to the intuitive sense that sentences are 'cut from the same pattern.' The concept of phrase structure in Chapter 3 carries this extension a step further.

In describing the structure of sentences such as *Fat giraffes cavort* and *Wooly bears love sticky honey,* we could use two separate patterns: 'ADJECTIVE NOUN VERB' and 'ADJECTIVE NOUN VERB ADJECTIVE NOUN.' However, this misses the fact that they have an initial section in common. It seems more economical to have some kind of notation (such as brackets) indicating an optional element and to combine them into a single pattern 'ADJECTIVE NOUN VERB {ADJECTIVE NOUN}.' Similarly, we notice that some elements can be repeated an indefinite number of times. If we want to represent the structures of *bears, wooly bears, ferocious wooly bears, hungry ferocious wooly bears,* etc., it is unsatisfactory to have a set of separate patterns:

Noun

Adjective Noun

Adjective Adjective Noun

Adjective Adjective Adjective Noun

Instead, we want another notation to represent optional repetition (we will use a '*') so we can combine them into a single pattern 'ADJECTIVE* NOUN.' By convention, the symbol '*' means 'zero or more repetitions,' so it covers the first pattern as well. In addition, we note that in place of a noun with preceding adjectives we might have a pronoun, as in *He loves honey.* We can use the logical symbol for 'or' ('$\vee$') to represent alternatives and parentheses to indicate grouping, so that for example '$(A \vee B)^*$' means a repeated sequence, each member of which is either A or B, while '$A \vee B^*$' is a choice between a single A and an indefinitely long sequence of B's. The choice between a noun with adjectives and a pronoun is expressed as 'PRONOUN $\vee$ (ADJECTIVE* NOUN).' Finally, combining all of these we can express a wide variety of structures in a single pattern:

(Pronoun $\vee$ (Adjective* Noun)) Verb {(Pronoun $\vee$ (Adjective* Noun))}

This kind of algebraic notation has been developed as part of the theory of formal languages. The specific form introduced here is the *regular language* formalism developed by Kleene. It is quite useful for proving things about languages and about the kinds of machines that can recognize them. However, from the point of view of specifying procedures for doing recognition and parsing, this kind of pattern is complex. It is difficult to deal with a pattern that contains in it symbols like '(' and '$\vee$' that do not match elements in the word string themselves but affect the matching of the other symbols.

Fortunately, there is a more usable notation that gives us the same power, called *state transition diagrams* or *finite state machines* in *automata theory,* a branch of mathematics that serves as a basis for much of the theory of computation. We will use *transition networks* (as these same structures are often called in computational linguistics) as a way of organizing processes both for the production and the analysis of linguistic structures. The rest of this chapter describes these networks and explains how they are used. The correspondence between networks and regular language expressions is covered in textbooks on automata theory and is explored in some of the exercises.

A transition network consists of a set of *states,* connected by *arcs.* Each arc represents a *transition* between two states. In figures, states will be represented by circles and arcs by lines between them, with an arrowhead indicating the direction of the arc. A transition network can be viewed as a pattern for recognizing or generating sequences of words. In both generating and recognizing, the process follows the form of the net in a step-by-step way—each transition along an arc corresponds to a single word in the sequence. The pattern is used by 'stepping through' the transitions from state to state, following the arrows. The stepping must begin in an *initial state* (one marked by a small arrow) and end in a *terminal state* (indicated by a double circle). Figure 2–12 is an example of a transition network, matching the same set of sentence patterns described in the long regular expression above. The letters in the circles for the states do not affect the way the network is used but are there for use in describing it.

The pattern corresponding to *fat wooly bears love honey* starts in state a and goes over a series of arcs 'a –ADJECTIVE→ a –ADJECTIVE→ a –NOUN→ b –VERB→ c –NOUN→ d,' while *they gobble it* would be 'e –PRONOUN→ b –VERB→ f –PRONOUN→ d.' Note that two verb arcs are needed, since if there were simply a pronoun arc connecting states c and d, the network would allow sequences of adjectives followed by a pronoun.

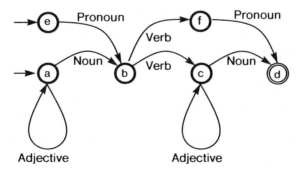

Figure 2–12. A simple transition network.

Describes: a formal structure combining a set of simpler patterns

Roles:

> **States:** a set of *states* §
>
> **Arcs:** a set of *arcs* §
>
> ^c**Initial states:** the subset of states categorized as initial
>
> ^c**Terminal states:** the subset of states categorized as terminal

Classes:

STATE

> **Describes:** a node of the network
>
> **Roles:**
>
> > ^c**Outgoing arcs:** the set of arcs in the network with this state as their starting state
> >
> > ^c**Incoming arcs:** the set of arcs in the network with this state as their ending state
>
> **Categories:**
>
> > **Initial:** {Yes No}
> >
> > *Only an initial state can be without incoming arcs.*
> >
> > **Terminal:** {Yes No}
> >
> > *Only a terminal state can be without outgoing arcs.*

ARC

> **Describes:** a transition in the network
>
> **Roles:**
>
> > **Label:** a word or a *lexical category*   2–10
> >
> > **Starting state:** a state
> >
> > **Ending state:** a state
> >
> > *An arc is a connection between two states. It can connect a state to itself, in which case its starting state and ending state are the same.*
>
> **Predicates:**
>
> > An arc matches a word if the label of the arc is:
> > - the word, or
> > - a lexical category to which *the word belongs.*   2–10
> >
> > **Background:** a *dictionary*   2–10

TRANSITION NETWORK

Procedures:

> *Generate a sentence using a network*   2–14
>
> Recognize a sentence using a network
>
> *Different versions will be presented in Figures 2–15, 2–19, and 2–21.*

Figure 2–13. Transition network.

Formal definition of a transition network

Figure 2–13 defines the structure of a transition network. New features of DL used in the figure include:

Roles. A network includes a set of states and a set of arcs. This is indicated by listing them both as 'Roles' associated with the network. Similarly, the roles associated with an arc are its label, starting state, and ending state. The use of the term 'role' is based on the metaphor of roles in a play. In any one performance of *Hamlet,* some person plays the role of Ophelia. Similarly, in any one arc, some particular symbol plays the role of 'label.'

Categories. States can be initial or terminal (or both). We could use the earlier notation and say that terminal state is a 'kind' of state, just as we said that variable pattern was a kind of pattern. But we do not need to give any additional definition of terminal states—all we really care about is that they are somehow identifiable as being terminal. In cases like this, we refer to the different kinds as *categories* and indicate the set of alternatives. A class of objects can be divided into categories along more than one dimension, as illustrated by having separate category sets for 'initial' and 'terminal.' The importance of this will become clear later on.

Computable roles. In addition to being able to talk about the states and arcs of a network, it is useful to be able to talk about its terminal states and initial states. These are in fact subsets of the states and the membership of a state in them is determined by its categories. If we included 'terminal states' and 'initial states' as roles with no further note, it would appear that they could be modified independently of what was in the states or how states were categorized. By marking them as *computable* (with a superscript 'c') we indicate that they can be computed from knowledge of the other roles and categories. Similarly, the incoming and outgoing arcs of a state can be determined by looking at the starting and ending states of the arcs.

There is a degree of arbitrary choice in deciding what is computed from what. We could have chosen instead to have the initial states and terminal states as separate roles (subject to the constraint that they be a subset of the states) and have the categories of a state be computable based on its membership in those sets. The reason for doing one or the other is to make it easier to specify the steps that an interpreter will take in operating with objects of these types. The reason for a particular choice is generally based on a feeling about what will produce the most understandable overall structure.

Using a knowledge base consisting of a dictionary, we can write algorithms that generate and recognize sentences using a transition network. Figure 2–14 describes a procedure for generation.

The definition in Figure 2–14 is different from the earlier definitions in one major way. It includes steps that call for *choosing* a member of a set and steps

---

Generate a sentence using a network (nondeterministic)

Purpose: Produce a sentence that matches the network

Background: a *dictionary*   2–10

Inputs: a *transition network*   2–13

Results: a sequence of words that is a sentence matched by the network

Working Structures:
  Current state: a state in the network
  Result: a sequence of words; initially empty

Basic Method:
  ■ Choose any initial state of the network and let it be the current state.
  ■ Keep repeating:
      ■Choose one of the outgoing arcs of the current state.
      ■If the label of that arc is:
          ■a word, then insert that word at the end of the result.
          ■a lexical category, then choose any word in the dictionary that
              belongs to the category and insert it at the end of the result.   2–10
      ■Assign the ending state of the chosen arc to be the current state.

Conditions: Whenever the current state becomes a terminal state:
  ■ If it has any outgoing arcs, choose either to continue or to return the
      result.
  ■ Otherwise return the result.

Figure 2–14. Schema to generate a sentence using a network.

that call for choosing whether to do something or not. The procedure definition in Figure 2–2 (for finding a match in a set of patterns) allowed an unordered search on the assumption that the answer would come out the same for any ordering. In Figure 2–14, different choices will lead to different results. In Figure 2–15, choices are even more critical in that some choices lead to failure of the procedure.

These definitions are not algorithms but *nondeterministic schemas* for algorithms. In saying that they are *nondeterministic,* we imply that they contain steps where choices are made, but we do not specify how to choose. In the schema for generation, this freedom allows for all of the different possible sentences based on the pattern to be generated. A schema containing possible failures is successful if there exists any possible combination of choices that leads to success. The recognition schema of Figure 2–15 will succeed if any set of choices leads to matching the sequence. Section 2.4 describes how a recognition schema can be turned into a fully specified algorithm. In many cases like this, it is easiest to explain what is going on by first describing the schema on the assumption that all the right choices will just happen to be made, and then to elaborate the description to specify how to do the choosing.

Recognize a sentence using a network (nondeterministic)	
Purpose: Test whether a network matches a sequence of words	
Background: a *dictionary*	2–10
Inputs: a *transition network* and a sequence of words	2–13

Working Structures:
   Current state: a state in the network
   Current arc: an arc in the network	

Basic Method:
■ Choose any initial state of the network and let it be the current state.
■ Step through words of the input doing:
  ■ Choose any of the outgoing arcs of the current state to be the current arc.
  ■ If the current arc *matches* the word, then assign the ending state of the current arc to be the current state. Otherwise fail.
	2–13

Conditions: ■ When the sequence of words runs out, if the current state is a terminal state, then succeed. Otherwise fail. ■ If at any time the current state has no outgoing arcs and the sequence of words is not finished, fail.	

Figure 2–15. Schema to recognize a sentence using a network.

A sample recognition

Instead of describing the structure of the recognition schema of Figure 2–15, we will illustrate how it applies to an example. For illustrating procedures in this section and the following one, we will use the sample input *The little orange ducks swallow flies* and the dictionary and network of Figure 2–16. This network differs from the one of Figure 2–12 in that it does not deal with pronouns but does handle the optional presence of determiners (definite and indefinite articles), as in *a wooly bear ate the honey*. Both state a and b are initial states of the network.

If we follow the recognition procedure through the sample sentence always making the right choices (the ones that will get us through the sentence), the resulting sequence of current states and current arcs is as shown in Figure 2–17. In indicating an arc, we combine its label with the letters indicating its starting and ending states, for example: $_a$DETERMINER$_b$ is the arc with label DETERMINER from state a to state b.

If a wrong choice is made along the way, it is possible to reach a state with no outgoing arcs that match the next word. For example, if we start in initial state b, there is no outgoing arc matching *the*. An example that goes further before failing is shown in Figure 2–18.

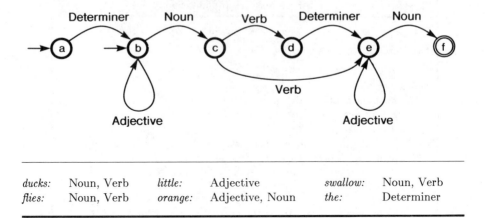

| ducks: | Noun, Verb | little: | Adjective | swallow: | Noun, Verb |
| flies: | Noun, Verb | orange: | Adjective, Noun | the: | Determiner |

Figure 2–16. A transition network and dictionary for examples.

If the word *ducks* had been matched by $_c$VERB$_e$ instead of $_c$VERB$_d$, the word *swallow* would have matched $_e$NOUN$_f$, leaving us in a terminal state with a word left in the input and nothing to do with it. This would also cause a failure.

2.4 Deterministic recognition with transition networks

In describing how a transition net can be used for recognition, we allowed the schema of Figure 2–15 to include steps with unspecified choices. If there were only one initial state, if each word were in only one lexical category, and if

Word matched	Current state	Current arc
the	a	$_a$Determiner$_b$
little	b	$_b$Adjective$_b$
orange	b	$_b$Adjective$_b$
ducks	b	$_b$Noun$_c$
swallow	c	$_c$Verb$_e$
flies	e	$_e$Noun$_f$
	f (a terminal state)	

Figure 2–17. Recognition with a network.

Word matched	Current state	Current arc
the	a	$_a$Determiner$_b$
little	b	$_b$Adjective$_b$
orange	b	$_b$Noun$_c$
ducks	c	$_c$Verb$_d$
swallow	d	—FAIL—
flies		

Figure 2–18. Failed recognition with a network.

no state had two outgoing arcs with the same label, then there would be no problem in choosing. There would always be exactly one thing to choose if the input was in fact a sentence, and there would be a failure otherwise. However, these restrictions are not realistic for natural language, and we need some way to handle multiple possibilities.

Much of Chapter 3 is concerned with techniques for exploring multiple possible parsings. This section uses simple transition nets as an example in laying out the two basic approaches: *parallel processing* and *backtracking*. The examples deal only with recognition, not parsing. The procedures do not produce results that indicate the structure of the input, but simply succeed if there is a match and fail if there is not.

Parallel processing of alternatives

In a parallel processing algorithm, when faced with a choice between alternatives, the processor takes all of them at once. It must maintain working structures that keep track of a set of current states, rather than a single one as in the procedures presented so far. Every time there is a choice to be made, a representation is produced that covers all of the alternatives.

Figure 2–19 defines an algorithm for a parallel process that recognizes sentences using a transition net. It makes use of a bookkeeping scheme based on sets of states of the network. At any point in going through the input, the 'current state set' contains all of the states that are consistent with the input thus far, for all possible choices. It is rather simple to keep track of this state set but, as we will see later, the records kept by a parallel processor can get quite complex for more complicated structures.

Figure 2–20 shows the succession of possible states in a parallel recognition of the sample sentence given in the previous section, using the dictionary and network of Figure 2–16. It shows a successful recognition, since the final state set includes state f, which is a terminal state.

Recognize a sentence using a network (parallel)

Purpose: Test whether a network matches a sequence of words

Inputs: a *transition network* and a sequence of words   2–13

Working Structures:

> **Current state set:** a set of states
> *At any time, this is the set of all states that could have resulted from any sequence of choices in advancing to the current position in the input sequence.*

Basic Method:

- Let the current state set be the set of all initial states of the network.
- Step through words of the input doing:
  - If the current state set is empty, fail.
  - Otherwise reassign the current state set to be the result of *advancing the current state set* over the word using the network.   §
- If the current state set contains any terminal states, succeed. Otherwise fail.

Procedures:

Advance a state set over a word using a network

Purpose: Produce a new state set resulting from all possible ways of taking arcs that start from members of the previous state set and that match the word

Inputs: a set of states, a word, and a transition network

Working Structures:

> **New state set:** a set of states; initially empty

Results: the new state set at the end of the process

Basic Method:

- For each state in the given set of states do:
  For each arc in the outgoing arcs of that state do:
  If *the arc matches the word*, add its ending state to the new   2–13
  state set.
  The primitive operation of adding an element to a set is defined such that duplicate elements are not added.

- Return the new state set.

Figure 2–19. Parallel procedure to recognize a sentence using a network.

Word matched	Current state set	Arcs that match	New state set
the	{a b}	$_a$Determiner$_b$	{b}
little	{b}	$_b$Adjective$_b$	{b}
orange	{b}	$_b$Adjective$_b$ $_b$Noun$_c$	{b c}
ducks	{b c}	$_b$Noun$_c$ $_c$Verb$_d$ $_c$Verb$_e$	{c d e}
swallow	{c d e}	$_c$Verb$_d$ $_c$Verb$_e$ $_e$Noun$_f$	{d e f}
flies	{d e f}	$_e$Noun$_f$	{f}

Figure 2–20. Trace of a parallel recognition.

Backtracking

A second strategy for dealing with choices is to plunge ahead with a single alternative while keeping track of the others that could have been selected and going back to them later if necessary. If at any point the process fails, it can *backtrack* to somewhere a previous a choice was made, take a different alternative, and try again. In the simplest method, called *chronological backtracking,* the most recently taken decision is the one that is changed. More sophisticated backtracking procedures have been developed and are discussed in Chapter 7, but for the purposes of this chapter and Chapter 3 we will use the simple form.

One of the critical factors in designing an algorithm is the way its work increases with the length of the input sentence. In using the parallel processing algorithm of Figure 2–19 with a transition network, the amount of work will be *linearly* proportional to the length of the sentence, since the processing at each step will never be larger than a constant factor times the number of states in the network. At each step through the input sequence, the set of states in the current state set (and in the new state set) must be a subset of the total set of states.

The backtracking algorithm of Figure 2–21 can do an amount of work that is *exponentially* related to the length of the sentence. The number of different *paths* that could be tried is multiplied by a constant factor for each additional word in the input, since it represents a new choice between a set of possible arcs that is independent of the set of choices made by the previous words in getting to that state.

Of course, if the ordering of the arcs is 'lucky,' the backtracking algorithm will go right through the sentence without considering any alternatives, while the parallel algorithm must follow all alternatives as it goes along with no chance of saving work. The tradeoffs between these strategies will be discussed in much more detail as they apply to the context-free grammars of Chapter 3.

Figure 2–21 defines an algorithm for recognition using backtracking, which keeps a *stack* of records indicating places where a choice was made. Each time the process advances to a new position in the input by matching an arc against

---

Recognize a sentence using a network (backtracking)

Purpose: Test whether a network matches a sequence of words

Inputs: a *transition network* and a sequence of words   2–13

Working Structures:

    Current arc: an arc

    Current position: an integer representing a position in the input
    sequence

    Stack: a stack of *records*; initially containing a single record with: §
        ■ position = 1
        ■ arcs-to-try = all arcs in the network whose starting state is an
           initial state

Basic Method: Keep repeating:

■ If the stack is empty, fail.

■ Assign the position from the top record on the stack to be the current
  position.

■ Remove the first arc from the arcs-to-try of the top record and assign
  it to be the current arc.

■ If the top record now has no arcs-to-try, pop it off the stack.

■ If *the current arc matches the word* at the current position in the input   2–13
  sequence then:
    ■ If the position is the last of the input sequence, then:
        ■ If the ending state of the current arc is a terminal state, succeed.
        ■ If it is not a terminal state, go on. (*This will be a backtrack*)
    ■ If it is not the last position, push onto the stack a new record
      with:
        ■ position = the current position + 1
        ■ arcs-to-try = the outgoing arcs of the ending state of the
           current arc.

    If the current arc does not match, the process goes on to the next arc.

Classes:

R **E** **C** **O** **R** **D**	**Describes:** a record used to keep track of alternatives that have not been tried yet
	Roles:
	Arcs-to-try: a sequence of arcs
	In order to put arcs into a sequence (rather than an unordered set) the network needs an ordering convention, as described in the text.
	Position: an integer
	The position in the input sequence that contains the word to be matched by one of the arcs

---

Figure 2–21. Recognition with backtracking.

a word, a new record is created showing all of the possible arcs that could be taken from the state just reached. This record is 'pushed' (added) at the 'top' of the stack. As arcs are tested for a match with the input word at the next position, they are removed from the top record, and when a record contains no more arcs it is 'popped' (removed) from the stack. When a record is popped from the stack, the process will continue trying arcs from the previous top record. Since this previous record was created for an earlier position in the sequence, the process has 'backtracked.' If an arc ever matches the last word of the sequence and ends in a terminal state, the recognition has succeeded. If the stack runs out of things to try, it fails.

In order to use a transition network with backtracking, there must be a convention for deciding in what order to try the arcs. This is a choice that can have significance in a real network, since much work can be saved by putting the more likely arcs first. However, it cannot change the final outcome of success versus failure. Since backtracking is a way of trying all alternatives, any successful combination of choices will be found eventually, no matter what the order. For demonstration purposes, we will take arcs in alphabetical order on the starting state, label, and ending state. For example, $_a\text{DET}_b$ precedes $_b\text{ADJ}_b$, $_b\text{ADJ}_b$ precedes $_b\text{NOUN}_c$, and $_c\text{VERB}_d$ precedes $_c\text{VERB}_e$.

Figure 2–22 on the following page follows the backtrack parser through the sample sentence *the little orange ducks swallow flies,* showing the working structures at each step of the processing. The stack is shown first, with the top record at the left. Records are printed as: '[n: $_i\text{CATEGORY}_j$ $_i\text{CATEGORY}_k$...],' showing the position and the sequence of arcs-to-try. The category names for determiners and adjectives are abbreviated to DET and ADJ. The current arc is always the first arc in the top record and the word is the word at the position indicated by that record. The result can be a 'match' (in which case the arc is removed from the top record, the record is popped if it is empty, and either the recognition is done or a new record is pushed onto the stack) or a 'no match' (in which case the arc is removed from the top record and that record is 'popped' if it has no more arcs).

For the first three steps of Figure 2–22, everything goes forward easily—the first arc tried always matches and the remainder are saved away on the stack. When $_b\text{ADJ}_b$ is matched against *ducks* it fails, but $_b\text{NOUN}_c$ succeeds and the forward process continues. Since there are no other arcs to try matching against *ducks,* the record is popped. When $_c\text{VERB}_d$ is matched against *swallow,* it becomes apparent that a wrong choice has been made, since the only arc from state d is for a DET, which will not match *flies.* When the record for position 6 (*flies*) is popped, the one for 5 (*swallow*) becomes the top again and a different arc, $_c\text{VERB}_e$, is tried and succeeds. When the terminal state f is reached at the end of the input, the process succeeds. It needed to backtrack only once due to the fortuitous ordering of the arcs.

Stack	Word	Current Arc	Actions
[1: $_a$Det$_b$ $_b$Adj$_b$ $_b$Noun$_c$]			
	the	$_a$Det$_b$	Match
[2: $_b$Adj$_b$ $_b$Noun$_c$][1: $_b$Adj$_b$ $_b$Noun$_c$]			
	little	$_b$Adj$_b$	Match
[3: $_b$Adj$_b$ $_b$Noun$_c$][2: $_b$Noun$_c$][1: $_b$Adj$_b$ $_b$Noun$_c$]			
	orange	$_b$Adj$_b$	Match
[4: $_b$Adj$_b$ $_b$Noun$_c$][3: $_b$Noun$_c$][2: $_b$Noun$_c$][1: $_b$Adj$_b$ $_b$Noun$_c$]			
	ducks	$_b$Adj$_b$	No match
[4: $_b$Noun$_c$][3: $_b$Noun$_c$][2: $_b$Noun$_c$][1: $_b$Adj$_b$ $_b$Noun$_c$]			
	ducks	$_b$Noun$_c$	Match and pop
[5: $_c$Verb$_d$ $_c$Verb$_e$][3: $_b$Noun$_c$][2: $_b$Noun$_c$][1: $_b$Adj$_b$ $_b$Noun$_c$]			
	swallow	$_c$Verb$_d$	Match
[6: $_d$Det$_e$][5: $_c$Verb$_e$][3: $_b$Noun$_c$][2: $_b$Noun$_c$][1: $_b$Adj$_b$ $_b$Noun$_c$]			
	flies	$_d$Det$_e$	No match and pop
[5: $_c$Verb$_e$][3: $_b$Noun$_c$][2: $_b$Noun$_c$][1: $_b$Adj$_b$ $_b$Noun$_c$]			
	swallow	$_c$Verb$_e$	Match and pop
[6: $_e$Adj$_e$ $_e$Noun$_f$][3: $_b$Noun$_c$][2: $_b$Noun$_c$][1: $_b$Adj$_b$ $_b$Noun$_c$]			
	flies	$_e$Adj$_e$	No match
[6: $_e$Noun$_f$][3: $_b$Noun$_c$][2: $_b$Noun$_c$][1: $_b$Adj$_b$ $_b$Noun$_c$]			
	flies	$_e$Noun$_f$	Match and succeed

Figure 2–22. A backtracking recognition.

In fact, (as explored in the exercises) even relatively simple networks can produce large amounts of backtracking. In particular, it is important to note that when backtracking happens, there are no records left around about any of the work that was done beyond that position, so it must be redone as the process goes forward again.

Further Reading for Chapter 2

Pattern-based computer programs. ELIZA is described in Weizenbaum (1966). A program that later developed the pattern concept in a much more elaborate way was Colby's (1976) PARRY, which played the role of a paranoid mental patient instead of a psychiatrist! Raphael's SIR program is described along with several other early natural language programs in *Semantic Information Processing,* edited by Minsky (1967).

Word classes. For more information on word classes from a traditional linguistic point of view, see any of the books listed in Chapter 1 as references for the history of linguistics. In particular, Chapter 5 of Lyons's *Introduction to Theoretical Linguistics* deals with many of these issues. For an encyclopedic account of word classes, see Quirk et al., *A Grammar of Contemporary English.*

Networks and regular languages. There are a number of texts describing finite state machines (transition networks) and formal languages from a mathematical point of view. Minsky's *Computation: Finite and Infinite Machines* is easy reading, while Hopcroft and Ullman's *Formal Languages and Their Relation to Automata* is more comprehensive and serves as a standard textbook for many courses. For a discussion of algorithms in general that will serve as background for the formalization of computational processes, see Knuth, *The Art of Computer Programming,* Volume 1.

Backtracking. Backtracking was proposed as a programming technique by Golomb and Baumert (1965). It is a standard feature of programming languages designed for use in artificial intelligence, as described in Bobrow and Raphael's 1974 survey of 'New programming languages for artificial intelligence research.' For a discussion of the problems inherent in chronological backtracking and a description of some more sophisticated alternatives, see Nilsson (1980).

Exercises for Chapter 2

Exercises for Section 2.1

2.1 It was pointed out in the text that the procedures described in Section 2.1 could be modified to use recognition-response pairs like those of ELIZA. Write a new version of the procedure in Figure 2–2 which takes a sequence of words and a set of 'pairs,' each containing two patterns with variables: a *recognition* pattern and a *response* pattern. It should find a pair whose recognition pattern matches the sequence and generate a response from the response pattern using the same bindings.

2.2 In Exercise 2.13, we will create a procedure for matching a pattern with variables that allows a single variable to match a sequence of words. For example, applying the recognition-response pair: 'My 1 is 2 → What if your 1 were not 2' to the sentence *My left arm is about to fall off* would produce *What if your left arm were not about to fall off*. Assuming such an extension, analyze carefully what the responses would be to the following inputs:

> *My head is on my shoulders*
> *My problem is that you hate me*
> *My problem is how to pay you*
> *My brother said your car is bigger than mine*
> *My job is working in the mine*

Describe the changes to the procedure that would be needed to produce responses that are syntactically appropriate (don't worry about their therapeutic appropriateness!). What kinds of problems stand in the way of a general solution within the framework of pattern-matching? The algorithm actually used by ELIZA gets three of these examples right and two of them wrong.

Exercises for Section 2.2

2.3 Give some arguments on both sides of the issue as to whether the English possessive *'s* should be considered a separate word or not. Consider sentences like *I saw the man you met in Ankara last year's brother*.

2.4 Consider the three linguistic frames:

> 1) *Miss Muffett ___ to eat whey with curd.*
> 2) *Sybill ___ her man to be a good cook.*
> 3) *Stu was ___ to be on time.*

a) Classify the following verbs according to which of these frames they can fill: *asked, preferred, condescended, believed, promised, wanted, tried, considered, accepted, forced, expected.*

b) Find frames that show that no two of the above verbs have the identical distribution.

c) Can you find a verb which, as far as you can tell, has the same distribution as 1) *promise*, 2) *ask*, 3) *believe?*

2.5 Try to identify every word in the following paragraph by its traditional word class.

> *It is of course true that quality is much more difficult to 'handle' than quantity, just as the exercise of judgment is a higher function than the ability to count and calculate. Quantitative differences can be more easily grasped and certainly more easily defined than qualitative differences; their concreteness is beguiling and gives them the appearance of scientific precision, even when this precision has been purchased by the suppression of vital differences of quality. The great majority of economists is still pursuing the absurd ideal of making their 'science' as scientific and precise as physics, as if there were no qualitative differences between mindless atoms and men made in the image of God.*

2.6 Explain how the concept of closed and open word classes relates to the fact that it is relatively easy to deal with some of the sex biases of language by creating new words such as *repairperson* and *congressperson*, but that it is extremely difficult to find an appropriate word to use in the sentence *When the chairperson brings the meeting to order, ___ must pound the gavel with vigor.*

Exercises for Section 2.3

2.7 Which of the following sequences can be described (recognized or generated) by this transition network:

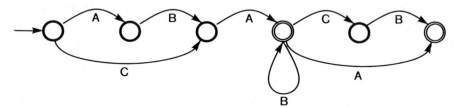

(1) ab (2) ca (3) cb (4) cabbb (5) ababa (6) bacb (7) cabcb (8) ababcbc

2.8 Write a regular expression corresponding to the transition network in the previous exercise. Use the standard convention for regular languages that an asterisk means *zero or more* repetitions and the superscript '+' is used to mean *one or more*. For example, 'a*b' matches the expressions 'b, ab, aab, aaab,...' while 'a⁺b' matches all but the first of them.

2.9 Draw a transition network corresponding to the regular expression:

$$(a \lor (b\ a\ b))^* (b^* \lor a)$$

2.10 Draw a transition network that will match the expressions for time of day in English, such as *one thirty-two and twelve seconds, half past three*, and *six fifteen a.m.*. The basic lexical categories will include things like:

> Hour-Number: *one, two,... , twelve*
> Minute-Number: *one, two,... , fifty-nine*
> Fraction: *quarter, half*

There will also be arcs whose labels are specific words such as *to, past, after, till, o'clock, a.m.*, and *p.m.*

2.11 (*For programmers*) If the definitions of this chapter were implemented in a straightforward way, there would be a data structure for a transition network that contained structures for arcs and states. Networks can be compiled into a more efficient form in which the states of the network correspond to states of the program. Describe or demonstrate how a transition network can be compiled so that a state corresponds to a location (e.g., a GO TO label) in a program.

Exercises for Section 2.4

2.12 If we had chosen a different convention for ordering arcs, the backtracking process described in Figure 2–22 would have gone differently. Assume reverse alphabetical order on each arc's starting vertex, label, and ending vertex. That is, the arcs of the network in Figure 2–16 are ordered: $_e$NOUN$_f$, $_e$ADJ$_e$, $_d$DET$_e$, $_c$VERB$_e$, $_c$VERB$_d$, $_b$NOUN$_c$, $_b$ADJ$_b$, $_a$DET$_b$. Generate a trace like that of Figure 2–22 using the same input sentence.

2.13 If we want variables in a pattern to match sequences of words, there is a problem in knowing what to do as we proceed from left to right. For example, the pattern '1 X Y' will match the sequence 'YXY' with the variable matching the first 'Y' and will match 'YXYXY' if the variable matches 'YXY'. If the procedure simply takes the element of the pattern and sequence in order, it will not be able to decide whether the first 'X' should be included in the variable or matched against the 'X' in the pattern.

a) Write a nondeterministic schema for matching a pattern with variables to a sequence of words, which allows a variable to match any sequence of *one or more* words in the input.

b) Write a backtracking procedure that deterministically matches the same kinds of patterns.

2.14 In introducing the problem of dealing with choices in networks, we commented that a network would be deterministic (involve no choices) if it had a single initial state, if no two arcs with the same starting state had the same label, and if no two arcs with different labels could match the same word. In fact, any transition network of the kind defined in Figure 2–13 can be used to produce a deterministic network that is *weakly equivalent* in that it will accept and reject exactly the same inputs. The new network will have a state for each subset of the states in the original and each of its arcs will match a particular word, not a lexical category. Describe how to derive this network from the original network and dictionary.

2.15 (*For programmers*) In a recursive language such as LISP, it is possible to use the internal stack on which variables are bound as the means of keeping the stack for backtracking. Write a recursive procedure for recognition with a transition network in which the stack is maintained this way.

Chapter 3

Context-free Grammars
and Parsing

This chapter introduces context-free grammar, a formalism for describing languages that has been widely used because of its simplicity and clarity. A formal linguist describes the structures of a language by devising a collection of *rules,* called a *grammar,* that can be used in a systematic way to generate the sentences of a language. The form and functioning of these rules differs among different forms of generative grammar. A context-free grammar provides an especially simple way of describing the structures of a language and of setting up a correspondence between the knowledge structures, the structures generated in producing or recognizing a sentence, and the processes of recognition and production.

Context-free grammars are also known as *immediate constituent grammars* (by traditional linguists), *Backus normal form* (by programming language designers), and *recursive patterns* (in some computer applications). They are one particular kind of a more general class of *phrase structure grammars* (described in Chapter 4), which are the basis for generative linguistics and for most computer systems that manipulate either natural language or computer languages.

As a background against which to view the details of context-free grammar, Section 3.1 introduces phrase structure and raises some general issues about how structures can be described. Section 3.2 gives a formal definition of context-free grammars and presents the concept of *derivation.* Sections 3.3 through 3.6 deal with the problem of *recognizing* and *parsing* sentences using a stored knowledge base of context-free rules. Those sections lay out the basic dimensions of parsing strategy and give examples of a number of parsing techniques that have been developed.

Difficulties arise in applying the basic ideas of phrase structure to complex languages (including all natural languages), but in this chapter we will ignore these and concentrate on what can be done with the formalism. Later chapters present some of the extensions that have been proposed to handle real languages. These extensions gain the power to describe more of the properties of language, often at the price of losing the simplicity of pure context-free grammars.

3.1 Three approaches to structure

The patterns described by the simple transition networks of Chapter 2 have a kind of 'flat' quality. Our intuitions about language call for some kind of *constituent structure* that is not captured by describing a sentence as matching a sequence of arcs through a network. Sentences are made up of 'chunks' or 'phrases,' and this structuring is important for how they communicate meaning.

One of the major themes of linguistics throughout its history has been an attempt to describe these structures and the ways in which they fit together. There have been many different formulations of the rules for language structure, and their details depend on a basic attitude towards how structures are best described. These views of structure are not particular to linguistics. They apply equally well to any study of objects (physical, mental, or social) that are describable as being made up of parts that in turn are made up of smaller parts.

The head and modifier approach

Many traditional presentations of grammar describe structures in terms of a basic simple pattern that is elaborated, or *modified*. For example, the underlying structure of a sentence can be thought of as a noun followed by a verb, with additional words (such as articles and adjectives) modifying the noun and others (such as adverbs) modifying the verb. Modifiers can themselves be modified (by words such as adverbs) to produce a multi-layered structure. At each level, there is a *head*, which is a single word and which may have one or more *modifiers*.

Figure 3–1 shows two different diagrams of a head and modifier analysis of the sentence *The glorious sun will shine in the winter*. The first is a traditional grammar school *sentence diagram* using a formalism devised toward the end of the last century by Reed and Kellogg. The second is a *dependency structure* based on a formalism called *dependency grammar,* which was originally developed in connection with early programs for machine translation. In both the diagrams of Figure 3–1, modifiers are placed below the word they modify and are connected to it by a line. In the dependency grammar version, even the subject of the sentence is viewed as a modifier. The head of the sentence is the verb *shine*, which conveys what it is that happens. The fact that the *sun* does the shining is a modification.

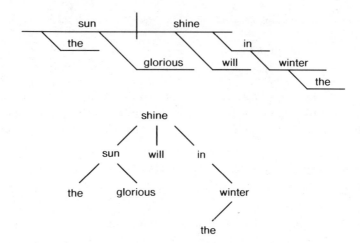

Figure 3–1. Head and modifier structures for a simple sentence.

The head and modifier approach has held an important position in linguistics for reasons involving both meaning and syntax. In trying to associate word patterns with meanings, we find that the concept of modification corresponds well to our intuitive notions of description. A noun tells what an object basically is, while adjectives provide further description. A verb tells what happened, while adverbs tell the manner, time, place, and other details of how it was done.

This correspondence between word structure and conceptual structure is very useful in looking at language as an integrated system for conveying meaning.

The head and modifier approach, as formalized in *dependency grammar*, formed the basis for some early approaches to question answering, such as Protosynthex I (Simmons, Klein, and McConlogue, 1964). It also influenced some of the current approaches to natural language, including Schank's (1975) *conceptual dependency* and Wilks' (1975a,b) *semantic templates*. Protosynthex I stored the sentences of a children's encyclopedia and when asked a question, it tried to retrieve an appropriate sentence as the answer. Both the stored sentences and the question were parsed into dependency structures. For example, the two sentences *Worms eat grass* and *Horses with worms eat grain* were represented by the structures of Figure 3–2. In the Protosynthex I version of dependency grammar, the main verb depended on the subject rather than the other way around.

When asked the question *What do worms eat?*, Protosynthex I found (by means of an index) all the sentences containing the two words *worms* and *eat*. It then checked to see if in any of them the word *eat* depended on the word *worms*, as in the leftmost tree of Figure 3–2, since a sentence whose dependency structure matched that of the question would be more likely to

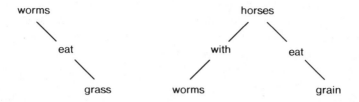

Figure 3–2. Dependency structures used for question answering.

provide a relevant answer. In this case, the sentence *Worms eat grass* would be printed out, but *Horses with worms eat grain* would not, since its dependency structure does not match. This was an extremely simplistic form of question answering. It could work only if the relevant answer appeared directly in the stored knowledge, and even then it knew only roughly whether the selected sentence was appropriate. But the use of dependency structures enabled the system to be more selective than a simple keyword search.

At a more purely syntactic level, many phenomena of language follow closely along the lines of head-modifier structure. Most languages have rules of *agreement* or *concord* that are conveniently expressed in terms of modification. For example, in Spanish both the adjective and determiner depend for their form on the number and gender of the noun they modify, as in: *la vaca morada, las vacas moradas, el caballo morado, los caballos morados (the purple cow, the purple cows, the purple horse, the purple horses)*. In each of these sentences, the determiner *(la, las, el, los)* and the ending on the adjective *morad-* are selected to match the noun. This feature of head and modifier analysis was a motivation for its use in the early programs for machine translation. It provided a direct handle on the choices that needed to be made in forming the detailed word structure and endings in the target language.

The formal theory of dependency grammar has emphasized ways of describing structures rather than how the system's permanent knowledge is structured or how a sentence is processed. It does not address in a systematic way the problem of finding the correct dependency structure for a given sequence of words. In systems that use dependency as a way of characterizing structure, the parsing process is generally of an *ad hoc* nature, as will be discussed in Chapter 7.

The immediate constituent approach

The simplest uniform way to describe constituent structures is to extend the notion of pattern as developed in Chapter 2 by making patterns *recursive*. The elements of a pattern are not limited to words and lexical categories, but can also include the names of other patterns. This allows common sequences to be factored out and provides a kind of nesting that captures some of the structure visible in the head and modifier approach. As a simple example, consider the sentence pattern represented of by the network of Figure 2–16, used as an example in Chapter 2. In regular expression form, it could be written as:

{Determiner} Adjective* Noun Verb {{Determiner} Adjective* Noun}

By creating a pattern for *noun phrase* (labeled 'NP'), we can define a sentence ('S') as:

$$\begin{aligned} \text{NP} &= \{\text{Determiner}\}\ \text{Adjective* Noun} \\ \text{S} &= \text{NP Verb \{NP\}} \end{aligned}$$

In matching a set of patterns like these against a sequence of words, we are in effect assigning the sentence a *phrase structure*, due to the nesting of sequences within one another. The sentence *The little orange ducks swallow flies* has three constituents: *the little orange ducks* (an NP), *swallow* (a VERB), and *flies* (another NP). In this case, each of these constituents is either a word or in turn made up of individual words. However, immediate constituent grammars allow any constituent itself to be a constituent structure. Figure 3–3 illustrates three different notations for representing constitutent structure, using a more complex set of patterns which will be introduced in Section 3.2. The bracketed text notation is used when for typographical reasons it would be inconvenient to use a two-dimensional form. A pair of brackets is labeled with the name of the pattern (appearing just after the opening bracket) and contains all of the elements that make up the instance of the pattern. When a pattern element is matched by a single word, that word appears. When it is matched by another whole pattern, the matching of that pattern is laid out within its own set of brackets.

The box notation illustrates graphically the fact that one pattern is made up of elements each of which can be another pattern. The more usual graphical notation uses *trees,* a formal structure with general applicability for representing a recursive organization based on two relationships—*constituency* and *order.* Each object bears the constituency relationship to a single object called its *parent.* Lines connect objects upward to their parent (or, conversely, downwards to their children). In this case, the children are the immediate constituents of their parent. The children of any one parent are ordered by the order relationship, in this case corresponding to the left-to-right order in which they appear in the sentence.

Figure 3–4 gives a formal definition of tree structures that will be used in the rest of this chapter. It includes a role for the 'contents' for each node, as well as its parent and children. In using tree structures to represent immediate constituent structure, each node corresponds to a word or phrase. The contents are a *label* indicating which pattern it corresponds to. Its children are its *immediate constituents*, which in turn represent words or other phrases made up of constituents.

Bracketed text

$[_S$ $[_{NP}$ the $[_{NP2}$ glorious sun $]]$

$[_{VP}$ $[_{VP2}$ will shine $]$ $[_{PP}$ in $[_{NP}$ the $[_{NP2}$ winter $]]]]]$

Nested Boxes

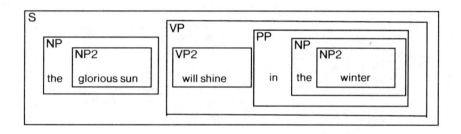

Tree Structure

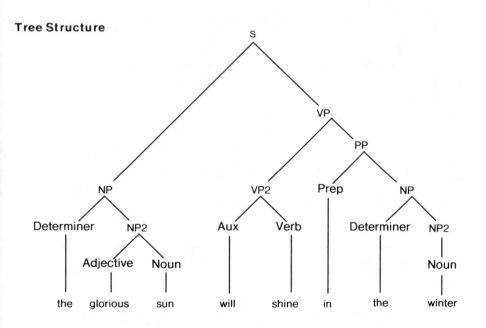

Figure 3–3. Representations for constitutent structure.

Describes: any formal object with a recursive branching structure

Roles:

   Nodes: a set of tree nodes with a *common root*   §

   ^c**Root:** the one *root node* in the tree   §

   ^c**Leaves:** the set of all *leaf nodes* in the tree   §

Classes:

> **Describes:** the basic component of a tree structure
>
> **Roles:**
>
>   **Parent:** a tree node or nothing
>   **Children:** a sequence of tree nodes each having this node
>   as its parent; possibly empty
>
>   *The children are ordered—a sequence, not just a set.*
>
> **Contents:**
>
> *Depends on the kind of tree node. Different subclasses of tree nodes will have different contents associated with each node. The simplest form of tree node has no contents and is used to represent just the branching structure.*
>
> **Predicates:**
>
> > A node is a <u>root node</u> if it has no parent.
>
> > A node is a <u>leaf node</u> if it has no children.
>
> > A node (A) is a <u>descendant</u> of a node (B) if either:
> > - the parent of A is B, or
> > - the parent of A is a descendant of B.
>
> > A node (A) is an <u>ancestor</u> of a node (B) if B is a descendant of A.
>
> **Kinds of Tree node:**
>
> *Dependency, Phrase structure, Role structure*   3–6

Predicates:

> A set of <u>nodes has a common root</u> if there is a node (A) in the set such that:
> - A is a root node, and
> - Every node in the set other than A is a descendant of A.

Figure 3–4. Tree structure.

The slot and filler approach

The motivation for analyzing the structure of a sequence of words is that the result is to be used in some further analysis or processing, such as translation or comprehension of meaning. The fact that there is a particular sequence of recognizable elements is one aspect of structure, but this does not capture *functional* relationships. For example, the pattern 'NP VERB NP' for sentences does not specify that the two instances of NP play different *roles*—one is the subject, and the other is the direct object.

In a slot and filler (or *role structure*) approach, the pattern for each kind of phrase is described as a sequence of named *slots* or *roles*, each of which corresponds to a *filler* in the sequence to which it is matched. Each pattern element specifies the kind of word or phrase it can match (as with the constituent structure approach), and also the name of a role that the word or phrase plays in the pattern as a whole. A role name can appear only once, but the objects filling different roles may be of the same kind. A slot and filler pattern lists all of the potential elements and will match phrases containing any combination of them in the right order. Patterns can have roles (such as the describers, classifiers, and qualifiers of a noun phrase) that are filled by a sequence of items, rather than by a single item.

Figure 3–5 illustrates a slot and filler pattern for English noun phrases. It makes use of an asterisk to indicate that a single slot is filled by a sequence of elements of the same type. Although it is still a simplification compared to the full range of English constructs, it covers a wide variety of phrases, including those with all slots filled, such as *All the last three successful game show contestants from Iowa,* and those with only some slots filled, such as *a tree* and *three blind mice.*

It is important to recognize that in a slot and filler analysis, role names are different from phrase types. Thus a word that is a NOUN can be the HEAD of a noun group or one of its CLASSIFIERS. This distinction between labels of

Role name	Filler type	Example
Pre-determiner	Pre-determiner	*all*
Determiner	Determiner	*the*
Ordinal	Ordinal	*first*
Cardinal	Cardinal	*three*
Describers	Adjective*	*big red*
Classifiers	Noun*	*steel fire*
Head	Noun	*hydrants*
Qualifiers	(PP or Clause)*	*without covers that you can see*

Figure 3–5. A slot and filler pattern for noun phrases.

function and those related to *form* will be discussed in Chapter 6. However, for classes such as ORDINAL and CARDINAL that have only one function, we have chosen for simplicity to use the same name for both the class and the role.

In a slot and filler analysis, there is still a recursive constituent structure. For example, in an analysis of the sentence *The glorious sun will shine in January*, there is a slot for SUBJECT filled by an NP, which in turn has slots filled for DETERMINER (*the*), DESCRIBERS (*glorious*), and HEAD (*sun*). If there were a simple one-to-one correspondence between slots and the sequence of elements in the constituent structure, this approach would be different only in providing a convenient way of referring to elements of the structure without mentioning their position. However, as we will see in the later chapters, it is often useful to postulate sets of slots along different dimensions, with the same element filling a slot in each dimension. Even along a single dimension, we may want to describe an element as filling more than one slot. In this sense, a slot and filler analysis deals with *roles*, rather than *parts*, as discussed in the description of DL in Section A.2.

The slot and filler approach has served as a standard form of linguistic description in traditional grammar and in much of the structural paradigm. Transformational linguists have not generally dealt with functional considerations (the explicit analysis of role structure), arguing that they add no syntactic information that is not already expressed in the constituent structure. Other formalisms, such as systemic grammar (described in Chapter 6), have made extensive use of a slot and filler approach. The computational paradigm, with

---

Dependency tree (head and modifier)

The contents of each node is a word, called the *head*. The children of the node are its *modifiers*.

Phrase structure tree (immediate constituent)

Each node has a sequence of children and has as its contents a *label*, which is either a syntactic category or a word. Leaf nodes have words as their labels and all other nodes have syntactic categories.

Role structure tree (slot and filler)

Each node has a sequence of children and a label, as with a phrase structure tree. In addition, it has a *role table* (called a *register table* in Chapter 5), which associates role names with other nodes, sequences of nodes, or symbols. Each key in the role table is called a *slot* and the corresponding entry is its *filler*.

Figure 3–6.   Three kinds of tree structure.

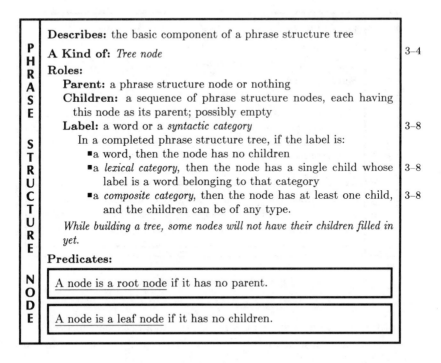

Figure 3–7. Node of a phrase structure tree.

its emphasis on integrating the analysis of different levels of language structuring, has reintroduced slot and filler notions in several forms. For the purpose of studying basic syntactic analysis strategies in this chapter, we will use context-free grammars, which deal only with immediate constituent structure. Chapters 5 and 6 describe uses of the slot and filler approach in dealing with more complex linguistic issues.

Summary of structure types

Figure 3–6 summarizes the different kinds of structuring, extending the basic formal definition of trees (Figure 3–4) by specifying the contents of a node in each type of structure. Only phrase structure trees are given a full DL definition in this chapter (in Figure 3–7), since we will be using them in defining procedures for recognition and parsing. In Chapter 5, a version of role structure nodes will be defined and used for parsing with augmented transition networks.

The labels associated with nodes in a phrase structure tree are either words or *syntactic categories,* a formalization of pattern names (like S and NP). Every

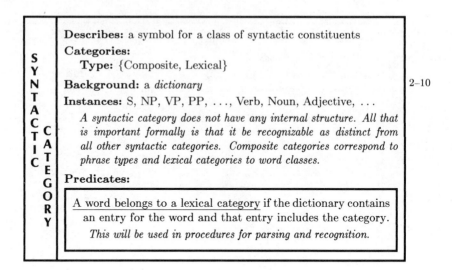

Figure 3–8. Syntactic categories.

word or phrase can be assigned to one or more syntactic categories. Figure 3–8 gives a DL definition which has little formal content, but specifies the existence of the class.

3.2 Rules and derivations

A context-free grammar consists of a set of *rules,* each representing a labeled pattern to be matched against a sequence of constituents. In the most commonly used notation, the pattern name is followed by an arrow, followed by the sequence of symbols (syntactic categories or words) that make it up, as illustrated in Figure 3–9. This simple grammar covers the same sentences as the network of Figure 2–16 in Chapter 2. It includes patterns for sentence (S),

$$
\begin{aligned}
\text{S} &\rightarrow \text{NP VP} \\
\text{NP} &\rightarrow \text{Determiner NP2} \\
\text{NP} &\rightarrow \text{NP2} \\
\text{NP2} &\rightarrow \text{Adjective NP2} \\
\text{NP2} &\rightarrow \text{Noun} \\
\text{VP} &\rightarrow \text{Verb} \\
\text{VP} &\rightarrow \text{Verb NP}
\end{aligned}
$$

Figure 3–9. A simple grammar.

noun phrase (NP), and verb phrase (VP), making use of the standard syntactic categories from transformational grammar. In addition, a separate pattern (NP2) is used to stand for a structure containing nouns and adjectives but no determiner. Rules for constituents like this one that are parts of the more traditional constituents are needed in writing a grammar that fully characterizes a language. A general definition for rules and context-free grammars appears in Figure 3–10.

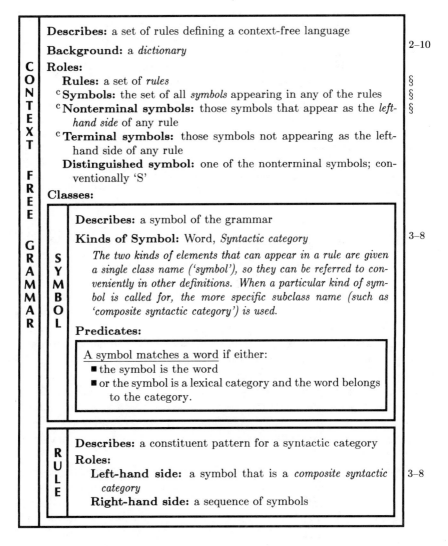

Figure 3–10. Context-free grammar.

Generate a phrase structure tree (non-deterministic)

Purpose: Produce a phrase structure tree using a context-free grammar

Background: a *context-free grammar*   3–10

Results: a *phrase structure tree*   3–7

Working Structures:
   Derived tree: a phrase structure tree; initially, a single root node
   with no children, having the distinguished symbol of the grammar
   as its label

Basic Method: Keep repeating:
- If all of the leaf nodes of the derived tree have terminal symbols of
  the grammar as their labels, then return the derived tree.
- Choose any node in the derived tree that has no children and whose
  label is a nonterminal symbol of the grammar.
- Choose any rule in the grammar whose left-hand side is the label of
  that node.
- Step through the sequence of symbols on the right hand side of the
  rule doing:
   - Create a new node with no children, whose parent is the chosen
     node, and whose label is the symbol.
   - Insert the new node at the end of the children of the chosen node.

Figure 3–11.   Schema to generate a phrase structure tree.

The derivation of sentences

Figure 3–11 gives a schema for the generation of a phrase structure tree whose
leaf nodes contain the words of a sentence. It is a schema, not an algorithm,
because it includes steps that call for making arbitrary selections—different
sentences will be derived for different choices. It is not intended as a model of
the process that actually goes on in generating a sentence for communication,
but more as a form for 'proof' that a sentence is in the language defined by
the grammar. Just as the rules of proof specify what the legal steps are but do
not say what steps to try, a grammar can be used to derive sentences. Each
application of a rule corresponds to the use of an axiom or rule of inference in
going from one step of a proof to the next. The result is a formal demonstration
that the sentence is grammatical. This idea of abstract generation is essential to
the generative paradigm and its approach to a language as a set of mathematical
objects.

Figure 3–12 illustrates how a structure for the sentence *The decorated
pieplate contains a surprise* could be derived using the grammar of Figure 3–9.
Notice that the generation as defined in Figure 3–11 is complete when all of
the leaf nodes have terminal symbols of the grammar as their labels. In order
to produce a sentence, an additional node would be produced for each of these,
containing a word belonging to the lexical class indicated by the label.

The sequence of trees in Figure 3–12 represents the first few steps of the derivation, based on a sequence of arbitrary decisions as to which unexpanded node should be worked on and which rule for it should be used. The rule is shown on the arrow between the trees representing steps in the derivation. The order of steps is partially determined, since a node must be expanded before any of its children, but there is some freedom, and the same sentence could have been produced by choosing to expand symbols in a different order. For example, the top level NP could have been expanded before its sibling VP.

The schema of Figure 3–11 builds up a tree structure which can be filled in with words to produce a sentence. It is also possible to generate sentences of the language without keeping a structural description, as in Figure 3–13. The working structure is a sequence of symbols, which includes both symbols of the grammar and words. As each rule is applied, one of the symbols is replaced with another symbol or sequence of symbols, eventually leading to a sequence containing only words. Figure 3–14 shows the steps of a derivation of the same sentence as in 3–12, in which we have chosen always to expand the leftmost symbol at each step.

In this example, the filling in of words for lexical classes is included as though there were rules such as 'Determiner → *the*.' In working with context-

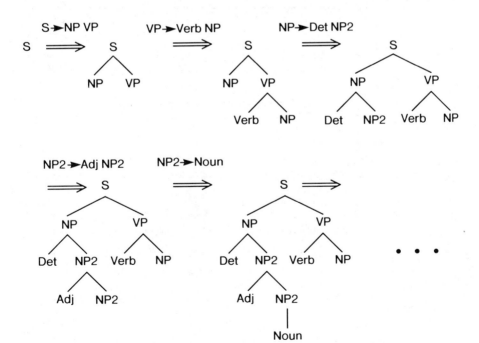

Figure 3–12. A derivation of phrase structures.

free grammars, it is sometimes convenient to think of the dictionary as a set of such rules. For each word, there is one rule for each word class (lexical category) to which it belongs. The left-hand side of the rule is the category and the right-hand side is the word itself. This allows the association of words with lexical categories to be carried out by the same mechanisms as the association of sequences of constituents with composite categories. However, in this chapter we will write the algorithms and schemas on the assumption that there is a separate dictionary associating words with word classes. This calls for slightly more complex definitions, but greatly simplifies the traces used to demonstrate their operation. We do allow a symbol on the right-hand side to be a word, so that words with special syntactic functions, such as *that, to, by,* and *which,* can be included directly in rules.

Choices and repetitive structures

In Chapter 2, we added facilities of looping and choice to the basic pattern mechanism by using transition networks. In a context-free grammar, the same

---

Generate a sentence (nondeterministic)

Purpose: Produce a sentence using a context-free grammar without deriving a tree structure

Background: a *context-free grammar* and a *dictionary*   3–10 2–10

Results: a sequence of words that is a sentence in the language

Working Structures:
   Derived sequence: a sequence, each member of which is either a syntactic category or a word; initially consisting of one occurrence of the distinguished symbol of the grammar

Basic Method: Keep repeating:
- If the derived sequence contains only words, return it as the result.
- Choose any position in the derived sequence that contains a syntactic category
- If the category is:
  - a lexical category, then choose any word in the dictionary belonging to that category, and replace the symbol at that position with the word.
  - a composite category, then choose any rule in the grammar having the symbol as its left-hand side, and replace the derived sequence with a new sequence that consists of:
    - the part of the sequence that was before the chosen position
    - the sequence of symbols specified by the right hand side of the rule
    - the part of the sequence that followed the chosen position.

Figure 3–13. Schema to derive a sentence without a tree structure.

Rule applied	Derived sequence
	S
S → NP VP	NP VP
NP → Det NP2	Det NP2 VP
Det → *the*	*the* NP2 VP
NP2 → Adj NP2	*the* Adj NP2 VP
Adj → *decorated*	*the decorated* NP2 VP
NP2 → Noun	*the decorated* Noun VP
Noun → *pieplate*	*the decorated pieplate* VP
VP → Verb NP	*the decorated pieplate* Verb NP
Verb → *contains*	*the decorated pieplate contains* NP
NP → Det NP2	*the decorated pieplate contains* Det NP2
Det → *a*	*the decorated pieplate contains a* NP2
NP2 → Noun	*the decorated pieplate contains a* Noun
Noun → *surprise*	*the decorated pieplate contains a surprise*

Figure 3–14. Derivation of a sentence without producing a tree.

effects are achieved by creating appropriate rules. By having more than one rule for a single symbol, we can account for choices and optional elements. For example, the rules of Figure 3–9 allow a noun phrase to contain a determiner or omit it, depending on the choice of the rule 'NP → DETERMINER NP2' or 'NP → NP2.' By allowing a rule to contain its own label as part of its right-hand side we can describe structures with repetition. The rule 'NP2 → ADJECTIVE NP2' can be expanded to produce an adjective followed by an unexpanded node that is still an NP2. This can be repeated any number of times to produce a string of adjectives before finally applying the rule 'NP2 → NOUN' to end the recursion.

A number of abbreviations have been developed to make it easier to combine similar patterns. One common abbreviation is to group together all rules with the same label, using vertical bars to separate their right-hand sides. Thus the two rules 'NP → DETERMINER NP2' and 'NP → NP2' could be written as 'NP → DETERMINER NP2 | NP2.' Another abbreviation allows the use of parentheses to indicate optional elements, as in 'VP → VERB (NP),' which replaces the two VP rules of Figure 3–9. Although such notations are convenient for writing complex grammars, we will not use them for the simple grammars of this chapter.

3.3 Parsing with context-free grammars

The schemas for sentence generation given in Section 3.2 are not directly applicable to the problem of how people (or computers) would go about generating sentences. To extend the abstract generation process to a model of sentence production, we would need a formalism for describing the factors that control the choice of individual rules. There is little that can be done on a purely syntactic level, and discussion of this problem will have to wait for the theories of semantics developed in the volume on meaning.

The problem of *parsing* (recognizing sentences and assigning them structures) can be dealt with more directly as a syntactic problem. Many techniques have been developed to apply generative grammars in a uniform way to analyze the structure of sentences. Figure 3–15 illustrates the relationship between stored knowledge and assigned structures in the use of a parser. It is a more specific example of the general organization discussed in Chapter 1 and illustrated in Figure 1–6.

A parser uses a parsing algorithm, along with a grammar and dictionary, to produce a phrase structure tree that corresponds to a given sequence of words. There is a direct correspondence between the rules of a grammar and the structures it assigns. As in the derivation trees of Section 3.2, each non-leaf node in the *parse tree* (the phrase structure tree produced in parsing) corresponds to a single rule in the grammar, whose left-hand side is the label of the node, and whose right-hand side corresponds to the children. Each leaf node is a word in the sequence. A *recognizer* is like a parser in its use of a grammar, but it does not produce a tree representing the analysis of the word sequence. Instead, it simply succeeds or fails for a given sequence of words, depending on whether it is or is not a sentence of the language defined by the grammar. Recognizers are, of course, not as useful since the reason for parsing is usually to get the resulting analysis. However, in our description of parsing algorithms in the rest of this chapter, we will often first present a related recognition algorithm, then add the additional steps needed to produce the parse tree.

The problem in designing a context-free parser is to use the correspondence between rules and structures as the basis for organizing the analysis process. Many different parsing procedures have been devised, each with its own kind of working structures and with particular properties of efficiency (in time and storage). In designing a specific procedure, one must make choices along a

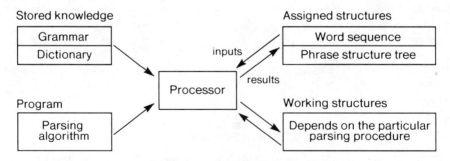

Figure 3–15. Stored knowledge and assigned structures in parsing.

number of different dimensions of parsing strategy, laid out in the rest of this section.

General issues in parser design

To begin with, many issues in designing a parsing procedure are not technical choices, but have to do with the overall approach to language and grammar. This chapter deals with context-free grammars and adopts a mathematical idea of grammaticality. This leads to a number of consequences:

Uniformity of processing. There is no inherent reason why the parsing process must correspond directly to the form of the grammar. By writing a procedure based on specialized knowledge of the language being parsed, it might be possible to do things more efficiently. On the other hand, if there is a simple uniform procedure for applying a set of rules, the job of writing a language understander is simplified. Once the rules have been put into the knowledge base, no further knowledge is needed for parsing. The correctness of the parsing procedure and the correctness of the grammar can be tested separately. Ideally, the same rules would be used in a uniform way for generation as well, although this has rarely been the case in practical systems. This chapter describes only uniform procedures.

Separate processing of levels. As discussed in Chapter 1, the stratified model of language *structure* (illustrated in Figure 1–5) does not imply a stratification of *processing*. It is possible to design systems in which the parsing of syntactic structures is intermixed with other processing levels such as word recognition and the analysis of meaning. Much of the difficulty of choosing rules in parsing can be avoided by letting knowledge from the other levels take part in the selection. Some of the more sophisticated computer systems for natural language understanding use a mixed strategy, and a number of experiments support the intuition that a human language understander operates on many levels simultaneously. All of the procedures in this chapter, however, are based on the assumption that the input is a sequence of words and that the parsing is completed without any appeal to meaning. The strategies for purely syntactic parsing will provide a framework for understanding more sophisticated procedures.

Precision. An obvious property of human language is that we can understand sentences that do not precisely fit a grammar. Even when we recognize a sequence of words as not being grammatical, we are often able to assign a structure to it anyway and figure out its meaning. Some computer systems for natural language are designed with an emphasis on this sort of flexibility. By looking for key words and using fairly unspecific patterns, they can accept a wider range of sequences than would be formally allowed by a grammar. The price they pay is in never producing a complete analysis that could be used to dig out the subtleties of meaning that can play such a large part in communication. They are limited to a rather vague notion of what a sentence is about, and as a result often make blunders in deciding on responses. The generative paradigm is based on an attempt to be precise, and our approach here is to follow that path first, looking at flexibility later as a way to relax the precision when forgiveness is called for, rather than eschewing it from the beginning.

Dimensions of parsing strategy for context-free grammars

Within the boundaries of purely syntactic, uniform, precise, context-free parsing, there are three major dimensions along which parsing strategies differ. In presenting the details of each, we will begin with a nondeterministic schema, in which one dimension of choice has been fixed but the others are still open. Any actual parsing procedure must make specific choices along all of these dimensions.

Parallel versus sequential treatment of alternatives. Chapter 2 presented two different procedures for recognizing sentences with a transition network. One followed multiple possibilities in parallel, keeping track of a set of simultaneous possible states. The other tried them in sequence, backtracking when its choices led to failure. This is one of the fundamental dimensions of strategy for every kind of procedure involving choices, and applies equally to procedures for reasoning and for the analysis of meaning.

Top-down versus bottom-up analysis. Parsing and recognition procedures for context-free grammars are similar to those of Chapter 2 in that they try to match successive elements of patterns (in this case, the right-hand sides of rules) to successive elements of the input sequence. The difference is that instead of a single pattern being matched to the entire sequence, a number of rules must be used with elements of one rule calling for the application of another. This leads to the problem of deciding which rules to try, and in what order. There are two basic strategies, corresponding to two different ways of finding answers to the question 'What should I do next?'

Basically, a top-down procedure begins by looking at rules for the desired top-level structure (usually a sentence), sees what constituents would be needed to make it up, looks for rules for those constituents, and in this way proceeds down the structure tree until it reaches words. A bottom-up procedure begins with the words and looks for rules whose right-hand sides match sequences of adjacent words that can then be combined into a constituent as identified by the left-hand side. It then tries to combine these with each other and the remaining words into larger constituents, and proceeds up the structure tree until it is able to combine constituents covering the entire input into a single structure labeled with the distinguished symbol.

The same structures are found by top-down and bottom-up parsing, but the amount of work done and the nature of the working structures are quite different. We will look at the advantages and disadvantages of each. The distinction between top-down and bottom-up strategies applies in a very general way to any kind of processing. It can be characterized as the difference between *goal-directed processing,* which is guided by the goals it is trying to achieve (in this case the recognition of a sentence), and *data-directed processing,* which is guided by the availability of specific data (in this case the words of the input sequence).

Choice of nodes to expand or combine. Within the context of working basically top-down or bottom-up, there are still decisions to be made as to which nodes to work on first, either by expanding them (in a top-down procedure) or by combining them (in a bottom-up procedure). There are two basic organizations used to make these decisions: moving systematically through the input in one direction (usually from left to right), or systematically taking chunks of increasing size. There are mixed strategies in which a basically directional organization has a size-oriented substructure. How much work will be done with a given grammar on a given input depends significantly on the details of this choice.

In the the rest of this chapter, we will generally use a left-to-right strategy with top-down procedures and a chunk-building strategy with bottom-up procedures. This is the simplest combination but not the only one. Many parsers for programming languages use left-to-right bottom-up procedures which can take advantage of special properties of the grammars. Some parsers used in speech understanding systems operate top-down but look for *islands* from which they work in both directions. For example, in looking for an NP they first look for a noun (which tends to be more clearly enunciated and more predictable from meaning) and then work to the left looking for adjectives and determiners and to the right looking for modifying phrases.

Even in working across in a single direction it is possible to go from right to left instead of from left to right, and some parsers adopt this ordering. As far as the formalism is concerned, there is no privilege to either direction, but it seems more natural to proceed in the same order that the words would be heard in spoken language. Parsers that operate primarily in this direction are more likely to be good psychological models than those that need to have the entire sequence of words available before beginning processing. Of course, the use of the term 'left-to-right' for temporal order is specific to the writing conventions of English and other European languages. A Hebrew or Arabic parser would naturally operate 'right-to-left.'

The problem of ambiguity

An obvious feature of natural languages is their ambiguity. The same sequence of words often has more than one interpretation. In those cases where this is

Grammar	Dictionary
S → NP VP *(statements)*	*an:* Determiner
S → VP *(commands)*	*arrow:* Noun
NP → Determiner NP2	*flies:* Noun, Verb
NP → NP2	*like:* Preposition, Verb
NP → NP PP	*time:* Adjective, Noun, Verb
NP2 → Noun	
NP2 → Adjective NP2	
PP → Preposition NP	
VP → Verb	
VP → Verb NP	
VP → VP PP	

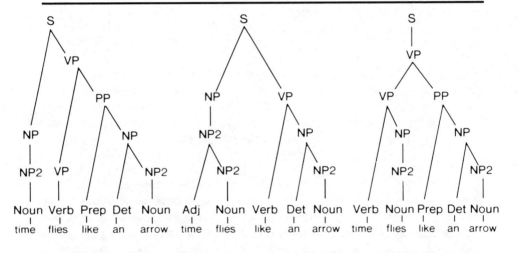

Figure 3–16. An example of ambiguity.

due simply to *polysemy* (multiple meanings) of individual words, it does not present a problem for parsing. The sentence *She walked towards the bank* must be interpreted in a context that makes it clear whether it is the bank of a river or a financial institution, but the syntactic structure is identical in the two cases.

However, there are many cases of ambiguity where the syntactic structure is ambiguous. A classical example is the phrase *the old men and women,* in which the modifier *old* can be associated with either *men* or *men and women.* Conjunctions such as *and* are a major source of structural ambiguity. The attachment of modifying phrases is another common problem, as in the sentence *I saw the man on the hill with a telescope.* There are at least three different ways to interpret the phrase, differing in whether I used a telescope, there is a telescope on the hill, or the man had a telescope. Other ambiguities arise from words that are in multiple word classes, as in the two parsings of *I saw that gasoline can explode.*

A context-free grammar is said to be *ambiguous* if it can be used to derive two different trees that have the same sequence of leaf nodes. A classical case of ambiguity is illustrated in Figure 3–16. Note that *time* is listed in the dictionary as a noun (*Time passes slowly*), a verb (*We are timing the marathon*), and an adjective (*Show me the time cards*).

A parsing procedure can be based on either of two basic attitudes towards ambiguity: it can search for a single interpretation and quit as soon as it has found one, or it can return all of the possible interpretations. In general, parallel procedures are better suited to returning all of the interpretations since they work on them all simultaneously. Backtracking procedures naturally stop as soon as they find a single parsing, but it is easy to produce all the parsings by forcing them to backtrack each time they succeed. In describing the procedures below, we will assume that the parser should stop as soon as one parsing is found. It is an easy exercise to modify them to continue until all parsings have been found.

3.4 A sampler of recognition procedures

This section describes several procedures for *recognition* of sentences with a context-free grammar. As mentioned above, these differ from parsing procedures for parsing in that they do not include the steps needed for saving the phrase structure tree, simply succeeding if there is some possible tree and failing if there is none. Section 3.5 describes the modifications that are needed to make these into parsing procedures.

Grammar			Dictionary	
S	→	NP VP	*a*	Determiner
NP	→	Determiner NP2	*an*	Determiner
NP	→	NP2	*cucumber*	Noun
NP2	→	Noun	*nibbled*	Adjective, Verb
NP2	→	Adjective NP2	*orange*	Adjective, Noun
NP2	→	NP2 PP	*rabbit*	Noun
PP	→	Preposition NP	*saw*	Noun, Verb
VP	→	Verb	*the*	Determiner
VP	→	Verb NP	*with*	Preposition
VP	→	VP PP		

Figure 3–17. Sample context-free grammar and dictionary.

The procedures will each be demonstrated recognizing the sentence *The orange rabbit nibbled a cucumber with a saw* using the grammar and dictionary of Figure 3–17. NP, VP, and PP stand for *noun phrase, verb phrase,* and *prepositional phrase,* respectively. In order to save space, some figures use the abbreviations ADJ, DET, and PREP for ADJECTIVE, DETERMINER, and PREPOSITION.

Schemas for top-down and bottom-up recognition

The first dimension of choice is between a top-down procedure, which works from a higher constituent looking for its subparts, and a bottom-up procedure,

---

Recognize a sentence top-down left-to-right (nondeterministic)

Purpose: Test whether a sequence of words is a sentence in the language defined by a context-free grammar

Background: a *context-free grammar* and a *dictionary*   3–10 2–10

Inputs: a sequence of words

Working Structures:
  Current position: an integer representing a position in the input sequence; initially 1
  Remainder: a sequence of syntactic categories; initially consisting of a single occurrence of the *distinguished symbol* of the grammar   3–10
  At any point in the recognition, this is the sequence of constituents that are yet to be found.

Basic Method: Keep repeating:
  ▪ If the first symbol of the remainder is a word or lexical category, then:
    ▪ If it *matches* the word at the position, then: 3–10
      ▪ Remove the first element from the remainder.
      ▪ If the current position is the last in the sequence, then
          If the remainder is empty, succeed. Otherwise fail.
      ▪ Otherwise increment the current position by 1.
  ▪ Otherwise:
    ▪ Choose any rule in the grammar having that symbol as its left-hand side.
    ▪ Set the remainder to a sequence consisting of:
      ▪ the right-hand side of the rule, followed by
      ▪ the remainder, omitting its first element.

Conditions:
  If the remainder is ever empty when the position is not the last of the sequence, fail.

Figure 3–18. Schema for top-down left-to-right recognition.

Position	Remainder	Rule chosen
1 *the*	S	S → NP VP
1 *the*	NP VP	NP → Determiner NP2
1 *the*	Determiner NP2 VP	*the* = Determiner
2 *orange*	NP2 VP	NP2 → Adjective NP2
2 *orange*	Adjective NP2 VP	*orange* = Adjective
3 *rabbit*	NP2 VP	NP2 → Noun
3 *rabbit*	Noun VP	*rabbit* = Noun
4 *nibbled*	VP	VP → VP PP
4 *nibbled*	VP PP	VP → Verb NP
4 *nibbled*	Verb NP PP	*nibhled* = Verb
5 *a*	NP PP	NP → Determiner NP2
5 *a*	Determiner NP2 PP	*a* = Determiner
6 *cucumber*	NP2 PP	NP2 → Noun
6 *cucumber*	Noun PP	*cucumber* = Noun
7 *with*	PP	PP → Preposition NP
7 *with*	Preposition NP	*with* = Preposition
8 *a*	NP	NP → Determiner NP2
8 *a*	Determiner NP2	*a* = Determiner
9 *saw*	NP2	NP2 → Noun
9 *saw*	Noun	*saw* = Noun

Figure 3–19. Trace of a nondeterministic top-down recognition.

which works from the available constituents seeing how they can be combined. We begin by defining nondeterministic schemas for both approaches and illustrating them for the sample sentence.

In the top-down procedure of 3–18, a sequence (called the 'remainder') is used to keep track of all the things that must still be found in order to complete a sentence. This is sometimes referred to as the *stack,* since elements are added to and removed from its beginning. When a rule is used, its left-hand side is removed from the remainder and replaced with all of the symbols on its right-hand side. Figure 3–19 is a trace of the recognition process of Figure 3–18 for a particular set of choices given the sample input. Each line represents one step of the repeated cycle, showing the position in the sentence, the contents of the remainder, and the rule that was chosen. The current position is indicated by number and by showing the word at that position. In this example, the choices result in a successful recognition. The PP *with a saw* is treated as a modifier of the VP *nibbled a cucumber.*

Figures 3–20 and Figure 3–21 define a schema (a procedure with arbitrary choices) for doing a bottom-up recognition. It operates by repeatedly finding a *handle* in the current sequence that matches the right-hand side of some rule and replacing it with the left-hand side of that rule. It succeeds if the

---

Recognize a sentence bottom-up (nondeterministic)

Purpose: Test whether a sequence of words is a sentence
Background: a *context-free grammar* and a *dictionary*
Inputs: a sequence of words   3–10 2–10
Working Structures:
   Current sequence: a sequence of symbols; initially the input
Basic Method: Keep repeating:
  ■ If the current sequence contains exactly one element which is the distinguished symbol of the grammar, then succeed.
  ■ Either:
    ■ replace a word in the current sequence with any lexical category in its dictionary entry
    ■ or *find a handle* in the current sequence and replace the current   3–21
sequence with a sequence consisting of:
      ■ the elements of the current sequence before the handle-start
      ■ a single element that is the handle-label
      ■ the elements of the current sequence following the handle-end.
Conditions: If there are no words left in the sequence and no handle can be found, fail.

Figure 3–20. Schema for bottom-up recognition.

Find a handle in a sequence (nondeterministic)

Purpose: Produce the start, end, and replacing symbol
Inputs: a sequence of symbols
Background: a *context-free grammar*   3–10
Results:
  Handle-start: an integer
  Handle-end: an integer
  Handle-label: a symbol of the grammar
Basic Method:
  ■ Choose any position in the sequence.
  ■ Choose any rule in the grammar.
  ■ Step in parallel through the right-hand side of the rule, and through the sequence beginning at the chosen position, doing:
    ■ If the corresponding elements are not the same, fail.
  ■ Return:
    ■ handle-start = the chosen position
    ■ handle-end = the last position in the sequence matched against the right-hand side of the rule
    ■ handle-label = the left-hand side of the rule.
Conditions: If the sequence runs out before the rule, fail.

Figure 3–21. Schema to find a handle for replacement.

sequence can be reduced to a single occurrence of the distinguished symbol of the grammar.

Figure 3–22 illustrates the sequence of steps that would result from applying one particular set of choices to the bottom-up recognition schema. Instead of making all the right choices, as in the example of top-down recognition, this trace demonstrates what happens when a wrong choice is made somewhere during the process. Notice that the process can continue for quite a while after the wrong path is taken, and when a failure finally occurs it may be difficult to analyze which choice was wrong.

Rule or dictionary entry used	Current sequence
	The orange rabbit nibbled a cucumber with a saw
rabbit = Noun	*The orange* Noun *nibbled a cucumber with a saw*
NP2 → Noun	*The orange* NP2 *nibbled a cucumber with a saw*
orange = Adj	*The* Adj NP2 *nibbled a cucumber with a saw*
NP2 → Adj NP2	*The* NP2 *nibbled a cucumber with a saw*
the = Det	Det NP2 *nibbled a cucumber with a saw*
cucumber = Noun	Det NP2 *nibbled a* Noun *with a saw*
with = Prep	Det NP2 *nibbled a* Noun Prep *a saw*
NP → Det NP2	NP *nibbled a* Noun Prep *a saw*
NP2 → Noun	NP *nibbled a* NP2 Prep *a saw*
nibbled = Verb	NP Verb *a* NP2 Prep *a saw*
a = Det	NP Verb Det NP2 Prep *a saw*
NP → Det NP2	NP Verb NP Prep *a saw*
VP → Verb NP	NP VP Prep *a saw*
S → NP VP	S Prep *a saw*

The choice to use this rule at this point will lead to failure since in the example grammar, S never appears on the right-hand side of a rule.

a = Det	S Prep Det *saw*
saw = Noun	S Prep Det Noun
NP2 → Noun	S Prep Det NP2
NP → Det NP2	S Prep NP
PP → Prep NP	S PP

No further handles can be found, so the procedure fails

Figure 3–22. Trace of an unsuccessful path for a bottom-up recognizer.

Recognize a sentence top-down left-to-right (backtracking)

Purpose: Test whether a sequence of words is a sentence

Background: a *dictionary* and a *context-free grammar*   2–10 3–10

Inputs: a sequence of words

Working Structures:
  Position: an integer representing a position in the input
  Rule: a rule of the grammar
  Remainder: a sequence of symbols
  Stack: a stack of *records*; initially containing a single record with: §
    ▪ position $= 1$
    ▪ remainder $=$ a single occurrence of the distinguished symbol of
       the grammar
    ▪ rules-to-try $=$ a sequence containing all of the rules of the gram-
       mar whose left-hand side is the distinguished symbol

Basic Method: Keep repeating:
  ▪ If the stack is empty, fail.
  ▪ Assign the position of the top record as the position.
  ▪ Remove the first rule from the rules-to-try of the top record and
     assign it as the rule.
  ▪ Set the remainder to a sequence consisting of the right-hand side of
     the rule, followed by all but the first symbol of the remainder from
     the top record.
  ▪ If the rules-to-try of the top record is empty, pop it off the stack.
  ▪ As long as the remainder is not empty, and its first symbol *matches*   3–10
     the word at the position, repeat:
    ▪ Remove the first symbol from the remainder and add 1 to the
       position.
  ▪ If the position is one greater than the length of the sequence and the
     remainder is empty, succeed.
  ▪ If the remainder is not empty and its first symbol is a nonterminal,
     then:
    ▪ Create a new record with position $=$ the position, remainder $=$
       the remainder, and rules-to-try $=$ all the rules in the grammar
       that have the first symbol of the remainder as their left-hand
       side.
    ▪ Push it onto the top of the stack.

Classes:

R E C O R D	**Describes:** alternatives to be tried
	Roles:
	  Position: an integer representing a position in the input
	  Remainder: a sequence of symbols
	  Rules-to-try: a sequence of rules

Figure 3–23. Algorithm for top-down left-to-right backtracking recognition.

Serial processing of alternatives by backtracking

The two schemas defined above are nondeterministic—they succeed only for a correct sequence of choices. We want to extend them to explore the choices systematically, using the techniques of parallel processing and backtracking described in Chapter 2. Figure 3–23 defines a top-down left-to-right backtracking recognizer. It is based on the top-down schema of Figure 3–18. When faced with a choice, it takes one alternative and keeps a record of the others in case it needs to go back and try them. If the backtracking procedure is extended to save an assigned tree structure, it must also save information about this structure in the records and replace the old tree whenever it backs up.

In order to explain details of the procedure, we will trace it in recognizing the sample sentence. Each block of the trace (between lines) represents one cycle through the outer sequence of steps indicated in the procedure. The lines within it represent steps through the inner cycle (the one beginning 'As long as the remainder is not empty...'). Records are represented by a list enclosed in square brackets, containing the position (indicated by a number and the word at that position) followed by the remainder (in parentheses) and the rules. To save space, the symbols for lexical categories will be represented by their first letters (e.g., V for VERB).

Stack	**Rule**	**Remainder**	**Posn**
[1 *the* (S): S→NP VP]	S→NP VP	NP VP	1 *the*

The recognition begins at the first position of the input with a single record in the stack, containing the rules for the distinguished symbol S and with that symbol as the remainder of the sentence yet to be found. It applies the rule for S, removing the record from the stack since it has no other rules to try, leaving a remainder of 'NP VP.'

	NP→D NP2	D NP2 VP	1 *the*
[1 *the* (NP VP): NP→D NP2, NP→NP2]	*the* = D	NP2 VP	2 *orange*

A record with the rules for NP is pushed onto the stack and the first rule (NP→DET NP2) is tried. Note that in each block of the trace, the rule tried is the one appearing as the first rule of the top record on the stack. In fact, the definition is somewhat arbitrary in stating that the rules always be taken in the same order. A more sophisticated procedure might include ways of deciding on an order by applying criteria such as meaning or previous experience. For simplicity we will assume that rules are always tried in the order of Figure 3–17.

In this case, application of the first rule to the previous remainder (appearing in parentheses in the top record) leads to a remainder of 'DET NP2 VP.' The first symbol is a terminal symbol, so it is matched against the word at the current position (1) of the sequence. Since *the* is a determiner, this succeeds. The position is advanced and the symbol DET is removed from the remainder.

[2 *orange* (NP2 VP): NP2→N, NP2→A NP2, NP2→NP2 PP] [1 *the* (NP VP): NP→NP2]	NP2→N	| N VP	| 2 *orange*
	orange = N	| VP	| 3 *rabbit*

The symbol NP2 is now expanded, with its record going on top of the one containing the other rule that was not used for NP. In this example, we will never go back and try this other rule, but the procedure saves all choices for possible backtracking. The first rule for NP2 calls for a noun and *orange* is one, so the procedure advances. This is not the right choice for this example, since *orange* is used here as an adjective modifying *rabbit*.

[3 *rabbit* (VP):
   VP→V, VP→V NP, VP→VP PP]
[2 *orange* (NP2 VP):
   NP2→A NP2, NP2→NP2 PP]
[1 *the* (NP VP): NP→NP2]
	VP→V	| V	| 3 *rabbit*

This time, the top of the remainder is a lexical category (VERB), but it does not match the word at the position (*rabbit*). Therefore the position is not changed and no new record is added to the stack. On the next cycle, a different expansion for VP will be tried.

[3 *rabbit* (VP): VP→V NP, VP→VP PP] [2 *orange* (NP2 VP): NP2→A NP2, NP2→NP2 PP] [1 *the* (NP VP): NP→NP2]	VP→V NP	| V NP	| 3 *rabbit*
[3 *rabbit* (VP): VP→VP PP] [2 *orange* (NP2 VP): NP2→A NP2, NP2→NP2 PP] [1 *the* (NP VP): NP→NP2]	VP→VP PP	| VP PP	| 3 *rabbit*

In the process of trying all of the expansions for VP, the system encounters the rule 'VP → VP PP.' This results in pushing a new record on the stack in an attempt to expand the VP on the right-hand side of that rule.

[3 *rabbit* (VP PP): VP→V, VP→V NP, VP→VP PP] [2 *orange* (NP2 VP): NP2→A NP2, NP2→NP2 PP] [1 *the* (NP VP): NP→NP2]	VP→V	∣ V PP	∣ 3 *rabbit*

At this point the process is in trouble. The lexical category VERB will never match the word *rabbit,* which is at position 3 in the sentence, but by applying the rule 'VP → VP PP,' we can continue indefinitely adding more PPs to the remainder and still be looking for a VERB. There are various ways to avoid this problem—later we will see how to rewrite this grammar without *left-recursive* rules like 'VP → VP PP.' Many parsers have special additional mechanisms to handle this sort of construction. For the moment, we will assume the use of some such mechanism without specifying exactly how it works. We will proceed on the assumption that the procedure got sent back to try the second rule for NP2 as recorded in the stack.

[2 *orange* (NP2 VP): NP2→A NP2, NP2→NP2 PP] [1 *the* (NP VP): NP→NP2]	NP2→A NP2 *orange* = A	∣ A NP2 VP ∣ NP2 VP	∣ 2 *orange* ∣ 3 *rabbit*
[3 *rabbit* (NP2 VP): NP2→N, NP2→A NP2, NP2→NP2 PP] [2 *orange* (NP2 VP): NP2→NP2 PP] [1 *the* (NP VP): NP→NP2]	NP2→N *rabbit* = N	∣ N VP ∣ VP	∣ 3 *rabbit* ∣ 4 *nibbled*
[4 *nibbled* (VP): VP→V, VP→V NP, VP→VP PP] [3 *rabbit* (NP2 VP): NP2→A NP2, NP2→NP2 PP] [2 *orange* (NP2 VP): NP2→NP2 PP] . . .	VP→V *nibbled* = V	∣ V ∣ –empty–	∣ 4 *nibbled* ∣ 5 *a*

In the immediately preceding step, the procedure has managed to empty the remainder, indicating that it has found a full sentence. In fact, *The orange rabbit nibbled* is a sentence according to the grammar. But it is not the full input, so the procedure must backtrack and try other choices that can cover the whole input sequence. When the stack is deeper than three elements, as in the last step, we will leave out the bottom and indicate it with '. . .' to save space.

[4 *nibbled* (VP): VP→V NP, VP→VP PP]
[3 *rabbit* (NP2 VP):
  NP2→A NP2, NP2→NP2 PP]
[2 *orange* (NP2 VP): NP2→NP2 PP]
...

VP→V NP	V NP	4 *nibbled*
nibbled = V	NP	5 *a*

[5 *a* (NP): NP→D NP2, NP→NP2]
[4 *nibbled* (VP): VP→VP PP]
[3 *rabbit* (NP2 VP):
  NP2→A NP2, NP2→NP2 PP]
...

NP→D NP2	D NP2	5 *a*
a = D	NP2	6 *cucumber*

[6 *cucumber* (NP2):
  NP2→N, NP2→A NP2, NP2→NP2 PP]
[5 *a* (NP): NP→NP2]
[4 *nibbled* (VP): VP→VP PP]
[3 *rabbit* (NP2 VP):
  NP2→A NP2, NP2→NP2 PP]
...

NP2→N	N	6 *cucumber*
cucumber = N	–empty–	7 *with*

Once again the remainder is empty, corresponding to the sentence *The orange rabbit nibbled a cucumber*. Note the importance of the order in which the rules are tried. If the rule 'NP2→NP2 PP' had been tried before 'NP2→NOUN,' we would not have hit this dead end. In fact, the ordering of the rules is extremely good for this example, and there is relatively little backtracking.

[6 *cucumber* (NP2):
  NP2→A NP2, NP2→NP2 PP]
[5 *a* (NP): NP→NP2]
[4 *nibbled* (VP): VP→VP PP]
...

NP2→A NP2	A NP2	6 *cucumber*

[6 *cucumber* (NP2): NP2→NP2 PP]
[5 *a* (NP): NP→NP2]
[4 *nibbled* (VP): VPC]
...

NP2→NP2 PP	NP2 PP	6 *cucumber*

[6 *cucumber* (NP2 PP):
  NP2→N, NP2→A NP2, NP2→NP2 PP]
[5 *a* (NP): NP→NP2]
[4 *nibbled* (VP): VP→VP PP]
[3 *rabbit* (NP2 VP):
  NP2→A NP2, NP2→NP2 PP]
...

NP2→N	N PP	6 *cucumber*
cucumber = N	PP	7 *with*

In taking the rule 'NP2 → NP2 PP,' we have followed the path in which the phrase *with a saw* is taken as a modifier of *a cucumber*. With further backtracking or a different ordering of the rules, it could also be parsed as a modifier of of the sentence as a whole.

[7 *with* (PP): PP→P NP] [6 *cucumber* (NP2 PP): NP2→A NP2, NP2→NP2 PP] [5 *a* (NP): NP→NP2] . . .			
	PP→P NP	| P NP	| 7 *with*
	with = P	| NP	| 8 *a*

[8 *a* (NP): NP→D NP2, NP→NP2] [6 *cucumber* (NP2 PP): NP2→A NP2, NP2→NP2 PP] [5 *a* (NP): NP→NP2] . . .			
	NP→D NP2	| D NP2	| 8 *a*
	a = D	| NP2	| 9 *saw*

[9 *saw* (NP2):
  NP2→N, NP2→A NP2, NP2→NP2 PP]
[8 *a* (NP): NP→NP2]
[6 *cucumber* (NP2 PP):
  NP2→A NP2, NP2→NP2 PP]
. . .			

	NP2→N	| N	| 9 *saw*
	saw = N	| –empty–	| –end–

Finally, the end of the sequence is reached at the same time the remainder is emptied, so the parse succeeds. The trace is quite long, but as mentioned above, it is short compared to traces produced for other possible rule orderings.

In this particular example, there is never more than one stack record with the same starting position. This is due to the particular grammar. For example, with the grammar of Figure 3–24, the stack would become quite deep before ever progressing beyond the first position.

Top-down parallel recognition

Top-down recognition and parsing can be done in parallel as well as with backtracking. It is another extension of the schema of Figure 3–18, in which the working structures consisted of a position in the sentence and a remainder of constituents that were yet to be found.

A parallel procedure can be written by having a *set of remainders,* each corresponding to one set of choices. In the nondeterministic schema, the basic step is to remove the first element of the remainder and replace it with the expansion of a rule for which it is the left-hand side. The corresponding step in a parallel procedure is to go through the entire current set of remainders, creating for each of them one new remainder for every rule whose left-hand side is the first element. Similarly, instead of simply removing a symbol from one remainder when it matches the next word in the sentence, we must try advancing all remainders whose top symbol matches the next word. By being

Grammar	Dictionary
S → A B	$x = X$
S → A X	
A → B	**Input**
A → B X	
B → C	$xxxx$
B → C X	
C → X	

[1 x (S): S → A B, S → A X]	S → A B I A B I 1 x

[1 x (A B): A → B, A → B X]	A → B I B B I 1 x
[1 x (S): S → A X]	

[1 x (B B): B → C, B → C X]	B → C I C B I 1 x
[1 x (A B): A → B X]	
[1 x (S): S → A X]	

[1 x (C B): C → X]	C → X I X B I 1 x
[1 x (B B): B → C X]	x= X I B I 2 x
[1 x (A B): A → B X]	
[1 x (S): S → A X]	

Figure 3–24. Example of a stack for backtracking.

careful about the sequencing, it is possible to keep all the remainders marching in lock step through the sentence so there is only one current position. This is done by cycling through the process of expanding remainders whose top symbol is a nonterminal until every remainder has a terminal symbol on top, then trying to advance all the remainders to the next position in the sentence, throwing out those whose first symbol does not match the next word.

The writing of the detailed procedure will be left as an exercise. It should be noted that the resulting recognizer does a great deal of duplicated work. Often two remainders will be created that begin identically but differ farther along. For example, a grammar might contain the rules:

$$S → NP\ VP$$
$$S → NP\ VP\ PP$$
$$NP → \ldots$$

The first step in a top-down parse is to ask 'What might a sentence be made up of?' This grammar offers two different answers, and the remainders 'NP VP' and 'NP VP PP' would both be put into the set. They would be expanded in parallel through all the details of the NP and VP, with all of the work being done twice. Finally, one or the other would be eliminated, depending on whether there actually was a PP at the end of the sentence. A number of techniques have been developed to avoid this kind of duplication, sometimes under the title *multiple path elimination*. One possibility is to replace the individual rules with a network (as we did in Chapter 2), so that the common initial sequence appears only once. Section 3.6 presents a more general solution to this problem using a device called a *chart*.

Another simplification of the procedure results from converting the grammar to one in which every rule begins with a terminal symbol. The resulting grammar is called a *predictive grammar,* or is said to be in *Greibach normal form.* At each cycle through the parallel process, each remainder can be expanded at most once before its first element is a terminal symbol. A single expansion pass through the set of remainders is done before trying to advance to the next position in the sentence, rather than the repeated expansions described above. Section 3.5 discusses this kind of grammar conversion.

Bottom-up parallel recognition

Figures 3–25 and 3–26 describe a procedure for bottom-up parallel recognition. It begins by finding all lexical categories that each word of the input could belong to, and then combining these in all possible ways consistent with the grammar to obtain larger constituents. The procedure as given does not avoid duplicated or unnecessary work. Many combinations of constituents will be computed and discarded because they are not even adjacent parts of the input; further combinations will be rejected because no rule in the grammar has such a sequence as its right-hand side. In addition, a new constituent found in an early cycle will be rediscovered on every later cycle as well. Section 3.5 presents a refinement that reduces the work by looking only for new constituents of increasing size. Section 3.6 will introduce a data structure from which sequences of contiguous constituents can be computed directly.

Figure 3–27 illustrates a bottom-up parallel recognition. Each clump of adjacent lines in the figure represents a set of structures added to the set of known constituents on a single cycle of finding new constituents. A constituent is represented by the positions of its first and last elements in the input string surrounding its syntactic category. For example, $(_1\text{DETERMINER}_1)$ is a one-element sequence at the beginning of the string, and $(_1S_9)$ is a sentence covering the entire input. For convenience in interpreting the trace, we also display the corresponding words of the input string.

Recognize a sentence bottom-up (parallel)

Purpose: Test whether a sequence of words is a sentence in the language defined by a context-free grammar

Background: a *context-free grammar* and a *dictionary*   3–10 2–10

Inputs: a sequence of words

Working Structures:

   Known constituents: a set of *constituents*; initially empty   §

Basic Method:

- Step through the words of the input sequence doing:
  - For each lexical category in the dictionary entry for the word:
    - Create a constituent whose start and end are both the position of the word, and whose label is the category.
  - Add the constituent to the known constituents.
- Keep repeating:
  - If there is a constituent whose start and end are the first and last positions of the input, and whose label is the distinguished symbol of the grammar, then succeed.
  - *Find new constituents* from the known constituents.   3–26
  - If any new constituents are found, add them to the known constituents. Otherwise fail.

Classes:

<table>
<tr><td rowspan="8">C
O
N
S
T
I
T
U
E
N
T</td><td>

Describes: a phrase structure constituent

Roles:

  Start: an integer representing a position in the sequence
  End: an integer representing a position in the sequence
  Label: a syntactic category or a word

Predicates:

<u>A constituent equals a constituent</u> if their start, end, and label are equal.

</td></tr>
</table>

Figure 3–25. Bottom-up parallel recognition.

Find new constituents from a set of constituents

Purpose: Produce a set of new constituents that can be built out of given ones

Inputs: a set of *constituents* 3–25

Results: a set of constituents

Background: a *context-free grammar* 3–10

Working Structures:

New constituents: a set of constituents; initially empty

Basic Method: For every subset of the constituents in the input do:

- Try to *order them into a contiguous sequence.* §
- If this succeeds, then for every rule in the grammar do: §

  If the *rule spans the sequence*, then:
  - Create a new constituent with:
    - start = the start of the first element of the sequence
    - end = the end of the last element of the sequence
    - label = the left-hand side of the rule.
  - If this constituent is not equal to one already in the input or in the new constituents, add it to the new constituents.

Procedures:

Order a set of constituents into a contiguous sequence

Inputs: a set of constituents

Results: a sequence of constituents

This will not be given in detail. It tries to find an ordering for the constituents such that the start of each constituent after the first is exactly one greater than the end of the constituent preceding it. If such an ordering can be found, it is returned. Otherwise the procedure fails.

Test whether a rule spans a contiguous sequence of constituents

---

Basic Method:

Step through the right-hand side of the rule and the sequence of constituents in parallel, doing:

If the symbol from the rule is the same as the label of the constituent, then go on. Otherwise fail.

Conditions:

If both sequences run out at the same time, succeed.
If one finishes before the other, fail.

Figure 3–26. Find new constituents from a set of constituents.

$(_1\text{Det}_1$ *the*$)(_2\text{Adj}_2$ *orange*$)(_2\text{Noun}_2$ *orange*$)(_3\text{Noun}_3$ *rabbit*$)$
$(_4\text{Verb}_4$ *nibbled*$)(_4\text{Adj}_4$ *nibbled*$)(_5\text{Det}_5$ *a*$)(_6\text{Noun}_6$ *cucumber*$)$
$(_7\text{Prep}_7$ *with*$)(_8\text{Det}_8$ *a*$)(_9\text{Noun}_9$ *saw*$)(_9\text{Verb}_9$ *saw*$)$

$(_2\text{NP2}_2$ *orange*$)(_3\text{NP2}_3$ *rabbit*$)(_4\text{VP}_4$ *nibbled*$)(_6\text{NP2}_6$ *cucumber*$)(_9\text{NP2}_9$ *saw*$)(_9\text{VP}_9$ *saw*$)$

$(_1\text{NP}_2$ *the orange*$)(_2\text{NP}_2$ *orange*$)(_2\text{NP2}_3$ *orange rabbit*$)(_3\text{NP}_3$ *rabbit*$)$
$(_5\text{NP}_6$ *a cucumber*$)(_6\text{NP}_6$ *cucumber*$)(_8\text{NP}_9$ *a saw*$)(_9\text{NP}_9$ *saw*$)$

$(_1\text{NP}_3$ *the orange rabbit*$)(_2\text{NP}_3$ *orange rabbit*$)(_3\text{S}_4$ *rabbit nibbled*$)$
$(_4\text{VP}_6$ *nibbled a cucumber*$)(_7\text{PP}_9$ *with a saw*$)$

$(_1\text{S}_4$ *the orange rabbit nibbled*$)(_1\text{S}_6$ *the orange rabbit nibbled a cucumber*$)$
$(_2\text{S}_4$ *orange rabbit nibbled*$)(_2\text{S}_6$ *orange rabbit nibbled a cucumber*$)$
$(_3\text{S}_6$ *rabbit nibbled a cucumber*$)(_4\text{VP}_9$ *nibbled a cucumber with a saw*$)$
$(_6\text{NP2}_9$ *cucumber with a saw*$)$

$(_1\text{S}_9$ *the orange rabbit nibbled a cucumber with a saw*$)$
$(_2\text{S}_9$ *orange rabbit nibbled a cucumber with a saw*$)$
$(_3\text{S}_9$ *rabbit nibbled a cucumber with a saw*$)(_5\text{NP}_9$ *a cucumber with a saw*$)$
$(_6\text{NP}_9$ *cucumber with a saw*$)$

Figure 3–27. Structures built in a bottom-up parallel recognition.

3.5 Refinements to the basic recognition procedures

In a practical system for parsing (or a model of human language understanding), the procedures defined in the previous section would be inadequate in several ways:

Generation of structure. So far we have dealt only with recognition, not parsing. The procedures need to be augmented in order to keep track of what they have found.

Efficiency. In defining a simple procedure, it is often useful to avoid complications that would make it run more efficiently. As a simple example, the backtracking procedures of Figures 2–21 and 3–23 build a record for backtracking even in those cases where there is only one arc or rule to try. A slightly more complicated procedure would avoid the extra work. A much more serious example is provided by the bottom-up recognition procedure of Figures 3–25 and 3–26. In the process of finding new constituents, there is an instruction:

> For every subset of the constituents in the input do:
>> Try to order them into a contiguous sequence
>> If this succeeds, then for every rule in the grammar do:
>>> If the rule spans the sequence. . .

When this is done, subsets of constituents are combined into sequences again and again, and we may apply the same rule over and over to the same constituents, only to discover that it does not match or that the result is already in the known constituents. The required amount of work at each step is exponential in the number of constituents already found.

There are many ways that procedures can be modified to make them more efficient while producing the same results. Often this involves setting things up so a particular computation can be done once and used in many places. Much of the work on context-free grammars in both computational linguistics and computer science has centered around designing efficient procedures, and a number of clever devices have been invented for keeping additional records of just what has been done and what its potential is for further expansion.

Avoiding problems. As mentioned in the discussion of top-down backtracking recognition above, there is a problem with left-recursive rules (those whose right-hand side begins with the symbol that is the left-hand side). If a straightforward top-down left-to-right procedure is applied to a grammar containing such rules (or containing more subtly recursive forms in which several rules are jointly recursive), it will go into an infinite loop. It is possible to avoid this by going right-to-left, but then right-recursive rules cause the same problem. In order for a parsing procedure to be fully general, it must deal with problems of this sort.

Taking advantage of special properties of particular grammars. For some grammars, there exist specialized parsing procedures that can operate much more efficiently. For example, some grammars make it possible to parse deterministically—to know exactly which rule to apply at each point. Although most natural language grammars do not have this property, there is a well-developed body of techniques for designing and using such grammars for computer languages.

There is an extensive theory of context-free parsing and recognition that deals with issues like those just listed. It is not the purpose of this book to survey the theory of formal grammars, but we will indicate the basic problems and techniques. In particular, we will describe the use of additional bookkeeping for building structures and the use of modified grammars with properties that suit particular parsing procedures. The reading list at the end of the chapter cites books that go into more detail on all of these topics.

Additional bookkeeping for generating structures

All of the procedures we have described so far are recognizers, which do not keep a full record of the structures they analyze. The extensions to the working structures needed to keep track of this structure depend on whether the process

---

Parse a sentence top-down left-to-right (nondeterministic)

Purpose: Produce a phrase structure tree corresponding to a parsing of a sequence of words as a sentence

Background: a *context-free grammar* and a *dictionary*   3–10 2–10

Inputs: a sequence of words

Results: a *phrase structure tree*   3–4 3–7

Working Structures:

  Distinguished node: a phrase structure node; initially a node with no parent, no children, and the distinguished symbol of the grammar as its label

  Nodes: a set of phrase structure nodes; initially containing just the distinguished node

  Current position: a position in the input sequence; initially 1

  Current node: a phrase structure node

  Remainder: a sequence of phrase structure nodes; initially containing the distinguished node

Basic Method: Keep repeating:

- If the remainder is empty, fail.
- Remove the first node from the remainder and assign it as the current node.
- If the label of the current node is a lexical category, then:
  - If the word at the current position belongs to that category, then:
    - Create a new node with no children whose label is the word and whose parent is the current node
    - Let it be the only child of the current node.
    - If the current position is the last in the sequence, then
        If the remainder is empty, return the nodes. Otherwise fail.
    - Otherwise increment the current position by 1.
  - If it does not belong to the category, then fail.
- If the label of the current node is a composite syntactic category, then:
  - Choose any rule in the grammar having that symbol as its left-hand side.
  - For each symbol in the right-hand side of the rule, create a new node with:
    - parent = the current node
    - label = the symbol
    - children = empty
  - Insert the sequence of new nodes (in the order they were created) at the front of the remainder.

Figure 3–28.   Top-down left-to-right parsing.

is parallel or backtracking and top-down or bottom-up. In general, the additional structure for a parallel process is easier to state but inefficient in its use of storage space, while with backtracking there are inefficiencies in processing effort, since the same structures are built over and over.

Figure 3–28 adds structures to a nondeterministic schema for top-down left-to-right parsing. Instead of keeping track of a sequence of symbols yet to be found, it creates a sequence of unfilled tree nodes, and fills them as it moves through the input from left to right. If it were applied to the sample sentence, making the same sequence of choices as in Figure 3–19, it would produce the tree of Figure 3–29. The maintenance of the information in a top-down backtracking or parallel schema is more complex, calling for maintaining multiple versions of the tree, and is left as an exercise.

The parallel bottom-up recognizer of Figures 3–25 and 3–26 already builds up some degree of structure in its set of constituents. However, these constituents preserve only the start, end, and label, without keeping track of parents and children. It is relatively easy to modify this procedure so that each constituent contains a list of the children that went into building it up as well. A tree can easily be generated from the results.

A bottom-up parallel parse may produce many more structures than the corresponding recognition. In recognition, after a new constituent is created, the procedure states: 'If this constituent is not equal to one already in the input or in the new constituents, add it to the new constituents.' This means that only one structure with a given start, end, and label will ever be created. If tree structures are to be saved, this is not sufficient. Two nodes can have the

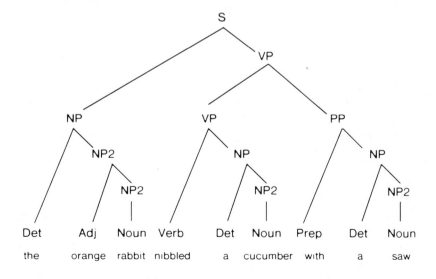

Figure 3–29. A parse tree produced for the sample sentence.

same start, end, and label, but different children. For ambiguous sentences, there will be alternative parsings that span the entire input.

Conversion of grammars

In the trace of a top-down backtracking recognition, it was pointed out that the rule 'VP → VP PP' was *left-recursive,* causing a problem for top-down left-to-right parsing. In trying to find a VP, the parser could try looking for this combined structure, which meant first looking for a VP, etc. Working from right to left would prevent this particular problem, but the same thing would then arise from the right-recursive rule NP2 → ADJECTIVE NP2. The grammar of Figure 3–17 can be converted as illustrated in Figure 3–30 to avoid left-recursion. Note that what we have done is to change one grammar to another. This is not something done at the time a sentence is parsed, but is a way of reorganizing the stored knowledge.

S	→	NP VP	NP3	→	Noun
S	→	NP VP PREPS	PREPS	→	PP
NP	→	Determiner NP2	PREPS	→	PP PREPS
NP	→	NP2	PP	→	Preposition NP
NP2	→	Noun	VP	→	Verb
NP2	→	Adjective NP2	VP	→	Verb NP
NP2	→	NP3 PREPS			

Figure 3–30. Grammar with left-recursion removed.

To eliminate the rule 'VP → VP PP,' we create a symbol for a sequence of prepositional phrases (PREPS), and then duplicate the rule for S to include one version with a sequence of prepositional phrases and one without. That is, the sentences formerly derived by using 'S → NP VP' followed by 'VP → VP PP' will now be derived by using 'S → NP VP PREPS' and 'PREPS → PP.'

The new grammar allows a top-down parser to operate without getting into infinite loops. It can be shown that it accepts exactly the same sentences as the original grammar. However, it is only *weakly equivalent*—that is, the old and new grammars will assign different structures for the same input sequence. Two grammars that always assign the same structures are said to be *strongly equivalent.* The importance of assigning the right structures is not apparent from the example grammar, but when we try to do an analysis of meaning, it is important to produce the analysis most appropriate to the use of the parsing rather than to be driven by technical details of what the parser can and cannot do. Computer languages are carefully designed so that problems such as left-recursion do not arise. Systems that try to parse natural language usually have a special mechanism that circumvents the uniform way of applying rules in order to produce the correct structures.

Grammar conversions are often necessary to take advantage of specialized parsing strategies, and the resultant grammar is said to be in *normal form* for the particular algorithm. In the previous section we mentioned that parallel top-down procedures could be simplified by putting the grammar into a normal form (predictive grammar) such that the right-hand side of every rule begins with a terminal symbol. Some parsers operate with a *binary grammar,* in which every rule has at most two symbols on its right-hand side. Others cannot use grammars in which a right-hand side contains only one symbol.

In each of these cases, a procedure can be devised that accepts any context-free grammar and produces a weakly equivalent grammar that meets the desired criteria. In some cases (such as producing a binary grammar), this is quite easy, while in others (such as eliminating left-recursion) the conversion procedure can be rather complex.

There are other specialized forms of grammar that cannot be produced for every language. For example, a useful property of some formal languages is that there exist context-free grammars for them that can be used deterministically. In a left-to-right top-down parse, it is always possible to decide which rule to use in expanding a symbol by looking ahead in the input sequence some fixed number of words. There is a large literature on variations of these *bounded-context grammars,* which describes how the choice of a rule can depend on varying amounts of lookahead and recall of what has been done so far. Natural languages do not apparently fall into this class, but it is reasonably easy to design bounded-context computer languages, thereby allowing the parser to operate very efficiently. There has been some recent research, such as Marcus (1980), described in Chapter 7, in which a more sophisticated concept of bounded-context has been applied in building a *deterministic* parser for English (one that can always tell which alternative to take as the parsing proceeds from left to right).

An example of a simple language that is not bounded-context is the abstract language consisting of a sequence of Xs followed by a Y followed by another sequence of Xs, where one of the sequences is of odd length and the other of even length. It is defined by the rules:

$$
\begin{array}{llll}
S & \rightarrow & \text{Odd Y Even} & \qquad \text{Odd} & \rightarrow & X \\
S & \rightarrow & \text{Even Y Odd} & \qquad \text{Odd} & \rightarrow & X \text{ Even} \\
& & & \qquad \text{Even} & \rightarrow & X \text{ Odd}
\end{array}
$$

Given a sentence of this language, there is no way of telling whether the initial X is part of an ODD or an EVEN without looking an unbounded distance ahead, since parity is a global property of the whole sequence.

Power, formal equivalence, and efficiency

In the theory of formal languages, one class of results deals with the *formal power* of different kinds of grammars. For example, it can be shown that there are languages that can be described with a context-free grammar that cannot be described with the simpler transition network formalism of Chapter 2. It was pointed out above that a deterministic (bounded-context) grammar cannot describe all of the languages that a general context-free grammar can, but it can also be shown that deterministic transition nets are fully equivalent to nondeterministic ones (see exercise 2.14). We will discuss the power of different grammar formalisms further in Section 4.2.

A second kind of result is the demonstration of *formal equivalence* between different grammars or different procedures. We have already described weak and strong equivalence in discussing the conversion of grammars from one form to another.

The third kind of result deals with the level of resources used by a given procedure in recognizing or parsing a sentence. In general, the question posed is 'For a given grammar, how does the amount of time it takes to recognize (parse) a sequence of words vary with the length of that sequence?' It is also possible to ask about the storage used or the variation of time with the size of the grammar, but most of the well-known results address the relationship between input length and parsing time. A particular procedure is said to be *quadratic*, for example, if the amount of time goes up in proportion to the square of the length of the sequence and *linear* if it goes up in direct proportion to the length.

As people have developed recognition and parsing procedures over the years, they have learned to sort out those sources of inefficiency that are due to a particular choice of how structures are stored or accessed from those that are inherent in the type of procedure. In the procedures described in this section, we have not been careful to optimize performance, and if they were programmed directly as described, they would be highly inefficient. For example, if an instruction that says 'If the new element is not equal to one already in the set' is implemented by simply checking against each member, it will require a length of time proportional to the length of the set. However, if a set is stored with elements indexed according to their contents, the check to see if an element is in the set can take an amount of time that is independent of the number of elements.

Section 3.6 describes a particular indexing structure that makes it possible to get the maximal theoretical efficiency in context-free parsing. It can be shown that a general parser will take a time proportional to the *cube* of the length of the input if the grammar allows ambiguities, or to its *square* if the grammar is unambiguous.

In all of the discussion of efficiency, it is important to remember that formal efficiency and practical efficiency are not the same. Although a quadratic procedure is likely to be more efficient than a cubic procedure for inputs of any significant length, these differences can be outweighed by differences in the way the procedure is implemented using particular data structures in a particular programming language on a particular machine. Often, for example, one parser is faster than another because it takes advantage of *pre-computations*, in which auxiliary tables or indexes are created that avoid computation steps as the parser runs.

Categorial grammar

There have been many variants of context-free grammar, each with its own specialized mechanisms. In general, such variants are not of interest, since they have the same generative power as a standard context-free grammar and do not support processing algorithms that are especially clear or efficient. However, a brief description is included here of *categorial grammar,* which has recently been used as the basis for *Montague grammar,* described in Appendix C.

In a categorial grammar, all the knowledge of syntactic structures is included in the dictionary, in the form of complex syntactic formulas associated with individual words. In some ways, categorial grammars can be thought of as a formalization of dependency grammars. In dependency theory, a noun can be replaced by a structure that has a noun as its head and a dependent modifier such as an adjective. If we designate nouns by the symbol N, and adjectives as N/N, we can imagine a kind of arithmetic cancellation. Just as 3/2 x 2 gives 3, we can think of the sequence 'ADJECTIVE NOUN' as the combination N/N x N, which cancels to leave N.

Going further, an adverb like *very* can be expressed as (N/N)/(N/N). It cancels with an adjective (N/N), with the result still an adjective. The phrase *very fine stuff* can be viewed as (N/N)/(N/N) N/N N. The first two elements cancel, leaving the sequence N/N N, followed by a second cancellation leaving N. The structure of the cancellations can be set into direct correspondence with a phrase structure tree, and it can be shown that for every categorial grammar there is a weakly equivalent context-free grammar and vice versa.

One problem with simple versions of dependency theory is that a phrase does not always play the same syntactic role that its head would alone. For example, a preposition with a noun depending on it is a complete modifying phrase, and can't be treated as though it were just an elaborate preposition. In linguistics, such constructions are called *exocentric,* as opposed to *endocentric* constructions, which can function as substitutes for their head. A structure in which an adjective modifies a noun is endocentric, since it can be substituted for a noun in order to elaborate a sentence further. On the other hand, noun-verb constructions are exocentric, since the resulting phrase is neither a noun nor a verb, but may be a sentence.

Categorial grammars express exocentric constructions by having categories such as S (for 'sentence'), which are not assigned to single words but can be the result of a cancellation. Most categorial grammars take noun and sentence as the two basic classes, deriving others from their dependencies on these. An intransitive verb like *sighed* can be thought of as S/N, or 'something that combines with a noun to produce a sentence.' A transitive verb is then (S/N)/N—something that combines with a noun (its object) to produce an intransitive verb. There are a number of further subtleties needed for a complete definition of a categorial grammar, such as specifying the left-right order of dependencies, and making use of subclassifications.

Logicians have been attracted to the categorial formalism because of its parsimony of mechanism. A single knowledge base (the dictionary with categorial formulas for each word) and a simple cancellation schema are all that is needed to define a language. The price paid for this simplicity of mechanism is a great deal of complexity in the category formulas assigned to individual words.

3.6 Charts and the active chart parser

The different parsing strategies outlined in this chapter each have advantages and deficiencies. In general, a top-down strategy avoids putting together combinations that would not fit into the overall structure of the sentence, while a bottom-up parser never tries building up structures that will fail to complete their later parts. A backup strategy duplicates many computations that are the same along separate paths, while a parallel strategy makes it possible to combine common subcalculations but involves extra bookkeeping.

However, it is possible to think of parsing in a more general way that avoids a commitment to any one strategy. By organizing the working structures to keep track of the progress of each constituent separately, we can define an algorithm that combines the advantages of all the strategies and leaves open the detailed choices of what rules will be tried in what order. This section describes such an algorithm (which we have chosen to call an *active chart parser*). It operates in a way that makes it possible to achieve the two principles of efficient parsing: only do what is relevant; and don't do anything more than once.

Well-formed substring tables (charts)

One of the basic inefficiencies in simple backtracking strategies is that the same work is often done over and over again along separate paths. To demonstrate this, consider a top-down backtracking parse of the sentence *The rabbit with a saw nibbled on an orange* using a version of our previous grammar which has no left-recursion, and which is simplified further by having no NP following the verb in a VP, as in Figure 3–31.

The parser begins by looking for an S, which (according to the first rule) can be found by finding an NP followed by a VP. After a large number of steps,

S	→	NP VP	NP2	→	NP3 PREPS
S	→	NP VP PREPS	NP3	→	Noun
NP	→	Determiner NP2	PREPS	→	PP
NP	→	NP2	PREPS	→	PP PREPS
NP2	→	Noun	PP	→	Preposition NP
NP2	→	Adjective NP2	VP	→	Verb

Figure 3–31. A grammar with no left-recursion.

including several backtracks, it will analyze *the rabbit with a saw* as an NP, followed by a VP consisting of the single word *nibbled*. At this point, another backtrack occurs because there are more words, but the remainder is empty, since both the NP and the VP have been found. The parser carefully retraces its steps through all of the saved records, trying all of the other possibilities. Finally it gets all the way to the bottom of the stack, finding the record '[1 *the* (S) : S → NP VP PREPS],' indicating that at the very beginning it could have used the second rule of the grammar instead of the first to expand the symbol S. The remainder then becomes 'NP VP PREPS,' and the parser begins once again finding the NP and VP with all of their substructure, redoing all of the work that was done before.

This process is highly inefficient. One of the basic advantages of a context-free grammar is the independence of its rules. A rule 'NP → ADJECTIVE NP2' applies regardless of how the NP itself is being used in other structures. Once a structure has been found in a top-down parse, it can be reused as a unit even though the constituent for which it was proposed as a member turned out to be wrong. Many parsers have bookkeeping mechanisms known as *well-formed substring tables* or *charts* for keeping track of constituents that were built up during part of the parse, but may be used by other rules.

The chart can be visualized as a network of *vertices* representing points in the sentence, linked by *edges* representing constituents. An edge names a constituent that begins and ends at the vertices it connects. The chart starts out containing only the edges corresponding to the individual words and their lexical categories, as in Figure 3–32. In a more sophisticated parser, entries for

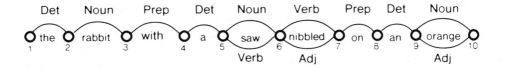

Figure 3–32. A chart initialized for parsing.

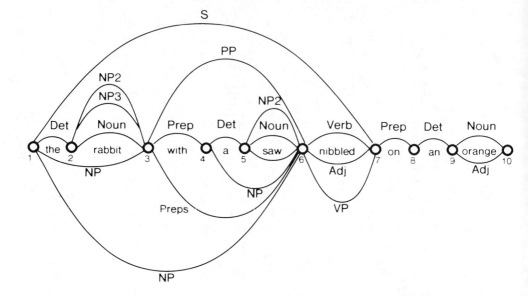

Figure 3–33. A chart containing a record of constituents found.

idioms could also be added directly to the chart, based on an idiom dictionary, and could then be used in the further parsing.

As a constituent is found by the parser, it is added to the chart. At the point in the parse described above where the second rule for S was tried, the chart would look like that of Figure 3–33.

The parser uses the chart by entering a new constituent whenever a rule succeeds and looking in it for constituents whenever there is a nonterminal at the beginning of the remainder. If there is an edge for the corresponding symbol at the current point in the chart, the parser can advance in the sentence to the point at the end of that edge without having to reparse the constituent. This can save a large amount of the combinatorial inefficiency of top-down parsing.

Actually, more information must be saved than what is shown in the chart. If a constituent succeeds with a particular parsing, but problems develop later on, there must be some way of knowing which rules have been tried and which haven't. The chart as described above keeps track only of those that succeeded, without indicating which rules were used. In the original chart parsers, such as Kay's (1967) 'powerful parser,' the rules were taken in an order that guaranteed that everything got tried, at the cost of some of the bottom-up problems of constructing things that could never be used. In the rest of this section we will see how a more elaborate kind of chart can save all of the necessary information.

Describes: a record of all constituents and partial constituents produced in the course of recognition

Background: a *context-free grammar* and a *dictionary*   3–10 2–10

Roles:

    Vertices: a sequence of *vertices*   §
    Edges: a set of *edges*   §
    Pending edges: a set of edges
    Pending edges have been proposed but not yet entered into the chart. There will be none when the chart is complete.

Classes:

> **Describes:** a constituent or partial constituent
>
> **Roles:**
>
>   **Starting vertex:** a vertex in the chart
>   **Ending vertex:** a vertex in the chart
>   **Label:** a *symbol*   3–10
>   **Remainder:** a sequence of symbols, possibly empty
>
> **Categories:**
>
>   **State:** {Active Complete}
>   An edge is complete if its remainder is empty. Otherwise it is active.
>
> **Predicates:**
>
> > Two edges are equal if their starting vertices, ending vertices and labels are equal, and their remainders contain the same symbols in the same order.

> **Describes:** a place in the sequence of words being parsed
>
> *Vertices correspond to the spaces between words (plus the beginning and end) instead of to the words themselves, so there will be one more vertex than there are words.*
>
> **Roles:**
>
>   [c]**Incoming edges:** The set of edges in the chart having this vertex as their ending vertex
>   [c]**Outgoing edges:** The set of edges in the chart having this vertex as their starting vertex

(Left margin label: **ACTIVE CHART**; inner box labels: **EDGE**, **VERTEX**)

Figure 3–34. An active chart.

Recognize a sentence using an active chart

Purpose: Test whether a sequence of words is a sentence in the language defined by a context-free grammar

Inputs: a sequence of words

Background: a *context-free grammar* and a *dictionary*   3–10 2–10

Working Structures:
    Chart: an *active chart*   3–34
    New edge: an edge

Basic Method:
- Set the chart to the result of *initializing* a chart for the input sequence.   3–36
- Keep repeating:
  - Remove any member of the pending edges of the chart and assign it as the new edge.
  - *Combine* the new edge with the chart.   3–38
    This may produce new pending edges.
  - If the new edge is active, *Propose* the first symbol of its remainder   3–37
    at its ending vertex in the chart.
    This may produce new pending edges.

Conditions:
    Succeed if at any time there is a complete edge in the edges or pending edges of the chart with:
- starting vertex = the first element of the vertices of the chart
- ending vertex = the last element of the vertices of the chart
- label = the distinguished symbol of the grammar.

If there are no pending edges when one is to be chosen, fail.

Figure 3–35. Recognition with an active chart.

An active chart parser

If we want to keep a complete record of what has gone on so far in a parse, we can best organize it as a chart that has a set of *active edges* in addition to the set of *complete edges*. Figure 3–34 defines an active chart. A complete edge represents a constituent that has been found. An active edge represents a point along the way in looking for a constituent. Its *remainder* indicates what still needs to be found.

In the text we will specify an edge by giving the numbers of its starting vertex and ending vertex, along with a representation of the grammar rule on which it is based and the remainder of that rule yet to be completed. The number of the ending vertex is used to separate the part of the rule that has already been matched from the remainder. For example, ($_4$NP → DET $_5$ NP2) represents an active edge beginning at vertex 4, ending at vertex 5, which is working on a constituent of type NP, has already found its DETERMINER, and still needs an NP2 to become complete. A complete edge will have the ending vertex number at the end of the rule, as in $(_4\mathrm{NP} \to \mathrm{DET}\ \mathrm{NP2}_6)$. In fact, this form contains more information than is actually in the formal structure, since there is no record of the part of the rule already matched. This additional information is needed for producing a parse tree, as discussed in exercise 3.21.

Figures 3–35 through 3–38 give a procedure for recognition with an active chart. The basic algorithm is a loop, in each cycle of which a new edge is *entered* into the chart. As part of this entering, there is a *combining* of the newly entered edge along with others already in the chart, and a *proposing* of other potential edges that the newly entered edge could combine with if they were found. At each stage, there is a list of *pending edges* waiting to be entered. The initialization of the chart puts some initial edges into this list, and both the searching and proposing activities can add new ones. The activity of combining is bottom-up in that it deals only with edges already in the chart. The activity of proposing is top-down, leading to a search for new edges on the basis that

---

Initialize a chart for a sequence of words

Purpose: Produce an active chart for the input sequence

Inputs: a sequence of words

Results: an *active chart* 3–34

Background: a *context-free grammar* and a *dictionary* 3–10 2–10

Working Structures:

   Chart: an active chart; initially an active chart with no edges or pending edges, and with a single vertex *(to represent the beginning of the word sequence)*.

Basic Method:

- Step through the words of the sequence doing:
  - Create a new vertex and insert it at the end of the vertices of the chart
  - For each lexical category in the dictionary entry for the word do:
    - Create a new edge with:
      - starting vertex = the next to last element of the vertices of the chart
      - ending vertex = the last element of the vertices of the chart
      - label = the lexical category
      - remainder = an empty sequence.
    - Add the new edge to the edges of the chart.
- *Propose* the distinguished symbol of the grammar at the first vertex 3–37
  of the chart.
  This will add at least one edge to the pending edges of the chart.
- Return the chart.

Figure 3–36. Initialization of an active chart.

Propose a syntactic category at a vertex in a chart

Purpose: Modify the chart by adding new pending active edges looking
for constituents of the category, beginning at the vertex

Background: a *context-free grammar*   3–10

Inputs: a symbol, a chart and a vertex in the vertices of that chart

Basic Method:

  If the symbol is a nonterminal symbol of the grammar and there is
  no edge in the edges or pending edges of the chart with the symbol
  as its label and with the vertex as its starting vertex,

  This will be false if the symbol has previously been proposed at that vertex.

  then for each rule in the grammar having the category as its left-
  hand side do:

  ■Create a new edge whose label is the category, whose remainder
  is the right-hand side of the rule, and whose starting and
  ending vertices are both the input vertex.

  ■Add this edge to the pending edges of the chart.

Figure 3–37. Propose new edges in an active chart.

they could be used to match the remainder of some active edge. By combining
the two directions in this way and keeping track of everything in the chart, we
avoid the inefficiencies of either approach taken alone.

There is a good deal of flexibility in choosing the order in which pending
edges will be processed. The definition in Figure 3–35 is actually nondeterministic in that it contains the step 'Remove any member of the pending edges....'
This is not the kind of nondeterminism that must be replaced with extra bookkeeping (as with the schemas in earlier sections), since any arbitrary strategy
(e.g., always take the edge that was put there first; always take the one put
there most recently) will result in a fully specified algorithm that has all of
the advantages of an active chart parse. The choice of strategy can be used to
modify the detailed behavior of the procedure, as discussed at the end of this
section. For the purpose of illustration, we will follow the strategy of always
taking the oldest edge from the pending edges.

We will follow an active chart parse of the sentence *The rabbit with a saw
nibbled on an orange,* using the original grammar of Figure 3–17, presented
again in Figure 3–39. The initialization process first produces the chart of
Figure 3–32, then proposes the symbol S at the first vertex. The proposing
mechanism drives the top-down aspects of the parse, setting up an attempt to
fill out the right-hand side of a rule, much as in a simpler top-down parser. The
proposal produces a new active edge for each rule whose left-hand side is the
symbol being proposed. Both the starting vertex and ending vertex of the edge
are the position at which it is being proposed, and the remainder is the entire

---

Combine an edge with a chart

Purpose: Modify the chart by adding a new edge and possibly new pending edges

Inputs: an *edge* and an *active chart*   3–34

Basic Method:

Add the edge to the edges of the chart

If it is:
- Complete, then for each of the active incoming edges of its starting vertex:
  - *Try to continue* the incoming edge with the edge.   §
- Active, then for each of the complete outgoing edges of its ending vertex:
  - Try to continue the edge with the outgoing edge.

Procedures:

Try to continue an active edge with a complete edge

Purpose: Produce a new edge

Inputs: an active edge and a complete edge whose starting vertex is the ending vertex of the active edge

Background: an active chart

Basic Method:

If the label of the complete edge is the same as the first symbol of the remainder of the active edge, then:

- Create a new edge with:
  - label = the label of the active edge
  - starting vertex = the starting vertex of the active edge
  - ending vertex = the ending vertex of the complete edge
  - remainder = a copy of the remainder of the active edge, with the first element removed.

  The new edge will be complete if there was only one element in the remainder of the active edge.

- Add the new edge to the pending edges of the active chart.

  The equality predicate defined in Figure 3–34 will be used in adding new members, so if an equal edge is already there nothing will be added.

Figure 3–38. Combine an edge with a chart.

right-hand side of the rule. In the grammar used here, there is only one rule for S, and the initialization creates a single pending edge, $(_1S \rightarrow {}_1NP\ VP)$.

In the first cycle through the basic algorithm, the initial edge is removed from the list of pending edges and entered in the chart. There is no way to combine it with anything, since the only edges in the chart are those put there by the initialization, which have lexical categories as their labels. According to the definition, a continuation would have to be a complete edge with label NP beginning at vertex 1. Since the new edge is active, the first symbol of its remainder (NP) is proposed at its ending vertex (1). Since there are two rules for NP, two new pending edges are created.

Step 1: Entering $(_1S \rightarrow {}_1NP\ VP)$

Pending edges created from proposing NP *at vertex* 1:

$$(_1NP \rightarrow {}_1DET\ NP2)\ \ (_1NP \rightarrow {}_1NP2)$$

The pending edges now contain these two new edges, and the first is selected for the next cycle. In this cycle, there is something to be combined, since the first symbol of the remainder (DET) matches a complete edge that was created for the word *the*. No proposing is done since the right-hand side of the rule begins with DETERMINER, a terminal symbol.

Step 2: Entering $(_1NP \rightarrow {}_1DET\ NP2)$

Pending edges created from combining the active edge: $(_1NP \rightarrow DET\ {}_2\ NP2)$

At this point, there are now two pending edges—the second NP edge proposed at vertex 1 and the new active edge just produced. Following our convention of always taking the oldest, we try the first of these, resulting in no combinations but a new proposal of NP2 at vertex 1.

Step 3: Entering $(_1NP \rightarrow {}_1NP2)$

Pending edges created from proposing NP2 *at vertex* 1:

$$(_1NP2 \rightarrow {}_1Noun)(_1NP2 \rightarrow {}_1ADJ\ NP2)(_1NP2 \rightarrow {}_1NP2\ PP)$$

At this point, we take the next pending edge, which was put there as the result of combining $(_1NP \rightarrow {}_1DET\ NP2)$ with the complete edge $_1DET_2$. The old active edge remains in the chart, which will have significance later. Since there are no edges with label NP2 beginning at vertex 2, a new edge is proposed for each rule expanding NP2.

Step 4: Entering $(_1NP \rightarrow DET\ {}_2\ NP2)$

Pending edges created from proposing NP2 *at vertex* 2:

$$(_2NP2 \rightarrow {}_2NOUN)(_2NP2 \rightarrow {}_2ADJ\ NP2)(_2NP2 \rightarrow {}_2NP2\ PP)$$

Note that the active edges whose labels are NP2 starting at vertex 2 are completely separate from the three NP2 edges created in step 3, which begin at vertex 1.

In the next two steps, no new pending edges are created since neither remainder begins with a nonterminal or can be combined with something already in the chart.

Step 5: Entering $(_1NP2 \rightarrow {}_1NOUN)$

S	→	NP VP	NP2	→	NP2 PP
NP	→	Determiner NP2	PP	→	Preposition NP
NP	→	NP2	VP	→	Verb
NP2	→	Noun	VP	→	Verb NP
NP2	→	Adjective NP2	VP	→	VP PP

Figure 3–39. Sample context-free grammar.

Step 6: Entering $(_1\text{NP2} \rightarrow {}_1\text{ADJ NP2})$

No proposing is done in the next step, even though the edge being entered has a remainder beginning with a nonterminal (NP2). This is because there are already edges with label NP2 beginning at vertex 1. This condition, as specified in the procedure for proposing a symbol for a vertex, is the key to avoiding problems with left-recursion.

Step 7: Entering $(_1\text{NP2} \rightarrow {}_1\text{NP2 PP})$

Step 8: Entering $(_2\text{NP2} \rightarrow {}_2\text{NOUN})$

Pending edge created from combining the active edge with one that was created for the noun rabbit: $(_2\text{NP2} \rightarrow \text{NOUN}_3)$

Step 9: Entering $(_2\text{NP2} \rightarrow {}_2\text{ADJ NP2})$

Step 10: Entering $(_2\text{NP2} \rightarrow {}_2\text{NP2 PP})$

Step 11: Entering $(_2\text{NP2} \rightarrow \text{NOUN}_3)$

Pending edges created from combining active edges with the newly entered complete edge: $(_2\text{NP2} \rightarrow \text{NP2 }_3\text{ PP})$ $(_1\text{NP} \rightarrow \text{DET NP2}_3)$

Step 12: Entering $(_2\text{NP2} \rightarrow \text{NP2 }_3\text{ PP})$

Pending edge created from proposing PP at vertex 3: $(_3\text{PP} \rightarrow {}_3\text{PREP NP})$

Step 13: Entering $(_1\text{NP} \rightarrow \text{DET NP2}_3)$

Pending edge created from continuing active edge with the newly entered complete edge: $(_1\text{S} \rightarrow \text{NP }_3\text{ VP})$

Step 14: Entering $(_3\text{PP} \rightarrow {}_3\text{PREP NP})$

Pending edge created from combining the new edge with one for PREPOSITION*:* $(_3\text{PP} \rightarrow \text{PREP }_4\text{ NP})$

Step 15: Entering $(_1\text{S} \rightarrow \text{NP }_3\text{ VP})$

Pending edges created from proposing VP at vertex 3:

$(_3\text{VP} \rightarrow {}_3\text{VERB})(_3\text{VP} \rightarrow {}_3\text{VERB NP})(_3\text{VP} \rightarrow {}_3\text{VP PP})$

Step 16: Entering $(_3\text{PP} \rightarrow \text{PREP }_4\text{ NP})$

Pending edges created from proposing NP at vertex 4:

$(_4\text{NP} \rightarrow {}_4\text{DET NP2})$ $(_4\text{NP} \rightarrow {}_4\text{NP2})$

Several steps later (it is left to the reader to fill in the details) there will be a pending edge which combines the active edge created in step 14 and entered in step 16 with a complete edge $_4NP_6$. This will result in a new complete edge $_3PP_6$ which will in turn combine with the active edge ($_2NP2 \rightarrow NP2\ _3\ PP$), which was created in step 11, resulting in another complete edge $_2NP2_6$. Looking in the chart, we find the active edge ($_1NP \rightarrow DET\ _2\ NP2$), which was created in step 2. This active edge was combined with an NP2 edge starting at vertex 2 once already (in step 11), but this does not remove it from the chart, and it can be combined again with the new constituent. One of the most important facts about this procedure is the way in which an active edge is kept active even though it has already been combined with a following complete edge, so that whenever a new complete edge is found, it can be used. This goes hand in hand with the fact that each complete edge is entered into the chart and can be combined with every new active edge at the proper place whose remainder begins with its label.

The parse continues in the same way through the sentence, and its completion is left as an exercise. If it is not apparent to the reader from the trace how greatly the duplication of work is reduced by this procedure, he or she should go back and simulate this parse for any of the other procedures!

It can be shown that with this algorithm, the amount of time taken to parse a sentence depends on the cube of its length if the grammar is ambiguous (i.e., it can assign two different parsings to the same sentence) and the square of the length otherwise. This is the fastest that parsing can be done (producing structures), although there exist somewhat faster recognition algorithms which are much more complex. As mentioned earlier, there exist special classes of context-free grammars, such as bounded-context grammars, for which faster parsing times are possible.

Control structure and agendas

In all of the procedures described in previous sections, some of the information about the state of the parse was implicit in the control structure—it was not explicitly recorded in the working structures just which rules had and had not been tried in which positions. The active chart provides a complete bookkeeping method for parsing. All of the information about what has been tried and what is yet to be tried can be derived from the chart. Therefore it is not necessary to cycle through the generation of new edges in the strict left-to-right fashion of the example described above. New edges can be entered in any order without losing the completeness of the parsing.

For example, if we were to always choose the pending edge that progresses furthest through the sentence (i.e., that has the highest numbered ending vertex of any pending edge), the procedure would try to finish an entire parse based on one rule choice before exploring alternatives. If we combined this with a stopping rule that terminated the parse as soon as it found a complete S edge from the start to end of the sentence, the parser would have some of the properties of a backtracking parser—stopping quickly when a successful parse is found. The strategy used above is much more like a parallel parser, doing the work for all of the different alternatives at one place in the input string before moving on to the next.

Parsers based on active chart parsing, such as Kaplan's GSP (General Syntactic Processor), make it possible to design flexible strategies for deciding the order in which to try rules. The pending edges, along with other pending tasks involving other levels of analysis, form an *agenda* of things to be done. At each cycle through the system, strategy procedures can be applied to decide which item to take next from the agenda. This simplifies the writing of systems that integrate syntactic processing with the other levels, including morphological analysis of words and semantic analysis. It is also possible to use different control strategies to build models of the human parsing process, and parsers of this sort have served as a basis for psychological theories and experiments.

Further Reading for Chapter 3

Linguistic structure and word classification. The ideas that have been presented in this chapter and the previous one are discussed clearly in Gleason's *Linguistics and English Grammar*. Lyons's *Introduction to Theoretical Linguistics* (Chapters 5 and 6) presents many of the details.

Theory of context-free grammars and parsing. Many of the techniques described here were developed for use in parsing computer programming languages. The theory is developed at length in Aho and Ullman's *The Theory of Parsing, Translation, and Compiling* (1972) and Hopcroft and Ullman's *Formal Languages and their Relation to Automata* (1969). A brief, clear introduction can be found in a paper on 'Translator writing systems' by Feldman and Gries (1968).

Parsing systems for natural language. The early approaches to parsing natural langauge are described in a 1967 collection of papers edited by Borko, entitled *Automated Language Processing.* It includes survey papers by Bobrow on syntactic analysis and by Simmons on question-answering systems, including Protosynthex I. The Harvard Syntactic Analyzer is described in detail by Kuno (1965). The 'powerful parser' is described by Kay (1967). Many of the later developments are included in a 1973 collection edited by Rustin entitled *Natural Language Processing.*

Active chart parsing. One of the first parsers to use a data structure like the active chart was Earley's 'An efficient context-free parsing algorithm' (1970). This algorithm used a fixed ordering of things to try. Kaplan's General

Syntactic Processor (1973a,b, 1975) extended the use of active charts to transition network parsers and introduced the concept of flexible scheduling. Sheil (1976) has proved a number of results about the efficiency of a class of algorithms related to the one described here.

Specialized grammars. Techniques for writing and using specialized grammars were developed by Floyd (1964) and Knuth (1968a), among others. They are described in the Aho and Ullman volume mentioned above.

Variants of context-free grammar. Dependency grammars are described in Hays (1964). Categorial grammars were first developed by logicians such as Adjukiewicz (1935) and are described in several of the surveys mentioned above. A good example of their recent use in Montague grammar is a paper by Lewis (1972), from which the example in exercise 3.18 was adapted.

Exercises for Chapter 3

Exercises for Section 3.1

3.1 Write a procedure for deciding whether a dependency tree contains a given pair, as described for Protosynthex I. The inputs are:

   A word which is the *above*.

   A word which is the *below*

   A *dependency tree* (see Figures 3–4 and 3–6) that is to be checked.

The algorithm should simply return with success or failure, depending on whether there are two nodes A and B such that A is an ancestor of B, the *above* is A's head, and the *below* is B's head. It may be easier to write a nondeterministic schema first, then modify it to be a fully defined algorithm.

3.2 For the phrase structure shown in Figure 3–3, list the following:

   a) The label of the root node

   b) The labels of the children of the root node

   c) The labels and contents of all the leaf nodes

   d) The labels of all the nodes that are ancestors of the node whose word is *glorious*.

3.3 Choose some kind of complex object with which you are familiar. It can be a mechanical object like a motorcycle, a conceptual object such as a computer program, or a social structure such as an academic department. Apply the three different structural approaches to it. Give examples of aspects of its structuring that are best brought out by each approach. For a good discussion of structures, take a look at Pirsig's *Zen and the Art of Motorcycle Maintainance.*

Exercises for Section 3.2

3.4 Derive some sentence from the grammar of 3–9 other than the ones derived in the examples. Try to derive one that fits the grammar but is not a sentence of English.

3.5 Write a context-free grammar for time-of-day expressions (as described in exercise 2.10). Demonstrate a derivation with your grammar, using both derivation procedures (with structures and with sequences).

3.6 It was mentioned in the text that with a context-free grammar we can avoid the need for a dictionary by simply letting lexical categories be nonterminal symbols and having rules like:

$$
\begin{array}{llll}
\text{Noun} & \rightarrow & \textit{horsecollar} & \text{Verb} \;\rightarrow\; \textit{fidget} \\
\text{Noun} & \rightarrow & \textit{newspaper} & \text{Verb} \;\rightarrow\; \textit{expectorate} \\
\text{Noun} & \rightarrow & \textit{wicket} & \text{Verb} \;\rightarrow\; \textit{impeach}
\end{array}
$$

How could we avoid the use of lexical categories in writing the transition network grammars of Chapter 2? Is it possible to produce a network in which the label of each arc is a word, that defines the same set of patterns as one that includes lexical categories as labels? What problems are there in doing so?

3.7 Write a context-free grammar that will derive all of the sentences in the left-hand column below, but none in the right-hand column. Make it reasonably general (i.e., do not have rules for just these specific sentences). Try to express in general terms any difficulty that arises in writing the rules succinctly.

She walks.	*She walk.*
He does walk.	*He does walks.*
Does she walk?	*Do she walk?*
They ride.	*They rides.*
We do walk.	*We does walk.*
Do they walk?	*Do they walks?*

Exercises for Section 3.3

3.8 Show how the terms *top-down* and *bottom-up* can be applied in describing how a detective goes about solving a murder. Consider questions like 'Who would profit from the death?' and 'Who wears size 18 herringbone tread running shoes?'

3.9 Estimate the number of different parsings for the sentence *Gravely concerned with spreading racial violence, President Kennedy used his press conference to issue counsel to both sides in the struggle.* Which types of ambiguity seem the hardest to eliminate? (This sentence was actually parsed by the Harvard Syntactic Analyzer, using a grammar with over 3000 rules, and there was ambiguity).

3.10 Figure 3–16 shows three of the four possible parsings for *Time flies like an arrow* with the given grammar. Show the fourth.

Exercises for Section 3.4

3.11 The trace of a top-down backtracking recognizer given in Section 3.4 ends when it has found one acceptable analysis of the sentence.

a) Draw a tree corresponding to the analysis it recognized (but did not record).

b) Draw a tree for a different parsing of the same sentence.

c) Give an ordering for the grammar rules that would produce this other tree first.

3.12 Section 3.4 discusses top-down parallel recognition but does not give a detailed procedure or a trace. Give the procedure and trace it through the recognition of the sample sentence with the sample grammar. *Warning:* this is straightforward but rather long, and the trace is tedious.

3.13 Write a procedure that does a bottom-up backtracking left-to-right recognition.

3.14 (Recognition procedures)

a) For each of the following grammars, decide which of the simple recognition procedures would be most and least efficient, and explain why. Remember that the question concerns which recognizer would best handle *this grammar.*

b) Consider the language described by each grammar, and find the most efficient algorithm and weakly equivalent grammar that will accept the same set of sentences. Lower case letters indicate terminal symbols; upper case indicate nonterminals. The distinguished symbol is S.

1.			2.		
S	→	X X	S	→	X
X	→	b X Y	X	→	X Y
X	→	a X Z	X	→	Z X
X	→	c	X	→	Y Z Z
Y	→	a a	Y	→	a Y
Y	→	b a	Z	→	Z a
Z	→	a b	Y	→	a b a
Z	→	b b	Z	→	a b b a

3.15 (*For programmers*) Write programs in a standard computer language such as LISP or PASCAL for some of the procedures in Section 3.4.

Exercises for Section 3.5

3.16 Write in detail the procedure for a top-down backtracking parse that produces a structure for every interpretation.

3.17 Give a procedure for converting any grammar that is not left-recursive into a *predictive grammar* (one in which the right-hand side of every rule begins with a terminal symbol).

3.18 Consider the following categorial grammar and examples. Show at least one successful tree of cancellations for each of the sentences. The rule formalism has been augmented here to indicate the order in which the components fit together. A word of category X/Y cancels with a Y on its right to produce an X, while Y\X cancels with one on its left. That is, the sequences 'X/Y Y' and 'Y Y\X both produce X. The basic categories are S (sentence), N (proper noun), and C (common noun).

Grammar:

a	N/C	*Petunia*	N
believes	(N\S)/S	*pig*	C
grunts	N\S	*piggishly*	(N\S)/(N\S)
is	(N\S)/N	*Porky*	N
loves	(N\S)/N	*yellow*	C/C

Examples:

A yellow pig loves Petunia.
Porky piggishly grunts.
Petunia believes Porky is a pig.

Exercises for Section 3.6

3.19 (Trace of an active chart recognition)

a) Finish the simulation of the active chart recognition as started in the text.

b) Repeat the trace using the opposite convention for deciding which pending edge to enter. Always take the one most recently added to the list instead of the one that has been there longest.

c) Do the same, but use the grammar in the opposite order. That is, when proposing rules for a symbol, put the alternatives on the list starting from the bottom of the grammar.

Note: For all of these, if you have access to a computer, you may find it more interesting to write a program that implements the active chart parsing procedure and let it do the work.

3.20 Modify the definitions in Figures 3–34 through 3–38 so that active edges are not put into the pending edges if the first symbol of their continuation is a terminal symbol and the corresponding terminal is not already in the chart at the right place. How many steps are removed from the trace given in the text by this modification? This is a simple form of lookahead like the one discussed in the section on bounded-context grammars.

3.21 The definitions of Figure 3–34 through 3–38 give a recognition procedure using an active chart. They do not create a phrase structure tree representing the analysis of a sentence, although all of the ingredients of such a tree are placed in the chart.

a) Modify the definitions of the active chart and of the procedures so that each edge has a set of associated phrase structure tree nodes, representing different parsings for the constituent corresponding to the edge. When the procedure is complete, each of the nodes associated with each edge labeled S spanning the entire input should be a distinct parsing for the sentence.

b) Leaving the definitions and procedures as they are, write a procedure that takes a completed chart as its input and produces a set of phrase structure trees, one corresponding to each distinct parsing of the sentence.

Chapter 4

Transformational Grammar

This chapter introduces the theory of transformational generative grammar, as developed by Chomsky and his followers over the past twenty-five years. This approach has come to dominate theoretical linguistics, especially in the United States, and its adherents have dealt with many issues that bear on our understanding of language as a cognitive process. The computational implications of transformational grammar are complex and have been the source of much debate and misunderstanding. After presenting the basic theory and describing how it has developed, we will attempt to draw connections to the approach taken in this book and to work in artificial intelligence. First, however, we will present the theory in its own terms.

It is important to be aware that three related but distinct things are at times labeled 'transformational grammar.' First, there is the general approach to linguistic theory (the generative paradigm) that was discussed in Chapter 1. Within this paradigm, the problem of linguistics is seen as that of understanding syntactic competence—the formal structure that underlies the intuitions of a native speaker about the grammatical structure of sentences. It emphasizes the formal characterization of grammaticality, and its research methodology is dominated by the development of syntactic formalisms that provide precise means for characterizing the set of sentences of a language. It is far from being a coherent, consistent paradigm with an agreed upon set of questions and methodologies at all levels of detail. Section 4.5 presents a number of different emphases within generative linguistics and Appendix C describes some of the many variations of generative theory that have been developed.

Second, there is a particular model of language within the generative paradigm that might be called the *transformational model*. It is described in detail in Section 4.3, and has served as the basis for much of the work in generative linguistics. However, it is not the only possible generative model, and much of the linguistic research that is described as 'non-transformational' (or even 'anti-transformational') argues against this model while maintaining the same generative approach to language and grammar. As a simple example, the basic ideas of context-free grammar presented in Chapter 3 are consistent with the generative paradigm but are not transformational.

Finally, within the transformational model there are several distinct formal mechanisms, described in Section 4.3. Among these mechanisms, there is one particular kind of rule called a *transformation rule*. Transformational grammar was so named because this kind of rule was an innovation, but it includes other formal devices as well. In fact, there are current attempts to limit the importance of transformations or to eliminate them altogether while preserving other parts of the overall transformational model.

This chapter proceeds in a roughly historical fashion, describing the origins of transformational grammar, its early standard form, and the motivations behind the more recent developments. Section 4.1 describes the background in which transformational grammar arose, demonstrating some ways in which immediate constituent grammars are inadequate for describing the properties of natural language. Section 4.2 introduces *generalized rewrite rules,* which are a formal link between the simpler grammars presented in Chapter 3 and the mechanisms of transformational grammar. Section 4.3 presents an idealized version of transformational grammar as it was seen in the mid-sixties, briefly mentioning some of the earlier versions. The remaining sections provide a framework for understanding more recent developments in transformational theory, which are discussed in Appendix C.

4.1 The inadequacies of phrase structure grammars

Transformational grammar developed in the context of structural linguistics, and to understand its formal development it is useful to look at the kinds of problems that were considered most relevant at the time. This was before the development of formal grammars of the kind presented in Chapter 3, and the discussion was couched primarily in terms of immediate constituent structuring as described in Section 3.1.

In describing a language, a linguist produced a set of rules such that an immediate constituent structure conforming to those rules could be assigned to every sentence of the language. The rules specified the composition of constituents (the children) allowed at a node of a given category. There were two basic assumptions made at that time about phrase structure that led to problems: *tree-like structuring* and the *locality of rules* (each rule dealt with a single node).

The assignment of structures to discontinuous constituents

Given a sentence like (1) below, we would naturally expect a structure like that of tree A of Figure 4–1, in which the phrase *a man wearing earrings* is a single constituent.

A man wearing earrings walked by. (1)

A man walked by wearing earrings. (2)

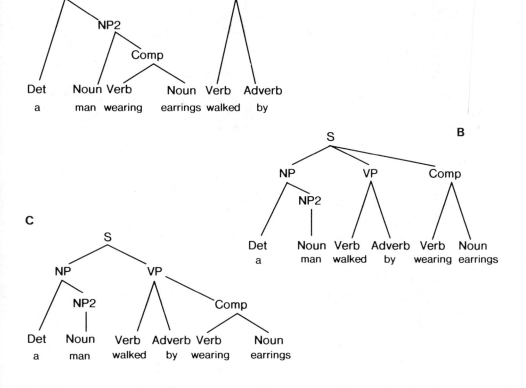

Figure 4–1. Immediate constituent structures for related sentences.

However, for (2) we are forced to assign either B or C, since there is no way to attach *wearing earrings* directly to *a man* without violating the ordered tree-like nature of the constituent structure or giving up the notion of a sentence as an NP followed by a VP. It is possible to write a grammar that generates all three trees of Figure 4–1 by including rules that allow modifiers like *wearing earrings* to appear in the relevant places, but it is awkward to do so and it leads to building structures that do not correspond to our intuitions about meaning. We understand *wearing earrings* as a modifier of *the man* regardless of where it appears and we would like the structural description to reflect this connection.

Similarly, we would like to treat both (3) and (4) as making use of a single lexical item (or idiom) *call up.*

He called up his poor old lonely mother.	(3)
He called her up long distance twice a week.	(4)

If we simply treat *called* and *up* as two unrelated words, the grammar fails to reflect the underlying structure in which they are really a single unit, and in a tree structure for (4) they cannot form a constituent by themselves, since *her* is interposed.

Agreement

A common phenomenon in most languages is the matching of attributes between a verb and one or more of the major nouns in the sentence, or between a noun and its modifying adjectives. English is relatively deficient in this area, but does demand agreement in number (singular versus plural) between subject and verb. A third-person singular subject demands a verb ending with some form of the suffix *-s,* as in *He plays,* while a plural subject takes the root form of the verb, as in *They play.* This distinction (and other syntactic distinctions like it) can be critical to analyzing the meaning of sentences, as in the pair *I know Danny and Toni knows me* versus *I know Danny and Toni know me.* Agreement does not just apply between adjacent constituents, but can involve a gap, as in:

What <u>architect</u> do you know who <u>likes</u> the balalaika?

What <u>architects</u> do you know who <u>like</u> the balalaika?

As with the examples above, there is no way to reflect this agreement in a tree structure that matches our intuitions about constituent structure. Of course, there are many other ways to describe the relationship of agreement, and linguistic analyses throughout the centuries have done so. The problem comes in trying to give a precise uniform account of grammatical rules based on constituent structure.

Internal word structure and paradigms

In trying to use ideas of constituent structure for morphology as well as for word-order syntax, people were led into analogies between word structure and sentence structure, and into a number of problems. In writing agreement rules, for example, we must have some way to generate the final forms of the words. In the case of simple endings like the *-s* in *plays* or the *-ing* in *enjoying,* the ordinary notions of constituent structure can be applied. But languages typically have much more intricate morphological structure. Even in English, simple constituency cannot handle forms like *ring, rang, rung.* Attempts were made within structural linguistics to preserve the notion of constituency by introducing discontinuous constituents, such as *r–ng* that could then be combined with other constituents by special grammar mechanisms. This was a limited improvement and it still had no obvious way to handle *paradigms* (sets of alternative forms) like *am, is, are, was,...,* in which the underlying structure is completely obscured by unrelated forms. Note that this use of the word 'paradigm' is completely different from the scientific paradigms described in Chapter 1.

The assignment of structures to related sentences

All of the problems described so far were recognized and discussed within the structural paradigm. Solutions were proposed with varying degrees of complexity, and it was assumed that through some amount of patching, the basic ideas of constituent structure could be extended. A major shift occurred after the publication of Chomsky's *Syntactic Structures* in 1957. He insisted that an entire dimension of linguistic structuring was being left out, and that the theories he proposed would illuminate this additional dimension as well as solve many of the detailed technical problems of constituency theory.

The phrase structure analysis that is directly associated with a sentence is superficial in that it is determined by the ordering of elements in the sentence. A native speaker has intuitions about the similarity of sentences that are not based solely on ordering, but are still based on syntactic structure rather than on meaning. For example, we recognize the first pair of sentences in Figure 4–2 as more closely related than the second pair, even though the two members of each pair can be seen as *paraphrases* (sentences with the same meaning). The connection depends on some intuition of underlying similarity of structure. The sentences of the third pair have different functions—one is a question and one is a phrase referring to an object, rather than a statement about it. Nevertheless, there is the same strong feeling of structural similarity as with the first pair, and language teachers have for many years used sets like these in exercises to teach the different forms of a language. A student is given one of the forms and asked to *transform* it to one of the others.

A porcupine nibbled that elm.
That elm was nibbled by a porcupine.

My car isn't working.
The automobile that belongs to me is out of order.

Which elm did the porcupine nibble?
...the elm which the porcupine nibbled...

Figure 4–2. Different forms with underlying similarity.

The members of each set of sentences in Figure 4–3 have similar forms but different meanings. Again, the problem seems to be not just one of words but of different syntactic structures. The phrase *flying planes* is ambiguous not only because there are multiple meanings for the noun *plane,* but also because the phrase can be interpreted as referring either to planes that are flying or to the act of flying them. In the sentences with *buying* and *falling,* other factors make it clear which interpretation is intended. In the sentences with *please,* the surface forms are identical but reflect different underlying relationships. In one, Warren is doing the pleasing, while in the other he is the one being pleased. A sentence like *The chicken is ready to eat* is ambiguous because it allows both interpretations.

Chomsky proposed that linguistic theory should deal with relations between structures by looking both at *surface structures,* which had been studied previously, and at *deep structures,* which capture the underlying similarities and differences. This was much more than a simple refinement of the ideas of constituency, since it meant dealing with structures that could not be observed in the data but that were postulated to have some kind of underlying mental reality. This appeal to mental entities and the corresponding need to use a native speaker's intuitions as data were the essential issues of debate in the shift from the structural to the generative paradigm. We will discuss the issue of the psychological reality of transformational grammar further in Section 4.5.

Flying planes can be dangerous.
Buying planes can be dangerous.
Falling planes can be dangerous.

Warren is eager to please.
Warren is easy to please.

Figure 4–3. Similar forms with underlying differences.

4.2 Generalized rewrite rules

The solution proposed by Chomsky for the problems of immediate constituent grammars grew out of his attempts to formalize the kind of analysis such grammars provided. A *grammar rule,* as defined in Chapter 3, is a formal object specifying a possible structural relationship among phrases and words in a sentence of a language. A formal definition of a grammar (like that of Figure 3–10) embodies assumptions about the nature of the structures, in this case the assumptions of tree-structured constituency and the locality of rules.

For the definition of Figure 3–10, we can describe the relation of grammar rules to linguistic structures:

> *A sequence of words is in the language defined by a grammar if there exists a phrase structure tree such that:*
>
> 1. *The leaf nodes of the tree correspond in order to the words of the sequence, with each word being the label of the corresponding node.*
> 2. *Every node whose label is a lexical category has a single child which has as its label a word belonging to that category.*
> 3. *Every other node in the tree corresponds to one rule of the grammar, with the label of the node being the left-hand side of the rule and the sequence of labels of its children matching the right-hand side.*

This description treats grammar rules as *constraints* on phrase structure trees. It does not say anything about how a sentence is analyzed or generated, but is a static characterization of what constitutes a valid analysis—a tree structure that describes the sentence in terms of constituents based on the grammar. In this sense, it does not give up the basic structural orientation. It differs from earlier approaches primarily in its formality and sparseness of mechanism.

The defects of phrase structure grammars described in Section 4.1 are really limitations on the usefulness of this kind of constraint. Phenomena like agreement must be handled by adding further constraints that are not conveniently expressed in terms of the sequence of constituents for a single node. The difficulties arise in providing precise forms for informally stated constraints like 'The subject and verb must agree in number and person.'

Instead of trying to add other kinds of constraints to the basic analysis of the constituent structure (an approach that many other people took and continue to explore, as we will see in Chapter 6 and in Appendix C), Chomsky proposed a shift in perspective. Instead of treating grammar rules as constraints on the structure assigned to a sentence, he noticed that they could be treated as rules for specifying the steps in a *derivation,* as described in Section 3.2. In a grammar consisting purely of context-free rules, this shift of view made no significant difference. A derivation is simply a process by which an analysis meeting the constraints is generated step by step. The derivation does not add information to the phrase structure analysis, since the final tree structure uniquely specifies which rules were applied, and the order in which the nodes are expanded in the course of the derivation has no effect on the structures that are produced. However, thinking of rules as steps in a derivation opened up possibilities for new kinds of rules that had no direct correlates in the phrase structure analysis.

A more general notion of derivation and *rewrite rule* permits structures to be manipulated in the course of a derivation without producing corresponding structures in the final result. The simplest generalization of rewrite rules does not involve trees at all, but is based on string derivation, as it was defined in Figure 3–13 and illustrated in Figure 3–14. Grammar rules specify the legal steps in a process of modifying a sequence of category symbols. At each step, one symbol of the sequence is replaced with a sequence corresponding to the right-hand side of some grammar rule.

Figure 4–4 illustrates a grammar based on a more general kind of rewrite rule that differs formally from our previous context-free rules in three ways. First, it allows a sequence of symbols, rather than a single symbol, on the left-hand side. Second, in addition to syntactic categories and words, it allows special *grammatical markers*. Third, it allows the right-hand side of a rule to be empty. Figure 4–5 gives a formal definition of a general rewrite grammar. Following the example of Figure 3–13, we can define a process of derivation for this kind of grammar, as shown in Figure 4–6.

As mentioned in Figure 4–6, we are considering morphemes like -*s* as words. This grammar does not deal with the problem of 'gluing together' the morphemes into actual English words. Figure 4–7 illustrates two different derivations using the grammar of Figure 4–4, making different choices of which rules to apply. At each step of the derivation, a rule is chosen whose left-hand side matches some sequence of adjacent symbols. That sequence is removed and replaced with the right-hand side of the rule.

Grammars like the one of Figure 4–4 are not *context-free*. They can be used to indicate context dependencies by putting more than one element on the left-hand side of a rule. Rule 6 is an example of a particular kind of rule called a

1.	S	→	NP VP
2.	NP	→	Determiner Noun Number
3.	Number	→	Singular
4.	Number	→	Plural
5.	Singular VP	→	Verb -*s*
6.	Plural VP	→	Plural Verb
7.	Plural	→	-*s*

Grammatical markers: Plural, Singular

Figure 4–4. A general rewrite grammar.

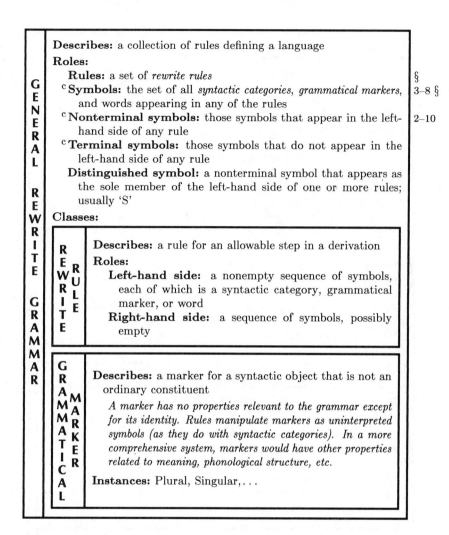

Figure 4–5. A grammar based on generalized rewrite rules.

context-sensitive rule. In a context-sensitive rule, the right-hand side is formed from the left-hand side by taking just one of the symbols and replacing it with a different symbol or sequence. Such rules are often written using a notation in which the left-hand side consists of the single symbol that is expanded, with the other symbols appearing in brackets as a *context* following the rule. Rule 6 would be written as 'VP → VERB[PLURAL ___].' The underline in the brackets indicates that the VP must appear following the marker PLURAL in order for this rule to apply. Note that rule 5 is not a context-sensitive rule, since both elements appearing in the left-hand side are replaced. A grammar

---

Generate a sentence (nondeterministic)

Purpose: Produce a sentence using a general rewrite grammar

Results: a sequence of words that is a sentence

Background: a *general rewrite grammar*   4–5

Working Structures:

    Derived sequence: a sequence, every member of which is either
a symbol of the grammar or a word; initially containing just the
distinguished symbol of the grammar

*A word may become part of the derived sequence in two ways: either by
lexical insertion (replacing a symbol for a lexical class it belongs to), or
by generation directly from a rule of the grammar. The latter way will be
used, for example, to generate suffixes that cannot stand alone. We allow
suffixes to be included as words (see the discussion in Section 2.2).*

Basic Method: Keep repeating:

- If the derived sequence contains only words, return the derived sequence.
- Otherwise, either *apply a rule of the grammar* to the derived sequence   §
  or *insert a lexical item* in the derived sequence.   §
- If this fails, then fail.

Procedures:

Apply a rule of a grammar to a sequence of symbols

Purpose: Modify the sequence in accordance with a grammar rule

Inputs: a general rewrite grammar and a sequence containing words
and symbols

Basic Method:

- Choose any subsequence of symbols in the sequence that is identical to the left-hand side of some rule of the grammar.
- Remove the subsequence from the sequence and replace it with a copy of the right-hand side of that rule.

Insert a lexical item in a sequence

Purpose: Modify the sequence in accordance with a dictionary entry

Background: a *dictionary*   2–10

Basic Method:

- Choose any symbol in the sequence that is a lexical category.
- Choose any word in the dictionary that is a member of that category.
- Replace the symbol in the sequence with the chosen word.

Figure 4–6. Derivation with a general rewrite grammar.

Rule	Derived Sequence
	S
1	NP VP
2	Determiner Noun Number VP
4	Determiner Noun Plural VP
6	Determiner Noun Plural Verb
7	Determiner Noun -*s* Verb
	...Lexical insertion steps...
	The willows sway
	S
1	NP VP
2	Determiner Noun Number VP
3	Determiner Noun Singular VP
5	Determiner Noun Verb -*s*
	...Lexical insertion steps...
	The willow sways

Figure 4–7. Derivations with a general rewrite grammar.

that generates the same sentences as Figure 4–4 could easily be written using only context-sensitive rules. However, as discussed below, there exist languages that can be generated by a general rewrite grammar but not by one containing only context-sensitive rules.

Rules that specify a sequence of symbols on their left-hand side can also be used to account for word paradigms. The grammar of Figure 4–4 could be augmented with rules like:

goose Plural → *geese*
be Singular Third-Person → *is*

In the course of the derivation, these could be applied when sequences matching their left-hand sides appeared. Otherwise, regular expansions for the grammatical markers (such as 'PLURAL → -*s* ') would be used.

The formal power of grammars

In extending the notion of rewrite rule beyond context-free grammars, we make it possible to provide mechanisms that build underlying structures that are intuitively more appropriate. For example, we can allow a combined constituent like *call up* to be generated as a unit and then use rewrite rules that interpose pronouns to produce sentences like *She called him up*. An obvious question to

Ch. types of grammars?

Type	Name	Restrictions on rule form	Languages
0	Unrestricted	None	*Any language whose sentences can be generated by any deterministic computational machine.*
1	Context-sensitive	The right-hand side consists of the left-hand side with a single symbol expanded (*see text*).	*Any language whose sentences can be recognized by a deterministic computational machine using an amount of storage proportional to the length of the input (called a linear bounded automaton).*
2	Context-free	The left-hand side consists of a single symbol.	*Includes languages involving embedding such as $X^n Y^k Z^n$ but not $X^n Y^n Z^n$ or WW, where W is an arbitrary string of terminal symbols and the two W's are identical.*
3	Regular	The right-hand side consists of a single terminal symbol or a terminal symbol followed by a single nonterminal symbol.	*Any regular language (a language that can be defined with a regular expression—see Section 2.3).*

Figure 4–8. The hierarchy of grammar types.

be asked is whether we also extend the class of languages for which we could write a grammar at all. Chomsky developed a formal theory of grammars in which such questions can be studied. He devised a classification of grammars into a hierarchy according to their *power*. There are four types of grammars (called *type 0, type 1, type 2* and *type 3*), each defined by the kind of rewrite rules it contains. Type 0 is the most powerful, and each increasing number is more restricted. For each grammar type, there is a class of languages that can be defined only by a grammar of that power or greater power—that is, there are languages that can be defined by a type 0 grammar but not by any type 1 grammar, others that can be defined by a type 1 but not type 2, etc.

Figure 4–8 lists the four types of grammars and gives examples of languages that can be generated by each type but not by any lower type. The transition network grammars of Chapter 2 are type 3 grammars, the context-free grammars of Chapter 3 are type 2, and in this chapter we are dealing with the more powerful (lower numbered) types.

The entries for rule restrictions in this table are cumulative—the rules of a type 3 grammar obey the restrictions for type 1 and type 2 as well. There is no standard name for type 0 grammars, although they are sometimes called *unrestricted rewriting systems* and described as having *Turing machine* power, since they are equivalent to the general kind of computational mechanism developed by the mathematician Turing. In Chapter 2 we did not introduce grammar rules, but there is an immediate translation, as defined in Figure 4–9, from transition networks to rules.

Pattern or network grammars of the kind described in Chapter 2 (which are type 3 grammars) are unable to generate many simple languages. For example, there can be no transition network that generates the language consisting of all sequences made up of a number of Xs followed by an equal number of Ys (often represented with the notation $X^n Y^n$). This language can easily be defined by a context-free grammar (type 2) with two rules: 'S $\rightarrow$ X S Y' and 'S $\rightarrow$ X Y.'

In a grammar for a natural language, this problem arises in dealing with *center embedding*, as in *The wallpaper the man your friend suggested put up is crooked*. Even in structures that do not have center embeddings, like *This is the cat that bit the rat that...*, the natural analysis may be the recursive one in which each constituent is part of the one starting to the left of it. Although many of the embedding phenomena of natural language can be changed into repetitive structures (using grammar modifications like those described in Section 3.5), this is done at the cost of losing the natural structuring of the meanings. It is an interesting feature of language comprehension that complex center embeddings can be extremely difficult to comprehend, although a careful paper and pencil analysis leads to recognizing how they fit together. This is especially the case when semantic clues do not provide information about the grouping, as in *The book the article the index listed mentioned quoted the Kama Sutra*.

Going up in the hierarchy, the classical example of a construction that cannot be handled properly by a context-free (type 2) grammar is the use of *respectively* in English. The sentence *Randy, Ken, and Charlotte are a doctor, a nurse, and a philosopher, respectively* contains dependencies that can be mathematically characterized as an instance of the sequence $x_1 x_2 x_3 \cdots y_1 y_2 y_3 \cdots$ where x_i and y_i are related for each integer i.

It is difficult to find examples in natural languages of structures that could not in some way be generated by grammars low in the hierarchy. The more relevant problem is that the natural intuitive analyses require the building of structures that cannot be the result of an analysis produced by a simple grammar. For example, the problem of subject-verb agreement can be handled in a context-free grammar by having parallel expansions, as in the grammar:

$$S \rightarrow S_{singular}$$
$$S \rightarrow S_{plural}$$
$$S_{singular} \rightarrow NP_{singular} \, VP_{singular}$$
$$NP_{singular} \rightarrow Determiner_{singular} \ldots$$
$$S_{plural} \rightarrow NP_{plural} \ldots$$
$$\cdots$$

Create a grammar from a transition network

Purpose: Produce a regular grammar that generates the same language as the network

Inputs: a *transition network*   2–13

Results: a *regular grammar*   4–5 4–8

Working Structures:

   Grammar: a set of grammar rules

Basic Method:

- *Convert the network* to have a distinguished initial state.   §
  This state will be the distinguished symbol of the grammar.

- For each arc in the network do:
  - Add a new rule to the grammar with:
    - left-hand side = the starting state of the arc
    - right-hand side = a sequence consisting of the label on the arc followed by the ending state of the arc.

  The states of the network serve as the nonterminal symbols of the grammar. The arc labels are the terminal symbols.

  - If the ending state of the arc is a terminal state of the network then add a new rule to the grammar with:
    - left-hand side = the starting state of the arc
    - right-hand side = a sequence containing just the label on the arc.
- Return the grammar.

Procedures:

Convert a network to have a distinguished initial state

Purpose: Modify the network to have a single initial state

Inputs: a transition network

Working Structures:

   Distinguished state: a state

Basic Method:

- Create a new state and add it to the states of the network.
- Assign it as the distinguished state.
- For each arc of the network whose starting state is an initial state do:

  Add a new arc to the network with:
  - starting state = the distinguished state
  - ending state = the ending state of the arc
  - label = the label of the arc.

Figure 4–9. Procedure for producing a grammar from a network.

Although this method makes it possible to define the language with a context-free grammar, it means that the distinction between plural and singular must be propagated through all of the constituents involved, duplicating all of the rules. If other distinctions are added (as in person agreement for the forms *I am, you are, she is,...*), the effect is to multiply the size of the entire grammar by the number of terms in each new distinction. Section 6.7 describes ways in which special rules called *meta-rules* can be added to the grammar to express this kind combinatorial effect succinctly. In this chapter, we will see alternative ways of handling the same problem.

In general, the motivations for using more powerful grammars go beyond *weak generative capacity* (the ability to specify a given language), but are based on a desire to have a grammar that is simple and that produces structures that correspond to our intuitions about other considerations, such as meaning.

Rearrangement of structures

By viewing a grammar as controlling the derivation process rather than as specifying the derived structures, we are now in a position to offer an attractive

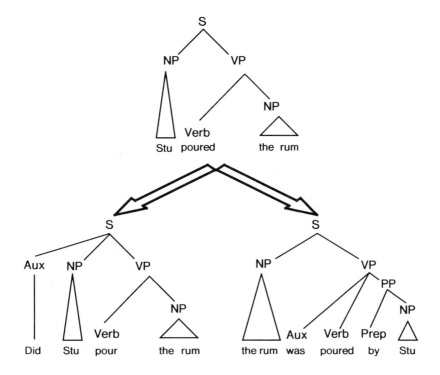

Figure 4–10. Sentences transformed from the same deep structure.

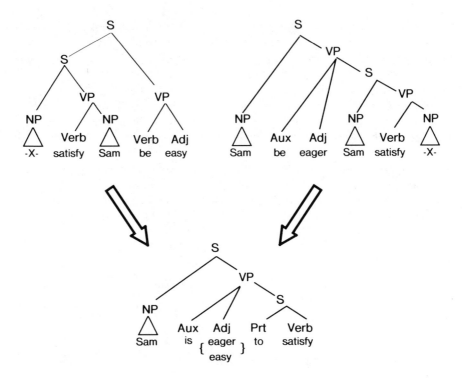

Figure 4–11. Sentences transformed into similar surface structures.

solution to the problems of similarity and difference illustrated in Figures 4–2 and 4–3. If two sentences have underlying similarities that are not apparent in their structure, we can postulate that at some earlier point in the derivation the similarity was explicit, and the application of later rules caused the difference in appearance. Conversely, two sentences that look alike might have differed in significant ways earlier in the derivation.

In order to express this formally, we can create grammars that perform derivations on structures. Instead of having rewrite rules that operate on sequences, we can have them operate on tree structures. We will not give the details of such rewrite rules until the next section, but their potential effects can be demonstrated in structures like those of Figures 4–10 and 4–11. The derivational process results (perhaps in several steps) in the conversion of the top tree (or trees) to the bottom one. One of the greatest appeals of transformational grammar has been its ability to represent such derivations clearly and simply.

These and some of the following figures use simplified versions of the phrase structures in order to more simply illustrate the basic issues, and they make use of the standard convention of drawing a triangle to represent a segment of the structure that is not shown in detail.

4.3 The basic transformational model

The generalized rewrite rules introduced in the previous section provide the formal capability to characterize a wide variety of languages. Of all the potential ways of organizing rewrite rules into a coherent system, some are better suited to describing what happens in natural languages, although others may be better suited for some mathematical or other formal languages. In the development of transformational grammar, it has been argued that by understanding the kinds of grammars that are best suited for human languages we will gain a key to understanding the structure of the human mind. Section 4.5 discusses the relationship between grammatical formalisms and mental capacities in more detail. In this section, we will look at the particular organization that was developed in the original form of transformational grammar.

The model presented here is close to what is often called the *standard theory* and corresponds roughly to the version described in Chomsky's *Aspects of the Theory of Syntax* (1965). This is sometimes called the 'Aspects model.' Our presentation is a simplification in the sense that it presents a cleaner-than-real view of the mechanisms. As a result, it is not adequate for handling all of the linguistic data but serves as a base on which to build extensions. In the following sections we will discuss the shortcomings of the standard theory and some of the extensions and modifications that have been proposed to overcome them.

The human language capacity

Figure 4–12 illustrates the basic generative model of the human language capacity. This model has three main components, the central one being the *linguistic competence* of the adult language user. This competence, along with extralinguistic factors, is the basis on which the *performance mechanism* carries out linguistic activities such as comprehension and production of sentences. Linguistic competence is also the source of our intuitions about grammatical structure, and therefore can be studied with a linguistic research methodology based primarily on *grammaticality judgments* by adult native speakers. The *language acquisition device* (often abbreviated as 'LAD') is the means by which a person comes to know a language. Its input is the *primary linguistic data* of utterances heard by the language learner and its output is the collection of cognitive structures that embody the knowledge of a particular language. These structures include the grammar as well as the rules that deal with sound patterns and meaning. As we will see in Section 4.5, there has been much discussion about the relationship of language acquisition to the form of linguistic knowledge.

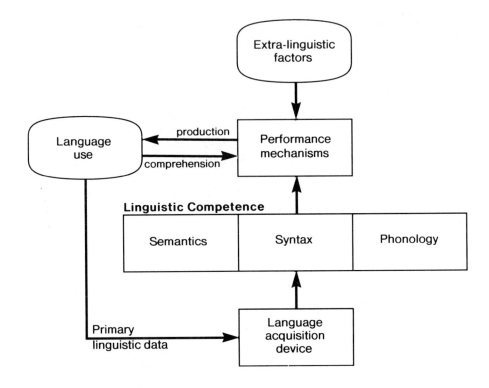

Figure 4–12. A model of the human language capacity.

One of the major ways in which the transformational model differs from most work in the computational paradigm is the assumption that the underlying competence can be described independently of the processes of comprehension and production. The context-free grammars introduced in Chapter 3 are a good example of such separability. We can formulate a context-free grammar for a language and understand it as a set of constraints on valid analyses of sentences without introducing questions of how these sentences are produced or understood. We can then build parsers and generators that make use of the grammar, keeping the details of their algorithms separate from the basic characterization of the language. As one obvious effect of separating the underlying structure from the processing, we can use the same grammar (with different procedures) for both parsing and generation.

In the transformational model, it is assumed that this property holds for the more complex syntactic formalisms of transformational grammar. The model distinguishes *competence* (the structures) from *performance* (the processes that make use of them). In justifying this separation, Chomsky pointed out that the details of how language is actually spoken or understood depend on phenomena such as memory limitations, changes of intention in the middle of speaking, and even physical states such as coughing or sleepiness, which according to him are not properly part of linguistic theory.

In many subsequent discussions, all issues of processing were dismissed as being too intertwined with these nonlinguistic issues and not at the appropriate level of idealization for linguistic theory. Two issues were confused in this characterization: *idealization* and *procedural description*. It is clear that in linguistics, as in any science, we create idealizations in order to study the central phenomena without hindrance from peripheral issues. A study of linguistics that included coughs and interruptions would be like a study of physics that began with bumpy objects moving on sticky surfaces. The other issue is whether a particular phenomenon is best understood in terms of a nonprocedural characterization of its results or in terms of a formal characterization of its processes.

The science of computation deals with theories of processing, while linguistics has typically dealt with characterizations of structures. It is an open question which of these approaches will provide the most revealing and useful theory of language. It is a central working hypothesis of transformational grammar (and almost all work in generative linguistics) that a non-processing characterization is desirable. The computational paradigm described in this book is based on a belief that by developing idealized theories of the processes, we will have a clear and revealing way of explaining the structure of their results. From this standpoint, the knowledge of syntax is an integral part of a body of knowledge organized around the information processing that goes on when language is produced and comprehended. Chapter 5 describes a syntactic formalism that is more oriented to processing, and in the volume on meaning we will discuss the issues of processing related to meaning and language use.

The transformational model of linguistic competence

Linguistic competence, as illustrated in 4–13, consists of three basic components: *syntactic, semantic,* and *phonological.* These three together make up a person's knowledge of his or her language. In the standard transformational grammar approach, it is assumed that these three components can be characterized separately. The *autonomy of syntax hypothesis,* as this assumption is called, has been mistakenly caricatured at times as a belief that meaning is unimportant in the study of language. Adherence to the autonomy principle has indeed led to a general atmosphere in which the study of syntax has been given priority, but in theory it is simply a methodological assumption about the degree of relatedness between meaning and syntax.

The essential claim is that an analysis of the structure of language (including sound patterns and meaning) will be best achieved by finding the structure of each component separately and then understanding their interactions. We can

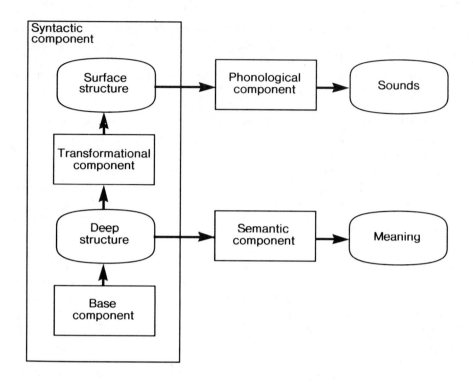

Figure 4–13. The transformational model of linguistic competence.

define syntactic structure and grammaticality purely in syntactic terms, mean-ingfulness in semantic terms, and sound patterning in phonological terms. We can then put them together by describing the correspondences between them. This basic idea of treating a complex system as *nearly decomposable* does not depend on total independence but on the fact that the interactions among com-ponents are much less crucial than the independent functioning within each one. As with the assumption about competence and performance, this assumption has been the source of much debate within linguistics. Some of the formalisms discussed in Chapter 6 take a more complex view of the decomposability of language capacity into nearly independent components.

Having thus dismissed (for the time being) questions of linguistic process-ing and questions of sound and meaning, the linguist can ask 'What is the nature of the syntactic structure of a language?' As discussed in Section 4.1, the simple ideas of phrase-structure grammar do not suffice for dealing with actual languages. It was observed that some sentences with the same apparent structure seem essentially different while others with differing visible structure seem closely related. The solution was to posit two levels of structure, *deep structure* and *surface structure,* which are related to one another by the grammar.

In the standard transformational model, the *base component* is a context-free grammar that generates deep structures. The deep structure of a sentence contains everything relevant to its meaning. For example, the deep structures corresponding to *Sam is easy to satisfy* and *Sam is eager to satisfy* look something like those that were illustrated in Figure 4–11, in which the subject of *satisfy* is made explicit.

The second component is the *transformational component,* consisting of a set of rewrite rules (called *transformation rules*) that operate on tree structures (called *phrase markers* or *P-markers*). The transformational component is used in a derivation process that begins with a deep structure produced by the base and results in a surface structure, which can be used to produce the actual sequence of sounds or letters in the sentence. A sequence of words is a sentence in the language defined by a transformational grammar if it can be generated by a derivation that produces a deep structure and then transforms it into a surface structure that has a sequence of leaf nodes corresponding to the sequence of words.

The transformational model has been misinterpreted at times as a computational model of how language is produced, since the process of derivation leads to the generation of a sentence. It has been clear to transformational linguists that the model is something else. It is a mathematical abstraction, intended to characterize formally the knowledge a person must have about the syntax of a language. There is no assumption that a person generates (or parses) sentences in a way that corresponds to the derivation process. Section 4.5 discusses the relation between derivation and processing and some of the theoretical issues that have been raised concerning it.

In the rest of this section, we will describe the basic functioning of transformations. In Section 4.4, we will introduce further subtleties concerning the structure of the base component and the transformational component and the way that they are integrated.

The form of transformations

Figure 4–14 gives some sample transformations that we will use in explaining the details of the formalism. They are included at the beginning in order to give some feeling for what transformations look like, and will be repeated as they are discussed later on. They include many features (such as the use of the symbols '#' and '>') that will be explained in the following sections.

There is no standardly accepted notation for transformation rules, and in this chapter we use a version that is adapted from Akmajian and Heny

---

Passive (Optional)

	SD: NP	Aux	Verb	NP
	1	2	3	4

SC: 4   2 > be + -en   3   by # 1

Stu was pouring the rum → The rum was being poured by Stu

Dative (Optional)

SD: Verb   NP $\left\{\begin{array}{c} to \\ for \end{array}\right\}$ NP

1   2   3   4

SC: 1+4   2   ∅   ∅

handed the bottle to Andy → handed Andy the bottle

Affix Hopping (Obligatory)

SD: $\left\{\begin{array}{c} \text{Pres} \\ \text{Past} \\ ing \\ en \end{array}\right\}$ $\left\{\begin{array}{c} \text{Modal} \\ \text{Verb} \end{array}\right\}$

1   2

SC: ∅   2 # 1

Past be -ing be -en pour → was being poured

Figure 4–14. Some transformation rules.

(1975). In fact, the problem of precise formal specification of transformation rules has been a continuing theme of disagreement and research in transformational grammar. In illustrating transformations (as in Figure 4–14), we include sample sentences or phrases that correspond roughly to the structure before and after the transformation. They are included to give a feeling for what the transformation does and are not a part of the formal specification of the transformation.

Figure 4–15 gives a formal definition for a transformation rule, leaving the detailed description of its parts for Figures 4–17 through 4–19.

A transformation rule consists of three components: a *structural description* (a pattern to be matched against the tree as derived so far), a *structural change* (an operation to be done on the tree structure when the rule is applied), and a

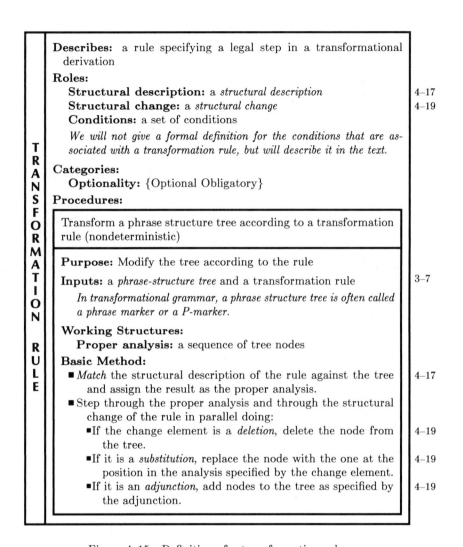

TRANSFORMATION RULE

Describes: a rule specifying a legal step in a transformational derivation

Roles:
Structural description: a *structural description* — 4–17
Structural change: a *structural change* — 4–19
Conditions: a set of conditions

We will not give a formal definition for the conditions that are associated with a transformation rule, but will describe it in the text.

Categories:
Optionality: {Optional Obligatory}

Procedures:

Transform a phrase structure tree according to a transformation rule (nondeterministic)

Purpose: Modify the tree according to the rule

Inputs: a *phrase-structure tree* and a transformation rule — 3–7

In transformational grammar, a phrase structure tree is often called a phrase marker or a P-marker.

Working Structures:
Proper analysis: a sequence of tree nodes

Basic Method:
- *Match* the structural description of the rule against the tree and assign the result as the proper analysis. — 4–17
- Step through the proper analysis and through the structural change of the rule in parallel doing:
  - If the change element is a *deletion*, delete the node from the tree. — 4–19
  - If it is a *substitution*, replace the node with the one at the position in the analysis specified by the change element. — 4–19
  - If it is an *adjunction*, add nodes to the tree as specified by the adjunction. — 4–19

Figure 4–15. Definition of a transformation rule.

set of *conditions* on the tree that is matched. The structural description (often abbreviated as 'SD') and conditions together correspond to the left-hand side of a generalized rewrite rule, since they control whether the rule is applicable. The structural change ('SC') is the right-hand side. None of the rules of Figure 4–14 has a condition, and the detailed explanation of conditions will be deferred until the following section. In the commonly used notation of Figure 4–14, the structural description and the structural change are written one above the other with corresponding elements lined up.

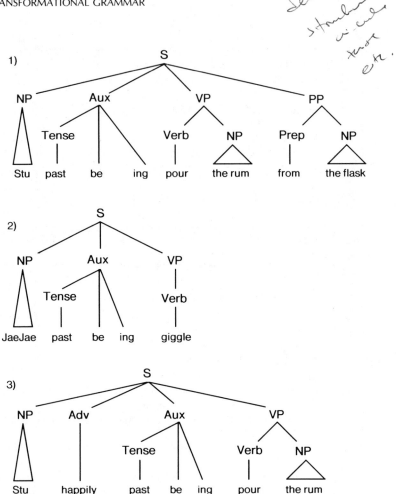

Figure 4–16. Trees to be matched by a transformation.

Generally (we will elaborate on other possibilities later), the structural description specifies a sequence of elements without giving the details of their relationship in the tree. The rule can be applied to a tree if it contains a corresponding sequence of nodes having the specified labels. For example, the structural description for the PASSIVE transformation of Figure 4–14 ('NP - AUX - VERB - NP') matches the first tree of Figure 4–16, but not the second or the third. In this figure, we have again used the standard convention of using a triangle to indicate that further details of structure are not shown because they are not relevant to the analysis at hand. The second tree does not match because there is no sequence of nodes having a VERB followed by an NP. The third does not match because there is an adverb interposed between the NP and the AUX. The first does match even though there is an extraneous PP at

S T R U C T U R A L D E S C R I P T I O N

Describes: the left hand side of a transformational rewrite rule

Basic Structure: a sequence of *description elements* 4–18

Procedures:

Match a structural description against a tree (nondeterministic)

Purpose: Produce an analysis of the tree corresponding to the description

Inputs: a structural description and a *phrase structure tree* 3–7

Working Structures:

Proper analysis: a sequence of tree nodes; initially empty
The order of the nodes in the analysis corresponds to the order of the elements in the structural description.

Results: a sequence of tree nodes, which is the final value of the proper analysis

Basic Method: Step through the elements of the structural description doing:
- If it is an *optional element,* choose either to go on to the next element or to continue. 4–18
- If it is the first element,
  - Then choose any node in the tree that *matches* the element. 4–18
  - Otherwise choose any node that matches the element and that is a *right-neighbor* of the node chosen for the previous element. §
- If no such node can be chosen, fail.
- Add the chosen node at the end of the proper analysis.

Predicates:

A tree node (B) is a right-neighbor of a tree node (A)
  if either:
- A and B are children of the same parent and B immediately follows A in the sequence of children, or
- A is the rightmost child of its parent (C) and B is a right-neighbor of C, or
- B is the leftmost child of its parent (C) and C is a right-neighbor of A.

Figure 4–17. The structural description of a transformation.

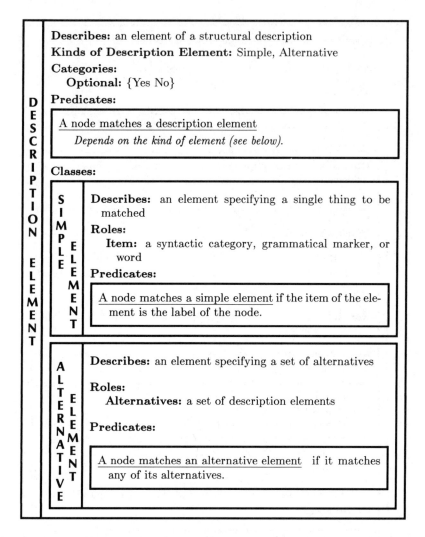

Figure 4–18. Element of a structural description.

the end, since the structural description need not specify the entire tree but only a sequence within it.

For a set of nodes to match, it is necessary that they all be neighbors, as defined more precisely in 4–17. For example, tree 1 of Figure 4–16 would not match the structural description 'NP - Aux - VP - NP,' since there is no VP node immediately followed by an NP. The NP node corresponding to the phrase *the rum* is a descendant, not a neighbor, of the VP node, and the NP *the flask* is not a right-neighbor of the VP, since the preposition *from* is interposed.

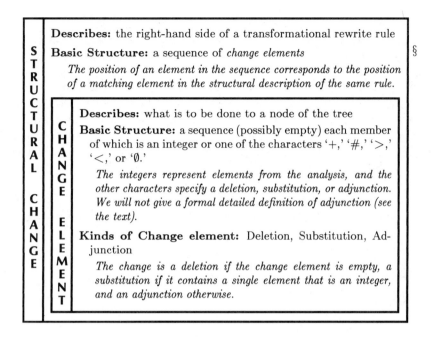

Figure 4–19. The structural change of a transformation.

In addition to specifying elements by syntactic category or by giving individual words or markers, the structural description can include *alternatives,* indicated by a set of items in curly brackets. This element matches if any one of the alternatives matches. For example, the DATIVE transformation given in Figure 4–14 matches if the third element is either the word *to* or the word *for.* In addition, elements can be optional, indicated by putting them in parentheses.

The structural change of a transformation rule specifies the actions to be taken on the tree once it has been determined to match the structural description. A number of notations have been proposed for specifying the resulting structure. They have been based on considerations of the basic transformational operations to be allowed. A transformation is not seen as taking a sequence of elements and scrambling them, but instead as performing a series of *elementary transformations* on the tree structure. Each elementary transformation is a *deletion,* a *substitution,* or an *adjunction.* Figure 4–19 defines the structural change associated with a transformation.

In writing transformations, deletion is normally indicated by putting the symbol '∅' (null) at the corresponding place in the sequence. The sequencing is indicated by lining up the change elements under the corresponding description elements in the transformation. For example, in the dative transformation as illustrated in in Figure 4–20, the tree nodes corresponding to the last two elements are deleted and the deleted NP is adjoined to the first element. The change element '1+4' indicates that the deleted NP is adjoined as a sibling of the verb, as explained below. This transformation converts trees underlying forms like *Stu handed the bottle to Andy* to forms like *Stu handed Andy the bottle*.

The different adjunction symbols control the way in which the new element is attached. In this case, we want to adjoin the moved element (the NP) as a sibling of the one previously there (the verb). In other cases, we may want to adjoin it as a child, or as a sibling of a parent (aunt/uncle). The plus sign is an example of the special notations used to indicate the kind of adjunction, indicating adjunction as a sibling. The PASSIVE transformation shown in Figure 4–21 illustrates other notations for adjunction.

The '+' indicates sibling adjunction. The '>' indicates that the node for *be* is to be adjoined as the rightmost child of the node to its left in the sequence,

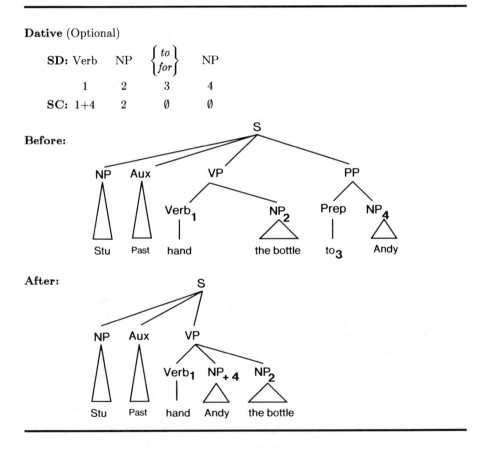

Figure 4–20. An example of dative movement.

Passive (Optional)

    SD: NP   Aux   Verb   NP

            1   2   3   4

    SC: 4   2 > *be* + -*en*   3   *by* #1

Before:

After:

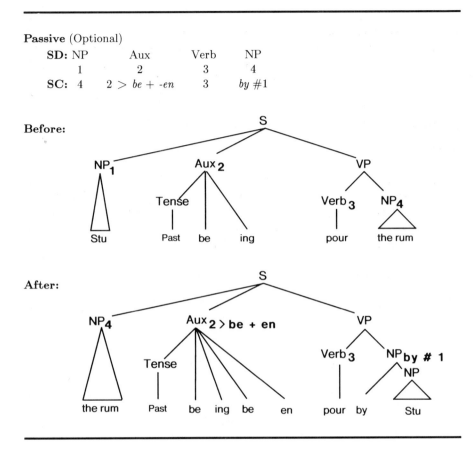

Figure 4–21. Structure changes specified in the passive transformation.

while '<' would indicate adjunction as the leftmost child of the node to its right. Finally, the '#' indicates *Chomsky adjunction,* in which the new node and the one already there are joined as children of a new parent node whose label is identical to the label of the node that was previously there. Following these conventions, the passive transformation operates on the first tree of Figure 4–21 to produce the second one.

This notation makes it possible to specify transformations precisely. However, it is not used widely or consistently. As one textbook on transformational grammar (Bach, 1974, p. 88) notes:

> *The reader should be warned that many discussions of transformations for various languages are stated in a very informal and rough way, so that the exact effect of a given transformation is often unclear.*

In general, arguments about the formulation of transformations do not hinge on fine points of the details of the produced structures, and can go on without a precise specification. In cases where it is necessary to be precise (for example, in computer implementations of transformational grammar like that of Friedman (1971)), it has turned out to be quite difficult to do so consistently.

Optional and obligatory transformations

Some transformations, such as PASSIVE, are *optional*. If they are applied in the course of deriving a sentence, the sentence will have a particular form. If they are not applied, it will have a different but equally grammatical one. Many transformations are not of this kind. They perform 'housekeeping' activities that must be done to get things into their appropriate final form, and if they are not applied, the result is not a grammatical sentence. Transformations for agreement are generally of this *obligatory* type.

A good example of an obligatory transformation is AFFIX-HOPPING, which can be applied more than once in a single sentence.

$$
\textbf{Affix-Hopping} \text{ (Obligatory)}
$$

$$
\textbf{SD:} \quad \left\{ \begin{array}{l} \text{Pres} \\ \text{Past} \\ ing \\ en \end{array} \right\} \quad \left\{ \begin{array}{l} \text{Modal} \\ \text{Verb} \end{array} \right\}
$$

$$
\begin{array}{ccc}
& 1 & 2 \\
\textbf{SC:} & \emptyset & 2 \,\#\, 1
\end{array}
$$

For a number of reasons, one is led to have the base component generate the elements of the verbal sequence in an order that is different from the order of appearance in the surface structure. The sentence *He has been carousing* is based on the sequence 'PRESENT *have -en be -ing carouse.*' Affix-hopping (applied three times) results in '*have*-PRESENT *be-en carouse-ing,*' in which the constituents have been reordered and grouped (because of the '#' in the structural change, indicating adjunction). This is then converted by the phonological component to *has been carousing.* Transformations like PASSIVE maintain the base ordering. As illustrated in Figure 4–21, the structural change of the PASSIVE rule inserts the sequence *be -en* before the verb *pour.* AFFIX-HOPPING reverses the order of *-en* and *pour* and combines them into a single constituent. The phonological component converts the sequence *pour -en* into the participle form *poured.*

In early versions of transformational grammar, there was a simple distinction between optional and obligatory rules. The housekeeping rules were obligatory and all others (such as QUESTION FORMATION, NEGATIVE, PASSIVE, and DATIVE) were optional. A rule for forming yes-no questions might have been stated as:

Yes-No Question Formation (Optional)

$$\textbf{SD:} \quad \text{NP} \quad \text{Tense} \quad \left(\left\{ \begin{array}{l} \text{Modal} \\ \textit{have} \\ \textit{be} \end{array} \right\} \right)$$

$$\qquad\qquad 1 \qquad\quad 2 \qquad\qquad\qquad 3$$

$$\textbf{SC:} \; 2+3 \qquad 1 \qquad\qquad\qquad \emptyset$$

Stu was pouring the rum → *Was Stu pouring the rum*

The element to be moved is the tense, along with the following modal or *have* or *be* if there is one. The parentheses in the structural description indicate that this last element may or may not be present. If it is not, the transformation leaves a naked tense in front of the NP, and another obligatory rule (known as 'DO SUPPORT') inserts a form of the auxiliary *do* to form questions like *Did Stu pour the rum?* In this original formulation, a sentence that was derived without optional transformations was called a *kernel sentence*.

Later versions of transformational grammar adopted the convention that all transformations were *meaning preserving*. If the deep structure captures all of the meaning of a sentence, then a transformation cannot turn a statement into a question. Instead, markers were generated in the base structure and the corresponding transformations were made obligatory. In the standard model, the grammatical marker Q (for question) is generated in the base structures, and there is an obligatory transformation:

Yes-No Question Formation (Obligatory)

$$\textbf{SD:} \; \text{Q} \quad \text{NP} \quad \text{Tense} \quad \left(\left\{ \begin{array}{l} \text{Modal} \\ \textit{have} \\ \textit{be} \end{array} \right\} \right)$$

$$\qquad\quad 1 \qquad 2 \qquad 3 \qquad\qquad\qquad 4$$

$$\textbf{SC:} \; 1 \qquad 3+4 \qquad 2 \qquad\qquad\qquad \emptyset$$

Q *Stu was pouring the rum* → Q *Was Stu pouring the rum*

Other transformations later delete the grammatical marker Q before the surface structure is reached. In the same manner, other meaning-changing transformations, such as those for negation and the formation of imperatives can be triggered by appropriate markers. Those that do not obviously change meaning (such as passive) remain as described before. Later we will see that even these can have an effect on meaning, and this led to further modifications to the framework.

---

1. Restrictions on transformations

   Explicit conditions
   Bracketing
   Variables
   Recoverability of deletion

2. Syntactic features

3. Extensions to the base

4. Rule ordering

Figure 4–22. Refinements in the standard theory.

4.4 Refinements in the standard theory

The previous section outlined the major components of the transformational model and described the basic operation of transformations. The model is not quite as simple as that section suggests, and in this section we will look at a number of refinements that are part of the standard theory. The further modifications described in Appendix C represent developments beyond the standard theory. The issues we will discuss here are summarized in Figure 4–22.

Basic restrictions on transformations

One of the principles of transformational theory is that all of the rules needed to describe natural language are *structure dependent*—the rearrangements can be stated in terms of phrase structure trees, not calling for arbitrary rearrangements of symbol strings. For example, we cannot write a transformation that deals differently with the words appearing at odd-numbered and even-numbered positions in the sentence. This has been viewed as reflecting a fundamental fact of human cognition and thereby illustrating the ways in which formal linguistic studies can shed light on the nature of mind (see Chomsky (1968) for a lengthy discussion).

The limitation that transformations must be structure dependent is enforced by the nature of the structural description—by the fact that it can only specify an analysis in terms of tree nodes. For some transformations, it is necessary to provide further limitations on the structure to be matched, as illustrated by the EQUI-NP DELETION transformation (often referred to as 'EQUI'):

Equi-NP Deletion (Optional)

SD: NP   X $\overline{S}[\left\{\begin{matrix} \text{Poss} \\ \textit{for} \end{matrix}\right\}$ NP $Y]_{\overline{S}}$

     1   2   3   4   5

SC: 1   2 $\emptyset$ $\emptyset$ 5

Conditions:

   1 $=$ 4

   With main verbs such as *want,* term 1 must be the subject of
      the verb; with verbs such as *force,* term 1 must be the object
      of the verb

Woodrow wanted $_{\overline{S}}$[*for Woodrow to dance*]$_{\overline{S}}$ $\rightarrow$
   Woodrow wanted to dance

Wilhelm forced Woodrow $_{\overline{S}}$[*for Woodrow to dance*]$_{\overline{S}}$ $\rightarrow$
   Wilhelm forced Woodrow to dance

This transformation produces structures like *Woodrow wanted to dance* from a deep structure having an embedded sentence corresponding to *for Woodrow to dance.* The subject of the inner sentence is deleted, since it is identical to the subject of the outer sentence, as indicated by the condition '1 = 4.' The other explicit condition prevents the sentence **Woodrow forced to dance* from being derived from the corresponding deep structure. Instead, other transformations apply to produce *Woodrow forced himself to dance.* On the other hand, *Wilhelm forced Woodrow to dance* could be generated from *Wilhelm forced Woodrow* $_{\overline{S}}$[*for Woodrow to dance*]$_{\overline{S}}$. We have followed here the standard convention of preceding ungrammatical examples with an asterisk (or 'star'). In conversation, such forms are often referred to as 'starred.'

    In addition to the conditions given explicitly, there is an additional notation illustrated in the structural description of EQUI: labeled square brackets. Instead of just specifying a sequence of elements, the structural description also includes a further indication of the tree structure. It requires that in addition to being neighbors, the last three elements must be descendants of some node whose label is $\overline{S}$ (we will explain what this symbol means later). This prevents the transformation from operating on structures like the one underlying *Seymour bought a house for Seymour's parents* to produce **Seymour bought a house's parents.*

    There is no standard agreement on the exact form that tree structure specifications can take within structural descriptions, and we will not pursue the issue in detail. A related issue illustrated by EQUI is the question of whether *essential variables* can appear in transformations. In the transformations described previously in this chapter, each element of the structural description specifies particular syntactic categories, markers, or words. In EQUI there is an element X standing for any intervening set of structures. It does not need to be matched against a single tree element, but can cover any number of nodes. This is necessary in order to have the transformation not only apply to the examples so far, but also to produce *Woodrow wanted to be asked to dance* from an underlying structure containing ₛ[*for Woodrow to dance*]ₛ. The variable X will match the intervening stretch *wanted to be asked* and the transformation will apply.

There are other ways to achieve this effect, and there has been a good deal of debate about whether a variable is needed for this transformation and whether such variables are needed in general. It might at first appear that variables are obviously needed to handle things like the intrusion of an adverb such as *happily* in the sentence *Stu happily was pouring the rum,* illustrated in Figure 4–16. However, this can be handled in either of two ways without variables: the structural description can contain an optional ADVERB element (as with the optional MODAL element illustrated in the QUESTION FORMATION transformations of the previous section), or the grammar can be written so that adverbs are generated elsewhere (for example, at the end of the sentence) and moved into position after transformations like PASSIVE have been applied. Of course, there are implicit variables at the beginning and end of every structural description, since it need not match the entire sentence but only a contiguous segment. We will not discuss the technical arguments concerning the role of variables in this chapter, but will use variables in our examples. They are not taken into account in the formal definitions of the parts of a transformation rule or the application of a transformation in the previous section. They are discussed further in Appendix C.

The condition that elements 1 and 4 be identical in EQUI is a specific instance of a more general restriction called the *recoverability of deleted structures.* A transformation can delete a phrase only if there is sufficient redundancy in the structure that no information is lost. This redundancy can happen in three different ways: another copy appears somewhere (as with the deleted NP in EQUI); the deleted item is a word or grammatical marker specified in the structural description (as with the *to* or *for* in DATIVE); or the deleted item is a dummy, or *pro-form,* that is inserted in the base structure to fill a node that will later be deleted. An example of the last possibility is illustrated by the AGENT DELETION rule. Beginning with a deep structure corresponding to the active form *Someone robbed Julie,* we can apply PASSIVE to get *Julie was robbed by someone,* then AGENT DELETION to derive *Julie was robbed.* The *someone* is not an actual lexical item but a special pro-form used to stand in for an NP. Thus when it is deleted, no information is lost.

It has been argued that through this and related restrictions, transformational grammars could express all of the generality of natural language with mechanisms formally less powerful than unrestricted type 0 grammars, and that this would represent an empirical fact about the human mental apparatus. There have been many different formulations of transformations that have been devised with this in mind. In general, the basic restriction of recoverability has been kept. Of the transformations we have specified so far, only EQUI deletes a component other than a specified word or grammatical marker without adjoining or substituting it somewhere else in the structure, and its condition guarantees that this will happen only when no information will be lost.

Syntactic features

In early versions of transformational grammar, phenomena like agreement were handled by introducing grammatical markers such as PLURAL, FIRST-PERSON, and MASCULINE, and moving them around with transformations. At some stage in the derivation, rules were applied to convert a sequence like 'PRONOUN PLURAL FIRST-PERSON' into *we*. This turned out to be clumsy in many cases. There were no good criteria for deciding on the relative ordering of these markers, and they tended to get in the way of transformations. Just as the adverb in Figure 4–16 blocks what would be the expected transformation, the grammatical markers cluttered up a number of rules.

In the standard theory, many of the same phenomena are treated instead by assuming that a tree node whose label is a lexical category can contain a set of *syntactic features* in addition. Instead of inserting a marker PLURAL next to the verb, an agreement rule might add the feature +PLURAL to the set of features for the VERB node. The REFLEXIVE transformation illustrates the notation:

Reflexive (Obligatory)

SD: NP	Aux	Verb	X	NP
1	2	3	4	5
SC: 1	2	3	4	5
				[+Reflexive]

Conditions:
1 = 5

Richard will put the blame on Richard →
Richard will put the blame on himself

The feature +REFLEXIVE is added to the node, eventually leading to its conversion (through other obligatory transformations) to the pronoun *himself*. Features are indicated in square brackets underneath an element of the structural description or the structural change. If they are in the structural description, the corresponding node in the match must already have that feature for the rule to apply and it will remain there afterwards. If features are in the structural change, they are added to the node when the change is applied. Features are binary, having a '+' and '−' value. For example, +PLURAL and −PLURAL are used for plural and singular, respectively. In addition to the agreement features for person, number, and gender, features are used for several other things. Nouns, for example, are classified as $\pm$COUNT. A +COUNT noun like *apple* cannot appear in the singular without a determiner, while a mass noun (–COUNT) like *wheat* can. We say *Wheat is being sold to Russia* but not **Apple is being sold to Russia.*

Using features, a rule for number agreement simply needs to copy the appropriate features from the place they are generated (in the NP) to the other places they are needed. Greek letters such as 'α' and 'β' are used in place of '+' or '–' to indicate that whatever value of the feature appears in the structural description should be copied to the structural change. When features are copied they are also left on the original node, even though this is not mentioned in the structural change.

$$
\begin{array}{ccc}
\textbf{Number Agreement} \text{ (Obligatory)} \\
\textbf{SD:} \quad \text{NP} & \text{VP} \\
\begin{bmatrix} \alpha \text{ Person} \\ \beta \text{ Plural} \end{bmatrix} \\
1 & 2 \\
\textbf{SC:} \quad 1 & 2 \\
& \begin{bmatrix} \alpha \text{ Person} \\ \beta \text{ Plural} \end{bmatrix}
\end{array}
$$

Extensions to the base

Up to this point, this section has described refinements to the transformational component of the grammar. However, the underlying phrase structure trees used in transformational grammar are not identical to those generated by the context-free grammars of Chapter 3. In order to simplify the transformational component, a number of extensions have been made to the base grammar, although formally it is still a context-free grammar.

Features. The use of features in transformations implies that the base component must generate nodes containing features as well as labels (categories, words, and markers). Formally, a set of features can be thought of as a complex symbol and does not increase the power of the grammar. However, the notation is much more convenient if it allows the different feature components (e.g., number, gender, and person) to be factored out. Features are discussed at greater length in Section C.3.

Embedded sentences. In the grammars of Chapter 3, the distinguished symbol S never appeared on the right-hand side of a rule, although the formalism does not preclude that possibility. In early forms of transformational grammar, the distinguished symbol was also used only once in a derivation. A sentence like *He wondered whether they had seen the damage he had done* was derived as three separate sentences, corresponding to *He wondered X, They had seen the damage,* and *He had done the damage.* These underwent transformations such as NUMBER AGREEMENT that could be applied to single sentences (called *singulary transformations*), then were joined into a single sentence through the action of *generalized transformations.*

In later versions of the standard theory, embedding and conjoining are not done by transformations. Instead, the base can generate S nodes as components of other nodes. These nodes are expanded using the same rules as for the S node at the top of the tree. The result is a single deep structure tree for the full sentence. A phrase marker containing embedded S nodes is called a *generalized phrase marker.* Somewhat later, a new symbol '$\overline{S}$' (pronounced '*S-bar*') was introduced for a constituent containing a sentence along with a *complementizer,* such as *for* or *that.* It is part of a larger notational generalization called the *X-bar convention,* described in Section C.3.

More abstract use of symbols. The PASSIVE transformation as stated in Figure 4–21 produces an NP node whose constituents are the word *by* and another NP. This node bears little structural resemblance to the kind of NP generated in the base. However, this enables the phrase *by. . .* to be manipulated by other rules as though it were an NP, making it easier to state certain transformations. In general, the motivation for using a particular symbol such as NP in our earlier grammars was an intuition about the kind of structure it had. In most transformational grammars, symbols are assigned in whatever way makes the statement of the rules easiest. Some further consequences of this are described in Section C.3 as well.

Lexical insertion. The transformational model of Figure 4–13 has two places where words might be inserted into the structure. We could think of the base component as having *lexical insertion rules* such as 'NOUN → *dog.*' In this case, the transformational component would begin with a tree having its lexical items included. These would need to be more abstract than actual words, since it is only after the transformations that we can determine the exact surface form, including irregular verbs, contractions, etc. The other approach is to have a base that produces leaf nodes containing lexical categories and other features, but to let the transformations insert the words. There are certain grammatical words (such as *by* in PASSIVE) that are inserted by transformations in almost all versions of transformational theory. For other words, in the standard theory it was assumed that there was a discrete phase of lexical insertion following the base generation and preceding all transformations. Only grammatical words could be introduced by transformations. This issue turned out to be a major

---

Bridget loves Bernie. $\underset{\text{Passive}}{\rightarrow}$ *Bernie is loved by Bridget.*

Bertrand is intelligent. $\underset{\text{Tag Formation}}{\rightarrow}$ *Bertrand is intelligent, isn't he?*

Boris loves my cousins.

$\qquad\qquad\underset{\text{Passive}}{\rightarrow}$ *My cousins are loved by Boris.*

$\qquad\qquad\underset{\text{Tag Formation}}{\rightarrow}$ *My cousins are loved by Boris, aren't they?*

Boris loves my cousins.

$\qquad\qquad\underset{\text{Tag Formation}}{\rightarrow}$ *Boris loves my cousins, doesn't he?*

$\qquad\qquad\underset{\text{Passive}}{\rightarrow}$ **My cousins are loved by Boris, doesn't he?*

Figure 4–23. A transformation ordering problem.

source of debate, as described in the discussion of *generative semantics* in Section C.1.

Rule ordering

In grammars with general rewrite rules (unlike context-free grammars), it is possible for the order in which the rules are applied to have a significant effect on the outcome of a derivation. There may be a possible derivation in which rule A is applied, followed by rule B. But if rule B is applied first, it may change the structure so that rule A is no longer applicable. As linguists examined the various transformations that were needed to describe English, they found tantalizing regularities in the consequences of choosing particular orderings. Much of the excitement in early transformational grammar came from the feeling that grammarians were discovering a set of rules with a natural underlying order, which therefore must have some kind of psychological reality. Figure 4–23 illustrates a simple transformation ordering problem. It does not give the detailed structures, but gives sentences representing structures to which we could apply the PASSIVE and a transformation called TAG FORMATION, which adds the tag to the end of sentences such as *He's going, isn't he?* We will not give a formal definition for TAG FORMATION, but simply note that form of the tag must agree in number and person with the subject of the sentence, so that we do not get **He's going, aren't they?*

If we allow PASSIVE to occur after TAG FORMATION, we get the unacceptable form **My cousins are loved by Boris, doesn't he?*, while the opposite

Dative Movement (Optional)
Equi NP Deletion (Obligatory)
Raising to Object (Obligatory)
Raising to Subject (Obligatory)
For Deletion (Obligatory)
Passive (Optional)
Agent Deletion (Optional)
Reflexivization (Obligatory)
Extraposition (Optional)
It Deletion (Obligatory)
Number Agreement (Obligatory)
There Insertion (Optional)
Tag Formation (Optional)
Negative placement (Obligatory)
Contraction (Optional)
Subject-Auxiliary Inversion (Obligatory)
Wh- Fronting (Obligatory)
Affix-Hopping (Obligatory)
Do Support (Obligatory)

Figure 4–24. Order of transformations (from Akmajian and Heny, p. 392).

ordering gives a grammatical sentence. As more rules were developed, it appeared that it was possible to impose a strict ordering on the entire set, such that each rule could be applied only when its turn in the sequence came. The *strict order hypothesis* motivated many of the internal details of transformations, since each one needed to be carefully formulated to fit properly into its place in the sequence.

Much of the material in transformational grammar textbooks consists of the introduction of a number of transformations and arguments concerning their ordering. The result is an ordering for the entire set, as illustrated by Figure 4–24. The lines indicate specific ordering arguments—cases where there is an example like the one of Figure 4–23 to motivate the ordering of that specific pair. There is not an argument for every pair, but the combination of all the pairwise orderings leads to a total ordering.

It soon became apparent that a simple linear ordering could lead to *ordering paradoxes* like the one illustrated in Figure 4–25, which makes use of the

---

They believed that Patty robbed the bank

$\underset{\text{Passive}}{\longrightarrow}$ *They believed that the bank was robbed by Patty.*

$\underset{\text{Raising}}{\longrightarrow}$ *They believed the bank to have been robbed by Patty.*

They believed that Patty robbed the bank.

$\underset{\text{Raising}}{\longrightarrow}$ *They believed Patty to have robbed the bank.*

$\underset{\text{Passive}}{\longrightarrow}$ *Patty was believed by them to have robbed the bank.*

Figure 4–25. A transformation ordering paradox.

RAISING TO OBJECT transformation, which converts the deep structure un-derlying *The leaders believed* $_\overline{\text{S}}$[*that Portia was a clandestine agent*]$_\overline{\text{S}}$ into one for *The leaders believed Portia* $_\overline{\text{S}}$[*to be a clandestine agent*]$_\overline{\text{S}}$.

The examples of Figure 4–25 show that legal sentences can be generated both by PASSIVE followed by RAISING and by RAISING followed by PASSIVE. If we do not allow both orderings, the grammar will fail to generate the sentences of the language. At first, this seems to preclude the possibility of including these two transformations in an ordered list. However, this kind of problem arises only when there is an embedded S node, and transformations are applied both to it and to the sentence containing it. This led to the postulation of a *transformational cycle,* in which rules are applied to the different S nodes in turn. There is still a linear ordering of the rules, but the entire sequence of rules is applied to each embedded S before any are applied to the S containing it. The grammar cycles through all of the rules once for each S node. Thus in the first pair of Figure 4–25, the PASSIVE in the cycle for the embedded S (*Patty robbed the bank*) precedes a RAISING in the outer S (*They believed. . .*), while in the second, RAISING and PASSIVE are both applied in the outer cycle. The rule ordering as given in Figure 4–24 holds within each cycle.

The transformational cycle neatly solved many problems of rule ordering, and most versions of transformational grammar have some form of it with a few further refinements. Some rules, such as TAG FORMATION, can be applied only to the outermost S. We cannot apply them to an embedded S to derive something like *She knows that they're in the bedroom, aren't they?* Such rules are called *last-cyclic.* There have also been proposals for *pre-cyclic* rules that apply to the entire tree before the cycle begins and *post-cyclic* rules that apply to the entire tree after the cycle ends (i.e., they are not ordered with respect to the cyclic transformations of the last cycle). It is not generally agreed which, if any, of these additional mechanisms are needed, and there is a good deal of variety in the details of how the cycle is formalized in different versions of transformational grammar.

4.5 Criteria considered in developing syntactic theories

One of the major appeals of early transformational grammar was that it could be used by linguists to predict syntactic intuitions about a large number of complex structures with a relatively simple formalism and a small number of rules. As more linguists began applying it to a variety of problems, it became apparent that many facts about English (in which most of the work has been done) demanded further additions to the theory, along with sets of specialized rules. The transformational cycle was an extension that covered a great deal of territory in a relatively elegant way, but other phenomena did not yield as easily.

There were a number of circumstances under which transformations that seemed quite general could not apply. For example, a general question formation transformation produces structures like *Whom did he buy it for?* from structures corresponding to *He bought it for X*. However, it cannot be allowed to generate *What did he order ham and?* from *He ordered ham and X* or *Whom did that we gave it to amaze him?* from *That we gave it to X amazed him*. Further rules and constraints had to be added. Each of these in turn faced the problem of having exceptions if stated in a general way and being inordinately baroque if it tried to account for all of the cases.

At each step, as new complexities have been added, there has been an attempt to keep the formalism as simple as possible (in the complexity of individual rules and principles), the grammar as small as possible (in number of rules), and the coverage as broad as possible (in the number of sentences properly assigned structures). Often these goals have been at cross purposes, and there has been heated debate as to whether various extensions were appropriate.

In order to understand the development of transformational grammar, it is important to recognize that in the process of developing the theory to cover more of the phenomena of language, researchers are guided by a diverse collection of motives and priorities. Although there is broad agreement about the basic goals, we see very different emphases when we compare the work of different researchers or look at the work of one person over a period of time. As a background for describing major schools or lines of thought in Appendix C, we will lay out a number of dimensions along which arguments are made concerning alternative developments of the theory. Although Figure 4–26 is not a complete list of all the issues that have been considered, it covers most of the major discussions.

1. Formal properties
   Generative power
   Learnability
   Processing mechanisms
2. Psychological reality
3. Relation to other language phenomena
   Acquisition
   Meaning
   Diachronic linguistics and dialect
4. Language universals
5. Simplicity of grammars and theories
6. Coverage of the data

Figure 4–26. Criteria for the development of syntactic theories.

Formal generative power

The theory of formal grammars was developed together with the early work
on transformational grammar. It led to a classification of different kinds of
abstract machines according to the class of languages they can recognize, as
we described in Section 4.2. Many people anticipated related results with
respect to natural language. From a computational viewpoint, the question
of cognitive psychology is 'What kind of machine is the human mind,' and one
obvious characteristic of human cognition is the ability to use language. If we
could derive a precise formal characterization of the class of 'possible human
languages,' we would have said something substantive about the nature of mind.
Chomsky has often described the central goal of linguistics as the discovery of
the *universal grammar* that is common to all human language. Of course, there
is no one grammar (in the sense of a particular set of rules) that is common.
The universality is in the structure of the overall model and the kinds rules and
operations it allows.

Over the years, this intuition has been a major force in the development
of syntactic theory. In proposing a change to the formalism, people often
argue that it is interesting because it in some way 'restricts the power' of the
mechanism. Chomsky has stated (1977a, p. 125) that 'Reduction of the class
of grammars is the major goal of linguistic theory,' and he characterized the
problem as (1972, p. 67):

> *The gravest defect of the theory of transformational grammar is its enormous lati-*
> *tude and descriptive power. Virtually anything can be expressed as a phrase-marker*
> *. . . virtually any imaginable rule can be described in transformational terms. There-*
> *fore, a critical problem in making transformational grammar a substantive theory*
> *with explanatory force is to restrict the category of admissible phrase-markers,*
> *admissible transformations, and admissible derivations.*

At first, there was hope that results on types of formal grammar could be applied directly—that the class of possible human languages could be characterized by something less powerful than a type 0 grammar. There have been a number of proposals for transformational formalisms with restricted formal power, but they have not generally been compatible with intuitions about the kinds of rules that best capture linguistic generalities. Current research has turned away from this particular formal notion of power, but the underlying attitude has remained strong.

Most attempts to justify new formalisms devote considerable attention to arguments that the proposal will result in 'stronger constraints' on the class of mechanisms that could underlie human language competence. It is difficult to judge these claims formally, since they do not correspond to precise notions of power and constraint. However, it is important not to underestimate their impact on those who develop the theories. Some of the formal concepts already described (such as the recoverability of deletion) were motivated to a large degree by intuitions about restricting the power of the formalism.

Formal learnability

In the 1970s, when it appeared that the formal classification of languages would not provide sufficient means for deciding among alternative formulations of transformational grammar, some researchers turned to a related set of formal questions concerning *learnability*. Looking back to the overall model of language illustrated in Figure 4–12, we can see that there are three basic components with three corresponding problems: abstract competence (the *characterization* problem); performance (the *realization* problem—discussed in the following section); and acquisition (the *projection* problem). The projection problem, formally stated is 'How can we find a way of predicting, from a person's primary linguistic data, a grammar that in turn correctly predicts his adult linguistic intuitions?'

Just as competence can be characterized without respect to psychological processes, formal learnability can be studied as an abstract property of grammars without concern for the cognitive processes that take place in human language learning. Given a syntactic formalism, we can formally characterize whether it is possible to devise a process that will be able to infer a grammar from a body of syntactic data. At some level this corresponds to what must go on when a child learns a language. He or she begins with some basic mechanisms and is exposed to utterances in a particular language. As a result, he or she develops a grammar that makes it possible to use the language and to have intuitions about grammaticality and structure that correspond to those of other speakers of the language.

It has seemed to a number of people that the requirements of learnability might provide a guideline for deciding among competing syntactic formalisms.

In order to be precise, assumptions are made concerning the learning process, and different grammar mechanisms are analyzed in terms of their effects on learnability under these assumptions. For example, Culicover (1976, p. 288) adopts one such set of assumptions:

> *The assumptions that we will make here about the learning procedure, called P, are the following: Whenever P encounters a sentence from the language that it cannot handle, it forms a new grammar by changing one rule of its old grammar so that the new grammar will account for this type of sentence.... P cannot remember previous sentences that were presented to it, but has available to it at any given time only the most recent grammar and the sentence that has just been presented to it. We also assume that the data are presented to P in such a way that over time P encounters a sequence of grammatical sentences of the language, and that no sentence is systematically withheld from the sequence...*

As with formal generative power, it has turned out to be quite difficult to come up with restrictions that give interesting formal results yet do not rule out all plausible grammatical formalisms. One particular result that has led to many speculations is that under the assumptions listed above (and many other similar sets of assumptions), a context-free grammar is not learnable. This means that formally one could not learn the base component of any language. This result has led to speculation that the base is part of the initial language capacity— that it is actually encoded in the genetically determined structure of the brain. Of course, this would have to mean that the base is the same for all human languages, having consequences discussed further in the section on language universals below.

The results of research on formal learnability are fragmentary and quite hard to relate to actual languages and problems of learning. The assumptions required for the formal learnability results (including the negative result about context-free grammars) include some that are psychologically quite implausible. But awareness of the issue has had a significant influence on the recent development of transformational syntax, just as questions of formal generative power did a few years earlier. Several of the developments described in Appendix C were motivated or justified by formal learnability considerations.

Formal processing mechanisms

The third problem listed above was the *realization problem*—the way that grammatical competence plays a role in the processes of language use. As with the preceding two considerations, we can look at generation and parsing from a purely formal point of view, leaving aside psychological issues, such as memory limitations and the interrelation of syntax and meaning. In particular, different kinds of grammar have quite different properties with respect to the efficiency of parsing. Type 3 grammars (regular expressions) can be parsed in a time that is directly proportional to the length of the input—that is, they take a constant amount of work per word parsed. Type 2 grammars (context-free) can be parsed in a time proportional to the square (if not ambiguous) or cube of the length of the input, as was discussed in Section 3.5. For some type 0 grammars, the length of time needed to parse grows exponentially with the length of the input, and for others there is no limit to the amount of processing it may take to find an analysis of a sentence, regardless of its length.

Much of the current research in generative grammar is influenced by the desire to use grammatical formalisms that lend themselves to effective parsing. If a formalism that is otherwise equally intuitive can be shown to permit a *polynomial* parsing time (one that is proportional to the length of. the input taken to some fixed power), it can be argued to be better than one for which an exponential amount of time is needed. As with the other formal critieria above, it is difficult to relate these abstract results to the real processing that goes on, since they intentionally avoid consideration of factors such as meaning, which play a central role in the production and comprehension of language.

Psychological reality

A continuing question in transformational grammar has been the relationship of the formal apparatus of syntactic theory to cognitive processes in the language user—the hearer, speaker, or learner of a language. Transformational grammar first appeared in an intellectual atmosphere that was dominated by the behaviorism advocated by Skinner. The behavioral paradigm emphasized the systematic analysis of observable data, discouraging any postulation of unobservable 'mental entities' as an explanation of behavior. Under this influence, linguistic methodology was strongly oriented toward observational generalizations that could be made on a corpus of recorded linguistic data. Chomsky argued that linguistics must deal with an underlying 'deep structure' that could only be discovered by systematically tapping the judgments of the native speaker. His review (1959) of Skinner's *Verbal Behavior* (1957) was highly influential in turning attention towards language as having cognitively determined structure.

In the early days of transformational grammar, it was assumed that psychologists would soon find experimental correlates of the specific entities (deep structures, transformation rules, etc.) postulated in the formalism. Experiments were carried out to test the *derivational theory of complexity*—the theory that the number of transformations operating in the derivation of a sentence provides a measure of the psychological complexity of comprehending or producing the sentence.

Early results seemed promising. Taking transformations such as PASSIVE, NEGATION, and QUESTION FORMATION, it was possible to demonstrate that sentences involving a transformation took longer to comprehend than corresponding untransformed sentences. Furthermore, there was a kind of additivity. Sentences that were both passive and negative took longer than sentences that were only one or the other.

It soon became apparent, however, that if one took into account the full range of different transformations needed to account for the structure of the language, the simple correlation between complexity and the number of transformations no longer held. Some transformations (such as deletions) made the sentences easier to comprehend by any of the available measures. Others were bookkeeping transformations (such as AFFIX-HOPPING), whose psychological correlates could not be sorted out from complexities of the base. As the theory developed further, even fairly obvious examples such as NEGATION became difficult to interpret, since the standard model postulated that there was not a transformation to make a sentence negative, but instead there was a grammatical marker for negativity that was generated in the base and only moved by transformations.

There was tension between those changes to the transformational formalism that would make it possible to preserve a derivational theory of complexity and those that would make it possible to cover an acceptably wide range of phenomena. The theory developed in the direction of wider coverage, and it has come to be generally accepted that transformations are not directly correlated to psychological mechanisms whose effects on language performance can be measured. The grammar formally *characterizes* a language, but it does not deal with the question of how the knowledge of a language is *realized* in psychological mechanisms.

Recently there has been a renewal of interest in the question of psychological reality, under the label *realistic transformational grammars*. Bresnan, who has been a central figure in transformational grammar, says (1978, p. 1):

> In the past ten years, linguistic research has been devoted almost exclusively to the characterization problem; the crucial question posed by the realization problem has been neglected—How would a reasonable model of language use incorporate a transformational grammar?

This recent concern has led to the development of grammars with attention to their relation to psychological models of language use. To some degree this is a natural extension of developments within the framework of transformational grammar over the intervening years, and to some extent it is the result of a continuing dialog between transformational grammar and computational theories. These two approaches seem in some respects to be converging, as we will discuss in Section 4.6.

Empirical relation to language acquisition

Just as questions of cognitive processing come up in looking at language use, it seems potentially relevant to ask how a formalism relates to the actual processes of language learning. Theoretical linguists (as opposed to the large number of practical linguists engaged in second-language teaching) have dealt mainly with the question of first-language learning. It is clear that the assumptions described above are not a realistic model of how a child learns a language, and there has been much discussion about what goes on in that process.

Transformational grammar has not provided the formal basis for most work on child language acquisition. There were some studies that looked for direct correlates, analogously to the derivational complexity experiments discussed above. They tested the assumption that the evolving pattern of language use by a child could be explained by assuming that the rules of the adult grammar are learned one by one over time. This hypothesis proved to be untenable and more recent studies, when they have used transformational grammar at all, have used it to characterize the competence of the child at one particular stage. However, intuitions about language acquisition have had some influence on the discussion of formal learnability:

Incremental learning. In his early work, Chomsky characterized the language acquisition device as performing a mapping from a set of sentences (as a whole) onto a set of possible grammars, followed by some kind of *evaluation procedure* by which a 'best grammar' was chosen. The more common current convention (quoted above) is that the learning process deals with sentences one by one, using them to modify an evolving grammar incrementally. At each step the evaluation procedure chooses among the possible modifications to the old grammar that would account for the new sentence. The newer version is much closer to our understanding of what a person does.

Negative evidence. Formal characteristics of learning processes are quite different when the data includes *negative evidence*—instances of non-sentences, designated as such. In earlier work it was assumed that utterances corrected by adults provided a large body of such negative evidence for the child learning a language, and therefore it was included in formal characterizations of the learning process. Careful analysis of recorded conversations revealed this was not true (Brown, 1977, p. 412):

> In general, the parents seemed to pay no attention to bad syntax nor did they even seem to be aware of it.... What parents generally correct is pronunciation, 'naughty' words, and regularized irregular allomorphs like 'digged' or 'goed'.... But [incorrect] syntax —the child saying, for instance 'Why the dog won't eat?' instead of 'Why won't the dog eat?'—seems to be automatically set right in the parent's mind, with the mistake never registering as such.

In light of this result, more recent work on formal learnability assumes the presence of only positive evidence.

Meaning. It is obvious that children do not learn a language primarily as a formal syntactic structure. They learn it as a vehicle for communication, and it seems likely that the properties of syntax learning are closely intertwined with 'learning how to mean.' Although the hypothesis of autonomous syntax weighs against bringing considerations of meaning directly into the mechanisms of syntactic learning, there has been some work in which it is assumed that the primary linguistic data consists not just of the utterances but of pairs containing an utterance and the corresponding deep structure or some kind of semantic structure for the sentence. Presumably, this deep or semantic structure would be known *a priori* by the child hearing the utterance, on some grounds of pragmatics or meaning. Although this assumption is clearly implausible in its simple form, it has served as intuitive motivation for discussing learning processes with paired inputs. These do in fact have different implications for the learnability of grammar formalisms.

Relation to meaning

As is apparent in the discussion above, the relation between syntactic structure and meaning has always been a problematic issue in transformational grammar. One of the most powerful appeals of transformational grammar is its ability to provide a formal account of perceived meaning similarities and differences that could not be explained on the basis of surface structure. However, with the autonomy of syntax as a methodological cornerstone, the edifice of syntactic mechanisms has been built without explicit resort to semantic arguments.

It remains the case, though, that the enterprise of understanding syntactic competence is one piece of a larger study of the entire language capacity, including meaning. The complexity of the hypothesized semantic component is determined to a large extent by the degree of correspondence between formal structures for meaning and the deep structures that serve as its input (or sets of structures, as in some of the more recent models described in Appendix C). When this is taken into account, a high priority is placed on the 'naturalness' of the deep structures and this in turn affects the detailed decisions made about the form of the transformations and the organization of the overall syntactic mechanism.

The desire to have the underlying structures systematically reflect meaning is probably the single most significant subliminal influence on the development of transformational theory. Although it may not be used as an explicit argument, it provides a background for the question of what forms are 'plausible,' from which it is hard to escape. It has also played an explicit theoretical role in major controversies. The *Katz-Postal hypothesis* that all transformations are meaning preserving was a major factor in directing the development of transformational grammars in the 1960s. The relation of syntax to meaning is a major area of difference in more recent debates between proponents of the standard theory and those advocating other formalisms, such as *generative semantics* and *Montague grammar*. As Partee (1976, p. 555) points out in discussing Montague grammar (which takes a particularly strong stand on the connection between syntax and semantics), '...the requirement that semantic interpretation rules correspond structurally to the syntactic rules can put very strong constraints on possible syntactic analysis.'

Diachronic linguistics and dialect

Looking at the concerns of linguists over the years, we see areas that were at one time of great importance but were dropped or relegated to obscurity in transformational grammar. In particular, there is the concern with *diachronic linguistics* (the change of language over time) and with the existence of different dialects within a language.

One could speculate that changes in the syntax of a language take place 'one rule at a time'—that historical developments might be shown to be built out of steps corresponding to the addition or modification of specific transformations or other rules in the grammar. Similarly, we might try to describe the syntactic difference between dialects in terms of sharing or not sharing particular rules. If these enterprises were central to the development of the grammatical formalism, we would expect them to have an influence on its details. A linguist would be motivated to prefer a particular formulation over another because he or she could thereby account for a particular historical change in terms of the grammar.

There have been some attempts (such as Closs, 1965) to bring together diachronic syntax and generative grammar, but they have not been influential in the theoretical developments. In reading through the core transformational literature, one often finds arguments for some version of the theory based on simplicity, learnability, and others of the issues discussed above, but almost never is an argument based on superior ability to account for some historical or dialect phenomenon.

Language universals

In the discussion of formal learnability, we mentioned the proposal that all languages share the same *universal base* grammar, and that this grammar is 'built in' to the human language capacity. At first hearing, this hypothesis sounds wildly implausible. We do not expect something as specific as a particular set of context-free rules to be part of our genetic inheritance. To understand why the suggestion was made (and is considered a serious hypothesis by many linguists), it is useful to understand the larger context of arguments concerning 'nature versus nurture,' in which Chomsky and his followers have been engaged throughout the years.

In the behaviorist-dominated atmosphere in which transformational grammar first emerged, it was assumed that the language learner began with a minimum of specific structure and a very general 'learning mechanism.' This assumption made it seem highly implausible that a system as intricate as transformational grammar could be learned. Chomsky argued instead that we have an *innate language capacity* that is highly specific to the nature of human language and that includes the components illustrated in Figures 4–12 and 4–13. He saw the goal of linguistics as the discovery of the structure of this *language faculty*.

In the behaviorist paradigm, the scientist looks for minimal mechanisms. Anything that cannot be proved to demand specialized structures is initially assumed to be explainable in terms of the basic notions of stimulus, response, and reinforcement.   Chomsky reversed the standards.   Under his research program, anything common to all human languages is assumed to be revealing of specific innate structures unless shown otherwise. This attitude has provided much of the motivation for the rather dry technical debate over the exact form of transformations and of the syntactic component as a whole. There has been much discussion of finding the principles of *universal grammar* through the search for both *formal universals* and *substantive universals*.

Formal universals. In proposing a basic syntactic formalism, one is making universal claims. For example, the claim 'Any human language can be described with a context-free grammar' is a formal universal. More theory-specific statements such as 'Transformations cannot change meanings' and 'Lexical insertion takes place before any transformations' also fall into the category of formal universals.

Substantive universals. Within an overall formalism there can be specific properties that are not determined by the formalism but that hold for all human languages. Examples of proposed substantive universals are: 'The base rules for all languages are identical;' 'Among the categories of the base rules are S, NP, and VERB, but not NOUN;' and 'There is a restricted set of rules for forming relative clauses, of the form....'

Substantive universals, like formal universals, are assumed to reflect the nature of the language capacity. One textbook, for example, argues in describing a particular constraint (Baker, 1978, p. 211):

> *Again, as with the complex-NP constraint, it appears that speakers of English are never confronted with any evidence, in the course of their acquisition of their language, that would provide a reason for incorporating the Rightward Movement Constraint into their system of rules for English. This fact gives us good reason to propose that this constraint belongs in our universal grammar rather than in our description of English proper. We are thus proposing that the constraint forms part of the general language faculty common to all humans, no matter what their native language happens to be.*

Although universality was always a theoretical concern, it had little direct effect on the details of transformational theory for many years. Recently there has been more concern with finding regularities among languages and with revising the formalism in a way that captures these regularities more systematically. Recent work on a descendant of transformational grammar called *relational grammar* is notable for its concern with cross-language generality. Most books on transformational grammar deal almost exclusively with English, using examples from other languages only occasionally to make detailed points. The major collection of works on relational grammar (Cole and Sadock, 1977), on the other hand, includes elaborate examples drawn from Achenese, Albanian, Algonquian (Fox), Arabic, Blackfoot, Breton, Cebuano, Chicewa, Chi-Mwi:ni, Coos, Coeur d'Alene, Dutch, Dyirbal, English, Eskimo, Greenlandic Eskimo, West Greenlandic Eskimo, Finnish, French, German, Classical Greek, Homeric Greek, Gugu-Yalanji, Hebrew, Hindi, Hungarian, Hurrian, Indonesian, Jacaltec, Japanese, Kannada, Kinyarwanda, Latin, Latvian, Luganda, Malay, Mandarin, Machiguenga, Malagasy, Classical Mayan, Mohawk, Palauan, Persian, Polish, Romansh, Samoan, Sanskrit, Siuslaw, Spanish, Tagalog, Tongan, Tzeltal, Vietnamese, Wappo, Welsh, Wichita, and Zeneyze.

Other work in transformational grammar has also turned more toward the issue of universality. Soames and Perlmutter (1979), for example, include in their textbook an argument based on Greek to demonstrate that the transformational cycle is not just a property of English but may be a formal universal.

Simplicity of grammars and theories

One of the major components of any syntactic argument is the attempt to 'capture the generalizations.' Given a set of data to explain, a theory that can cover several aspects with one rule or mechanism is considered better than one requiring two. There are a number of classical arguments (such as Halle's (1959) argument that there is no independent level of phonemes) based on the demonstration that an approach being criticized would require two separate accounts of something that the other approach could do in one stroke. However, one of the most difficult things to understand in reading the generative grammar literature is the mixed role that simplicity has played. The arguments seem to go in both directions—sometimes stating that a particular alternative is better because it is simpler, and at other times arguing that one is better because it contains more specific and restrictive mechanisms. For example, Postal (1972, p. 137) considers general questions of theoretical parsimony in science and argues:

> . . . given the same theoretical base, on general grounds one must choose that theory with the most restricted theoretical makeup. With respect to all competitors, such a theory must be held to be privileged, only to be abandoned in favor of some conceptually more complex alternative in the face of direct empirical evidence showing the need for such additions.

Under this view, only the failure of a simpler theory to cover the linguistic data would lead to building a more complex one. On the other hand, Chomsky has often argued (as described above) for the value of finding more restrictive formalisms, which are generally also more complex. He begins from the assumption that the human brain is a uniquely complicated object and that a major goal of linguistic theory is the discovery of its particular properties. Each time a restriction can be shown to be consistent with the set of possible human languages, one can hypothesize that it corresponds to a property of the human language faculty. Since there is such a large gap between formal results (on generative power and learnability) and intuitions about the 'powerfulness' or 'restrictiveness' of mechanisms, arguments in this area tend to be imprecise and vociferous.

A further complication arises when we consider the different perspectives of the linguist and of the language learner. In the standard model of language acquisition, the learner is choosing at each point between a number of grammars, all of which account for the data and are within the constraints determined by the underlying mechanisms. Some kind of *evaluation metric* must be postulated in order to explain how a particular grammar gets chosen over the alternatives. It has generally been assumed that this metric involved simplicity—that the language learner, like the scientist, preferred parsimony. As with the other considerations discussed above, there has been little success at formulating precise measures of simplicity or complexity, but linguists (like all scientists) have a personal tacit understanding of complexity and are motivated by the attempt to find those explanations that to them seem simpler.

Coverage of the data

Linguistics is an empirical science. The goal of the linguist is to explain the observable phenomena of people using language. From this standpoint, we would expect all of the meta-theoretical issues discussed above to be secondary to the primary problem of accounting for all of the data. However, the issue is not so obvious when we recall the discussion of scientific paradigms in Chapter 1. One of the major defining characteristics of a paradigm is the implicit agreement as to just what will be considered relevant data. What for one paradigm might seem to be a crucial experiment might for another seem quite peripheral. In the process of developing a new theory, there is a basic pressure to account for the phenomena that other people have observed, but there is a good deal of room for interpretation and maneuvering. There are several dimensions along which differences can arise:

The choice of central phenomena. Different schools within transformational grammar have at times differed in their attitudes towards what data should serve as the basic material for consideration. For example, the generative semanticists (see Section C.1) draw many examples from colloquial speech (e.g., the grammaticality of *I'll be damned if you'll get away with it* but not

He'll be damned if you'll get away with it). Others saw this as peripheral to the basic rules of the language.

At a less controversial level, everyone agrees that no existing theory gives a satisfactory account of *conjunction, ellipsis,* and *comparatives.* There are extremely complex regularities in the grammaticality and interpretation of sentences such as:

> *John believes that Bill won the race and Mary the pole vault.*
> * *... and that Mary the pole vault.*
>   *... and that Mary almost did.*
>
> *I have never seen a man taller than Mary.*
> *John is taller than Bill is fat.*
> *They have many more enemies than we have friends.*
>
> *More students flunked than thought they would.*
> *More students flunked than they thought would.*
> * *More students flunked than the instructor thought they would.*

The failure to provide a set of rules for such sentences is not taken as a critical weakness of the theory. It is assumed that eventually they will be covered, and for the time being they are left as data unaccounted for.

The assignment of phenomena to other components. Since the study of syntax is only one part of the study of language, there is much variability in the decision as to which phenomena to treat syntactically. The problem of pronouns (discussed further in Appendix C) provides a good example of shifts in assignment. In initial versions of transformational grammar, there was a transformation that converted other noun phrases into ones with pronouns. As more and more problems became apparent in this approach, it was gradually agreed that pronominalization should be treated by the semantic component and not dealt with primarily as syntax. Some recent proposals within Montague grammar bring much of the mechanism of pronominalization back into syntax, along with some changes to the structure of that component. The desire that a phenomenon be included usually goes hand in hand with ideas for mechanisms that can handle it.

The fuzziness of grammaticality. The early problems addressed in transformational grammar allowed the linguist to use intuitions about grammaticality in a fairly straightforward way. The rules of a grammar distinguished sentences that were clearly grammatical from those that were equally clearly ungrammatical. As the work proceeded, this distinction became harder to make, and many articles included hedges about the fact that a particular judgment was based on the writer's *idiolect* (individual dialect) and might not correspond to the judgments of any other speaker. Arguments have hinged on such difficult judgments as the difference in grammaticality between pairs like:

When you put former cheerleaders in a room, they discuss their numerous-
    ness.
When you put former cheerleaders in a room, they discuss their own
    numerousness.

In choosing data to attack or defend a particular theory, the linguist can decide
how far to go in claiming that there are clear grammaticality judgments. It is
clear that grammaticality cannot be identified with acceptability to the normal
speaker. As pointed out in Section 4.2, there are forms of center-embedding that
make sentences incomprehensible although they are syntactically correct. In the
other direction, it has been suggested (Langendoen and Bever, 1973) that some
sentences (such as those involving collocations like *not unhappy*) are best viewed
as ungrammatical but acceptable in order to avoid inordinate complication to
the grammar.

4.6 Computational implications of transformational grammar

Throughout the history of transformational grammar, there has been an uneasy
relationship between linguists working within the transformational paradigm
and researchers in artificial intelligence, who adopt a more computational orientation. It is easy to find statements made on both sides to the effect that the
work done by the opposing camp is irrelevant, nonsensical or just plain wrong.
Briefly, the arguments have centered around a few basic topics:

The relationship between syntax and other mental capacities. One
of the central methodological principles of transformational grammar is the
autonomy of syntax. It is assumed that the human mental capacities underlying
syntactic competence are the result of specialized mechanisms (the *language
faculty*) that are not shared by other animals (including other primates such
as chimpanzees) and are to a large extent distinct from the rest of our mental
processes. For this reason, the study of syntax is seen as a relatively unique
opportunity to isolate the operation of one component of mental processing and
understand its special structure.

Within artificial intelligence, on the other hand, the goal has been the
identification of the general principles and mechanisms that underlie all thought
processes. Instead of looking for specialized faculties (except in obvious cases
like visual processing in the retina), researchers formulate general theories of
representation and problem solving that can be applied to a wide range of
information processing activities. A particular kind of competence (such as
syntax or even the motor skills underlying juggling) is assumed to share the
same basic structure unless there is explicit need to postulate otherwise.

This difference in starting point has led to accusations in both directions.
The AI researchers argue that transformationalists propose highly specialized
'kludges' (complex gadgets) to account for properties of language that are the
result of more general cognitive principles. The rejoinder from those working

in transformational grammar is that all of the mechanisms proposed in AI are so general that they cannot serve as a theory of the human mind at all.

The proper use of formalism. Along with the difference in assumptions about generality and specificity, there is a deep difference in the way that formalisms are used. The computational paradigm grew out of computer programming, and the formal structures are seen as analogous to programming languages and data structures. They are good to the extent that they make it possible (and easy) to model the observed phenomena of language use. Often a particular mechanism will be preferred because it is *more powerful* than its predecessors, since this allows it to cover more of the phenomena.

In transformational grammar, on the other hand, the intuitions grew out of mathematics and the physical sciences. A theory is not something to be 'programmed,' but a terse set of axioms that can be used to predict the data. One theory is better than another because it is more restrictive, or as often stated, *less powerful*. Much of the meta-theoretical discussion in transformational grammar deals with questions of how to limit the power of the formalism so that it can serve as a more precise theory of the capacities it models. From this point of view, most AI models are hardly theory at all.

Attention to problems of processing. The most obvious difference between the two approaches is in the amount of attention paid to issues of the mental processes that go on when language is used. One of the main theoretical bases of transformational grammar has been the distinction between *competence* and *performance* discussed above. Early in its development, the theory went in the direction of handling a wider range of syntactic problems with a succinct formalism, at the expense of processing concerns. As has been pointed out many times, generative grammar 'generates' only in the most abstract sense and the formalism has little or nothing to say about what goes on when a person produces or comprehends an utterance.

The computational approach takes the opposite starting point. The information processing that goes on in the mind of a person using language is taken as fundamental. It is assumed that this process makes use of stored structures (such as a grammar) that are not themselves procedural, but whose form is constrained by the way they are used in procedures of production and comprehension. From this viewpoint, it seems that a characterization of abstract competence will inevitably fail to capture the appropriate generalities about language since it does not deal with what is 'really going on.'

Of course, this short account does not do justice to either view and this book is not the place for a history of the debate or a thorough exposition of the issues. Interested readers are referred to the papers listed at the end of the chapter.

Uses of transformational grammar in a computational approach

In light of the history of separation and conflict between the two paradigms, it may seem odd that a book on *Language as a Cognitive Process* devotes so much space to transformational theory. Indeed, it has been much more typical for training in artificial intelligence to exclude serious attention to the details of transformational grammar. There are many reasons why, even in light of the differences, it is important for any serious student of language within the computational paradigm to understand both the history and the direction of current work in transformational grammar.

Direct applicability of the formalism. Although early attempts to find psychological correlates of the mechanisms of transformational grammar failed, it is still possible that some version of the theory may in the end serve as part of a comprehensive theory of language processing. There have been some attempts (described in Section 7.3) to use transformational theory directly in the design of computer systems. This has been a difficult venture with debatable results, but has been seen by at least some researchers as a profitable path to follow.

Applicability of parts of the formalism. Even if the overall transformational model does not serve as a psychological theory or as a basis for computer programming, it is quite likely that some of the mechanisms that have been developed as parts of that model will prove useful. Many of the computer systems described in Chapter 7 make use of some kind of 'transformation' procedure, often within a rather different overall framework. Other systems have made use of many formal devices developed in transformational grammar, such as complexes of binary features for lexical items, abstract phrase structure elements, and even the basic distinction between surface structure and some kind of deep structure. A familiarity with the different versions of transformational grammar can serve as a valuable source of ideas for developing other theories and models.

Example of well-developed formal mechanism. The fact that so many different variations have been suggested for transformational grammar makes it of interest both for the variety of ideas (as mentioned in the previous paragraph) and as an example of how a complex unified framework can serve as the basis for a broad field of formal explorations. As the listing in Appendix C makes painfully obvious, a theory can be extended and modified in many different ways to suit many different purposes. Within linguistics (and cognitive science in general) transformational grammar is the formalism to which the greatest number of people have devoted the largest amount of effort. An understanding of its development (including the technical details) provides a valuable perspective on what it means to develop a formal theory to account for a complex collection of data.

Language for characterizing problems. The fact that so much work has been done within transformational grammar makes it important for another reason—its role as a *lingua franca* in which different phenomena have been described and discussed. The many linguists developing the theory and its terminology over the years have given names to many phenomena of importance, and a knowledge of the terminology is necessary for communicating within linguistics. Even those linguists who work within different frameworks find it useful to be able to discuss issues like 'heavy NP shift' or 'raising' and to be able to refer to the problem through the transformational literature. Most attempts to compare the coverage of different computer grammars have used transformational terms in characterizing the data, even though the programs are not based on transformational grammar.

Wealth of non-obvious data. An obvious correlate of the amount of work that has gone on within the transformational approach is the identification of many syntactic phenomena that would not be apparent to the casual observer of language. Anyone who is developing a grammatical formalism, whether for a computer or not, will find that a quick glance at an issue of a journal or collection on transformational grammar will provide examples that lead to important additions or changes to the grammar. Even if none of the theoretical apparatus is adopted, the transformational literature is a rich source of sentences raising syntactic problems that must be faced by anyone attempting a comprehensive syntactic account of English.

Convergence of the approaches. Finally, there are currently several research projects in which transformational and computational approaches are being brought together. Work on realistic transformational grammars mentioned in the previous section is being combined with work on augmented transition networks (described in Chapter 5), which grew out of computational considerations. In the synthesis, some elements of each are preserved and the overall framework combines aspects of both. In order to understand the development and future promise of this work (some of which is described in Section 6.6), it is necessary to be familiar with the transformational background as well as with the computational sources.

Further Reading for Chapter 4

Basic works. The basis of all work on transformational grammar appears in two major books by Chomsky, *Syntactic Structures* (1957) and *Aspects of the Theory of Syntax* (1965). Some of the more theoretical issues are discussed in his *Language and Mind* (1968), *Reflections on Language* (1975), and *Language and Responsibility* (1977b).

Textbooks. Textbooks on transformational grammar have a rather short lifetime, as the theory changes rapidly. There are a number of good recent books, including *An Introduction to the Principles of Transformational Syntax,* by Akmajian and Heny (1975), which was the primary influence on the form of the standard theory presented in this book. It is formally clear and gives a complete account of many issues. Jacobson's *Transformational-generative Grammar* (1978) is perhaps the best introduction to the field. It follows Akmajian and Heny in its formalism, but does not attempt to be as complete in its detail. It is easy to read and puts transformational grammar into a broader context of linguistic study. Newmeyer's *Linguistic Theory in America* is also quite readable. Other texts include Bach, *Syntactic Theory* (1974), Baker, *Introduction to Generative-transformational Syntax* (1978), Culicover, *Syntax* (1976), Soames and Perlmutter, *Syntactic Argumentation and the Structure of English* (1979), and Stockwell, *Foundations of Syntactic Theory* (1977).

Research papers. Much of the literature in transformational grammar has appeared in unpublished mimeographs and in the proceedings of meetings such as those held by the Chicago Linguistic Society (CLS), the New England Linguistics Society (NELS), and the Berkeley Linguistics Society (BLS). These volumes are usually referred to by number, e.g., 'CLS9,' and sometimes have colorful subtitles such as 'The great Chicago which hunt,' and 'You take the high node and I'll take the low node.' The journal *Linguistic Inquiry* is the basic journal for people working in the transformational paradigm, but papers also appear in the older, more structurally oriented journal of the Linguistic Society of America, *Language.*

There have been a number of books collecting relevant papers, of which some are from a specific conference, and others are selected by the editors from the literature. The following collections do not exhaust the literature but provide pretty good coverage: Reibel and Schane, *Modern Studies in English: Readings in Transformational Grammar* (1969), Jacobs and Rosenbaum, *Readings in English Transformational Grammar* (1970), Steinberg and Jakobovits, *Semantics* (1971), Peters, *Goals of Linguistic Theory* (1972), Anderson and Kiparsky, *A Festschrift for Morris Halle* (1973), Partee, *Montague Grammars* (1976), Cole and Sadock, *Syntax and Semantics 8: Grammatical Relations* (1977), Culicover, Wasow and Akmajian, *Formal Syntax* (1977), Halle, Bresnan, and Miller, *Linguistic Theory and Psychological Reality* (1978), and Wexler and Culicover (1980), *Formal Principles of Language Acquisition.*

Transformational grammar and the computational paradigm. There have been many contributions to the debate and a particularly coherent exchange is found in a series of papers by Dresher and Hornstein (1976, 1977a, 1977b), Schank and Wilensky (1977), and Winograd (1977). Petrick (1973) and Plath (1976) have used transformational grammar as the basis for a computer parsing system, and Friedman (1969) developed a computer system to generate sentences from a transformational grammar.

Exercises for Chapter 4

Exercises for Section 4.1

4.1 Describe several English structures other than those mentioned in the text whose intuitive analysis seems to call for discontinuous constituents.

4.2 Consider English phrases of the form 'DETERMINER NOUN VERB *-ing* NOUN,' such as *a man eating tiger* and *a man eating peanut butter*. Informally describe the different underlying structures that lead to the ambiguity.

Exercises for Section 4.2

4.3 The grammar of Figure 4–4 handles agreement between the noun and verb, but does not deal with other kinds of number agreement.

a) Some determiners in English (such as *this/these, that/those*) must also agree with the noun. Rewrite the grammar to include these facts. You will need to use rules that combine symbols to produce single words, like the *'goose* PLURAL $\rightarrow$ *geese'* example in the text. Derive the following sentences to test your grammar:

> *These willows follow that stream.*
> *That willow sways.*

b) Include quantifiers such as *every, each, all*, etc., and numbers, as in *the three willows sway*.

4.4 The following grammar was written to handle the same phenomena as the grammar of Figure 4–4:

1.	S $\rightarrow$	NP VP
2.	NP $\rightarrow$	Determiner Noun Number
3.	Number $\rightarrow$	Singular
4.	Number $\rightarrow$	Plural
5.	Singular VP $\rightarrow$	Singular Verb Singular
6.	Plural VP $\rightarrow$	Plural Verb
7.	Noun Singular $\rightarrow$	Noun
8.	Plural $\rightarrow$	*'-s'*
9.	Singular $\rightarrow$	*'-s'*

a) Show that the sentences *The willows sway* and *The willow sways* can be derived with it.

b) Show that ** The willows sways* can also be derived.

c) Describe an ordering rule for controlling which rules can be taken in what order to prevent the bad derivations.

4.5 Modify the network of Figure 2–16 to accept sentences like *The fire burned the stick that beat the dog that bit the cat that ate the kid*.

Exercises for Section 4.3

4.6 Which of the following structural descriptions match the first tree of Figure 4–16?

a) NP - S - PP

b) *be* - *ing* VERB

c) AUX - *pour* - NP - PREP

d) NP - TENSE - AUX - VP

4.7 The 'after' tree of Figure 4–21 includes elements such as *be, -ing,* and *-en* in an order that does not correspond to the surface form of the sentence. The AFFIX-HOPPING transformation given in Figure 4–14 should convert this to a different order.

a) Informally describe the series of 'hops' and the resulting sequence.

b) Draw a new tree structure which contains the same leaf nodes as the 'after' tree of Figure 4–21 and which also has enough additional intermediate nodes so that the AFFIX-HOPPING rule as formally stated can be applied.

c) Describe the difficulties that arise in trying to write the PASSIVE transformation so that this structure is produced as its output. This kind of difficulty is typical of many of the detailed analyses in transformational grammar. The form that makes one rule the simplest may not give the right structure for other rules to apply.

4.8 Show the surface structure tree that results from applying PASSIVE to the 'after' tree of Figure 4–20. Is this what you would expect? If not (hint, it shouldn't be), reformulate the rule so that it works for the case in Figure 4–21 and also for your case.

Exercises for Section 4.4

4.9 Transformation ordering

a) Show the result of applying the PASSIVE transformation to the 'before' tree of Figure 4–20.

b) Show the result of applying the DATIVE transformation to the result of **a**. Give both the tree and the corresponding sentence that would be generated by applying all the other relevant obligatory transformations.

c) Note that the statement of the PASSIVE transformation does not generate a PP with the preposition *by*, but rather uses Chomsky adjunction to produce an NP whose two constituents are *by* and an NP. How did the decision to do this affect the possibility of the transformation in **b** in this exercise? Interactions like this play a large part in determining the form of transformations.

4.10 The IMPERATIVE transformation takes deep structures whose subject is an NP corresponding to the pronoun *you* and deletes the subject. It produces *Drink your milk* from *You will drink your milk*. Give examples and informal arguments to justify ordering it before or after each of the following transformations:

a) PASSIVE: *Jack saw Jill.* → *Jill was seen by Jack.*

b) TAG FORMATION: *He wants it.* → *He wants it, doesn't he?*

c) REFLEXIVE: *He cut him.* → *He cut himself.* (where the two NPs refer to the same person).

4.11 The overall process of derivation with a transformational grammar is described in this chapter, but there is no DL definition pulling it all together. Write a nondeterministic derivation procedure, making use of the procedures given in the chapter and any others you need. Include things like the operation of the cycle, lexical insertion, etc.

Exercises for Section 4.5

4.12 Describe briefly the kind of data (either linguistic or from psychology experiments) that you would look for to back up the claim that a particular grammar formalism was better than its competitors because it was:

a) A more realistic basis for comprehension

b) A structure that could be learned in a natural way

c) A theory that could help explain dialect differences

4.13 What kind of formal theory would you need in order to back up the claim that greater simplicity was achieved by:

a) A particular grammar for a language, compared to others for the same language, given a common framework (e.g., the standard theory)?

b) An overall grammar framework (such as the standard theory) compared to other such frameworks?

Exercises for Section 4.6

4.14 Consider the knowledge that a person must have in order to do ordinary arithmetic—addition, subtraction, etc. Describe how it could be characterized in terms of competence and performance, with the competence based on some kind of axiomatic system. What would be included in a computational model that would not be included in the formalization of competence?

4.15 Consider the knowledge that a person must have in order to drive a car. How much of it can be described in terms of abstract competence? What kinds of procedural accounts would describe what the person does?

4.16 Compare the knowledge needed by a person who appropriately uses a natural language to the examples of arithmetic and and car-driving. What kinds of theories would the two analogies lead us to look for?

Chapter 5

Augmented Transition Networks

Chapter 3 described a basic formalism for grammars (context-free) that was easily incorporated into computational processes of parsing and generation. Chapter 4 described the much more elaborate formalisms developed in transformational grammar to account for the complexities of natural language. As discussed in that chapter, transformational linguists have been primarily concerned with accounting for linguistic intuitions and their theories have not generally been directly concerned with the processes of language use. As pointed out in Section 4.6, it is difficult to describe processing algorithms of any kind that make direct use of transformational theory.

In the same period during which transformational grammar emerged, a series of developments within artificial intelligence followed a different approach. Instead of taking the process of abstract *derivation* as a starting point, they took the process of *parsing*. Starting with a basic top-down left-to-right parsing scheme like the one described in Section 3.4, mechanisms were added to handle more complex syntactic problems. There were a number of systems of this type, several of which are discussed in Chapter 7. The clearest formulation was in terms of *augmented transition networks* (ATN), as presented in this chapter. Augmented transition networks and their descendants are currently one of the most common methods of parsing natural language in computer systems. They have also served as the basis for psycholinguistic theories and experiments.

This chapter is intended to serve two complementary purposes. First, it presents the augmented transition network formalism and explains how it is used in parsing. In addition, it provides detailed analyses of some substantial syntactic problems in English. Chapter 3 dealt only with extremely simplified grammar examples in order to concentrate on the mechanisms. Chapter 4 discussed more realistic linguistic phenomena, but did not describe the transformational formalism in enough detail for students to follow the detailed analysis of examples. The ATN formalism is clear enough to be grasped and followed easily, while providing mechanisms that make it possible to deal with complex phenomena. Therefore it is used here as the vehicle for building some insight into the problems that arise in trying to write a comprehensive grammar for a language. This chapter does not give a full or definitive grammar, but goes into a variety of issues that are typical of those that have been dealt with in other theories and in computer systems. The grammar that is developed throughout the chapter is summarized for reference in Section D.2.

The ATN formalism as presented here does not correspond exactly to any of the existing versions. It draws both from the original ATN (Woods, 1970) and from later modifications by Kaplan (1975). In particular, the structures produced by these networks are similar to those in Kaplan's version, although they have been influenced by some ideas from systemic grammar, as described in Chapter 6.

Section 5.1 introduces the concept of a *recursive transition network,* which is formally equivalent in power to a context-free grammar but provides a foundation on which to build augmented transition networks. Section 5.2 describes the basic ATN mechanism and the process of parsing using an ATN. Sections 5.3 through 5.6 present a series of problems in English syntax, both introducing the required ATN mechanisms and illustrating the kind of analysis that is needed to write grammars that cover the linguistic data. Finally, Section 5.7 discusses the implementation of ATN parsers on computers.

5.1 Recursive transition networks

Chapter 2 described a formalism based on *transition networks* that made it possible to specify patterns involving optional elements, choices, and repetitions. We noted in Section 4.2 that a transition network is equivalent to a type 3, or regular grammar. In this section we describe an extension of the network formalism (recursive transition networks) that has the power of a type 2 or context-free grammar.

Instead of being made up of rules, a recursive transition network (RTN) grammar consists of a set of labeled networks. These are like the simple transition networks defined in Chapter 2 (Figure 2–13) except that each network has a label and each arc is labeled with a word, a lexical category, or a syntactic category that is the label of some network in the grammar. As with a simple transition network, an arc whose label is a word or lexical category can be traversed if it matches a single word of the input.

The arcs labeled with composite syntactic categories are the main new feature of recursive transition networks. The label of such an arc will also be the label for a network. The arc is traversed by matching a sequence of input symbols to this other whole network. To match an arc labeled NP, for example, we call the recognition process recursively, with the word string, the current position, and the network for NP as inputs. If this process succeeds in recognizing the desired constituent (as indicated by stopping in a terminal state), then processing returns to the original network, going to the state at the end of the arc and continuing with the current position moved beyond the elements 'used up.'

We have also added a new kind of arc called a *jump arc* (indicated with the label 'JUMP') that can be taken without matching a word of the input. Any time a generation, recognition, or parsing process is in the starting state of a jump arc, it can move to the ending state of that arc without any other changes. This does not change the formal power of the networks, but it makes it more convenient to write them.

Figure 5–1 shows a simple context-free grammar (the one introduced in Figure 3–19) and a recursive transition network that defines the same language (i.e., matches the same set of word sequences). As with simple transition networks, we show the states as circles, the arcs as arrows (from starting state to ending state), and the labels next to the arcs. Initial states are indicated by a small arrow coming in and terminal states by a double circle.

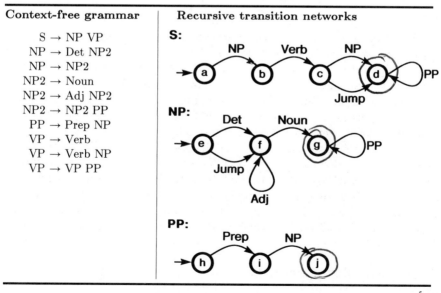

Figure 5–1. Equivalent context-free and RTN grammars.

A. Context-free grammar

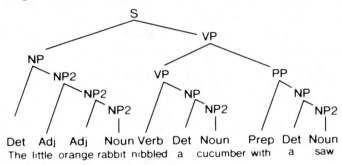

B. Recursive transition network grammar

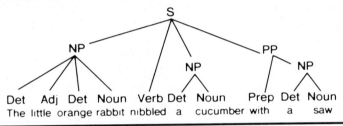

Figure 5–2. Analyses produced by weakly equivalent grammars.

The two grammars are *weakly equivalent* in that they accept the same sequences but assign different structures. For example, given the sentence *The little orange rabbit nibbled a cucumber with a saw,* the context-free grammar produces two parsings, one of which is shown as tree A of Figure 5–2. If we represent the result of an RTN recognition by placing the label of a network on a node and putting the sequence of arcs followed in going through the network as its children, we get trees like tree B instead.

It is possible to produce an RTN that is *strongly equivalent* to a given context-free grammar (see exercise 5.2), but the natural tendency in making full use of the power of networks is to produce 'flatter' networks rather than having one for each of the many nonterminal symbols. For example, in the context-free grammar of Figure 5–1 it is necessary to introduce the symbol NP2 in order to allow repetition of adjectives, while in the network it is done with a loop.

Parsing with RTN grammars

Recursive transition network grammars can be used to parse sentences with small modifications of the schemas and algorithms given for context-free gram-

---

Parse a sentence top-down left-to-right (nondeterministic)

Purpose: Produce a tree structure corresponding to a parsing of a sequence of words as a sentence in the language defined by an RTN grammar

Background: a *dictionary* and an *RTN grammar*   2–10 5–4

Inputs: a sequence of words

Results: a *phrase structure tree*   3–4 3–7

Working Structures:
    Root: a phrase structure node; initially with null parent and no children, having the distinguished symbol of the grammar as its label

Basic Method:
- *Match* the network whose label is the distinguished symbol of the grammar against the input sequence, beginning at position 1 and expanding the root.   5–5
- If the match succeeds and the position returned is one greater than the length of the input sequence, return the tree consisting of the root and all of its descendants. Otherwise fail.

Figure 5–3. Top-down nondeterministic parsing with an RTN grammar.

mars in Chapter 3. A nondeterministic schema for top-down left-to-right parsing with an RTN grammar is given in Figure 5–3, making use of the definition of a grammar in 5–4 and the one of matching given in Figure 5–5. The parser for ATN grammars will be an extension of these definitions. This is a parsing schema, not just a recognition schema—its result is a phrase structure tree corresponding to the sentence.

In adapting a schema from grammar rules to networks, each occurrence of 'Choose a rule' is replaced by 'Choose an arc.' In most implementations of RTN parsers (and the ATN parsers developed from them), the arcs are assigned an order so that a backtrack strategy can be more efficient by trying the more likely ones first.

In a bottom-up strategy, the networks would be used nonrecursively. Each occurrence of 'Test whether a rule spans a contiguous sequence of constituents' must be replaced with 'Test whether a network accepts a contiguous sequence of constituents,' and the networks are treated like simple transition nets, with each arc matching either a single word or the label of a single previously known constituent. Recursive transition networks lend themselves nicely to an active chart strategy of the kind described in Section 3.6. Instead of having a remainder that is part of the right-hand side of a rule, each active edge indicates a state in a network. An active edge can be combined with a following complete edge whenever the label of the complete edge is the same as the label on one or more outgoing arcs from this state.

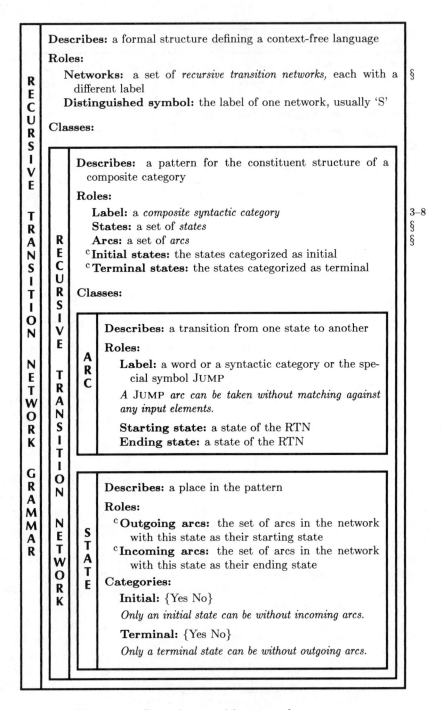

Describes: a formal structure defining a context-free language

Roles:

> **Networks:** a set of *recursive transition networks,* each with a different label
>
> **Distinguished symbol:** the label of one network, usually 'S'

Classes:

> **Describes:** a pattern for the constituent structure of a composite category
>
> **Roles:**
>
>> **Label:** a *composite syntactic category*
>> **States:** a set of *states*
>> **Arcs:** a set of *arcs*
>> ^c**Initial states:** the states categorized as initial
>> ^c**Terminal states:** the states categorized as terminal
>
> **Classes:**
>
>> **Describes:** a transition from one state to another
>>
>> **Roles:**
>>
>>> **Label:** a word or a syntactic category or the special symbol JUMP
>>>
>>> *A JUMP arc can be taken without matching against any input elements.*
>>>
>>> **Starting state:** a state of the RTN
>>> **Ending state:** a state of the RTN
>>
>> **Describes:** a place in the pattern
>>
>> **Roles:**
>>
>>> ^c**Outgoing arcs:** the set of arcs in the network with this state as their starting state
>>> ^c**Incoming arcs:** the set of arcs in the network with this state as their ending state
>>
>> **Categories:**
>>
>>> **Initial:** {Yes No}
>>>
>>> *Only an initial state can be without incoming arcs.*
>>>
>>> **Terminal:** {Yes No}
>>>
>>> *Only a terminal state can be without outgoing arcs.*

Figure 5–4.   Recursive transition network grammar.

Match an RTN against a sequence of words, beginning at a position and expanding a phrase structure node (nondeterministic)

Purpose: Test whether a network matches the sequence beginning at the given position

Background: a *dictionary* and a *recursive transition network grammar.*   2–10 5–4

Inputs: a network, a sequence of words, an integer and a *phrase structure node*   3–7

Results: an integer representing a new position in the sequence

The position following the words matched by the network

Side Effects: modify the parse tree by adding children to the node

Working Structures:
   Position: an integer representing a position in the sequence; initially the input position
   State: a state; initially any initial state of the network
   Arc: an arc in the network
   New node: a phrase structure node

Basic Method: Keep repeating:
- If either the position is larger than the length of the sentence or the state has no outgoing arcs, then fail.
- Choose any outgoing arc of the state and assign it as the arc.
- Assign the ending state of the arc as the state.
- Create a new tree node with no children, whose parent is the input node and whose label is the label of the arc, and assign it as the new node.
- If the label of the arc is:
  - JUMP, then go on.
  - a word that is the same as the word at the position in the input sequence, then increment the position by 1.
  - a lexical category to which the word at the position belongs, then:
    - Increment the position by 1.
    - Create a node with the word as its label, no children, and the new node as its parent, and let it be the only child of the new node.
  - any other word or lexical category, then fail.
  - a composite category, then:
    - Match the network whose label is the category against the word sequence beginning at the position, expanding the new node.
    - If the match succeeds, then assign the position it returns as the position. Otherwise fail.
- If the label of the arc is not 'JUMP', then add the new node at the end of the children of the input node.
- If the state is terminal, either succeed and return the position or go on.

Figure 5–5. Matching with a recursive transition network.

Network	Position	Arc	Node Modified
S	1	*the*	$_aNP_b$	S (NP$_1$)
NP$_1$	1	*the*	$_eDet_f$	NP$_1$ (Det)
	2	*orange*	$_fAdj_f$	NP$_1$ (Det Adj)
	3	*rabbit*	$_fNoun_g$	NP$_1$ (Det Adj Noun)
	4	*nibbled*	$_bVerb_c$	S (NP$_1$ Verb)
	5	*a*	$_cNP_d$	S (NP$_1$ Verb NP$_2$)
NP$_2$	5	*a*	$_eDet_f$	NP$_2$ (Det)
	6	*cucumber*	$_fNoun_g$	NP$_2$ (Det Noun)
	7	*with*	$_gPP_g$	NP$_2$ (Det Noun PP)
PP	7	*with*	$_hPrep_i$	PP (Prep)
	8	*a*	$_iNP_j$	PP (Prep NP$_3$)
NP$_3$	8	*a*	$_eDet_f$	NP$_3$ (Det)
	9	*saw*	$_fNoun_g$	NP$_3$ (Det Noun)

Figure 5–6. Parsing with an RTN grammar.

In the parser of Figures 5–3 and 5–5, whenever an arc whose label is a network label is to be taken, a new node is added before checking to see if the arc can be successfully matched. Since the schema is nondeterministic, this simply means that in case of failure a useless structure will be built. In implementing a deterministic algorithm, the check would be done before building the new node. In this section and most of the rest of this chapter, we will give nondeterministic schemas, putting off the question of trying multiple alternatives for Section 5.7.

The operation of the recursive parsing process is illustrated in Figure 5–6. The trace represents a successful parsing of the sentence *The orange rabbit nibbled a cucumber with a saw* using the networks of Figure 5–1. Nodes of the phrase structure tree being constructed are shown with the label of the node followed in parentheses by the labels of its children. The three different NP nodes built in the course of the parsing are distinguished by subscripts, which are not part of the formalism, but are included to clarify the table.

In the building of node structures by an RTN parser, we no longer have the simple correspondence that exists between the sequence of symbols in a context-free rule and the sequence of elements in a constituent produced using that rule. A single arc (for example, a loop) can contribute a series of constituents to a parse, while a jump arc contributes none. As mentioned above, the structures assigned by an RTN grammar like that of Figure 5–1 will in general be flatter than those produced by a corresponding context-free grammar.

Some terminology

Chapter 3 introduced *grammar rules* and *tree structures*. Taken together, these provide the formal mechanisms by which a grammar can *generate* a language. It also introduced mechanisms for *parsing,* and in particular the use of an *active chart.* Chapter 2 introduced *transition networks* as a more convenient way of encoding a set of sequential patterns for syntactic elements. This section combines the idea of tree structures with that of networks. We have not given detailed definitions for charts or for any other formalism in connection with RTN grammars for keeping track of what has and has not been tried, as would be needed for a deterministic parsing procedure. In most of this chapter we will be ignoring the contents of the last sections of Chapter 3 and going back to improve (in the sense of better natural language coverage) on the basic ideas of writing grammars.

At this point, before going on to the additional complexities of augmented transition networks, it is useful to take note of some terms that can be difficult. It is easy to confuse them, since several different kinds of structures are depicted as labeled nodes connected by lines, and all of the structures have syntactic categories of the grammar appearing as labels.

Rule. Each rule in a context-free grammar represents a possible structure for a phrase. It consists of a *left-hand side* (a *nonterminal symbol* that can be thought of as the *label* of the rule), and a *right-hand side,* which is a sequence of symbols. A rule is usually represented by writing the left-hand side followed by '→' followed by the right-hand side.

Phrase structure tree. A tree is used to represent the assigned *constituent structure* of a sentence. Each *node* of the tree has a *label* and a (possibly empty) sequence of *children,* each of which in turn is a tree node. There is a one-to-one correspondence between the structure of a constituent and the rule that produced it, in which the label is the left-hand side and there is one child for each symbol on the right-hand side. A phrase structure tree does not tell us anything about how it was built up, such as the order in which things were added, or the set of other things that were tried. It is purely a result, and in fact different strategies (e.g., bottom-up and top-down) lead to producing it in different ways. Trees are drawn by writing the labels of the nodes and connecting a parent to each of its children by a downward line.

Transition network. A *transition network* is used in place of rules to define a language, either by itself (a single network as described in Chapter 2) or as one of a set of networks in an RTN or ATN grammar. A network consists of a set of *states* connected by *arcs.* States can be designated as *initial states* and as *terminal states.* A simple transition network grammar consists of a single network whose arcs are labeled with words or lexical categories. A recursive transition network grammar contains a network for each nonterminal symbol of the grammar. Its arcs are labeled with terminal and nonterminal symbols. An augmented transition network grammar is similar, but allows some special kinds of arcs, one of which (*send arcs*) is used instead of terminal states. A network is not used to store information about a particular parse. It represents a pattern to be matched against potential sentences. All kinds of transition networks are represented graphically with circles for states and arrows connecting the circles representing arcs. An arrow is used rather than just a line, in order to distinguish the starting from the ending state of the arc. The label of the arc is usually written alongside the arrow.

Chart. A chart is used as a *working structure* to keep track of what has been tried so far in parsing a particular input. It consists of a set of *vertices* connected with *edges*. Vertices correspond to positions in the input sequence. Edges represent completed or partial constituents and are labeled with the label of that constituent (terminal or nonterminal). Whereas networks are parallel to rules (both are part of defining a grammar), charts are parallel to phrase structure trees in that they are used to represent the analysis of a particular sentence. A parse tree or chart is built up in parsing an input and does not exist as a permanent part of the language user's knowledge. However, the chart is complementary to the parse tree. Since each edge corresponds to a constituent, there must be some way to store the internal structure of that constituent, and the easiest way is to 'hang' a tree node from each edge. The children of that node will in turn correspond to other edges in the chart. A chart is represented by a set of circles (one for each vertex) and lines connecting these (one for each edge). Each line has a label indicating the contents of the edge. In some cases, this will simply be the label for the corresponding constituent, while in others it will be more complex. Although edges distinguish their starting and ending vertices, they are typically drawn as lines without arrowheads.

In a complex parsing system, several of these structures can be used. There will be a set of rules or networks representing the grammar. In the course of parsing, tree structures will be built, which in turn will be entered into a chart.

5.2 Augmenting the network

The recursive transition networks described in the previous section have the same formal power as context-free grammars but are a more convenient form to work with. This section describes the *augmentation* that allows ATN grammars to handle the more complex syntactic phenomena described in Chapter 4. The augmentation centers around the addition of *conditions* and *actions* associated with the arcs of a network. Conditions restrict the circumstances under which an arc can be taken, while actions perform feature-marking and structure-building operations. Conditions and actions make use of *registers* for roles and features, associated with the nodes of the parse tree being constructed. Registers are similar to the variables of a programming language, each having a name and storing some information. In transformational grammar, a single formal mechanism (transformation rules) could be used for a number of different things. In a similar vein, conditions and actions making use of registers can also be applied in many ways.

Conditions can depend on constituents that have already been found, on special properties of the word or constituent to be matched against the arc, and on properties of the entire structure that has been built up so far. Actions are used both to generate the ultimate structures that result from the analysis and to provide temporary information that can be used by conditions on other arcs.

This section describes in general how conditions and actions are used and defines *register structures,* which are built by the particular style of augmented transition network presented in this book. Formal definitions for the structures of an ATN grammar and the corresponding processes for recognition and parsing are given in Section D.1, in the appendices. The following sections introduce the mechanisms in a less formal way, making reference to the definitions given there.

Register structures

In our presentation of ATN grammars, we will be working with a kind of syntactic structure that is different from the phrase structure trees of Chapters 3 and 4, and more closely related to the *role structure trees* discussed in Section 3.1. Woods' original ATN formalism, as well as many current ATN parsers, use more standard tree structures. The *register structures* used here are similar to those introduced by Kaplan (1975) and are closely related to those of systemic grammar, as described in Chapter 6. The *features* and *functions* of systemic grammar correspond to the contents of *registers,* and we use the term 'register structure' in place of 'role structure' to emphasize this connection. Structure building in other forms of ATN grammar is discussed in Section 5.7.

A register structure is made up of nodes, each having a label (as in phrase structure trees) and a *register table,* as defined in Figure 5–8. A register table associates *feature dimensions* and *role names* with particular values. The entry for a feature dimension will be a feature chosen from the possible values for that dimension, and the entry for a role name will be a node or sequence of nodes. For example, the feature dimension NUMBER has choices PLURAL and SINGULAR, while the role SUBJECT will be filled by an NP node and the role DESCRIBERS by a sequence of ADJECTIVE nodes. Feature dimensions are defined formally in Section 5.3.

Figure 5–7 is an example of a register structure for the sentence *We have been given a firm deadline by the secretary.* Each node is represented by a box, with the label in the upper left-hand corner and the words of the corresponding phrase along the top edge. The entries of the register tables appear in the boxes, with features listed directly and roles indicated by lines to the appropriate other boxes. A horizontal line is drawn to separate the features from the roles, although formally they are all part of the same table. In addition to having the extra feature markings and role labels, these structures differ from tree

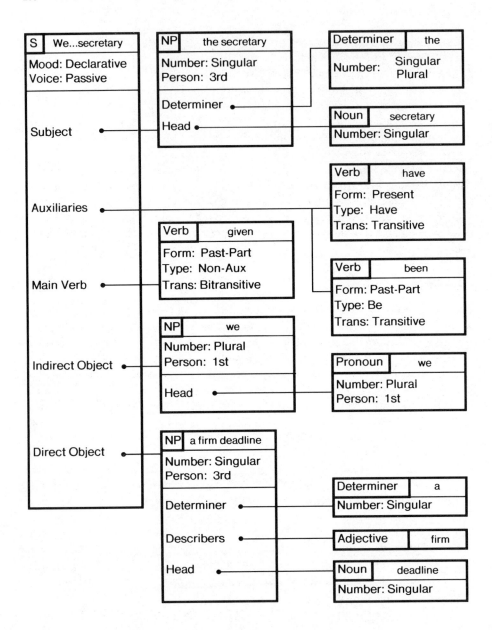

Figure 5–7. A sample register structure.

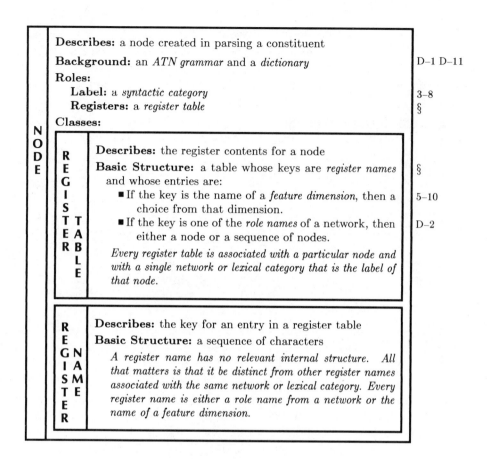

Figure 5-8. Register structure node.

structures in that no ordering is specified for the role fillers and the same node can play more than one role, as we will see in Section 5.5.

In the structures associated with individual words, such as *have* and *the,* the features are those associated with one particular entry in the dictionary (as defined later). For example, *firm* is both an adjective and a noun and is used here as an adjective, while *the* (which is both SINGULAR and PLURAL) is parsed here using the entry for SINGULAR.

Basic elements of an ATN grammar

An augmented transition network (defined formally in Figure D-2) is quite similar to a recursive transition network (as defined in Figure 5-4), with a few additions:

Feature dimensions and role names. Associated with each network there is a set of feature dimensions and a set of role names. When a phrase is parsed using a network, the register table of the resulting node will contain entries whose keys are the feature dimensions and role names for the network named in its label.

Conditions and actions. The most important addition is the association of conditions and actions with the arcs of the grammar. In order for an arc to be taken, its condition must hold for the current state of the parsing (along with the normal arc-applicability requirements, as for an RTN). When an arc is taken, the associated action is carried out, causing the contents of registers to be set. Figure 5–9 summarizes the possible conditions and actions and the objects with which they operate. It includes all of the basic operations, but most ATN grammar formalisms allow extensions to these, as described in Section 5.7. The detailed explanation of items like 'dummies' and 'copies' will appear in the following sections. The appendix does not include a formal definition of the structures needed to represent conditions and actions, but they can be derived in a straightforward way from the other definitions and the information in Figure 5–9.

Initializations. When an arc is followed that calls for parsing with a network, some of its registers can be initialized to contents derived from the status of the parsing so far. The use and form of initializations are discussed in Section 5.5.

Classification of arcs. An augmented transition network can contain four different kinds of arcs. A *category arc* (often referred to as a 'CAT Arc') is matched against a single word of the input. Its label is a lexical category. A *seek arc* (called a 'PUSH arc' in the original ATN grammars) specifies a recursive call to a network (possibly the one in which it appears). Its label is the label of that network or of a state in it. A *send arc* (originally called called a 'POP arc') is labeled with the symbol 'SEND' and has a starting state but no ending state. The starting state of a send arc can be thought of as a terminal state of the network, and the effect of following a send arc (as defined in Figure D–10) is to successfully complete the recognition of that network. This change makes it easier to associate actions and conditions with the successful matching of a network, since they can be attached to a send arc just as to any other arc. *Jump arcs* (labeled with 'JUMP') are taken without parsing any elements of the input, as described in Section 5.1. They can have associated conditions and actions, often simplifying the writing of networks. The formal definitions of the different kinds of arc appear in Figures D–7 through D–10.

Parsing with an ATN

The schema for parsing with an ATN grammar (Figures D–3 through D–6) is a modified version of the schema for an RTN grammar described above. In the

Actions that can be taken are:

A feature register is set to a choice for its dimension
A role register is set to a node
A node is appended to the end of a role register containing a sequence of nodes

Conditions on accessible values that can be tested are:

Two features are identical
A role register is empty
A node is of a specific category
A node is a dummy node (created by an action)
The word associated with a node is a specific word
Any logical combination (using *or, not, if...then,* etc.) of the above

Initializations consist of:

A **key**, which is the name of a register in the network being initialized
A **value**, which accesses features or nodes in the configuration
           from which the initialization is being done

Features and sets of features that can be accessed are:

Values explicitly given in an action or condition
The contents of a feature register of the current configuration
The contents of a feature register of some accessible node

Nodes that can be accessed are:

The contents of a role register of the current configuration
The most recently parsed constituent
The contents of a role register of some accessible node
The first or last element of an accessible sequence
Dummy nodes explicitly created in actions
A copy of the current node (used in relative clauses)

Sequences of nodes that can be accessed are:

The contents of a role register of the current configuration
The contents of a role register of some accessible node

Figure 5–9. Actions, conditions, and initializations in an ATN.

RTN parser, one of the inputs is a phrase structure tree node, which is used to keep track of the results as arcs are followed. In the ATN parser, we have created a new kind of temporary structure called a *configuration,* as defined in Figure D-3. A configuration includes the register table for the constituent being built, along with a current network, state, position, and the node most recently parsed. A node is not actually built until the parsing with the network is finished (when a send arc is taken), at which time the register table of the configuration is incorporated into the node.

By having a single structure incorporating all of this information, it is quite easy to modify the schema to do deterministic parsing. A backtracking scheme would save configurations in order to go back to them, while a parallel scheme would keep track of a number of alternative configurations simultaneously. There are two places where nondeterminism arises in the schema. One is in the step of choosing an arc to follow out of the current state, as shown in Figure D-6. The other is in the choice of a word sense in the dictionary entry for a word being matched by a category arc, as shown in Figure D-7. This isolating of all the nondeterminism into two places simplifies the job of keeping appropriate choice records.

The parsing process proceeds almost exactly like that for RTN grammars, except that the actions put contents into registers and the conditions constrain which arcs can be taken. Rather than following an example in detail here, the features are introduced gradually in the following sections.

5.3 The use of registers in ATN grammars

The previous section introduced the idea of registers associated with networks and of conditions and actions associated with arcs. This section describes the use of registers in more detail.

Feature registers

One of the simple syntactic problems described in Section 4.1 was *number agreement.* In transformational grammar, this was originally handled by adding special grammatical markers for SINGULAR and PLURAL and having them be manipulated by transformations. Later versions, as illustrated by the NUMBER AGREEMENT transformation illustrated in Section 4.4, used features associated with individual lexical items. In an ATN grammar of the kind defined here, features can be used in a somewhat more general way, allowing features that have multiple choices (instead of being binary) and associating feature registers with networks as well as having features on individual words.

As mentioned above, the use of features as described here is not exactly as it appears in papers on ATN grammars. It has been formalized in a style that is closer to systemic grammar in order to emphasize and clarify the linguistic

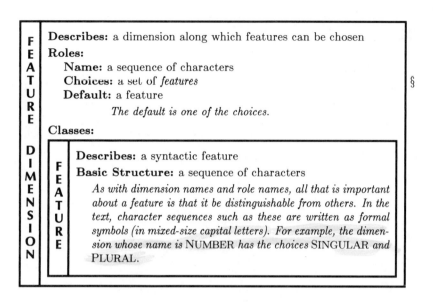

Figure 5–10. Feature dimension.

concepts instead of describing them in terms of a computer implementation. It is based on a formal structure called a *feature dimension* defined in Figure 5–10. Each dimension has a *name*, a set of *choices*, and a *default* choice to be assumed initially.

We will first illustrate number agreement in the NP network, as illustrated in Figure 5–1, leaving the problem of subject-verb agreement until after we have introduced ways of handling roles like SUBJECT. The data to be handled are exemplified by:

this kumquat	*this kumquats	the kumquat	the kumquats
*these kumquat	these kumquats	this fish	these fish

Two things need to be considered. First, we need a way of characterizing the differences among the determiners *this, these,* and *the* and between the nouns *kumquat* and *kumquats* in terms of a NUMBER feature associated with each word. Second, we need to include conditions and actions in the NP network to enforce agreement between the noun and the determiner.

The dictionary described in Chapter 2 (Figure 2–10) associates with each word a set of *lexical categories* to which it belongs. For ATN grammars, we will use an extended kind of dictionary that still assigns words to lexical categories, but also has for each lexical category a set of feature dimensions, as illustrated in Figure 5–11. The feature dimensions listed here do not include all of those needed in a comprehensive grammar, but are those used in the examples. Other

Category	Dimension	Choices	Default
Adjective	—		
Complementizer	—		
Determiner	Number	Singular, Plural	Singular, Plural
	Question	Yes, No	No
Noun	Number	Singular, Plural	Singular
	Case	Subjective, Objective	Subjective, Objective
Preposition	—		
Pronoun	Number	Singular, Plural	Singular
	Person	1st, 2nd, 3rd	3rd
	Case	Subjective, Objective	Subjective, Objective
	Question	Yes, No	No
Proper	Number	Singular, Plural	Singular
	Case	Subjective, Objective	Subjective, Objective
Relative	—		
Verb	Form	Infinitive, Present, Past, Past-Participle, Present-Participle, 3rd-Singular-Present	Present, Infinitive
	Transitivity	Intransitive, Transitive, Bitransitive	Transitive
	Type	Be, Do, Have, Modal, Non-Aux	Non-Aux

Additional verb dimensions would be needed to handle all the forms of 'be.'

Figure 5–11. Lexical categories used in this chapter.

dimensions will be added as exercises. There are also radical simplifications (for example, in the treatment of transitivity) that will be discussed below.

Figure D–11 formally defines the kind of dictionary used in the ATN grammars of this chapter. As illustrated in Figure 5–12, a word can have several *word senses,* each of which is assigned to a category and a choices along each of the feature dimensions for the category. The same word may belong to several categories and have different features in each. For example, the word *fish* can be a singular noun, a plural noun, a present tense verb (as in *They fish in the ocean*) or an infinitive verb (as in *I like to fish*).

Two devices have been used to keep the dictionary smaller and to express regularities. First, when there are several senses differing only in feature choices, they are combined on a single line. For example, *fish* is listed as a noun with NUMBER features of both SINGULAR and PLURAL, standing for the two different entries mentioned above. When there are multiple choices along several feature dimensions, the cross-product is intended. For example, *persuaded* has a single line representing four entries with the feature combinations {PAST

Word	Category	Features
a	Determiner	Number: Singular
been	Verb	Form: Past-Part; Type: Be, Non-Aux
Ben	Proper	
Carol	Proper	
by	Preposition	
caught	Verb	Form: Past, Past-Part
dance	Verb	Transitivity: Intrans
deadline	Noun	
entertain	Verb	
firm	Adjective, Noun	
fish	Noun	Number: Singular, Plural
	Verb	Transitivity: Intrans
given	Verb	Form: Past-Part, Transitivity: Bitrans
have	Verb	Type: Have, Non-Aux
having	Verb	Form: Present-Part; Type: Have, Non-Aux
kumquat	Noun	
kumquats	Noun	Number: Plural
persuaded	Verb	Form: Past, Past-Part; Trans: Trans, Bitrans
secretary	Noun	
that	Complementizer Determiner Pronoun Relative	
the	Determiner	
these	Determiner	Number: Plural
this	Determiner	Number: Singular
to	Complementizer Preposition	
want	Verb	Transitivity: Trans, Bitrans
we	Pronoun	Number: Plural; Person: 1st; Case: Subjective
were	Verb	Form: Past; Type: Be, Non-Aux
which	Determiner Relative	Question: Yes
who	Pronoun Relative	Case: Subjective; Question: Yes
whom	Pronoun Relative	Case: Objective; Question: Yes

Figure 5–12. Sample dictionary entries.

TRANSITIVE}, {PAST-PARTICIPLE TRANSITIVE}, {PAST BITRANSITIVE}, and {PAST-PARTICIPLE BITRANSITIVE}.

The second economy lies in the use of a *default* for each dimension, which will be assumed to hold for any word sense for which a value along that dimension is not specified. For example, in the categories defined by Figure 5–11, a noun will be assumed singular unless otherwise marked, while a verb will be assumed NON-AUX (not an auxiliary). When more than default is given, there is a word sense for each. For example, a verb that does not specify FORM is assumed to have one sense for INFINITIVE and one for PRESENT. These devices are related to the it redundancy rules discussed in Sections 6.6 and C.4.

Figure 5–12 is a sample dictionary, including words used in examples in this chapter and based on the categories of Figure 5–11. It includes separate entries for irregular forms, such as *been* and *were,* as well as for regular forms, such as *kumquat* and *kumquats.* In most formal accounts and computer parsing systems, the entries for regular forms are generated from the corresponding root entries.

Given the feature dimensions defined for nouns and determiners in Figure 5–11, we can put actions onto the arcs of the NP network to check number agreement, as shown in Figure 5–13. The network is a simplified version of the NP, which will be expanded later. It lists all of the arcs in the NP network that have a condition (indicated by 'C:') or an action (indicated by 'A:'). In the rest of the chapter, a state is indicated by a state name prefixed by a network name (e.g., S.a for state a in the S network). We have previously represented arcs by their label, surrounded by the letters for the start and end state. Since we now have multiple networks, we will prefix the name of the network to this notation. In addition, an ATN can contain two different arcs with the same starting state, ending state, and label, but with different conditions and actions. To avoid confusion, we will give each arc a number and include the number of the arc in the notation as well. The arc referred to as 'NP-6:ₓPROPERₕ' is arc number 6 in the NP network, going from state NP.f to state NP.h and labeled PROPER.

Figure 5–13 illustrates several aspects of the ATN formalism:

Jump arcs. As in the recursive transition networks on which they are based, ATNs can contain arcs labeled JUMP, which are taken without matching any of the input sequence. A jump arc can have actions and conditions, although in this simple network the one jump arc does not. Jump arcs (and the process of matching them) are defined formally in Figure D–9.

Send arcs. Instead of having terminal states, an ATN contains one or more arcs labeled SEND, which can be matched without matching any of the input sequence and which have no ending state. When a send arc is taken, the matching of the network terminates successfully. The reason for this change is to allow conditions and actions to be associated with the completion of a network. In our simple example there are no actions or conditions on the send

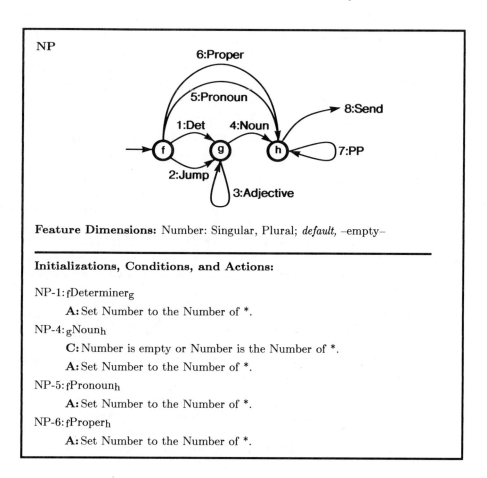

Feature Dimensions: Number: Singular, Plural; *default,* –empty–

Initializations, Conditions, and Actions:

NP-1: fDeterminerg

    A: Set Number to the Number of *.

NP-4: gNounh

    C: Number is empty or Number is the Number of *.

    A: Set Number to the Number of *.

NP-5: fPronounh

    A: Set Number to the Number of *.

NP-6: fProperh

    A: Set Number to the Number of *.

Figure 5–13.   Number agreement in the NP Network.

arc. Send arcs (and the process of matching them) are defined formally in Figure D–10.

Category arcs. The rest of the arcs in the network of Figure 5–13 (except for the jump and send arcs) are *category arcs*, each specifying the lexical category of the word it will match. When a category arc is encountered in parsing with a network, a new node is created and contents are assigned to it as defined in Figure D–7. The register contents for the new node are taken from the appropriate word sense for the word in the dictionary.

Feature dimensions. Associated with the network for NP there is a feature dimension for NUMBER. Each NP node will have an entry in its register table containing one of the choices SINGULAR or PLURAL. In this case, the same dimension also applies to individual words. Later we will see examples of feature dimensions that are associated with networks but do not appear in the dictionary. Following the name of the feature dimension is a list of all of the possible choices, followed by the default, which serves as an *initial setting* when the network is entered. In this case, an NP is assumed to have no feature marking its number before its elements are parsed.

Feature assignment. One kind of action that can be associated with an arc is to set the choice in some feature register. The action 'Set NUMBER to ....' specifies that the register for NUMBER is to be set to a given value.

Most recent node. Often an action on an arc needs to refer to the node that was created in the matching of the arc. In the case of an arc whose label is a lexical category, this will be a node whose label is the lexical category and whose feature choices are those in the corresponding part of the dictionary entry for the word matched by the arc. In the case of a seek arc (described below), it will be a node whose label is the name of a network and whose contents are the registers for that network. In both cases, the symbol '*' is used to refer to this entire node.

Feature extraction. In referring to the node just parsed, we want to look specifically at the NUMBER features associated with it. In general, when we want to refer to a particular set of features from a node, we use the name of the feature dimension in a phrase like 'the Number of *.' The contents of the corresponding register of the node are used.

The actions shown in 5–13, along with the dictionary of 5–12, will correctly handle the data given above. In the case of ungrammatical phrases like *these kumquat,* there will be no choice of word senses for the individual words that allows the conditions to be satisfied. In the case of words with multiple entries (such as *the*), a phrase that calls for a particular choice (e.g., *the kumquat*), will succeed with some choices and fail with others. Since the ATN formalism is nondeterminsitic, a phrase is grammatical as long as one successful combination of choices exists. In ambiguous cases like *the fish,* there will be more than one potential successful result. If the NP consists of a pronoun (i.e., results from taking the NP-5: ₍PRONOUN₎ arc) or a proper noun, the number feature of the NP as a whole will be that of the word. There are no actions or conditions associated in this example with the arcs for modifiers such as adjectives and PPs, since they do not affect number agreement in English (although they do in many other languages). Later figures will include actions related to keeping track of modifiers.

Role registers

Figure 5–14 describes some actions associated with the S network to handle the phenomenon of *passive voice*. We would like to capture the fact that the sentences *An aardvark ate an artichoke* and *An artichoke was eaten by*

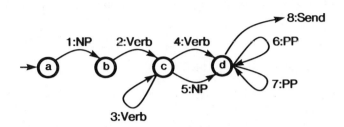

Roles: Subject, Direct-Object, Main-Verb, Auxiliaries, Modifiers

Feature Dimensions: Voice: Active, Passive; *default,* Active

---

Initializations, Conditions, and Actions:

S-1: $_a$NP$_b$

    A: Set Subject to *.

S-2: $_b$Verb$_c$

    A: Set Main-Verb to *.

S-3: $_c$Verb$_c$

    C: The Type of the Main-Verb is Be, Do, Have, or Modal.

    A: Append Main-Verb to Auxiliaries. Set Main-Verb to *.

S-4: $_c$Verb$_d$

    C: The Form of * is Past-Participle and the Type of Main-Verb is Be.

    A: Set Voice to Passive.

       Append Main-Verb to Auxiliaries. Set Main-Verb to *.

       Set Direct-Object to Subject. Set Subject to a dummy NP.

S-5: $_c$NP$_d$

    A: Set Direct-Object to *.

S-6: $_d$PP$_d$

    A: Append * to Modifiers.

S-7: $_d$PP$_d$

    C: Voice is Passive and Subject is a dummy NP and the word in the Prep of * is *by.*

    A: Set Subject to the Prep-Object of *.

S-8: $_d$Send   *No initializations, conditions, or actions*

Figure 5–14. Active and passive voice in the S network.

an aardvark have the same underlying structure. To do this, we associate a SUBJECT register and a DIRECT-OBJECT register with the S network and let them be assigned by actions as shown. Once again, this is a simplified network that will be expanded later on. It deals only with transitive verbs (those that take a direct object).

Some further mechanisms are introduced in Figure 5–14:

Declaring roles. Associated with each network there is a set of *role names.* When the network is called in parsing, part of the structure created is a *register table,* which contains both feature registers and role registers. Before any arcs are taken, initial values can be given to both feature and role registers. In this example, we do not make use of these *initial settings.*

Assigning contents to role registers. After parsing an NP to satisfy the arc S-1:$_a$NP$_b$, we assign that NP to a register named SUBJECT, as indicated by the action 'Set SUBJECT to *..' This is like an assignment in a programming language—from this point until another assignment is made to the same register, its contents will be the NP node just parsed (indicated by the '*'). If an assignment action is taken when a register has already been assigned (as with the action setting the SUBJECT to a dummy on arc S-4:$_c$VERB$_d$ and the one assigning the object of the PP to be the subject, on arc S-7:$_d$PP$_d$), the old entry is replaced with the new one.

Appending to role registers. When there is a loop in the network, we want a role register to be filled by a sequence of constituents rather than by a single constituent. The auxiliaries and modifying phrases of a sentence are examples of such constituents in our grammar. An action like 'Append MAIN-VERB to AUXILIARIES.' changes the contents of the AUXILIARIES register to be the result of appending the current contents of the MAIN-VERB register to the end of the previous contents of AUXILIARIES. If the register was previously empty, it is set to a sequence consisting of just the new item.

Conditions. On the S-3:$_c$VERB$_c$ arc there is a condition specifying that the current MAIN-VERB must be a possible auxiliary, as determined by its TYPE. Unless this condition is met, the arc cannot be taken—the match fails. A condition can specify any Boolean combination (using *and, not, or, if...then,* etc.,) of tests, exactly like a program step in DL (see Section A.4.3.2 in Appendix A).

Extracting contents of registers. Just as the notation 'the NUMBER of ...' refers to the contents of the NUMBER register for some node, 'the PREP of ...' refers to the contents of the PREP register. Since it is a role register, not a feature register, the result will be another node (in this case the node for the PREPOSITION within a PP). This notation can be nested. For example, if we have just taken an arc that parses a sentence (i.e., has S as its label), we could use the notation 'the NUMBER of the SUBJECT of *' to mean the choice in the

NUMBER register in the node filling the SUBJECT register in the sentence just parsed.

Extraction of contents from a sequence. In order to access registers containing sequences of elements, we use phrases like 'the first element of...' and 'the last element of....' We do not need to access arbitrary positions within the sequence (such as 'the third element of...') in order to write reasonable grammars. This fact is related to the notion of *structure dependence* that was formulated for transformations.

Dummy nodes. We have used the phrase 'a dummy NP' to indicate an NP node with no register contents, constructed to represent an unknown subject. Such nodes would be treated specially in the semantic analysis of the parsed sentence, but for the purposes of this chapter we will simply assume that they have no relevant properties except for the label NP.

Arcs differing only in conditions and actions. Finally, note that a PP with preposition *by* may be parsed by a special PP arc, S-7:$_d$PP$_d$, instead of by the arc intended for modifiers, S-6:$_d$PP$_d$. This is necessary because there must be separate paths through the network for *by* phrases that specify agents, as in *The wood was burned by the fire,* and those that do not, even though they appear in a passive sentence, like *The wood was stored by the fire.* An ambiguous sentence will have multiple parsings, each corresponding to a different sequence of arcs taken in matching the networks.

Figure 5–15 illustrates the operation of this network in going through an active sentence and through passive sentences with and without an agent. It does not show the contents of the MODIFIERS register or give the details of parsing the constituent NPs and PPs. It uses the dictionary entries of Figure 5–12.

The network of Figure 5–14 manipulates register contents so that the DIRECT-OBJECT register will end up containing the 'deep direct object' (in this case, *the fish*), regardless of whether the sentence is passive or active. The SUBJECT register will contain the deep subject (if it was given in the sentence) or a dummy NP if the sentence is an agent-deleted passive like *The fish have been caught.*

We have also used a register for MAIN-VERB, which is assigned on three different arcs. It is initially assigned on the S-2:$_b$VERB$_c$ arc (which takes the first verb), and then reassigned for each match of the S-3:$_c$VERB$_c$ arc (which takes subsequent verbs in a sequence like *will have caught*) and for the S-4:$_c$VERB$_d$ arc if it is taken. The resulting entry for this register is the last verb encountered, which is always the main verb of the sentence (in the sense of bearing the meaning of the action or relationship being described). In the meantime, the AUXILIARIES register contains a list of all of the auxiliary verbs preceding the main verb.

Arc	Words parsed	Subject	Direct-Object	Main-Verb	Auxil-iaries

The secretary caught a fish by the deadline

Arc	Words parsed	Subject	Direct-Object	Main-Verb	Auxil-iaries
S-1:$_a$NP$_b$	the secretary	the secretary	.	.	.
S-2:$_b$Verb$_c$	caught	the secretary	.	caught	.
S-5:$_c$NP$_d$	a fish	the secretary	a fish	caught	.
S-6:$_d$PP$_d$	by the deadline	the secretary	a fish	caught	.
S-8:$_d$Send					

The fish have been caught

Arc	Words parsed	Subject	Direct-Object	Main-Verb	Auxil-iaries
S-1:$_a$NP$_b$	the fish	the fish	.	.	.
S-2:$_b$Verb$_c$	have	the fish	.	have	.
S-3:$_c$Verb$_c$	been	the fish	.	been	have
S-4:$_c$Verb$_d$	caught	–dummy–	the fish	caught	have been
S-8:$_d$Send					

The fish were caught by the secretary

Arc	Words parsed	Subject	Direct-Object	Main-Verb	Auxil-iaries
S-1:$_a$NP$_b$	the fish	the fish	.	.	.
S-2:$_b$Verb$_c$	were	the fish	.	were	.
S-4:$_c$Verb$_d$	caught	–dummy–	the fish	caught	were
S-7:$_d$PP$_d$	by the secretary	the secretary	the fish	caught	were
S-8:$_d$Send					

Figure 5–15. Parsing active and passive sentences.

This treatment of verbs and auxiliaries is in fact too simple. For example, it lumps modals like *will* with verbs like *eat* and allows sequences like *be will having is go*. This is discussed further in Section 5.6.

5.4 The ordering of actions and conditions

The conditions and actions in an ATN are designed with a specific parsing order in mind. It is assumed that the parser will work left-to-right and top-down. This means that an action that sets a register will affect conditions on arcs to the right, but not those to the left that were previously traversed. This assumption is both an advantage and a limitation. It is a limitation because it removes flexibility in the design of a parser. If there is reason to operate in bottom-up or not purely left-to-right fashion, it is necessary to modify the formalism, as discussed in Section 5.7. However, it can make it possible to provide in a relatively simple and elegant way for the interactions between different syntactic phenomena. In this section, we will use subject-verb agreement and transitivity to demonstrate this aspect of ATN grammars.

Modifications to the NP network (Figure 5–13)

Additional feature dimension: Person: 1st, 2nd, 3rd; *default,* 3rd

Additional conditions and actions:

NP-5: ₍Pronoun₎ₕ

    A: Set Person to the Person of *.

Modifications to the S network (Figure 5–14)

Additional conditions and actions:

S-2: ᵦVerb꜀

    C: Either: the Type of * is Modal

    or the Form of * is Past

    or the Form of * is 3rd-Singular-Present and the Number of Subject
    is Singular and the Person of Subject is 3rd

    or the Form of * is Present and either the Number of Subject is
    Plural or the Person of Subject is 1st or 2nd.

Figure 5–16. Conditions and actions for subject-verb agreement.

Subject-verb agreement

So far we have discussed agreement within the NP network, but we have not dealt with agreement between subject and verb. This could be handled in a number of ways, as is often the case in writing the rules of a grammar. We will make use of role registers to provide the necessary information. The actions and conditions added to the grammar in 5–16 are to be applied in addition to the ones in Figures 5–13 and 5–14.

In dealing with number agreement in the NP, we had a NUMBER and a condition on the NP-4: ₉NOUN₎ₕ arc that tested that register. Figure 5–16 has an agreement condition on S-2: ᵦVERB꜀. The condition is somewhat complex, since the set of forms for verbs do not line up neatly with the person and number categories for nouns and pronouns. MODAL forms (as in *I may* and *he may*) and PAST forms (as in *she went* and *we went*) are identical for all person and number choices. There are two present tense forms: 3RD-SINGULAR-PRESENT (as in *she walks*), used with NPs that are both 3RD and SINGULAR; and a general PRESENT form (*you walk*) used with all other combinations. In fact, the condition as stated here is not yet adequate, as it does not properly handle the verb *be*.

One motivation for having multiple verb arcs in the S network (one for the first verb of the sequence and others for the rest) is that it provides a clear place for the agreement check—agreement always applies to the first verb, whether it is the main verb (as in *A salmon swims*) or an auxiliary (as in *You are being watched*). Often decisions about the states and arcs of the network are determined by this kind of consideration.

It is important to note the interaction between subject-verb agreement and the actions associated with passive voice. There is an agreement condition on the S-2:$_b$VERB$_c$ arc that makes use of the SUBJECT register, and an action on the S-4:$_c$VERB$_d$ arc that can potentially change the contents of that register. It is clear that the condition needs to apply to the SUBJECT before the change. In a sentence like *Some pears were picked by a platypus*, it is the plural surface subject, *some pears*, that agrees with the verb *were*, not the deep subject, *a platypus*. This happens naturally, since the arcs are taken in the left-to-right sequence indicated in the network. Phenomena like this are closely related to the *rule ordering* mechanisms of transformational grammar, but are somewhat more natural, since the order is imposed by the order of the phrases in the sentence rather than by a less intuitively guided choice of ordering for derivation rules.

Transitivity and the use of jump arcs

The grammar as we have developed it so far does not distinguish among different verbs according to their transitivity. It would accept *They caught* and *They arrived the fish* and does not allow *bitransitive* sentences (with two objects) like *I gave my love a cherry*. We would like to account for (at least) the following data:

I slept.	**I slept you.*	**I slept him the blanket.*
*I like.	*I like you.*	**I like her a book.*
*I brought.	*I brought an eggplant casserole.*	*I brought her a rose.*
I ate.	*I ate the eggplant casserole.*	**I ate her an apple.*

In fact, the data concerning transitivity are very complex and have not been fully handled in any grammar formalism. We will discuss them further in the context of systemic grammar and case grammar in Chapter 6. For the moment, we will assume that associated with the lexical category of VERB there is a feature dimension TRANSITIVITY that includes the choices INTRANSITIVE (no objects), TRANSITIVE (one object), and BITRANSITIVE (two objects). In the examples above, *sleep* is INTRANSITIVE, *like* is TRANSITIVE, *eat* is both INTRANSITIVE and TRANSITIVE, and *bring* is TRANSITIVE and BITRANSITIVE.

In order to handle this data, we need to add some new states and arcs to the S network, along with the associated conditions and actions. This is done in the network of Figure 5–17, which also handles the phenomena of *dative*. It will assign the same final register structure to pairs like *We gave them the fish* and *We gave the fish to them*.

In this and the following networks, the newly added arcs and states will be drawn darker, and the previously defined actions and conditions will not be shown. Except where explicitly mentioned, we assume that all of the previously given conditions and actions continue to apply. In this case, several arcs have been renumbered in order to accommodate an intervening state: the two PP arcs and the send arc previously starting in S.d have been replaced with equivalent arcs starting in S.e. For reference, Appendix D contains a summary of the networks developed in this chapter, incorporating the conditions, actions, and initializations from all of the figures.

New mechanisms used here include:

Jump arcs. The new network uses jump arcs (defined formally in Figure D–9) to account for the different possible combinations of transitivity, voice, and datives. After the main verb is found (in the active case), the S-5:$_c$NP$_d$ arc can be taken to find a first object, or the S-8:$_c$JUMP$_e$ arc can be taken to skip past the finding of objects. Once a first object has been found, S-6:$_d$NP$_e$ will find a second object if there is one, while S-7:$_d$JUMP$_e$ handles the case where there is not. The first object found is stored (by arc 5) as the DIRECT-OBJECT and remains there if the S-7:$_d$JUMP$_e$ arc is taken. However, if a second one comes along, the first is moved (by arc 6) to INDIRECT-OBJECT and the new one becomes the DIRECT-OBJECT.

Conditions on send arcs. The network of Figure 5–17 parses as many objects as can be found, even if the transitivity features on the verb do not allow them. The checking for appropriate transitivity is done on the final send arc, allowing the conditions to be stated all together. The send arc (as defined in Figure D–10) does not match an element of the word sequence or call another network, but simply provides a convenient place for such final conditions and actions.

Once again, ordering is important. The checking of the transitivity features takes place on the send arc, after all other arcs have been taken. Therefore an indirect object that is found in a PP starting with *to* or *for* (by taking arc S-11:$_e$PP$_e$) will cause failure unless the verb is bitransitive. If the transitivity check were done earlier, it would fail to interact properly with this kind of dative. This use of the send arc for checking transitivity will lead at times to attempting unnecessary parses. Additional checking could be done before taking the arcs with NP labels (for example, not bothering to look for objects if the verb is only intransitive) at the expense of making the conditions and actions more complex.

5.5 Non-local context and hold registers

This section introduces the mechanisms that have been used in the ATN framework to handle syntactic phenomena involving information 'passed down' from a higher node to one of its constituents. The first example is the problem of

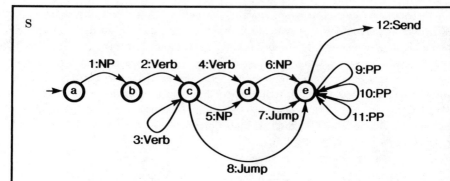

Roles: Subject, Direct-Object, Indirect-Object, Main-Verb, Auxiliaries, Modifiers

Feature Dimensions: Voice: Active, Passive; *default,* Active

---

Initializations, Conditions, and Actions:

Arcs 1–4 *See Figure 5-14 as extended in Figure 5-16.*

S-5: $_c$NP$_d$

   A: Set Direct-Object to *.

S-6: $_d$NP$_e$

   A: Set Indirect-Object to Direct-Object. Set Direct-Object to *.

S-7: $_d$Jump$_e$ and S-8: $_c$Jump$_e$: No conditions or actions

S-9: $_e$PP$_e$

   A: Append * to Modifiers.

S-10: $_e$PP$_e$

   C: Voice is Passive and Subject is a dummy NP and the word in the Prep of * is *by*

   A: Set Subject to the Prep-Object of *.

S-11: $_e$PP$_e$

   C: The word in the Prep of * is *to* or *for* and Indirect-Object is empty

   A: Set Indirect-Object to the Prep-Object of *.

S-12: $_e$Send

   C: If Indirect-Object is not empty, then the Transitivity of Main-Verb is Bitransitive.
   If Indirect-Object is empty but Direct-Object is not empty, then the Transitivity of Main-Verb is Transitive.
   If Direct-Object is empty, then the Transitivity of Main-Verb is Intransitive.

Figure 5–17. S network with actions for transitivity and dative.

assigning the correct structure to sentences like *Woodrow wants to dance.* As discussed in Chapter 4, this sentence has a deep structure in which Woodrow does the dancing as well as the wanting. In transformational grammar, this is handled by having identical NP nodes in the two places and deleting one of them through EQUI-NP DELETION. In an ATN grammar, registers are used for the same purpose.

In order to do this, the basic grammar must be extended to allow embedded clauses like *to dance* to serve as subjects or objects. There are several different ways of doing this, and there are many different kinds of clauses to be considered, each with its own distribution (see Section B.1.3). The network of Figure 5–18 does not attempt to provide full generality, but it deals with a number of cases in which both subjects and objects are embedded sentences, such as:

> *Carol wanted to sing.*
>
> *Ben told Carol to dance.*
>
> *For her to argue would have upset him.*

It introduces a number of conventions that have not been used before:

Specific words on category arcs. The new category arcs S-13: $_x$PREP(for)$_y$ and S-15: $_z$COMP(to)$_c$ have conditions that allow them to match only specific words. This is indicated visually by including the word along with the lexical category on the arc label and in the arc-naming notation. Formally, this requires no mechanisms that have not already been used. The condition that an arc match a particular word can be handled like any other condition. In some versions of ATN grammar, there is a separate kind of arc called a 'LEX arc' (because it specifies a particular lexical item) for this purpose. There is a slight difference in that a LEX arc specifies a word without needing to name a category, while the use of category arcs requires one. In some ATN implementations there is also a 'MEM arc,' which specifies a list of words and is conditional on the word parsed being a member of that list.

Multiple entry points into a network. The new state S.x is not reachable from the normal initial state of the S network (S.a). However, the S-16: $_a$S/x$_b$ arc specifies that the S network is to be matched, beginning in S.x instead of the initial state. An arc specifying a starting state need not start with a special one introduced off to the side such as S.x, but can jump right into the middle of the network, as we will see later in dealing with relative clauses.

In parsing the sentence *For her to argue would have upset him,* we start as always in S.a. The first arc taken is S-16: $_a$S/x$_b$, which recursively calls on the S network starting in state S.x to parse the phrase *for her to argue.* This entire S is put into the subject register and the parsing of *would have upset him* continues from S.b. The embedded sentence *for her to argue* does not begin with the normal sequence of a subject followed by a first verb, but with a *for. . . to*

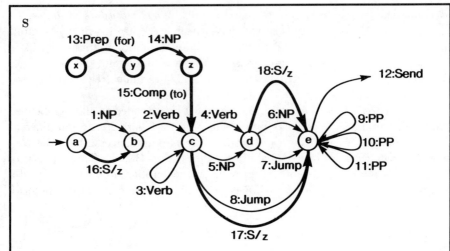

Roles: Subject, Direct-Object, Indirect-Object, Main-Verb, Auxiliaries, Modifiers

Feature Dimensions: Voice: Active, Passive; *default,* Active

---

Initializations, Conditions, and Actions:

Arcs 1–4: *See Figure 5-14 and Figure 5-16.* Arcs 5–12: *See Figure 5-17.*

S-13: $_x$Prep(for)$_y$

    C: The word in * is *for.*

S-14: $_y$NP$_z$

    A: Set Subject to *.

S-15: $_z$Comp(to)$_c$

    C: The word in * is *to.*

    A: Set Main-Verb to a dummy verb with Type = Modal.

S-16: $_a$S/x$_b$

    A: Set Subject to *.

S-17: $_c$S/z$_e$

    I: Initialize Subject to the Subject of ↑.

    A: Set Direct-Object to *.

S-18: $_d$S/z$_e$

    I: Initialize Subject to the Direct-Object of ↑.

    A: Set Indirect-Object to Direct-Object. Set Direct-Object to *.

Figure 5–18. S network including 'to' complements.

Arc taken	Words	Role register contents
S-1: $_a$NP$_b$	*Carol*	Subject: *Carol*
S-2: $_b$Verb$_c$	*wanted*	Subject: *Carol* Main-Verb: *wanted*
S-17: $_c$S/$_z$e		

-initialization-		Subject: *Carol*
S-15: $_z$Comp(to)$_c$	*to*	Subject: *Carol* Main-Verb: dummy modal
S-3: $_c$Verb$_c$	*sing*	Subject: *Carol* Auxiliaries: dummy modal Main-Verb: *sing*
S-8: $_c$Jump$_e$ S-12: $_e$Send		

		Subject: *Carol* Main-Verb: *wanted* Direct-Object: *(Carol) to sing*
S-12: $_e$Send		

Figure 5–19. Register assignments in an embedded sentence.

phrase. The words after *to* in the embedded S have the usual possibilities for auxiliary verbs, a main verb, and a sequence of objects, depending on the transitivity of the main verb, as in *for her to have given him an argument.* By joining the network in S.c after finding the *for. . . to* phrase, all of this structure can be shared. The action on S-15: $_z$COMP(to)$_c$, which sets the MAIN-VERB register to a dummy verb, causes proper agreement between adjacent verbs to be checked—i.e., the verb following *to* must be in the INFINITIVE form, as would a verb following a MODAL such as *will* or *could.* Since the normal subject-verb agreement check is on the S-2: $_b$VERB$_c$ arc, it is bypassed in this case. Note that in this case (as well as the ordinary case), it is possible to take one of the arcs out of S.c when the main verb register contains a modal. In this case the parse will fail when the transitivity check is tried at the end.

Initial settings for role registers. The second major mechanism introduced here is *register initialization.* In those cases where the network is entered in S.x, the SUBJECT and MAIN-VERB registers will be set by the time S.c is reached. However, in sentences like *Carol wanted to sing,* the embedded sentence consists just of *to sing,* which is matched by the S-17: $_c$S/$_z$e arc. Its subject (from the point of view of meaning) is the subject of the outer sentence. This is handled by having an initialization (indicated in the figure by an '**I:**') associated with the

S-17:$_{c}$S/z$_{e}$ arc. It states that the new node created by that arc (the embedded S) is to have its subject register initially contain the contents of the subject register in the S that called it. The symbol '↑' is used to indicate the node from which the recursive call was made. Previously, we have had initial settings (defaults) for feature registers, but these have been the same every time the network was matched. In this case, the setting is done in the particular context—the subject register of the inner S will start out with contents taken from the outer one. The results of parsing *Carol wanted to sing* are illustrated in Figures 5–19 and 5–20. The S-18:$_{d}$S/z$_{e}$ arc handles sentences such as *Ben told Carol to dance,* in which *Carol* is both the indirect object of the outer sentence and the subject of the inner one. It moves the previous direct object (in this case *Carol*) to the indirect object register after parsing an embedded sentence in which it is initialized as the subject.

In previous cases, such as the handling of passive voice, contents were moved from one register to another but not left in both. This is the first case in which an action has resulted in two registers set to the same contents. It leads to structures like that of Figure 5–20, in which a single node fills a role in more than one other node. This is why register structures as defined in Section 5.2 are not trees, but more general graph structures. The initial register setting is only one of a number of possible ways to establish this connection. It might at first seem more natural to simply parse the embedded sentence without a subject and then to have an action on the S.z arc insert the appropriate subject. However, this alternative solution would not work properly when combined with passive voice. Figure 5–21 illustrates the parsing of another sentence, in which the embedded sentence is passive. The subject needs to be in place initially so that it can participate in the actions that move it into the DIRECT-OBJECT register.

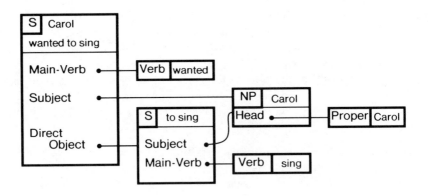

Figure 5–20. A structure including a shared component.

Arc taken	Words	Register contents
S-1:$_a$NP$_b$	*Ben*	Subject: *Ben* Voice: Active
S-2:$_b$Verb$_c$	*wanted*	Subject: *Ben* Voice: Active Main-Verb: *wanted*

S-17:$_c$S/$_z$e

–initialization–		Voice: Active Subject: *Ben*
S-15:$_z$Prep(to)$_c$	*to*	Voice: Active Subject: *Ben* Main-Verb: dummy modal
S-3:$_c$Verb$_c$	*be*	Voice: Active Subject: *Ben* Auxiliaries: dummy modal Main-Verb: *be*
S-4:$_c$Verb$_d$	*entertained*	Voice: Passive Subject: dummy NP Auxiliaries: dummy modal, *be* Main-Verb: *entertained* Direct-Object: *Ben*
S-7:$_d$Jump$_e$ S-12:$_e$Send		

Subject: *Ben*
Voice: Active
Main-Verb: *wanted*
Direct-Object: *(Ben) to be entertained*

S-12:$_e$Send

Figure 5–21. Register assignments for an embedded passive.

This is a good example of how the careful ordering of arcs with their initializations and actions can do some of the same work as the ordering of transformations and mechanisms like the transformational cycle. However, as discussed in the exercises, this analysis is not complete and would need to be refined to handle the data of English. Among other problems, the network as we have presented it *overgenerates*. In addition to accepting real sentences, it accepts ones like **Carol told to dance*, **Ben hoped Carol to dance*, and **Carol was wanted to dance*. It also assigns an indirect object in sentences such as *Ben wanted Carol to dance*, in which our intuitions about meaning do not call for one (as opposed to sentences with verbs like *tell* or *persuade*). These problems are dealt with in Exercise 5.12.

Questions

The network of Figure 5–22 includes new registers and arcs that deal with different forms of questions, such as:

> *Did you catch a fish?*
>
> *Which secretary caught a fish?*
>
> *Which fish did the secretary catch?*
>
> *What river was it caught in?*
>
> *Whom did you want Arthur to tell to catch a fish?*

The feature dimension MOOD has choices DECLARATIVE, INTERROGATIVE, and IMPERATIVE. All of the sentences we have dealt with so far are DECLARATIVE, which is the default choice. Questions like the examples above are INTERROGATIVE, and commands (see the following section) are IMPERATIVE. These terms are used rather than the more obvious 'question,' 'statement,' and 'command' to indicate that the feature concerns the form of the sentence, not its use. The sentence *You're really going?* spoken with a rising intonation, is a question, although its form is declarative, while *Am I hungry!* is a statement whose form is interrogative.

The new state S.q and its two associated arcs, S-19: $_a$VERB$_q$ and S-20: $_q$NP$_c$, handle the *subject-auxiliary inversion,* which marks the interrogative mood. The first verb of the sequence appears in front of the subject, rather than after it, as in <u>Would</u> *she have been caught?* The mood check will prevent this arc from being taken in embedded sentences (like relative clauses) as defined below. However it will be taken following an initial question element, as in *Which fish did they catch?* and *In what river did they find it?* Once the auxiliary and subject are parsed, the rest of the sentence continues as usual. The condition to check for subject-verb agreement is duplicated on the S-20: $_q$NP$_c$ arc, since the ordinary S-2: $_b$VERB$_c$ arc will not be taken and we need to eliminate mismatches like **Was they apprehended?* In most ATN implementations, a complex condition like the one for agreement can be written together as a unit (a procedure in the underlying programming language) and called from both places. One of the motivations in the development of lexical-functional grammar (described in Section 6.6) was to avoid having to put in such special mechanisms by handling condition checking in a more general way.

The QUESTION-ELEMENT register is added to contain the questioned-element in *wh-* questions like *Who caught the fish?* In such a sentence, knowing what was questioned is a key element of the meaning and needs to be part of the analysis produced by parsing. The S-21: $_a$NP$_b$ arc handles the simple case

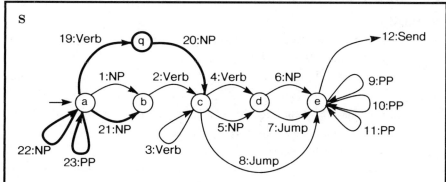

Roles: Subject, Direct-Object, Indirect-Object, Main-Verb, Auxiliaries, Modifiers, Question-Element

Feature Dimensions:

Voice: Active, Passive; *default,* Active

Mood: Declarative, Interrogative, Imperative; *default,* Declarative

---

Initializations, Conditions, and Actions:

Arcs 1–4: *See Figures 5-14 and 5-16.* Arcs 5–12: *See Figure 5-17.*

Arcs 13–18 (not shown): *See Figure 5-18.*

Additional actions and conditions on S-1: $_a$NP$_b$

    C: The Question of * is No and Mood is not Interrogative.

Additional actions and conditions on S-12: $_e$Send

    C: Hold is empty.

S-19: $_a$Verb$_q$

    C: The Type of * is not Non-Aux and Mood is Declarative or Interrogative.

    A: Set Main-Verb to *. Set Mood to Interrogative.

S-20: $_q$NP$_c$

    C: *Subject-verb agreement check (see* S-2: $_b$Verb$_c$ *in Figure 5-16)*

    A: Set Subject to *.

S-21: $_a$NP$_b$

    C: The Question of * is Yes and Mood is Declarative.

    A: Set Subject to *. Set Question-Element to *.

    Set Mood to Interrogative.

Continued in Figure 5-23

Figure 5–22. S network including questions.

S-22: aNPa

    C: The Question of * is Yes and Mood is Declarative.

    A: Set Question-Element to *. Set Hold to *.

        Set Mood to Interrogative.

S-23: aPPa

    C: The Question of the Prep-Obj of * is Yes and Mood is Declarative.

    A: Set Question-Element to the Prep-Obj of *. Set Hold to *.

        Set Mood to Interrogative.

Figure 5–23. S network including questions (continued).

in which the subject of the sentence is a QUESTION NP. We have added a feature dimension labeled QUESTION with choices YES and NO that applies to NPs, to pronouns, and to determiners. YES applies to NPs consisting of question pronouns like *who* and *what* and to those with a question determiner such as *which* or *how many*. The necessary extensions to the NP network are shown later in Figure 5–25. The conditions on the S-21: aNPb arc and the added condition on the S-1: aNPb arc work together to guarantee that a sentence with a QUESTION subject will be parsed as a question. The condition on the mood on S-1: aNPb forces any sentence with an initial question element that is not treated as the subject to follow the path through S.q, eliminating *In what river they fished?* The mood condition on S-21: aNPb eliminates ungrammatical forms like *In what river who fished?*, while the corresponding conditions on S-22: aNPa and S-23: aPPa forbid multiple question elements caused by looping, as in *With what whom what did they give?*

Long-distance dependencies and hold registers

The two arcs (S-22: aNPa and S-23: aPPa) in Figure 5–22 that we have not yet explained are used in parsing questions like:

Which fish did Shoshana catch?	(1)
In what river was it caught?	(2)
What river was it caught in?	(3)
Whom did you want Arthur to tell to catch a fish?	(4)

These sentences are all similar in that they begin with a question element and exhibit subject-auxiliary inversion. However, they differ in the role that the initial *wh-* phrase plays in the sentence. In (1) it is an NP which is the direct object of *catch;* in (2) it is a PP modifier of the sentence as a whole; in (3) it is the object of the preposition *in;* and in (4) it is the object of an embedded sentence (with main verb *tell*) and the subject of another (with main verb *catch*). This kind of *long-distance dependency* is one of the most complex phenomena of syntax, and is described at length in Section B.1.4 in the Appendices. As we discussed in Chapter 4, it has been a major motivation for many of the mechanisms of transformational grammar, and it is the source of much debate in current linguistics, as discussed in Appendix C and Sections 6.6 and 6.7.

In transformational grammar, this kind of data has often been handled by a *movement transformation* that takes the questioned constituent out of its original home in the deep structure and moves it to the front of the sentence. In ATN grammars (and in some of the newer formalisms described in Chapter 6), we can think of finding a questioned constituent at the front of the sentence and saving it to be inserted somewhere later when a 'hole' is found into which it could fit.

At first, it might seem that this could be handled with initial register settings, like the embedded sentences handled by the network of Figure 5–18. In that network, a subject was found (from the higher sentence) and put into a register before parsing with the S network began for the embedded sentence. However, questions are not as simple, since the passed-down phrase is not limited to a particular role (the subject) but can appear anywhere within the S, including within an embedded constituent to any level of depth. The problem here can be thought of as one of communication between the higher constituent, where the held item originates, and the lower ones, where its presence allows an NP or PP to be missing. The communication must flow in both directions, since the lower phrases depend on the details of the initial question element, and also on whether a previous constituent has used it. A simplistic implementation which communicated only downward (not letting the higher network know whether a lower one had used the item) would accept a phrase such as **Which secretary did you tell to control?* putting *which secretary* as both the subject and object of *control*.

Three basic approaches have been taken to this problem of communication, all of which have benefits and drawbacks. We will call them the *explicit communication* mechanism, the *context search and modification* mechanism, and the *global register* mechanism.

Explicit communication. The straightforward way to handle this problem is to use the initial register-setting mechanisms already present in the ATN formalism. The element can be passed down to any constituent that might use it or that in turn could pass it down to one of its constituents. The held item can be put into a special role register associated with every type of constituent.

In the constituent that actually uses it, this register will be reset to be empty. On the arc that called for that constituent, there must be an action that checks to see if an item was passed down and not returned, and if so the corresponding register in the calling network must also be emptied, and so on recursively.

Context search and modification. Rather than passing items, we can wait until a constituent looks for a constituent and cannot find it, then let it search through the chain of constituents above it looking to see if one has a constituent of the appropriate kind in an appropriate register. If so, it can use it and remove it from the register it was in. This mechanism has been used in several parsers, but involves adding special operations for searching context and for setting registers of a constituent other than the one currently being parsed. It interacts in complex ways with issues of choice and multiple alternatives, since the non-local structure modifications it allows can have unwanted side effects. It is not well suited to a system that is purely syntactic, since often it is not obvious that an NP is missing. Many verbs are both transitive and intransitive, and allow optional second objects, so it takes an analysis of meaning to decide whether there is indeed a missing NP and whether a higher constituent could fill its place.

Global registers. In order to avoid the complex search needed to see if the current constituent is embedded somewhere in a constituent that is holding something, we can have a single register that does not belong to any one constituent, but to the sentence being parsed as a whole. An arc that finds an item such as an initial NP of a question puts it into this global *hold register,* and an arc that corresponds to a missing element can take it out. All conditions and actions that involve hold registers operate on this common one, regardless of what network they appear in. However, items put on hold can be nested (as we will see in dealing with relative clauses below) and can only be used by constituents below where they were put on. Therefore a global hold register must actually be a list and must be expanded and contracted as nets are entered and left. For this reason, it is often called a *hold list.* For example, the phrase *the cat that the dog I bought bit* includes a held item *the cat,* which becomes the object of *bit* and which in turn is modified by a phrase in which *the dog* is held to become the object of *bought.*

The solution used here is a modification of the first alternative—the explicit passing of held constituents. There is a hold register (not a list) associated with each call to match a network to the word sequence, but this register is treated specially. Since items are held only for temporary purposes (they must be taken out of the hold register somewhere in the sentence), the hold register is not part of the register table that goes into the node structure. In addition to leaving it out of the resulting structure, the hold register is special in two other ways:

Automatic emptying. Ordinarily, when the contents of a register are accessed, they do not change. A hold register is emptied (the entry removed) whenever its contents are used to set another register. Thus the check 'HOLD is an NP' does not change the contents, but 'Set SUBJECT to HOLD.' both sets the subject register and empties the hold register. This mechanism forces a held item to be used only once. The condition that hold be empty at the end (on the S-12:$_e$SEND arc) makes sure that once something is put into the hold register, it will be used somewhere.

Automatic inheritance. When a network is matched as a result of taking a seek arc, its hold register is initially the hold register from the network in which that arc was taken. This is different from the simple initialization of registers as described above in that the register is actually *shared*. If the called network empties it, it is empty when parsing returns to the calling network. This makes it possible for a network to 'use up' a held element that is passed down to it.

In the network of Figure 5–22, the actions associated with the S-22:$_a$NP$_a$ and S-23:$_a$PP$_a$ arcs do the first part of the job. When there is an initial *wh-* phrase (either an NP or a PP whose head is a QUESTION NP), it is parsed and put into the hold register. The other half of the work is done by the PP and NP networks. Figures 5–25 and 5–24 contain versions of these, which include both the features mentioned above for distinguishing question forms and the actions for saving all of the constituents in appropriate registers.

The NP-9:$_f$SEND and PP-4:$_i$SEND arcs start in the initial states of their networks, and since they are send arcs, they successfully terminate the parsing of the network without matching any words. They use the element from the hold register, and their conditions guarantee that it will be a constituent of the right kind. They make use of a new kind of action, described as 'return....' Instead of going through the normal structure building for a send arc, they simply take the indicated node (the one in the hold register) and return that structure as the result of parsing with the network. Arcs of this kind are related to the arcs originally called 'VIR arcs' because they parse a 'virtual' element instead of one found at the current position in the sequence of words. They differ in that they appear in the network for the constituent found on the hold list, while the original VIR arcs appeared in the network from which the constituent was being sought. The formulation here makes it easier to treat them in a general way. They are also related to the *traces* appearing in some current versions of transformational grammar, as discussed in Section C.1.

Figure 5–26 shows the sequence of arcs that would be taken in parsing *Which secretary did they persuade to catch the fish?,* and Figure 5–27 shows the resulting structure. The NP *which secretary* ends up filling three roles: it is the INDIRECT-OBJECT and QUESTION-ELEMENT of the outer S, and the SUBJECT of the inner one. It is instructive to follow through the steps, seeing that the sequence of register settings does lead to the final structure.

By following through some examples, one can demonstrate that the network has the right interactions with passive and dative at multiple levels of embedding and will correctly assign structures to sentences like:

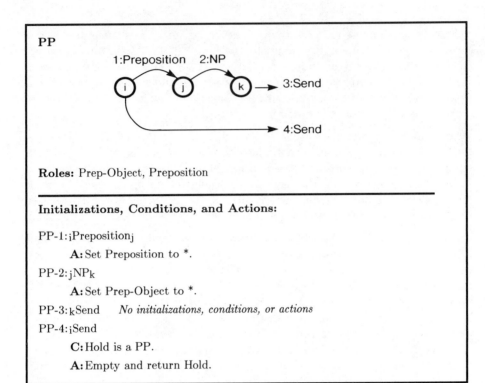

Figure 5–24. The PP network.

Whom was the fish caught by?

By whom was the fish caught?

By whom was the fish expected to be caught?   (5)

Whom was the fish expected to be given to?

The ambiguity of (5) and of modifier questions like *On what day did he tell you to catch it?* can be accounted for by the fact that the question element can be taken out of the hold register by an arc in either of two embedded sentences.

There are a number of ways in which the network of Figure 5–22 fails to capture the data. For example, it does not deal with NP modifiers as in *Which day did you catch it?* and assigns structures to ungrammatical sequences such as *Which hat did the man with catch a fish?* It also cannot deal with questions containing multiple question elements, such as *Who caught which fish?* and *At what time on what day did she do it?* Further conditions and arcs are needed to refine the set of sentences accepted.

NP

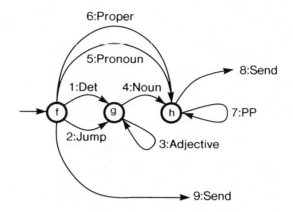

Roles: Determiner, Head, Describers, Qualifiers

Feature Dimensions: Number: Singular, Plural; *default,* –empty–
    Person: 1st, 2nd, 3rd; *default,* 3rd.   Question: Yes, No; *default,* No

---

Initializations, Conditions, and Actions:

NP-1: $_f$Determiner$_g$
    A: Set Determiner to *. Set Number to the Number of *.
        Set Question to the Question of *.

NP-2: $_f$Jump$_g$ *No initializations, conditions, or actions*

NP-3: $_g$Adjective$_g$
    A: Append * to Describers.

NP-4: $_g$Noun$_h$
    C: Number is empty or Number is the Number of *.
    A: Set Head to *.. Set Number to the Number of *.

NP-5: $_f$Pronoun$_h$
    A: Set Head to *. Set Number to the Number of *.
        Set Person to the Person of *. Set Question to the Question of *.

NP-6: $_f$Proper$_h$
    A: Set Head to *. Set Number to the Number of *.

NP-7: $_h$PP$_h$
    A: Append * to Qualifiers.

NP-8: $_h$Send   *No initializations, conditions, or actions*

NP-9: $_f$Send
    C: Hold is an NP.
    A: Empty and return Hold.

Figure 5–25. The NP network extended for questions.

Arc taken	Words parsed
S-22: $_a$NP$_a$	*which secretary* $\rightarrow$ Hold
NP-1: $_f$Determiner$_g$	*which*
NP-4: $_g$Noun$_h$	*secretary*
NP-8: $_h$Send	
S-19: $_a$Verb$_q$	*did*
S-20: $_q$NP$_c$	*they*
NP-5: $_f$Pronoun$_h$	*they*
NP-8: $_h$Send	
S-3: $_c$Verb$_c$	*persuade*
S-5: $_c$NP$_d$	*(which secretary)*
NP-9: $_f$Send	*(which secretary)* $\leftarrow$ Hold
S-18: $_d$S/z$_e$	*to catch the fish*
S-15: $_z$Comp(to)$_c$	*to*
S-3: $_c$Verb$_c$	*catch*
S-5: $_c$NP$_d$	*the fish*
NP-1: $_f$Determiner$_g$	*the*
NP-4: $_g$Noun$_h$	*fish*
NP-8: $_h$Send	
S-7: $_d$Jump$_e$	
S-12: $_e$Send	
S-12: $_e$Send	

Figure 5–26. Parsing with the hold list.

Relative clauses

The last phenomenon we will deal with at length is the presence of *relative clauses* as *qualifiers* following the head of an NP. There are several different kinds, as described in Section B.1.3 and exemplified by:

> *an architect having lunch in the portico*
> *the answer that they were looking for*
> *a cake the likes of which I had never seen*
> *the deity in whose image we were created*

There must be additional arcs in the NP network that match relative clauses, and new states and arcs in the S network that deal with their specialized form. We can divide relative clauses into two general groups, one of which can be dealt with in a manner similar to the embedded sentences of Figure 5–18, and the other requiring the use of hold registers. An arc for each kind is added as a loop on the final state of the NP network, as shown in Figure 5–28.

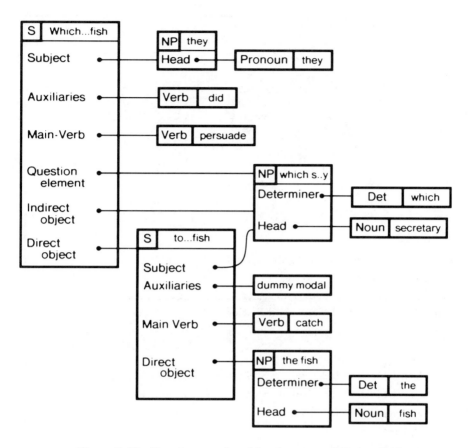

Figure 5–27. Structure produced by the parse of Figure 5–26.

This network makes use of the previous S network, but with an expanded set of MOOD choices, including RELATIVE and WH-RELATIVE. The arc labeled NP-10: $_hS/c_h$ is for a relative clause like *having lunch*, which begins with a verb in the present participle form. It enters the S network in state S.c, with the subject and main verb initialized and with a mood of RELATIVE. In the phrase *an architect having lunch*, the relative clause *having lunch* closely resembles the sentence *An architect is having lunch*, missing the subject and a first auxiliary, which is a form of the verb *be*. By putting them in on the initialization, the rest of the sentence can be parsed as usual. Since we enter after the subject-verb agreement check, the exact form of the verb is unimportant and is not specified. This initialization corresponds almost exactly to the transformation called 'whiz-deletion,' by which the same phenomena are handled in transformational grammar. In the course of generation, whiz-deletion removes a subject marker and a following form of the verb *be*. Since an

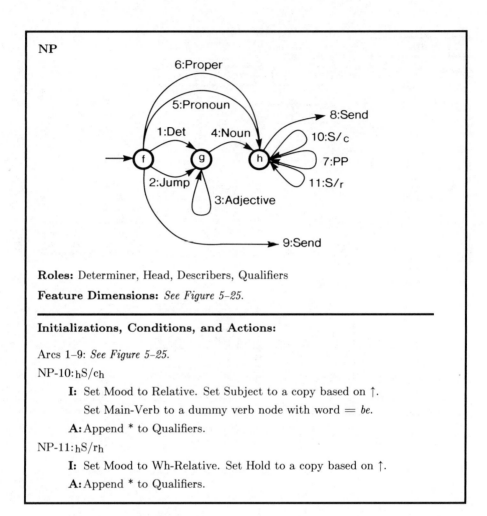

Roles: Determiner, Head, Describers, Qualifiers

Feature Dimensions: *See Figure 5–25.*

Initializations, Conditions, and Actions:

Arcs 1–9: *See Figure 5–25.*

NP-10: hS/ch

    I: Set Mood to Relative. Set Subject to a copy based on ↑.

        Set Main-Verb to a dummy verb node with word = *be*.

    A: Append * to Qualifiers.

NP-11: hS/rh

    I: Set Mood to Wh-Relative. Set Hold to a copy based on ↑.

    A: Append * to Qualifiers.

Figure 5–28. NP modified for relative clauses.

ATN operates by parsing rather than by generating, it must insert them. The reader should verify that this addition allows the parser to handle the example above, as well as more complicated clauses, as in *the windows broken in the scuffle* and *a baby being given a bath.*

    There is a new mechanism being used here in initializing the subject. In our earlier networks, the element used in an initialization was available in one of the registers of the outer sentence (its subject or direct object). In this case, the missing subject is in some sense identical to the NP in which the S is embedded. In *It was ordered by an architect having lunch,* the object of *by* is the same as the subject of *having lunch.* However, no node has yet been constructed for the

NP, and if there were one its use would result in a circular structure in which the subject of *having lunch* is the NP *an architect having lunch*. To avoid this, we construct a node that contains the register contents of the NP being parsed, as they are when the arc is taken. This node is marked as a copy so that programs dealing with the meaning of the sentence can connect the structures appropriately. This is indicated by the phrase 'a copy based on ↑' for the value to be put into the register. The result is illustrated in Figure 5–29.

Figure 5–30 extends the S network to handle the other kind of relative clause, in which there is a 'hole' to be filled in by the copied parent NP, as in:

The crook who ⏝ put the overalls in Ms. Murphy's chowder
The book that the inquisitors burned ⏝
The shelf that you stashed the stuff on ⏝

The new NP network contains an arc for matching a relative clause after the head (NP-11:hS/rh), which enters the S network in state S.r. It sets the hold register to a copy of the NP. If the first element of the S is a relative pronoun (as in *the fish that they caught*), it is parsed by the S-24:rRELa arc, and no change is made to the hold register. Later in the parsing, some NP arc (in this case, the one looking for the object of *caught*) uses the element from the hold register, just as in a question. If there is no relative pronoun (as in *the fish they didn't catch*), the first element of the relative clause will be the

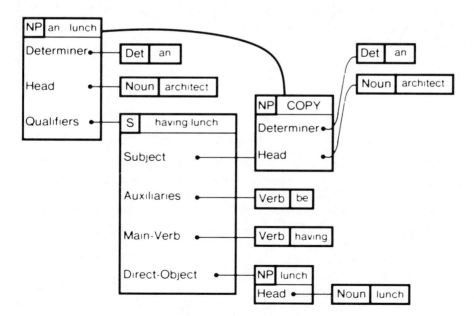

Figure 5–29. A structure with a copy.

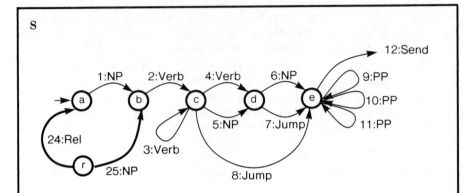

Roles: Subject, Direct-Object, Indirect-Object, Main-Verb, Auxiliaries,
Modifiers, Question-Element

Feature Dimensions:

Like Figure 5–22 except Mood *includes* Relative *and* Wh-Relative.

Initializations, Conditions, and Actions:

Arcs 1–4: *See Figures 5–14, 5–16 and 5–22.* Arcs 5–12: *See Figure 5–17.*
Arcs 13–18 (not shown): *See Figure 5–18.* Arcs 19–23 (not shown): *See Figure 5–22.*
Additional conditions on S-12: $_e$Send *(replacing condition added in Figure 5–22).*

    C: If Mood is Interrogative or Wh-Relative, then Hold is empty

S-24: $_r$Rel$_a$ *No initializations, conditions, or actions*

S-25: $_r$NP$_b$

    A: Set Subject to *.

Figure 5–30. S network with relative clauses.

subject of the embedded S and is parsed by the S-25: $_r$NP$_b$ arc. It is put into
the SUBJECT register, while the hold register is left unchanged for later use.
We cannot deal with missing relative pronouns by simply having a jump arc
from S.r to S.a because this would result in treating the phrase *the secretary
caught it* as containing a relative clause (parallel to *the secretary who caught
it*), since the item in the hold register could be used by the NP parsed by the
S-1: $_a$NP$_b$ arc. The held item can be the subject of the embedded S only when
a relative pronoun is present, as in *the one that got away.*

    By using the same hold mechanism as for questions, we get the same degree
of generality for embedded use of the held items, as in parsing *the fish that
they thought you had told me not to bother with.* One of the major influences

on the design of the ATN formalism was the desire to capture this kind of generalization in an intuitively pleasing way. The setting of the mood to WH-RELATIVE in a relative clause prevents any of the initial question arcs (such as S-21:$_a$NP$_b$ or S-22:$_a$NP$_a$) from being taken, which would lead to forms like *the eclipse that did you see* and *the people who which house do live in*. This is a standard use of a feature register as a kind of 'switch' to allow parts of the network to be shared among different kinds of structures while making sure that each takes its own path.

Changes to the formal mechanism

As mentioned above, the hold register cannot be treated as simply another register. In order to incorporate it properly into the definitions of Appendix D, it is necessary to make a number of modifications.

Separate table. Since the hold register does not form part of the final node structure produced by a parse, it needs to be kept separately. A 'hold table' can be added to the definition for a configuration (Figure D–3), which will potentially contain an entry for HOLD.

Passing down values. Since a held item can be used by an embedded phrase (as in *the man I told you to ask her to see*), it is necessary for the hold register to be passed down as seek arcs are taken. The procedure for matching a seek arc (Figure D–8) needs to include an extra argument in its call to 'Match a network...,' which is its current hold table. The definition of 'Match an ATN...' (Figure D–6) needs to accept this additional input and put it into the configuration it is building. The top level call to match a network with the distinguished network (in Figure D–4) specifies an empty hold table to start with.

Emptying when used. As mentioned above, the contents of a hold register are accessible in a special way. When its contents are used to set some other register, it is emptied—the entry in hold table is removed. This is the means of assuring that a held item will be used only once. The key to communication is the fact that what is passed down is not the *contents* of the hold register, but the entire *table*. Thus, if an embedded phrase removes the item from the table, the higher node (which passed it down) will have an empty table after the lower network returns.

Displacement. Any action or initialization that sets a hold register operates differently from a normal register setting. With all other registers, the entry in the register table is changed, but the table itself (with all of its other entries) remains the same. To carry out an action or initialization of the form 'Set HOLD to ....,' the entire hold table is replaced by a new table with the item as its entry. This means, for example, that if there is a relative clause within a question (as in *What did the man that you saw catch?*), the initialization on the NP-11:$_h$S/r$_h$ arc will 'displace' the hold table that is inherited from the question with a new one having the appropriate entry (a copy of the NP *the man*). This will also happen when relative clauses are nested, as in *the cat that the dog that your friend bought bit*. Because of displacement there can be different hold registers associated with different levels of the structure currently being parsed, achieving the effect of a *hold list*.

In the networks presented here, the initializations ensure that a relative clause will have its own hold register (rather than an inherited one), the emptying ensures that an item will be used only once, and the condition that the hold register be empty (for INTERROGATIVE and WH-RELATIVE S's) on the S-12:$_e$SEND arc guarantees that a held item will be used up within the constituent in which it was put onto hold.

The grammar as extended in Figure 5–30 combines mechanisms for handling questions, embedded sentences of other kinds, passive, and datives. A bit of study is needed to see the subtleties, for example how subject-verb agreement is correctly established with the higher NP when it is the subject. However, many phenomena are not dealt with by the networks given here.

There has been a good deal of work in transformational grammar on the kinds of additional *constraints* needed to eliminate ungrammatical sentences, as discussed in Section C.2. In general, it is possible to find ATN correlates of the transformational constraints, without significantly more (or less) complication. Current work on functional and lexical-functional grammars (as described in Section 6.6) is further refining an ATN-like approach to make this kind of constraint more natural.

Some of the exercises deal with modifying the networks to account for additional syntactic complexities.

5.6 Further syntactic issues

The previous sections have described the basic mechanisms of ATN parsing. However, they are not sufficient for handling all of the phenomena of a natural language. As with other syntactic formalisms, there is a 'basic theory' and then an ever-growing collection of changes and extensions as people try to cover more of the data. In this section, we will briefly review a number of problems raised by English that were not dealt with in the previous sections. Some of them can be readily handled with the existing mechanisms by adding new arcs and states to the grammars. Others call for more radical modifications of the formalism. One of the main goals of this section (along with describing more of English grammar) is to illustrate some typical ways the ATN formalism is used. Extensions made in this section with numbered arcs are included in the grammar of Appendix D. Extensions illustrated with arcs having labels but no numbers are not.

Appendix B gives more detail on the problems that must be dealt with in a comprehensive grammar. For practical uses of ATN grammars, one picks out a subset of structures that will be handled and simply ignores the others. The hope in doing so is that the subset will be 'habitable' in that a particular system handling only that subset will be convenient for a person to converse with.

Case agreement

Sections 5.3 and 5.4 introduce actions and conditions to check for person and number agreement. However, there are other kinds of agreement in English that have not been dealt with, and the grammars defined would accept sequences like *Him told I to talk to they. As we will see in Section 6.5, English has a limited form of *case marking* that applies to pronouns but not other forms of NP. Many languages have distinct noun forms as well and have many more cases.

This phenomenon can be handled with no new arcs by adding a feature dimension 'CASE' with choices OBJECTIVE (sometimes called 'accusative'), SUBJECTIVE (sometimes called 'nominative'), and POSSESSIVE, as discussed below. An NP is initialized with no case choice. The choice is set by the SEND arcs—the normal exit sets it to the case of the head (which may be a noun, proper noun, or pronoun) and the posessive send arc (see below) sets it to POSSESSIVE. The pronouns *he, she, I, who,* etc., are marked SUBJECTIVE, *her, us, them,* etc., are OBJECTIVE, and *my, your, her,* etc., are POSSESSIVE. Some pronouns (such as *it* and *her*) have senses with different features. Each common noun and proper noun has senses for both SUBJECTIVE and OBJECTIVE, since this distinction is not reflected in the form of English nouns. The changes to the NP network are shown in Figure 5–36 below.

Each arc that parses an NP must have a condition specifying the appropriate feature. For example, S-1:$_a$NP$_b$, which parses the subject of an ordinary sentence, has a condition 'the CASE of * is SUBJECTIVE,' while S-5:$_c$NP$_d$ and PP-2:$_j$NP$_k$ have 'the CASE of * is OBJECTIVE.' Arcs dealing with simple relative pronouns and questions allow either case (as in *Who brought him?* and *Whom does he know*), since agreement will be checked by the arc using the NP that removes the element from the hold list. These changes are not shown in this chapter but are included in the networks of Appendix D.

It is interesting to note that sentences involving *who* and *whom* are not treated uniformly by most English speakers. In spoken conversation, few people insist on the phrase *the English teacher whom you never liked* in place of the more common *the English teacher who you never liked*. This is a typical phenomenon, in which a realistic grammar (one that accounts for what actually occurs) demands more special cases and is not as regular as an idealized one.

The verb sequence

The network as defined so far will accept any sequence of auxiliaries followed by a main verb. This would include obvious nonsense such as *He is be had will will had were gone.* The restrictions on possible ordering are basically conditions on the S-3: cVERBc arc, such as: 'If the TYPE of MAIN-VERB is HAVE, then the FORM of * is PAST-PARTICIPLE.' However, there are a number of complexities about just what order things occur in, and whether phrases like *is going to leave* and *used to work* should be treated as containing auxiliaries. This problem is described at length in Section B.1.5, and the rules described there can be implemented in an ATN without new mechanisms. A simple form is shown in the grammar of Appendix D.

There is also a need to handle *multi-word verbs* made up of a verb and particle (as in *pick up*) or a verb in combination with a preposition (as in *account for*). Verb-preposition combinations can be parsed with the grammar as it now stands, but the transitivity features will not be handled properly. We want to reject *Mitchell couldn't account* on the basis that *account* is not a simple intransitive verb, but accept *Mitchell couldn't account for the missing funds.* Verb-particle combinations are more complex, as they allow a particle either before or after an object, as in *Mitchell called up Dean* and *Mitchell called Dean up.*

The basic solution is to put in extra arcs to parse particles and PPs and to put actions on both those arcs that modify the MAIN-VERB register to reflect the combination. These arcs need to check that the verb and particle or preposition can be combined. For example, *up* is not a particle in *He climbed up the stairs,* as shown by the ungrammaticality of *He climbed the stairs up.* The dictionary needs to be extended to include entries for such pairs, having the appropriate transitivity features and a definition reflecting the meaning of the

---

Additional arcs:

S-26: cParticlec

    C: There is a dictionary entry for Main-Verb combined with *.

    A: Set Main-Verb to the entry.

S-27: dParticled *Same as S-26*

S-28: ePPe

    C: Direct-Object is empty and there is a dictionary entry for Main-Verb combined with the Prep of *.

    A: Set Main-Verb to the entry. Set Direct-Object to the Prep-Object of *.

Figure 5–31. Additions to the S network for multi-word verbs.

Type	Examples
Adverb	*(Fortunately,) we did it (quickly).*
(For-)To- clause	*(To get in) you have to wait (for someone to answer).*
-ing clause	*(Thinking nobody was watching,) she walked out (carrying the bag).*
Bound clause	*(After the food came,) we ate it (before it got cold).*
Time NP	*(Last year) we finished (the first day of October).*
Adverb group	*(Quicker than a wink,) they built it (as well as they could).*

Figure 5–32. Sentence modifiers.

combination. For example, for each such combination there could be a separate word sense for the verb. The send arc in the S network would have to check that these special senses only appeared with the proper particle or preposition. Another solution is to have such entries not available when a normal category arc is taken with category VERB, but to have them available to replace the verb entry when the particle or preposition is found. The special entry (with its own feature choices) is put in place of the previous main verb, and would also provide the basis for procedures dealing with the meaning of the sentence. The formalism for conditions and actions also needs to be extended (beyond those shown in Figure 5–9) to allow the appropriate entry to be found and used, as shown in Figure 5–31.

Only one combination will be allowed in parsing an S, since the word sense resulting from taking one of these arcs will not be combinable with an additional particle or preposition. In order to forbid a pronoun following a verb-particle pair (as in *Mitchell called up him*), we need an additional condition on the S-5:$_c$NP$_d$ arc stating 'If MAIN-VERB is a verb-particle combination, then the HEAD of * is not a pronoun.' The reader should check that the modifications as given interact properly with passives, questions, etc., and allow bitransitive sentences like *He'll pick me up a sandwich when he goes to lunch.*

Modifiers

The network for S so far accepts prepositional modifiers at the end, but does not include them at the beginning. It also does not include any of the other many types of modifiers that can appear at both beginning and end, as illustrated in Figure 5–32. Loops (not included in Appendix D) can be added to states S.a and S.e for each of these kinds of modifiers, with an action appending the result to the MODIFIERS register. However, there are some complications:

Subject initialization. The loop for a modifier like *thinking nobody was watching* would have label S.c, while the one for *to get in* would have S.z. We have already introduced arcs with each of these labels: NP-10:$_h$S/c$_h$ for *the* architect _having lunch_ and S-17:$_c$S/z$_e$ for _Carol wanted to dance_. However, in those cases there was a register that could be used to initialize the subject of the embedded S, while in the case of a sentence modifier there is none. Generally, the subject is the same as the (surface) subject of the S, as in the example of Figure 5–32, but it can also be the speaker (as in _Speaking frankly, he doesn't stand a chance_) or the object (as in one interpretation of _I saw him coming in the door_). If the modifier appears at the end, then we need to account for all of the possibilities. If it appears at the beginning, we are faced with the problem of initializing it to something that hasn't been parsed yet. This cannot be done without a significant revision of the ATN formalism.

These examples raise the general question of how much detail should be handled by the syntactic formalism and how much should be left to the semantics. One of the basic assumptions underlying the networks of this chapter (and most of the work in transformational grammar) is that the syntactic component should account for intuitions such as the one that the object of _see_ in _Which movie did you see?_ is _which movie_. It is possible to take an opposing view, in which the connection is captured by the semantic component instead, making it easier to deal with cases like those mentioned above, where the appropriate syntactic connection is unclear or missing. However, this can only be done properly if the syntactic and semantic components work closely together, so that the kinds of connections we have been demonstrating in the earlier parts of the chapter are properly accounted for. This is done in many of the newer grammar formalisms described in Chapter 6 and Appendix C.

Questions and relative clauses. Adverbs and time NPs can be used as question elements and can have relative clauses, as in:

> _When did it happen?_   the place _where she buried it_
> _What month will it erupt?_   the night _they drove old Dixie down_

The loop for parsing an initial adverb needs to note if it is a question form (which in turn must be marked in the dictionary entry) and if so, set the hold register and the question-element and mark the sentence as INTERROGATIVE. Either of the loops for a time NP will automatically pick up an item from the hold list to handle the other cases.

Overgeneration. The network with the added loops accepts many sentences that seem too contorted to be really acceptable, such as ?_The man who to get away cut the bars didn't succeed_. If the modifier _to get away_ were at the end of the relative clause it would sound much more natural, but it is overly restrictive to forbid modifiers of this kind at the beginning of such a clause, since they seem acceptable in other sentences like _I won't go to any movie that to get into you have to stand in line_. Constraints of this kind are complex and not fully handled in any existing formalism. ATN grammars are usually written in a style that accepts many questionable constructs in order to have the generality to handle the sentences intended by the designer.

In addition to initial and final modifiers, sentences can have adverbs in the middle (as in *They soon discovered the truth*). Adverb loops (which append to the MODIFIERS register) have to be added to states S.b (*She quickly recovered*) and S.c (*She will soon be working*). For the grammar of some speakers, there needs to be a check that the previous element is not *to* to avoid *split infinitives* like *?We wanted to immediately start work*. Formally, we need to check that the main verb is not the dummy modal inserted when a clause beginning with *to* is parsed.

An adverb cannot be the last thing parsed before leaving state S.c. We can have *He soon will have finished it, He will soon have finished it, He will have soon finished it* and *He will have finished it soon* (which uses the adverb loop in state S.e), but not *He will have finished soon it*. There are several ways that this can be handled, and they are a good illustration of the kinds of choices faced by someone developing an ATN grammar:

Additional mechanism. We can add a mechanism that keeps track of the previous thing parsed. The conditions on the arcs leaving state S.c can include a check that it is not an adverb. Note that this is not the same as the most recent constituent '*', but is the constituent preceding it. In general, we want to avoid complicating the basic ATN formalism with special devices if the same effects can be achieved with something that already exists. This is both for the practical reason of keeping the implementation simpler and for theoretical considerations of the kinds discussed in Section 4.5.

Additional feature registers. A register could be added with a feature dimension ENDS-WITH-ADVERB with choices YES and NO. It would be set by the arcs that parse verbs and adverbs and could be checked in conditions. Some grammar writers feel free to create any number of such specialized registers that do not have any significance for the final register table resulting from the parse, but are useful in controlling it. In a sense, they are treating the ATN more as a programming device than as a structural grammar. As described in Section 5.7, the original ATN grammars treated the building of structure as completely independent from the use of registers while parsing, and registers were often used in this style. More recent uses of ATN grammars tend to encourage a structural justification for registers and to avoid adding them in this kind of case.

Additional role registers. In a similar vein, we could add a role register LAST-VERB-OR-ADVERB that is set by the same arcs. The conditions would then check the word class of its contents rather than checking a yes-no feature. The issues are the same as for feature registers in that many ATN grammar writers are reluctant to add registers whose contents are used solely for some temporary purpose.

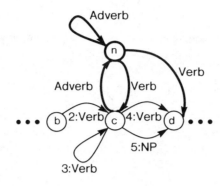

Figure 5–33. A fragment of the S net for adverbs.

Additional states and arcs. A final solution is to create a more complicated network in which state S.c is replaced with more than one state, as illustrated in Figure 5–33.

When an adverb is first found, the parser goes to state S.n, remaining there as long as adverbs continue to be found. When a verb is found, it goes back to S.c (or to S.d if it is the main verb of a passive). In S.c it can find any number of additional verbs before either encountering another adverb or proceeding on to the end of the sentence. This network allows verbs and adverbs to be mixed in an arbitrary order, except that the last thing must be a verb. It is typical of the kind of complication that is added to a grammar to account for syntactic subtleties. It is also typical of a case in which it is not clear what the grammar should allow. As written, it accepts multiple adverbs between verbs, as in *They will then immediately quickly proceed to the next room.* However, this will also allow questionable sequences like *We quickly soon happily left.* As discussed in the section on noun phrases below, there are many places like this in a grammar where the data are difficult to pin down.

Finally, the adverb *not* is different from other adverbs in that it cannot appear in a *double negative* and its contracted form *-n't* appears where other adverbs cannot, as in *Didn't you know?* In addition to preventing multiple uses of *not* (as in **He can't not have not done it*), the grammar must prevent it from appearing with a negative noun phrase (as in **Nobody didn't say nothing*). A NEGATIVITY feature dimension needs to be added not only to S and to the dictionary entries for adverbs and verbs (contractions like *can't* can be treated as negative verbs), but also to NP and to entries for quantifiers (*no*) and pronouns (*nobody*). The register in each network needs to be set to NEGATIVE whenever a NEGATIVE constituent is parsed, and conditions need to be added that prevent this from happening more than once. This involves putting new actions and conditions on a number of arcs. It is an example of a phenomenon that is more easily described globally ('No more than one constituent can be negative') than by dealing with the steps that actually put the constituents together. The addition of such global conditions would be a substantial change to the ATN formalism.

The structure of the NP

The NP network as defined so far can deal with common NPs and with those whose head is a pronoun or proper noun. It accepts PPs and two kinds of relative clauses following the head, even if the head is a proper noun or a pronoun, as in *Jeannie with the light brown hair* and *he who hesitates*. It also has a special arc to deal with the hold list. However, it does not deal with the variety of modifiers preceding the head in an ordinary noun phrase like *The last three remaining broken roof pillar supports*. They can include numbers (*three*), past participle verbs (*broken*), present participle verbs (*remaining*), nouns (*roof, pillar*), and other words in special categories such as *last*. Figure 5–34 shows some arcs added to the NP network to handle these.

This network includes a loop for each kind of modifier, allowing an arbitrary mixture following the determiner and preceding the head. Each arc has an action 'Append * to DESCRIBERS.' and conditions to check for the appropriate form (e.g., it cannot be an infinitive verb or a plural noun), as shown in Figure 5–36 later in the section. Clearly, this is general enough but allows many combinations that should not be accepted, such as *the old three stone four roof broken pillars*. Ordinarily we expect numbers first, followed by adjectives and verbs, followed by nouns, as indicated in the slot and filler analysis illustrated in Chapter 3 and Section B.2. However, this is not always the case, as in *the big three universities* and *the stone supporting pillar*. As described in Section B.2, the rules for ordering modifiers in an NP are quite difficult to describe in any formalism.

In general, ATN grammars offer two basic ways of dealing with ordering. There can either be a *chain,* in which the sequence is specified by the order of the states and arcs, or a *daisy* structure like the one of Figure 5–34, in which the loops can be taken in any order and the precise ordering constraints appear as conditions. For example, if we want to allow a number either first or after a single modifier that is not a noun, we can put a condition on the NP-12:gNUMBERg arc that checks the contents of the DESCRIBERS register to see that it is empty or that there is only one element of the right kind. Any ordering constraint that can be specified with states and arcs can be done

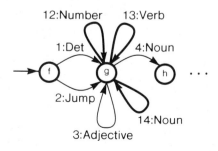

Figure 5–34. Additional arcs for NP modifiers.

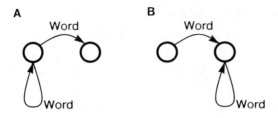

Figure 5–35. Different kinds of loop structure.

instead with conditions and actions (assuming appropriate registers are added), and there have been some proposals (such as Lakoff and Thompson's *cognitive grammar*) to have each network consist of a single daisy, putting all of the syntactic details into the conditions and the actions of the arcs.

One other thing worth noting is the treatment of a sequence of nouns like *hatch cover support strut holder*. The NP-14:gNOUNg arc parses a noun and appends it to the describers and the NP-4:gNOUNh arc parses the head. A sequence of nouns can be succesfully parsed only if all but the last are taken by the loop, and the last by the other arc. If the last is taken by the loop, there is no way to proceed further, and if any but the last is, the left-over nouns will block continuation. Because we treat the networks nondeterministically, we do not need to worry about how to detect that the last noun is coming. Given a sequence there will be precisely one successful path, and it will have the structure we want. In practical (deterministic) parsers there are often special mechanisms to avoid the creation of ultimately unprofitable paths.

It is interesting to compare this structure to the one used for parsing the sequence of auxiliary verbs in Figure 5–14. In both cases, there is a sequence of words of the same type (noun and verb respectively), which must contain at least one entry. In the NP there is a loop followed by a single arc, while in the S network there is a single arc followed by a loop. These are shown schematically in Figure 5–35.

In deciding which structure to use, one considers the associated actions and conditions. If, for example, the first item of the sequence is to be saved in a separate register while the rest are combined, structure B allows the actions to be put onto the two arcs independently. In the case of the NP, all the nouns but the last are to be appended to the describers while the last becomes the head, so A is used. In the case of the verb sequence, it is the last element (the main verb) that is saved separately, yet B has been used in our network. This is because of the need to check subject-verb agreement and the proper sequence of auxiliaries and verb forms (as described above). The agreement check applies only to the first verb and does not apply at all in cases where the S network is entered in states S.x and S.z. The auxiliary sequence check applies in parsing all but the first verb. These can be much more easily stated by having a separate arc for the first verb (as in structure B). The main-verb register is set to the last verb by resetting it each time a verb is found, appending the previous value to the auxiliaries. The final contents of the auxiliaries and main verb are then just as though structure A had been used.

The NP network as extended with the arcs of Figure 5–34 still does not cover the full structure of the NP. For example, it does not deal with *pre-determiners* (as in <u>all</u> *the old reasons*), *quantifiers* (*every day*), *partitives* (*some of the time*), *quantified pronouns* (*everything he says*), or with the details of number agreement among determiners, quantifiers, numbers, and nouns. These are all discussed in Section B.2 and dealt with in some of the exercises. It also does not deal with possessives, as discussed below.

Possessives

The most straightforward way of handling possessives would be to add the arcs of Figure 5–36 (which also includes the loops for DESCRIBERS and the CASE register discussed in previous sections). This network has been drawn in a simplified form in which several loops from the same state are indicated by a single loop with several labels. NP-15:$_f$NP$_g$ allows a possessive NP (like *my* or *the author's*) to be used in place of a determiner. The action on the pronoun arc NP-5:$_f$PRONOUN$_h$ will cause an NP whose head is a possessive pronoun (as marked in the dictionary) to be possessive. Finally, the NP-16:$_h$('s)$_p$ arc creates a possessive NP out of an ordinary one by matching *'s*. A separate send arc (NP-17:$_p$SEND) is needed because if the arc that matches -*'s* returned to state NP.h, additional modifiers could be added after it. This send arc sets the CASE to POSSESSIVE, instead of to the case of the head. The grammar as written allows modifiers to be parsed before the -*'s*, as in *the man I told you about's mother*, which is common in spoken English although not used in writing. The conditions mentioned earlier for dealing with case on arcs that use an NP will prevent a possessive NP from being used in any place other than on the NP-15:$_f$NP$_g$ arc. Some further additions would be necessary to handle possessive pronouns such as *mine* and *yours*.

However, in some ATN implementations this solution is not satisfactory because of the left-recursion—the first state in the NP network has an arc labeled NP in its outgoing arcs. As we saw in Section 3.4, there are problems for some top-down left-to-right parsers in handling left-recursive constructions. The ATN formalism is oriented towards top-down left-to-right parsing. The setting of registers and use of their contents in specifying conditions must take place in the proper order, or the results will be totally garbled. Therefore, either special mechanisms must be added to the parser, or another means must be found for handling possessives.

One possibility is to add an arc as shown in Figure 5–37. The new arc operates after a head has been found, parses a -*'s,* and goes back to the state

NP

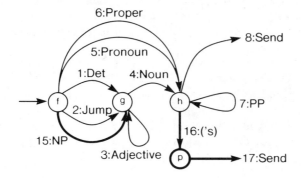

Roles: Determiner, Head, Describers, Qualifiers

Feature Dimensions:

　　Number: Singular, Plural; *default,* –empty–

　　Person: 1st, 2nd, 3rd; *default,* 3rd

　　Question: Yes, No; *default,* No

　　Case: Subjective, Objective, Possessive; *default,* –empty–

Initializations, Conditions, and Actions:

Arcs 1–9: *See Figure 5–25.* Arcs 10–11: *See Figure 5–28.*

NP-12: gNumberg

　　A: Append * to Describers.

NP-13: gVerbg

　　C: The Form of * is Pres-Part or Past-Part.

　　A: Append * to Describers.

NP-14: gNoung

　　C: The Number of * is Singular.　　**A:** Append * to Describers.

NP-15: fNPg

　　C: The Case of * is Possessive.　　**A:** Set Determiner to *.

NP-16: h('s)p

　　C: Head is not a Pronoun.

NP-17: pSend

　　A: Set Case to Possessive.

Figure 5–36. An NP network that handles possessives.

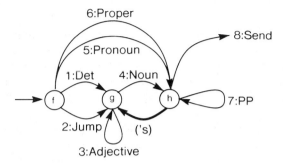

Figure 5–37. A specialized way of handling possessives.

normally reached after a determiner has been found. It has an associated action that creates a node for the NP as parsed so far and puts it into the determiner register. In addition, it sets all of the other registers (feature and role) back to the values they would have at the beginning of an NP. None of the mechanisms described in the formal definition of Section 5.2 can handle this kind of operation. We need to create a new node, then create a new configuration for the network that called it.

From a linguistic point of view, this seems much more complex than the solution of Figure 5–36. However, for someone writing a practical parsing system, it offers the possibility of getting rid of left-recursion, thereby making a top-down left-to-right parsing strategy feasible. Since ATN grammars have been developed in building practical systems, there has been a relatively large amount of such special manipulation of the grammar in light of processing considerations. The fact that special actions must be taken that are not part of the normal mechanism does not present an insuperable problem, since most ATN parsers are written in a programming language (such as LISP) that makes it possible to take direct actions on the underlying implementation. Actions like this are specified outside of the grammar formalism as calls to a program that operates directly on the data structures used to represent networks and configurations.

Other clause structures

As outlined in Section B.1, there are many forms of sentence (embedded and top-level) that are not covered by this grammar. Some of them can be added with a few simple arcs. For example, *imperative* sentences like *Shut the door* can be added by putting a single new arc into the S network:

S-29: ₐVerb꜀

    C: The Form of * is Infinitive and Mood is Declarative.

    A: Set Subject to a dummy NP with Head *you.*

    Set Main-Verb to *. Set Mood to Imperative.

In place of the usual subject-verb sequence, the sentence begins with a verb in the infinitive form (as in *Be sharp*) and the subject is an implicit *you*. Once again we use a dummy node inserted by an action, where the corresponding imperative transformation would delete an item of that form. The check on mood prevents this arc from being taken within a question, relative clause, or other form of embedded S. By explicitly putting *you* as the subject, we provide a structure containing the appropriate information for an analysis of meaning and also make it possible to handle syntactic phenomena like tag questions, in which some other constituent has to agree with the subject:

> *He ate it all, didn't he?*
>
> *Have some of this cake, won't you?*

Bound clauses like *while we were going* and *that we did it* can be handled by adding a new state S.t in which they begin (i.e., they are parsed by an arc whose label is S.t):

> S-30: $_t$Binder$_a$
>
> **A:** Set Binder to *. Set Mood to Bound.

We have added a new role register to hold the BINDER (a word such as *while* or *that*) and a mood choice BOUND to indicate the kind of S and to prevent a binder from being followed by an imperative verb, question form, etc. The only arc leading out of state S.a that has a mood condition compatible with BOUND is the standard subject arc S-1: $_a$NP$_b$ with its condition 'MOOD is not INTERROGATIVE.'

The addition of arcs calling for bound clauses is complex. They depend on the particular binder, among other things. For example, the subject of a sentence can be a bound clause beginning with *that* or *whether* but not *while*. The relevant arcs will not be added here, but the issues are discussed in Appendix B. Other forms of embedded S include:

> *They criticize <u>whatever we do</u>.*
>
> *We insisted <u>that he be there</u>.*
>
> *<u>Sitting on the side</u> will make you tired.*
>
> *A fish is <u>what we want to catch</u>.*

Some of these (like *sitting on the side*) can be parsed using states and arcs already in the network. The problem is in specifying just when they can be used. Others (like *that he be there,* in which the verb is in an unusual form) require further modifications. With all of these, it is relatively easy to modify the network so that it will accept a wide range of structures. The problem is overgeneration—unless the networks are made very complex, they will accept sequences that are not grammatical as well.

Finally, in our presentation of questions and relative clauses above, we did not account for relative clauses in which the first element is not a relative pronoun but an NP or a PP that contains *which, whom,* or *whose* embedded somewhere within it, as in:

the person by whom the fish was caught

a fish the likes of which you have never seen

those reports the height of the lettering on the covers of which is prescribed
   by the government (6)

Example (6) is an example of a phenomenon known as *pied piping,* in which material from the rest of the clause can be embedded into the initial phrase. It is described further in Section B.1.4, as are many of the syntactic structures discussed in this section.

These can be handled with an extension of the use of hold registers, in which held elements can be used by an arc that parses a relative pronoun when it occurs in the initial phrase of a wh- relative clause. This requires more than a single hold register (or hold list), since the two different ways of using held items (to match a relative pronoun or to fill a gap) must be kept separate. This problem is discussed in Exercise 5.20.

Transitivity

In the grammar given above, we have assumed that each verb can be classified as one or more of INTRANSITIVE, TRANSITIVE, or BITRANSITIVE, according to whether it can appear followed by zero, one, or two objects, respectively. Transitivity is in fact a much more complex phenomenon, as discussed in Section 6.5 and Section B.1.6. The grammar needs to be modified to account for *complements* that appear after the verb but are not ordinary objects, as in *He was delirious* and *They drank the bottle dry.* It must handle verbs like *put* that demand a locational object in addition to a direct object (**He put the book*) and others that take apparently ordinary objects but do not allow passive voice and other such rearrangements, as with **A fool was thought him by them* and **A good idea was seemed by what he said.*

In general, only the simplest kinds of transitivity phenomena have been handled directly within the ATN formalism. Those parsing systems that deal with it in a more comprehensive way combine ATNs with some kind of case grammar analysis, as described in Sections 6.5 and 7.5.

Conjunction, comparatives, and ellipsis

There remain classes of phenomena that present great difficulties for all syntactic formalisms, including ATN grammars. Among the most important of these are *conjunction* (*He bought a peach and ate it*), *comparatives* (*Bertha is wider than Debby is tall*), and *ellipsis* (the leaving out of implied constituents, as in the response *Ted thinks vanilla* to *What kind of ice cream does Carol like?*).

At first, it might seem that conjunctions might be handled by adding more arcs to the grammar, but this is not feasible since they can occur at almost any place in the structure, as in:

> *Paul and Joy came to dinner.*
>
> *They brought some yellow and purple flowers.*
>
> *They gave Joan a kiss and Eileen a hug.*
>
> *We opened and drank some wine and ate falafel.*
>
> *Paul liked to play tunes on the guitar, and Joy on the mandolin.*   (7)
>
> *He played and she sang every old tune in the book.*   (8)

The intuitive explanation of how conjunctions should be treated can be summarized as 'When you see a conjunction, start parsing a new phrase that matches some phrase you are in the process of parsing, and combine the two as a conjoined constituent. If there are gaps in the new one, fill them in with the corresponding elements from the old one.'

Several systems have had ways of implementing such instructions, allowing the presence of conjunctions in the input sequence to trigger special operations rather than being parsed by the ordinary operations of matching arcs in the network. They have been adequate for handling some of the simple cases, but have not been able achieve broad generality. The difficulties lie in appropriately specifying how the system is to look through the set of phrases it has been parsing and to decide what is an appropriate match. Often the section of the input that is matched is a partial constituent (as in (8)) or one with gaps (as in (7)).

As with other phenomena discussed above, there are two ways of looking at the problem. From a formal syntactic point of view, we want to put in mechanisms that assign appropriate structures to sentences and reject non-sentences. From a practical point of view, conjunction raises another issue. It often leads to large amounts of potential ambiguity, since there are a number of different ways in which the structures following the conjunction could be matched against the ones preceding it. The phrase *the old men and women* has been traditionally used as an illustration of a word sequence with two different structural interpretations, but the problem is compounded in a case like *The President indicated his concern with spreading violence and growing....* The word *growing* could be the beginning of a phrase parallel to several of the previous ones:

> *...spreading (violence) and (growing)...*
>
> *...with (spreading violence) and (growing frustration)...*

...*his (concern with spreading violence) and (growing displeasure with...)*

...*indicated (his concern with spreading violence) and (growing public outrage...)*

...*The President (indicated his concern with spreading violence) and (growing angry called for...)*

(The President indicated his concern with spreading violence) and (growing pressures caused him to...)

If a grammar is built to accept all of the possibilities, every appearance of a conjunction will create an explosion of paths for the parser to follow, and when more than one conjunction appears, the number of possibilities grows exponentially. Therefore in practical systems, there has been a tendency to limit the generality of the conjunctive mechanisms and to make use of criteria based on meaning to limit exploration to a small number of paths. In looking at naturally occurring sentences, we find that a great many of them have apparent ambiguity (if we consider only syntactic structure), but that a normal speaker of the language will not be aware of this and will immediately adopt a single parsing. This is based not only on meaning but also on subtle effects of parallelism between structures, involving features such as their length, syntactic complexity, and the sorts of modifiers. A quick reading of the sentence *We vehemently urge that he resign and heartily applaud the efforts of the committee* does not give a feeling of ambiguity, even though it can perfectly well be interpreted (both syntactically and in its meaning) as containing the structure *he resign and heartily applaud the efforts of the committee.*

In order to handle these phenomena properly, the system needs some notion of *matching* a new structure to an existing one. The basic ATN approach can be seen as matching a new structure against a pattern that specifies all possible structures (the network), but this has a very different character from matching against an actual set of structures already parsed.

Rather than matching an individual word or phrase against an abstract class name or constituent label, we are matching it against a phrase with which it differs in some specific ways. For example, a decision must be made as to whether to match an NP with a single adjective against one with two adjectives or match a clause in the present tense against one in the past tense. The decision must be based on some metric of similarity and a notion of *best match,* rather than the strict yes-or-no decisions provided by the networks.

Comparatives present similar problems in that they are also combined with ellipsis. *I bathed Emma faster than you* could mean ...*than I bathed you* or ...*than you bathed Emma,* and might be continued instead ...*than you washed the car.* The dimension of comparison need not be the same, as in *Mine is longer than yours is tall.* Although many ATN grammars include arcs to handle simple cases of comparatives, they have not dealt with the problem in a general way.

Special phrases

Looking at the large ATN grammars that have been developed, one is struck by the fact that a large proportion of the arcs do not deal with general syntactic phenomena of the kind we have been considering, but deal instead with specialized phrases such as times of day, dates, airline flights, amounts of money, and chemical compounds. In developing a *semantic grammar* (as described in Chapter 7), one includes arcs, states, and lexical categories that are tailored to the specific subject matter. However, even in an ordinary syntactic grammar there must be many specialized phrases.

Anyone who has tried to write a substantial grammar is aware of the frustration that comes from picking up a piece of text from a magazine or newspaper and asking 'How many of the sentences does my grammar handle properly?' There are a surprisingly large number of sentences whose basic structure has been accounted for but that include one or more special combinations associated with particular words. A speaker of a language has a large *phrasal lexicon* that associates both meanings and specialized syntactic structures with particular combinations of words. For example, the structure of a phrase like *old enough to know better* is peculiar to the word *enough*, while *We were just about to leave* includes both *just* and *about* in structures that are not general. Therefore the grammar given here (and any grammar of similar size and generality) will fall short of handling natural text and must be augmented with a good deal of more specialized structure.

The form of resulting structures

ATN grammars as presented here produce *register structures* as described in Section 5.2. As mentioned there, this is not a property of all ATN grammars and in fact was not part of the original development. In the procedure for matching a network against a sequence of words (Figure D–6), the final steps create and return a node containing the register table. In other versions of ATNs, this is not done uniformly for all nodes. Instead, the grammar writer includes 'BUILDQ' actions on the arcs of the network (usually on the send arc) that take the register contents and build some kind of structure. Since the details of this structure are under the control of the grammar writer, it can conform to any version of linguistic theory.

The early ATN grammars built phrase-structure trees that corresponded to the deep structures of transformational grammar. For example, the S network would build a tree of the kind shown in Figure 5–38, filling in the contents from the indicated registers.

Other ATN implementations have built case structures, tagmemic structures, dependency structures, stratificational analyses, and a number of variations on register structures. In most cases, there has not been a tight theoretical coupling between the details of the networks and the form of the structure

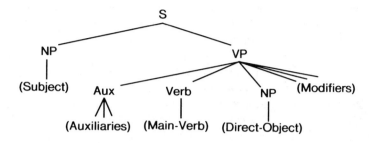

Figure 5–38. Deep structure produced by the original ATN grammars.

produced. There have been a collection of primitive structure-building actions available to the grammar writer, who treated them as a programming language for building whatever seemed most appropriate in each network.

5.7 Implementation of ATN parsers

In order to implement a parser based on ATN grammars, it is necessary to replace the nondeterminism of the parsing schemas defined in Section D.1 with fully defined procedures. Throughout this chapter, we have left aside matters of choice, thinking of networks in a nondeterministic way. The possibility of dealing separately with the underlying structure of the computation (the non-deterministic schema) and the *scheduling strategy* is an important theoretical property of the ATN formalism. Unlike parsers that are tied to a specific processing order (such as the procedural parser of SHRDLU (Winograd, 1972)), an ATN parser can make use of a grammar that was written without a specific processing regime in mind.

As we have mentioned, the way that registers are typically used forces a strong orientation towards left-to-right top-down processing. However, some current descendants of ATN grammar (see Section 6.6) replace registers with *functional structures* that avoid this directional bias, and even with an ordinary ATN grammar there is still a great deal of latitude in how the alternatives are explored. There have been some ATN parsers that work in parallel, others that use backtracking, and others (designed for use in speech understanding systems, as described in Bates, 1978) that do not work left-to-right, but expand phrases out from *islands* that have already been analyzed.

The flexibility of ATN parsing has made ATN grammars an attractive basis for models of human language processing. Experiments have been carried out (such as those described in Wanner and Maratsos, 1978) assuming that a person uses an ATN-like grammar and seeking experimental evidence as to whether the parsing strategy is parallel, serial, or some more complex mixture. The General Syntactic Processor (Kaplan, 1973b) is a computer implementation of a flexible parsing strategy. It uses an active chart scheme (as described in Section 3.6) that has an *agenda* of active edges to expand. Rather than taking a fixed order for trying items on the agenda (as we did in Section 3.6), it allows the programmer to include strategy procedures that take other factors into account in deciding what to expand when. It has been used to test detailed psychological hypotheses about human syntactic processing.

In the rest of this section, we will not discuss general issues of processing strategy. The basic concepts are those described in Chapter 3, and their psycholinguistic implications are beyond the scope of this book. A number of more specific issues are discussed which have importance both for the construction of efficient computer parsers and for the development of plausible theories of comprehension. Section 7.5 gives details of some existing ATN systems that deal with these issues.

Sharing of structures

One of the important sources of inefficiency in a simple implementation of a parallel or backtracking parser is that new structures are built for each of the alternatives even though they have a great deal in common. For example, in the course of parsing a sentence, there may be a choice of two arcs. In order to keep the choices separate, each one must work with a separate copy of the register table, since a register may be modified along one arc in a different way than it would along the other. In a backtracking parser, the contents of the table before the choice was made must be preserved so that they can be restored if the other choice is tried. In a parallel parser, the different alternatives must work with different tables so that an action setting a register in one does not affect the other. However, it will generally be the case that only one or a few registers will differ, while the rest will continue to hold their same contents along the two paths.

Instead of creating a complete copy of the register table each time a choice is made, many implementations use a data structure that enables the common parts to be shared. In a backtracking parser, this can be done by using an *association list* instead of a table. An association list is a sequence of pairs, each consisting of a key and an entry. However, instead of having only one entry per key (as a table does), there can be any number of pairs with the same key. An entry is put in by adding a new pair at the end of the sequence, whether or not there is already a pair with the same key. An entry is found for a key by searching *backwards* from the end of the sequence for the most recent pair with that key.

The register table in a configuration can be replaced with an association list. Each time a choice is made, all that needs to be saved is the current end position of the association list. All actions that take place will affect the list beyond that point only. If it is necessary to backtrack, all that needs to be done is to restore the end position to its former value.

For a parallel parse, it is necessary to use a slightly more complex structure, since new additions need to be made independently along parallel paths. Instead of a linear list, we can use a tree structure, in which each node contains a table. Whenever a choice point is encountered, the current node is given a child for each choice. These child nodes initially have empty tables, and a different one is used in continuing the parse along each branch. Whenever a register is set, the contents are entered in this child node, and will not be seen by the other alternatives. However, when a lookup is done, anything not found in a node will be looked for in its parent, allowing all of the previous settings to be shared.

These are just two of many possible techniques to avoid doing copying when exploring multiple alternatives. They are easy to implement in *list structure languages* like LISP, and have been applied in many systems.

Feature sets

In the version of ATNs given here, a feature register contains a single choice from a dimension. In the case of multiple possibilities (as for the NUMBER of *the fish*), each possible combination will be the result of a different path through the parse. However, in such cases it is possible to improve efficiency by preserving the nondeterminacy in the structure. We can allow a feature register to contain a set of possibilities instead of a single one. Thus the determiner *the,* the noun *fish,* and the NP *the fish* would all have both SINGULAR and PLURAL as their number. The sentences *The fish are jumping* and *The fish isn't fresh* would both make use of a single parsing of the NP, with the subject-verb agreement check picking out the appropriate feature.

This additional mechanism cuts down the number of cases in which multiple alternatives are generated, with one or more being eliminated by later checks. The formalism for setting and using feature registers must be modified slightly in order to allow sets of choices, and the specific conditions and actions in the grammar must be modified accordingly. Many practical ATN parsers have used feature sets.

Charts

As discussed in Section 5.1, it is relatively easy to modify the active chart parsing procedure of Chapter 3 to handle recursive transition networks. In trying to extend the same technique to augmented transition networks, there is a significant problem caused by context-dependence. The reason that the procedure can operate so efficiently with a context-free grammar (or RTN) is that it can avoid doing the same thing more than once. When a constituent has been proposed at a particular place in the input sequence, the work done on that proposal is shared by all rules or arcs that would look for a constituent of that category at that position. The use of registers makes this sharing more difficult. If the arc that parses a constituent has an initialization, then the result can only be shared with other cases where the contents of the relevant registers were identical. As an obvious example, an embedded S that is parsed with an initial register setting for its SUBJECT cannot be used along a different path where the SUBJECT register would be initialized differently.

One way to solve this would be to share work only when there is identity not only of the constituent type and location, but also all of the register contents. Unfortunately, this defeats the whole purpose of the chart, since it will be relatively rare for the register contents to be identical along two paths. A more complex implementation would sort out those register differences that are relevant to the parsing of a particular constituent. This is further complicated by having hold registers that are inherited so that actions in a lower network can change the contents of a higher one. Several approaches have been taken:

Don't use a chart. The simplest solution is obviously not to have a chart at all. Many of the early ATN parsers did not use one.

Use a chart only for 'simple' constituents. Most constituents do not make use of non-local context. For example, an NP that does not make use of something on a hold list when it is entered can be parsed and saved away to be used in other structures. By carefully avoiding those constituents that do use non-local context, the chart can function as a *well-formed substring table*.

Use a chart normally and treat the register contents as filters. A third solution is to treat the ATN as though it were an RTN. Constituents are first parsed without regard to the register contents, and then the conditions and actions are applied to throw out those for which there is no consistent sequence of assignments. In this case, the efficiency gained from using the chart must be traded off against the extra structures that are produced and then rejected. To improve this, the conditions can be factored into two kinds—those that use non-local context and those that do not. Those that do not can be applied normally, while those that do are used as final filters.

Index the chart on non-local context as well. The entries in a chart normally specify a place in a grammar (rule or network) and a place in the sequence being parsed. We can add to this the contents of registers that were initialized, including the hold register, allowing a parsing to be shared if these are the same as well. In principle, this could add an arbitrary amount to the complexity of the chart. In practice, it is rare for two constituents of the same type starting at the same point to differ in initializations, so in fact most of the efficiency of a simple chart is preserved.

As mentioned in Section 5.6, things like conjunction have been handled by additional mechanisms in the parser that go completely outside the normal protocol of following arcs and building nodes corresponding to networks. When this happens in a chart parser, the special routines become very complex in order to preserve the integrity of shared structures while performing actions that violate the norms. Also, in some ATN implementations, it is possible for an action to affect the contents of registers other than those of the node currently being parsed by the network in which the action appears. When this happens, the change will have an impact on any other parsing that shares any of the nodes that are changed.

Compiling

Once a basic parsing strategy has been selected, it is often possible to take advantage of its special properties to increase the speed at which sentences can be parsed. Since ATNs have been the basis for a number of computer systems, there have been many proposals for such efficiency-motivated mechanisms. In computer science there is a broadly applied concept of *compiling* that can be loosely formulated as 'Once you know what is actually used, you can write a procedure that does it more efficiently than one designed to handle everything.' There may be a program that executes a particular ATN grammar very efficiently, which can be produced either by hand or by a general grammar compiler. The details of the compilation process are dependent on the specific implementation of the ATN system, and are not pursued here. However, it is important to recognize that there may be cases in which the use of certain combinations of ATN mechanisms makes it impossible to compile something as efficiently, and that the grammar writer may take this into consideration in developing a grammar.

Arc ordering

In systems that explore alternatives serially, it is necessary to choose some order in which to try the alternatives. In some ATN parsers, this has been taken as an opportunity to increase efficiency by ordering the arcs so that those more likely to lead to a successful parsing will be tried before those that are needed for more rarely occurring structures. Through careful choices of ordering, the grammar writer can 'shape' the direction the parser will take. Since this is combined with some kind of backtracking, it will not prevent the other arcs from being taken eventually if they are needed, but it can increase the speed with which common structures are parsed.

In a more sophisticated version, arcs can be given *weights* that are used to assign a total value to a path. Parsings can be explored in parallel, with the effort always going to the path with the highest value of combined weights. Factors of meaning can also be used in determining the value of a path.

A simpler method that has been used is the *grouping* of arcs into sets such that if any one member of the set succeeds, it is certain that all the others will fail and need not be tried. This can cut the search space without losing generality.

Explicit structure manipulation

In discussing possessives in Section 5.6, we mentioned the possibility of having actions that directly manipulate the underlying data structures of the implementation. This has been commonly done in ATN parsers, since it provides a relatively 'cheap' way of dealing with non-standard structures. In addition to those uses mentioned in the previous section (possessives, conjunction, and the building of result structures), structure manipulation has also been used in techniques for ambiguity reduction.

In a network that includes right-recursive structures, there is the potential for a large degree of ambiguity. As discussed in Section B.3.1, a string of PPs, as in *I saw the man on the hill with a telescope,* can lead to many alternative parsings. In some ATN grammars, such strings have been handled by putting conditions onto the NP-7:$_h$PP$_h$ and S-9:$_e$PP$_e$ arcs that prevent them from being taken under certain conditions, for example when the NP or S they are in is already the rightmost descendant of a PP. Thus a single *canonical structure* such as that of Figure 5–39 will be be produced for a sentence like *I saw the cheese on a plate with a crack.* The actions associated with the send arc on S would then call other programs (including those taking meaning into account) to decide how to distribute the modifiers among the embedded phrases, possibly leading to more than one parsing. This calls for a good deal of explicit modification of the structures built by the parser and must be carefully integrated with the strategy for serial or parallel exploration of alternatives.

Further Reading for Chapter 5

The basic idea of augmenting transition networks was proposed by Thorne, Bratley, and Dewar (1968) and developed further by Bobrow and Fraser (1969). ATN grammars are most widely known as they were formulated by Woods

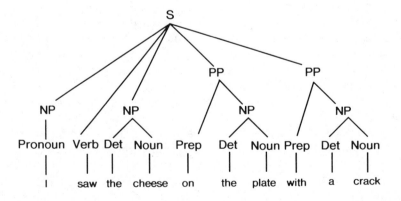

Figure 5–39. Flattened structure for right-recursive modifiers.

(1970, 1973a). The particular form presented in this chapter is closer to later developments by Kaplan (1972, 1973a, 1975), who has used ATN grammars as the basis for psychological models of sentence processing. Kaplan (1975) gives a brief and clear introduction to the psychological concerns. Winograd (1972) discusses the similarities between ATN grammars and procedural grammars. Bates (1978) gives a good overview of the issues that must be considered in building an ATN parser, including an example of a fairly extensive grammar and a section of practical advice on how to go about writing grammars.

Exercises for Chapter 5

Exercises for Section 5.1

5.1 Write a recursive transition network grammar corresponding to the following context-free grammar:

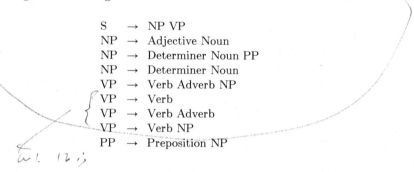

$$
\begin{aligned}
S &\rightarrow NP\ VP \\
NP &\rightarrow Adjective\ Noun \\
NP &\rightarrow Determiner\ Noun\ PP \\
NP &\rightarrow Determiner\ Noun \\
VP &\rightarrow Verb\ Adverb\ NP \\
VP &\rightarrow Verb \\
VP &\rightarrow Verb\ Adverb \\
VP &\rightarrow Verb\ NP \\
PP &\rightarrow Preposition\ NP
\end{aligned}
$$

5.2 Consider the problem of converting back and forth between context-free grammars and recursive transition networks.

a) Show that the RTN formulation never needs more networks than the number of CFG rules.

b) Give an example that shows that there must sometimes be more rules than networks.

c) Describe how an RTN can be produced that has *strong equivalence* with a given CFG.

5.3 Describe in detail the changes that would be needed in the procedures given for the active chart parser in Section 3.6 so that it would use recursive transition nets instead of a context-free grammar.

Exercises for Section 5.2

5.4 Write an ATN grammar that accepts strings of the form $a^n b^n c^n$ for every positive integer n.

5.5 The register structure of Figure 5–7 illustrates the fact that register structures are closer to the *deep structure* as defined in transformational grammar than to the *surface structure*.

a) Draw a surface-structure tree for the given sentence as it might be produced by a context-free grammar that stayed as close as possible to the surface ordering.

b) Draw a deep-structure tree corresponding to the analysis in the figure.

Exercises for Section 5.3

5.6 Follow through the parse of the S network for each of the following sentences, using the ATN grammar given in Figure 5–14 and showing the required dictionary entries. Indicate each point at which registers are set or their contents changed. Do not give the details of parsing the NPs.

a) *The cat was chasing birds by the open window.*

b) *The fenders were wrinkled by the impact.*

c) *That book was given to me by the author.*

5.7 Agreement between the determiner and noun is not entirely guaranteed by the compatibility of their number features. If we allow words like *all, each, some, many,* and *much* to serve as determiners, the network of Figure 5–13 will accept combinations like **much book* as well as *much snow*. To prevent this, we can use a feature dimension of COUNTABILITY for both nouns and determiners, with the possible choices COUNT and MASS. Make the appropriate changes to the lexical category definitions of Figure 5–11 and write some sample dictionary entries for both nouns and determiners using the NUMBER and COUNTABILITY features. Try to ensure that your choices for each word allow all and only the grammatical combinations to be accepted. (Keep in mind usages like *the snows of Kilimanjaro.*)

Exercises for Section 5.4

5.8 As mentioned in the text, the lexical categories and agreement condition of Figure 5–16 do not properly handle the verb *be*, which has more forms than other English verbs. Make the modifications needed to all of the relevant networks and dictionary entries to deal with it properly (i.e., accepting *I am* and *he is* while rejecting **I is*).

5.9 The network of Figure 5–17 does not deal with *copulative* verbs such as *be* that appear in sentences like *They are friendly*. Modify the network (and the necessary new feature choices and dictionary entries) to account for the following data:

> They are friendly.   They seem friendly.   * They catch friendly.
> They are fish.   * They seem fish.   They catch fish.

5.10 Put extra conditions into the network of Figure 5–17 as suggested in the text so that there will never be an attempt to parse an object for a verb that is only INTRANSITIVE or a second object for one that is not BITRANSITIVE. What is the appropriate corresponding check for passives?

5.11 What final role register assignments will the network of Figure 5–18 produce for each S of the following sentences? Describe the changes needed to produce a more appropriate structure from the point of view of meaning.

a) *This book was given me by a cousin.*

b) *They believed Patty to have robbed the bank.*

c) *The bank was believed to have been robbed by Patty.*

Exercises for Section 5.5

5.12 The network of Figure 5–18 will accept all of the following sentences. Indicate the changes needed to the network and dictionary (including new arcs and a feature dimension associated with verbs) to discriminate the good from the bad.

> I wanted to go.   *I forced to go.   I hoped to go.
> I wanted her to go.   I forced her to go.   *I hoped her to go.
> *She was wanted to go.   She was forced to go.   *She was hoped to go.

5.13 The conditions listed for the S-19:ₐVerb_q arc in Figure 5–22 are not quite thorough enough. By checking for NON-AUX verbs, we allow *Is the President signing it?* while forbidding **Signed the President it?* However, the condition also allows the ungrammatical **Did he the laundry yet?* and the question *Have you any tea?,* which is normal in British English but sounds strange to most Americans. Correct the condition for American speakers.

5.14 For each of the following sequences, indicate whether or not it would be accepted as a sentence by the grammar of Figures 5–22, 5–25, and 5–24. If not, indicate which condition in the networks or what feature of the hold mechanism blocks them.

   a) **Who in what did Moses see?*

   b) **Joshua did Moses see?*

   c) **Who did Joshua see Moses?*

   d) **Who did Moses tell to catch?*

5.15 Show the series of register settings in the S networks used in parsing *To whom did he give the tablets?* and *By whom did he want them to be inscribed?*

5.16 For each of the following sequences indicate whether or not they would be accepted as an NP by the grammar of Figures 5–24, 5–28 and 5–30. If not, indicate which condition in the networks or what feature of the hold mechanism blocks them.

   a) *the man the woman you saw saw*

   b) **the man the woman you told to see*

   c) **the chair that the man sitting on coughed*

Exercises for Section 5.6

5.17 Which of the following sentences would be accepted by the grammar as modified in Figure 5–36? What changes need to be made to block the unacceptable ones? Would they be accepted by the solution of Figure 5–37?

   a) **Which man did you see's brother?*

   b) **Which man's did you see brother?*

5.18 Give some arguments that contractions like *don't* and *wouldn't* should be treated as single verbs with a NEGATIVE feature, rather than as a verb followed by an adverb. Consider the placement of adverbs in general, the treatment of negative imperatives like *Don't do that!,* and the unacceptability of sequences like **He will haven't gone.*

5.19 Include the additional case choices, dictionary entries, and conditions to deal properly with the following data and the corresponding sentences for pronouns of other number and person:

They bought my house.   They bought his house.   * They bought mine house.
* They bought my.   They bought his.   They bought mine.

5.20 In the text it was mentioned that the grammar does not handle relative clauses whose first element (a PP or an NP) contains an embedded relative prounoun (as in *a person whose name you don't know*). Within such an element, the held item can be picked up to match the relative pronoun, and when the element is complete, it goes on the hold list to be used to fill a gap later in the clause. This gap may be a PP, rather than an NP, as in *The woman by whom the example was invented*. Show how to extend the grammar to handle this phenomenon, including sentences in which it is mixed with the other kind of hold register use, as in *What did the man the name of whom you forgot want to buy?* You may find it necessary to alter the formal treatment of the hold register, as well as adding new arcs, conditions, and actions.

Exercises for Section 5.7

5.21 Give DL definitions for association lists and trees of tables, as discussed in the section. Include the procedures for entering new items and looking up values.

5.22 Write a procedure for doing top-down left-to-right backtracking parsing with an ATN, making use of association lists.

5.23 Write a procedure for doing top-down left-to-right parallel parsing with an ATN, making use of a tree of tables.

Chapter 6

Feature and Function Grammars

This chapter introduces several grammar formalisms that were developed independently but have a common basis in their use of *feature choices* and *functional roles*. These mechanisms have been integrated most clearly in *systemic grammar*, a theory developed by M.A.K. Halliday and his colleagues, primarily in England. Systemic grammar developed somewhat independently of American generative linguistics and it approaches language structure from a different starting point. It emphasizes the functional organization of language—how it presents speakers with systems of meaningful options as a basis for communication. This chapter begins by presenting the concepts of systemic grammar and then relates them to a number of other formalisms.

Section 6.1 introduces the basic goals of systemic grammar, contrasting them to those of the formalisms presented in the previous chapters. Sections 6.2 and 6.3 introduce the basic mechanisms: choice systems and functional description. Section 6.4 introduces the concept of *realization* that provides the formal basis for integrating the components of a systemic grammar. It describes the use of *realization rules* in a systemic grammar and shows how realization applies to other theories of language as well. Section 6.5 relates systemic ideas to those of *case grammar*, a form of grammatical analysis dealing with the participants in a relation or action described by a verb. Case grammar is quite similar in some ways to systemic grammar and has been introduced into many linguistic frameworks, including ATN grammars and transformational grammars. Finally, Sections 6.6 and 6.7 discuss some new formalisms that have evolved outside of systemic grammar but share much of its orientation to structure and realization and are best understood in the context of this chapter. Section 6.6 deals with *functional* and *lexical-functional* grammars, while Section 6.7 describes *generalized phrase structure* grammars and *definite clause* grammars.

6.1 The goals of systemic grammar

In order to put systemic grammar into the context of this book, it is useful to contrast its approach with the one taken here—language *as a cognitive process.* In the cognitive paradigm, language is viewed as a psychological-computational phenomenon, and the linguist is concerned with discovering the knowledge structure and processes of the individual language user. As pointed out in Chapter 1, this is only one possible approach to language. In studying language evolution, for example, it is necessary to look at processes that have a time-scale and scope far beyond any individual.

The linguists who developed systemic grammar have not taken cognitive processing as their fundamental starting point. Their work grew out of *scale-and-category linguistics,* an approach developed in the early 1960s (e.g., Halliday, 1961), which in turn owed a great deal to still earlier work of Firth (1957). Its roots were in anthropology and sociology, not in mathematics or formal logic. The questions that motivated its development were not those of grammaticality or the acquisition of linguistic competence, but those of language as a social activity: *What are the social functions of language? How does language fulfill these social functions? How does language work?*

The approach to language as doing, not knowing, led to examining the structure of *linguistic behavior potential* as a property of a speech community, not an individual. It makes use of the kind of structural analysis that formed the basis for the structural paradigm, but it emphasizes the importance of context and situation in the analysis of each utterance or text.

Classification and linguistic resources

A linguist studying language in a social setting observes regularities in the patterning of what is said and done. Utterances can be classified in terms of the roles they play in interactions, on the basis of the consequences they have for further action and interaction. As a simple example, utterances might be classified as 'questions' (which call for a relevant verbal response), 'commands' (which call for some action that may or may not be verbal), and 'statements' (which call for no further action on the part of the hearer). At a more subtle level, one might classify the different ways in which a parent tries to achieve desired behavior in a child, as illustrated by Figure 6–1, based on Halliday (1973).

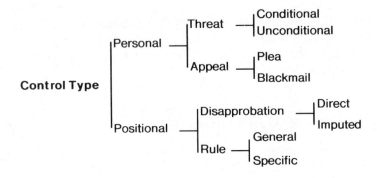

Figure 6–1. Classification of potential meanings in a specific situation.

The utterance *If you do that again, I'll spank you* would be classified as a 'conditional threat;' *Nice boys don't do things like that* involves the use of a 'general rule;' and *I'm trying to get the dishes done* is a 'plea' when said as a means of getting cooperation. It is clear from this example that the categories are social. The difference between a 'threat' and an 'appeal' is not a simple matter of the form of the utterance, but depends in subtle ways on the situation and on the backgrounds and social roles of the participants in the conversation. The sentence *The circus is coming next week* is superficially the statement of a fact, but might well be used as a promise or a threat depending on the context.

If there were no sensible correlation between the form of an utterance and its social meaning, analyses like that of Figure 6–1 might be of interest to the sociologist, but would hardly be of interest to the linguist. Of course, this is not the case. The essence of language is that there does exist a correlation (albeit a complex one) between form and meaning. If utterances are classified according to their intonation patterns (e.g., rising, falling, or complex), there is observed to be a correlation with their classification in terms of social function. In the patterns of words, there will be other obvious correlations. The pattern 'NOUN VERB NOUN' will tend to be a statement (as in *Henry helped Helen*); the pattern 'AUX NOUN VERB NOUN' will be a question (*Did Ruth tell Joe*); and 'VERB NOUN' a command (*Call Debbie*). Of course, things are more complex, but the basic idea of relating form to meaning can be extended.

From this point of view, a language can be seen as providing a collection of *syntactic resources* that the speaker can draw upon in order to successfully achieve a meaning. There are three kinds of immediate resources:

Choice of items. There is a finite vocabulary of individual items (such as phonemes, words, and idiomatic phrases) known to speaker and hearer. Every utterance is built up out of them.

Sequential arrangement. The basic organization of language is sequential. Words are spoken one after another and the arrangement of symbols on a written page mirrors this organization in left-to-right (or right-to-left), top-to-bottom sequences. Nonsequential arrangements of symbols are used for communication (for example, in schematic drawings) but do not correspond to natural language.

Prosody. Structure beyond the choice and sequential arrangement of symbols is provided by the particular medium, such as stress and pitch in spoken language or punctuation and typography in written language.

As discussed in the introduction to Chapter 2, it is possible to construct artificial languages (as in diplomatic code books) in which meanings are correlated to simple sequential patterns of elements. Natural languages have a more complex structure that can be analyzed in terms of three additional dimensions of patterning:

Classification. Much of Chapter 2 is a description of how patterns can be described as sequences of elements chosen from identifiable classes. The most obvious example is the traditional classification of words into categories like 'noun' and 'verb.' Classification can apply to other resources (such as prosodies) as well.

Grouping. The basic idea underlying the grammars of Chapter 3 is that sequences of words can be viewed as having a constituent structure—the sequence can be divided into non-overlapping contiguous groups and the pattern described as a sequence of groups. These groups can in turn be classified and described in terms of their own constituent groups.

Function. The third dimension of organization is the relation of one element (possibly a group) to another in terms of functional roles. In speaking of the 'subject' of a sentence, we are using a functional term, not a classification. The role of functional description in the grammars we have studied so far is relatively small, but it will be developed further in this chapter.

An utterance can be described in terms of the three primary resource dimensions and the way they are structured along the three dimensions of organization. This description is separate from the description of meaning potential illustrated in Figure 6–1. It deals with *form,* not *communicative function.* A systemic linguist is interested in three interrelated kinds of analysis: the description of meaning potentials in situations; the description of utterances (on the basis of form); and the characterization of the correspondence between these two.

Tools for formal description

For each dimension of organization, one can design formalisms that describe the structure both of individual utterances and of the potential resources within the language. Several basic ingredients of such formalisms have already been presented in other chapters and are used in essentially the same form in systemic grammar. Others are more particular to the systemic approach.

Selection of items. In a systemic grammar, there is a *lexicon* of individual vocabulary items, much like those of other theories. These include composite items (like idioms) that are single units at one level of analysis while being made up of several units at another.

Sequence. The basic sequential organization of language must be at the bottom of any analysis. As we will see in Section 6.4, systemic grammar treats rules for describing sequence in quite a different way from ordinary constituent grammars, even though the underlying concept of sequence is the same.

Prosody. The formalisms for describing prosodic features in systemic grammar attempt to deal with high-level structure, rather than reduction to small atomic elements. For example, intonation is described in terms of an overall pattern applied to a tone group (which may include several words and even span across sentences) instead of by the assignment of pitch levels to individual words or syllables. This analysis is not presented in this book, but is discussed in some of the references listed at the end of the chapter.

Classification. The classification of both meaning potential and forms plays a major theoretical role in systemic grammar. As we will see in Section 6.3, a systemic grammar is organized around a collection of *system networks* that make the structure of alternatives explicit. This concept is applied at every level of systemic analysis.

Grouping. The basic notion of immediate constituency is the same in systemic grammar as in the other formalisms, but it is used somewhat differently. First, constituent structure is described in terms of *units* that correspond to meaningful elements (as discussed in Section 6.3) and that are less broken up than those of transformational grammar. The finer details of analysis reflected by constituency in other grammars are described in terms of functional organization in systemic grammar. Second, a systemic analysis of an utterance will include constituent structures in different dimensions. For talking about some properties, a grouping into sentences, phrases, and words is used. For talking about others (such as the information structure), a grouping into *tone groups, feet,* and *syllables* is needed. The following sentences differ only in this second kind of structure and the prosodic features (emphasis and intonation) associated with it:

> //*Joe said/Beth was a re/<u>pub</u>lican,//then she in/<u>sul</u>ted him.//*
> //*Joe said/Beth was a re/<u>pub</u>lican,//∧ then/<u>she</u>//∧ insulted/<u>him</u>. //*

The second sentence includes an extra tone group as indicated by the notation, which indicates tone groups (double slashes) made up of rhythmic feet (single slashes) made up of syllables. Since this book does not deal with the properties of spoken language, this aspect of linguistic organization will not be developed in our presentation.

Function. The concept of function plays a central role in systemic grammar. Like classification, it can be applied to different aspects of description. It is possible to talk about the function of an utterance in a conversation and the way that certain forms (e.g., questions of a particular sort) serve this function. It is also possible to talk about the function of a noun group as the 'subject' of a clause or the function of a phrase as the 'theme' of a sentence. The function of conveying a particular aspect of meaning is correlated with syntactic function, but not identical to it. Section 6.2 describes the formalization of functional organization.

Consequences of the overall goals

It is important to recognize that systemic grammar differs from the other formalisms in more than its particular choice of mechanism and detail. The emphasis on language in a social context has led to a distinctive set of concerns.

For one thing, the principle that all linguistic choices are meaningful leads one to pay attention to aspects of language structure that have been relegated to a peripheral role in most forms of generative grammar. As an example, the following sentences differ in their *thematic structure*:

> *For my birthday my husband embroidered this jacket.*
>
> *My husband embroidered this jacket for my birthday.*
>
> *This jacket was embroidered by my husband for my birthday.*
>
> *This jacket, my husband embroidered for my birthday.*
>
> *This jacket is what my husband embroidered for my birthday.*
>
> *What my husband embroidered for my birthday was this jacket.*
>
> *What my husband did for my birthday was embroider this jacket.*
>
> *It was my husband that embroidered this jacket for my birthday.*
>
> *It was this jacket that my husband embroidered for my birthday.*
>
> *It was for my birthday that my husband embroidered this jacket.*

Although these sentences all describe the same fact, they vary in the organization of the participants. The syntactic devices by which they do so (such as passivization, fronting, clefting, etc.) can be described individually, but in a systemic grammar it is important to analyze the system of alternatives and their role in discourse. To a large extent, the reason these areas have not been studied in generative grammar is that the phenomena are complex and quite difficult to formalize. Discussions about thematic relations tend to be informal and descriptive rather than formulated in precise, testable rules. Systemic grammarians are generally more willing than transformational linguists to deal with non-discrete phenomena—those involving scales of acceptability rather than a yes-or-no distinction of grammaticality. There has been some attempt to deal with such continua or *clines* in generative grammar, for example, the *squishes* mentioned in Section C.3.3. However, these have remained much more peripheral than are the corresponding considerations in systemic grammar and in related approaches such as the *functional sentence perspective* of the Prague School (Mathesius, 1961, Sgall, Hajičová, and Benešová, 1969).

Since systemic grammar is not centered on a concern with formal rules, the general attitude is that it is better to say something less precise about an important aspect of language than to ignore it completely because it does not yield to the available formal tools. It is possible to provide descriptions that are structured (i.e., they include formal representations like system networks, not just descriptive text) but that are not generative in the strong sense of providing rigorous rules. Much of systemic grammar follows this course.

One consequence of accepting imprecise descriptive structure is an increased ease of dealing with multiple dimensions of analysis. In describing a text, one might independently describe its organization as a speech act, its organization as a logical proposition, and the cohesion relationships among its parts, without exploring the detailed interactions between these analyses. The problem of describing the *realization* of simultaneous choices along different dimensions is quite complex, and in the existing research there is an inverse relationship between the degree to which it is a concern and the degree to which independent dimensions like theme and information structure are considered in the analysis.

Finally, a quick glance through the literature on systemic grammar will indicate a broad interest in language functions. There is a relatively high proportion of papers on literature (the syntactic devices that give a text its texture), on register (the differences in syntax that mark different styles of speaking, such as casual conversation and formal lectures), and on coherence (what makes a discourse 'hang together'). Although these phenomena could be studied within a generative grammar framework, the differences of emphasis encourage different kinds of explorations.

Relation to cognitive and generative approaches

Given the difference in motivation for systemic grammar, it seems appropriate to ask why it is relevant to the study of language as a cognitive process and to the design of computer programs that deal with natural language. It should be apparent from the discussion so far that the relationship is both substantial and complex. The fact that ideas from systemic grammar found their way into the ATN grammars of Chapter 5 is one obvious connection. It is more than just an opportune borrowing—the systemic mode of analysis has deep cognitive significance.

In describing the role of classification in systemic grammar, we have carefully been using words like 'classify,' 'alternatives,' and 'describe,' avoiding the term 'choice,' which is more commonly used. This was to emphasize the fact that the classification is being imposed by an observer—by someone who is describing the form and use of utterances. One can talk about the classification of animals by a biologist, but it hardly seems appropriate to talk about a system of 'choices' in the sense of an active choosing. Similarly the categories and features assigned by a systemic grammar are not a hypothesis about a structure that exists in the mind of a language user who makes choices in putting together a sentence or in understanding one that is heard.

There are many philosophical issues involved in the distinction between choices represented within a cognitive system and alternatives as viewed externally, and it is beyond the scope of this book to explore them. The description given here of the details of systemic grammar is based on the standard assumption of cognitive modeling—that the observable organization of language results from corresponding cognitive structures of the speakers of the language. Having taken this stance, we can explore the possibilities for representing choice systems and functional structures in the same style we have studied the representation of grammars, rules, dictionaries, and all the other theoretical constructs of cognitive linguistics. Many of the ideas of systemic grammar can be applied within a cognitive processing approach, and this chapter presents such an adaptation.

In fact, the description of structure in terms of classification, grouping, and function is useful far beyond the discussion of syntax, and is broadly applicable to many kinds of cognitive models. It will appear again in the discussion of cognitive representations of the world the language-user talks about and in the discussions of the meaning and use of words and utterances in the volume on meaning.

Choice systems are related to the basic ideas of *information theory*. One of the fundamental tools of thought and communication is the classification of a potentially infinite set of objects into a small number of distinct categories. Properties can be associated with a category in general and inferred to hold of its members. A category assignment is often a sufficient discrimination for identifying an object in a context.

Functional description is also a basic cognitive tool. Consider the problem of writing a 'grammar for animals'—a formalism that describes what their pieces are and how they fit together. In doing this, biologists look for functional systems, such as the skeletal system, the muscular system, and the circulatory system. Individual structures are then described in the context of these different systems and the roles they play in them. Indeed, anatomy could be studied without any reference to this 'physiological' level of description. An animal can be seen as a complex interweaving of cords, tubes, bones, fibers, etc. But to do so would make the structure seem impossibly complex and arbitrary. The key to understanding the complexity of the structure lies in recognizing its functional organization. The old adage that 'form follows function' can serve as a framework for understanding language.

From a narrower point of view, we will explore the use of systemic ideas in representations of syntax. The grammars of Chapter 5 drew on ideas from systemic theory, and many computer systems are based on them to some degree. A number of the current proposals within generative linguistics have also been influenced by systemic grammar. It would be misleading to imply that there currently exists a comprehensive, well-developed systemic generative grammar that can be 'implemented' in a computer program. However, as we will see in Sections 6.4 and 6.6, there is a possibility that such a grammar might be developed. Hudson (1976) has described his *daughter dependency grammar* (a close descendant of systemic grammar) as 'better at doing the things transformationalists want to do,' and the formalisms described in Section 6.6 are being developed in keeping with the traditional goals of generative linguistics— the precise and concise formal characterization of syntactic intuitions.

In pushing systemic grammar into the cognitive or generative paradigm, we run some risk of distortion. As mentioned above, it was not originally intended as a hypothesis about the structure of mind, but as a descriptive system for use in characterizing texts and utterances. The consumers of systemic grammar have more often been practical language teachers and sociologists than psychologists or computer programmers. The formal mechanisms were designed to be used by human interpreters, so the rules for applying them can call for judgment and interpretation. In moving to a mechanically applicable rule system, the natural tendency is to lose sight of those aspects of language that do not fit. As discussed in Chapter 1, this is the consequence of any choice of paradigm—in focusing on one way of understanding a complex phenomenon like language, we need to let go of others. The rest of this chapter presents a narrowed view of systemic grammar, but one that is nevertheless relevant to the questions posed throughout the book.

6.2 Functions and systems

In order to express the underlying structure of sentences in Chapter 5, there were registers such as SUBJECT, INDIRECT-OBJECT, and DIRECT-OBJECT, whose contents were manipulated by actions on the arcs of the grammar. The choice of registers was based on intuitions about what would be useful in expressing regularities among related sentences and in analyzing meaning. A systemic analysis of a language includes a more systematic examination of how constituents fill functions in syntactic units and of the relationship between functions and features.

In the grammars of Chapter 5, there are two kinds of registers. *Feature registers* provide a classification of the constituent and will be discussed further in Section 6.3. *Role registers* provide a *slot and filler* analysis of the kind discussed in Section 3.1. In such an analysis, each constituent is viewed as instantiating a slot and filler pattern, with a register table associating role names with the children of the node. The registers associated with an NP in the networks of Chapter 5, for example, include HEAD, DETERMINER, DESCRIBERS, and QUALIFIERS. The result of parsing an NP using the network is an assignment of each constituent to one of these functions.

However, in the network for sentences, there are registers intended to capture an underlying analysis that does not correspond to the surface ordering. For example, the SUBJECT register is filled by *Stu* in *The rum was poured by Stu,* by *a dog* in the embedded sentence, *that purrs,* of *I invented a dog that purrs,* and by a dummy NP in agentless passives like *The rum was poured.* In using the register in this way, we are in effect saying that every sentence has something that serves (conceptually) as its subject, even when there is no corresponding constituent.

However, there is a problem with the analysis provided there. Consider the use of *tag questions:*

The duke gave my aunt this teapot, didn't he?

My aunt was given this teapot by the duke, wasn't she? (1)

These two sentences would be given almost identical analyses according to the grammar of Chapter 5. In (1), the SUBJECT register would initially contain *My aunt,* but the operations associated with passive voice would transfer her to the INDIRECT-OBJECT register, putting *the duke* as the SUBJECT. A properly formed tag question must agree not with the contents of the SUBJECT register at the time the tag is parsed, but with its initial contents. Even though *the duke* is the underlying subject, one cannot say:

*My aunt was given this teapot by the duke, wasn't (didn't) he?

In transformational grammar, this is handled by having the transformation responsible for tag questions operate at a different time in the derivation from the one concerned with deep subject-object relationships. But there is another way of looking at the problem. Instead of shifting things in and out of the subject register, it makes sense to think of two different functions (or registers): the *superficial subject,* which agrees in number and person with the verb, matches the tag, etc., and the *underlying subject,* which is concerned with the roles of the participants in the action or situation described by the verb. The superficial subject is filled in just like the SUBJECT register in the networks, but once filled in, it never changes. The underlying subject is filled in either by using the superficial subject (for an active sentence) or by using the object of the by-phrase (for a passive with an agent) or a dummy (if there is none).

Looking at examples like the following, there is yet another distinction.

This teapot, the duke gave my Aunt.

In English (especially spoken English), one can take one of the objects and *prepose* it without otherwise changing the structure of the sentence. Usually this is done with a strong intonational marking on the initial phrase. It is most likely to occur in contrastive texts (e.g., followed by ...*but the other one, she bought herself*). It is clear that the teapot is still the object, not the subject of the underlying action. It is also not the superficial subject, as demonstrated by the fact that tag questions still agree with *the duke*:

> *This teapot, the duke gave my Aunt, didn't he?*
> * *This teapot, the duke gave my Aunt, didn't (wasn't) it?*

This teapot is playing some other function. It is the 'subject' of the sentence, in the sense of 'what is being talked about.' This might be called a *thematic subject*. Sentences that differ only in the *thematization* of one of the participants can have differing interpretations. There is a systematic difference in meaning between pairs like:

> *Everyone in this room knows two languages.* (2)
> *Two languages are known by everyone in this room.* (3)

Example (2) is normally interpreted as implying that each person knows some two languages (possibly different from those known by other people), while (3) implies that some particular two languages are known jointly by everyone. Examples like these prompted the abandonment of the hypothesis that meaning is determined by the deep structure, since passives were seen as having the same deep structure as the corresponding active forms. But although (4) is not a passive, its interpretation is like the passive—in fact, even more strongly.

> *Two languages, everyone in this room knows.* (4)

In most contexts, it would demand an interpretation in which everyone knows the same two languages. The other interpretation could be forced only by a contrastive context, such as *Why are you so impressed that he knows two languages? Two languages, everyone in this room knows. Five or six languages would be impressive!*

In general, the thematic subject is much more likely to be interpreted as a definite referring phrase, rather than as a phrase corresponding to a quantified variable. These issues are discussed further in the volume on meaning. The important thing to note here is that it is useful to have a way of talking about the special function played by the theme.

The systems of the English clause

So far, we have simply been adding new functions into our description of the sentence, recognizing that they can overlap—that the same constituent can fill more than one function. One key observation of systemic grammar (from which it takes its name) is that these functions are not a haphazard mixture, but can be analyzed as belonging to different *systems* that operate simultaneously in determining the structure of a sentence. These systems can be thought of as operating in orthogonal dimensions, each with its own structure.

There are four basic systems in the structure of the English clause. (The term 'clause' is used in a general way in systemic grammar corresponding to S in generative grammar.) Our examples so far have illustrated the *transitivity* system (which includes the underlying subject), the *mood* system (the superficial subject), and the *thematic* system (the thematic subject). The fourth, the *information* system, deals with aspects of sentence organization that have not yet been discussed, interacting primarily with the prosodic features of spoken language.

Every clause can be analyzed by assigning its constituents to functions in each dimension, as illustrated in Figure 6–2, which introduces a number of new functions and shows the division of a clause into components for the four systems:

The mood system. The most obvious dimension of organization of the clause is its overall structuring to form a question, a command, a statement, or an embedded clause of several possible types. This structure depends on the relative positioning of elements, in particular the one called the 'superficial subject' above and the SUBJECT in Figure 6–2. This constituent is involved in person-number agreement, in the formation of tag questions, and in the subject-auxiliary inversion relating a statement like *This gazebo was built by Sir Christopher Wren* to a question like *Was this gazebo built by Sir Christopher Wren?*

The transitivity system. Every sentence involves some process or relationship (specified by the verb) and one or more participants (specified by clauses and noun phrases). In a loose sense, this structure represents the underlying

	• This gazebo	• was built	• by	• Sir Christopher Wren •
Mood	Subject	Predicator	Adjunct	
Transitivity	Goal	Action		Actor
Theme	Theme	Rheme		
Information	Given	New		

Figure 6–2. Systemic-functional analysis of a clause.

propositional content of the sentence—who did what to whom. The basic functions include ACTOR (the one doing the action) and GOAL (the one undergoing it). There is a general correspondence between mood functions and transitivity functions, in which the SUBJECT is the ACTOR and the DIRECT-OBJECT is the GOAL, but this is not the case in all sentences. In passive sentences like that of Figure 6–2, the SUBJECT is the GOAL and the ACTOR is included as part of an ADJUNCT. Transitivity is much more complex than it appears in this simple example, and is discussed at length in Section 6.5.

The thematic system. Much of the complexity of natural language grows out of the fact that in every sentence the speaker can specify much more than the simple 'Who did what to whom.' There is freedom to indicate which part of the information is the THEME and to mark the degree to which that theme is being emphasized. This aspect of sentence structure has been largely ignored in traditional and transformational grammar, and in most computational systems as well. Transformations and register setting are used to eliminate the variation in ordering caused by thematic choices. In a systemic grammar analysis, each sentence begins with a constituent functioning as its THEME, followed by the rest of the clause, called the RHEME. This structuring is largely independent of the transitivity structure and is linked to (but not determined by) the mood structure. In the sentence *This teapot, the duke gave my aunt*, the THEME is neither the SUBJECT nor the ACTOR. This sentence has a *marked theme,* since it has a mood element other than the normal one functioning as THEME.

The information system. In addition to highlighting one element of the sentence as its theme, a speaker imposes a structure indicating what part of the message is intended to be treated as NEW information, and what part as the GIVEN information, which should already be known by the hearer. The information system is the one interacting the most prominently with intonation in spoken language. Although a default information structure is provided by the ordering of constituents, it is often overridden by choices of stress and intonation. The proper unit of analysis for information structure is not the clause or sentence, but the *tone group,* as described in Section 6.1. The normal English intonation pattern for a declarative sentence places a downward pitch shift on the last major constituent. This is the *unmarked* form, and does not give any special information about what is new and what is given. Thus *Steve bought a new car in Denver* can be used in a context where all of the information is new, for example at the beginning of a discussion. By placing the tone shift on another constituent in the sentence, that constituent is marked as the new information. Thus, *Steve bought a car* has *Steve* as the new information and must be used in a context in which it is taken as given that someone bought a car, as in *No, Ed doesn't have a car, Steve bought a car.* This sequence in turn is likely to appear only in a context where a car has been mentioned, for instance in response to *Look at Ed's new car.*

There are grammatical forms that allow different constituents to appear at the end, which is the unmarked place for new information. For example, passivization moves the ACTOR out of its normal place as SUBJECT at the front of the sentence, putting it optionally in a *by* phrase at the end. The sentence *This jacket was embroidered by my husband* allows the identity of the embroiderer to be highlighted as new information and could be said in response to the question *Who embroidered that jacket?* It would be unnatural in response to the question *What did your husband do for your birthday?*, since in this case his identity is part of the given information, and either the jacket or the act of embroidering it should be marked as new.

As with transitivity, theme and information structuring is quite complex. It is discussed further in Section B.1.7.

Properties of functional description

The analysis illustrated in Figure 6–2 is similar to traditional immediate constituent analyses. It describes a syntactic entity (in this case, a sentence) as made up of a sequence of smaller entities, each of which in turn has its own analysis (which is not shown in the figure). However, it differs in several ways:

Multiple dimensions. A functional analysis can include several independent dimensions, each specifying its own roles. In a standard constituent structure analysis, all of the relationships between elements must be inferrable from the constituent tree structure. In a sense, the development of transformational grammar can be seen as a clever device to get out of the straitjacket imposed by this single-structure formalism. By allowing the tree to go through transformations, different relations can be expressed at different times in its history. Instead of having two dimensions of analysis (one dealing with the subject/verb relationships for agreement and the other dealing with the transitivity relationships among participants), a transformational grammar has one way of representing the subject role (by position), but has the 'deep subject' in that position at one point of the derivation and the 'surface subject' at a later point. A functional analysis makes these different dimensions explicit in simultaneous structures.

Functional labeling. In a functional analysis, the elements composing a larger structure are identified by the roles they play instead of by the kinds of elements they are. In a context-free grammar, a rule like 'S → NP VERB NP' identifies three elements, one of which is a verb and the other two of which are noun phrases. A functional description, on the other hand, involves a set of roles like SUBJECT and GOAL, without explicitly indicating what kind of syntactic unit can fill each role.

Less emphasis on order. Functional analyses are generally less tied to the order of constituents. The context-free rule above specifies that the three elements appear in precisely that order, and the roles they play (for example, as a part of a meaning analysis) can be determined only by identifying their place. It has been argued within transformational grammar that the notion 'subject' is precisely equivalent in meaning to 'the NP appearing as the first constituent of an S' at a certain point of the derivation. A functional description of a sentence deals only with the presence of elements like the SUBJECT, leaving for a more delicate level of description the precise rules governing the order in which they appear.

Shared structure. One of the basic mathematical properties of a tree structure is that every node has at most one parent (the root node has none). In most forms of functional analysis, this criterion is not adhered to. If the analysis is multi-dimensional, a single element (e.g., an NP in a sentence) will fill roles in different dimensions (e.g., THEME, SUBJECT, etc.) simultaneously. However, even within a single dimension it is often useful to think of an element as playing roles in two different parts of the structure. For example, in dealing with a sentence like *Walter wants to retire,* the NP *Walter* is the subject both of the main clause (with verb *wants*) and the embedded clause (with verb *retire*). This was done in the register structures of Chapter 5 and, as mentioned there, it is avoided in transformational grammar by moving constituents or by having identical constituents, one of which is deleted. There have been a number of grammar formalisms proposed for use in computational linguistics, such as Hudson's (1976) daughter dependency grammar (mentioned above), Lytle's (1979) *junction grammar,* and McCord's (1980) *slot grammar,* which are based on tree-like structures that allow sharing (a node can be a child of two other nodes). Some of these formalisms are close to systemic grammar in other ways, while others are more like transformational grammar except for this view of structure.

Advantages of functional description

There has been an ongoing debate in theoretical linguistics between those advocating functional descriptions and those favoring immediate constituent descriptions. A number of arguments have been given in favor of functional description:

Stating syntactic rules. Many linguists believe that syntactic regularities are stated more naturally and economically within a functional framework. They argue that grammatical relations such as 'subject of' and 'direct object of' play a central role in the syntax of natural languages, figuring directly in the statement of grammatical rules and universal principles, and serving as primitives in linguistic theory. In stating rules within a constituent framework, a linguist can be forced into imposing additional levels of structure in order to capture functional similarity. It has been suggested that, particularly in languages less dominated by word order than English, grammar formalisms based on roles can give much simpler descriptions than those primarily tied to the order and syntactic category of constituents.

Cross-language generalizations. In comparing the grammars of different languages, there are generalizations about syntactic patterning that seem best stated in functional terms. For example, in many languages there is some kind of phenomenon like the English passive, in which the order of participants can be varied and the variation signaled by syntactic markings. A number of linguists have worked on a formalism called *relational grammar,* which describes syntactic structures at a level of abstraction that makes it possible to compare mechanisms across languages. In relational grammar, there is a *hierarchy* of sentence participants, usually referred to simply by number (1 being the highest). In the English clause, the SUBJECT is 1, the DIRECT-OBJECT is 2, and the INDIRECT-OBJECT is 3. The passive can be described as *promoting* 2 to 1 (DIRECT-OBJECT to SUBJECT), leaving the previous 1 element 'unemployed' (the technical term used is *chômeur,* the French word for 'unemployed'). The chômeur can then find its way into an adjunct phrase or be dropped entirely. It has been postulated that movement rules like this in all languages can be seen in terms of role hierarchies, and obey very general principles like: *A rule that alters the status of an* NP *within its clause must increase its rank.*

Analysis of meaning. One of the most significant motivations for a functional analysis is its relevance to an analysis of meaning. Language is used to communicate, and the details of syntax have evolved to serve this end. The functional assignments illustrated in Figure 6–2 are obviously related to issues of meaning: the transitivity structures can be mapped onto logical representations of the event; the theme structures onto the focus and goals of the speaker; and the information structure onto the relation of the sentence to the context in which it is uttered. It is important to keep in mind that a syntactic functional analysis is not in itself semantic. It provides a syntactic description that is convenient for analyzing meaning but it is nevertheless syntactic, dealing with the form and arrangement of elements, and it is justified on the basis of observable regularities in form. Functional analysis has generally been more readily adopted in research that emphasizes the integration of syntax and meaning (including work in artificial intelligence and sociolinguistics) than in the generative school, with its emphasis on pure questions of syntactic intuition.

Structural function and macro-functions

In descriptions of systemic grammar, the word *function* is used in two compatible but not identical ways. In describing structures, we talk about the functional roles played by different constituents. A clause or an NP can *function* as the SUBJECT or THEME of a clause, a clause can *function* as a MODIFIER in a clause or NP, and so forth. At the same time, we can talk about the *function* of a particular constituent (or a particular choice of features on a constituent) in conveying meaning or in tying together the parts of the discourse. The first notion of function is local and syntactic, describing relationships among structures. The second operates at a broader level, involving meaning and the interaction between participants in a language situation.

Halliday refers to the second sort of functioning as *macro-function*. He distinguishes three major communicative macro-functions in adult language: the *ideational, interpersonal,* and *textual.* Every sentence expresses all of these functions simultaneously.

Ideational. The ideational function is what is traditionally referred to as meaning. In this dimension, an utterance can be thought of as saying something about the world. It expresses propositions about objects, properties, and states. The transitivity structure of a clause is primarily ideational.

Interpersonal. The interpersonal function deals with why the utterance is there—to communicate a fact, request an action, express a reaction or just to indicate to the listener that the speaker is still communicating according to the conventions their society imposes. Much of the syntactic structure of language comes from the need to combine this 'what for' message with the ideational message. The mood structure of a clause is its major way of embodying the interpersonal function.

Textual. The textual function is the additional glue that holds communication together. It is based on the need to indicate to the hearer how the information is connected—what is new and what he or she is expected to already know; what is important and what is secondary; what topic will guide the choice of what to say next. Both the thematic and information structure dimensions of the analysis in Figure 6–2 are concerned with the textual macro-function.

It is possible to express facts about syntactic structure without ever referring to the importance of syntax in communication. However, it is a tenet of systemic grammar that concern with the macro-functions provides a base for deeper understanding of how the structures are put together. Recall the example given earlier of developing a 'grammar' for living things. A simple structural analysis would be based on laying out maps of organs, what they connected to, and what tissue structures appeared in which areas. A functional analysis would involve a study of physiology, viewing the body as an intertwined set of systems (such as the circulatory system and the respiratory system) and describing individual organs and internal structures in terms of the functions they serve in each of these systems. A macro-functional analysis would include an understanding of the functions these systems serve in preserving the individual and the species. The organs and structures can be described in terms of the way they contribute to one or more of the necessary macro-functions (which have been succinctly characterized as 'feeding, fleeing, fighting, and reproduction').

6.3 Choice systems

In the augmented transition network formalism of Chapter 5, each network and lexical category has a set of *feature dimensions* associated with it. Each dimension represents a choice among alternatives such as SINGULAR and PLURAL. Systemic grammar formalizes the notion of *choice* and the organization of features into *systems* of interdependent choices (which we will call *choice systems* to distinguish them from other uses of the word 'system'). Section 6.1 discussed the importance of distinguishing *alternatives* (as seen by an observer) from a process of *choosing* as part of the operation of a cognitive system. However, the term 'choice' is standard in discussions of systemic grammar and we will use it here in spite of its connotation of intentionality.

The simplest examples of choice systems are those provided by *word paradigms,* such as the different forms of a verb (determined by person, number, tense, and aspect) or of a noun (number, gender, and case). The memorization of these paradigms is a central part of language learning. The knowledge used by a speaker of a language must include the set of alternatives and the ways in which some choices depend on others.

A clear example of such choice systems is provided by pronouns. In older forms of English, there were also highly developed paradigms for nouns and verbs, but in modern English, only the pronoun and the verb *be* have retained a wide variety of forms. We can classify the personal pronouns in a multi-dimensional space, with partitions for choices along each dimension and with a pronoun filling each intersection of partitions, as illustrated in Figure 6–3. Possessive determiners (like *my* and *your*) are included even though they are not simple pronouns, since they obviously exhibit the same patterning.

For purposes of drawing, the figure is limited to three dimensions. An additional choice system (that of gender) is indicated for third person pronouns but is not drawn as an independent dimension. The figure does not include the question pronouns (*who, whom, whose, what,...*) or demonstratives (*this, that, these,* and *those*), which would call for additional dimensions as well.

A quick look at such an array reveals two kinds of relations among the dimensions:

Simple dependence. Some choices are relevant only within a particular 'slice' of the space. In Figure 6–3, the dimension of gender is not represented as an orthogonal dimension, but as a sub-classification within the row representing third person singular. English (unlike many languages) does not distinguish gender in the first and second person (*I, you,...*) or in the plural (*they, them,...*). The dimension of gender has as an *entry condition* the choices of THIRD-PERSON and SINGULAR in their respective dimensions.

Multiple appearance. The words included in Figure 6–3 do not fill the boxes neatly. There is not always a unique word for each combination of features, and many words appear in more than one place. This would be even more

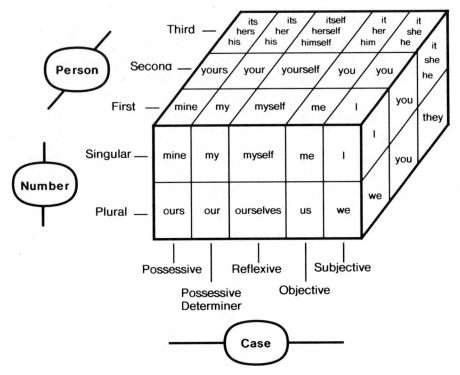

Figure 6–3. Feature dimensions for English personal pronouns.

prevalent if a dimension with entry conditions (such as gender) were included as an independent dimension. Except for third person singular, every word would appear three times—as the masculine, feminine, and neutral forms. In other cases, the redundancy is more complex. For example, *you* is used for both singular and plural. The distinction of number is *neutralized* when second person is chosen, but is operative for both first and third person. There is even more irregular variation in looking at the different cases. *Her* is both OBJECTIVE and POSSESSIVE, while *his* is both POSSESSIVE and POSSESSIVE-DETERMINER. Historical reasons can often be found for these complexities, but in the knowledge of a language user at one moment in history, they must be included as specific irregularities. Rather than say that there is no choice between OBJECTIVE and POSSESSIVE for third person singular feminine pronouns, we will simply observe that a given word (such as *her*) can *realize* more than one combination of choices.

System networks

The interdependencies among dimensions and choices can be represented in formal structures known as *system networks*. They convey an explicit analysis of the alternatives available within a language and are one of the key ways in which systemic grammar differs formally from immediate constituent grammar and its descendants such as transformational grammar.

A systemic analysis of an utterance includes the identification of different functional roles, as described in Section 6.2, along with the classification of each element according to choices represented by the system networks. System networks are written in a simple graphic notation, the basic elements of which are illustrated in Figure 6–4.

A single *choice system* is represented by a set of feature names aligned in a column to the right of a vertical bar, as in Figure 6–4A. There are two complementary ways of talking about choice systems—as sets of mutually exclusive feature labels, or as classifications for the objects to which those labels can be applied. Saying that an object has the feature A is equivalent to saying that the object is in the class A. We will use both ways of referring to objects and their features, since there are different contexts in which one or the other is clearer. A choice system describes an exhaustive partitioning. Every object to which it applies can be assigned to one and only one of the subcategories— i.e., it possesses exactly one of the features. When desired (for purposes of exposition), the entire choice system can be given a name, which is written above a horizontal line extending to the left of the vertical bar. In Figure 6–4A, the system named **X** has four mutually exclusive choices, A, B, C, and D.

The simplest way in which choice systems are related is by a hierarchical dependency, like the 'Phylum > Family > Genus > Species' hierarchy of biological classification. A particular feature in one choice system is a necessary condition for the applicability of another choice system. In classifying animals,

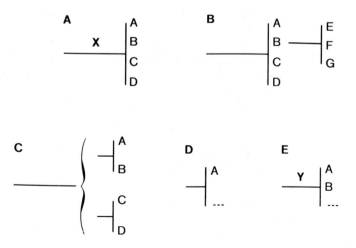

Figure 6–4. Notations for system networks.

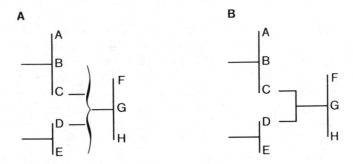

Figure 6–5. Notations for complex entry conditions.

the choice between CAT and DOG is dependent on the presence of the feature MAMMAL. Each choice system is said to have an *entry condition* determining whether it is applicable to a given object, and the dependence is represented by connecting the necessary feature to the dependent system, as in 6–4B. The choice among E, F, and G is applicable only to objects having the feature B.

Often there are two orthogonal sets of choices to be made (e.g., a choice of species and a choice between MALE and FEMALE), both depending on the same entry condition. This is represented with a bracket, as in 6–4C. An object satisfying the entry conditions for this network must have one of the four feature combinations {A C}, {A D}, {B C}, or {B D}.

Finally, the choice system in Figure 6–4D illustrates a convention that can be used for indicating an *unmarked* alternative. In a choice system with two alternatives, it is often more natural to classify objects as A or –A, rather than giving a distinct name to the second alternative. In such a system, the positive choice is *marked*—it will generally be the choice having special properties— while the *unmarked* choice (indicated in the diagram by a sequence of dashes) is the default. Binary choices are the only kind used in the feature systems of transformational grammar, as described in Section 4.4 and discussed further in Section C.3.2. A system with several alternatives can also have an unmarked choice, as illustrated in Figure 6–4E. A constituent classified by that diagram would have one of the features A or B, or be of 'unmarked Y.'

In a simple hierarchical categorization system, the notations of Figure 6–4 would be sufficient. However, additional complications such as neutralization arise, as discussed above. There are cases where the entry condition for a particular choice system involves the simultaneous selection of particular features in two dimensions, and there can be a choice system whose entry condition is satisfied by either of two feature assignments. The same basic connectors— vertical bars and brackets—are used facing to the left as illustrated in Figure 6–5. A bar is an 'or,' indicating that at least one of the features is necessary, while a bracket is an 'and,' indicating that all of them are. In 6–5A, the choice among F, G, and H is applicable if *both* C and D are selected, while in 6–5B, it is applicable if *either* C or D is selected.

Figure 6–6 is a system network for English pronouns, including the choices displayed in Figure 6–3 and also including question and demonstrative pronouns. The words *this, that, these,* and *those* are called *demonstrative* when used as pronouns (as in *I suspected that,* and *Those will be fine*) rather than as determiners (as in *that grape* and *those objections*). They are classified as NEAR (*this, these*) or FAR (*that, those*). The question pronouns (*who, whom, whose, what,...*) distinguish between ANIMATE and –ANIMATE. Some examples of pronouns and their corresponding features are:

I	Personal Singular First Subjective
us	Personal Plural First Objective
she	Personal Singular Third Feminine Subjective
her	Personal Singular Third Feminine Objective, *and*
	Personal Singular Third Feminine Possessive
this	Demonstrative Near Singular
those	Demonstrative Far Plural
whom	Question Animate Objective
what	Question –Animate

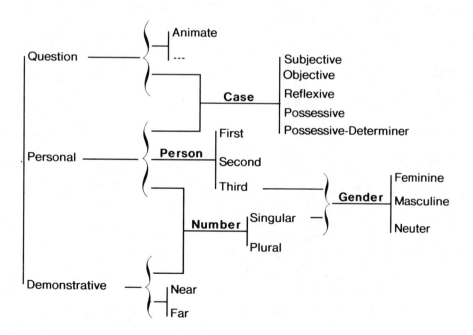

Figure 6–6. System network for English pronouns.

The system network precisely specifies the interdependencies among the choice systems. Personal pronouns are selected along all three basic dimensions while, for example, the choices of case and person are not applicable to demonstrative pronouns. There is no DEMONSTRATIVE POSSESSIVE-DETERMINER (which might look like *those's or *this's). As discussed above, a single pronoun can be used for several different combinations of features. This does not mean that the features are not distinct, but that there can be ambiguities, just as a word like *bank* can have multiple meanings.

Choice systems for composite constituents

So far in this chapter, two rather different kinds of analysis have been introduced. For composite syntactic categories (like the clause), there is an analysis in terms of roles and constituents, while for lexical classes (like pronoun), there are system networks describing interrelated choice systems.

The unifying formal principle of systemic grammar is that classification by system networks applies to syntactic categories of all kinds, and is connected to the functional analysis and constituent structure by *realization* relationships. The concept of realization is discussed further in Section 6.4. First we will look at system networks for composite categories—in particular, the clause.

Figure 6–7 presents a simplified version of the mood choices available in the English clause. The following examples illustrate different choices. In each example, the features are those of the clause in brackets.

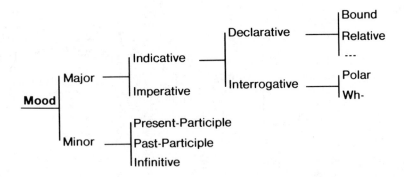

Figure 6–7. A system network for Mood in the English clause.

[The cat is on the mat.]	Major Indicative Declarative
He didn't see the cat [that chased the rat.]	Major Indicative Declarative Relative
It only hurts [when I laugh.]	Major Indicative Declarative Bound
[Has anybody seen my gull?]	Major Indicative Interrogative Polar
[When will they ever learn?]	Major Indicative Interrogative Wh-
[Don't be ridiculous.]	Major Imperative
You'll enjoy [having more free time.]	Minor Present-Participle
He had a face [weathered by the years.]	Minor Past-Participle
The hard part is [to do it without smiling.]	Minor Infinitive

The obvious question to be asked about such a network is *What are the criteria for making the classification?* There are different dimensions along which clauses could be discriminated and many ways of dividing each dimension into separate categories. In designing a system network like that of Figure 6–7, one is following (either consciously or unconsciously) some organizational principles. There are several potential answers, each having some degree of validity.

At first examination, the choice systems of Figure 6–7 seem closely related to the meanings of the clauses they apply to, and in particular to the *interpersonal function.* Categories like IMPERATIVE, DECLARATIVE, and INTERROGATIVE are named in accordance with the general classification of utterances into commands, statements, and questions. But this is only an approximate correspondence. The syntactic form of an utterance is not correlated in a one-to-one way with its use as a *speech act.* The sentence *You're going with him?* if said with a rising intonation pattern, is a question, even though its form is declarative. The sentence *What was I gonna do?* is used most often not as a question (as its form would indicate), but as a *rhetorical question*—a statement conveying my feeling that I had no alternative to the action I chose.

The system networks described here are syntactic, not semantic. *What was I gonna do?* is classified an interrogative form, and that classification is used in discussing its function in conversation. Even though many of the feature names have strong semantic connotations (and high degrees of correlation with categories of meaning and use), they are based on structure rather than meaning. INTERROGATIVE is associated with the structural property of having the first auxiliary verb preceding the subject, as in *Are you coming?* The features assigned in syntactic feature networks are classifications based on the *form* of the constituent, just as the taxonomy of plants and animals assigns them to classes purely on the basis of their form.

Unfortunately, there are problems with this criterion. In the classification of pronouns at the beginning of the section, form is not the determining factor. The assignment of a common feature of FIRST PERSON to *I, we, us, me,* etc., is clearly not the result of similarity in the forms of the words. It has much more to do with meaning. Considering a case feature like OBJECTIVE, there isn't even a clear uniformity of meaning. In the sentences *I hope he will win* and *I want him to win,* the choice between *him* and *he* depends on the specific verbs and does not seem related to any difference in meaning. However, in all those places where *he* would be chosen, so would *she, they* and *we,* while in place of *him* there would be *her, them,* and *us.* The feature OBJECTIVE can be thought of as grouping together those words that can *function* in the same places. On the other hand, the inclusion of possessive determiners like *my* and *his* in the classification of pronouns is not based on the fact that they function as pronouns, but is because they have clearly related patterns of variation.

There has been a certain amount of confusion in discussions of systemic grammar because of the different possible criteria for assigning features. If asked to justify a particular analysis, a linguist may give reasons that lie along quite different lines from those offered in favor of a competing analysis. System networks can be thought of as a purely formal mechanism to be used in different ways at different times.

In fact, this situation is not peculiar to systemic grammar. The very basis for language lies in the ability to use a single word such as *chair* to stand for many different objects. These categories have the same kind of multiple motivation as the ones discussed above. Something is assigned to the category *chair,* possibly because of its form, and possibly because of its function. One can talk of a tiny chair (that is too small to sit in), or of a beanbag chair (which looks nothing like the typical chair). Ordinarily this raises no problems, since the context in which the word is being used makes it clear which is relevant.

In this chapter and in Appendix B, we have followed (with a few minor modifications) the classifications developed by Halliday. There is no systematic attempt in this book to justify them on theoretical grounds.

Delicacy of description

As with any classification system, a system network for syntactic objects can go to varying levels of detail. In biology, an organism that is assigned a species feature is more precisely described than one assigned only to a family or genus. The more precise the classification, the more information is available about the object. In systemic grammar, this scale of precision is called *delicacy,* and feature descriptions can be assigned to sentences at varying degrees of delicacy, depending on the purpose.

It is worth noting that the idea of delicacy represents an orientation in contrast to that of the generative paradigm. It is not well-suited to looking at grammaticality as a precise notion analogous to mathematical deduction. A mathematical formula cannot be true to some level of delicacy—either it is true or false based on the set of axioms and rules of deduction. Delicacy is much more suited to an approach in which the emphasis is on how syntactic choices are used to communicate meaning. It may well be that for analyzing some particular aspect of meaning, a rough classification gives all of the necessary information, and further precise specification of the syntactic detail is unnecessary.

The units of language function

In order for a classification system to be integrated with a constituent analysis, there must be an analysis of each composite object (e.g., an utterance) in terms of its constituent *units,* each of which can in turn be classified. In a simple context-free grammar, the units correspond to the nodes of the parse tree—if there is a rule 'X → A B C' then there will be a unit of class X, made up of three smaller units, of classes A, B, and C. In going from a rule-based formalism to a network-based formalism in Chapter 5, structures were grouped into networks. For example, instead of having rules like NP2 → ADJECTIVE NP2, which creates a new NP2 unit for every additional adjective, there is a loop within the network for NP, adding successive adjectives to a sequence held in a register. Similarly, even though most context-free and transformational grammars of English contain the rule 'S → NP VP,' the grammar of Chapter 5 does not include a VP network, choosing instead to include the details of VP structure in the S network.

In a systemic grammar, there is an explicit identification of the *functionally relevant units* of a language. Rather than having 'nodes' and 'words' (terminal and nonterminal symbols) as the only structures, the linguist analyzes the vocabulary of basic structures for the particular language.

English has been described in terms of five levels of structure (or *ranks*). From lowest to highest, they are: morpheme, word, group, clause, and sentence.

Morpheme. The basic syntactic units of a language are the *morphemes* that make up individual words. In our discussion of systemic grammar (as with our earlier grammars) we will not emphasize this level, beginning the analysis at the word level. Morphemic structure is discussed in Section B.4.5.

Word. Chapter 2 gave reasons for wanting a basic level at which a sentence is analyzed as a sequence of words and discussed some of the problems in doing the necessary analysis. In context-free and transformational grammars, it is assumed that the syntactic component deals with sequences of words, each having a dictionary entry classifying it in terms of lexical categories. Although languages differ in detail, every language seems to have some level that corresponds roughly to our intuitive notion of words, and the basic idea of word categorization can be applied.

Group. The NP and PP networks of Chapter 5 described the structure of two kinds of *groups,* and to these we add in Appendix B an AP (adjunct phrase), which includes structures such as *as big as...* and *greener than....* Typically, groups have a single element that serves as their *head* (as indicated by the names used for groups) and a rather simple constituent structure.

Clause and sentence. The *clause* is the major unit of English, corresponding to the category S in transformational grammar and ATN grammars. A sentence can consist of a single clause or a sequence of clauses. In most discussions of generative grammar, the word 'sentence' (or the symbol S) is used for both traditional 'complete' sentences and for embedded sentences. In systemic grammar, the term 'clause' is used instead, since there is less tendency to confuse it with the notion of sentence as a function in discourse (the one that grammar teachers refer to as 'expressing a complete idea'). The clause shows a great deal of variety and complexity in its structure, and the greatest part of work in systemic grammar is at the clause level. Much of Appendix B is devoted to describing its properties.

The ranks are not purely hierarchical. It will not always be the case that a clause is made up of groups, which are in turn made up of words. Clauses can be parts of groups, groups parts of other groups, words directly part of clauses, and so on. The point of distinguishing the units is not to impose a rigid layered structure on every sentence, but to provide a way of talking about the similarities and differences among the basic units of which structures are built. The term *rank shift* is used to indicate the use of a unit as part of a 'lower level' unit. It does not represent some action of 'shifting,' but simply makes explicit note of the fact that the rank of a unit does not immediately determine the rank of the units in which it can take part.

The register structures produced by the ATN grammar of Chapter 5 were organized in terms of units close to those of systemic grammar. For example, in Figure 5–7 there is a single clause containing a number of words and groups, where the groups in turn contain words and other groups.

There are a number of issues in deciding just what constitutes a unit, and often the considerations of syntactic detail reinforce intuitions about meaning. In general, units of a single type will appear in a particular set of roles or functions (like those used as the distributional criteria of structural linguistics) and will also have a kind of semantic coherence in presenting a unified description or proposition. Typically, an NP describes an object or set of objects, a clause describes a single event or relationship, and so on. In an integrated system for language understanding, the organization of the meaning analysis process is strongly influenced by the units of the language. Typically, the processes for analyzing the meanings of all NPs will be grouped in a single program, those for analyzing the meaning of words in another, of clauses in another, and so on.

In addition, although there are a variety of possible structures for a single kind of unit, they will have much more in common with each other than with the structures of different kinds. A single network for S can capture many of the properties that are true in common for the different forms of clauses, but could not easily include as well the structure of an NP, even though they have some features in common.

6.4 Realization

The description of systemic grammar so far in this chapter has shown what various aspects of a systemic analysis of a sentence would look like, but has not described how they are integrated into a coherent whole. There are feature classifications associated with constituents at all ranks and functional descriptions (along multiple dimensions) associated with groups and clauses. Clearly, these are not independent—the features of one unit will constrain the possible functional roles it can play, as well as the functions that need to be filled within it. The interaction between the feature and function analyses and between units of different ranks can be formalized in terms of a relationship of *realization*. This section describes the systemic approach to realization, first providing some background by reviewing the basic idea of *stratification*.

Stratification

Throughout this book, we have generally assumed the model of Section 1.3, in which linguistic structure is described in terms of distinct components, such as those labeled 'phonological,' 'syntactic,' and 'semantic.' There are two kinds of rules: those that operate within a single component (like the base rules and transformations of transformational grammar), and those relating structures in one component to those in another (like the *projection rules* relating syntax and semantics).

In most work on generative grammar, the rules within each component have received most of the attention and the rules relating components have been left somewhat ill-specified. As pointed out in Appendix C, there is now a trend within transformational grammar towards considering more actively the rules relating syntax and semantics, simplifying the syntax and putting a larger share of the burden of characterizing what is a sentence onto the semantics. However, there have been other forms of grammar in which the different components and the rules relating them have been the central focus. The most general characterization comes from *stratificational grammar*. Stratificational grammar was developed by Lamb (1966) at approximately the same time as transformational grammar and systemic grammar. It is a different attempt to account for the 'deep structure' relationships that were not expressible in the immediate constituent framework generally accepted at the time.

Figure 6-8 illustrates the stratificational model. There are four *strata* (corresponding to what we have called components). The lexemic and morphemic strata together make up what is usually considered syntax. Within each stratum, there are basic elements (the '*-emes*') and *tactic patterns* specifying the well-formed combinations of the elements. Between each pair of adjacent strata, there are *realization relationships* prescribing how patterns on one stratum correlate with patterns of the other. The relationships within a stratum include those of constituency (one structure having others as parts), but those across

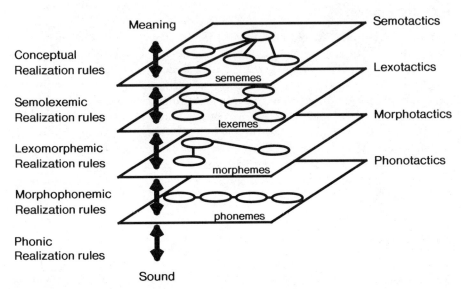

Figure 6–8. The stratificational model.

strata do not. A morpheme is not made up of phonemes. Rather, it is made up of smaller elements on the morphological stratum (called *morphons*) that are *realized* by phonemes. This realization need not be a direct one-one mapping. Lockwood (1972) characterizes eight kinds of relationships that can apply at each level of realization, as illustrated in Figure 6–9.

In these examples we have used *lexomorphemic* relationships. Similar examples can be found for each adjacent pair of strata. It is important to note that the elements in the two columns are of different kinds, even when they are closely correlated. To indicate this, we enclose morphemes in slashes. The lexeme GO is not the morpheme /GO/, but is realized by that morpheme in some contexts. The different kinds of realizations include the *simple* relationship, in which each item on one stratum corresponds directly to an element on the other. In addition, there are cases in which a single element on one stratum corresponds to different alternatives on the other (*diversification* and *neutralization*); those where it corresponds to a sequence of elements (*composite, portmanteau*); those where there is no corresponding element (*zero, empty*); and finally, a case in which the elements are in a one-to-one correspondence, but with a change of ordering (*anatactic*). This last type is more common as a morphophonemic relationship and is not illustrated in the figure.

By having independent sets of tactic rules in different strata, stratificational grammar makes explicit the underlying relationships that are not visible in the final surface form. By devising a uniform way of characterizing the tactics and realization rules, the syntactic formalism can encompass everything from

Lexical	↔	Morphological

Simple

$$go \leftrightarrow /go/$$

Diversification

$$good \leftrightarrow /good/ \ (in\ isolation),\ /bet/\ (in\ context\ \text{-}er)$$

Neutralization

$$bank_1\textit{(river)},\ bank_2\textit{(money)} \leftrightarrow /bank/$$

Composite

$$die \leftrightarrow /pass/ + /away/$$

Portmanteau

$$go + past \leftrightarrow /went/$$

Zero

$$sheep + plural \leftrightarrow /sheep/$$

Empty

$$I + not + know \leftrightarrow /I/ + /do/ + /not/ + /know/$$

Anatactic *see text*

Figure 6–9. Realization relationships between two adjacent strata.

semantics to phonology with a single notation and formal mechanism. The detailed formalism developed by Lamb and others was based on the metaphor of signals propagating through electronic logic networks made up of elements corresponding to the logical connectives *and, or,* and *not.* Not only was the same notation used at all strata, but it was also used for expressing both *syntagmatic* (constituency) and *paradigmatic* (choice) relationships. The resulting formalism was not easily understood or used, and the detailed form of stratificational grammar has not had a significant impact on linguistics. However, the general concept of independent strata of analysis linked by realization relationships is broadly applicable.

Realization in systemic grammar

Systemic grammar is also based on an analyis in terms of distinct strata (although in this chapter, as in most of the book, we have looked almost exclusively at the syntactic stratum), but within a single stratum there are three different kinds of analysis: *functional role assignment, feature assignment,* and *constituent structure.* Figure 6–10 illustrates these for the sentence *Has the elephant been delivered by Macy's?*

Most of the analysis in Figure 6–10 has already been discussed. We have not given explicit choice networks for features other than mood—the choices of transitivity will be described in Section 6.5 and the choices for the other

Constituent Structure

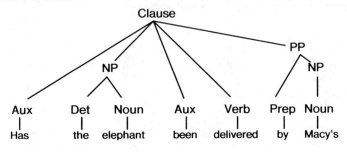

Functional Structure

Theme: *has*; Rheme: *the elephant been delivered by Macy's*
Actor: *Macy's*; Action: *deliver*; Goal: *the elephant*
Subject: *the elephant*; Auxiliaries: *has been*; Predicator: *delivered*;
    Adjunct: *by Macy's*

Feature Structure

Mood: Major Indicative Interrogative Polar
Voice: Passive Explicit-Agent
Transitivity: Action
Theme: Polarity-Theme
Information: Unmarked

Figure 6–10.   Three analyses of a sentence.

three are simple: VOICE (with choices ACTIVE and PASSIVE) is as described
in writing an ATN grammar; a sentence with POLARITY-THEME is one whose
polarity (whether the answer is 'Yes' or 'No') is the thematic element; and the
UNMARKED information choice indicates that no elements are marked as given
or new—the intonation pattern has its stress on the last major element of the
clause.

In a systemic grammar, as depicted in Figure 6–11, the idea of realization
is applied both between strata and in a 'horizontal' dimension, not crossing
the strata.   Each kind of analysis has its own tactic rules, and the three
separate analyses within a stratum are linked by *realization rules*. The tactic
rules of the constituency component are the ordinary phrase structure rules of
immediate constituent grammar. The tactics of the feature component are the
choice systems and dependencies among features specified by the networks of
Section 6.3. The tactics of the functional component deal with the independent
functional dimensions and the assignment of elements to functional roles in each
of them.

Within this general framework there are a large number of possible kinds of rules. There are three strata, each with three components. There can be tactic rules within a component of a single stratum, realization rules between components in a stratum, and realization rules from a component of one stratum to a component of another. If we attempted to describe a language using all possible kinds of rules, the result would be bewilderingly complex.

In practice, only a subset of the possible interconnections are used. For example, relations between one stratum and another may be expressed only between the constituent components of the two strata, or a stratum may be specified without using one component at all. In fact, the framework is general enough that many grammatical formalisms that were not developed in the stratificational or systemic approach can be described in its terms.

Generative systemic grammar

As mentioned in the introduction to this chapter, systemic grammar has not been developed with a primary emphasis on formal generative rules. It was

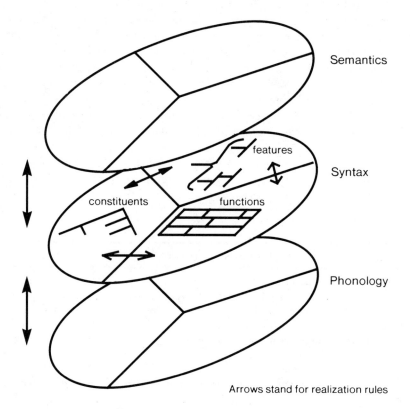

Figure 6–11. Realization in systemic grammar.

intended to provide a means of describing utterances that would elucidate the relationship between their form and their function—the way they could be used in situations. It did not have the generative emphasis on precision and instead was concerned with making it possible to talk systematically about issues like style, register, and the use of language in a social setting. However, the concepts of function and feature analysis that we have been describing can be made precise and formal, and a number of linguists have pursued the possibility of devising a grammar that satisfies the demands of generativity while also capturing the kinds of generalizations and insights that motivated the systemic approach.

The structure of choice networks can easily be formalized using the mechanisms of Boolean logic. The assignment of functional rules to constituents can be treated in a manner analogous to the use of role registers in our ATN grammars of Chapter 5. The difficult part is the formalization of the realization rules.

The basic organization is provided by associating a set of realization rules with each feature choice. These rules specify properties that must hold for any constituent having that feature. Different versions of systemic grammar differ in the exact form of these rules, but in general there are five kinds. Two kinds of rule associate features of a constituent with the functions it contains: an *inclusion* rule specifies that a particular function must be present, while a *conflation* rule specifies that two distinct functions will be filled by the same constituent. *Categorization* and *agreement* rules deal with the features of the children of the constituent to which they are applied. Categorization rules specify that the constituent filling a particular function must have a particular feature, while agreement rules specify that the constituents filling two distinct functions must agree in some choice system. Finally, *ordering* rules specify order relations that must hold among the constituents filling particular functions. Unlike most generative grammars, systemic grammar makes constituent ordering a fairly peripheral consideration. Most of the content of the grammar

Stage in the generation of a constituent	Rules used
1. Choose all of the features for the constituent	Choice network
2. Add all of the components required by these features	Inclusion
3. Combine components conflated by the features	Conflation
4. Assign features to each component	Categorization
5. Fill in the realization of each component	*Recursive generation*
6. Choose an ordering	Ordering
7. Check the agreement conditions	Agreement

Figure 6–12. Generation with a systemic grammar.

Abbreviations for rules:

+X	Inclusion of function X
X=Y	Conflation of functions X and Y
X/A	Classification of function X with feature A
X,Y//S	Agreement of functions X and Y for choice system S
X>Y	Ordering of function X before function Y
+X=Y	combines +X and X=Y
+X/A	combines +X and X/A
+X>Y	combines +X and X>Y

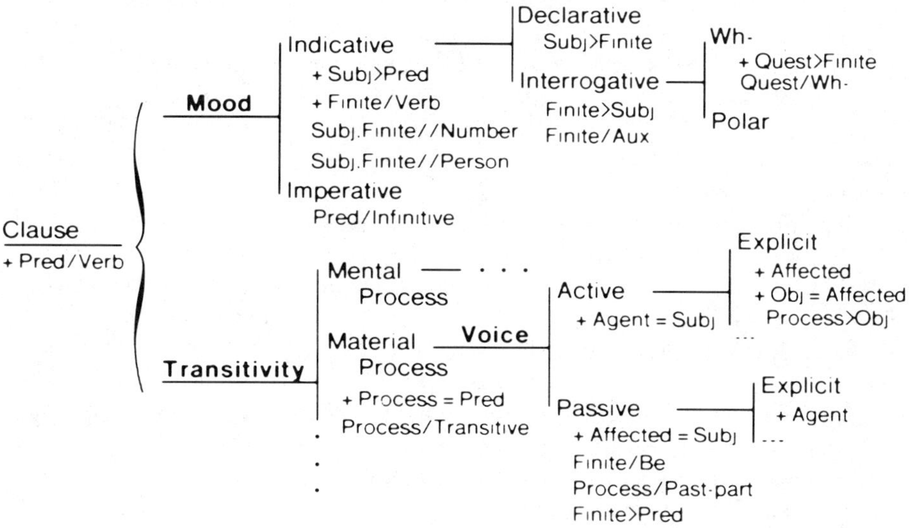

Figure 6-13. System networks with realization rules.

is in the interaction between features and functions, and ordering is a kind of afterthought.

A procedure for generating a constituent can operate in stages, as illustrated in Figure 6–12. In the fifth step, each of its component constituents is in turn either generated or taken from a lexicon (dictionary) of items, each with a set of features assigned to it. It is possible to design generation procedures that make use of realization rules of the same basic kinds but do not operate in this kind of lock-step, but the complexities of interactions between rules make it harder to understand their functioning. We will not give formal definitions for the different kinds of rules and their operation, but will illustrate them with the simplified clause network of Figure 6–13, using the notation indicated in the figure.

The rule associated with the entry condition (CLAUSE) specifies that there must be a constituent filling the role of PREDICATOR, and that it must be classified as a VERB. This will apply to every clause. The conditions associated with the MOOD choices are more complex. An INDICATIVE clause must a have a SUBJECT which precedes the PREDICATOR. It must have a FINITE element, which is a VERB (this will be the verb or auxiliary bearing the tense and agreement). The SUBJECT and FINITE must agree in person and number. Note that the order of FINITE and SUBJECT is not specified by these rules, since it will differ for different kinds of INDICATIVE. An IMPERATIVE clause has no SUBJECT or FINITE element, and its PREDICATOR is an infinitive.

The additional rules for distinguishing DECLARATIVE from INTERROG-ATIVE fix the order of SUBJECT and FINITE, producing *He will succeed* (DE-CLARATIVE) and *Will he succeed?* (INTERROGATIVE). They also specify that the FINITE element of an INTERROGATIVE must be an AUXILAIARY. WH- questions have a QUESTION element preceding the FINITE, as in *When will he succeed?*

The presence of objects is determined by the choices for TRANSITIVITY. The figure shows only the choices for a MATERIAL-PROCESS clause (see Section B.1.6 for a definition). For this kind of clause, there is a PROCESS role which is filled by the same element as the PREDICATOR, which must be TRANSITIVE. If the clause is ACTIVE, then the SUBJECT is its AGENT. If it is PASSIVE, then the SUBJECT is the AFFECTED and the AGENT is either unspecified or is included in a PP with *by* (through rules not shown here). The additional rules on PASSIVE deal with the structure of the verb sequence.

Figures 6–14 and 6–15 illustrate the generation of sentences using the rules of Figure 6–13. In the example of Figure 6–14, we have taken decisions at each point that will end up being successful. A set of features is chosen for the clause, according to the system networks, and the rules are applied in the order given in Figure 6–12. First a set of functions is included, then conflated (functions realized by the same constituent are adjoined with a period). The classification rules add features (in parentheses) to the constituents, but do not specify all of their features. The constituents are then filled, either by finding lexical items in the dictionary or by generating constituents using the generation process with the appropriate network for the constituent. The features that were added by the classification rules provide the initial features for the generation. The generated item is indicated in italics and the features generated for it (or found in the dictionary) appear below it. Finally, an ordering is chosen and the ordering and agreement rules are checked.

In filling in the constituents, many independent decisions affect the satis-faction of agreement rules. In Figure 6–15, features are chosen that generate a sentence with different structures from those of Figure 6–14. For illustration, we have made incompatible decisions in choosing the NUMBER features of the SUBJECT and FINITE, leading to failure of an agreement rule.

Features chosen:
Clause Indicative Declarative Material-Process Passive –Explicit

Realization Rules:

Feature	Rules	Result (Constituents)
Inclusion		
Clause	+Pred	
Indicative	+Subj, +Finite	
Material-Process	+Process	
Passive	+Affected	Pred Subj Finite Process Affected
Conflation		
Material-Process	Process=Pred	
Passive	Affected=Subj	Pred.Process Subj.Affected Finite
Classification		
Clause	Pred/Verb	
Indicative	Finite/Verb	Pred.Process
Material-Process	Process/Transitive	(Verb Past-Part Transitive)
Passive	Process/Past-Part	Subj.Affected ()
	Finite/Be	Finite (Verb Be)

Filling the constituents		
	Dictionary	Pred.Process — *generated*
		(Verb Past-Part Transitive)
	Network for NP	Subj.Affected — *a sentence*
		(NP Singular Indefinite Third-Person)
	Dictionary	Finite — *was*
		(Verb Be Singular Past Third-Person)

Ordering		
Indicative	Subj>Pred	
Declarative	Subj>Finite	
Passive	Finite>Pred	*a sentence* > *was* > *generated*
Agreement		
Indicative	Subj,Finite//Person	
	Subj,Finite//Number	**OK – Successful generation!**

Figure 6–14. Generation of a sentence using a systemic grammar.

It is quite easy to find ways in which the grammar of Figure 6–13 is inadequate. It generates non-sentences and fails to generate many grammatical

Features chosen:
Clause Indicative Interrogative Wh- Material-Process Active Explicit

Realization Rules:

Feature	Rules	Result
Inclusion		
Clause	+Pred	
Indicative	+Subj, +Finite	
Wh-	+Quest	
Material-Process	+Process	
Active	+Agent	|Pred Subj Finite Quest
Explicit	+Affected +Obj	| Process Agent Affected Obj
Conflation		
Material-Process	Process=Pred	
Active	Agent=Subj	|Pred.Process Subj.Agent
Explicit	Obj=Affected	| Finite Quest Affected.Obj
Classification		
Clause	Pred/Verb	|Pred.Process (Verb Transitive)
Indicative	Finite/Verb	|Subj.Agent ()
Interrogative	Finite/Aux	|Finite (Verb Aux)
Wh-	Quest/Wh-	|Quest (Wh-)
Material-Process	Process/Transitive	|Affected.Obj ()

Filling the constituents		
	Dictionary	Pred.Process — *plant*
		(Verb Transitive)
	Network for NP	Subj.Agent — *the pelicans*
		(NP Plural Definite Third-Person)
	Dictionary	Finite — *does*
		(Verb Aux Singular Third-Person)
	Dictionary	Quest — *when*
		(Wh- Adverb)
	Dictionary	Affected.Obj — *potatoes*
		(NP Plural Mass Third-Person)

Ordering		
Indicative	Subj>Pred	
Interrogative	Finite>Subj	
Wh-	Quest>Finite	*when > does > the pelicans >*
Explicit	Process>Obj	* plant > potatoes*

Agreement		
Indicative	Subj,Finite//Person	
	Subj,Finite//Number	**No – Generation fails!**

Figure 6–15. Attempted generation of a sentence.

sentences. Some of the problems could be patched up by making it only a little more complex, while others point to deeper difficulties with the formalism:

Association of rules with single features. The grammar as specified has an ordering rule associated with INTERROGATIVE indicating that the finite element appears before the subject. This applies both to POLAR (*Are you listening?*) and WH- (*When did you discover the leak? Whom did you tell?*). However, it is not correct in the case where the question element (QUEST) is conflated with the subject, as in *What can prevent it?* In order to correct this, we either need to remove such sentences from the class of interrogatives or to make the ordering rule depend on a particular combination of features. This can be done, but it adds to the complexity of the grammar.

Underspecification. In most generative formalisms, the underlying base creates a sequence of constituents in a fixed order. The problem is how to allow them to be omitted or to have flexible ordering. In systemic grammar, functions are included and ordered on a one-by-one basis. The problem is how to make sure everything gets accounted for. As a simple example, our grammar as stated will not generate a simple sentence like *The mouse ate the cheese.* The problem is that the appropriate combination of features will generate a set of components including PROCESS,PREDICATOR, and FINITE. These must be generated separately, since in either the case of a passive or an interrogative (as demonstrated in Figures 6–14 and 6–15 respectively) the FINITE will be an auxiliary. We need a rule that says in essence 'If nobody else wants the FINITE function, it should be given to the PREDICATOR.' It is, of course, possible to have a conflation rule stating 'FINITE=PRED,' but the problem is where to attach it. It is to be applied when none of a set of other things happen. In this case, there are only two—not passive and not interrogative—so it could be attached to the combination of these choices. In general, however, the cases in which something does not happen will be complex. It seems necessary to add another kind of rule specifically dealing with this problem.

Constituency and discontinuity. The model of constituency on which the examples are based is straightforward—a structure is made up of a sequence of non-overlapping contiguous parts. There are many phenomena for which it is much more natural to think of overlapping and discontinuous constituents. The rules presented here do not deal with the kind of multiple constituency represented in Figure 6–2, which shows elements filling functions along different dimensions. The situation becomes even more complex in dealing with dimensions of analysis that involve the phonological constituency structure, which is not divided up into clauses and groups at all, but cuts across the kind of constituency we have been describing.

Agreement across systems. We mentioned above that the agreement rules used here are oversimplified. One of the observations that has played an important role in systemic grammar (and in its predecessors in the British tradition) is the *polysystemic* nature of language. If systems are carefully defined in terms of alternatives in the language, we cannot assign the same feature choices to different classes, such as noun groups and verbs. The noun group (including those containing pronouns) has number and person features as laid out in Figure 6–6. Verbs do not have the same set of alternatives. One form is used for third-person singular (*she talks*) and another for other singulars and all plurals ({*I, you, we, they*} *talk*). The one exception is the verb *be,* which has a variety of forms. It is not particularly satisfying to say that every regular verb like *talk* has multiple entries in the lexicon, one for first-person singular, one for second-person singular, one for first-person plural, etc., all of which happen to be identical. It is much more natural to posit a two-choice system for verbs (other than *be*) and to complicate the statement of agreement to show the appropriate combinations of verb features and noun group features.

It is clear that each of these problems can be attacked by refining and extending the grammar formalism—by including more kinds of rules, more sophisticated sequencing of rule application, etc. Since the amount of effort that has been spent developing systemic grammar is substantially smaller than what has been spent on transformational grammar, it is difficult to compare the results. At the moment, there is no comprehensive generative systemic grammar that can compete in breadth and clarity with existing versions of transformational grammar.

Realization in procedural parsers

This section has described realization rules from a theoretical perspective. There have been a number of computer systems that embody realization rules in their programs in a less systematic but nevertheless effective way. Going back to the ATN grammars of Chapter 5, the conditions and actions on arcs can be viewed as a kind of 'encoding' of realization rules. From this standpoint, each rule is of the form:

> *If the constituent has a combination of features and components that would enable it to reach this state in the grammar, and also has the combination of functions and features specified in the condition, then add new components and classify the constituent with new features, as specified in the action.*

The parser in SHRDLU (Winograd, 1972) was of this kind, making explicit use of the function and feature notation in representing structures, but with realization rules only in this implicit form. Its grammar covered a relatively wide range of English phenomena, but it was complex and difficult to modify, since the interactions among rules were implicit in the order that things got done in the program.

Cognitive grammar (Lakoff and Thompson, 1975) went a step further towards independently meaningful realization rules, specifying a grammar as a collection if individual *strategies*. Each of these specifies a set of conditions (on the function assignments and the constituent structure) under which it would apply and a set of new *relational hypotheses* specifying new function assignments. Cognitive grammar is based more on the relational grammar model than on the ATN model and does not have an underlying network structure in which one state follows another. Instead, the strategies are written so that the applicability of each one can be determined on the basis of the structures that have been assigned so far. This makes grammars more general but much more difficult to write, and no grammars of any significant complexity have been developed.

Another similar system is *slot grammar* (McCord, 1980). In this formalism, each constituent has a set of potential functions (called *available slots*) that are filled in the course of a parse. Rather than proceeding in a simple left-to-right order like a standard ATN, a slot grammar contains a sequence of states that work their way out in both directions from the head of a construction. Thus, for example, the NP network is called when a noun is found and specifies words and phrases that can be adjoined to its left (adjectives, determiners, etc.) and to its right (prepositional phrases, relative clauses, etc.). Slot grammar makes use of fairly simple versions of the systemic grammar ideas we have been describing, but it is different in its particular use of a state-condition-action combination as a way of embedding the realization rules. As with the other formalisms, it has not been developed to a degree where a judgment can be made as to its success in providing clear and succinct accounts of complex syntactic phenomena.

6.5 Case grammar

As mentioned in the introduction to this chapter, systemic grammar developed largely independently of American generative (transformational) grammar. In most aspects of syntax, the transformational analysis was of a very different style from the systemic analysis. However, in one area there was a functional-systemic 'flavor' to work done by linguists within the generative school. A collection of theories dealing with the transitivity system discussed in Section 6.2 flourished and came to be known as *case grammar*. Case grammar has not become a mainstream part of generative grammar, perhaps because the phenomena it deals with do not yield to the kind of neat formal analysis that the paradigm demands. There has been a tendency to push the issues off by arguing that they are 'semantic' rather than to deal with them in the syntax. However, case grammar has been widely discussed and has influenced the design of many computer systems for natural language.

This section first describes case grammar from the point of view in which it was developed—as a style of analysis within transformational generative grammar. It then describes some of the ways case grammar has been used in computational systems and relates it to the parallel work in systemic grammar.

Case as a deep structure relationship

One of the main advantages of the generative paradigm over the immediate constituent paradigm was the ability to reflect deep similarities between superficially different structures and to assign different deep structures to superficially identical ones. The permutation of subject and object through the use of passive voice and the dative structure (e.g., *Tabby brought him the paper* and *Tabby brought the paper to him*) were among the phenomena that motivated transformational grammar and the use of registers in ATN grammars.

However, there are other regular patterns that are not covered by the same mechanisms. The two pairs of sentences below have underlying similarities much like pairs of corresponding passive and active sentences. In (5) and (6), the same event is described, but with a different choice of subject and no marking of passive voice. Example (8) is like a passive form of (7), except that the subject *the crowbar* is moved to a PP beginning with *with* instead of *by*.

We parked the orange truck easily.	(5)
The orange truck parked easily.	(6)
A crowbar could open that door easily.	(7)
That door could be opened easily with a crowbar.	(8)

There is a also a problem in the other direction. Identical structures involving subject and verb can have quite different meanings. The subject plays a different role in each of the following sentences.

We baked every Wednesday evening.
The pecan pie baked to a golden brown.
This oven bakes unevenly.

Cyril liked spaghetti.	(9)
Cyril ate a meatball.	(10)
Cyril got a bellyache.	(11)

We could think of the first three sentences as based on the same scenario having a fixed set of participants (the ACTOR, AFFECTED, and INSTRUMENT) with the subject playing each of these roles in turn. In the second three, different roles are involved. In (9), Cyril is in a certain state, in (10) he performs an act, and in (11) he undergoes something. There is also no simple set of role assignments that uniformly describes the different roles played by the direct objects in these sentences. It seems inappropriate to assign the same role to something being liked as to something being eaten if the role structure is to be the basis for determining meaning.

In the following sentences, the same verb is used for two totally different event scenarios, an ambiguity exploited in the old vaudeville repartee: **A.** *Call me a taxi.* **B.** *OK, You're a taxi.*

> *The sultan made Abdul the keeper of the harem.*
> *The waiter made Abdul a hot fudge sundae without nuts.*

Finally, the following sentences all use the preposition *with,* but with a diversity of underlying meanings.

> *He built it with mahogany.*
> *He built it with a sledge-hammer.*
> *He built it with an experienced carpenter.*
> *He built it with the other furniture.*
> *He built it with difficulty.*
> *He built it with no purpose in mind.*

One way to look at these phenomena is to see the sentence structure as a window onto an underlying scenario. The speaker has in mind some interrelated set of actions, perceptions, or properties, and wants the hearer to know about them. Phrases that refer to participants in the underlying scenario must be arranged into clauses, each of which has three primary positions for noun phrases (subject, direct object, and indirect object) and optional places for any number of prepositional phrases. The grammar must provide a systematic way to carry out this mapping so the hearer will know which object plays which role and what kind of scenario is intended.

It could be argued that this problem is not properly a part of syntax and instead should be viewed as semantic interpretation. Indeed, the whole issue of transitivity roles lies in the fuzzy region between those things that can be dealt with using the mechanisms of syntax and those that cannot. However, phenomena like those illustrated in the following sentences have led even those linguists who believe in the autonomy of syntax to look at case structure.

> *You were baking. I was baking.*
> *You and I were baking.*
> *The quiche was baking. I was baking.*
> ** The quiche and I were baking.*
>
> *The chef made me an avocado salad. The chef made the kitchen a mess.*
> ** The chef made me an avocado salad and the kitchen a mess.*

Conjunctions of sentences whose underlying role structures do not match are ungrammatical, even if there is a sensible way to interpret their meaning.

The traditional analysis of case

English relies primarily on the order of constituents in a clause to indicate their roles, for example in distinguishing between *Your dog just bit my mother* and *My mother just bit your dog.* In many languages, explicit markings (such as particles and the morphological structure of words) are used to represent the relationship between participants and an action or state. A choice system of *cases* is applied to nouns and noun groups, and a clause consists of a verb with one or more noun phrases (or embedded clauses), each indicating its role by exhibiting a particular case.

In Russian, for example, we have the two sentences: *Professor uchenika tseloval* (the professor kissed the student) and *Professora uchenik tseloval* (the student kissed the professor). There is a choice system of six cases called *nominative, genitive, dative, accusative, instrumental,* and *prepositional.* There is a complex set of rules for assigning endings to nouns in different cases, depending on the particular noun, its number and gender. There is another set of rules describing how the different cases are used. For example, the instrumental is used both for instruments, as in *She covered herself with a towel,* and to express temporary state, as in *She was a student.*

The syntactic cases in a language have a certain degree of correspondence with meanings, but it far from a simple one-to-one relationship. The same case is used for a variety of meanings, and often things that seem similar are expressed with different cases. Comparing case systems across languages, we find there is even more variation. Languages have different numbers of cases and differ widely in how they divide up the choices of meaning to be conveyed. It is therefore important to recognize that *surface case,* as these systems are called, does not directly reflect conceptual meaning, but rather is a mechanism used to connect conceptual relations to surface structure.

Applying case to English

In English, there is an extremely limited surface case system (operating only for pronouns, as described in Section 6.3), but there is a sense in which the surface positions of constituents and the prepositions used to attach extra clause participants can be viewed as reflections of underlying conceptual cases. In an influential paper entitled 'The case for case' (1968), Fillmore argued that a set of cases could be defined for English deep structure and that many linguistic phenomena could be explained in terms of general principles for combining cases and realizing them in surface structure.

Fillmore pointed to sentences like the following examples, arguing that the variety of forms should not be viewed as a special fact about the word *open,* but could be applied at least in part to a whole class of verbs, including *break, buy,* and *shatter.*

The chef opened a can of sardines for me with a key.

The chef opened me a can of sardines.

The big key easily opened the can of sardines.

The can of sardines opened easily.

He postulated an underlying deep *case frame* containing an AGENT, DATIVE, OBJECT, and INSTRUMENT, and a general set of rules determining which of these could be deleted and which could appear where in the surface structure. Each verb in the language has one or more ways of setting up a correspondence between the things in the conceptual scenario it describes and the underlying case frames provided in the grammar. The detailed structuring of the clause is specified by general case-manipulating rules.

Fillmore proposed some very general principles, such as hypothesizing that only one representative of any case could appear in a clause and that the cases within a case frame could be viewed as a simple linear hierarchy in which the deletion of a higher element causes it to be replaced in the structure by a lower ranked one. For example, the instrument can be the subject only in sentences where the agent is not specified and the object can become the subject only when neither the agent nor the instrument is specified. There are no prepositions in English that could be used in *The window broke ⎯ John ⎯ a hammer* to assign the appropriate roles to the actor and instrument.

The connection between verbs and cases

The verb plays a central role in determining the structure of a sentence. Each verb can specify one or more case frames, restrictions on what surface structures can be used, and prepositions that can be used for specific roles. There are several issues to be considered:

Multiple frames. The examples given earlier with the verb *make* illustrate different frames that can be selected, reflecting two different meanings. One frame (*I'll make you a milkshake*) involves AGENT, BENEFICIARY, RESULT. The other (*I'll make you a star*) involves AGENT, OBJECT, and ATTRIBUTE. In colloquial English, *make* can take another case frame involving only AGENT and OBJECT, with a sexual meaning. This kind of ambiguity is found for many verbs, and is similar to other kinds of polysemy (multiple meaning).

Restrictions on structure. Although there are general principles governing how cases are represented in surface structure, there is also a good deal of irregularity. Verbs that are closely related in meaning can differ arbitrarily in how they appear in clauses. The sentences *Cinderella broke the mirror* and *Cinderella polished the mirror* have much in common, both in their surface structure and in the underlying scenario of an actor performing an action that changes the state of an object. However, the sentence *The mirror broke* seems normal, while *The mirror polished* doesn't. This is further confounded by the fact that the thing polished could be the subject in a more elaborate sentence, such as *Silver utensils polish more easily than ones made from brass.* Such details have led to the invention of elaborate hypotheses about case structure rules. Perhaps the intentionality of polishing something distinguishes it from an unintentional breaking, or there is a difference between beneficial and destructive effects. There have been many attempts to find semantic principles that can explain differences in how verbs accept cases, but there seems to be a great deal of irreducible idiosyncracy.

Special prepositions. Many verbs enter into special combinations with certain prepositions. In some cases, the verb cannot be used at all without the appropriate preposition. For example, *account* is a verb in *How can you account for that weird sentence?,* but is not normally used without the preposition *for.* In other sentences, the presence or absence of a preposition changes the way in which the central participants (subject and objects) are interpreted, as illustrated by the following sentences.

> The ruling class blamed the depression on Thatcher.
>
> The ruling class blamed Thatcher for the depression.
>
> *The ruling class blamed on Thatcher for the depression.
>
> The ruling class blamed Thatcher.
>
> The ruling class blamed the depression.

In sentences whose main verb is *blame,* the direct object is the unfortunate event if the preposition *on* appears. If the preposition *for* appears, the direct object is the cause. Both cannot appear at the same time, and if neither appears, the direct object is interpreted as the cause.

Cases proposed for English

Within the general framework of case grammar, many different detailed analyses have been proposed. These differ in their choice of case names, the way they divide up the different roles, and most importantly in the way case assignments are expected to interact with the rest of the syntactic and semantic analysis. In order to give some feeling for the variety of detail, we will present some representative sets of cases. Several of these were done before Fillmore's formal notion of case grammar, and some degree of liberty has been taken in recasting them into a form suitable for comparison.

Fillmore (1968). The best known work on cases was Fillmore's original paper, which contained the set shown in Figure 6–16. A later version is shown in Figure 6–17. These two sets are typical of many of the case systems that have been proposed, both in the number of cases and the general style.

Agentive	Animate instigator of action
Instrumental	Inanimate force or object involved
Dative	Animate being affected by action
Factitive	Object resulting from action
Locative	Location or orientation
Objective	Everything else

John opened the door. The door was opened by John.

> Agentive: *John*; Objective: *the door*

John opened the door with the key.

> Agentive: *John*; Objective: *the door*; Instrumental: *the key*

John used the key to open the door.

> Agentive: *John*; Objective: *the door*; Instrumental: *the key*

The key opened the door.

> Objective: *the door*; Instrumental: *the key*

Chicago is windy.

> Locative: *Chicago*

We made him a jacket.

> Agentive: *we*; Dative: *him*; Factitive: *a jacket*

Figure 6–16. Fillmore's original cases.

Agent	Instigator of an event
Counter-agent	Force or resistance against which an action is carried out
Object	Entity that moves or changes or whose position or existence is in consideration
Result	Entity that comes into existence as a result of the action
Instrument	Stimulus or immediate physical cause of an event
Source	Place from which something moves
Goal	Place to which something moves
Experiencer	Entity that receives or accepts or experiences or undergoes the effect of an action

Figure 6–17. A later set of cases by Fillmore.

Simmons (1973). A smaller set of cases was developed by Simmons and Celce and used in a computer program for generating English sentences. There are only five cases: CAUSAL-ACTANT, THEME, LOCUS, SOURCE, and GOAL. These correspond loosely to Fillmore's cases, with CAUSAL-ACTANT including both the AGENT and INSTRUMENT, LOCUS serving as LOCATIVE, and THEME used to cover a variety of participants including OBJECT. In this system, the same role can be filled more than once. For example, the sentence *John broke the window with a hammer* is interpreted as having two CAUSAL-ACTANTS, *John* and *the hammer*.

Schank (1975). Schank developed a representation for meaning (called *conceptual dependency*) that is based on language-independent conceptual relationships between objects and actions. His set of conceptual roles bears a strong resemblance to the more syntactically motivated notions of case. The fundamental difference is that roles are filled by conceptual entities (objects and acts) rather than syntactic ones (NPs and clauses). Some roles require an act as their filler. For instance, an object like a key is not allowed to appear as the instrument of an action. Rather, the instrument is some other action (such as turning the key), in which the object is a central participant.

Conceptual dependency is described further in the volume on meaning. The cases are listed here to contrast them with other proposed sets. Other people's terms (such as ATTRIBUANT and ATTRIBUTE for the attribution of a property to an object) are used for roles to which Schank does not give explicit names, but represents with a pictorial notation (such as a triple-shafted two-headed arrow). The list of Figure 6–18 is derived from Schank (1975), but

---

Case roles filled by objects

  Actor, Object, Attribuant, Recipient (*paired* Recipient — Donor)

Case roles filled by conceptualizations (other acts)

  Instrument, Attribute, Attribuant, Cause, Reason, Enablement

Case roles filled by other conceptual categories

  Time: Time

  Location: Location, Direction (*paired* Source — Destination)

  State: Attribute, State Change (*paired* Initial — Final)

John handed Mary a book.

  Actor: *John*; Donor: *John*; Recipient: *Mary*; Object: *book*;
  Instrument: *an action of physical motion with:* [Actor: *John*; Object: *hand*]

Figure 6–18. Cases used in conceptual dependency.

the approach was developed beginning in 1967, largely independently of what was being done in linguistics.

Chafe (1970). Chafe uses a simple set of cases to describe the underlying structure of sentences. They were developed before case grammar was widely known and differ in minor ways. The term PATIENT is used as a neutral way of describing the object something happens to, and COMPLEMENT is used for cases in which the syntactic object is not really an object having something done to it, as in *Tom sang the Star Spangled Banner.*

Grimes (1975). Grimes developed a theory of *semantic role structure,* discussing both the history of case-like formalisms and his own version as summarized in Figure 6–19. The cases are divided into several groups, and part of Grimes's discussion is an attempt to find an underlying more abstract set (including FORMER and LATTER) that unify similar pairs like SOURCE – GOAL and MATERIAL – RESULT. As illustrated in the figure, a single participant can play more than one role.

Criteria for deciding on cases

It should be apparent from the preceding examples that there are no well-defined criteria for distinguishing cases and deciding how objects should be assigned case roles. There have been extended debates, for example, about whether *the wind* in *The wind opened the door* should be identified with the role ACTOR, as in *Tommy opened the door,* or with the role INSTRUMENT, as in *The key opened the door.* The arguments have centered on two basic issues: *syntactic patterning* and *meaning.*

Syntactic patterning. From one viewpoint, case is an extension of the syntactic mechanisms of transformational grammar. Cases can be used in a systematic way to represent deep structure relationships, using transformation rules to produce the corresponding surface forms. Discussions about the particular cases and their application must be framed within the goal of designing a system of rules that accounts for the data with the greatest overall simplicity. Arguments based on this viewpoint hinge on whether a particular case assignment would lead to valid predictions about other sentences that might occur. Thus *the wind* might be assigned as the actor, since we say *the door was opened by the wind* instead of *the door was opened with the wind,* and we would like to have a regular rule relating an actor to *by* and an instrument to *with.*

Meaning. Another view of case is based on its ability to express meaningful relationships among the constituents representing participants in an event or a relation. Assigning a constituent of a sentence as the actor or beneficiary is not simply syntactic, but reflects a regularity in how the object described in that constituent is related to the event. There are regularities in the facts that

---

Orientation Roles

  Object, Source, Goal, Range, Vehicle

Process Roles

  Patient, Material, Result, Referent

Agentive Roles

  Agent, Instrument, Force

Benefactive Roles

  Beneficiary

This idea came to me from Austin Hale.

  Object: *this idea*; Goal: *me*; Source: *Austin Hale*

She makes dresses from flour sacks.

  Agent: *she*; Patient, Result: *dresses*; Material: *flour sacks*

She makes flour sacks into dresses

  Agent: *she*; Patient, Material: *flour sacks*; Result: *dresses*

The gangster killed the girl.

  Agent: *the gangster*; Patient: *the girl*

Malaria killed the girl.

  Force: *malaria*; Patient: *the girl*

We carried the supplies all the way up the cliff for them on our backs with a rope.

  Agent, Source: *we*; Object: *the supplies*; Goal: *all the way up*; Range: *the cliff*; Beneficiary: *them*; Vehicle: *our backs*; Instrument: *a rope*

Figure 6–19. Grimes's semantic roles.

can be inferred from the statement of an action, and these regularities can be organized around the case assignments.

Thus, for example, acts are typically done for reasons and it can be inferred that the actor had a motivation for doing the act, while there is no need to assume that the beneficiary or object did. Systems such as those of Schank (1975) and Norman and Rumelhart (1975) treat case as a systematization of a conceptual organization for describing actions and events. They model human memory with network structures that are linked using case relationships, and assume that reasoning and inference are organized along those lines.

Arguments based on this view hinge on the inferences that could be drawn from an assignment, rather than the precise syntactic forms that could or could not appear. Thus *the wind* (or more precisely, the act of *the wind blowing*) could be argued to be an instrument rather than an actor, since the system would have a regular rule connecting an actor but not an instrument to inferences about intentionality and motivation.

Integrating case into formal syntax

Our discussion of case so far has been rather informal, emphasizing the intuitions that led people to examine case structures. In order to make use of case in a formal grammar or computer system, it must be more formally specified. From this point of view, the term 'case grammar' is somewhat of a misnomer, since it is not a full-scale grammatical theory like transformational grammar or systemic grammar. Case grammar deals with one particular set of phenomena within a language and must be embedded within another overall formalism. Several approaches have been taken:

Transformational. Case grammar served as the basis for at least one major transformational analysis of English, the UCLA Grammar (Stockwell, Schachter, and Partee, 1973). There were four kinds of relevant rules: *base rules* that inserted case elements into the base structures; *lexical rules* associating case frames with individual verbs, using feature marking; *redundancy rules* capturing generalizations applying to several verbs; and *transformation rules* that generated conventional surface structures from the deep structures. Figure 6–20 illustrates some of these rules.

We will not examine the rules in detail, but several things are worth noting. The cases follow more or less along Fillmore's analysis, adding the ESSIVE for the complement in a sentence like *That man is a good teacher*. The NEUTRAL case corresponds to his OBJECTIVE, handling all of those things that are specific to verbs and are least interpretable independently of the verb. Case structures are assigned to the NP as well as to sentences in order to analyze phrases like *the destruction of the environment by the corporations*. Rather than treating this as an embedded sentence that is transformed, the case structure is created in the base for the NP. The dictionary entry for each word specifies those cases that must appear (marked with a plus), and those that cannot (with a minus). Those that are not marked with either may or may not appear. In addition, there is a preposition associated with each case. This can either appear explicitly in the verb entry (as with *blame*) or if it does not, the *natural* (unmarked) preposition for the case is assumed (e.g., *by* for AGENT, *to* for DATIVE, *with* for INSTRUMENTAL). A redundancy rule specifies that any verb having a particular combination of features (+ESS in the example) will have a further set of features, as listed on the right-hand side.

Case roles are generated in the deep structure as a node whose children are a preposition and an NP. If the node undergoes no special transformation, it ends up as a PP in the surface structure. Transformations move case elements into surface syntactic positions like the subject and direct object, deleting their

Cases used

Agent, Dative, Essive, Instrumental, Locative, Neutral

Base rules

$$
\begin{aligned}
\text{S} &\rightarrow \text{Modal Proposition} \\
\text{Modal} &\rightarrow \text{(Negative) Auxiliary (Adverb)} \\
\text{Proposition} &\rightarrow \text{Verb (Ess) (Neut) (Dat) (Loc) (Ins) (Agt)} \\
\text{Agt} &\rightarrow \text{Prep[+Agt] NP[+Agt], } \textit{etc.} \\
\text{NP} &\rightarrow \text{Determiner Nominal} \\
\text{Nominal} &\rightarrow \text{Noun (Neut) (Dat) (Loc) (Ins) (Agt)}
\end{aligned}
$$

Lexical Rules

give   [+Neut +Dat –Loc –Ins +Agt]
open   [+Neut –Dat –Loc]
blame   [+Neut (Prep *for*) +Agt +Dat (Prep *on*) –Loc –Ins]

Redundancy Rules

$$
\begin{bmatrix} +\text{Verb} \\ +\text{Ess} \end{bmatrix} \rightarrow [+\text{Neut} -\text{Dat} -\text{Loc} -\text{Ins} -\text{Agt}]
$$

Transformation Rules

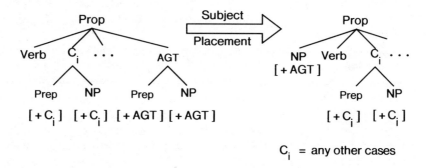

Figure 6–20. Rules from the UCLA Grammar.

prepositions. Thus the subject of a simple transitive sentence is dominated by an AGENT node and has a *by* preposition in the deep structure, which is deleted by a SUBJECT-PLACEMENT transformation if the sentence is active, and left in if it is passive.

Augmented transition networks. A number of ATN grammars have made use of case-like systems. To some degree this has been necessary because other formalisms have almost nothing to say about the prepositional phrases that appear as modifiers of sentences and noun phrases and that carry much of the information about what happened and who the participants were. In order to make sense of a sentence, the grammar must be able to assign each modifier to a role, often in situations where simple syntactic rules allow a good deal of ambiguity. By having case frames included in the dictionary entries for verbs, the parser has an additional source of knowledge to guide the analysis of the input sentence into a constituent structure.

A verb entry lists specific prepositions that are known to fit with the frame (such as *on* and *for* with *blame*), and often also includes semantic restrictions on the role fillers (the subject and objects of the sentence and the objects of the prepositional phrases). Thus, for example, the verb *bring* might have an entry indicating that a modifying phrase with the preposition *to* represents a BENE-FICIARY if the object is animate, and a DESTINATION if it is a place. The network for sentences (and also for NP if cases are used for nominalizations as described above) contains registers for each of the case names, and the conditions and actions make use of these registers.

There are two ways of using case analysis in parsing. In one, the case registers are used in the normal way as the parse proceeds. There are actions that fill case registers both on the arcs for major participants (SUBJECT, OBJECT, etc.) and on arcs that parse prepositional phrases. These actions must check for previous fillers and for the appropriate case frame associated with the verb. This means that they cannot be done before the verb has been seen. In English word order, there is generally one participant before the verb (the subject), and the rest follow. The subject can be initially placed in the AGENT register, then switched out if the verb so specifies. There are some problems with this. For example, an initial prepositional phrase may specify a participant that needs to be assigned a case role, as in *With this key we may be able to open it.* Special actions need to be taken to check back for prepositional phrases once the verb is found. The other method (used, for example, in GUS (Bobrow et al., 1977)) is to do the parsing in two phases. The first uses a more conventional set of registers (e.g., SUBJECT, DIRECT-OBJECT, INDIRECT-OBJECT) and simply puts prepositional phrases into a list of modifiers. The result is then analyzed using the case frame from the verb to produce a structure in which participants are assigned to cases. By doing this, all of the NPs and prepositional modifiers are available simultaneously as inputs to the case analysis.

Computational implementations. In systems that do not make use of a standard syntactic formalism or parsing strategy, case structure can be used as a way of representing the underlying structure of sentences and can be filled in by whatever computations can be made to work. In some parsers (like Kay's 'powerful parser' described in Section 7.4), case structures and the associated prepositions are treated in a style similar to the transformational analysis above. In others (like the MARGIE parser (Riesbeck, 1975) described in Section 7.7), there is no uniform treatment of syntactic forms, but the analysis procedures build case-like structures as an ultimate result.

Since most computational systems in the available literature have been built to analyze English, not much has been done in them to relate computational uses of case to the phenomena of surface case. In a system for analyzing a language with a more developed case system, like Russian or Japanese, the use of verb-centered case analysis would be of even more benefit. In these languages, the parser cannot rely on the order of constituents, looking for a sequence like 'SUBJECT VERB OBJECT.' It must operate by picking up components of the sentence and fitting them into case slots, using the surface case information to decide which constituent fills which role. The MIND grammar (Kay, 1973) for Korean made use of cases in this way.

It should be remarked that in all of the formalisms and systems described here, there has never been a large-scale satisfactory coverage of English verbs. In systems that deal with a limited vocabulary and limited domain, case structure has proved useful, but there is no candidate for a comprehensive case grammar of English, and the attempt to integrate it into transformational grammars did not succeed well enough to be adopted in the mainstream of research.

The relationship of case grammar to systemic grammar

It should be apparent from the preceding discussion that case grammar shares some basic philosophical assumptions with systemic grammar:

Functional analysis. The most obvious similarity is in the use of a functional (rather than immediate constituent) analysis of the participants in a clause. Cases provide a set of role names for the constituents, without regard to where they appear in the structure.

Multiple systems. Although not explicitly stated, it is clear that a case grammar can only be integrated into a formalism that has multiple dimensions of functional analysis, of which the case structure is only one. Many of the difficulties in trying to incorporate case ideas into transformational grammar grew out of the need to fit them into an overall system where each dimension of structure must be explicit in the shape of the tree at some point in the derivation.

In fact, systemic grammar has contained a case system from the very beginning. This system has been called 'transitivity' rather than 'case,' and we have used that terminology in spite of the danger of confusing this notion of transitivity with the more familiar superficial classification of verbs as *transitive* or *intransitive,* according to the number of surface objects they can take.

The systemic analysis differs from the case grammar approach primarily in that it makes use of additional mechanisms of systemic grammar, in particular those of *classification*. Rather than positing a single set of cases, clauses

---

Action clauses:

Central Roles
  Actor
  Goal   (Goal, Resultant)
  Beneficiary (Beneficiary, Recipient)
  Instrument (Instrument, Force)
  Range

Circumstantial Roles
  Location

He washed the clothes for me with detergent.

  Actor: *he*; Goal: *the clothes*; Beneficiary: *me*; Instrument: *detergent*

We walked twenty miles.

  Actor: *we*; Range: *twenty miles*

I sent the message to Garcia for the President.

  Actor: *I*; Goal: *the message*; Beneficiary: *the president*; Recipient: *Garcia*

The key opened the door.

  Instrument: *the key*; Goal: *the door*

The wind opened the door.

  Force: *the wind*; Goal: *the door*

Ergative clauses: Causer, Affected

The general marched the soldiers.

  Causer: *the general*; Affected: *the soldiers*

Mental process clauses: Processor, Phenomenon

I like your eyes.

  Processor: *I*; Phenomenon: *your eyes*

Attributive clauses: Attribuant, Attribute

John seems happy.

  Attribuant: *John*; Attribute: *happy*

Equative clauses: Variable, Value

The leader is John.

  Variable: *the leader*; Value: *John*

Figure 6–21. Transitivity roles for English clauses.

Sentence	Clause type	Role
Cyril likes spaghetti.	Mental Process	Processor
Cyril ate a meatball.	Action	Actor
Cyril got a bellyache.	Ergative	Affected
Cyril looks a little ill.	Attributive	Attribuant

Figure 6–22. Roles played by the subject.

are classified into several basic types and cases defined appropriate to each type. The case names are also structured in a hierarchical way, with some cases as further specifications of more general ones. Figure 6–21 describes the roles associated with the transitivity system in an early version of systemic grammar (Halliday, 1967). A more recent version is the basis for the analysis of transitivity given in Section B.1.6.

By having different sets of cases for different kinds of sentences, the system avoids identifying roles associated with different kinds of actions. Figure 6–22 shows the clause types and roles for one set of examples from the beginning of the chapter. In each case, the role listed is the one played by the subject (*Cyril*).

From the macro-functional point of view, the transitivity system is the primary system related to the *ideational* function of the clause—its message about who did what to whom. The volume on meaning will re-examine case structure, looking at it as a means of providing a kind of *perspective* on an event, and relating it to the use of *frames* in the representation languages developed in artificial intelligence.

6.6 Functional grammars

Our discussion of syntax began in Chapters 2 and 3 with the the concepts of *pattern* and *constituent structure*. The subsequent chapters have explored the structure of language, showing in many places the inadequacies of these simple concepts. They have described a sequence of formalisms of increasing complexity and abstractness, each attempting to deal with the facts of language. Generative grammar has arrived at a point where the concepts of 'rule' and 'generation' are extremely distant from naive intuitions of how we produce and understand linguistic patterns.

Some recent work has focused on the question of whether we can regain some of the advantages of simpler formalisms without losing the precision and power of complex generative grammars. Although this work has been done from several different starting points, all of the variations make substantial use of features and functions, in a way that is consistent with our development of those concepts in this chapter. In this section, we will look at two systems that are similar in formal structure but are based on different metaphors: *overlapping partial descriptions* and *simultaneous equations*. Before presenting the formalisms in detail, the motivation behind them can be better understood if we review some desiderata for grammar formalisms.

Desiderata for a grammar formalism

As discussed in Section 4.5, many different criteria can be applied in choosing among competing formalisms. Several have guided the development of functional grammars:

Perspicuity. The most immediate advantage of a formalism based on simple patterns or rules is that the facts they express about language are directly visible in their form. A syntactic pattern such as 'NP VERB NP NP' states an obvious fact about a sentence to which it applies—it must be constructed of four elements, of the given types, in the given order. In contrast, a transformation rule that moves an abstract marker from one place in a tree structure to another has no immediate interpretation in terms of the sentences that the grammar generates. Its consequences are implicit in its interactions with the other rules and may be incomprehensible on inspecting the rule.

The beauty of context-free grammars is that every rule is also a pattern. The rule 'S → NP VP' can be used in a process of derivation, but it can also be read as a statement that any constituent of type S consists of two adjacent parts, one an NP and one a VP. In adding a new rule to such a grammar, the linguist is asserting that some pattern appears (for the sentence as a whole or for some constituent) that was not previously accounted for. It is easy to see when such an addition is needed and to understand its consequences.

Recursive transition networks maintain this kind of transparency. It is possible to interpret a path through the arcs of the network as a pattern of constituents, and the addition or deletion of an arc represents a direct change in the set of patterns. Once augmentations such as conditions, actions, and registers are added, the perspicuity is no longer guaranteed, although the network still provides an overall structure. The importance of a particular arc may lie not just in the constituent it covers (there will not even be one if it is a jump arc), but in actions such as setting or using the contents of a hold register.

In the systemic grammars of this chapter, the effects of a particular realization rule can be seen as a direct statement of the form of the constituent to which it applies, but because the rules can interact in complex ways to derive the final structure, they are not perspicuous in the same sense as a context-free rule. In the functional grammars of this section, there is a return to simpler rules which are more immediately structural.

Nondirectionality. One consequence of the kind of perspicuity just discussed is the possibility of using the same set of rules in both the generation process and the parsing process. In writing simple patterns or a context-free grammar, one need not be concerned with the direction in which it will be used. The grammar is a neutral characterization of the possible structures. Neither transformational grammars nor ATN grammars meet this condition. As discussed in Chapter 4, a transformational grammar 'runs' only in the direction of generation, and it is quite difficult to apply the formalism in parsing. An ATN is somewhat more general (and simpler transition networks are in fact nondirectional), but the use of conditions and actions forces a left-to-right ordering (since registers can be accessed only after they are set) and the use of initializations requires a top-down process (since contents of a lower node are passed down from a higher one). Much of the work that led to lexical-functional grammar grew from an attempt to modify the ATN formalism to get rid of order dependencies.

Correspondence with meanings. In a simple pattern-based communication system, there is a one-to-one mapping from patterns to meanings. Even in a phrase structure system, it is often possible to describe a single meaning rule corresponding to each syntactic rule. For instance, corresponding to 'NP2 → ADJECTIVE NOUN' we might have a rule: 'The NP2 refers to the intersection of the set of objects referred to by the noun and those referred to by the adjective.' Thus the phrase *colorful ball* refers to the intersection of all things that are balls and all things that are colorful.

This approach of setting up a direct correspondence between syntactic rules and meaning rules is one of the standard techniques for defining the semantics of mathematical and programming languages. One common feature of the formalisms described in this section is their systematic linking of syntactic and semantic rules.

Multiple dimensions of patterning. As pointed out in the earlier sections of this chapter, there are many aspects of language structure that call for an analysis of a constituent along separate dimensions. As discussed, we can think of a transformational grammar as achieving this by having different dimensions represented in the structure of the phrase marker at different points in the derivation. However, it is more perspicuous to express the different dimensions explicitly.

Functional grammar

Section 6.4 described the full analysis of a sentence as being made up of the following parts:

Constituent structure. Some kind of constituent structure tree or net that can be mapped onto the sequence of words appearing in the sentence. This is often called the *surface structure*.

Functional description. A collection of dimensions, each of which has an associated set of function roles. The roles in a dimension can be in a one-to-one correspondence with constituents, but they can also allow a single constituent to play more than one role and can include deep structure constituents not appearing on the surface (such as the implicit *you* subject of an imperative).

Feature description. A set of features assigned to each constituent, selected from some collection of choice systems.

Lexical content. Each constituent is either made up of other constituents or filled by a lexical item chosen from some vocabulary.

Semantic structure. Corresponding to the syntactic analysis there is a semantic analysis of the sentence, built up of elements in the semantic stratum. In most systems, there is at least a partial correspondence between syntactic elements and semantic elements, but it need not be one-to-one.

Phonological or graphological structure. Finally, there is a structure on the stratum below syntax, corresponding to sounds or marks. Although this can be quite complex (particularly if we take into account prosodic features like stress and intonation), it is not dealt with in the formalisms described in this section, and we will simply assume a straightforward mapping from sequences of lexical items onto sequence of characters (their spellings).

All of the different kinds of rules in a grammar (and its companion dictionary) can be thought of as *constraints* or *conditions* on what constitutes a well-formed analysis. A constituency rule such as 'S → NP VP' says that a constituent structure is well-formed if its label is S and there are two children with labels NP and VP respectively. A dictionary entry such as *'person =* NOUN SINGULAR' states that a component filled by the word *person* must have the features NOUN and SINGULAR. The more complex kinds of realization rules described in Section 6.4 can all be cast in this mold as well.

In *functional grammar,* Kay (1979) applies this uniform way of thinking about structures and rules as constraints. A functional grammar contains only one kind of formal structure, used both for rules and for the analyses of specific sentences. This structure is a pattern specifying a combination of features, function assignments, lexical items, and constituent orderings. Figure 6–23 illustrates an analysis of the sentence *She smashed a brick.*

Each box in this figure describes a constituent (possibly the same as that described by some other box). The order in which the contents appear in the box is irrelevant, since each item can be thought of as a partial description that applies independently. In the interest of notational economy, functional grammar makes use of the same notation for functions, features, and lexical realization—a name followed by an equal sign followed by a filler. For functions, the name is the function name and the filler is the constituent filling that function. For features, the name is the choice system and the filler is the feature

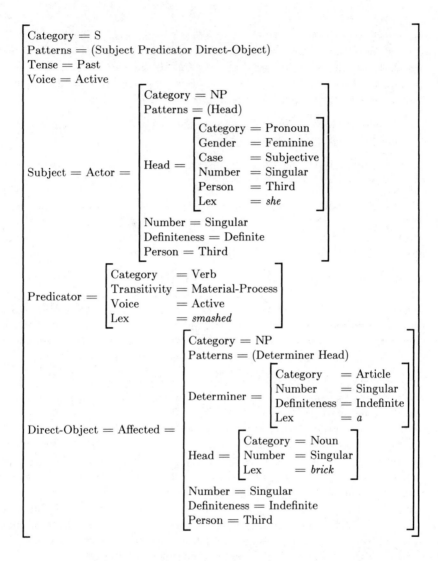

Figure 6–23. A functional grammar description of a sentence.

selected from it. The special choice system CATEGORY stands for the basic categorization of all constituents into syntactic categories. For lexical items, the symbol 'LEX' appears before the equal sign, followed by the word. Constituent structure is represented by the nesting of boxes and by a collection of sequence patterns, each in parentheses, as explained further below. In Figure 6–23, we have included these as a filler following the special symbol 'PATTERNS' to complete the regularity of the notation, although in the original form they simply appear at the top of the box without a label. In a complete analysis, every box must contain either PATTERNS or LEX, depending on whether it is a composite or lexical constituent.

We can now state rules of the language using the same notation. For example, active and passive voice can be represented by the three patterns of Figure 6–24. The first describes the active voice, the second describes passives with an agent, and the third covers agentless passives. They are in *alternation*—only one of them can apply to a given constituent. Of course, not every constituent is covered by one of these descriptions. The choice will not apply to an NP or to an S whose verb is not MATERIAL-PROCESS. The grammar notation includes a means of indicating the part of the description that is common to all of the alternatives (in this case, the part characterizing the constituent as a sentence whose verb is MATERIAL-PROCESS) and a set of choices of which one must be selected whenever the common part applies. This can be thought of as a generalization of the *entry conditions* of systemic grammar.

The constituent patterns associated with descriptions in functional grammar are also based on incremental partial description. The purpose of patterns is to identify constituents and to state constraints on the order of their occurrence. Rather than specifying a complete sequence (as grammar rules or ATNs do), a functional description includes a fragmentary order relation, more like the ordering rules of systemic grammar. For example, the description for a declarative clause would include the fragment '(... SUBJECT PREDICATOR ...),' while the one for a polar interrogative would include '(FINITE SUBJECT ...),' and the one for a transitive sentence (as illustrated in Figure 6–24) includes '(... PREDICATOR DIRECT-OBJECT ...). Just as the functional parts of the description are built up piece by piece, so are the patterns. Two descriptions cannot be applied to the same constituent if their patterns conflict, and when they are applied the result is the intersection of all the orderings they represent. The final constituent ordering for a declarative active sentence is the combination of the two patterns, resulting in '(... SUBJECT PREDICATOR DIRECT-OBJECT ...).'

There are several additional notations used in functional descriptions. The description of a passive with an agent (the second functional description in Figure 6–24) includes the filler '<AGENT>' for the OBJECT function in the prepositional phrase. This means that the filler is the AGENT of the whole S. Similarly, subject-verb agreement would be handled by having a description like that of 6–25. In this description, the sequence '<SUBJECT NUMBER>' means the filler of the NUMBER function in the constituent that fills the SUBJECT function in the S. There are also notations for referring to non-local constituents for characterizing constructs like relative clauses, which we will not describe.

Active

$$
\begin{bmatrix}
\text{Category} = \text{S} \\
\text{Patterns} = (\dots \text{Predicator Direct-Object} \dots) \\
\text{Subject} = \text{Actor} = \begin{bmatrix} \text{Category} = \text{NP} \end{bmatrix} \\
\text{Direct-Object} = \text{Affected} = \begin{bmatrix} \text{Category} = \text{NP} \end{bmatrix} \\
\text{Predicator} = \begin{bmatrix} \text{Category} & = \text{Verb} \\ \text{Transitivity} = \text{Material-Process} \\ \text{Voice} & = \text{Active} \end{bmatrix} \\
\text{Voice} = \text{Active}
\end{bmatrix}
$$

Passive with agent

$$
\begin{bmatrix}
\text{Category} = \text{S} \\
\text{Patterns} = (\dots \text{Predicator} \dots \text{By-Adjunct} \dots) \\
\text{Subject} = \text{Affected} = \begin{bmatrix} \text{Category} = \text{NP} \end{bmatrix} \\
\text{Agent} = \begin{bmatrix} \text{Category} = \text{NP} \end{bmatrix} \\
\text{Predicator} = \begin{bmatrix} \text{Category} & = \text{Verb} \\ \text{Transitivity} = \text{Material-Process} \\ \text{Voice} & = \text{Passive} \end{bmatrix} \\
\text{By-Adjunct} = \begin{bmatrix} \text{Category} = \text{PP} \\ \text{Prep} = \begin{bmatrix} \text{Category} = \text{Preposition} \\ \text{Lex} & = by \end{bmatrix} \\ \text{Object} = <\text{Agent}> \end{bmatrix} \\
\text{Voice} = \text{Passive}
\end{bmatrix}
$$

Passive without agent

$$
\begin{bmatrix}
\text{Category} = \text{S} \\
\text{Subject} = \text{Affected} = \begin{bmatrix} \text{Category} = \text{NP} \end{bmatrix} \\
\text{Agent} = \text{None} \\
\text{Predicator} = \begin{bmatrix} \text{Category} & = \text{Verb} \\ \text{Transitivity} = \text{Material-Process} \\ \text{Voice} & = \text{Passive} \end{bmatrix} \\
\text{Voice} = \text{Passive}
\end{bmatrix}
$$

Figure 6–24. Three alternative transitivity patterns.

$$
\begin{bmatrix}
\text{Category} = \text{S} \\
\text{Subject} = \begin{bmatrix} \text{Category} = \text{NP} \end{bmatrix} \\
\text{Predicator} = \begin{bmatrix}
\text{Category} = \text{Verb} \\
\text{Number} \quad = <\text{Subject Number}> \\
\text{Person} \quad = <\text{Subject Person}>
\end{bmatrix}
\end{bmatrix}
$$

Figure 6–25. Subject-verb agreement in a functional grammar.

A functional grammar consists of a collection of constituent descriptions organized into sets of alternatives. These include syntactic patterns like those we have been looking at so far and word-defining patterns as illustrated by the three entries for *saw* illustrated in Figure 6–26.

The grammar can be used for either generation or parsing. The goal is to produce a complete functional description of some sentence. The starting point in parsing is a sequence of words, and in generation either the symbol S (if the generation is purely syntactic) or some semantic characterization of the sentence. This initial specification is written in a 'chart' that records all of the structure and is then augmented step by step by adding pieces of description according to the patterns allowed by the grammar (a process called *unification*). The whole process is additive—each partial description that is added remains, and this serves to constrain the possibilities for what further descriptions can be included.

There are many technical problems involved in developing a generative functional grammar of any significant size. There are problems of dealing with

$$
\begin{bmatrix}
\text{Category} \quad = \text{Verb} \\
\text{Tense} \quad = \text{Past} \\
\text{Transitivity} = \text{Mental-Process} \\
\text{Root} \quad = see \\
\text{Lex} \quad = saw
\end{bmatrix}
$$

$$
\begin{bmatrix}
\text{Category} = \text{Noun} \\
\text{Number} \quad = \text{Singular} \\
\text{Lex} \quad = saw
\end{bmatrix}
\begin{bmatrix}
\text{Category} \quad = \text{Verb} \\
\text{Tense} \quad = \text{Infinitive} \\
\text{Transitivity} = \text{Material-Process} \\
\text{Root} \quad = saw \\
\text{Lex} \quad = saw
\end{bmatrix}
$$

Figure 6–26. Dictionary entries in a functional grammar.

alternatives in cases when more than one pattern in a set of choices could apply, problems of making sure that everything in the initial specification gets 'covered' properly, and problems in making fragmentary ordering patterns work correctly to generate a constituent structure. There may be complex interactions that make it impossible to specify the patterns simply while forcing them to interact properly. At this time, functional grammar provides an interesting metaphor for the characterization of grammatical rules and an open direction for exploration.

Lexical-functional grammar

A closely related approach to formalizing a grammar as a set of simultaneous patterns grew out of work by Bresnan (1978) on *realistic transformational grammar* and Kaplan (1975) on augmented transition networks and the *General Syntactic Processor*. Bringing together ideas from current transformational linguistics and computational linguistics, they devised a system that incorporates many of the ideas we have been discussing in this chapter. It is called *lexical-functional grammar* because it emphasizes the role of the lexicon.

Like functional grammar, it is an attempt to solve problems that arise in transformational and ATN grammars by using *additive description*. Instead of allowing trees to be transformed or the contents of registers to be changed, it provides a multi-layered description that applies in a *transparent* style—nothing in any of the layers contradicts anything in any of the others. Each layer can only augment what the others contain.

In a lexical-functional description of a sentence, there are two separate components, a *constituent structure* and a *functional structure*. The constituent structure is a standard context-free surface parse of the sentence. The grammar it is based on covers all possible surface strings, so it is much looser than the typical base context-free grammar of a transformational system. It allows many structures that are not grammatical, which are filtered out because they do not have a corresponding well-formed functional structure. The functional structure is generated by *equations* associated with the context-free rules. It is very much like the functional descriptions described above, including function and feature specifications under a common notation. One difference is that there is no pattern included in the functional description, since constituent structure is handled by the context-free grammar. Realization relationships crossing to the semantic stratum are explicitly represented, with *semantic forms* allowed to fill specially designated functions in each category of functional structure. Thus the filler for any role name can be a feature (if the role designates a choice system like NUMBER), a functional structure describing another component (e.g., the SUBJECT), or a semantic form.

In most of the grammars we have been discussing, there have been functions in different dimensions to account for the distinction between surface par-

Grammar rules:

S →   NP   VP
        ($\uparrow$ Subject)=$\downarrow$ $\uparrow$=$\downarrow$

NP → Determiner Noun

VP → Verb $\left(\begin{array}{c} \text{NP} \\ (\uparrow \text{Object})=\downarrow \end{array} \left(\begin{array}{c} \text{NP} \\ ((\uparrow \text{Object-2})=\downarrow) \end{array}\right)\right)$

       $\uparrow$=$\downarrow$

Lexical entries:

a	Determiner	($\uparrow$ Definiteness) = Indefinite ($\uparrow$ Number) = Singular
baby	Noun	($\uparrow$ Number) = Singular ($\uparrow$ Predicate) = 'Baby'
girl	Noun	($\uparrow$ Number) = Singular ($\uparrow$ Predicate) = 'Girl'
handed	Verb	($\uparrow$ Tense) = Past ($\uparrow$ Predicate) = 'Hand$<$($\uparrow$ Subject), ($\uparrow$ Object), ($\uparrow$ Object-2)$>$'
the	Determiner	($\uparrow$ Definiteness) = Definite
toys	Noun	($\uparrow$ Number) = Plural ($\uparrow$ Predicate) = 'Toy'

Figure 6–27. Some rules and lexical entries of a lexical-functional grammar.

ticipant roles in a sentence (SUBJECT, DIRECT-OBJECT,...) and the under-lying participant roles (AGENT, AFFECTED,...). Lexical-functional grammar leaves open the set of underlying participant roles on the belief that they are of semantic, not syntactic relevance. A lexical item is associated with one or more semantic predicates (for its distinct senses or meanings), and each seman-tic predicate has its own set of participants. The dictionary associates surface roles with the predicate's *argument positions*.

In place of the uniform partial description notation of functional grammar, lexical-functional grammar has two kinds of rules: context-free rules (with as-sociated functional equations) and lexical rules (the dictionary and redundancy rules that generalize across dictionary entries). Figure 6–27 illustrates some simple rules, the details of which are explained below.

The derivation of a sentence takes place in three steps. First, a tree is generated using the context-free grammar, ignoring the equations appearing below the symbols of the grammar rules. This proceeds exactly as described in Chapter 3 (Figure 3–12) until the leaves of the tree all have lexical categories as their labels. Next, each leaf node (called a *pre-lexical node*) is filled in by choosing a word of the appropriate category from the dictionary. Then, for

Context-free phrase structure and lexical insertion (C-structure):

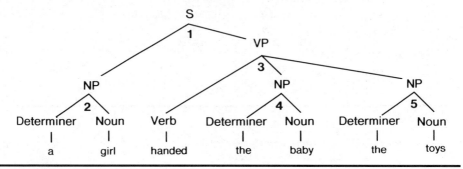

Equations:

Rule or word	Instantiations
S → NP VP	$(x_1 \text{ Subject})=x_2$, $x_1=x_3$
VP → Verb NP NP	$(x_3 \text{ Object})=x_4$, $(x_3 \text{ Object-2})=x_5$
a	$(x_2 \text{ Definiteness})=\text{Indefinite}$, $(x_2 \text{ Number})=\text{Singular}$
girl	$(x_2 \text{ Number})=\text{Singular}$, $(x_2 \text{ Predicate})=\text{'Girl'}$
handed	$(x_3 \text{ Tense})=\text{Past}$,
	$(x_3 \text{ Predicate})=\text{'Hand}<(x_3 \text{ Subject}), (x_3 \text{ Object}), (x_3 \text{ Object-2})>\text{'}$
the	$(x_4 \text{ Definiteness})=\text{Definite}$
baby	$(x_4 \text{ Number})=\text{Singular}$, $(x_4 \text{ Predicate})=\text{'Baby'}$
the	$(x_5 \text{ Definiteness})=\text{Definite}$
toys	$(x_5 \text{ Number})=\text{Plural}$, $(x_5 \text{ Predicate})=\text{'Toy'}$

Solutions (F-structure):

$$x_1 = x_3 = \begin{bmatrix} \text{Subject} & = x_2 \\ \text{Object} & = x_4 \\ \text{Object-2} & = x_5 \\ \text{Tense} & = \text{Past} \\ \text{Predicate} & = \text{'Hand}<\text{Girl, Baby, Toy}>\text{'} \end{bmatrix}$$

$$x_2 = \begin{bmatrix} \text{Definiteness} = \text{Indefinite} \\ \text{Number} & = \text{Singular} \\ \text{Predicate} & = \text{'Girl'} \end{bmatrix}$$

$$x_4 = \begin{bmatrix} \text{Definiteness} = \text{Definite} \\ \text{Number} & = \text{Singular} \\ \text{Predicate} & = \text{'Baby'} \end{bmatrix}$$

$$x_5 = \begin{bmatrix} \text{Definiteness} = \text{Definite} \\ \text{Number} & = \text{Plural} \\ \text{Predicate} & = \text{'Toy'} \end{bmatrix}$$

Figure 6–28. Derivation of a sentence using a lexical-functional grammar.

each node that was generated and each word that was inserted, the equations appearing under the symbols are *instantiated* (having the appropriate variables filled in for the arrows), producing the *functional description,* which is a set of equations. These equations, along with those associated with the dictionary entries, are finally solved to produce a *functional structure* or *f-structure.* If the set of equations has at least one solution, the result is a grammatical sentence, whose analysis includes both the original phrase structure tree and the assignments that result from solving the equations. If there is no solution, the generation fails. If there is more than one, the sentence is ambiguous with each solution corresponding to an interpretation.

Figure 6–28 illustrates the generation of the sentence *A girl handed the baby the toys* using the rules of Figure 6–27. A unique variable (indicated by x_n for any number n) is assigned to each node except the pre-lexical nodes. Each '↑' is replaced by the variable for the parent node (the one matching the left-hand-side of the rule) and each '↓' by the variable for the child node matching the symbol under which the equation appears. The equation can be thought of as 'sitting on the line' connecting the parent and child nodes, with the arrows pointing to the two ends of the line. Thus, for example, the rule 'S → NP VP' has two associated equations: one under the NP stating that the subject of the functional structure corresponding to the S is equal to the structure for NP, and one under the VP stating that the functional structures for the S and the VP are equal. In the sentence of Figure 6–28, this results in the equations '$(x_1$ SUBJECT)$=x_2$' and '$x_1=x_3$.' For dictionary entries, the equations are applied to the pre-lexical node (the one whose label is the word class). The '↑' refers to the parent of the pre-lexical node and the '↓' to the node itself. This can be thought of as having the equation from a lexical entry applied as though it belonged to the pre-lexical node. For example, the equation '(↑ TENSE) = PAST' associated with the word *handed* describes the tense of the *parent* of the VERB node (the VP node). Note that the leaf nodes in this analysis are the pre-lexical nodes, whose labels are lexical categories, not words.

In a lexical-functional grammar, the correspondence between constituents and elements of the functional structure is not one-to-one. The equations specify, for example, that a single functional structure corresponds simultaneously to the verb, the VP, and the sentence. Many phenomena of agreement are handled directly by this 'squashing together' of the constituent tree in the functional structure. For example, the rule for expanding S gives a value for its subject, the rule for VP determines the objects, and the rule for the verb itself specifies the mapping of these onto a semantic form. All of these are combined through the equality of their variables. Similarly, the NUMBER features of the determiner and noun in an NP are forced to agree with each other (and with the NUMBER of the NP as a whole) by setting the variables all equal to each other.

The PREDICATE function is handled specially, resulting in the instantiation of a semantic representation of the sentence. We will not discuss it in detail, but it is based on a straightforward notion of substitution into forms, much like the solution of the functional equation but in the semantic stratum with its own structure. The semantic forms act as realization rules relating syntax to semantics.

Long-distance dependencies in lexical-functional grammar

One of the motivations in the development of lexical-functional grammar was the desire to handle cleanly phenomena that require *movement rules* in transformational grammar. Figure 6–29 contains a grammar designed to deal with more complex sentences, omitting issues of number, definiteness, and tense in order to highlight the new issues. A full grammar, of course, would have to include these as well.

A number of new things have been added. The use of a $\overline{\text{VP}}$ to represent a sentential complement allows sentences like *I want to kiss the baby,* in which the complement of *want* is a $\overline{\text{VP}}$. The entry for the verb *want* specifies that one of the arguments to its semantic form must be the VCOMP of the S in which it appears. The equation '($\uparrow$ SUBJECT)=($\uparrow$ VCOMP SUBJECT)' associated with *want* in the dictionary causes its subject to be identified with the subject of its complement, in this case the subject of *kiss*. The same functional constituent plays a role in two different structures. This achieves the same effect as rules like EQUI-NP DELETION in transformational grammar and the initialization of the SUBJECT register in parsing the embedded clause in an ATN grammar. These equations are particular to *want*. A sentence like **I kiss to kiss the baby* would not have a solution, since the semantic form for *kiss* calls for an OBJECT instead of a VCOMP.

Figure 6–30 illustrates the analysis of the sentence *I want to kiss the baby,* using the grammar of Figure 6–29. The constituent structure includes a $\overline{\text{VP}}$ as the complement of *want*. The solutions to the equations contain four independent f-structures, one for *I,* one for *the baby,* one for the VP whose main verb is *kiss,* and one for the sentence with *want*. All of the variables refer (as a result of the equations) to one of these structures. The fact that *I* is the subject of *kiss* is not reflected in the constituent structure of the VP in which it appears, but in the assignment of the variable x_6 as the subject in the corresponding f-structure.

The new second rule for S in Figure 6–29 is included to handle questions like *Which baby did the girl kiss?* It is not fully general, and would need to be somewhat more complex in a full grammar. However, this version is sufficient to illustrate the use of a new notation, the *distant binding* arrows '$\Uparrow_{\text{NP}}$' and '$\Downarrow_{\text{NP}}$.'

In the examples so far, equations have been produced from the rules and lexical entries by instantiating $\uparrow$ and $\downarrow$ with the variables corresponding to the

Grammar rules

S → NP VP
(↑ Subject)=↓ ↑=↓

S → NP Aux NP VP
↓=⇓$_{NP}$ (↑ Subject)=↓ ↑=↓
(↓ Q-Form)=+

NP → Determiner Noun

NP → Pronoun

NP → ∅
↑=⇑$_{NP}$

VP → Verb $\left(\begin{array}{c} \text{NP} \\ (\uparrow \text{ Object})=\downarrow \end{array} \left(\begin{array}{c} \text{NP} \\ (\uparrow \text{ Object-2})=\downarrow \end{array}\right)\right)$

VP → Verb $\overline{\text{VP}}$
(↑ Vcomp)=↓

$\overline{\text{VP}}$ → $\left(\begin{array}{c} \text{Particle} \\ (\uparrow \text{ Prt-Type=To}) \end{array}\right)$ VP
↑=↓

Lexical entries

baby	Noun	(↑ Number) = Singular
		(↑ Predicate) = 'Baby'
did	Aux	
girl	Noun	(↑ Number) = Singular
		(↑ Predicate) = 'Girl'
I	Pronoun	(↑ Q-Form) = –
		(↑ Predicate) = 'I'
kiss	Verb	(↑ Predicate) = 'Kiss<(↑ Subject), (↑ Object)>'
the	Determiner	(↑ Q-Form) = –
to	Particle	(↑ Prt-Type) = To
want	Verb	(↑ Predicate) = 'Want<(↑ Subject), (↑ Vcomp)>'
		(↑ Subject) = (↑ Vcomp Subject)
which	Determiner	(↑ Q-Form) = +
who	Pronoun	(↑ Q-Form) = +

Figure 6–29. A more complex lexical-functional grammar.

nodes at the top and bottom of a single line in the tree. The symbols ⇑$_{NP}$ and ⇓$_{NP}$ are instantiated with variables that can span over a distance in the tree. Each occurrence of ⇓$_{NP}$ must be matched with an occurrence of ⇑$_{NP}$ that

Context-free phrase structure and lexical insertion (C-structure):

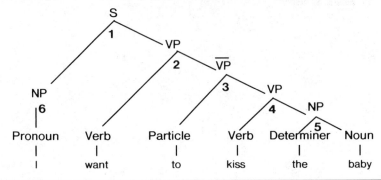

Equations:

Rule or word	Instantiations
S → NP VP	$(x_1 \text{ Subject}) = x_6,\ x_1 = x_2$
VP → Verb $\overline{\text{VP}}$	$(x_2 \text{ Vcomp}) = x_3$
$\overline{\text{VP}}$ → Particle VP	$x_3 = x_4,\ (x_3 \text{ Prt-Type}) = \text{To}$
VP → Verb NP	$(x_4 \text{ Object}) = x_5$
I	$(x_6 \text{ Q-Form}) = -,\ (x_6 \text{ Predicate}) = \text{'I'}$
want	$(x_2 \text{ Predicate}) = \text{'Want} < (x_2 \text{ Subject}),\ (x_2 \text{ Vcomp}) >,\text{'}$
	$(x_2 \text{ Subject}) = (x_2 \text{ Vcomp Subject})$
to	$(x_3 \text{ Prt-Type}) = \text{To}$
kiss	$(x_4 \text{ Predicate}) = \text{'Kiss} < (x_4 \text{ Subject}),\ (x_4 \text{ Object}) >\text{'}$
the	$(x_5 \text{ Q-Form}) = -$
baby	$(x_5 \text{ Predicate}) = \text{'Baby'}$

Solutions (F-structure):

$$x_1 = x_2 = \begin{bmatrix} \text{Subject} & = x_6 \\ \text{Vcomp} & = x_3 \\ \text{Predicate} & = \text{'Want(I, Kiss(I, Baby))'} \end{bmatrix}$$

$$x_3 = x_4 = \begin{bmatrix} \text{Subject} & = x_6 \\ \text{Object} & = x_5 \\ \text{Prt-type} & = \text{To} \\ \text{Predicate} & = \text{'Kiss(I, Baby)'} \end{bmatrix}$$

$$x_5 = \begin{bmatrix} \text{Q-Form} & = - \\ \text{Predicate} & = \text{'Baby'} \end{bmatrix}$$

$$x_6 = \begin{bmatrix} \text{Q-Form} & = - \\ \text{Predicate} & = \text{'I'} \end{bmatrix}$$

Figure 6–30. Derivation of a sentence with non-local context.

Context-free phrase structure and lexical insertion (C-structure):

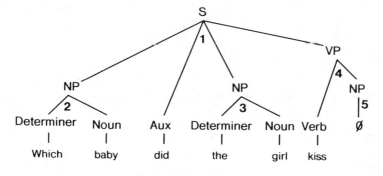

Equations:

Rule or word	Instantiations
S → NP Aux NP VP	$x_2 = x_5$, $(x_2$ Q-Form$) = +$, $(x_1$ Subject$) = x_3$, $x_1 = x_4$
VP → Verb NP	$(x_4$ Object$) = x_5$
which	$(x_2$ Q-Form$) = +$
baby	$(x_2$ Predicate$) = $ 'Baby'
the	$(x_3$ Q-Form$) = -$
girl	$(x_3$ Predicate$) = $ 'Girl'
kiss	$(x_4$ Predicate$) = $ 'Kiss$<(x_4$ Subject$)$, $(x_4$ Object$)>$'

Solutions (F-structure):

$$x_1 = x_4 = \begin{bmatrix} \text{Subject} & = x_3 \\ \text{Object} & = x_5 \\ \text{Predicate} & = \text{'Kiss(Girl, Baby)'} \end{bmatrix}$$

$$x_2 = x_5 = \begin{bmatrix} \text{Q-Form} & = + \\ \text{Predicate} & = \text{'Baby'} \end{bmatrix}$$

$$x_3 = \begin{bmatrix} \text{Q-Form} & = - \\ \text{Predicate} & = \text{'Girl'} \end{bmatrix}$$

Figure 6–31. Derivation of a sentence with distant dependencies.

appears within a part of the tree called the *control domain* of the constituent under which it appears. In the grammar of Figure 6–29, $\Downarrow_{\text{NP}}$ appears in one of the equations under the first NP of the S rule used to generate questions. This NP is also marked (by the other equation) as having the feature 'Q-FORM=+,' which will be satisfied only by question noun phrases, like *who* and *which baby*. An $\Uparrow_{\text{NP}}$ appears in the null expansion for NP, the last NP rule in the

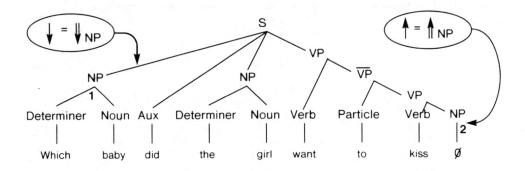

Figure 6–32. A structure with distant binding.

grammar. In Figure 6–31, the node assigned variable x_2 (*which baby*) is matched with the $\Downarrow_{\text{NP}}$, and the node assigned x_5 (the null object of the VP) with $\Uparrow_{\text{NP}}$. This produces the equation '$x_2 = x_5$' associated with the S rule. In solving the equations, the question phrase becomes identified with the object of the verb *kiss*.

This is a good example of the use of the functional structure to filter out overgeneration by the context-free grammar. The rule 'NP → ∅' allows any NP node to be expanded with an empty constituent. Since the grammar is context-free, any number of different NPs in the same structure could be null. However, only one is allowed to use the $\Downarrow_{\text{NP}}$ to match the $\Uparrow_{\text{NP}}$ in its equation, so any structure with too many null NPs will fail to have a functional solution.

The precise definition of control domains depends on a concept of *bounded domination*, which we will not describe in detail. It is carefully designed to allow certain structures and prevent others, just as the rule of *subjacency* (see Appendix C) captures many of the constraint phenomena discovered in trans-formational grammar. It deals with embedded sentences of a variety of kinds. For example, the sentence *Which baby did the girl want to kiss?* would have a structure like that of Figure 6–32, in which the functional structures associated with x_1 and x_2 would be equated, leading to a semantic form in which the baby was the object of the kissing.

This presentation has been somewhat oversimplified. There are many other features of lexical-functional grammar, which attempts to achieve or surpass the precision and coverage of transformational grammars. Unlike some of the other formalisms discussed in this chapter, it has been developed with a generative orientation, placing major emphasis on the precise characterization of the gram-matical sentences of a language. Unlike most other forms of generative gram-mar, it was motivated by considerations of processing and has been shaped by criteria of formal (computational) processability and psychological plausibility. It is being developed with the hope that it can serve as a theoretical model for the knowledge structures and processes of a human language user. We will not go into further detail here, except to note two other areas: the role played by the lexicon, and the problem of parsing.

The lexicon. The dictionary entry for *want* given above is highly specialized. It is applicable to the use of *want* in sentences like *I want to kiss the baby,* containing a complement that is a $\overline{\text{VP}}$. It would not cover *I want a round-trip ticket to Kabul* or *I want you to hold the baby.* In most grammar formalisms, it is assumed that a single dictionary entry can cover a number of such forms and that the grammar rules supply the variation. In a lexical-functional grammar, dictionary entries are highly specific and a single word like *want* will have several different entries corresponding to the different forms. This also applies to such phenomena as passive voice. Rather than having a syntactic rule or a pattern relating passive and active constituent structures, each verb can have both passive and active entries. The active entry relates the first argument of a predicate like KISS to the SUBJECT, while the passive entry relates it to a BY-OBJ.

There has been much argument within transformational grammar as to whether it is better to deal with phenomena like passivization through grammar rules or in the lexicon. One argument for treating them lexically is that there are many irregularities as to exactly which verbs can take what forms. For example, there are verbs that do not allow a passive, such as *seem.* On the other hand, it seems strange to have closely related passive-active pairs for the majority of verbs in the lexicon without any rule showing the generalization relating them. In lexical-functional grammar (and some other current forms of transformational grammar, as described in Appendix C), this is handled by the addition of *redundancy rules.* A redundancy rule specifies that an entry can be generated from another entry in the absence of specific information that it should not apply. A typical redundancy rule would produce a passive form for *kissed* from the corresponding active form.

Parsing. One of the major advantages of using a context-free grammar as a basis for parsing surface structures is that the techniques of Chapter 3 can be applied directly. By putting the additional relationships into the functional component, they are not restricted (as are the conditions and actions of an ATN) to being processed in a particular order. By adopting a processing algorithm like the active chart described in Section 3.6, it is possible to use flexible scheduling in which the context-free parsing can be intermixed with the instantiation and solution of the functional equations. The originators of the formalism hope that it will provide a good basis for the formulation of psycholinguistic models that can be tested experimentally, and that it can also be implemented in practical parsing systems. As of now, this work is still to be done.

6.7 Generalized phrase structure grammars

The grammars described in this chapter have all introduced a *functional* component, in which constituents are described as having relationships to other constituents that go beyond the basic parent-child relationship of immediate constituent structure. There is another body of current work that adopts some of the ideas presented here, but does not posit a distinct functional component.

Two quite different forms have been developed. One came from work in theoretical generative linguistics, and is often referred to as *phrase structure grammar,* or PSG, because it makes use of an underlying context-free grammar. The other, called *definite clause grammar,* was devised in the context of computer deduction systems and makes use of predicate logic.

Phrase structure grammar

The PSG formalism, developed by Gazdar (1979) and his associates (Gazdar, Pullum, and Sag, 1980), is based on an extension of context-free grammars. PSG is a descendant of transformational grammar, but differs in that it does not make use of transformations. To an outsider, this development seems somewhat surprising, since it was the invention of transformation rules that gave form to the entire paradigm of generative linguistics. In order to understand the implications of eliminating transformations, it is useful to summarize the different kinds of generalizations they have been used to formalize.

Agreement and morphology. Section 4.1 described the problems that were being faced in the earlier forms of phrase structure grammar. Among these were the difficulty of analyzing phenomena like agreement, which call for interdependencies that are not local to a single phrase. One of the earliest applications of transformation rules was to the kind of problem discussed in that section.

Related forms. Another important application of transformations was the formalization of the relationship between different surface forms such as the passive and the active or between a statement and the corresponding question. This was done by showing that sentences with similar deep structures could exhibit different surface structures. Some forms of transformational grammar have also used transformations to account for the relation of nominalized forms like *his criticism of the press* to the corresponding sentences.

Structural ambiguity. The ambiguity of sentences like *The chickens are ready to eat* was accounted for by postulating different deep structures that could be transformed into the same surface structure.

Unbounded movement. In order to account for sentences like *Which bank did your uncle tell you to have the check made out to?*, it is necessary to formalize the 'movement' of a phrase (in this case *which bank*) from an embedded component over an arbitrary distance.

One of the major attractions of transformational grammar was that a single new kind of rule (the transformation rule) could do all of these things. However, as the theory developed, it became more difficult to come up with a clean formulation of transformation rules that could handle all of the phenomena that were discovered. It became necessary to add new complexities to the form of rules and to their application (as described in Chapter 4 and Appendix C), and even with these, many problems remained.

In the course of these extensions, it was noted that some of the required additions made it possible to handle the same phenomena without using transformations at all. For example, the use of complex features associated with nodes made it possible to state rules for agreement without using feature-moving transformations. In the interest of overall parsimony, linguists continually ask 'What parts of the formalism could be left out without losing generality?' and it has appeared to some that the answer is 'Transformations.'

In order to do this, it is necessary to show how each of the problems originally handled by transformations can be handled by some other part of the formalism and to argue that since this other part is needed anyway, it cannot be left out in favor of transformations. There is also a desire, due to considerations of formal power (as discussed in Section 4.5), to eliminate transformations in hopes of coming up with an overall formalism that is formally more constrained.

There are three major ways in which the work done by transformations can be replaced: features, meta-rules, and semantic rules.

Features and derived categories

As mentioned above, the addition of feature complexes to phrase structure nodes makes it possible to handle many phenomena that were originally stated in terms of transformations. In PSG, nodes at all levels are assigned features, similar to those described in Section 6.3, which are used to handle phenomena like agreement. A special use of features (called *derived categories*) enables the grammar to generate sentences with 'holes' of the kind produced by long-distance dependencies.

Given a sentence like *Which friend did you want him to leave it with?*, the standard transformational theory would postulate a deep structure like that of Figure 6–33, which is then transformed by moving the NP dominating *friend* to the front of the sentence.

In the phrase structure model, the surface structure is generated directly by the base, as shown in Figure 6–34. In addition to the usual rules, there is a top level rule 'S → NP[+Q] AUX NP VP/NP,' which makes use of the derived category VP/NP, which stands for 'a VP that has a hole for an NP somewhere within it.' For any ordinary symbols A and B of the grammar, a node labeled A/B will be the ancestor of a structure identical to one for A except that: somewhere in every subtree of the A/B type there will occur a node of the form

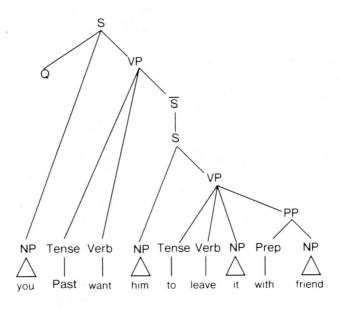

Figure 6–33. Deep structure for a question.

B/B dominating an empty constituent; and every node linking A/B and B/B will be of the X/B form. Intuitively, A/B labels a node of the type A which dominates material containing a 'hole' of type B.

The addition of these derived nodes and derived categories makes it possible to write a context-free grammar that accepts sentences like those of the figure and correctly rejects ones such as *Which friend did you go to the store?* (which has no hole in the VP) and *Which friend did you like with?* (which has too many holes). This calls for duplicating the rules of the grammar. If there is a rule of the form 'X → Y Z' and a possible hole of type A, we need to add the rules 'X/A → Y/A Z' and 'X/A → Y Z/A.' However, this does not change the power of the grammar since each rule is still context-free, and the use of meta-rules (as described below) makes it possible to express this multiplication of rules in a general and parsimonious way.

Note that the context-free version does not indicate any kind of meaning correspondence between the questioned NP and the hole. In this model, the correspondence is established by semantic interpretation rules, not as a part of the syntactic component.

Meta-rules

In order to introduce derived categories into a grammar systematically, it is necessary to make use of rule-generating rules. For example, we want to have

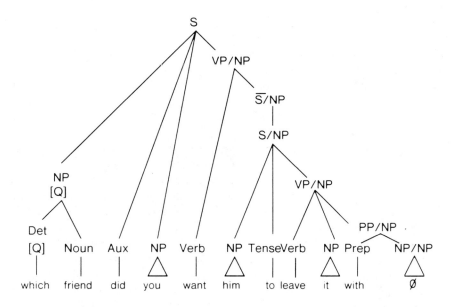

Figure 6–34. Context-free structure for a question.

a general rule specifying that for any rule of the form 'A → B C' and for any category X that can be displaced, there are rules 'A/X → B/X C' and 'A/X → B C/X.'

By introducing *meta-rules,* which apply to rules and produce other rules, it is possible to do this and also to capture many other generalizations previously handled by transformations. Formally, it is necessary to introduce *rule schemas* of two kinds: *finite* rule schemas like the one just given, and *infinite* rule schemas. Finite rule schemas do not change the generative power of the grammar and therefore leave it context-free. Infinite rule schemas do change the power and are less understood but appear to be necessary for describing phenomena such as conjunction.

We will not describe rule schemas in detail, but it is worth noting that they can be used to express the interactions between forms like passive and dative. Instead of having a lexical redundancy rule relating active to passive forms (as in lexical-functional grammar), PSG uses meta-rules that produce new context-free rules from other ones. For example, there might be a meta-rule that produces a rule for matching a passive S from one that matches the corresponding active S, and another that produces one for dative. Other meta-rules might apply to produce rules matching relative clauses and other embedded clause forms. The grammar resulting from the application of the meta-rules will contain a rule for each possible form (for example, a relative clause that is both passive and dative).

Semantic rules

One of the reasons for moving away from immediate constituent grammars was their inability to express relationships underlying intuitions such as the one that *Which baby* is the object of *kiss* in *Which baby did the President want to kiss?* Much of the motivation for the functional component of the grammars described in this chapter lies in its ability to capture these intuitions. In lexical-functional grammar, for example, an analysis that is valid from the context-free standpoint can fail because there is no solution to the functional equations. In phrase structure grammars, such relationships are simply not part of the syntax. There are associated semantic rules that cause the appropriate connections to be made in the logical form, but their operation is parallel to the syntax, not a part of it. An analysis includes both a syntactic derivation and the corresponding instantiation of the semantic rules, and a derivation can be blocked because of semantic rule failure. It is only through the joint action of syntactic and semantic rules that the grammaticality of a sentence is determined. In formulating such a grammar, many of the phenomena that have been treated syntactically can be seen as semantic. For example, in a sentence like *Woodrow wants to dance,* the embedded sentence *to dance* is not generated with a subject equal to *Woodrow,* which is then deleted, but simply has a semantic variable that is identified at a semantic level with the subject of the main sentence.

In the original formulation of generative grammar, there was a concept of grammaticality that was independent of meaning. A sentence could be judged as grammatical or ungrammatical purely on the basis of syntactic knowledge, without appeal to the semantic component. In lexical-functional grammar, phrase structure grammar, and many other current versions of generative grammar, this division has been dropped, or at least softened. In lexical-functional grammar, for example, the non-grammaticality of **The girl handed* or **I kiss to want the baby* results from a mismatch in the predicate forms associated with the functional description. These forms are intended to be part of the semantics—they follow conventions for predicate logic and could be used in processes of inference. Similarly, in phrase structure grammars and Montague grammars (see Appendix C), the structure associated with the semantic rules is a major factor in accepting or rejecting strings of words as grammatical sentences.

In discussing case grammar, we noted a related uncertainty as to whether the assignment of case roles should be thought of as syntactic or semantic, and in our discussion of systemic grammar, we raised the problem of sorting out the criteria used in identifying the choices that go into a choice system—some dealt more with form, and others more with meaning.

Each of these grammars raises the issues in different ways, but all seem to call for a re-evaluation of the roles played by syntax and semantics in an integrated formal theory. Since the preponderance of existing research and discussion is based on the older model of autonomous syntax, it is not yet clear just what the advantages are of shifting more of the work to the semantic component and what prices will have to be paid. However, it does appear that there is a significant trend away from the earlier concept of autonomous syntax, visible in a number of widely differing approaches to grammar.

Definite clause grammar

In the introduction to Section 6.6, the rules of a context-free grammar were described as 'constraints' on well-formed analysis trees. This way of looking at rules has led to the development of grammars in which the rules are just specific instances of logical formulas. For example, the rule 'S → NP VP' can be thought of as the formula:

$$\forall x,y,z \ NP(x) \wedge VP(y) \wedge Concat(x,y,z) \supset S(z)$$

The variables x, y, and z refer to sequences of words in the language. The predicate NP is true of any sequence that is a well-formed NP. The predicate CONCAT is true if its third argument is the concatenation of its first two. This formula therefore states that any sequence consisting of an NP followed by a VP is an S. For each word in the language there are atomic propositions representing its lexical categories, such as 'NOUN(*dog*)' and 'DETERMINER(*the*).'

A context-free grammar stated in this form can be used for parsing with a *theorem prover*. In order to prove a statement like 'S(*The dog chased a chicken*),' a series of proof steps must be produced that correspond directly to the parse tree. This makes it possible to integrate the syntactic formalism (including processing) with the deductive formalism used in dealing with meaning.

By translating grammars into logic, augmentations can then be added in a straightforward way, using the ordinary mechanisms of first order logic. For example, subject-verb agreement can be stated by having rules like:

$$\forall x,y,z,n \ NP(x) \wedge VP(y) \wedge Concat(x,y,z) \wedge Number(x,n) \wedge Number(y,n)$$
$$\supset S(z)$$

$$\forall x,y,z,n \ Verb(x) \wedge NP(y) \wedge Concat(x,y,z) \wedge Number(x,n)$$
$$\supset VP(z) \wedge Number(z,n)$$

$$\forall x,y,z,n \ Det(x) \wedge Noun(y) \wedge Concat(x,y,z) \wedge Number(x,n) \wedge Number(y,n)$$
$$\supset NP(z) \wedge Number(z,n)$$

The variable n refers to a possible choice of number, and NP and VP must agree in order for the condition of the first rule to be true. The number of the VP is that of its verb, and that of the NP must be held by both its determiner and noun. The dictionary contains propositions such as:

$$Number(\textit{tooth, } Singular)$$
$$Number(\textit{teeth, } Plural)$$
$$Number(\textit{the, } Singular)$$
$$Number(\textit{the, } Plural)$$

In a similar way, roles can be assigned. For example, we can have:

$\forall x,y,z$ NP(x) $\wedge$ VP(y) $\wedge$ Concat(x,y,z)
$\quad \supset$ Subject(z,x)

$\forall x,y,z$ Verb(x) $\wedge$ NP(y) $\wedge$ Concat(x,y,z) $\wedge$ Active(x)
$\quad \supset$ Obj(z,y) $\wedge$ Main-Verb(z,x)

$\forall v,w,x,y,z$ NP(x) $\wedge$ VP(y) $\wedge$ Concat(x,y,z) $\wedge$ Obj(y,w) $\wedge$ Main-Verb(y,v)
$\quad \supset$ Obj(z,w) $\wedge$ Main-Verb(z,v)

Since conditions in an ATN are logical tests on the contents of registers, it is possible to implement most of them directly. This includes the possibility of hold registers, although the formulas needed to guarantee that a held item is used once and only once are somewhat complex. The one major problem lies in the ATN's ability to change register contents after they have been established. For example, passive sentences are treated by putting the initial NP into the SUBJECT register when it is encountered, then shifting it to the DIRECT-OBJECT register when the passive verb form is found. In logic, things can't be 'taken back.' If the proposition SUBJECT(a,b) has been proved, then it stands. In order to handle this, the augmentations need to be written in a style that does not call for reassigning registers. For example, the initial NP can be assigned as the THEME in the rule for expanding S, and formulas establishing equality between THEME and SUBJECT or THEME and DIRECT-OBJECT can include a test on the form of the verb. In this sense, definite clause grammars are more similar to the other grammars of this chapter, with their emphasis on *transparency.*

The structures built by a definite clause grammar can be of different kinds. For example, if we want to build case structures we can include rules of the form:

$\forall x$ Verb(x) $\wedge$ Passive(x) $\supset$ VP(x) $\wedge$ Main-Verb(x,x)

$\forall v,x,y,z$ S(z) $\wedge$ Main-Verb(z,v) $\wedge$ Subj(z,x) $\wedge$ Obj(z,y) $\wedge$ Active(v)
$\quad \supset$ Agent(z,x) $\wedge$ Affected(z,y)

$\forall v,x,z$ S(z) $\wedge$ Main-Verb(z,v) $\wedge$ Subj(z,x) $\wedge$ Passive(v)
$\quad \supset$ Affected(z,x)

These rules are simplified—they deal only with agentless passives, treat the verb sequence as a single element, etc. However, they illustrate the basic idea of converting conditions and actions into logical formulas, using predicates for the features and role names and quantifying over phrases of the language.

There are a number of technical problems in writing grammars that capture the linguist's intuitions and also fit into the definite clause form (which is not the one used in the examples here). Although any formula can be translated into one or more formulas of the appropriate form, the translation may make it much less comprehensible. The grammars that have been written (see Pereira and Warren, 1980) do not use the simple kinds of encoding that we have presented, but rearrange things to make them more suitable for efficient use in parsing.

As with functional and lexical-functional grammar, there are many details of the new phrase structure and definite clause grammars that we have not mentioned and that are needed in order to make the system work—to generate all and only the sentences of the language. In all of these grammars, current research is at an early stage and is far from being able to supply a comprehensive account of English. However, they are likely to play an increasingly central role in the study of syntax in the coming years.

Further Reading for Chapter 6

Systemic Grammar. Systemic grammar was developed initially by Halliday and his colleagues while he was at the University of London. Kress's (1976) *Halliday: System and Function in Language* collects a number of his papers. The original series of papers entitled 'Notes on transitivity and theme in English' (1967) is extensive but difficult. Halliday's paper in Lyons's *New Horizons in Linguistics* (1970) is a good short introduction, and his more recent books, *Explorations in the Functions of Language* (1973), *Cohesion in English* (Halliday and Hasan, 1976), and *Language as a Social Semiotic* (1978) give more detail. They convey much of the spirit of systemic grammar but do not give a detailed account of the theory that would be satisfying to most grammarians. Berry's (1975, 1977) *Introduction to Systemic Linguistics* presents the basic ideas in a style intended for university students of English. There is a fairly extensive introduction intended for computer scientists in Winograd's *Understanding Natural Language* (1972), an account of a computer program for language comprehension (SHRDLU) that was designed using principles of systemic grammar. Hudson's *English Complex Sentences* (1971) is a good example of an extended application of systemic grammar to a set of problems in English, and his more recent *Arguments for a Non-transformational Grammar* (1976) describes his modified version of systemic grammar, daughter dependency grammar. Two forthcoming books will provide a general introduction (Halliday, *A Short Introduction to Functional Grammar*) and a survey of current research (Halliday and Fawcett (eds.), *New Developments in Systemic Linguistics*).

The Prague School. The 'functional sentence perspective' of the Prague School is described in Mathesius' *A Functional Analysis of Present Day English on a General Linguistic Basis* (1961, English translation 1975) and in *Topic, Focus, and Generative Semantics* by Sgall, Hajičová, and Benešová, 1969.

Case Grammar. The original paper that aroused interest in case grammar within generative linguistics was Fillmore's 'The case for case' (1968). It still serves as the best introduction to the basic issues. The use of case grammar in computational systems is described by the individual authors cited in the section and the early work is summarized by Bruce (1975). The attempt to integrate case grammar into transformational grammar is described in the extensive (845 pp.) UCLA grammar of English (Stockwell, Schachter, and Partee, 1973) called *The Major Syntactic Structures of English.*

Stratificational Grammar. The original formulation is described in Lamb's *An Outline of Stratificational Grammar* (1966). Lockwood's *Introduction to Stratificational Linguistics* (1972) is a more readable presentation designed for students.

Functional and lexical-functional grammar. The name *Functional Grammar* is used by Dik (1978) to describe a system that is based on many of the same underlying intuitions as systemic grammar, but is not as fully worked out. Functional grammar as described here is presented in Kay (1979). The formal and intuitive specification of lexical-functional grammar is provided by Kaplan and Bresnan (forthcoming), in a volume edited by Bresnan, entitled *The Mental Representation of Grammatical Relations.* This volume also includes papers arguing for the linguistic adequacy of the theory and papers considering how it might be embedded in psycholinguistic models of language acquisition, comprehension, and production.

Phrase structure grammars. The work on phrase structure grammars will appear in a volume edited by Jacobson and Pullum, entitled *The Nature of Syntactic Representation.* The major papers are Gazdar's 'Phrase structure grammar' and Gazdar, Pullum, and Sag, 'A phrase structure grammar of the English auxiliary system.' The idea of meta-rules was drawn from work on programming languages by Van Wijngaarden (1965), and was used in program language specification by Cleaveland and Uzgalis (1977), who call them 'double-level grammars.' Definite clause grammars were first proposed by Colmerauer (1978) and developed by Pereira and Warren (1980).

Related forms of grammar. Slot grammar (McCord, 1980), junction grammar (Lytle, 1979), cognitive grammar (Lakoff and Thompson, 1975), and relational grammar (Johnson, 1977) were also mentioned in the chapter.

Exercises for Chapter 6

Exercises for Section 6.1

6.1 In the text, we pointed out the difference between classifications based on meaning and those based on form.

a) Draw a network that classifies meaning potentials (like that of Figure 6–1) in a situation where the speaker wants possession of a toy that the hearer has.

b) Draw a network that classifies the form (like that of Figure 6–7) of the corresponding utterances. A given meaning option (for example, REQUEST) may be realized by different forms such as *Please give me the toy* and *Would you please give me the toy?*, while one form (e.g., *Would you give me the toy?*) can serve more than one semantic function (REQUEST and CHECK-POTENTIAL-WILLINGNESS).

6.2 Write as many different thematic rearrangements as you can think of for the sentence *The man who owned it expected them to pay him $20.* Example: *What the man who owned it expected them to pay him was $20.*

Exercises for Section 6.2

6.3 In the sentence *The duke gave my aunt this teapot,* the functions filled by each NP are:

> Theme=Subject=Actor=*the duke*
> Beneficiary=Indirect-Object=*my aunt*
> New=Direct-Object=Goal=*this teapot*

Give a sentence exhibiting each of the following combinations. Each NP will fill other functions in addition to those mentioned.

the duke	my aunt	this teapot
a) Actor	Bene=New	Theme=Goal=Subject
b) Actor=New	Bene=Subject	Theme=Goal
c) Bene=Subject=New	Actor	Theme=Goal

6.4 Think of your academic department as a system. There are functions it must serve with respect to the outside world (getting money, giving degrees, etc.) and an internal organization that involves a number of functions (teaching, planning, etc.). Describe it in functional/systemic terms, explaining the different systems of functional roles.

Exercises for Section 6.3

6.5 Which of the following feature combinations are allowed by the network of Figure 6–6?

      a) Personal Animate Subjective
      b) Personal Objective Second Plural
      c) Personal Third Plural Masculine
      d) Demonstrative Near Singular Neuter
      e) Question Reflexive
      f) Question Demonstrative Near Animate

It is allowable to have a feature description that does not make a choice from a particular system. Such a description is said to be less *delicate* than one that gives further choices, and it cannot then specify anything for which the missing choice would be a part of an entry condition.

6.6 Draw a system network that accounts for the following possible feature combinations.

Accept: CDE, DEG, BCD, BDG, BDGI, BDGK
Reject: AD, DI, AB, AG, IB, IG, DBE, DCG, BDGIK, BCDI, DEGK

6.7 Write a network like the one of Figure 6–7 to classify phrases describing times of day, such as *midnight, four o'clock, three fifteen p.m.,* and *a quarter till noon.* You do not need to specify formally how the classification is realized in the choice and ordering of constituents, but the feature systems you choose should be designed to make this correspondence as simple as possible (i.e., categorize by form, not meaning).

Exercises for Section 6.4

6.8 Show the steps (in the style of Figures 6–14 and 6–15) in the generation of the sentences *Plant the potatoes!* and *Were the potatoes planted?*

6.9 Extend the network of Figure 6–13 to cover sentences with beneficiaries by creating a new choice system called BENEFACTION that applies in parallel to VOICE in MATERIAL-PROCESS clauses (just as MOOD and TRANSITIVITY apply in parallel to CLAUSE). Show how your realization rules work on *We gave them the papers, Did they gave the papers to us?* and *The papers were given to us by them.*

6.10 The process of derivation as defined in the section involves doing all of the rules of one type (e.g., conflation) before any of the next type. Discuss how the content of the different rule types would have to be changed if we wanted to allow them to be applied in any order.

Exercises for Section 6.5

6.11 For each of the verbs *make, give, feel,* and *think,* give the different case frames specifying the major participants (i.e., ignoring prepositional phrases). Each frame should specify what roles are filled (e.g., ACTOR and AFFECTED or ATTRIBUTOR, ATTRIBUANT, and ATTRIBUTE) and which of the major constituents (subject, direct-object, indirect-object, and complement) fill them. Two frames are different if they have different numbers of participants, different role assignments, or if they seem to convey different meanings (as in the examples with *make*). Use role names from any of the case systems in the chapter that seem most appropriate.

6.12 Consider the general rule that a beneficiary (or recipient) in English can appear either as the indirect object (as in *I gave her the book*) or in a modifying prepositional phrase as in (*I gave the book to her*). Give examples of role patterns in which:

a) The beneficiary can appear as indirect object, or in a *for* phrase.

b) There can be a *to* phrase, but not an indirect object.

c) There can be an indirect object but not a *to* phrase.

The pattern will include both a verb and some of the participants. For example, *I won the race for him* allows a *for* phrase but cannot have an indirect object, as in **I won him the race*. Describe how these differences might be accounted for in terms of different meaning-roles played by the NP we have been calling the BENEFICIARY.

6.13 In the introduction to the section there is a series of examples containing the word *with*. Choose case names that are intuitively useful for you, such as INSTRUMENT, MATERIAL, and CO-AGENT. For each case, find an example of a verb that does not allow *with* to be used to fill that role.

6.14 Find a short text in a magazine or newspaper and assign case roles to the NPs in each clause (including embedded clauses) following the classification schemes shown for clause types and roles in Figure 6–21. Some NPs will be parts of adjuncts that do not play a direct role in the case structure and can be ignored. **Note:** You are likely to have difficulty with some of the clauses. Discuss any modifications to the scheme that might help.

Exercises for Section 6.6

6.15 Give functional grammar descriptions for declaratives, imperatives, and polar (yes-no) questions. Include the functions SUBJECT, PREDICATOR, and FINITE and the feature dimension MOOD. Use Figure 6–24 as a model for what the descriptions should look like, and Figure 6–13 for the content.

6.16 Give a functional analysis (in the style of Figure 6–23) for the sentence *She wanted to kiss the baby.*

6.17 Make additions to the grammar and lexicon of Figures 6–27 and 6–29 to handle the sentence *Which baby did she want the boy to kiss.* Give an analysis of the sentence in the style of Figure 6–28.

Exercises for Section 6.7

6.18 Describe how derived categories relate to the distant binding arrows of lexical-functional grammar, indicating what aspects they do and do not cover.

6.19 Informally describe the meta-rule that would be needed to handle simple cases of conjunction (without deletion, gapping, etc.).

6.20 Definite clause grammars:

a) Write a set of axioms in predicate calculus that correspond to the context-free grammar and dictionary of Figure 3–17, in the style shown in Section 6.7.

b) Give a proof of the theorem 'S(*the orange rabbit nibbled a cucumber with a saw*).'

c) How can the ambiguity of the sentence be related to the possibility of finding different proofs? Note that the existence of more than one proof is not equivalent to the presence of ambiguity.

Chapter 7

Computer Systems for Natural Language Parsing

The previous chapters have presented a body of concepts related to syntax and parsing. In the interests of clear presentation, they have been organized conceptually rather than historically—we have not tried to give a coherent picture of the order in which they were developed or the ways in which they have been used in computer systems. This chapter describes what has been done from a more pragmatic point of view, discussing the approaches that have been taken to designing practical natural language systems. In doing so, we are adopting the standpoint of the engineer rather than the natural scientist—the question is 'How can we build effective systems?' rather than 'How do we understand the systems we observe naturally?'

The systems described here cover a time period from the late 1950s to the present. They are among the best known and most developed currently in the literature, but they are a cross-section and not a full catalog—there may well be systems of equal interest that are not mentioned. Of course, all that can be given here is an overview. In order to get a deeper understanding of the systems and the variety of language data to which they have been applied, it is necessary to read the original papers.

Figure 7–1 lists the systems mentioned in this chapter and the basic references for each of them. A number of other papers, which are not presentations of specific syntactic systems, are referred to in the chapter but not listed in the figure. Since changes in the area of applied systems are much more rapid than in those basic theory, the reader interested in keeping up with the cur-

BASEBALL (Green et al., 1963)	MIND (Kay, 1973)
BORIS (Dyer, 1981)	Mitre Transformational Parser
CA (Birnbaum and Selfridge, 1981)	(Zwicky et al., 1965)
DIAMOND (Paxton, 1978)	NLP (Heidorn, 1976)
ELI (Riesbeck, 1978)	PARRY (Colby et al., 1974;
ELIZA (Weizenbaum, 1966)	Parkison et al., 1977)
EPISTLE (Miller,	PARSIFAL (Marcus, 1980)
Heidorn, and Jensen, 1981)	PHLIQA1
FLEXP (P. Hayes	(Scha, 1976, Landsbergen, 1976)
and Mouradian, 1980)	PLANES (Waltz, 1978)
FRUMP (DeJong, 1979)	Powerful Parser (Kay, 1967)
GUS (D. Bobrow et al., 1977)	PROGRAMMAR (Winograd, 1972)
GSP (Kaplan, 1973)	REL (F. Thompson et al., 1969)
HAM-RPM (Hahn et al., 1980)	REQUEST (Plath, 1976)
Harvard Syntactic Analyzer	ROBOT (Harris, 1977)
(Kuno and Oettinger, 1962)	RUS (R. Bobrow and Webber, 1980)
HEARSAY-II (Lesser et al., 1977)	SAD-SAM (Lindsay, 1973)
INTELLECT (see ROBOT)	SHRDLU (Winograd, 1972)
JETS (Finin,	SOPHIE (Burton and Brown, 1979)
Goodman, and Tennant, 1979)	SPEECHLIS (Bates, 1978)
KLAUS (Haas and Hendrix, 1980)	STUDENT (D. Bobrow, 1967a)
LADDER (Hendrix, 1978)	SYSTRAN (Toma, 1977)
LIFER (Hendrix, 1977)	TALE-SPIN (Meehan, 1981)
LINGOL (Pratt, 1975)	TORUS (Mylopoulos et al., 1979)
Linguistic String Parser (Sager, 1981)	TQA (Damerau, 1978; Petrick, 1981)
LNR (Norman et al., 1975)	UNDERSTAND
LUNAR (Woods, 1973b)	(J. Hayes and Simon, 1975)
Machine Translation System	USL (Lehman, 1978)
(Wilks, 1973, 1975a)	Word Expert Parser (Rieger and
MARGIE Parser (Riesbeck, 1975)	Small, 1979; Small, 1981)
MCHART (H. Thompson, 1981)	Writer's Workbench (Cherry, 1981)

Figure 7–1. Systems discussed in this chapter.

rent technology will need to look at recent technical reports and conference proceedings.

This can be difficult. Original research papers are often confusing, since a system is presented as a whole, with its unique features (rather than the common ideas) emphasized, and with the important ideas mixed with implementation details. The goal of this chapter is to provide a framework for understanding the details found in the literature.

Computer systems dealing with natural language syntax can be divided into several basic groups:

Machine translation. The first computational work on natural language was done in the pursuit of machine translation, an effort that was heavily supported during the 1950s and early 1960s. That work predated much of the work on formal linguistics (and contributed to it), so from our current standpoint the computational techniques and theories of syntax look chaotic and outdated. With a few exceptions we will not describe the early translation systems here. After a long period during which there was little active work in machine translation, there is currently a renewed interest, as described in Snell (1979): 'Machine translation has re-emerged after a long period in limbo.' Commercial systems, such as SYSTRAN, are being developed and King (1981) describes current efforts to specify a major translation system to be built under the sponsorship of the European Economic Community.

Integrated question-answering systems. From the mid 1960s to the mid 1970s, much of the new work was centered around the development of comprehensive systems that integrated syntax, semantics, and reasoning to carry out some kind of question-answering or cooperative task. The focus in these systems was on the integration of all kinds of linguistic knowledge and on trying to achieve a broad coverage of linguistic phenomena, including complex syntax. Much of the material presented in this book grew out of those efforts. Toward the end of the period, there was a concerted project to develop speech understanding systems, which again focused on the integration of multiple knowledge sources. In addition, some question-answering systems have been integrated into systems for computer aided instruction, such as SOPHIE. We will deal with all of these systems more extensively in the volume on meaning, limiting our discussion here to their syntactic components.

Data base retrieval. In the last five years, there have been two different kinds of work in natural language on computers. One trend has been towards pursuing the deeper problems of meaning and conversation, concentrating on issues other than syntax. This work will be the basis for much of the material in the volume on meaning. The other trend has been towards systems that have a limited capacity to handle complex syntax and deduction, but can be used as a practical *front end* for a data-retrieval system. These systems have generally made use of well-understood techniques to cover a subset of natural language that is incomplete but *habitable* in that a person using the system will quickly learn what kinds of things are handled and which others to avoid. Experience has shown (Finin, Goodman, and Tennant, 1979) that the semantic and reasoning limitations of the overall systems are much more constraining than their relatively simple syntax.

Many natural language data base interfaces (such as LIFER, PHLIQA1, REQUEST, and INTELLECT) are designed to operate as front ends for commercially available data base systems, while others (such as the much earlier REL system) were developed with their own data base formalism. The economics of computation are just now beginning to reach the point where practical natural language data-retrieval systems can be put into use. Systems are being developed by IBM, Phillips, Burroughs, Sperry Univac, SDC, Hewlett-

Packard, and a number of other companies and university research groups. These are beginning to be marketed and it is likely that within the next two to five years many such systems will be available.

Text analysis. There have been a number of applications that are not interactive, but involve the syntactic processing of bodies of text. One purpose is to provide a basis for information retrieval, in which the analysis can be used either to retrieve pieces of text or to extract a structured data base directly from textual information such as medical records. The Linguistic String Parser was developed primarily for such applications. Systems designed to aid in writing (such as EPISTLE and the Writer's Workbench) use syntactic analysis techniques to find possible errors in text being prepared. They do only a limited form of parsing, but are able to detect certain classes of error, such as improper subject-verb agreement and pronoun cases (as in *I are here* and *Him hit me*). Speech understanding is being applied to the problem of *transcription* (the conversion of speech to printed text), which must include syntactic and semantic analysis along with the signal processing techniques.

Text generation. There has been some work on the *generation* of text by computers, including the output of question-answering systems (Simmons and Slocum, 1972), paraphrase generation, (Goldman, 1975), and story generation (Meehan, 1981). Friedman (1969) developed a generator based on transformational grammar, to be used in testing grammars. Bates and Ingria (1981) also use transformational grammar in a system that generates sentences in a tutorial program for teaching English to hearing-impaired children. Some speech generation systems (e.g., Levine and Saunders. 1979, Melby, 1977) make use of syntactic analysis in order to generate appropriate intonation patterns. The difficult problems in generation are those of meaning and context rather than syntax. Typically, a program for generation can get by with a repertoire of output structures that is much more limited than full English, handled by a simple finite state or phrase structure generator. We will discuss generation systems in a later volume and limit our concern in this chapter to systems for parsing.

Theory-motivated systems. Throughout the history of computational linguistics, there have been projects dealing with parsing as a theoretical problem, not associated with a particular application. One of the best known early projects was the Harvard Syntactic Analyzer, which was an early version of a top-down backtracking context-free parser. This project first developed the technique of *path elimination,* discussed under the heading of *well-formed substring tables* in Chapter 3. A grammar of over 3000 rules was developed for English. A series of projects at the Rand Corporation (described by Hays, 1967) produced many of the early implementations of the parsing strategies presented in Chapter 3. The General Syntactic Processor, Definite clause grammars, and

MCHART are examples of more recent attempts to define a parser for a particular class of grammars.

There has always been a dual motivation in developing computer systems for parsing. On the one hand, they have practical uses. On the other, they can be viewed as hypotheses about the nature of human language processing, and their mechanisms can be a basis for psycholinguistic theory. Systems primarily motivated by theoretical considerations (such as PARSIFAL) do not emphasize wide coverage or practicality, but they attempt to capture in their design the same kinds of generalizations that linguists and psycholinguists posit as theories of language structure and language use. Although psychological and linguistic theory has always been a source of motivation, a much wider gap between this approach and the more pragmatic approach has developed over the past few years.

Language learning. There have been some programs that attempt to learn the grammar of a language through examples. In general, these have been based on assuming that the underlying grammar is very simple (finite state or context-free with only a few rules), and have made no attempt to deal with the complexities of real language. Anderson (1977, 1981) has developed theories of acquisition based on augmented transition networks, and has described computer implementations. Pinker (1979) gives an excellent review of formal models (including computer models) of language learning. Many systems have allowed the user to enter new vocabulary items and specify their meaning and syntactic class. Some infer the class of a new word by assuming it is in the class that would make a sentence grammatical (for example, inferring that *glitc* must be a noun in *Pick up a glitc*). Others, such as KLAUS, use an English-like dialog to allow someone to define new words and their syntactic properties (including the case frames associated with verbs) without needing to know the linguistic formalism underlying the program.

7.1 Issues in the design of a parsing system

In designing a computer system for analyzing natural language inputs, there are a number of different issues to be addressed. There are tradeoffs of power versus efficiency and simplicity, decisions as to what constructs need to be handled, and different aspiration levels for the generality of the system outside of its specific intended use. The decisions are interrelated, each having consequences in a number of areas. This section discusses the issues outlined in Figure 7–2 and describes the range of approaches that have been taken. Only those issues related to syntax and parsing are discussed in this volume. Issues of representation, meaning, and language use are left for the volume on meaning, including the kind of reasoning the system does, its treatment of pronouns and items whose meaning depends on context, and the organization of its discourse.

Completeness

>   Full parse
>   Partial analysis

Basic framework

>   Augmented phrase structure grammar
>   Transformational grammar
>   Chart rewrite
>   ATN
>   Pattern matching
>   Situation-action rules

Form of assigned structures

>   Annotated surface structure
>   Deep syntactic structure
>   Systematic non-syntactic structure
>   Arbitrary structure building

Ambiguity and search

>   Parallel parsing
>   Chronological backtracking
>   Explicit backtracking
>   Deterministic parsing

Syntactic coverage

>   Grammaticality checking
>   Complex clause embedding
>   Complex noun phrases
>   Phrases and idioms
>   Conjunction, ellipsis and comparatives

Domain specificity

>   Special patterns
>   Semantic lexical categories
>   Special structures produced

System engineering

>   User interface
>   Grammar-writer amenities
>   Efficiency

Figure 7–2. Issues in the design of a computer parsing system.

Completeness

Throughout the years there have been systems whose parsing is not based on a systematic approach to grammar and syntax. Instead, they contain a collection of algorithms and strategies that perform a sufficient analysis for the purpose of the overall system. We can distinguish between systems designed explicitly for *partial analysis* and those that aspire to a full analysis.

There are those who argue that full syntactic analysis is not necessary in practical systems, since semantic considerations can lead to a full analysis in cases where the syntactic structure is not too complex. DeJong (1979) describes a system (FRUMP) for analyzing newspaper stories that '...does not need a very complete knowledge of syntax,' since 'Text analysis is motivated by predictions of conceptual items. Syntactic knowledge in general is used only to find the general sentence location of the desired word.' Wilks (1973) similarly proposes that a translation program can operate with an ad hoc syntax when it is guided by the matching of a stock of *semantic templates*. These claims are difficult to evaluate, since the systems supporting them have generally been applied only to very simple inputs. The general attitude in the field is that although partial analysis can be useful (and sufficient for some specialized tasks), any fully general language system will need a syntactic parser that uses a large grammar based on a systematic formalism.

In doing a partial analysis, there is a tradeoff between *specificity* (assigning structures only when they are appropriate) and *exhaustiveness* (assigning structures to as many inputs as possible). A system with low specificity will often assign structures that are not appropriate to an input. In some cases, the structure assigned will be plausible but the information that was thrown away would have clearly pointed to a different structure intended by the speaker. Systems doing partial analysis are most useful in applications where high specificity is not required, such as document retrieval (Salton, 1975). One good example is the PARRY program for psychiatric interview simulation. PARRY carries on a dialog with an interlocutor in which it simulates the responses of a mental patient suffering from paranoia. The system needs only to be able to do *something* for every input, and if the response is out of line, there is no high penalty (in fact, it may serve to reinforce the image of craziness).

Basic framework

The most far-reaching technical decision is the choice of a basic theoretical framework—the overall architecture of the system and grammar. The remaining sections of this chapter will examine these architectures one by one. The following short summary serves as a background for examining the other design issues:

Augmented phrase structure grammar. One of the most common approaches is to augment context-free grammar in the same way that ATNs augment recursive transition networks. These augmentations associate features and/or registers with nodes and specify conditions and/or actions associated with rules. There are many variations, as discussed in Section 7.2.

Transformational grammar. There have been some attempts to make use of transformational grammar directly in a parsing system. The major advantage of this approach is that there exists a large body of work within the transformational framework that could be used to build systems covering a very wide range of syntactic phenomena. Some systems, like REQUEST, attempt to be 'pure' implementations, while others, such as PHLIQA1, adapt the idea of transformations to a different framework. There are a number of problems in making transformations computational, discussed in Section 7.3.

Chart rewrite. One group of systems has developed in parallel to the others described here, along rather different lines. These systems make use of a chart (from which the active chart of Chapter 3 evolved) and a collection of rewrite rules that can add new edges to the chart, as described in Section 7.4. They grew out of early work that went under the name 'computational linguistics' as opposed to 'theoretical linguistics' (transformational grammar) or 'artificial intelligence' (ATN and many of the augmented phrase structure systems). The chart ideas were later incorporated into other systems, but the original mechanism is still the basis of systems like REL and USL.

ATN. The ATN formalism has been used in a number of systems. Some, such as LUNAR and GUS, use ATNs explicitly. Others, such as SHRDLU, use a different notation but are closely related. Chapter 5 briefly discussed computational issues like parallel versus serial parsing and the efficiency of grammar interpreters. It presented a composite notion of the ATN that combines ideas that were actually derived from a number of different systems and were not part of the initial formulation. Section 7.5 addresses these issues.

Pattern matching. Some systems are organized around simple ideas of pattern matching like those described in Chapter 2, along with additional *ad hoc* processing techniques. These are generally systems that do only a partial syntactic analysis, in conjunction with some kind of semantic analysis. They are described in Section 7.6.

Situation-action rules. In standard parsing, there is some kind of grammar describing the structures to be found and a parsing process that uses that grammar. It is possible to organize the system around a set of procedural situation-action rules instead, each of which can be triggered independently by features of the situation and can act to change that situation. Such systems tend to be less structured than standard grammars, and are often used for partial analysis or in cases where semantic considerations drive the analysis process. They are discussed in Section 7.7.

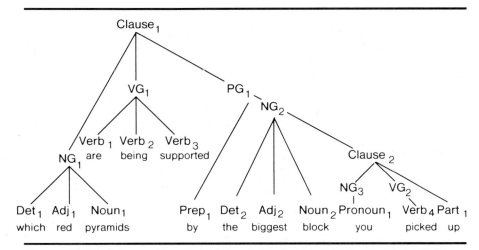

Clause₁ (*Which red pyramids are being supported by the biggest block you picked up?*) Clause
  Major Question Wh- Transitive Passive (Present in Present) Subject-Question
  Agent
NG₁ (*Which red pyramids*) NG Determined Indefinite Question Plural Subject
  Det₁ (*Which*) Determiner Question-Determiner Singular Plural
  Adj₁ (*red*) Adjective
  Noun₁ (*pyramids*) Noun Plural
VG₁ (*are being supported*) VG Finite Passive (Present in Present)
  Verb₁ (*are*) Verb Auxiliary Intensive Be Plural Present
  Verb₂ (*being*) Verb Auxiliary Intensive Be Ing
  Verb₃ (*supported*) Verb Transitive Past-Participle
PG₁ (*by the biggest block you picked up*) PG By Agent
  Prep₁ (*by*) Preposition By
  NG₂ (*the biggest block you picked up*) NG Definite Singular Prep-Obj
    Det₂ (*the*) Determiner Definite Singular Plural
    Adj₂ (*biggest*) Adjective Superlative
    Noun₂ (*block*) Noun Singular
    Clause₂ (*you picked up*) Clause Secondary Qualifier Wh-Rel NG-Relative
        Object-Relative Transitive Active Particle (Past)
      NG₃ (*you*) NG Plural Subject Pronoun-NG
        Pronoun₁ (*you*) Pronoun Plural Subject Object
      VG₂ (*picked*) VG Finite (Past)
        Verb₄ (*picked*) Verb Finite Past
      Particle₁ (*up*) Particle

Figure 7–3. Annotated surface structure produced by SHRDLU.

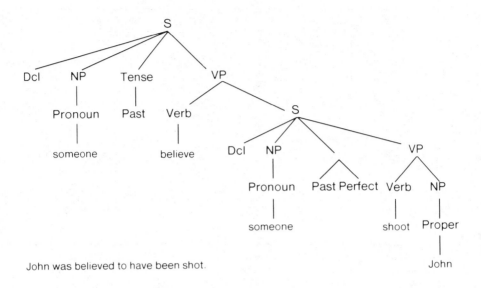

Figure 7–4. Deep structures produced by an ATN system.

The form of assigned structures

In building a computer parsing system, one usually has in mind some purpose for the parsing. Some other component of the system will make use of the analysis to answer questions, find documents, store information, generate sounds, or produce a translation. There is a good deal of latitude in how the work is divided up among components. The syntactic analysis can be 'surfacey,' leaving more work to the semantic analyzer, or can provide a 'deeper' analysis that is more immediately useable in carrying out the activities of the system. It can be more complete, trying to preserve all of the information about the sentence, or can be boiled down, leaving only that which is known to be relevant for further analysis. There are four general types of strategy:

Annotated surface structure. The most straightforward result of a parser is a tree structure corresponding to the parse. This is the result that has been produced by many of the parsing algorithms described in this book. In a simple context-free system, the result is a phrase structure tree. In an augmented system, this tree can be annotated with features. The PROGRAMMAR system used in SHRDLU, for example, produced structures like that of Figure 7–3, in which each node has a list of features, based on a systemic choice network. The subject *which red pyramids* and prepositional agent *by the biggest block...* are left in their surface positions in the tree—the syntactic parser does not move them around, but simply adds the feature PASSIVE to the node containing them. The semantic analyzer notes this feature and uses the correct elements for the deep subject and object of the verb.

Deep syntactic structure. In order to simplify the semantic analyzer, many systems do some kind of transformation of the surface structure tree to produce a syntactic structure in which phenomena like passive voice and implicit subjects have been accounted for. In some systems (such as LUNAR), the generated structure is an ordinary phrase structure tree like the deep structures of transformational grammar, as illustrated in Figure 7–4. In others (such as GUS), the structure is based on role registers and is more akin to the role and feature structures of Chapter 5. One particular kind of structure generated by a number of parsers is based on *case frames,* as described in Section 6.5. Rather than return a clause structure containing a subject, objects, and prepositional modifiers, these systems combine them when possible into a case structure based on the particular verb, as illustrated in Figure 7–5.

Systematic non-syntactic structure. In many systems, there is no need to produce a complete syntactic analysis. Each constituent can be analyzed for its 'content' as it is parsed, and that content used to build up an overall semantic analysis. In systems like MARGIE, the structure is based on a semantic theory and each syntactic constituent simply contributes its part to the evolving semantic structure. In data base systems, the structure being built up may be a request in some *query language* associated with the data base. In general, systematic non-syntactic systems are organized to produce an overall structure that is determined by the syntactic pieces but is not organized along syntactic lines.

Arbitrary structure building. Systems like LIFER and LINGOL do not attempt to provide any systematic resulting structure at all. They allow the

---

I want to go to San Diego on May 28

```
(Client Declare
    (Case for want/e (Tense Present)
        Agent = Dialog.Client.Person
        Event = (Case for go (Tense Present)
            Agent = Dialog.Client.Person
            To-Place = (Case for City
                          Name = San-Diego)
            Date = (Case for Date
                       Month = May
                       Day = 28))))
```

Figure 7–5. Case structure produced by GUS.

grammar writer to associate a structure building procedure with each rule, using the underlying implementation language (in these cases, LISP). A particular grammar writer could choose to write actions that produced annotated surface structures, deep structures, semantic structures, or anything else. These systems are simpler and have a greater generality while placing a correspondingly higher design burden on the user.

Ambiguity and search

Chapter 3 raised a number of issues related to nondeterminism and ambiguity. In designing any practical parsing system, one must make concrete decisions about them. They can be initially grouped into two basic issues: how to deal with multiple successful parsings (ambiguity), and how to explore the space of alternatives in searching for a successful parse.

In dealing with ambiguity, there are three choices: Banish it (insist that the grammar give only one parse for any grammatical sentence); use the first parsing found (perhaps providing clues to the parser as to the order in which to try things); and find multiple possibilities (to choose among). All of these approaches have been used, and under the third category there have been a number of ways of resolving the ambiguity. The simplest is to respond to all of the interpretations, or to present the alternatives to the person who entered the input and to let her or him indicate which was intended. A somewhat more sophisticated solution is to first try generating a response for each interpretation and eliminate those for which there is no sensible response (e.g., a command that cannot possibly be carried out). The user is required to choose only when there is more than one sensible alternative.

The issue of search is more complex, and all of the approaches described in Chapter 3 have been used:

Parallel parsing. Systems based on chart rewrite rules and many of the systems based on augmented phrase structure rules make use of parallel parsing techniques. In general, it is relatively easy to write a parallel system if one is not concerned with efficiency issues. However, with grammars more complex than context-free grammars, it can be quite difficult to provide for the sharing of common elements that makes some parallel implementations relatively efficient.

Chronological backtracking. One of the simplest strategies to implement is chronological backtracking, as described in Section 3.4. Parsers making use of more complex grammar formalisms (such as ATNs) have often taken advantage of this simplicity to keep the overall system from going beyond reasonable complexity bounds. Systems like ROBOT have made use of the natural recursive structure of LISP to implement the backtracking involved in keeping track of register assignments. Some have also used *arc ordering* to lead the parser into the exploration of more likely alternatives first. Such ordering would be irrelevant in a parallel parser, since it explores them all.

Explicit backtracking. Some systems, such as PROGRAMMAR, do not have a uniform means of keeping track of choices, but instead include explicit actions in the grammar to go back and try something different. Thus, for example, in the grammar for the noun group there is a loop that accepts noun sequences such as *butcher knife handle*. In a sentence such as *Does this butcher knife handle frozen foods too?,* the loop can be taken once too often, treating *handle* as a noun when it is actually the main verb. If the main verb is missing, the system explicitly goes back and (if possible) removes the last noun from a preceding noun group and recognizes it as the verb. This strategy runs more efficiently than uniform backtracking, since it does not keep choice records at every alternative. It is a more difficult grammar formalism to work with, since the grammar writer must anticipate those places where wrong paths can be taken and must carefully undo all the effects of following them before going back. It does not distinguish knowledge about the structure of grammatical sentences from the process of parsing as cleanly as does the ordinary ATN formalism.

Deterministic parsing. Section 3.5 mentioned the use of *bounded-context* grammars for artificial languages such as programming languages. There have been several parsers that treat natural language in a bounded-context style, assuming that at every choice point it is possible to choose the right alternative deterministically. As was pointed out in the original discussion in Chapter 3, no simple notion of bounded-context will suffice for English. Given sentences like *Have the students who were tardy take the exam* and *Have the students who were tardy taken the exam?,* we cannot tell whether the initial *have* is a main verb or an auxiliary until we see the form of *take*. The intervening phrase *the students who...* could be arbitrarily long. However, with a few extensions to the basic mechanism (described in Section 7.7), it can be argued that the parser will make wrong choices only in those *garden path sentences* that would confuse a human hearer or reader, such as *The boat floated down the river sank,* in which *(that was) floated down the river* modifies *the boat*.

The choice of a strategy for exploring multiple alternatives is often guided by the way that the syntactic parser will be integrated with the other components of the system. For example, if semantic analysis is done on a phrase-by-phrase basis as the parsing goes along, then a backtracking strategy will often work well, since the semantic analysis eliminates false paths early. On the other hand, if all of the parsing is done before any further analysis, some kind of parallel strategy is called for, since all of the alternatives must be available. In discussing individual systems in the following sections, we will point out how they integrate syntax with other levels of analysis.

Syntactic coverage

No computer system (or linguistic analysis) covers all of the phenomena of natural language. The designer must decide which things are critical and which can be ignored, and this decision is guided both by theoretical concerns and by practical experience. There is a tradeoff between having a larger, more complex grammar and having a less complete system. Some applications (such as the use of the SYSTRAN machine translation system to translate repair manuals) have involved the writing of specially constructed grammars that eliminate constructs that are difficult to parse. Writers and editors who do pre-processing of the text to be translated learn a 'customized' form of English. For example, they are taught to replace the sentence *Center cam follower with snubber cam and secure.* with *Put cam follower in center of snubber cam and secure cam follower.* For some applications, this can allow a relatively limited system to perform useful work. In others (such as interactive question answering with naive users), the system cannot depend on special limitations on the constructs used.

In deciding on the breadth of coverage to be attempted, there are a number of issues that have generally been considered:

Grammaticality checking.   In the formal grammars of Chapters 3 and 4, there was an emphasis on having the grammar precisely characterize the sentences of the language. Any string of words that was not a legal sentence would be rejected by the recognizer or parser. For practical systems, this ability is not vital. A system that accepted ill-formed sentences in place of the corresponding correct ones would be even better—if it were accurate in assigning the right corresponding form.

There have been strong arguments for and against precise grammars. Those who argue against them draw analogies to the human capacity for understanding a wide range of 'ungrammatical' utterances. Those who argue for precision point out that grammar serves a vital function—that for any rule of grammar, no matter how apparently obscure, there exist sentences that would be ambiguous if the rule were not taken into account, but whose structure is not in fact ambiguous. As an example, the sentences *The man who knew him was going left* and *The man who knew he was going left* are both meaningful and contain the same words, differing only in a subtle syntactic marker. But one is interpreted as *The man who was acquainted with him was going leftward* and the other as *The man who knew that he was going went out.* If the message is to be properly deciphered, the complexities of the syntactic structure need to be accounted for.

In speech understanding systems, grammaticality checking can be even more important, since there is uncertainty about the very words of which the sentence is formed. A sequence of hypothesized words that can be parsed only as an ungrammatical sentence is probably incorrect in its hypothesis about one or more of the words. Finally, there is the question as to whether less precise systems can adequately assign structures, or whether they will make mistakes (compared to a human interpreter). Most imprecise systems have avoided dealing with the kinds of complex structures discussed below, working reliably only for short simple sentences. A number of techniques for dealing with ungrammatical inputs are discussed in a survey by Kwasny and Sondheimer (1981).

Complex clause embedding. Much of the work in transformational grammar has been motivated by the analysis of complex embedded sentences like *List all the ships the cargoes of which include only what the chief officer authorized the loading of.* In designing a practical system, one has the choice of simply rejecting such sentences, insisting that the user give a series of simpler sentences in their place. Those systems built from a more theoretical perspective (in general, using transformational grammar or ATNs) tend to include these complexities, while those built with practical applications in mind (often using augmented phrase structure grammars) do not.

Complex noun phrases. As with clauses, noun phrases can be analyzed as having an intricate syntactic structure, including quantifiers and numbers of various kinds, as in *most of the first hundred successful prize winners.* They also can introduce quantifier scope ambiguity, as illustrated by the difference between:

> *Take down the name of every person here.*
>
> *Greeley, Colorado is the hometown of every person here.*

Systems differ in their attempts to deal with these complexities, often allowing only the simplest kinds of quantification and numeration.

Phrases and idioms. Much of our everyday language is made up of stock phrases that are not understood by a direct analysis of their structure. Some, such as *Could you please tell me...,* could be syntactically analyzed but are used so frequently that they act like atomic vocabulary items. Others, such as *the more the merrier,* have a specialized syntactic form. In theoretically oriented systems, these have tended to be ignored. In practical systems, people have discovered that a moderate-sized stock of phrasal items can account for a great deal of the complexity encountered in the inputs given by naive users. Some systems, such as PARRY, have taken an extreme position, building most of the syntactic knowledge as a collection of thousands of patterns. Others, such as LUNAR, PLANES, and REQUEST, use a more standard syntactic parser, but have preprocessors that recognize standard phrases and convert them to a canonical form.

Conjunction, ellipsis, and comparatives. Some of the most problematic areas of syntax, as mentioned in earlier sections, are conjunction, ellipsis, and comparative constructions. They all raise similar problems in that they allow gaps to appear in what would be the normal unreduced form, as in:

Laurie wants to visit next week, and Peter the week after.

Do you know what kind of ice cream Haj likes? George thinks vanilla.   (1)

This Honda is bigger than Ron said.

In all three cases, there is an implicit filling in of the final clause, based on material in the previous context:

. . . and Peter (wants to visit) the week after (next week).

George thinks (that Haj likes) vanilla (ice cream).

. . . Ron said (this Honda is X big).

There are no adequate general theories as to just what can be omitted and how it can be filled in. Linguists concerned with theoretical syntax have at times looked at these problems, but they have generally relegated them to the category of 'hard issues to be looked at later.' However, in practical systems, naive users will often use such constructions and will find it particularly constricting to have them forbidden, ignored, or misinterpreted. Therefore most computer systems include facilities to handle some standard cases. We can distinguish *whole phrase* conjunction or comparatives from the *elliptical* cases given above.

Whole phrase conjunction and comparison are relatively easy to implement. At the simplest, one can simply include rules (or their equivalent in the grammar formalism) for 'NP → NP CONJ NP,' 'S → S CONJ S,' 'PP → PP CONJ PP,' etc. Loops or recursive rules can handle lists like *Shadrack, Meshack, and Abednego*. In some systems (including PROGRAMMAR and LUNAR), rather than having a separate conjunction rule for each syntactic category in the grammar, there is a special process associated with conjunctions that produces the same effect. This leads to a shorter grammar but one requiring a more complex parser.

In handling ellipsis of the kinds shown in all three examples above, there are three basic approaches, all of which have been used in computer systems. First, it is possible to include explicit rules for phrases that contain less than the normal set of constituents. For example, the following grammar fragment would accept the sentences *I gave Fernando tea and Gloria coffee* and *Pablo showed me his answer and told Rodrigo nothing*:

S	→	S Conjunction Reduced-S
S	→	NP Verb NP NP
Reduced-S	→	NP NP
Reduced-S	→	Verb NP NP

Such a grammar would be augmented by actions that produced an underlying structure in which the appropriate pieces were filled in from the first conjunct. Such an approach is simple to implement but demands explicit rules for every possible deletion. It becomes too complex to handle in cases of embedding like *George thinks vanilla,* where the fragments are from different clause levels.

Rather than putting in explicit rules for reduced forms, it is possible simply to apply the grammar in its non-elliptical form, along with additional rules allowing deletions. These rules sit outside the regular grammatical framework and are generally built up on the basis of watching what happens in a number of sentences, rather than on the basis of a formal theory. In LUNAR, for example, whenever a conjunction appeared, the parser went into a special mode where it could go back to any previous node it had crossed in the networks and start a new parse forward from that node, using special rules as to what paths could be followed. This approach is more general in that it allows missing elements to be filled in at whatever level, but it is quite difficult to come up with the right rules for deciding what arcs to allow. In (1), for example, it is necessary to take an arc calling for an embedded S with missing constituents *(that Haj likes...),* even though the surface structure has no indication that such a clause exists. In allowing all the relevant possibilities, the grammar generates a large number of ambiguities and an even larger number of false paths.

A more direct approach, which goes even farther outside the normal notion of parsing, is to analyze a potentially elliptical construct by matching it against the context preceding it. Often its phrases will line up more or less directly against a subset of the phrases in the preceding sentence or conjunct, allowing gaps for the missing constituents. This is particularly true if semantic information is taken into account in doing the matching, lining up elements from the same semantic category. Thus we would align:

> *I gave Fernando a cup of tea and*
> *...   Gloria   ...   coffee*

This alignment is not always so simple. In (1), *George thinks vanilla* must be aligned against the deep structure *You know that Haj likes what kind of ice cream* rather than the surface structure of the question. However, surface structure plays a large role in determining what elliptical constructions sound natural, and surface-oriented matching strategies handle a large number of cases.

Domain specificity

In designing a system for a specific application, one has the possibility of taking advantage of peculiarities of that application or its subject domain in order to make the system work better. The earliest natural language systems, such as BASEBALL, SAD-SAM, and STUDENT, were designed specifically for a single problem area. For example, STUDENT analyzed every sentence as a linear algebraic equation, since its task was to solve algebra word problems. Later systems have attempted to be more general in their treatment of syntax while remaining domain-specific in their treatment of meaning and the overall organization of their interactions with a user. However, there are a number of ways in which specific knowledge of the subject area can be used in building an effective parser.

Special patterns. In any subject area, there will be phrase forms and idioms that need to be treated specially. As an obvious example, any system that deals with times and dates needs to be able to handle phrases like *Monday February 24, 1946, Thursday morning,* and *half past three,* which do not fit the ordinary patterns for an NP. Rather than adding a great deal of complexity to the grammar for the ordinary constituents, it is usually more straightforward to introduce new categories such as DATE-SPECIFICATION and TIME-OF-DAY. In a similar vein, the purpose of the system (for example, to answer questions from a data base) can lead to the common use of standard phrases like *Could you tell me ...* and *What about....* As mentioned above, special treatment of these can serve to handle a large number of inputs that would otherwise require a more complex grammar.

Semantic lexical categories. In addition to having syntactic categories that represent special classes of phrases, it is possible to organize the dictionary so that words are classified according to semantic as well as syntactic criteria. In a program dealing with medicine, for example, the words *potassium, finding,* and *heart* might all appear in separate noun subclasses, and the rules for agreement in constituents can depend on these subclassifications. The sentence *I don't agree with her finding about the potassium balance* would be judged grammatical, while *I don't agree with her potassium about the heart balance* would be rejected *on syntactic grounds.* Grammars based on a *science-specific vocabulary* have been used for many years in programs like the Linguistic String Parser, and have more recently been widely adopted under the slightly misleading rubric *semantic grammars.* They are in fact syntactic grammars (unlike the truly semantic grammars underlying systems like MARGIE) which make use of semantic criteria in determining lexical categories.

By writing a grammar that is specific to a particular topic domain, one can let the syntactic component do more of the work, producing fewer proposed parsings for semantic analysis. With some system organization strategies, this reduces the problem of ambiguity, makes the overall process more efficient, and (as discussed above) makes possible an effective matching strategy for handling ellipsis. The importance of introducing semantic categories into the grammar is related to the use of a system organization in which parsing and semantic analysis are done in separate stages. A system that does semantic well-formedness checks on constituents as they are being built up (such as

SHRDLU and RUS) can have the same effects on parsing while keeping syntactic categorization distinct from semantic categorization.

The use of semantic subcategorization is an extension of the lexical categorization done in transformational grammar, such as the $\pm$ABSTRACT feature on nouns, which causes *Sincerity admires John* to be classed as ungrammatical. The major difference is that in computer systems, the classification is generally more extensive, more specific to a subject domain, and developed through a pragmatic methodology (what works) rather than by carefully marshaled theoretical argumentation.

System engineering

The final issue lies largely outside the theoretical domain of language and grammar but is of critical importance in building a useable system. In comparing the relative merits of different systems, theoretical issues often take a back seat to the more practical considerations of what it is like to use the system. There are two different classes of users to be considered: the ultimate end users (who will interact with the system in natural language) and the specific application designers (who will build grammars and enter knowledge for topic domains). It would seem that a one-use system could to some extent ignore the second class, since the system designers are themselves the application engineers. However, for anything but a one-person one-shot project (such as a dissertation), it is always important to consider the needs of a variety of programmers and, even in the lone-wolf case, time spent on building tools that make it easier to develop grammars and programs is often more than repaid in the saving of programming effort.

User interface. For the end-user, there are a number of features that are extremely convenient, such as the ability to go back and edit a request and the presence of a spelling corrector. Often (as in LIFER) it is possible to make use of facilities built into an underlying programming environment such as INTERLISP (Teitelman, 1978) and make them directly accessible to the natural language user. Systems built on a more primitive base need to include their own versions of these capacities, and the degree of user acceptance can depend to a large extent on their success. Even a system with a marvelous grammar will not be convivial if it demands that a person type a full line with no typographical errors.

Grammar-writer amenities. A grammar is a complex artifact that is created and debugged. A system can provide a wide range of tools to help in this process. These include basic interfaces (e.g., editors and graphic printers for the grammars), grammar structuring aids (e.g., cross-references, mechanisms for producing a number of rules from a common pattern), and debugging aids (e.g., statistical tools for keeping track of what is being used how often and tracing facilities for monitoring the effect of particular rules during the parsing process). In this area, as with the previous one, there are often facilities available in the programming system in which the natural language system is built. However, they usually need modification—tracing a grammar rule is not exactly like tracing a subroutine, an editor for a network grammar is not exactly like an editor for a list-structured programming language, etc.

Even with a well-engineered system, the writing of a complex grammar can be quite difficult. In describing the application of LIFER to a data base system, Slocum (1981, p. 1.) observed:

> *After more than two years of intensive development, the human costs of extending the coverage began to mount significantly. The semantic grammar interpreted by LIFER had become large and unwieldy. Any change, however small, had the potential to produce 'ripple effects' which eroded the integrity of the system.*

Efficiency. Chapter 3 discussed the theoretical efficiency of different parsing strategies. When we design a practical system, this kind of efficiency needs to be taken into account, but is only half the story. The theory of computation deals with the gross order of efficiency—whether it is linear, logarithmic, polynomial, exponential, etc. This is measured with respect to the length of some particular input. In this analysis, constant factors are not usually considered. Two different implementations may be equivalent in the sense that they both take a time proportional to the square of the length of the input, but one of them might be tens or hundreds of times faster than the other.

In an implemented system, many decisions are made that affect these constant factors. One basic issue is the choice of an implementation language. Many systems (SHRDLU, LUNAR, PLANES, LIFER, MARGIE,...) have been built in LISP because it makes the job of system building much easier. Others (the Linguistic String Parser, REL, USL,...) have been built in more primitive languages such as FORTRAN and assembly language in order to gain efficiency. Within a given language, the grammar can be used *interpretively,* computing with the same form of grammar rules that the grammar writer sees, or can be *compiled,* converting the grammar into some more efficient form for parsing. Many systems (SHRDLU, DIAMOND, SOPHIE,...) have put a good deal of effort into grammar compilers, while others (such as LINGOL) have concentrated on having an efficient interpreter, thus keeping the system simpler from the standpoint of the grammar-writer, who need not worry about compiling and can trace the effect of individual rules more easily.

There is an extremely wide range in the efficiency achieved by different systems. The literature includes parsing times from 150 milliseconds for sentences of 8 to 12 words (SOPHIE) to 36 minutes for an eleven word sentence (the Mitre Transformational Parser). In judging these figures, it is important to recognize the different goals of the system builders. Speed is often gained at the cost of generality, and there are many external contributing factors, such as the specific machine on which the processing is done and the amount of effort that has been devoted to optimization. Most systems are designed for interactive question answering, so the important constraint is that the time needed to produce a response be acceptable—in the range up to ten or twenty seconds. In most cases, the syntactic analysis constitutes only a fraction of the overall response time, so optimization is not important in terms of the system as a whole. In some applications (such as processing text for retrieval), the speed of the parser is much more critical and the systems are correspondingly more tuned to efficiency considerations.

7.2 Augmented phrase structure grammar systems

The augmented transition network grammar formalism was presented in Chapter 5 in two steps. Section 5.1 introduced *recursive transition networks,* which are formally equivalent to context-free grammars but can be a more convenient form for writing complex grammars. The augmentations (role and feature registers, conditions, and actions) were then added to RTNs. It is also possible to augment context-free grammars directly, without using a network form. Many of the practical natural language systems in use today are based on this approach. It has also been used in a number of systems dealing with computer programming languages, following the original paper on *attribute grammars* by Knuth (1968a).

The basic idea is a straightforward adaptation of the mechanisms described in Chapter 5. For each composite syntactic category (such as S and NP), there is a set of potential features and roles (often called *attributes*). Associated with each rule of the grammar there are conditions and actions. A condition can make use of the information in the attributes and can prevent a rule from being applied if its test fails. The actions can set the attributes associated with nodes of the parse tree. These settings provide the basis for the testing of further conditions and can also be used to generate result structures that are 'deeper' than the parse tree created by the natural operation of the context-free parser. Attributes based on information from the parent node are called *inherited attributes* and those based on attributes of child nodes are called *synthesized attributes.*

By beginning with a context-free grammar, it is possible to make direct use of the many available algorithms for context-free parsing. However, the addition of conditions and actions interferes with the freedom of choosing strategies because of assumptions about the order in which things are done. The basic issue is that in associating a set of conditions and actions with a rule, it is necessary to know what other information will be available at the time the rule is applied. A condition that depends on knowledge of the parent of a node (i.e., makes use of inherited attributes) can be applied only in a top-down parser, since in a bottom-up parser a node is completed before any attempt is made to fit it into a parent. If actions are taken only on the completion of an entire node, then they cannot be used to allow knowledge of one constituent to affect the parsing of a following one (as they are in mechanisms like the hold list of ATNs). If they are associated with individual elements of a rule (corresponding to the arcs of an ATN), they may depend on parsing the constituents in a left-to-right order.

Each system based on augmented phrase structure grammar provides a parsing strategy and a particular set of augmenting mechanisms that are compatible with that strategy. Therefore, although they are all based on the same principles, they differ in the detailed nature of conditions and actions and in their efficiency and convenience.

The Linguistic String Parser

One of the earliest computer parsing systems was the Linguistic String Parser, developed for parsing sentences from scientific and technical texts as a basis for information retrieval. Its grammar consists of phrase structure rules, augmented with a set of conditions (called *restrictions*) stated in a *restriction language* that allows Boolean combinations of feature comparisons. Features are associated both with lexical items and with higher nodes of the parse tree. Earlier versions had no role registers, but the set of phrase categories was expanded to carry much of the information handled in registers by an ATN grammar. For example, the NP that is the subject of the sentence is assigned on the basis of restrictions to a category NP-SUBJECT, while one that is the object is assigned to NP-OBJECT. Later versions allowed more general registers, conditions, and actions like those of ATN grammars. All conditions are written on the assumption of left-to-right top-down parsing, never using checks on constituents to the right of the one being constructed. In practice, this has been combined with a backtracking parser.

The system uses explicit *locating relations* to find appropriate elements of non-local context, thereby handling structures dealt with by hold registers in an ATN. The condition for subject-verb agreement in a relative clause, for example, can explicitly check the number feature on the NP that is the parent of the clause being parsed. In practice, the restrictions mainly check that the words corresponding to terminal symbols have compatible attributes, such as number agreement of subject and verb and the proper case of pronouns. The output of the basic parser is modified by the application of a small number of *string transformations,* which are specialized procedures for phenomena such as conjunction expansion and the replacement of the dummy element in a relative clause with the appropriate higher constituent. There are explicit rules for constructs involving ellipsis, indicating what can be omitted.

As mentioned in Section 7.1, the grammars built for this parser have made heavy use of semantic categories in order to reduce the number of alternative parsings. These categories were generated by an empirical study of the texts rather than by an *a priori* analysis. Word classes are formed by grouping together words occurring in similar syntactic environments. For example, *X-ray* and *film* are grouped together since they both occur as the subject of the verb *show* in the texts. Similarly, *reveal* and *show* are grouped into a class because they both occur with the subject *X-ray*.

There have been several implementations of the Linguistic String Parser. Since it was designed for processing quantities of text (rather than interactive question answering), efficiency has been a consideration and low level languages such as IPL-V, assembly language, and FORTRAN have been used. Early versions did not have a systematic restriction language, but called on the grammar writer to do feature checking and structure locating directly in the list structure language.

General-purpose systems: LINGOL and LIFER

Two augmented phrase structure systems have been advertised in the artificial intelligence community as potential 'off the shelf' subsystems to be used by application designers. LINGOL emphasizes issues of parsing efficiency and is closely related to the augmented phrase structure systems used in *compiler compilers* and other programming language systems. It contains three sets of rules: a binary context-free grammar (each rule has at most two symbols on the right-hand side), a set of *cognitive* functions that operate somewhat like conditions, and a set of *generative* functions that are used for structure building actions.

Both the cognitive functions and the generative functions assume a basically bottom-up parser. They operate on an entire node when all of its constituents are present and do not make use of inherited features. Rather than having a separate mechanism for registers, LINGOL makes use of the standard variable bindings of LISP (in which it is built). The generative function associated with a rule can bind any number of variables as well as make use of the built-in variables for the left and right constituents parsed by the rule. Each node is expected to produce a *value* which then serves as one of these two arguments to the generative function for its parent node.

Parsing is done with a complex and highly efficient parsing algorithm that combines the Earley algorithm with the Cocke-Kasami-Younger algorithm (see Aho and Ullman, 1972, for a description). In order to use these, the grammar must be in a normal form in which there are at most two symbols on the right-hand side of a rule. In the original system, users had to provide extra symbols and rules to meet this restriction. In later versions, there is a pre-processor that takes an initial grammar and converts it to this form. Although a LINGOL grammar is not compiled, parsing is quite fast because of the restriction on its form and the efficiency of the algorithm.

LIFER is based on INTERLISP and makes available the user conveniences provided by that system. Of all the parsers, it is the one most developed in terms of system engineering, and includes features like spelling correction and interactive facilities for specifying a grammar. The basic context-free grammar allows the right-hand side of a rule to include individual words, LISP predicates to be applied to strings, and non-terminal categories that appear on the left-hand sides of other rules. The entire set of rules for a non-terminal symbol is compiled into a *transition tree,* an equivalent but more efficient form. This is referred to as the *sub-grammar* for the symbol. Compilation is incremental, so the addition of a single new rule in the course of developing a grammar does not require recompiling the entire grammar.

Associated with each rule there is a construction pattern, specifying a structure to be produced for the node. The following rules are examples:

$$
\begin{array}{ll}
\text{S} \;\rightarrow\; \textit{How}\ \text{Adjective}\ \textit{is}\ \text{Person} & \text{(GETP Person Adjective)} \\
\text{People} \;\rightarrow\; \text{Person} & \text{(LIST Person)} \\
\text{People} \;\rightarrow\; \text{Person People} & \text{(CONS Person People)}
\end{array}
$$

The construction patterns build up the LISP structures needed for answering the questions in which these phrases appear. The construction pattern '(GETP PERSON ADJECTIVE)' in the first rule uses LISP property lists as a representation for adjectival modifiers. The other two rules illustrate how the basic list structure operations (LIST and CONS) are used in conjunction with grammar rules to parse a list of arbitrary length.

The category names used in the construction pattern are replaced with the corresponding elements from the rule application. The value produced by substitution in the pattern becomes the value for the corresponding element in the pattern for the parent node. A special value is designated as the failure marker, and this can have the effect of blocking a rule because a condition is not met. Because the category names are used as variables, it is necessary to generate a new category if there would be a conflict, as in the rule 'S → *Is* PERSON1 COMPARATIVE-ADJECTIVE *than* PERSON2.'

In the case of rule elements matched by words, the dictionary entry for the word is produced as the value for the element. In the case of arbitrary LISP predicates, it is whatever LISP value the predicate returns.

The parser is top-down, left-to-right. To allow left-recursion, it traps rule applications that would cause the level of left-recursion to exceed a given depth (initially set to 6). The computation of the value of a node is delayed until the parse is complete to avoid doing useless work when a particular parse fails. The initial version took the first parse found, but later versions produce all possible parses for an input.

Since the parser is general purpose and has no 'core' grammar, there is no restriction on the categories that can be used. However, grammar writers are encouraged to make use of semantic categories. In the application of LIFER to a data base system (called LADDER) dealing with naval vessels, the categories include things like SHIP and SHIP-POSSESSIVE, and rules for the distinguished symbol S do not contain the familiar 'S → NP VP,' but instead have specialized patterns like 'S → *What is the* ATTRIBUTE *of* SHIP.'

LIFER contains a special mechanism for ellipsis, which compares an input to the previous input, looking for a match with any contiguous substring of words. The match is based on matching categories (which are usually semantic), and takes the first possible match at the least depth of recursion. Thus if the previous utterance was *Which ships have captains?*, the utterance *Submarines?* would be interpreted as *Which submarines have captains?* The usefulness of this mechanism for ellipsis depends a good deal on the presence of semantically based categories. In the same context, the utterance *First-mates?* would be interpreted as *Which first-mates have captains?* unless (as would likely be the case) there is a lexical category mismatch between *first-mate* and *ship*.

LIFER does not have the ability to pass down context from higher nodes, or to use locating relations to find nodes anywhere in the tree outside the node being currently processed. It is therefore weak in dealing with phenomena like relative clauses and questions containing long-distance dependencies (such as *Which ships does the admiral think the fourth fleet can spare?*). It is intended for applications in which it is not necessary to deal with complex inputs.

DIAMOND

The parser DIAMOND, used in the speech understanding system at SRI International, is based on an augmented phrase structure grammar, but with several innovations. It is designed to operate in an overall system that does not process a sentence top-down left-to-right, but rather tries to put pieces together in whatever order it can, using multiple knowledge sources. This is necessary since it may not even be possible to make a decision as to what words are present without using context from a later part of the sentence.

The parsing algorithm is based on the active chart algorithm described in Section 3.6. In order to make the conditions and actions independent of the order in which things are done, the parser uses a special discipline for testing, in which a test is done as soon as the pieces of information it uses are available, even if other parts of the constituent are not yet complete.

The basic English grammar used by the speech system has 10 rules and 10 pages of procedures. The rule language allows multiple alternatives to be included in a single rule, thereby gaining much of the efficiency of transition networks. Figure 7–6 illustrates a typical rule.

This rule handles questions like *How many ships are there?* and *What ships does the navy use?* It illustrates a number of features. The first part is a context-free rule that uses alternatives and options to combine the rules:

$$S \rightarrow NP1\ VP1$$
$$S \rightarrow NP1\ Do\ NP2\ VP1$$
$$S \rightarrow NP1\ Be\ VP2$$
$$S \rightarrow NP1\ Be\ NP3$$
$$S \rightarrow NP1\ Be\ there$$

The constructs following the BEGIN in the figure are conditions and actions. The conditions associated with the rules can set registers (such as MOOD) to values which include a special marker, UNDEFINED. This is important in allowing conditions to be checked when full information about the constituent is not yet available. The next condition 'IF OMITALL...' is a special rule for dealing with ellipsis. It indicates that certain combinations are not allowed. The final condition ('IF MOOD...') is a special kind of rule in this grammar, called a *variable rule*. Rather than specifically allowing some constructs and prohibiting others, it assigns a numerical factor that is generated from a set of alternatives used by the grammar writer, including GOOD, OK, UNLIKELY, and IMPOSSIBLE. In doing the parse, these factors are combined using arithmetic to give an estimate of how good the particular parsing is so work can be focused on the most likely alternative. The particular rule here indicates that Wh-questions are to be assigned a factor of GOOD, since they are highly likely to occur in the context of the parser (part of a question-answering system).

The overall system uses semantic categorization of words and compiles the grammar into a kind of transition net. It uses only synthesized features (not inherited features) in order to avoid a top-down orientation. A recent DIAMOND grammar, called DIAGRAM (Robinson, 1980), is more general and includes several hundred rules.

Rule.Def S1 S = NP1 <(Do NP2) VP1 | Be {VP2 | NP3 | 'There'}>;

Begin

Mood = If Deix(NP1) Eq 'Wh Then 'Wh
   Else If Deix(NP1) NotEq 'Undefined Then 'Declarative
   Else 'Undefined;

If OmitAll(VP1,Be) and Subcat(NP1) Eq 'Pronoun
   and Mood Eq 'Declarative
  Then F.Reject(F.Prosent);

If Mood Eq 'Wh Then F.Mood = Good;

End

Figure 7–6. A rule from a DIAMOND grammar.

Other phrase structure systems

The extended phrase structure grammars described in Section 6.7 are relatively new and the parsing systems for them are experimental. One that has been described in the literature is MCHART, a parser designed for the phrase structure grammars developed by Gazdar, using an active chart algorithm. Definite clause grammars, on the other hand, were motivated by the desire to make use of existing deductive systems for first-order logic. There exist programming systems such as PROLOG (Kowalski, 1974, Warren and Pereira, 1977), which can take a set of logical axioms in a standard form (called *definite clause form*) and treat them as a program, executing them to produce a proof. If a definite clause grammar is executed as a PROLOG program, the interpreter behaves as an efficient top-down parser for the language described by the grammar. Definite clause grammars have been used to write natural language question-answering systems and compilers (as described in Colmerauer, 1978, and Pereira and Warren, 1980).

There are a number of other systems based on augmented phrase structure grammars. Some, such as PHLIQA1, combine this with some form of transformations, and are discussed in Section 7.3. The NLP system developed at IBM and used in EPISTLE employs a fairly straightforward version of the ideas presented in this section, doing analysis bottom-up. A grammar containing 300 English *decoding rules* and 500 *encoding rules* (structure building, both syntactic and semantic) has been developed for it. Many of the European systems described in Rahmstorf and Ferguson (1978) also use the same approach.

7.3 Systems based on transformational grammars

The main appeal of context-free grammars is their simplicity and versatility. The same rule can be used by a generation process or by a uniform parsing process, and all of the knowledge of the syntactic structure of a language can be included in the set of rules. In addition, each rule corresponds in a natural way to a piece of the assigned structure.

In the more complex derivation rules of transformational grammar, the advantages of simple context-free rules are lost. Individual pieces of the structure no longer correspond to individual rule applications and there is no uniform way to apply the rules to do parsing instead of abstract derivation. However, since there is an extensive literature on the details of English syntax based on transformational grammar, a number of researchers have looked into the problems of applying transformational grammar directly to parsing. Several techniques have been attempted, with only partial success.

Since generative grammars are designed to generate sentences, it was pointed out in early discussions of computer parsing (Matthews, 1962) that one could systematically generate all possible structures from the rules, checking to see if

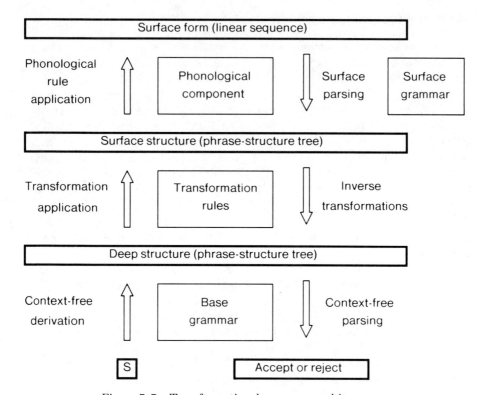

Figure 7–7. Transformational grammar and its reverse.

the surface form of any structure produced matches the sentence that is to be analyzed. It is theoretically possible to do this *analysis by synthesis,* but the process is one of those (like exploring all possible plays of a chess game) that would take vast amounts of computation, far beyond what is imaginable for computers we could build.

A somewhat more realistic approach is based on using transformational grammar in reverse, as diagrammed in Figure 7–7, using the rules to parse instead of generate. The stages of the derivation are done in reverse order, with each one appropriately inverted. In this process, transformational inverses are applied in an order precisely opposite to that in which their forward counterparts would be invoked in sentence generation. That is, inverses of postcyclic transformations are applied first, starting with the latest and ending with the earliest; then inverses of the cyclic transformations are applied (also in last-to-first order) working down the tree from the main S until the most deeply embedded S nodes have been processed. The inverse of the context-free base derivation is a context-free parsing using the base rules of the grammar.

This approach has been taken in several systems, the earliest of which were the Mitre Transformational Parser and Petrick's (1973) transformational parser. There is at least one major question-answering system (IBM's TQA system, formerly called REQUEST) that has been based on this technique and applied in practical data base uses, as described in Petrick (1981). Grishman (1976) describes the basic algorithms in detail. In general, these systems have been complex and difficult to construct. There are several problems in using existing forms of transformational grammar:

The need for a surface grammar. In a transformaticnal derivation, the transformations operate on trees to produce other trees. The final tree is then the input to phonological rules which produce the surface form. In order to operate transformations in reverse, it is first necessary to obtain a surface structure tree for the input. However, there is no component in the transformational model that characterizes surface structures, and it is necessary to create a new component—the *surface grammar*—so that the input can be parsed into a tree on which to apply the transformations. This has generally been a standard context-free grammar. In the Mitre system, the surface grammar was produced in an ad hoc fashion. In other systems, it has been written more systematically, so that it corresponds to the structures the transformations could actually produce, but in practice some hand-tailoring has been necessary. It is interesting to speculate whether current ideas in transformational theory (such as Emonds' (1976) structure preserving constraint discussed in Appendix C) will make it easier to provide this component.

The need for search in finding the right inverse transformations. As we saw in studying context-free grammars, a parser must provide some mechanism for searching alternatives. In a derivation, a sequence of rules is applied. In parsing, we need to find the sequence that produced a particular sentence. In order to apply inverse transformations, we must search for an appropriate sequence (or all such sequences in the case of ambiguity) that could have produced the surface structure. Since there is likely to be ambiguity in the surface grammar as well, the result is a very large set of possibilities, which can be explored only with a good deal of computation. The search is exponentially dependent on the length of the derivation (not the length of the sentence), and for grammars with a reasonable scope, it is large enough to make the technique infeasible. The Mitre system was reported as taking 36 minutes of computation to parse an 11 word sentence. The REQUEST system deals with a limited subset of English for which it is possible to write transformations leading to less search.

The design of inverse transformations. In the simple version of the method, as outlined in Figure 7–7, the inverse transformations are simply the ordinary transformations applied in reverse—the structural change becomes the structural description and vice versa. In practice, this does not work, and the inverse transformations must be specially designed and carefully tailored. In some systems, the inverse transformations are 'looser' than the corresponding forward transformations. A series of inverses can be applied to a surface structure to produce a deep structure when the corresponding series of forward transformations would not actually be valid. In these systems, there is a pass after doing the inverse transformations to check whether there is a corresponding forward derivation and if not, the parse is rejected.

Transformation rules for parsing

It is possible to apply the general framework described above without basing it on a well-formed forward transformational grammar. One can have a surface parser that produces a tree that is then modified by transformations to build an appropriate deep structure. These transformations are not one-to-one inverses of ordinary forward transformations, but are specifically designed to operate in the direction needed for parsing. One system of this type is PHLIQA1, which first parses a surface structure using an augmented phrase structure grammar like those described in Section 7.2 and then applies transformations.

Passive-active transformation

$Condition_1$:

　　branching-category(SEM_L) = nucleus *and*

　　SEM_L.obj.val = PASSIVE *and*

　　SEM_L.ind-obj.val $\neq$ PASSIVE *and*

　　$\forall i : SEM_L$.prepobs.i.obj.val $\neq$ PASSIVE *and*

　　$\exists k : SEM_L$.prepobs.k.prep = BY

$Action_1$:

　　$SEM_R := SEM_L$ [obj.val := SEM_L.subj.val ;

　　　　　　　subj.val := SEM_L.prepobs.k.obj.val ;

　　　　　　　delete k-th element from list of prepobs]

$Condition_2$:
$Action_2$:　*Analogous transformation for a passivized indirect object*

$Condition_3$:
$Action_3$:　*Analogous transformation for a passivized prepositional object*

$Condition_4$: SEM_L is not a nucleus or a nucleus without a passive

$Action_4$: $SEM_R := SEM_L$

Figure 7–8. A transformation group from PHLIQA1.

The transformation rules are organized into *transformation groups* and applied in a pattern that is the inverse of the cyclic derivation described in Section 4.4. A typical transformation group (for dealing with the various forms of passive) is illustrated in Figure 7–8. Note that there is less attempt at generality than in most transformational accounts, and more willingness to write separate transformations that have a good deal in common but differ in specifics (in this case, which element is passivized). This more pragmatic approach to the problem of 'capturing generalizations' is common to almost all computer parsing systems.

The symbols SEM_L and SEM_R represent the semantic representation associated with the left-hand side of the rule (the tree before transformation) and the right-hand side (after transformation). These semantic representations are based on role registers like those of Chapter 5. Associated with each transformation there are conditions for application and an action that produces the new representation. The first transformation, for example, indicates that if the constituent is a clause of the right type for passivization (NUCLEUS), and in the surface parsing the direct object was filled in with a dummy (PASSIVE) and none of the other elements (indirect object or prepositional objects) were, and there was a prepositional phrase with preposition *by,* then the new structure is derived from the old one by taking the surface subject as the object, the object of the *by* phrase as the subject, and deleting the *by* phrase from the set of modifiers. In order to apply these, the surface grammar must have rules that allow dummies to be assigned for missing constituents. This can be done in a context-free way (i.e., allowing a dummy to be assigned to any element independently of whether one has been assigned to another element), since the conditions on the transformation will block their application in any case where more than one has been assigned. No transformation in the group will apply, and therefore the parse will be rejected. The last transformation in the group is included to handle the case where there is no passive at all.

7.4 Chart rewrite systems

Several computer systems have been based on a very general parsing scheme, originally used in a system called the Powerful Parser. This parser extends the notion of bottom-up parallel parsing to grammars that are not context-free, allowing the grammar writer to include more powerful rewrite rules. Before discussing the systems we will describe the basic idea of charts.

Charts and parsing

The active chart parser of Section 3.6 was based on two ideas: the use of *charts* as an indexing scheme for constituents; and the presence of *active edges* representing partial constituents. In its simple (non-active) form, a chart is simply

Before passive rules

After passive rules

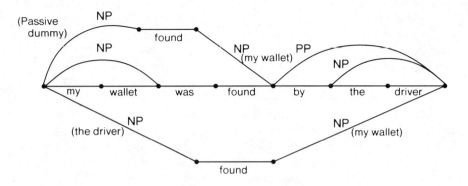

Figure 7–9. Chart rewriting for passive voice.

a way of recording the constituents that have been found. By having a data structure that records for each position in the sentence all of the known constituents beginning and ending at that position, it is possible to be more efficient in bottom-up parsing based on the recognition schema defined in Figures 3–25 and 3–26.

As discussed in Section 4.2, the notion of a rewrite rule can be extended to cover grammars other than context-free. We can think of the rule as specifying an arbitrary replacement for one or more symbols. The basic idea of the Powerful Parser is to allow a rule to match a sequence of edges in the chart and to enter a new *sequence of edges* in addition. The pattern (corresponding to the right-hand side) can specify not only a sequence of labels on the edges it matches, but also the contents of each edge (the sets of constituents making it up). The replacement (corresponding to the left-hand side) can construct an arbitrary set of edges and nodes, based on the the constituents matched in the pattern.

As an example, let us once again consider the problem of passive voice, as illustrated in Figure 7–9 (which includes the charts in a simplified form including only the relevant information). The chart on the bottom represents two different parsings of *My wallet was found by the driver*. In one parsing the driver found it, while in the other he was in a nearby location. The upper chart is produced just as it would be in a bottom-up context-free parser. It is then matched by two rules of the grammar: One has a right-hand side 'NP AUX VERB' with appropriate conditions on the constituents. Its left-hand side builds new edges and nodes using a dummy NP to represent the unknown subject of a passive. The other rule matches 'NP AUX VERB *by* NP' and builds the reordered structure at the bottom of the figure. These rules do the same kind of work that is done by inverse transformations, reordering the constituents to reflect an underlying structure. The difference is that the result is added to the chart, along with the earlier edges, instead of producing a new phrase marker, as is done by both forward and inverse transformations.

This use of constituent sequences to represent a deeper analysis of the sentence is an important feature of most grammars used in chart rewrite parsers. However, the formalism of the chart rewrite parser is extremely general and allows a variety of different styles of grammar writing. For example, in some versions, constituent sequences are used to represent the kind of analysis done in case grammars. A preposition is assigned to each case and sentences are converted to make the preposition explicit. The sentence *Dorothy gave me a cookie* would be rewritten as 'SUBJ *Dorothy gave to me* OBJ *a cookie.*' In the rewritten sentence, an explicit *to* is put in before the indirect object, and pseudo-prepositions SUBJ and OBJ are inserted before the appropriate noun phrases. This can be carried further, using information associated with individual words, so that sentences such as *This key opens the tomb* and *The door opened* would be rewritten as '*with this key* SUBJ DUMMY *opens* OBJ *the tomb*' and 'SUBJ DUMMY OBJ *the door opened.*'

The problem with parsers of this general sort is the difficulty in controlling the interactions among rules. Since any rule can put arbitrary constituents into the chart, it is quite easy for a rule to operate in a situation for which the grammar writer did not intend it. The rule was written with a particular set of conventions in mind, but a later rule changed those conventions in a way that interacted. The general problem of ordering rewrite rules (discussed in Section 4.2) has been handled by using a strict ordering convention, usually with successive rules finding larger and larger constituents, working in one direction through the sentence.

There are many techniques for controlling the application of rules, such as the use of special markers. One rule can put into the chart a special marker that prevents a constituent from being constructed until some other rule finds and removes the marker. Individual rules specify conditions under which they apply, and if a constituent is not well-formed, the parser will eventually reach a point where no rules apply. This kind of *blocking* can be used explicitly to establish control over the rules. Of course, this means that all other rules must be written to take into account the possible presence of this marker.

There are also questions about the exact form of the conditions that can be specified in the pattern to be matched and the primitives for constructing new edges and nodes as the result of a match. Each chart rewrite parser has its own special language and conventions for these operations. In general, systems based on chart rewrite parsers contain grammars of Byzantine complexity that are quite difficult to understand and modify, although some of them have obtained a reasonably broad coverage of English after many years of work.

Systems based on chart rewrite parsers

The earliest use of chart rewrite parsing in a practical system was in the MIND system for machine translation. A good description of the algorithms it used are found in Kaplan (1973a). There are several existing practical systems using chart rewrite parsers, the most notable (and earliest) of which is REL (which stands for Rapidly Extensible Language). REL combines a data base formalism with an English parser, and is designed for general use, with the user supplying specialized vocabulary for a particular subject domain. It employs a modification of the basic chart rewrite algorithm, including features as well as transformations of the kind described. It uses features associated with verbs for a case-like transitivity scheme similar to the one described above. The subset of English it can handle is called *REL English* and includes questions with a complexity like that of *The per capita gross national product of which South American nations exceeded 50 in the last three years?*

Other current systems based on chart parsers are being done in Germany, including USL, which has an 800 rule German grammar and operates from left to right instead of in reverse, as is more common with chart rewrite parsers.

7.5 ATN-based systems

One of the earliest parsers to go beyond context-free grammars was a rudimentary augmented transition net developed by Thorne, Bratley, and Dewar (1968). The formalism was further refined by Bobrow and Fraser (1969), then systematized and first used with an extensive grammar by Woods (1970) in the LUNAR system.

LUNAR

LUNAR is a question-answering system that responds to questions based on data about the mineral samples brought back from the moon, using a large data base provided by NASA. It uses an ATN grammar that was motivated by transformational grammar theory and therefore produces deep tree structures rather than register assignments (see Figure 7–4). Registers are thought of as temporary holding places for use during the parsing of a constituent.

The send arc for each constituent has an associated *tree-building action* which takes selected register contents and substitutes them into tree patterns. Thus, for example, at the end of parsing a passive sentence, the deep subject (the constituent ending up in the subject register) would be placed as the initial NP, and the deep object as a constituent inside the VP. Registers are used for features as well as constituents, but not in a systematic way. Each register can hold an arbitrary LISP pointer, so that pointers to constituents and to feature names (represented by LISP atoms) can be mixed. Conditions and actions are pieces of the LISP program, containing whatever the grammar user chooses, but generally based on a small set of standard primitives provided by the formalism. Since register contents are not returned as part of the final analysis, there is no attempt to provide linguistic or formal justification for the specific use of registers. Linguistic justifications (based on transformational grammar) are given primarily for the formalism used in encoding the results in the deep structure trees.

Parsing is done left-to-right top-down. Some versions of this system have used backtracking and others use a parallel scheme. In both cases, use is made of a likelihood ordering on the arcs leaving any state. Given a choice, the system takes the more likely one first in order to increase the probability of finding the right path early in the process. In some versions, a cumulative measure of goodness is kept for each parse, so the choice of which alternative to work on can be made on a best-first basis. The system includes a special mechanism for handling conjunction, as described in Section 7.1. When a conjunction is encountered (in the left-to-right parse), new alternatives are set up for each of the states that have been traversed so far in the parse, attempting to continue forward from that point with the new conjunct. Thus a phrase like *the old men and women* would have two parsings, one based on going back to the node for parsing a noun, and the other going back to the NP node. This technique leads to a great many possibilities, especially if there is more than one conjunction in a sentence. The system includes some special heuristics to avoid large combinatorial searches.

PROGRAMMAR

The PROGRAMMAR parsing system was designed for use in SHRDLU, an integrated system that simulates a simple robot, allowing a person to give commands, state facts, and ask questions concerning a series of actions being displayed on a CRT screen. In appearance, a grammar for PROGRAMMAR is quite different from a transition network—it is a program specifying a series of steps to be taken. In fact, it is quite close to an ATN grammar. The calls to the PARSE subroutine in a PROGRAMMAR program correspond to the arcs of an ATN, and the steps within the program correspond to the conditions and actions. Program variables correspond to registers. Figure 7–10 shows a PRO-

Program Step	Success	Failure
DEFINE S		
PARSE NP	–	–
PARSE VP	–	RETURN
DEFINE NP		
PARSE Determiner	–	ADJ
Copy the features {Singular Plural} from *		
and mark the NP Determined	–	–
ADJ		
PARSE Adjective	ADJ	GO ON
PARSE Noun	–	–
If the current node is Determined then intersect its		
features {Singular Plural} with those of *		
Otherwise copy the features {Singular Plural} from *	RETURN	–
DEFINE VP		
PARSE Verb	–	–
Take the intersection of the features {Singular Plural}		
with those of * and those of the NP preceding *	–	–
Is * Transitive?	–	INTRANS
PARSE NP	RETURN	–
INTRANS		
Is * Intransitive?	RETURN	–

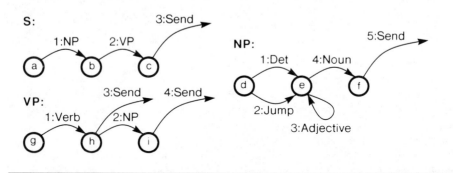

Figure 7–10. A PROGRAMMAR grammar and corresponding ATN.

GRAMMAR program and the corresponding ATN (not including the conditions and actions). The original LISP syntax has been put into a more easily readable form.

    With each step of the program, there are actions to be taken if it succeeds or fails. A dash is used in the figure to stand for the normal action—if the step succeeds, GO ON to the next step; if it fails, the parse FAILS. Other possibilities are to RETURN (equivalent to a send arc) or go to a specific place in the program. For example, the step that parses an adjective goes on to the next step (looking for a noun) if no adjective is found, but loops back to the same step again if one is found, achieving the same effect as the looping arc in the ATN. Several properties of the formalism are apparent from the example:

Mixing of parsing steps, conditions, and actions. The steps of a PRO-GRAMMAR program include the equivalent of arcs, conditions, and actions all mixed together. A condition or action is not connected directly to a particular parsing step, but simply appears in the code following it. The only connection is that the current constituent pointer (indicated with '*') always refers to the last constituent parsed in the same definition. In an implicit way, all of the code between two calls to PARSE constitutes the conditions and actions on the first call. This orientation towards explicitly describing the parsing process rather than specifying a skeleton of the structures makes it easy to include special mechanisms for problems like conjunction, since programs can be triggered by information associated with individual words in the dictionary, as well as top-down by the general course of the parsing.

The use of tree descriptions instead of registers. PROGRAMMAR uses features, but has only a few special role registers. Instead of having a register called SUBJECT, for example, it uses a tree-description mechanism (represented in the simplified form of the example by the phrase 'the NP preceding *') to refer to the appropriate constituent to be checked. There is a similar device used in the conditions associated with the context-free grammar of the Linguistic String Parser described in Section 7.2. PROGRAMMAR does have a role register for the main verb, and in sentences containing a multi-word verb (like *pick up*) it is reset after finding the particle to contain a special dictionary entry for the combination, as described in the ATN grammar of Section 5.6. The structures built are trees of constituents, usually in the surface order in which they are found, with features serving to identify their functional roles, as was illustrated in Figure 7–3.

PROGRAMMAR was strongly influenced by systemic grammar and therefore makes extensive use of feature marking on both words and constituents, organizing them into explicit choice systems. The overall SHRDLU system emphasizes the integration of syntactic, semantic, and reasoning processes, and this is facilitated by the fact that conditions and actions are arbitrary LISP procedures that can deal with information of any type, based on either syntactic features or semantic analysis. Meaning checks (involving the current state of the robot's world as well as its general knowledge) are interspersed into the parsing process. These programs can be used not only to reject the possibility of finding a certain constituent, but also to make strategy decisions about which arcs should be tried in what order. The system therefore was designed to generate only the first possible parsing, but in the process, it eliminated alternatives that were well-formed syntactically but failed semantic tests.

There is no automatic mechanism for trying multiple alternatives. The grammar is a deterministic program, designed to try the most likely alternative first, using semantic considerations to avoid false paths, and including explicit backup operations written to fit the likely wrong paths that the parser might take (e.g., assuming that a prepositional phrase modifies an NP when in fact it modifies a structure containing that NP). This strategy is made feasible by the intermixing of syntactic and semantic processing, since the semantic constraints tend to eliminate wrong paths before further action has been taken that would need to be undone.

The General Syntactic Processor (GSP)

The General Syntactic Processor was designed on the basis of experience with both the LUNAR system and the MIND system. It combines the mechanisms of ATNs and charts in a way that is close to the model of ATN grammars presented in Chapter 5. It includes a parser that is similar to the active chart parser described in Section 3.6. GSP (as its name implies) leaves a great deal of latitude in the exact parsing process and form of the structures, giving the user a chance to combine independently and explicitly a number of the strategies and features we have described. In trying to maintain the maximum generality

---

I want to go to San Diego on May 28

```
(S: Mood = Declarative
    Subject = (NP: Head = (Pronoun: Case = Nominative
                                      Number = Singular
                                      Root = I))
    Pverb = (Verb: Tense = Present, Root=Want)
    Object (S: Mood = ForTo
               Subject = I
               Pverb = (Verb: Tense = Present, Root = Go)
               Modifiers = ((PP: Preposition = (Preposition: Root = To)
                            PrepObject =
                                (NP: Head = (ProperNoun:
                                             ProperType = CityName
                                             Root = SanDiego)))

                           (PP: Preposition = (Preposition: Root = On)
                            PrepObject =
                                (NP: Head = (ProperNoun:
                                             ProperType = DateName
                                             Month = May
                                             Day = 28))))))
```

Figure 7–11. Role structure produced by GUS.

and flexibility, it does not provide specific decisions for many of the issues of parsing, leaving these to the user. It is a kind of 'parsing workbench' that can be used in different styles. For example, a version of GSP (programmed in POP-2) was used by Eisenstadt (1979) to implement a version of the MARGIE parser (Section 7.7) as well as a more conventional ATN.

GSP is the syntactic processor in the GUS system, using a grammar similar to that developed in Chapter 5. The grammar generates role structures like the one shown in Figure 7–11, which are then converted by another component (making use of information associated with individual verbs) into case structures like the one that was shown in Figure 7–5.

As illustrated by the example, the grammar includes special arcs and states for dealing with things like city names and dates. Other than this, it does not use semantic categories. It also has a special mechanism for recognizing sentence fragments as the answers to questions. If the system asks *When do you want to return?*, it treats the answers *I want to return on June 1, on June 1,* and *June 1* as equivalent. It does this by transforming the question into a statement and allowing the parser to make use of an initial sequence of this statement as a prefix to the response.

GSP also formed the syntactic base for the LNR system, using several different case-based grammars in different aspects of the research program.

SOPHIE

The SOPHIE system for teaching principles of electronic circuit debugging makes use of computer programs for natural language interaction and for circuit simulation. It interprets statements and questions within its subject domain using an ATN grammar based on semantic lexical categories. The phrase *voltage across capacitor C2* is handled not by rules like 'NP → NOUN PP' and 'PP → PREPOSITION NP,' but by one like:

Measurement → Measurable-quantity Preposition Part

This system is one of the few that has been the result of a good deal of effort to optimize the efficiency of the grammar, since it needed to produce quick responses if the larger goal of teaching students about circuits was to be met. In early versions, the grammar was hand coded into LISP, and a sentence of 8 to 12 words took 150 milliseconds. In the later versions, there is an ATN compiler that converts the ATN to LISP code, which is then run in parsing. The result is only about half as fast, but the grammar is more understandable and can easily be modified.

The system allows some special cases of ellipsis, making use of semantic categorization to figure out what role the remaining elements play. It uses the INTERLISP facilities of spelling correction and editing.

SPEECHLIS and RUS

One of the most highly developed ATN systems is SPEECHLIS, a modification of LUNAR used in the BBN speech understanding system. The main grammar written for it (which may be the largest existing ATN grammar) contains 448 states, 881 arcs, and 2280 actions. However, since it uses semantic categories and includes many special phrases relevant to the domain of the speech system (travel-expense reports), it is more limited in the variety of constructions it can accept than a more general 83 state, 202 arc, 386 action grammar that was written for the same system.

The ATN parsing procedure was modified to avoid the purely left-to-right orientation, allowing the parser to find a *partial parse path* starting anywhere. This strategy (also called *island driving*) enables the system to work its way out from 'islands' that are securely understood into areas where the phonological hypotheses are less secure. The only accommodation that the grammar writer needs to make to this system is to mark actions that use register contents with the state or states where the original setting could have taken place. This makes it possible to avoid trying to use registers whose contents are not available, or that might possibly change by the point in the sentence being parsed.

The grammar is preprocessed, producing an index by which all arcs that call for a particular lexical category can be found. Therefore, when a word is hypothesized by the lower-level processes, parsing can begin with those arcs.

RUS is a related ATN parser, designed to interface with concurrent semantic analysis. As with SHRDLU, the semantic interpretation of an utterance is generated incrementally during the parsing process and is used to guide the operation of the parser. The grammar uses case frames and functional labeling along multiple dimensions, of the kind described in Section 6.3. The functional relationships are used to communicate with the semantic component, which can accept or reject a proposed functional assignment on semantic or pragmatic grounds. Semantic acceptability can be one of the conditions on an arc, so if the assignment is rejected, another arc will be tried. The parser also has heuristics to guide it down the most likely path, which along with the selectivity provided by semantic processing makes it possible to parse without backup in most sentences. The current RUS grammar is more complete than the LUNAR grammar, and is not oriented to a specific domain.

Data base systems using ATN grammars

A number of current data base systems use versions of ATN parsing. Each of them has its own special features and makes some kind of simplification in the range of language constructs it can handle. We will summarize the syntactic features of several such systems. Each of them has other properties (such as the handling of pronouns and the use of the data base in semantic analysis) that will be discussed in the volume on meaning.

PLANES. PLANES is an English language question-answering system for a large relational data base on Navy aircraft maintenance. Its limited domain results in a small vocabulary with no lexical ambiguity, and leads users to offer few complex sentences. Since the system is built with a good *a priori* idea of what the users will want to know, it can deal with some kinds of ellipsis and non-grammatical sentences. When it fails to interpret an input, it asks for a rephrasing.

It is based on a slightly different use of ATNs. There are *subnets* for different kinds of phrases that make up sentences, but not for a sentence as a whole. PLANES contains a separate subnet for each kind of semantic object in its world (e.g., plane type, date, time period, malfunction, maintenance type, and aircraft component). The parser does a phrase-by-phrase match and uses specially programmed heuristic techniques for locating the boundaries of noun groups and relative clauses. It then strings together the phrases using *concept case frames,* each of which consists of an act and a list of noun phrase types that can occur meaningfully with the act. For example, the frame for *require* specifies that its objects must be of a PLANETYPE and a MAINTENANCETYPE. The cases are not based on general roles of the kind discussed in Section 6.5, such as AGENT and INSTRUMENT.

There is a pre-pass that incorporates a spelling corrector and throws out phrases like *please tell me, can you tell me, would you let me know,* and *could you find.* It recognizes a number of general patterns for embedded clauses and simply matches these to the request sentence. Like LIFER, it has a number of facilities for aiding the grammar writer, such as a network editor that takes a phrase and adds the minimum number of new arcs and states needed to match this phrase to a specified subnet. The JETS system, which is the successor to PLANES, differs primarily in its treatment of meaning and use of the data base, and uses the same syntactic methods.

INTELLECT. The INTELLECT system (formerly called ROBOT) uses an ATN with backtracking (implemented using LISP recursion). It generates all possible interpretations, then calls another component (called 'WEED') to distinguish those that are semantically possible, directly using the information in the data base. INTELLECT is designed to work with any data base of the right form, without a special dictionary. It therefore uses the contents of the data base itself as a way of determining what types of objects can go with what relations. It performs spelling correction and handles phrases (idioms) through special mechanisms. There is an explicit separate ATN for sentence fragments, which is called only if the attempt to parse the input as a full sentence fails. Conjunction is handled with explicit arcs in each place it is allowed to occur. As of this writing, INTELLECT is one of the few systems that has already been marketed and is being used on a commercial basis.

7.6 Pattern matching systems

Most of the early natural language systems in artificial intelligence used a simple pattern matcher to interpret their inputs, as described in Chapter 2. A typical example is the ELIZA program, which simulated a non-directive psychiatrist interviewing a patient. ELIZA matched its inputs against a stock of patterns containing *key words* and phrases, such as *dream that...* and *computer*. It produced responses keyed to those patterns, such as *Do you ever wish that...?* and *Do machines frighten you?* Since the goal of the program was simply to produce a generally relevant response, this level of precision was sufficient for most inputs.

The development of formal syntax and grammars could be thought of as a further development of the idea of pattern matching. However, there have also continued to be systems based on pattern matching that do not follow any of the standard syntactic formalisms. In general, these are systems that need only partial analysis, either because of the way they carry out their task (as with ELIZA) or because it is assumed that other components of the analysis (e.g., semantics) can fill in what the syntax misses.

There are several large systems based essentially on pattern matching techniques:

PARRY. The PARRY program is a direct descendant of ELIZA, but instead of playing the doctor it simulates a paranoid patient. Like ELIZA, it does not attempt to do a full analysis, but simply needs to provide a response that would be judged as plausible (given that the patient is crazy). It is probably the most comprehensive pattern based system, having an elaborate sequence of processing stages and a dictionary with hundreds of idioms and thousands of patterns. Figure 7–12 gives a list of the different processing stages, some of which are explained further below.

---

1. Standardize input
2. Identify word stems
3. Condense rigid idiomatic phrases
4. Bracket noun phrases using a transition network grammar
5. Simplify verb phrases
6. Replace flexible idioms
7. Locate simple clauses
8. Embed subordinate clauses
9. Determine relevance

Figure 7–12. Processing stages in PARRY.

Wilks's machine translation system. This machine translation system is based on a pattern match analyzer that uses *templates* whose elements include semantic categories. The processor has several stages that include grouping, reordering, matching to templates, and then special processes for extending and tying together the phrases that have been found. Some of the early translation systems used related techniques, but in a less coherent way and without the same degree of emphasis on semantics.

UNDERSTAND. A combination of pattern matching and grammar-like techniques are used in the UNDERSTAND system, which is intended to produce a problem description from a natural language text. It includes phases of segmentation and integration along with a rule-based grammar.

FRUMP. FRUMP is designed to skim newspaper stories and summarize the major information. It has a collection of patterns for stock phrases used in reporting certain kinds of events (such as accidents and natural disasters), and processes only those sentences or sentence fragments that match one of the phrases. For example, given the input *A passenger train carrying tourists, including some Americans, collided with a freight train in the rugged Sierra Madre of northern Mexico, killing at least seventeen persons and injuring 45, the police reported today,* it gleans the facts that a train hit a train in Mexico, with 17 dead and 45 injured. It simply ignores much of the content, including modifiers (such as *carrying tourists* and *at least*) and makes use of semantic knowledge (e.g., that Mexico is a place) to fill in connections for which its syntactic analysis is inadequate.

FLEXP. The Flexible Parser uses linear patterns based on semantic categories designed for a limited domain. It has been applied to the parsing of an English-like computer command language, as described by Carbonell and Hayes (1981). By using a case-frame like analysis, it can interpret the command *Edit the programs in FORTRAN* as indicating that programs written in FORTRAN are to be edited, while *Edit the programs in TECO* implies that programs are to be edited using TECO (which is a text editor, and is so categorized in the lexicon). The system has specialized parsing techniques for each type of construction and specialized ambiguity representations for each type of ambiguity that a particular construction can give rise to, as described in Hayes (1981).

Mechanisms used in pattern match systems

The basic organization of these systems is to do some kind of pattern match, based on a stock of phrase and sentence patterns. There are many thousands of such patterns in systems attempting broad coverage. At various stages in the processing, the work is done by a pattern matcher similar in character to those described in Chapter 2. Some systems make use of compiling techniques to convert these into a *pattern tree* that can be matched more efficiently. This is similar to converting a set of context-free rules into an equivalent transition network, but without allowing paths to converge (thus making the matching process simpler).

In extending the basic pattern matcher to handle more of the complexities of natural language, a number of techniques have been applied:

Idiom recognition and substitution. Most systems begin with an initial pass over the input in which they find word sequences that are recognizable as fixed patterns. They then substitute some indicator of the pattern as a whole, for example substituting *despite* for *in spite of.* The same technique can be used in reverse, in order to allow more general patterns to apply to lexicalized structures. PARRY replaces the word *insane* with the sequence *not sane,* and then can apply its patterns involving *not.*

Canonical forms. In addition to converting phrases to words and vice versa, pattern-match programs often convert words into a canonical form. The input string *I am here* would be converted to *I be here,* so that general patterns involving *be* can be applied without worrying about the verb forms. This process often includes replacing inflected forms with their roots, eliminating words considered irrelevant (such as *so* and *well*) and replacing all members of a set of synonyms with a single canonical member. If idiom recognition is done after canonicalization, the system can recognize *flexible idioms* such as *it be strange that...,* in which the form of the verb *be* and the synonym of *strange* (e.g., *funny, weird*) can vary. One simple form of canonicalization is spelling correction—converting unrecognizable words to the dictionary entry that is closest in spelling.

Grouping strategies. Most of the patterns used in a program like PARRY or Wilks's translation system are intended to cover a single clause or noun phrase. It is useful to do a rough grouping of the input into units of the right size to provide boundaries for the matching. There are many different heuristics used for this kind of grouping. Particular words (like *the, that,* and *which*) are fairly reliable markers of boundaries, as are some punctuation marks. PARRY uses an ATN-like grammar for noun phrases (not for clauses) to do an initial grouping. There is a special grouping mechanism for dealing with relative clauses, but they are not handled fully. Wilks inserts boundaries after words like *say* and *want* which typically are followed by embedded clauses. The word *of* is treated specially by many systems because it is very common and can be used to piece together the structures of noun phrases. Wilks does a special scan for *of* phrases, and PARRY uses them (and no other prepositional phrases) in its attempt to find noun groups. Each system includes some combination of strategies that achieves a level of accuracy in grouping which (although far below 100 per cent) is deemed acceptable. In general, complex relative clauses and other such constructs cannot be correctly analyzed all of the time.

Fuzzy matching. Since all of the previous steps can introduce distortions, and since the system does not have enough patterns to cover all eventualities, it is often faced with the situation of no exact match. If the requirements on specificity are sufficiently low, it can fall back on some partial match strategy such as allowing one or more elements to be mismatched, absent, or interposed. This opens up very large possibilities of getting an undesirable match, but there are applications for which it is useful.

These same techniques are also used in some form or another within other kinds of systems. For example, most systems use some kind of simple program or pattern technique to convert the input into a standardized form, dealing with punctuation, capitalization, hyphenation, misspelling, etc. Some (such as REQUEST) do an initial pass looking for idioms, or *multi-words*. Some (such as PLANES) supplement a simple grammar with specialized grouping techniques for more complex phrases, such as relative clauses.

Again, as discussed above, it is important to recognize that some of the differences in syntactic processing strategies really represent decisions about how work is divided up in the overall system. For example, the replacement of synonyms with a standard form in the syntactic processing phase achieves the same effect as having a canonical form in the representation language used in the semantic analysis.

7.7 Situation-action parsers

The concept of parsing as developed in the study of formal grammars is based on a separation of the *declarative* description of forms in the language and the *procedural* details of the parsing process. One of the reasons that context-free grammars are so easy to parse and transformational grammars so difficult is that a context-free grammar has a straightforward interpretation as a set of constraints on possible syntactic structures. In attempting to deal with more complex grammars, formalisms like ATNs bring the parsing process itself into the form of the grammar. The setting of a register happens at a particular moment and any condition using that register after that moment will make use of the new result. The basic framework, however, is still oriented towards a description of the patterns.

There is a group of parsing systems that go one step further, making all of the declarative structure *implicit* and writing the grammar as a collection of *situation-action rules,* each of which specifies an action to be taken on a set of structures that are being built up in the course of parsing. The action is triggered by some particular configuration of the structures being built. The system maintains a catalog enabling it to decide which actions are to be taken at any given time, and some kind of control discipline for deciding how to go about applying them. Such systems provide a tremendous amount of flexibility, with a corresponding tendency towards unstructured results and impromptu organization. They have been described under a variety of different names, such as *expectation-based, data-driven,* and *expert-based.* These names emphasize the fact that the grammar is a collection of separate situation-action patterns ('experts'), each of which is triggered when a certain situation arises ('expectation,' 'data-driven').

Within this general class of parsers, there are wide differences in the approach to syntax. Before explaining the organization of this kind of parser in detail, we will describe a few of the best-known systems.

Conceptual dependency parsers. A series of programs developed by Schank and his associates (Schank, 1975, Schank and Abelson, 1977, Shank and Riesbeck, 1981) have been based on a formalism called *conceptual dependency.* The theory on which the programs are based de-emphasizes the role of syntax, concentrating on the processes by which meaning structures are constructed during language comprehension. The parsers associated with these systems (MARGIE, ELI, CA, and BORIS) integrate parsing with semantic analysis and do not use systematic grammars. There has been little attempt to handle complex syntactic constructions, and the parsers have been used either to parse very simple inputs or in systems where a partial analysis is considered sufficient.

The MARGIE parser was the first of the series, and handled only very simple sentences. It operated in a data-driven (bottom-up) style, in which the processing at each moment was based on a program associated with the word just input. ELI was more top-down, accepting a structure for processing only if it satisfied a prior expectation. ELI's capabilities were expanded by the addition of special routines designed to handle complex noun groups and relative clauses. CA (Conceptual Analyzer) integrated these routines into a more coherent framework. The BORIS system does not have a distinct parser, but runs as a single module: all tasks such as event assimilation, inference, memory search, and question answering occur as an integral part of the parsing process.

PARSIFAL. At the other end of the spectrum of attitudes towards syntax lies PARSIFAL, a parser designed to elucidate the interactions between parsing, human linguistic processing, and syntax as studied in transformational grammar. It is one of the computer parsing systems most closely aligned with the study of formal generative syntax. One of the major assumptions underlying its structure is that it is possible to parse natural language deterministically—that parallel or backtracking schemes are unnecessary for handling normal sentences. This *determinism hypothesis* is discussed further below.

Word Expert Parser. The Word Expert Parser is like the conceptual dependency parsers in its focus on semantics. It has a more elaborate organization, bringing in complex semantic analysis (such as word sense discrimination) as an integral part of the parsing process. It is still in an early stage (dealing only with combinations of a few words) and has not been developed to the point where it could be used in integrated systems.

HEARSAY-II. The HEARSAY-II system for speech understanding integrates a number of *knowledge sources* (of which syntax is one) into a situation-action rule framework that makes use of a *blackboard* to keep track of the overall analysis. The parser itself uses standard context-free techniques, called as a result of new information being put onto the blackboard. The detailed parsing analysis is not put onto the blackboard, but success at parsing a phrase (which need not be a complete sentence) can serve to trigger other knowledge sources.

Issues in the organization of a situation-action parser

Figure 7–13 lists the basic issues in the design of a situation-action parser and outlines some of the alternative choices that have been made.

Available structures

The coherence of a situation-action parser is provided by the structures that it builds and uses in recognizing situations to trigger actions. These differ widely from parser to parser.

What kind of structures are available?

    Input string
    Syntactic structures
        Parse being built
        Unassigned constituents
    Semantic structures
    Control information

How are rules activated?

    Individual words
    Explicit actions
    Association with stack
    Content and context

How are rules chosen for application?

    Arbitrary ordering
    Queuing
    Numerical priorities

How are rules de-activated?

    Self-deleting
    Explicit

Figure 7–13. Issues in the design of a situation-action parser.

Input string. Of course, the parser must have the input available. In all of the systems mentioned above, the input is introduced one word at a time. To a large extent, the organization of the process as a whole is the result of this left-right ordering, which is usually justified on psychological grounds. As each successive word is entered, the system looks up the situation-action rules associated with it (as a specific dictionary entry) or with its lexical category, and adds these to the collection of rules to be considered for running before the next word comes in. In some cases, words are divided into morphemes (such as *give* and *-en* for *given*) and treated as two items. The Word Expert Parser deals with such combinations in the reverse of the normal order. In others, like PARSIFAL, the description of situations and actions makes use of features on the words. One could imagine a situation-action parser in which the entire input string was available from the beginning, but such systems have not been implemented.

In most systems, there is no explicit list of the words that have been seen. Each word simply has its effect when its time comes, leaving information around in the other structures. In the Word Expert Parser, a program associated with each word remains in a *word bin* and other parts of the program can access it.

Syntactic structures. In a syntactically based system, the final result is a parse structure like those we have studied throughout the book. In general, these are 'deep' structures, since one of the advantages of a parser of this kind is its flexibility in deciding just where to attach new elements as it builds. Instead of continually adding to a single structure, most situation-action parsers work with a collection of structures organized into sequences or stacks. This makes it possible to delay decisions about how they are to be connected until the relevant information is available. CA, for example, keeps a list of conceptual structures that have been built but have not yet been fit into a larger structure. Figure 7–14 illustrates how PARSIFAL makes use of two major data structures: a pushdown stack of incomplete constituents called the *active node stack* and a three-place *constituent buffer* which contains constituents that are not yet complete and whose higher level grammatical function is as yet uncertain. It shows the structures resulting from the initial steps in parsing the sentence *John should have scheduled the meeting.*

At this point, four words have been processed. The first two have resulted in the building of two syntactic structures, a sentence, S1, and an auxiliary sequence, AUX1. The NP *John* has been assigned as a constituent of S1 and the modal *should* as a constituent of AUX1. The second two have been put into the buffer, waiting to see how the sentence will continue. The lists of features associated with the words were the result of dictionary entries. Those associated with other constituents are produced with actions similar to those used in ATN grammars. The bracketed lists following '/' deal with rule activation and will be explained below.

Active Node Stack:

> S1 (S Declarative Major S) / {Parse-Aux Cpool}
> NP : *John*
>
> Aux1 (Modal Past Verb-Singular-Plural Auxiliary) / {Build-Aux}
> Modal : *should*

Buffer:

> 1 : Word3 (*Have Verb Tenseless Aux-Verb Present 3rd-Singular) : *have*
> 2 : Word4 (*Schedule Comp-Obj Verb Infinitive-Obj 3rd-Singular
> Past Past-Participle) : *scheduled*

Figure 7–14. Syntactic structures in PARSIFAL.

The words in the buffer are generally used in first-in first-out order, but need not be. The ability to keep words in a buffer makes it possible to delay decisions. For example, the role of the word *have* is quite different in:

Have the students who missed the exam taken the makeup?

Have the students who missed the exam take a makeup.

It cannot be decided whether *have* is a main verb or auxiliary until the form of *take* has been taken into account. It can be kept unassigned in a buffer while the detailed processing of the NP *the students who missed the exam* is completed. A buffer cell can contain a full grammatical constituent as well as single word.

Semantic structures. The conceptual dependency parsers and the Word Expert Parser do not attempt to systematically build a syntactic structure, but instead allow the actions taken in parsing to directly produce conceptual structures of some kind. The work that is usually divided into parsing and semantic analysis is combined in a single component. A rule can specify particular configurations of the semantic structure that must be present for the rule to apply, and can specify actions that modify the structure. Figure 7–15 illustrates the situation-action rules associated with one of the senses of the word *give* in the MARGIE parser. It makes use of a case-frame semantic structure (based on abstract verbs like 'ATRANS,' which represents a transfer of possession) and a set of simple semantic categorizations (like HUMAN and PHYSICAL-OBJECT) associated with words in the dictionary. The form shown here is a simplified pedagogical version of the original LISP structures used in writing the grammar.

The actions specify what to do with the next noun encountered in the sentence. If it is a word for a human, it is to be assigned the RECIPIENT role in the structure. If it is a physical object, it is assigned the OBJECT role. A special definition is substituted for *to* so that a subsequent phrase describing a

Feature Sense Human	→	Choose Recipient Sense
Feature Sense Physical-Object	→	Choose Object Sense
		Redefine To = To1
Feature Sense Physical-Object	→	Replace Concept with
		[Atrans
		Actor = Subject
		To = Recipient
		From = Subject
		Object = Object
		Time = ?
		Mode = ?]

Figure 7–15. A meaning of *give* in MARGIE.

human will be interpreted as specifying the RECIPIENT. A case frame is set up, with some of the items filled in and others left to be added as more words come along. This approach works well for simple sentences like *John gave Mary a present,* but there is difficulty with more complex structures like *Did the party John gave present Mary with any problems?*

Control information.   In order to provide the needed degree of control, most situation-action parsers allow the rules to deal explicitly with information structures representing the current state of the parser. The Word Expert Parser, for example, has a *control workspace* that contains parser control state data that can be explicitly accessed and changed. The MARGIE parser, ELI, and CA allow the actions associated with rules to add, delete, or modify other rules or the actions associated with them.

The activation of rules

In describing the operation of a situation-action parser, it is useful to distinguish three states a rule can be in: *active, applicable,* and *applied.* At any given moment, there is a collection of active rules, each specifying some situation that must be present in order to trigger the rule. If that situation comes into effect, the rule is applicable. At any one moment, a subset of the active rules is applicable. The parser has some means of choosing an applicable rule and applying it. This entails running the actions associated with the rule and (possibly) deleting it from the list of active rules.

In the discussion so far, we have indicated that new rules become activated as successive words of the sentence are processed. In addition to this word-based activation, there are other ways that rules can be added to the set of those whose conditions are being checked.

(RULE Imperative in Packet SS-Start
    [=tenseless] →
        Label C to be S, Imperative, Major.
        Insert the word 'you' into the buffer.
        Deactivate SS-Start. Activate Parse-Subj.)

(RULE Aux-Inversion in Parse-Subj
    [=auxverb] [=np] →
        Attach 2nd to C as NP.
        Deactivate Parse-Subj. Activate Parse-Aux.)

(RULE Start-Aux in Parse-Aux
    [=verb] →
        Create a new Aux node.
        Label C with the meet of the features of 1st and vspl, v1s,
                v+13s, vpl+2s, v-3s, v3s.
        Label C with the meet of the features of 1st and pres, past,
                future, tenseless.
        Activate Parse-VP. Deactivate Parse-Aux.)

Figure 7–16. Some rules from PARSIFAL.

Explicit activation. There can be an explicit action taken in the application of one rule which activates another rule or collection (sometimes called a *packet*) of rules. This requires that the individual rules or packets be given names and be available in some kind of catalog. The names appearing in brackets in the PARSIFAL structures shown in Figure 7–14 (PARSE-AUX, BUILD-AUX, and CPOOL) are names of rule packets. In PARSIFAL, rules are always activated or deactivated as a whole packet, rather than on an individual basis. Three typical rules (one from each of three packets) are illustrated in Figure 7–16. Rules in PARSIFAL are written in PIDGIN, an English-like formal language that is translated into LISP by a simple translator.

The first rule is in a packet SS-START, activated at the start of parsing a sentence. It is the rule that handles imperative sentences like *Be serious*. The first line specifies the situation under which it will apply, listing the contents of the buffers. The IMPERATIVE rule states that the first element of the buffer must be a tenseless verb (like *be* or *go*). The associated actions label the sentence (the current structure C) as IMPERATIVE and MAJOR (not an embedded sentence), and place the word *you* into the buffer. This corresponds to the action in an ATN of creating a dummy subject for an imperative, as described in Section 5.6. Finally, the sentence-starting packet is deactivated and a new packet PARSE-SUBJ is activated. This is the packet normally used to parse a subject. Since the word *you* was placed into the buffer (not into a syntactic structure), it will then be treated just as though it had appeared at the beginning of the sentence.

The second rule deals with subject-auxiliary inversion, specifying that if the buffer contains an auxiliary followed by an NP, the NP can be attached to the current structure (as a subject) and the packet that normally parses an auxiliary is called. Once again, since the auxiliary is left in the buffer and the NP has been removed, this new packet will operate exactly as it would in the usual non-inverted case. This second rule would never apply in the same sentences in which the first rule did, since the required buffer configuration would not occur.

The third rule is intended to parse the initial member of the auxiliaries—the one that has to agree in number and person with the subject. It illustrates a use of feature registers.

In this example, the activation of successive packets operates almost exactly like stepping through the sequence of states in an ATN. Each rule checks some conditions, does some actions and then moves to a new state by deactivating the old packet and activating a new one. However, in more complex grammars the correspondence is not as simple. Several packets can be active at one time, and an action can add to the pool or remove from it. One way of thinking of such a system is as a factored transition network—one in which the current state is a combination of components rather than a unitary element.

Stack activation. In addition to explicitly activating packets, PARSIFAL makes use of stack operations. When a new constituent is pushed onto the stack of structures being built, all of the rules that were active become inactive and are saved away. When a structure is completed and the previous element returned to the top of the stack, its rules are reactivated. The packet names listed in Figure 7–14 are those associated with the stack elements. For example, if a sentence is being parsed and a determiner like *the* is found, it pushes a new NP onto the stack and activates those rules relevant to parsing an NP. The sentence rules rest in abeyance until the NP is completed, at which time they return to active duty.

In CA, there is a special use of stacking, implemented to handle noun phrases. When a noun phrase is entered, the rules associated with the higher level component are deactivated until the end of the noun phrase is found. Thus, in parsing *John bought apple pies*, the rule associated with *bought* that is looking for an object will not take *apple*, but will wait until the entire phrase *apple pies* is complete. There are complex heuristics for deciding just when a noun phrase is being started or has been completed.

Semantic and contextual activation. In systems based on semantics, additional activation is done on the basis of the semantic structures being built or semantic features of the context. In some cases, these will be individual rules, while in others there are packets organized around topics.

Choice of rules for application

At any particular moment, there is a collection of structures and a list of active rules. The system checks the conditions associated with each active rule to determine whether it is applicable. This test is usually a set of simple conditions. The Word Expert Parser organizes these into a discrimination net (a tree of multiple-choice questions) for efficient checking of multiple conditions. If no rules are applicable, the parse fails. If only one is applicable, it is applied. If more than one is applicable, one of the potential candidates must be selected. There are several basic strategies.

Arbitrary choice. The system can be built with no systematic procedure for deciding. Of course, any actual implementation will have some specific way of doing things, but the grammar writer cannot make assumptions about it and must write the rules so the right things happen regardless of the order.

Queuing. A systematic regimen can be prescribed for choosing among candidates. The simplest is to take them in the order they were first activated, or the order in which they became applicable. Some parsers take the most recent first, and others group them by recency and have additional heuristics to apply within a recency group.

Numerical priorities. The most sophisticated scheme is that of PARSIFAL, in which each rule has a numerical priority and the highest valued candidate is always chosen.

Deactivation of rules

As illustrated in Figure 7–16, it is possible to have the deactivation of rules or rule packets as an explicit action taken by a rule. It is also possible to distinguish between *self-deleting* rules, which are deactivated after being applied (e.g., those that look for the subject and object), and others that can be applied more than once (e.g., looking for modifiers). In practice, the problem of deactivation can be quite significant, since a rule that was activated at an earlier stage of the parse can be an unwelcome intruder at a later stage when its effects were not anticipated by the grammar writer. In general, the 'traffic control' of rules is a major problem in all situation-action parsers. To the degree that they go through a regular sequence of activating and deactivating packets, they are similar to an ATN. To the degree that they allow many different packets to be operating in parallel, they lead to complex unexpected interactions and can be difficult to debug and understand.

Ambiguity and the exploration of alternatives

Any parsing scheme can be modified to explore multiple alternatives, either in parallel or by backtracking. All that is needed is a bookkeeping scheme that makes it possible to keep a record of the entire relevant state of the parser just before a choice was made and to use this record to try a different path. With situation-action parsers this is difficult to implement, since the relevant state of the parser includes the entire set of structures being built, the set of rules that have been activated, and the control state. In general, these parsers have been built on the assumption that the exploration of multiple alternatives is unnecessary. Those who build semantically based systems argue that semantic considerations will force the right choice, while those who build syntactically based systems make use of special mechanisms (like the buffers of PARSIFAL) that allow decisions to be delayed until the relevant information is available.

PARSIFAL is intended to demonstrate that there is a theoretical significance to the *determinism hypothesis*—that with certain well-defined mechanisms, parsing is deterministic. Arguments are given (in the style of the formal capacity arguments discussed in Section 4.5) as to why the particular formal details of the system might correspond to interesting innate properties of the human language capacity. It is difficult to evaluate this hypothesis so far, since the mechanisms proposed do not yet handle phenomena like conjunction, prepositional phrase attachment, and lexical ambiguity.

Further Reading for Chapter 7

Primary sources. The primary references for the systems described in this chapter are listed in Figure 7–1. A number of other papers are mentioned within the text.

Surveys. The chapter on natural language in Barr and Feigenbaum (1981) gives an overall survey, including a good short summary of the early work on machine translation. Waltz (1978) contains more than fifty brief summaries of current natural language systems. Grishman (1976) surveys syntactic analysis procedures, including detailed accounts of several approaches. Rahmstorf and Ferguson (1978) describe a number of the European systems.

New research. As new systems are developed, they are usually presented at one of several conferences, primarily the biennial IJCAI (International Joint Conference on Artificial Intelligence) and the annual meetings of the AAAI (American Association for Artificial Intelligence), COLING (International Conference on Computational Linguistics), and ACL (Association for Computational Linguistics). More complete descriptions of systems appear in journal articles and books, but a scan of the conference proceedings can provide a good overview of what is going on.

Related areas. Many issues of syntactic processing are discussed in the literature on psycholinguistics, surveyed by Clark and Clark (1977). The problems of information retrieval are discussed by Sparck-Jones and Kay (1974) and Salton (1975). The issues in speech understanding are summarized by Newell (1975).

Exercises for Chapter 7

Exercises for Section 7.1

7.1 Read the reference given for one of the systems listed in Figure 7–1 and categorize it in terms of the issues outlined in Figure 7–2.

7.2 Give a deep structure in the style of Figure 7–4 corresponding to the annotated surface structure of Figure 7–3, and vice versa.

7.3 Write a context-free grammar that includes rules for REDUCED-S to handle the following sentences:

> *I thought she would go, but John predicted she wouldn't.*
> *I wanted her to fix this one immediately and the other one*
>   *by tomorrow.*
> *This one will be easy to fix with glue but that one won't,*
>   *even with epoxy.*

Exercises for Section 7.2

7.4 Write a bottom-up nondeterministic parser for an augmented context-free grammar, assuming that nodes have only synthesized attributes and a rule has conditions to be checked that deal with the features of its children.

7.5 Write a top-down left-to-right nondeterministic parser for an augmented context-free grammar. Assume that each node can have both inherited and synthesized attributes and that there are primitive operations for assigning features to nodes and checking conditions. You will have to put restrictions on just when feature values are assigned and checked.

7.6 Give some examples of places in a question-answering system where variable rules of the kind used by DIAMOND would be useful.

Exercises for Section 7.3

7.7 Analysis by synthesis was discussed as a theoretically possible way of parsing with a transformational grammar. Write a procedure for the related but simpler task of doing analysis by synthesis with a context-free grammar. It should take a sentence and a grammar, and systematically generate sentences using the grammar until either the input is found or all sentences of its length have been tried (in which case it fails).

7.8 Explain why the process described in the previous exercise will not work with a general rewrite grammar.

7.9 Write a transformation in the general condition–action style of Figure 7–8 (not following the details of the notation) that can deal with EQUI-NP-DELETION, as in *Woodrow wanted to dance.*

Exercises for Section 7.4

7.10 One of the rules used to rewrite the chart in Figure 7–9 could be represented as:

$$\text{NP}_1 \ \text{Verb}_1 \ \text{Verb}_2 \to \text{NP}_2 \ \text{Verb}_3 \ \text{NP}_3$$

      Verb_1 is a form of *be*
      Verb_2 is a past participle
      Verb_3 is Verb_2 with the tense of Verb_1
      NP_2 is a dummy
      NP_3 is a copy of NP_1

In this kind of rule, the right-hand side is added to the chart along with the left-hand side, rather than replace it as in the rewriting procedures of Section 4.2.

Give the rule that produces the other structure added in Figure 7–9.

7.11 Give a rule that would deal with yes-no questions, producing the corresponding declarative form preceded by a marker QUESTION.

7.12 Give rules for handling wh- questions in which the questioned element is the subject or object of the sentence. The question marker should precede the questioned element, which should appear in the appropriate 'hole' in the structure.

Exercises for Section 7.5

7.13 Write a PROGRAMMAR grammar that covers the same data as the ATN for NPs given in Appendix D. Use reasonable English-like sentences to state the conditions and actions.

7.14 Give a set of lexical categories that could be used in a semantic grammar for a system that makes airline reservations. Give examples of some network fragments that make use of these categories in recognizing specialized phrases like *American Airlines flight 27 to Chicago on the tenth.*

7.15 Give formal definitions for case frames associated with individual verb senses in the dictionary, and for a procedure that uses them in putting together structures like that of Figure 7–5, as described for the GUS system.

Exercises for Section 7.6

7.16 Make a list of all the stock patterns you think it would be useful for a parser to have in order to parse the contents of Section 7.6.

7.17 Write a procedure that takes a set of independent patterns with lexical categories and constants (as defined in Figure 2–9) and produces a structure in which all shared initial sequences are merged. For example, given the patterns 'A B C' and 'A B D E,' the parsing of the initial 'A B' would be shared, with a split at the next element. This is like a transition network, except that paths never come back together.

7.18 Write a procedure that recognizes patterns using an extended version of the structure of the previous exercise. Given an input sentence, it should return a set of pattern identifiers, one for each pattern that matches (empty if there are none). For example, if the patterns included '1: NOUN fly' and '2: birds VERB,' both would match *birds fly* and the result would include the identifiers '1' and '2.'

Exercises for Section 7.7

7.19 For each of the following sentences, describe the decision that must be delayed in order to decide on the correct parsing. For example, in the sentence *Have the students who missed the exam take(n) the makeup,* it cannot be decided whether *have* is the main verb or an auxiliary.

a) *Can the butcher knife handle burned foods? Can the butcher knife handle burned in the accident be repaired?*

b) *We realized that fish was spoiled. We realized that fish were jumping.*

c) *To his mother he told nothing. To his mother he told us to leave his stocks and bonds.*

7.20 Give an example of a sentence that would be assigned the wrong structure by the MARGIE rules of Figure 7–15.

7.21 In the text, it was mentioned that there was a close correspondence between ATN states and rule packets.

a) Describe how any ATN could be converted into a set of rule packets that have the equivalent effect.

b) Describe how any set of rule packets could be converted into an ATN. (Note, this is tricky and can involve duplicating information).

c) Give a simple example of rule packets that could not be converted into an ATN without having to duplicate information.

Appendix A

A Language for Describing Objects and Procedures

Contents of Appendix A

The previous chapters contain many descriptions of procedures used in language processing. These descriptions are written in a notation called DL, which was designed specifically for use in the book. It is intended to be comprehensible to students with little background in computer science while being precise enough so that programs written in it could be mechanically translated and carried out on a computer. This appendix describes the language in sufficient detail for understanding the procedures and writing similar ones. It does not deal with implementation issues that would arise in building a compiler or interpreter for the language.

Section A.1 introduces the language and explains the basic orientation underlying it. Sections A.2 and A.3 illustrate some of the details of the language through a series of examples. Section A.4 gives a full specification, to be used as a reference. Section A.5 defines some of the basic classes of objects used in the definitions throughout the book.

A.1 Programming and description

The motivations for DL differ from those for normal programming languages in a fundamental way. In creating a language intended primarily for the running of programs, it is important to make things easy for the machine. Design choices are made that simplify the automatic analysis of the structure of the program, make its operation more efficient, and simplify the design of an interpreter or compiler. For the purposes of a textbook, the ease of implementing a language and the speed at which programs run are of little importance. It is more important that the programs be easy for people to read and to understand.

The syntactic form of DL is based on natural language discourse and on standard conventions for writing. It takes advantage of the fact that these conventions are already familiar and easy for anyone who can read. For readers who have had a great deal of practice with standard programming languages it may seem awkward—once the skills of reading terse notation have been mastered, it has many advantages over a more verbose English-like form. This book was written on the assumption that its readers are not programmers, and that the familiarity of natural language provides a useful pre-understanding of the programming language.

More important than its syntactic form is DL's way of organizing programs to elucidate their conceptual structure. In designing a programming language, there are two potentially conflicting sources of criteria for organization—things can be classed as alike because they are implemented with the same underlying mechanism, or because they have a conceptual similarity for the language user. In most programming languages, the balance lies towards the implementation side. In DL it has been pushed in the other direction. At times, this leads to distinguishing things that are lumped together in other languages, and at other times it leads to bringing together things usually kept distinct. For example,

DL has logical expressions (which can be evaluated to produce a truth value), procedure invocations (which specify a procedure to be carried out and will succeed or fail), and referring phrases (which can be evaluated to produce an object). In many languages, this distinction is not made.

On the other hand, there has been an attempt in DL to achieve a uniformity beyond that of most programming languages when the differences are due to implementation rather than the conceptual structure. As a simple example, DL has a primitive class, *table,* for pairing keys and entries. In another language, one might have association lists, property lists, and hash tables, each having the basic properties of a table but making different efficiency tradeoffs. In DL this level of implementation is not visible. The computer is thought of as operating on *descriptions* rather than on *data.*

In the traditional view of programming, programs operate on data—on objects (bits, numbers, records, or whatever) stored in the computer. To understand or explain a program, we look at how data is being input, created, changed, and moved around. This is a limited view. It is a bit like viewing a business office as an organization for creating and processing business forms. Indeed, much of what goes on in the office consists of writing information on pieces of paper, passing them around, storing them, and modifying them. An analysis of the 'paper flow' can give a useful insight into how an office functions, but it is not the right starting point. The office is doing business, and that business exists in a world outside of the paperwork. An understanding comes first from knowing what the forms and files describe.

The same insight applies to programming. A program can be seen as manipulating data, but it can better be seen as operating with descriptions of things that lie outside the computer system. The procedures in this book operate on data that are descriptions of linguistic objects—of words and sentences, grammar rules and logical formulas. When we define a class for representing a sentence as a data object, what we are really doing is choosing to describe those aspects of a sentence that are relevant to the procedure being described. The data structure is not itself a sentence—it is one description of a sentence.

It is important to recognize that not all of the objects we want to describe exist in the hard physical world. In the business office, some of the forms describe real things and events, but there are other forms, and even whole areas of business, where existence is in a nonphysical domain. The stockbroker's forms describe objects and transactions that exist only on paper. The 'things' of that world are stocks and bonds, debentures, and options. The physical stock certificate is not the stock. If you ask me about a stock I own, I talk about the price and the dividends, not about the color of its paper or the pattern of swirls printed on its edge. If the piece of paper gets burned, I still own the stock.

Similarly, programs operate with descriptions of objects existing in a physical world, such as actual utterances of sentences, and also with descriptions of things whose existence is abstract, such as grammar rules and semantic networks. In dealing with these abstract objects, we should remember that the specific data structures are still a description of some conceptual object. The focus should be on the properties of the object that result from its place in a conceptual system, not on the form of the object's description.

The structure of DL reflects this view of programming. It places equal emphasis on notations for describing procedures and notations for describing objects. It pays relatively little attention to details of how data is stored in the computer, concentrating instead on how different data structures can best reflect the relevant structure of the objects being described. The notation is organized around definitions of *classes* of objects, logical *predicates* that can be true or false of those objects, and *procedures* that operate on records describing objects of each class.

A computer system for running DL programs would be relatively complex. To interpret the English sentences used in definitions, it would have to do syntactic and semantic analysis of the kind needed for natural language processing. In order to manipulate the descriptions with reasonable efficiency, it would need a 'smart compiler' doing operations usually thought of as 'automatic programming.' No such system now exists, although one close to it could be built using currently understood techniques.

A.2 Classes and objects

One of the three basic kinds of entities making up DL programs is the *class definition,* which specifies a form for describing objects of a particular kind. The definition for a class can include the properties and internal structure of its objects, relationships between an object of the class and other objects, and procedures done with objects of the class. In some cases, the definition will include things relevant to several different procedures. This is like a shoe store having a standard stock form on which all of the potentially relevant information about each pair of shoes is recorded. In other cases, it is useful to have a class definition that calls for only part of the information so that the description of the objects can be simplified. In the shoe store, this would be like having an inventory card for a pair of shoes, listing only its size, style, and color, and ignoring its price, its cost, where it came from, when it arrived, etc.

DL includes a few 'built-in' class definitions for objects that are common enough for their descriptions to be part of the basic language. These include numbers, characters, sequences, and sets, as defined in Section A.5. In writing a procedure definition, new classes are defined for the other relevant objects. In the chapters of this book, classes are defined for patterns, trees and charts, network nodes and links, logical formulas, grammar rules, and many others.

Figure A–1 shows a sample class definition (for a COURSE) that might be part of a computer program used by a university registrar. A class definition is

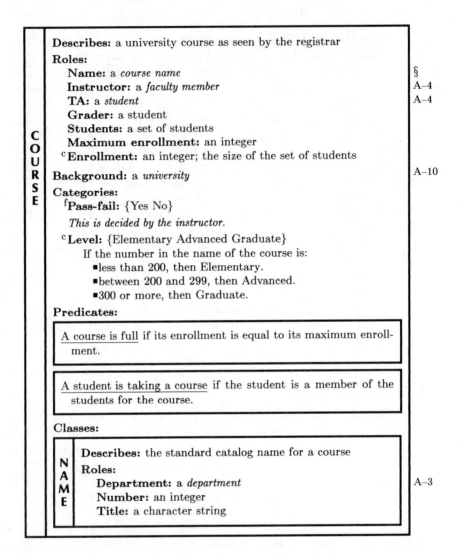

Describes: a university course as seen by the registrar

Roles:

    Name: a *course name*   §

    Instructor: a *faculty member*   A–4

    TA: a *student*   A–4

    Grader: a student

    Students: a set of students

    Maximum enrollment: an integer

    ᶜ**Enrollment:** an integer; the size of the set of students

Background: a *university*   A–10

Categories:

    ᶠ**Pass-fail:** {Yes No}

    This is decided by the instructor.

    ᶜ**Level:** {Elementary Advanced Graduate}

        If the number in the name of the course is:

            ■less than 200, then Elementary.

            ■between 200 and 299, then Advanced.

            ■300 or more, then Graduate.

Predicates:

> A course is <u>full</u> if its enrollment is equal to its maximum enrollment.

> A student is <u>taking a course</u> if the student is a member of the students for the course.

Classes:

> **Describes:** the standard catalog name for a course
>
> **Roles:**
>
>   **Department:** a *department*   A–3
>
>   **Number:** an integer
>
>   **Title:** a character string

(Left label: COURSE; inner class label: NAME)

Figure A–1. Class definition for a university course.

displayed in a box, with the name of the class as a label along the left side. As discussed above, this class definition is not a full account of what a course is. For example, it does not include the time it is being given or the prerequisites or anything about the content. In creating a definition, we specify particular aspects as relevant to the purposes of a procedure or collection of procedures. Figure A–1 illustrates several of the standard components of a class definition (for a more complete list, see Section A.4):

Description. Associated with each definition, there is some class of objects being described. Otherwise we would not bother to write the definition. Each class definition starts with a piece of English text intended to convey to the reader a basic idea of what the class is.

Roles. In describing any object as a member of a class, we specify the other objects that play specific roles associated with it. For each role, the class definition provides a *declaration* consisting of a role name and a description of the object or objects that can fill the role. The description specifies the class of the object, and can also include further descriptions that must be satisfied by any object that fills it. The class definition for a course in Figure A–1 lists a number of roles, including an instructor, students, and a maximum enrollment. Each of these is described as being an object or set of objects of a particular class, such as a faculty member, student, or integer. Each of these other classes must be defined in turn.

When a definition uses a class (or predicate or procedure) defined elsewhere, the number of the figure in which that other definition appears is included in the right-hand margin. If the other definition appears in the same figure, a '§' appears. Italics indicate which word or phrase is being cross-referenced. A cross-reference is omitted if it has already appeared in the same definition, or if it is a class standardly defined in DL (listed in Section A.5).

Background. Often an object is part of a larger context. In this case, the course is being offered at a particular university. A program that dealt with several universities would need to associate a UNIVERSITY role with each course. In order to make this context explicit without having to include it as a role with each object, it is listed as background.

Categories. Often the objects belonging to a particular class can be partitioned among a set of mutually exclusive categories. Procedures related to these objects may depend on the classification. Figure A–1 includes two classifications: a course can be either pass-fail or not and it can belong to one of three levels of difficulty. Every course must belong to exactly one of the categories along each dimension. A categorization can include any number of categories and has a name, like PASS-FAIL or LEVEL. Categories are referred to in phrases like *'If the course is (is not) pass-fail...'* and *'If the level of the course is advanced....'* A category name can also be used as a noun in referring to objects that belong to that category. Some categories (such as PASS-FAIL in the example) are simply assigned to objects and remain fixed (as indicated by the superscript 'f'). Others (like LEVEL) can be computed from the roles and other categories of the object (indicated with the superscript 'c').

Predicates. In a class definition, it is useful to define predicates for relationships involving objects in the class. *One-place predicates,* which are true or false of a single object, are similar to *binary categories* having the choices YES and NO. Saying that a predicate is true or false of the object is equivalent to saying that the object is or is not in the positive category. The predicate *'a course is full'* is a one-place predicate. There are also predicates relating several objects, as illustrated by the predicate *'a student is taking a course.'* The class definition can either give a definition of the predicate in terms of roles and categories (as in this case) or provide a procedure for testing whether the predicate holds. In this example, the definition is particularly simple and is only a slight convenience in referring to the relationships. For relationships with more complex definitions, it is vital to be able to introduce a name for the relationship.

Nested class definitions. In defining a form for describing courses, we specify that each course has a name and further define this name to have roles for a department, number, and title. This kind of nesting is a common occurrence—in the definition of one class, procedure, or predicate it is useful to define others that represent the more detailed structure. Putting one definition box inside another graphically indicates that the inner definition (in this case NAME) is relevant because of its use in the outer one. In addition, it provides a way of using more general names for specific cases. As illustrated by Figure A–2, people as well as courses have names, but these names have a different structure.

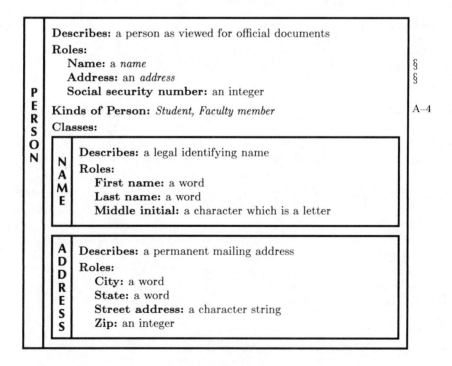

Figure A–2.   Class definition for describing a person.

When we speak about the name of a course, the definition in Figure A–1 is applicable, while in speaking about the name of a person we mean the one of Figure A–2. When there is any chance of confusion, we will use cross references to the definition that contains the appropriate definitions, or multiple word phrases like PERSON NAME and COURSE NAME.

In the particular examples here, it is not obviously necessary to create a new class for a name. We might instead, for example, simply include department, number, and title in the roles associated with a course. The goal of dividing them off into a separate definition is to point out (for the reader) that they are closely related, and to make it simpler to write procedures in which they are all operated on together.

Some additional features of class definitions

So far, we have described the basic elements that go into a class definition. There are a number of additional features illustrated in the examples:

Multiple roles. It is possible for an object to play more than one role with respect to another object. For example, the TA and the grader for a given course might be the same student. It is important to remember the difference between 'roles' and 'parts.'

When an object is thought of as built up out of parts, each part is distinct from the others. When it is thought of as related to a set of other objects by role-relations, it makes sense for multiple roles to be filled by the same object. Often two objects are related by playing mutual roles for each other, when neither can be thought of as a part of the other. Figure A–3 gives a definition of a department that contains roles filled by courses and faculty members. The definitions for these in turn, as given in Figure A–1 and Figure A–4, specify roles filled by the department.

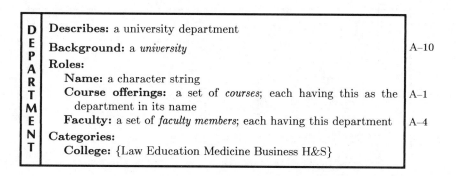

Figure A–3. Class definition for a university department.

Computable roles and categories. Often there are attributes of an object that are not independent, but are determined by the other attributes. The enrollment of a course is just the size of the set of its students. It is useful to have a separate role name because procedures that use the description of a course will include references to its enrollment. It would be clumsy to have to refer to this always as *'the size of the set of students.'* Similarly, the level can be computed from the number that is a part of the name of the course. Numbers less than 200 indicate elementary courses, numbers in the 200s indicate advanced courses, and those of 300 and higher are for graduate courses. *Computable* roles and categories are indicated by a superscript 'c' preceding the name. A definition specifying a computable role or category will also include a logical expression or a procedure for determining it, as discussed further in Section A.4. If a role is not marked computable, it is assumed that there can be steps in a procedure that involve assigning it to some particular object. Similarly, a non-computable categorization can be marked as one of the categories.

Fixed roles and categories. If a role or category is marked with a superscript 'f,' it is *fixed*. Once it has been assigned, that assignment cannot be changed

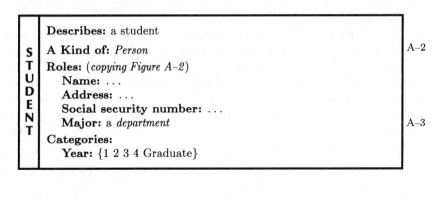

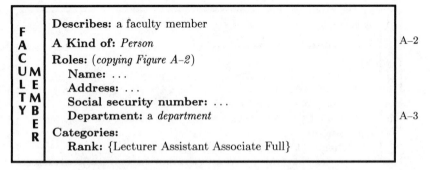

Figure A–4. Class definitions for describing students and professors.

by further steps of the procedure. In Figure A–1, the PASS-FAIL categorization
is so marked. Of course, this description is relative to a particular set of
procedures. The PASS-FAIL option can be changed in reality, but it is marked
so that it will not be changed by any of the procedures that use the definition.
Roles and categories will be marked as fixed only when it seems useful to point
out that they do not change. Each of the definitions so far includes roles and
categories that are unlikely to be changed by procedures we write (such as the
name of a department or person) but are not explicitly marked as fixed.

Kinds (subclasses). Often there will be a class of objects that is a specialized
version of a more general class. Categories can be thought of as a simple kind of
specialization, since they divide the class up into separate groups. Sometimes,
however, each subclass has special attributes to be considered. For example,
both students and faculty members are people and have the attributes described
in Figure A–2. But a faculty member has a department and rank, while a
student has a year and a major. If a class is defined as a *subclass* of another,
it includes a *kind-of declaration,* as illustrated in Figure A–4. Any object in
a subclass (STUDENT or FACULTYMEMBER) will have all of the roles and
categories of the superclass (PERSON) and may have additional material as
well.

In order to avoid copying all of the material from the definition of a
superclass to each of its subclasses, we can use ellipses ('. . .') to indicate places
where material is to be copied directly from the superclass. This abbreviation
is also used when a definition is a revised version of an earlier one and all that
is being described is the change.

Records

The notations presented so far are for class definitions. The procedures in
the book are written at this level—defining classes of objects, predicates, and
procedures on them. When the procedures are carried out, they operate with
descriptions of individual objects. In writing a program to deal with courses, for
example, we are defining their properties (and those of students, departments,
etc.) in general. When the procedures are run, they will create *records* for individual courses, students, and departments. Each course will be an *instance* of
the defined class.

Each record can be thought of as a form that follows the layout specified
by the class definition and is filled in with information about a particular
individual. Thus, for the course Linguistics 101, there will be a record based
on the definition of COURSE with *fillers* for the roles and categories. The fields
corresponding to categories are filled in by 'checking off one of the boxes'—that
is, by indicating one category along each dimension. The fields corresponding
to roles are filled in by naming *another record* that contains the information
about the object filling the role.

Course-17

Name	CourseName-82
Instructor	FacultyMember-33
TA	Student-655
Grader	Student-655
Students	Set-466
Maximum enrollment	Integer-406
Pass-Fail	No

CourseName-82

Department	Departmert-7
Number	Integer-47
Title	CharacterString-2537

Department-7

Name	CharacterString-1140
Course offerings	Set-5534
Faculty	Set-56
College	H&S

Figure A–5. Records for a particular course and some associated objects.

Each record has an identifier that is made up of the name of the class and an arbitrary number not shared by any other record of that class. The identifier for the record describing Linguistics 101 might be COURSE-17. A record can be mentioned in any number of other records and can play any number of roles. If Leonard Bloomfield teaches several courses, the record for each of these courses will have its field for instructor filled by the identifier of the record describing him (e.g., FACULTYMEMBER-33). Every object is described in DL with a record. Every number, every string, every set occupies a record just like any user-defined class, and every role-filler is a pointer to a record (indicated by its unique identifier).

When records are printed out directly, as illustrated in Figure A–5, they are hard to read. The details about any object are spread through records for each of the objects filling its roles. For more convenient reading, three special modes of printing are provided. It is important to remember that these are not relevant to the internal structure of records. Within a record, each field is filled by an internal reference to another record or records (or a basic object such as an integer or character). The printing modes have an effect only when printing (on paper or on a screen) the contents of the records.

Class	Print form	Example
Character (A–21)	Surrounded by single quotes	'a'
Character string (A–22)	Surrounded by double quotes	"a string"
Integer (A–15)	Ordinary numerical notation	1492
Sequence (A–18)	The items in order, separated by commas	a, b, c
Set (A–16)	Surrounded by braces Commas are used if needed.	{1 4 9}
Stack (A–23)	The items in order, with top element first	a, b, c
Table (A–20)	Aligned columns, separated with colons	*See below*
Word (A–22)	In italics	*dog*

Example of print form for tables (A–20)

17: *seventeen*
6:   *six*
50: *fifty*

Figure A–6. Print forms for the standardly defined classes.

Standardly defined objects. Each of the classes of objects standardly defined in DL has its own special way of appearing, as shown in Figure A–6. When a field is filled with one of these, this form will normally be used. The numbers are those of the figures containing the corresponding class definitions.

Identifying names. Often there will be instances of a class that are important enough to be given unique names more readable than CHARACTERSTRING-2537. A unique name can be given to any instance, such as DETERMINER. If the name is to be made up of several words, they are glued together, as in THINGWITHLONGNAME, to indicate that it is a single name.

Print forms. Usually objects are not given identifying names, but a small amount of the information about them would be sufficient for the reader to know their identity. In this case, a *print form* can be associated with a class, specifying which of the role and category fillers are to be mentioned and how they are to be arranged. There may be more than one print form for a class. For example, the print form for an address will be different for typing envelopes and for filling out an address book.

Figure A–7 gives examples of print forms for some of the definitions in this section and illustrates their use (along with the standard forms) in printing the same record as in Figure A–5. Print forms will not be defined formally, but their use in the examples in the chapters of the book should be fairly self-explanatory. In both Figure A–5 and A–7, the computable roles and categories (such as ENROLLMENT and LEVEL) are not printed out. They are not stored in the records, but are recomputed when needed from the other roles and categories according to the definition.

Print forms

Print course name as: Department Number: Title
    Where a department is printed as its name without the quotation marks

Print faculty member by printing: LastName, FirstName MiddleInitial.
    of the name, using no quotation marks or italics

Print student by printing: FirstName LastName
    of the name, using no quotation marks or italics

Course-17

Name	Linguistics 101: "Introduction to linguistics"
Instructor	Bloomfield, Leonard G.
TA	Alan Turing
Grader	Alan Turing
Students	{James Carter, Arturo Toscanini, Julia Child}
Maximum Enrollment	4
Pass-Fail	No

Figure A–7. Printing the contents of a record using print forms.

A.3 Descriptions of procedures

The formalism described so far is static. It provides for records that are filled out according to a class definition to describe objects of a class, but it does not account for how these records are created or changed. Of course, the whole point of a language for describing procedures is that something happens. DL also has a procedural side—a set of forms and conventions for specifying what is to be done.

Figure A–8 illustrates a simple procedure that might be used by the registrar in recording the courses that a student has signed up for. It takes two inputs, a student and a set of courses, and has two different kinds of results. For the successful part of the registration, it modifies the records for the courses. Future procedures that access those course records will find this student. For the unsuccessful part, it builds up and returns a PROBLEM SHEET, which tells the student which courses he or she did not get into. This example illustrates a number of the features of DL procedure definitions:

Procedure definition. Like a class definition, a procedure definition is shown in a box. It has a label along the top, naming the procedure and the objects it operates on. Within the box, the various parts of the definition are written out, with labels like 'Inputs' and 'Basic Method' indicating what each one is. Some of these parts are in turn drawn in boxes, while others are written as a sequence of lines of text following the label, using indentation and square dots

---

Register a student for a set of courses

Purpose: Modify the course records

Inputs:
    Student: a *student*   A–4
    Courses: a set of *courses*   A–1

Results: a *problem sheet*   §

Working Structures:
    Problem courses: a set of courses; initially empty

Basic Method:
  ■ For each of the courses do:
    ■ If the student *qualifies* for the course and the course is not *full*, § A–1
      then add the student to its students.
    ■ Otherwise add the course to the problem courses
  ■ Return a new problem sheet with:
    ■ student = the student
    ■ courses = the problem courses.

Predicates:

A student qualifies for a course when:
  If the year of the student is:
    ■ 1, then the course is elementary.
    ■ 2 or 3, then the course is elementary or advanced.
    ■ 4, then the course is any level.
    ■ Graduate, then the course is not elementary.

PROBLEM SHEET

Describes: a report to be sent back to the student

Roles:
    Student: a student
    Courses: a set of courses

Figure A–8. A procedure for registration.

to indicate which things go together. Elements starting at the same indentation level belong together, just as in the standard form for an outline. The dots are simply used to make the grouping more visually apparent.

Basic method. The heart of the definition describes a sequence of steps to be carried out. It is labeled *'Basic Method,'* and in the example of Figure A–8 it consists of two steps, *'For each of the courses do...'* and *'Return a new problem sheet....'* Each of these has its own internal structure as described below. A procedure is carried out by going through the sequence in order, doing each step and recording its results so they can be referred to in later steps. When the end of the sequence is reached, the procedure is done.

Actions associated with primitives. Steps within a procedure can describe actions on DL records. For example, '... *add the course to the problem courses'* describes the addition of an element to a set. For each of the primitive classes (sets, sequences, tables, etc.,) there is a collection of basic operations, listed in Section A.5.

Iteration. The first major step of the procedure in Figure A–8 is not a simple action, but is itself a sequence of steps to be carried out for each member of the courses. This structure is just one of many different forms for describing *iteration* in DL. An iteration has three basic elements: a *body,* a *stepper,* and a *stop test.* The body (in this case, the two lines starting *'If the student...'* and *'Otherwise add...'*) is carried out once for each go-round of the iteration. The stepper determines what is changed on each go-round—in this case, the procedure deals with a different element of the set of courses each time around. The stop test determines when to end the entire iteration. In the case of stepping through a set, the procedure stops when the set is exhausted. However, there can be iterations with more complex stop tests, such as ones that do the body a specific number of times or that continue going round again and again until some condition becomes true.

Conditionals and case selection. The body of the iteration is itself a special form called a *conditional.* It specifies a *logical expression* (in this case *'the student qualifies for the course and the course is not full'*), a step to be done if this expression is true in the given case (i.e., for the particular element on that go-round), and a different step to be done if it is false. As with iterations, there are many different forms of conditionals, some specifying a step to be done if true with nothing being done if it is false, others specifying a sequence of *'Otherwise if... then...'* pairs, of which the first one whose condition is true is taken. The definition of the predicate *'a student qualifies for a course'* makes use of a slightly different conditional form, a *case selection.* In this form, there is a set of alternative descriptions of an object, and each description is coupled with a particular result. An object is specified (in this case, *'the year of the student'*) and the first description that applies to it determines the result.

Logical expressions. One element of a conditional is a logical expression. As illustrated by the example, this expression can be composed of smaller expressions with connectives like *'and,' 'or,' 'not,'* and *'if ...then.'* There are primitive predicates known by the system, such as equality and category membership, as in *'the enrollment equals the maximum enrollment'* or *'the course is elementary.'* In addition, any predicate that has been defined (such as *'a student qualifies for a course'*) will be applied when the phrase used in defining it matches a phrase appearing as a logical expression.

Record creation. One of the basic operations known to the system is the creation of a new record for an object of a given type. This can be done with an explicit step of the form *'Create...'* or with a phrase using the modifier *'new,'* like *'. . . a new problem sheet with. . . .'* In specifying the creation, there can be a set of *bindings* for the objects filling the roles of the newly created object. These are represented by having the role name followed by '=' followed by the desired filler.

Procedure variables. So far we have been looking at the basic method of a procedure—the steps to be carried out. Another part of the definition is the declaration of the records with which it will work. In any particular case of applying the procedure, there will be a particular student and set of courses, and a particular problem sheet will be produced. Just as a class definition defines a set of roles that will be filled for each individual object, a procedure definition declares a set of variables, each of which will be filled for each application of the procedure. These are grouped into four categories: *inputs, results, working structures,* and *background.* The inputs are given in calling the procedure— they are there before it begins work. The working structures are created for use during the running of the procedure. They are temporary results and will disappear when the procedure is done. The results are produced at the end of running the procedure and are used for further processing by the procedure of which it is a part. Finally, the background (not illustrated here) contains structures used jointly by all of the procedures in the system. Rather than explicitly including them as inputs to each procedure that uses them, they are declared as part of a shared background, and any procedure can include declarations (under the heading *'Background'*) specifying that it will use them. In the chapters on parsing, a grammar and a dictionary are often included as a background to the parsing procedures, rather than as an input. The means by which a particular object (e.g., a particular university or grammar) is set up as the background for a DL system are not specified in detail, but in the examples used in the book, it is always clear what is intended.

Declarations. Variables are specified with a *declaration,* which gives a name to be used in the text and a description of the objects that can fill the variable. Although the system actually has a variable declaration for every variable, the declaration need not appear in the printed form if it is obvious from the context. In this example, the line *'Results: a problem sheet'* implicitly contains a declaration for a variable whose description is *'a problem sheet.'* In fact, the input declarations in this case were not really necessary, since they were implicit in the procedure's title, *'Register a student for set of courses.'* As with many things in DL, the writer has a choice between a shorter form and one including more explicit (possibly redundant) information that makes it easier to understand the definition. A declaration must always include the class of its filler (or the class of each element of the filler if the filler is a set, sequence, or table), and it can also include other descriptive information that applies to all possible fillers. This is also true for the role declarations of class definitions (in fact, they use the identical form).

Initial values. A declaration can include not only a general description of the filler, but also a specific description of the filler to be used at the start of carrying out the procedure. In the example, the *'Problem courses'* is initially an empty set and is possibly added to by later actions.

Embedded definitions. As with class definitions, a procedure definition can contain further definitions to be used within it. In this case, the definition of the predicate *'A student qualifies for a course'* is included, but the class of *'Problem sheet'* is not. Since the problem sheet is to be returned as a result and used in some other procedure, its definition is not special to the procedure of registering a student.

An extended example

The definitions in Figures A–9 and A–10 illustrate some additional features of the language. They produce a collection of report cards (one for each student) from a set of grade sheets (one for each course). For purposes of illustration, the grade sheets associate grades with student-identifying numbers (social security numbers), for which the corresponding student records need to be found. This is done by searching through the entire list of students. Of course, a realistic program would use some more efficient way of keeping records.

These new procedures and the accompanying class definitions illustrate a number of additional features:

Nested iterations. The basic method of this procedure includes an iteration (through the grade sheets), each of which in turn involves an iteration (through the grades on the grade sheet). These 'wheels within wheels' can go to any depth of nesting and are specified by simply including one iteration in the body of another. Within a nested iteration, a phrase like *'the grade sheet'* can be used when it unambiguously refers to one of the elements on one of the levels.

Assignment to working structures. Within the procedure there is a working structure given the name *'Current card,'* which is used to keep track of the card that was just found or created for the student whose grade is being recorded. The step *'...assign it as the current card'* causes the phrase *'the current card'* to become associated with the particular card referred to by *'it,'* so that a later step *'Add the grade...to...the current card...'* will operate on the record for that card. Once an assignment is made, it holds until another assignment is made to the same variable. In this case, each time another identifier-grade pair is considered there will be a new assignment of *'Current card.'*

Procedure calls. In the earlier definitions, each step within a procedure was either an iteration, a conditional, or a primitive action such as adding something

---

Make report cards from a set of grade sheets

Purpose: Produce a set of report cards, one for each student

Inputs: a set of *grade sheets*   A–10

Results: a set of *report cards*   A–10

Working Structures:
  Grade table: a table whose keys are integers and whose entries are
    report cards; initially empty
  Current card: a report card

Basic Method:
  ■ For each of the grade sheets do:
    ■For each *identifier-grade pair* do: A–10
      ■If there is an entry in the grade table for the identifier, then
        assign it as the current card.
      ■Otherwise:
        ■*Find a student having the identifier*. If this fails, go on to the   §
          next pair.
        ■Create a new report card with student = the student and
          assign it as the current card.
        ■Add it as an entry in the grade table with the identifier as
          its key.
      ■Add the grade as an entry to the grades of the current card
        with the course of the grade sheet as its key.
  ■ Return the set of entries in the grade table.

Procedures:

Find a student having an identifier

Purpose: Produce a student whose social security number is the
  identifier

Inputs: an integer

Results: a *student*   A–4

Background: a *university*   A–10

Basic Method: For each student in the university do:
  ■ If the input is the social security number of the student, then
    return the student.

Conditions:
  If all students are checked and none returned, then fail.

Figure A–9. A more complex procedure definition.

to a set. Steps can also be calls to other procedures. In Figure A–9, for
example, the procedure to enter a grade includes a step *'Find a student having
the identifier.'* This is not a primitive action in DL, but is defined in a procedure

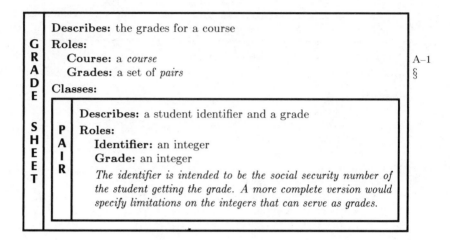

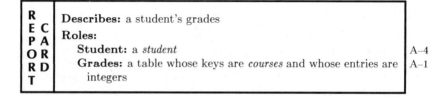

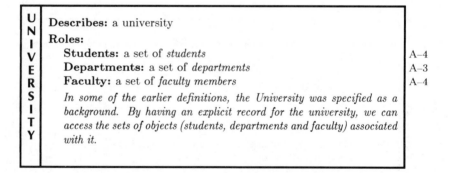

Figure A–10. Some class definitions for grading.

definition, in this case within the same figure (as indicated by the '§' in the margin). A procedure call is executed by carrying out the procedure specified in the definition, using the inputs specified in the *invocation* (the phrase saying it is to be done). For example, the phrase *'the identifier'* will be associated with a particular integer at each go-round of the iteration through the pairs, and the call to *'Find a student...'* on that go-round will have that integer as its input.

Success and failure. The definition for *'Find a student...'* illustrates another possible outcome of a procedure. Instead of succeeding and producing results, it can *fail* and produce no result. The procedure that invokes it must check for failure, either in the following step or as a condition (described below).

Conditions. Often there are special occurrences that can come up in carrying out a procedure that need to be taken into account but are not part of the normal flow. If these are specified as part of the basic method, they clutter it up and make it hard to get the basic idea of what is being done. In DL they can be separated out into another section of the definition, the *conditions*. Each condition specifies a particular test (e.g., *'all students are checked...'*) and an action to be taken if it is true. Conditions can be thought of as being tested at every point where they might become true, and their action being taken immediately if they are. The decision as to whether to include a particular check as part of the basic method or as a condition is one of clarity and readability. In some cases, the logic of the procedure is easier to understand if the checking is specified in exactly the place where it might be relevant. In others, clarity is maintained by putting it aside.

Returns from loops and procedures. Often in carrying out a procedure or iteration, there comes a point where the stepping along should not continue to the end, but should stop then and there. In Figure A–9, the process of looping through the students looking for one with the right social security number should stop as soon as one is found. The phrase *'...return the student'* indicates that the loop (through the students) and the procedure containing it should be stopped and a result returned to the one that called it.

Tables. Figure A–9 contains the first example of using tables, a primitive object of DL. A table contains paired *keys* and *entries* (like the words and entries of a dictionary) and is used for representing correspondences. Entries can be added, removed, and looked up. In this example, a table is used to keep track of the report cards associated with the identifying numbers for which students have already been found. A more efficient program would use a table for associating students with numbers once and for all instead of just keeping a list of students.

Purposes and side effects. Just as every class definition contains a description of the objects in the class, each procedure definition has a statement of its *purpose*. Each procedure is defined as having one of three basic purposes, to *modify* one or more descriptions, to *produce* some description, or to *test* a logical expression. However, some procedures may accomplish more than one thing. For example, the registration procedure modifies the course records and also produces a problem sheet. It is possible (as in this example) to have results specified for a procedure whose basic purpose is to modify. It is also possible to describe *side effects* that are modifications of records made by a procedure whose basic purpose is to produce a result, test an expression, or do some other modification. These are listed with the heading *'Side Effects.'*

Schemas and choice

In describing procedures that operate on objects of linguistic interest (such as phrase structure analyses of a sentence), it is often necessary to describe a procedure that requires making choices at various points. There may be no easy way to make the right choice, but it is easy to specify what the basic process is and what would happen if (by some magic) one could always make the right choice. In order to describe this kind of *nondeterministic* procedure, DL has primitive steps for making arbitrary choices.

In the procedure defined in Figure A–11, a student specifies not a set of courses but a set of COURSE GROUPS, with the desire that he or she be signed up for one course out of each group. The procedure of Figure A–8 is 'first come, first served'—when a particular student's registration is dealt with, he or she is signed up for any desired course that is not already full, and is rejected if it is full. In the procedure of Figure A–11, the goal is to find some set of course assignments that satisfies every student. For example, imagine that every course is limited to one student and the input is:

Jill	{Trigonometry Algebra} {Dance Drama}
Joe	{Trigonometry Arithmetic} {Dance Chorus}
Jared	{Trigonometry Arithmetic} {Drama Chorus}

If the procedure starts from the top of the list of students and takes the courses in order in each group, it will sign Jill up for trigonometry and dance, Joe for arithmetic and chorus (since his first choices are both full), and then discover that Jared cannot find an open math course. On the other hand, by anticipating the consequences of the choices, Jill could be signed up for algebra instead of trigonometry and everyone could have two courses.

Figure A–11 defines a *nondeterministic schema* for this example. Two elements of this definition are critical. First, it has a step involving an arbitrary choice, *'Choose a course from the course group.'* Second, when it finds that a course it has chosen is full, it fails. If the procedure were to be carried out somehow making compatible choices, it would succeed. Any wrong choice along the way would cause it to fail. In general, a nondeterministic schema succeeds if there exists *any possible sequence of choices* for which it would succeed. It is often much easier to describe a schema of this sort than to define a procedure that keeps track of all the possible choices so it can try another when one goes wrong. For many of the procedures in the book, we first define a schema to illustrate the basic idea and then later describe how to deal with problems of making choices and keeping track of alternatives.

Two other aspects of this definition deserve note:

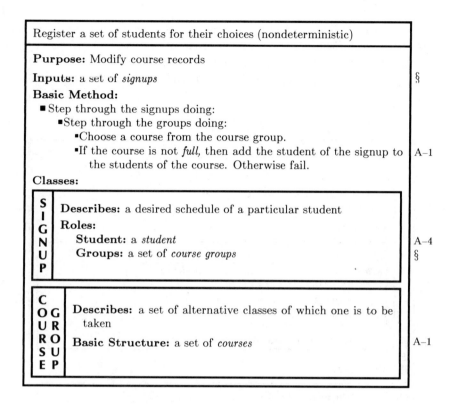

Figure A–11. A schema for registration.

Iteration through sets. An iteration like *'Step through the signups doing:...'* involves taking each of the elements one at a time. If the collection being stepped through is a sequence, this is obviously done in the order of the sequence. If it is a set, there is no standard order. A DL procedure that iterates through a set is assumed to work only if it works regardless of the particular order chosen. In the case of a nondeterministic schema like that of Figure A–11, this is simply another dimension of choice. In the case of an ordinary (deterministic) procedure like that of A–8, the order may just be irrelevant. For example, in stepping through all of the courses a student is registering for, it does not make any difference what order is taken, since each course will either be successfully enrolled in or put on the problem sheet independently of what happens with the other courses.

Basic structure. The class definition for COURSE GROUP does not include any roles, but instead has a description under the heading *'Basic Structure.'* A course group is simply a set of courses, and as such it would not even be necessary to define a class for it—each time *'a course group'* appears it could be replaced with *'a set of courses.'* However, in making the procedure definition understandable, it is useful to have a name for this particular way of using a set of courses. The *'Basic Structure'* declaration allows a class name to be given to a class of collections (sets, sequences, or tables) of elements. It is used in the text, for example, in defining a pattern as a sequence of elements.

Describes: a person as viewed for geneaology

Roles:

   Mother: a person; possibly null
   Father: a person; possibly null

Predicates:

A person (A) is an ancestor of a person (B) if either:
- The mother of B is not null and either:
  - A is the mother of B or
  - A *is an ancestor* of the mother of B.
- The father of B is not null and either:
  - A is the father of B or
  - A is an ancestor of the father of B.

§

P
E
R   **Procedures:**
S
O   Find the ancestors of a person
N

Purpose: Produce a set containing all of the person's recorded ancestors

Inputs: a person

Results: a set of people

Working Structures:

   Ancestors: a set of people; initially empty

Basic Method:

- If the person's mother is not null, then:
  - Add the person's mother to the ancestors.
  - *Find the ancestors* of the person's mother and add each of them to the ancestors.
- If the person's father is not null, then:
  - Add the person's father to the ancestors.
  - Find the ancestors of the person's father and add each of them to the ancestors.
- Return the ancestors.

§

Figure A–12. A genealogical definition of a person.

Recursion

DL shares with most other programming languages (although not FORTRAN or BASIC) the ability to specify *recursive* procedures and predicates, as illustrated in Figure A–12. In this definition, there is a predicate '*A person...is an ancestor...*' and a procedure '*Find the ancestors...,*' both of which are recursive. In order to decide whether A is an ancestor of B, the same predicate definition is used to decide if A is an ancestor of B's mother or father. Similarly, in producing a list of a person's ancestors, the procedure includes making a list of the ancestors of the person's mother and father. For purposes of illustration, the procedure and predicate are independent of one another, although one could write them in terms of each other.

It is important to recognize that for each *invocation* of a recursive predicate or procedure, a separate set of variables is produced. For example, in the course of finding the ancestors of someone's father, that person's ancestor list as produced so far is not affected. There are several other features introduced here:

Proper names in a heading. In the previous definitions, inputs to a procedure were given names in the '*Input*' declarations. This can also be done in a predicate, but in a case where there are two or more inputs of the same class, there can be confusion as to which is which. Names can be included (in parentheses) in the heading of a procedure or predicate in order to be clear, as in '*A person (A) is an ancestor of a person (B).*'

Null elements. If every record for a person included a father and mother, there would have to be an infinite collection stretching back to creation. Clearly, in any real program, some people would have parents listed, while others would not (even though they had parents). When items can be missing from a record, this is explicitly marked in the declaration and must be taken into account by procedures or predicates that make use of the filler that would otherwise be there. The procedure for finding ancestors will run for a time and then terminate when it reaches the 'top' of the family tree (people with no listed parents). Any recursive procedure or predicate must have some such way of terminating.

Set operations. It may well be that the same ancestor will be found more than once (as an ancestor of both father and mother if they are related). However, the primitive operation of adding an element to a set does not produce duplicates— if the element is already there, the set is unchanged. If the procedure produced a sequence instead, it could contain duplicates (the same element appearing at more than one position), which is appropriate for objects such as a sentence, which can contain the same word in two positions.

<u>A person is local</u> if either:
- The person is a student and the state of the person's address is *California*, or
- The person is a faculty member and the city of the person's address is *PaloAlto*.

Figure A–13.   A predicate that distinguishes subclasses.

Variants

One final example will illustrate the use of *variant* procedure and predicate definitions. Assume that there is some notion of being 'local' that is important in a university procedure (e.g., sending out mailings), but that is different for students and faculty. A definition like that of Figure A–13 (using only the notations introduced so far) could be included in the definition of PERSON.

In this simple case, such a definition would suffice. However, in dealing with more complex kinds of objects (as with the different kinds of pattern elements in Chapter 2), there are several predicates (and procedures), each of which treats the different kinds (subclasses) differently. It makes the overall definition more understandable if the specific definition for each subclass is included in the definition of that subclass, as illustrated in Figure A–14. In the definition of the more general class, a declaration is included that specifies the phrase used for the predicate but does not give a definition for it. In each of the subclasses, a definition is given for the same predicate (substituting the subclass name for the class name). In an exactly parallel way, a procedure can be defined within each subclass and declared in the superclass.

A note on input and output

Students accustomed to dealing with ordinary programming languages will have noted by this point that there is an important area that has been omitted—the use of input or output statements to read in data or write out results. Everything described so far assumes that the procedure operates on some pre-existing set of internal records, modifying them and possibly creating new ones, and then 'produces' one or more records as a result. The print forms described at the end of Section A.2 are not relevant to the operation of the procedures, but are used in writing text that describes what is going on.

If the procedures of this section were to be used in a real situation for university registration, they would need to account for the fact that the inputs would be in the form of punched cards or computer files, which are not organized according to the internal structures of DL. For example, a grade sheet might be a sequence of punched cards, each containing a sequence of characters representing the student number followed by a blank or tab, followed by a

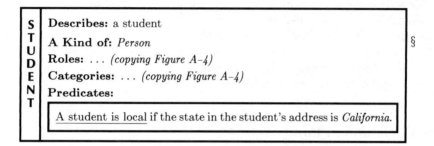

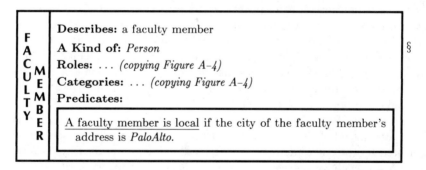

**P
E
R
S
O
N**

Describes: a person as viewed for official documents
Roles: ... *(copying Figure A-2)*
Kinds of Person: *Student, Faculty member*   §
Classes: ... *(copying Figure A-2)*
Predicates:

> A person is local
> > *Depends on the kind of person*

**S
T
U
D
E
N
T**

Describes: a student
A Kind of: *Person*   §
Roles: ... *(copying Figure A-4)*
Categories: ... *(copying Figure A-4)*
Predicates:

> A student is local if the state in the student's address is *California*.

**F
A
C
U
L
T
Y M
E
M
B
E
R**

Describes: a faculty member
A Kind of: *Person*   §
Roles: ... *(copying Figure A-4)*
Categories: ... *(copying Figure A-4)*
Predicates:

> A faculty member is local if the city of the faculty member's
> address is *PaloAlto*.

Figure A–14. Variant definitions of a predicate.

sequence of characters representing the grade. Before the work defined in this section is done, this other structure would have to be converted into the appropriate internal records. Similarly, once a report card is produced (as a record structure), it needs to be printed in some textual form (with rows and columns, etc.) to be sent to the student.

Although the handling of input and output is crucial for practical computer languages, it does not play a significant role in describing abstract procedures at a conceptual level, as is done in this book. Once it is clear just how the grades will be produced from the grade sheets, for example, it is of secondary importance just how they are arranged on the input cards or output reports. Therefore DL as defined here does not include the specification of any input or output activities. The procedures defined throughout the book deal strictly with the internal record forms. If they were implemented in a higher level language, there would be a mapping (using print forms) specified from these structures to the existing input-output primitives and formats of that language.

A.4 A specification of the language constructs

This section gives a systematic listing of the elements used in building descriptions in DL. It is intended to be used in the style of a manual and does not include explanations and justifications of all the structures. Sections A.2 and A.3 gave a more tutorial introduction and Section A.5 will define the primitive classes of the language (along with the procedures and predicates defined for them) and some further standard classes built out of them.

A.4.1 Definition forms

There are three kinds of definitions: class definitions, procedure definitions, and predicate definitions. Each appears in a box with a label. A class definition has the name of the class along the left edge. A procedure definition has the title of the procedure along the top edge. A predicate definition has its title underlined on the first line in the box. Definitions can be included as parts of other definitions, indicated by nesting the boxes. A definition can copy part of the material from another definition, indicated by ellipsis dots (see Figure A-4 and the corresponding explanation).

Each type of definition has a fixed set of potential parts. In any individual definition, not all of the parts need to be present. If a part is present, it will be indicated by the corresponding heading (in boldface), followed by its contents. Some parts (such as '*Purpose*') have a single component, while others (such as '*Roles*') can have a sequence of components. Indentation alignment is used in DL to indicate parallel structures. Whenever it seems useful, small boxes ('■') are included before items to give a visual impact to the fact that they form a sequence.

The ordering of the parts within a definition follows a standard convention (the order used below), but the order can be altered whenever a different ordering would make the definition clearer to read. In addition to the standard parts, a definition can contain explanatory comments (in italics) anywhere within it.

In general, the language has been designed to avoid unnecessary redundancy. When something is 'obvious' from the context, it can be omitted in the printed form. Of course, the definition of obviousness is complex and intuitive and would have to be more formally specified to build a real compiler or interpreter. A typical example is the omission of explicit input declarations when the title of a procedure makes it clear what the inputs are and no further description is to be given.

A.4.1.1 Class definition

Class definitions have a dual aspect. First, they define a means for describing *objects* belonging to a class. Second, by specifying the form of the description, they define a type of *data structure,* where each instance of the data structure is to be thought of as record describing an object in the class. When we speak of a *record* of a class, we refer to the data structure; when we speak of an *object* or an *instance* of a class, we refer to the thing that the data structure describes. The potential parts of a class definition are:

Label. A word or phrase for the class being defined, appearing vertically along the left-hand edge of the box. It must always be present.

Describes. An explanation of the kind of thing the class includes. This is for exposition only and is not used in a formal way.

Background. A set of objects that are in the global background of a whole body of definitions and that are referred to in the definition.

A Kind of. A set of class definitions for superclasses of this class (i.e., classes of which it is a subclass).

Kinds of. If there are subclasses of a general class, the definition of the more general class can (but need not) contain a list of them. It is not assumed that the list is complete.

Roles. Any number of role declarations, each giving a name for the role (indicated in boldface) and information about the object or objects that can fill it. The information must specify the class of the object (or its elements if it is a set, sequence, or table) and can include further description as well, for example, specifying that an integer is in a particular range, or that the object filling the role must be of a particular category within its class.

   Roles can be *changeable* (no special mark), *fixed* (marked with a superscript 'f'), or *computable* (marked with a 'c'). If a role is fixed, it can never be changed once assigned. If it is computable, the definition must include a predicate, procedure, or comment describing how to compute it from the other roles and categories, and it is computed each time it is needed. If an initial filler is specified for a role, it is given that filler when a record for an object of the class is created.

Basic Structure. Often it is useful to have a class for an object that is a set, sequence, or table made up of other objects. The definition of COURSEGROUP in Figure A–11 is an example. When this is used in a class definition, there are no other roles or categories except computable ones.

Categories. A definition can include any number of categorizations, each having a name and a set of alternatives. A binary category is indicated by using the choices *'Yes'* and *'No.'* Like roles, categorizations can be changeable, fixed, or computable.

Predicates. A class definition can contain any number of predicate definitions, each of the form described in A.4.1.3 below. At least one of the arguments of the predicate should belong to the class in order for it to be included.

Equality predicate. There is special use made of a predicate (if one exists), defining what it means for two members of a class to be equal. For example, equal members will not be added to a set. There is no special syntax, with the equality predicate simply included among the predicates with a title of the form *'A...equals a....'*

Procedures. Any number of procedure definitions can be nested within a class definition. In general, this will be done if the procedure is specific to operating on instances of that class.

Classes. Any number of other class definitions can be nested within a class definition. In general, this will be done if the inner class is used only in conjunction with instances of the outer class.

Instances. Instances can be created for any number of specific objects of the class. In general, this will be done for special cases or for classes having a small fixed number of elements. Often we give a list of typical instances to give the idea of what they are, without listing all instances. If the list is complete, the header will be *'All Instances.'*

A.4.1.2 Procedure definition

As with class definitions, there is a list of potential parts for a procedure definition.

Title. A phrase appearing in the top border of the box, which will match the calls to the procedure. Every procedure definition must have a title. The title includes a *referring phrase* for each of the inputs. Having defined a procedure such as *'Apply a rule to a situation,'* we can write DL programs that include phrases like *'...the result of applying the rule to the situation...'* and *'Return a new situation to which the rule has been applied.'* There are good reasons in natural language why forms like the passive and relative clause are available, since they make it possible to convey a particular assignment of objects to a verb while putting different ones into the focus position.

Purpose. An explanation of what the procedure is primarily for. Every procedure must be stated to *produce* an object or objects, to *modify* an object or objects, or to *test* a predicate. If a procedure does more than one of these, one is chosen as the purpose (the choice is almost always obvious) and the others specified as *side effects*.

Side Effects. An explanation (in unstructured English) of what happens when the procedure is run, in addition to its main purpose.

Inputs. A procedure can have any number (including zero) of declarations specifying its inputs. Each can be given a name or can simply be referred to by its class if there can be no confusion. If a name is given, it is followed by additional information about the objects that can be input, as with role declarations in class definitions. The procedure can be invoked only with the exact number of inputs of the right classes.

Background. There can be any number of declarations chosen from the declarations in the global background, specifying objects from that background that will be referred to in the procedure.

Results. A procedure can have any number (including zero) of results. Each can be given a name, or can simply be referred to by its class if there can be no confusion. If a name is given, it is followed by a description like those for roles in class definitions. Normally, a procedure with results will have *produce* as its purpose, but there can be cases (as is common in LISP) where the main purpose is to modify a structure, and there are results passed back as a corollary. The results of one step of a procedure can be referred to in later steps and conditions by their names or classes, or by phrases like *the result* whenever the intended referent is clear. An invocation of a procedure has an *outcome* of *'Success'* or *'Failure'* and produces its results only when the outcome is success.

Working Structures. A procedure definition can contain declarations for any number of temporary results to be used while operating. Each is given a name and a description, as with the roles of a class definition. They can also be given initial values (as with *'Problem Courses'* in Figure A–8) using the phrase *'; initially...'* following the normal declaration.

Basic Method. The activities carried out by the procedure are specified in a sequence of steps according to the rules described below in Section A.4.2. Every procedure has a basic method. If there are variants of the procedure according to the class of one of its arguments (see the example in Figure A–14), the more general class may have a procedure whose method is replaced by the phrase *'Depends on the kind of....'*

Conditions. In addition to the basic method, there can be any number of special conditions, as described below in A.4.2.5.

Procedures. Any number of procedure definitions can be nested within a procedure definition. In general, this will be done if the inner procedure is invoked only by the outer one.

Classes. Class definitions can be nested in procedure definitions. This will generally be done for classes of objects that are of use only in the course of running the procedure.

A.4.1.3 Predicate definition

The following are the potential parts of a predicate definition.

Title. A phrase appearing underlined in the first line of the box, which will match the logical expressions using the predicate. The title includes a *referring phrase* for each of the arguments. Logical expressions based on the predicate allow ordinary English variation. For example, we might include in an algorithm '...*if the course is being taken by the student...*,' making use of the definition in Figure A–1 for '*a student is taking a course.*' Every predicate has a title.

Body. The body of a predicate is either a logical expression (see A.4.3 below) or the definition of a procedure whose purpose is to test the predicate and whose result is a truth value, '*True*' or '*False.*' These are distinct from success and failure—they are both results produced by a successful process. Rather than including the entire syntactic form of the procedure, its parts—omitting its inputs (the arguments of the predicates), purpose (to test), and results (a single truth value)—appear in the predicate definition box. Every predicate definition contains a body.

Working Structures. If the body is a logical expression, it can make use of any number of working structures, declared just as in a procedure definition.

Background. There can also be any number of declarations that match declarations in the global background, specifying objects from that background that will be referred to in the logical expression that is the body of the predicate definition.

A.4.2 Process invocations

The central element of a procedure is its basic method, which is a sequence of items, each describing something to be done. We will use the term *process* in referring to what happens when the procedure definition is run, and *invocation* to refer to the form appearing in the definition that specifies what is to be done. There are four basic kinds of invocations, those for procedures, sequences, conditionals, and iterations. A procedure invocation matches the title of a procedure definition, either built into DL (for an *elementary process*) or given as part of the program. A sequence, conditional, or iteration invocation includes one or more invocations among its parts. Among the elementary processes are a few that directly affect the control of the processing, which we call *process control operations.*

A.4.2.1 Elementary processes

The elementary processes are the ultimate basis of the work that gets done. All composite processes must sooner or later get down to doing these things. If we were concerned with describing procedures for computers operating in a physical world, there would be descriptions of elementary processes for activating physical devices (like printers and terminals). Since we are concerned in this book with describing algorithms in a more abstract way, the fundamental 'actions' include only the creation and changing of records.

Create record. In describing a record to be created, we give its class and can specify the fillers for any of its roles or values for its categories. As a result of this process, a new record exists and can be used in further computation. Example (in Figure A–9): *'Create a new report card with student = the student.'*

Assign role. This covers the assignment of fillers, both to roles in instances and to variables in a procedure. As a result, the role or variable acquires a different filler (or a new one if there was no previous filler). Example (A–9): *'...assign it as the current card.'* In general, we will describe assignments using the word 'assign,' but at times it is clearer to use phrases like *'Let the...be...'* or *'Set the...to....'* An assignment cannot be made for a computable role and cannot be made for a fixed role if it already has a filler.

Mark category. The result of this process is the identification of an object as being in a category along one dimension of categorization. Example: *'... mark the course as pass-fail.'* A computable category cannot be marked, and a fixed category cannot be marked to become different from a previous value.

A.4.2.2 Procedure invocation

As a single step in one procedure, we can invoke another entire procedure. This is specified by a sentence that matches the title of the procedure, assigning appropriate inputs. Example (A–9): *'Find a student having the identifier.'* If the purpose of the procedure is to modify structures, this happens. If its purpose is to produce results, they are generated and can be referred to in the steps following the procedure call (see details of reference in A.4.4 below). A procedure whose purpose is a test will be called only as the test of a conditional, and returns a truth value. Any procedure can fail instead of performing its normal activity.

A.4.2.3 Composite invocations

We can describe a process in terms of other processes that make up its parts.

A.4.2.3.1 Sequence invocation

The simplest composite invocation is a sequence of invocations. It describes the process resulting from doing them one at a time in order. Depending on the complexity of the individual descriptions, a sequence is indicated either by using ordinary language conventions with words like *'and'* and *'then,'* or by putting each step on a separate line, all at the same level of indentation. Example (A–9): *'Create a new report card... and assign it....'*

A.4.2.3.2 Conditional invocation

There are two kinds of conditionals, those based on logical expressions (an expression that can be evaluated as true or false) and those specifying a set of alternative descriptions of some object. Section A.4.3 lists the different kinds of logical expressions used as tests. The words *if, then, else, otherwise,* etc., are used in ordinary sentences and sequences of sentences, in whatever form best clarifies the intention. When there is potential ambiguity, indentation alignment is used, as in:

> If the course is full, then:
> > If the student's year is 1, then fail.
>
> Otherwise create a petition card....

In this case, the petition card is created whenever the course is not full. If the third line were indented to line up with the second, the petition card would be created only if the course is full and the student's year is not 1.

In a *case statement,* there is some object being tested or compared, with a different action specified for each alternative description. There is an initial phrase *'If... is:'* followed by any number of alternatives, each specifying a description. Following all of the alternatives there may be a line indicating *'anything else...'* or *'otherwise....'* If not, then when no alternative matches, nothing is done. In the case where more than one of the tests is true, the first one in the list is taken.

A.4.2.3.3 Iteration invocation

Whereas a sequence invocation specifies each of its component invocations separately, an iteration includes a *body,* which is an invocation to be applied over and over. An iteration specifies this process and indicates how to decide on the repetition. There are two basic types of iterations.

Enumeration. Given a set or sequence, or any object whose basic structure is a set or sequence, we can specify a process to be done to each member. The elements of a sequence are taken in order. It is assumed that for iteration over a set, the ordering is irrelevant. To indicate an enumeration, we generally use the phrase *'For each...'* for sets, and *'Step through...'* for sequences. Example: *'For each student of the course do:....'* In a sequence, a beginning and ending position can be specified. If we want to do something a fixed number of times, the integers can be treated as a sequence, as in *'Step through the integers from...to...,'* which can be abbreviated as *'Count from...to....'*

Repetition on condition. Instead of specifying a set or sequence, we can specify that a process is repeated over and over until some condition is met. This condition can be explicit in the iteration statement, using *'while,' 'until,'* or *'as long as'*; it can be the result of a termination statement within the process that is being repeated (see part A.4.2.4 below), or it can be stated in the conditions associated with the procedure definition as a whole (as described in A.4.2.5). If the condition is explicit in the iteration statement, it is tested at the beginning of each iteration. If there is no explicit condition in the iteration statement, the statement is of the form *'Keep repeating: ....'*

Any iteration can be done in parallel with another. For example, we can say *'Step through the students of the course and the integers from 3 simultaneously, doing: ....'* The conditions of the procedure generally specify what to do if one iteration terminates before the other. If not, it simply continues until the first one terminates.

A.4.2.4 Process control operations

There are several other basic process descriptions used in the language.

Termination. At any point in a procedure description, there can be a statement that the entire procedure (or some iteration within the procedure) terminates. The statement can simply indicate that the procedure or iteration stops, or in the case of procedures, it can indicate that it fails (stops with outcome of failure) or succeeds (stops with outcome of success, producing any results). A successful termination within a procedure for producing results can explicitly name the results to be produced. Otherwise, the description of the results must specify how they are determined when the process stops successfully. Example: *'If...then fail. Otherwise succeed, returning the grade table.'*

Continuation. At any point in an iteration, there can be a statement of the form *'Go on to the next...'* indicating that the process for that round of the iteration should stop, and the iteration should continue to its next step. Example (A–9): *'If this fails, go on to the next pair.'* If there is no explicit indication of what to go on to, the iteration most closely nested to the continuation is assumed.

Choice. In specifying nondeterministic schemas, we allow steps that make arbitrary choices. The basic classes, such as set and sequence, have choice operations defined on them (as described in Section A.5), but it is also possible to include as a control description a choice of things to do, such as *'Either stop or go on.'* The schema as a whole is considered to succeed if there exists any possible sequence of choices that leads to success. Choices cannot appear in deterministic algorithms.

A.4.2.5 Process conditions

One element of a procedure definition is a set of conditions. These are separated from the basic method in order to make the overall structure of the procedure clearer. Each condition is of the form *'If...then...,'* giving a logical expression and an invocation, just as with a conditional. The action specified by a condition is applied whenever its test becomes true. It is not necessary to specify exactly when the test should be tried, but it needs to be something that could be effectively computed whenever it is relevant. It can be assumed that each condition is checked after every step (except for the steps involved in checking other conditions, to avoid infinite regress). Of course, in a direct implementation, this would be horribly inefficient. In almost all cases, there are only a small number of places where the condition could become true, and it is necessary to check only in those places. In a real implementation, this could be done either by adding a way of indicating where those places are (a kind of 'footnote'), or by having the compiler deduce it from the contents of the conditions. Example: *'If the number of students in the course is ever 17, then....'* A condition can be associated with an iteration, of the form *'If the sequence runs out...,'* to be applied when the iteration ends if it was not terminated by a termination statement.

A.4.3 Logical expressions

Conditions and conditionals are based on combining some kind of test with alternative actions, depending on the result of the test. The result of any test is a truth value (i.e., *'True'* or *'False'*) produced by the application of a predicate or by a logical combination (a composite expression).

A.4.3.1 Predicates

There are three basic classes of predicates. The form for using them is the same—a sentence that matches the form given in defining the predicate.

Primitive predicates. There are a small number of predicates associated with the classes, instances, and procedures of the basic language. Three of these predicates apply to instances and are stated using the verb *be:*

Being an instance of a class: If the element is a character...
Belonging to a category: If the course is pass-fail...
    If the level of the course is advanced...
Equality: If the character is 'x'...

These can be mixed in a case statement, as in:

> If the character is:
> '!', then...
> a letter, then...
> otherwise....

Class membership applies to subclass members (i.e., a member of a class is a member of any superclass of that class). Equality is defined for the built-in classes and can be defined by providing an equality predicate for any defined class. In general, numbers and characters follow the usual notions of equality. Sets are considered equal if they have the same (equal) members, in sequences if they have equal elements in the same order. If no equality predicate is defined for a user-defined class, it is assumed that no two distinct records describe equal instances.

The other primitive predicate refers to processes, dealing with the outcome of invocations. The outcome of a procedure is *'Failure'* if it terminates as the result of an explicit failure termination. Otherwise it is *'Success.'* These can be referred to in following steps. Example: *'If it fails....'*

Predicates on objects of built-in classes. Associated with the built-in classes of the system (such as those for sets and tables), there are predicates (such as set membership). These appear in the definitions of Section A.5, but are not given logical or procedural definitions. These basic built-in predicates for primitive classes are taken as given and can be used to define others.

Defined predicates. As described above, predicates can be defined by giving a predicate definition. There is a title indicating how the predicate name will be used in tests, followed by a logical definition (possibly composed of other tests) or a procedure for testing.

A.4.3.2 Composite logical expressions

English (like all natural languages) provides words for expressing logical relationships, such as *and, but, or, if,* and *not.* Tests can be made up of other tests through combinations of these.

Boolean expressions. DL allows any expression that can be represented in formal logic using the Boolean connectives *'and,' 'not,'* and *'or.'* Example: *'... if the course is full and the student's year is not 1, then....'* If the expression is complicated enough to need bracketing for disambiguation, it is lined up using indentations and dots, just as for the steps of a procedure.

Quantified expressions. Any expression can be used that can be represented in the quantificational calculus with the formal quantifiers '∀' and '∃,' where the quantification is over some set or sequence that can be referred to as a data structure. Example: *'If every student in the course has Biology as a major, then....'* Note that this does not include quantifying over all members of a class, unless a set has been explicitly kept into which all new members are entered as they are created. Also, it cannot be assumed that tests involving quantification take a constant amount of processing time.

A.4.4 Referring phrases

One of the greatest differences between DL and standard programming languages is the use of ordinary language *referring phrases* in place of variable names. In most programming languages, each variable is given a name that is unique within its scope, and all references to the object use that name. In natural language, we rarely give things proper names (people being the major exception), referring to them instead with generic phrases like *the chair* or *the other student.* In DL, variable names can be assigned and used as in other languages, but objects can also be referred to with a phrase containing their class (*'the student'*) or some role they play in the processing (*'the input,' 'the result'*). Each referring phrase has a head element, and possibly a modifier.

A.4.4.1 Head elements

In ordinary programming languages, a variable name is often chosen to indicate the class of the object it refers to, such as *'string1'* or *'newRule.'* In DL, it is possible to use proper names (see below), but the more general practice is to use definite referring phrases like *'the student,'* where the head of the phrase is a noun. This noun can be from one of several sources:

Class name. In the most common case, the class of an object is sufficient in context to know which object is being referred to. A phrase like *'the course'* can be used if there is no confusion as to which course is intended. A head can be used with modifiers if there is more than one.

Role or category name. The roles and categories of a class and the variables of a procedure (its inputs, results, background, and working structures) are associated with names that reflect their function. These can be used preceded with *'the'* anywhere within the definition where they are declared. In addition, the result role names from a procedure definition can be used in a procedure that invokes that procedure. For example, a procedure containing a step to *'find a student having an identifier'* can refer in the following steps to *'the student.'*

Proper name. If it seems more natural to use a proper name instead of a common noun, a proper name can be placed in the definition after the class name or role name, in parentheses. For example, if one of the inputs to a procedure were given the role name *'Foo,'* the algorithm might later say *'If the foo is....'* If it were given the proper name *'Foo,'* we would say *'If Foo is....'* Example (A–12): *'A person (A) is an ancestor of a person (B).'*

Built-in name. There are a few nouns whose meaning is related to the general way of describing procedures. They (like the other head elements) can be used with modifiers if they do not have a unique referent. They are:

Input: The input to the procedure
Result: The result of the procedure last called before 'result' appears
Element: The current element in an iteration in which 'element' appears
Position: The position in a sequence in an iteration

Pronoun. The pronouns *'it,'* *'this,'* and *'that,'* and substitute nouns like *'one'* (as in *'the other one'*) can be used whenever their intent is clear. Substitute nouns will usually appear with modifiers. Pronouns can refer both to instances and to processes. For example, following a procedure call there may be a conditional: *'If it succeeds, then....'*

A.4.4.2 Modifiers

The head of a referring phrase can be combined with a modifier when the head alone is not unique, or when the modifier provides extra useful information. There are two kinds of modifiers:

Classifiers. Classifiers appear before the head and are typically a single word. They can be of several kinds:

Explicit (the first word of a two-word role name): *the current card...*
Procedure-related: *the input character, the resulting integer...*
Text-related: *the former student, the other student...*
Creation: *the new thing, the old thing...*
Possessive: *the course's instructor, the student's name*

Qualifiers. A qualifier goes after a head and places it into relation to another object. For example, we can refer to *'the rank of the instructor of the course'* or to *'the element of the character string.'* In the first of these, the head is a role name and the qualifier indicates the instance for which it is a filler. In the second, the head indicates an iteration and the qualifier indicates which sequence. A possessive classifier, as in *'the student's address,'* has exactly the same meaning as an *'of...'* qualifier.

A.5 Standard definitions

This section contains definitions for the primitive classes and procedures of DL. In these definitions, there are declarations for the procedures and predicates that deal with instances of the primitive classes. In each of these, the body (the specification of how it is to be calculated) is left out. These are the primitives of the language, and in building an interpreter, we would *implement* each of them in the underlying machinery. The definitions just specify what procedures and predicates there are, what inputs they take, and what results they produce.

The choice of what to consider primitive is guided by the desire to maximize the understandability of the language. It would be possible, for example, not to have a primitive notion of table, and to use sets and sequences for tabular information. The primitives are chosen to provide an intuitive basis for algorithms of the kind presented in this book. There are many other things that could be included (such as non-integer numbers) that are omitted because they are not relevant for our purposes.

In thinking about the computational efficiency of an algorithm, we need a measure of computational work. We will make the assumption that all of the primitive operations and tests defined in this section can be done in a single unit of time. This means, for example, that in considering the efficiency of an algorithm that uses sets, we can assume that the operation of adding a member to a set takes a single unit of time regardless of the size of the set. It would take complex implementations of the data structures to guarantee this timing property. In fact, for some of the operations on sequences, there is no single coding that would make all of the operations take a time independent of the length of the sequence. However, for the algorithms we describe, an advanced compiler could in principle choose representations with the needed efficiency properties for each of the places where sequences are used.

Primitive classes

<table>
<tr>
<td>I
N
T
E
G
E
R</td>
<td>

Describes: the standard mathematical integers

An integer is printed in standard mathematical notation.

Predicates:

All of the standard arithmetic predicates, such as odd, even, prime, equal, greater than, less than, etc.

Procedures:

All of the standard arithmetic operations, such as plus, times, etc.

</td>
</tr>
</table>

Figure A–15. Definition of integer.

Describes: a finite set

A set is printed by listing its elements between brackets ('{}'), separated by commas if they improve readability.

Roles:

^{c}**Size:** a non-negative integer; zero if the set is empty

Predicates:

A set is empty *Primitive*

An object is a member of a set *Primitive*

If an object is equal to a member of a set, it is considered a member.

A set (A) equals a set (B) if:
- Each member of A is a member of B
- Each member of B is a member of A.

Procedures:

Add an element to a set

Purpose: Modify the set so the object is a member

Inputs: a set and an object

If the object is already a member, nothing changes. If not, the size is increased by 1.

Choose an element from a set

Purpose: Produce a member of the set

Inputs: a set

Results: an element of the set

Conditions: If the set is empty, fail.

This produces an arbitrarily selected member. It can be used only in nondeterministic schemas. The set is unchanged.

Continued in Figure A–19

Figure A–16.   Definition of set.

Continued from Figure A–16

Procedures:

Remove an element from a set

Purpose: Modify the set so the object is not a member

Inputs: a set and an object

Conditions: If the element is not in the set, fail.

If the element was in the set, it is no longer, and the size is reduced by 1.

Copy a set

Purpose: Produce a new set record

This is a top-level copy. It creates a new record that describes a set with the same members. The elements themselves are unaffected. The copy is equal to the set, but later operations (addition and deletion of elements) operate on the two records independently.

Figure A–17. Definition of set (continued).

Describes: an ordered finite sequence of elements

A sequence is printed by listing its elements in order, separated by commas.

Roles:

[c]**Length:** A non-negative integer; zero if the sequence is empty

Predicates:

a sequence is empty *Primitive*

an object is a member of a sequence *Primitive*

A sequence (A) equals a sequence (B) if:
- The length of A equals the length of B
- For each integer (N) from 1 to the length of A, the Nth element of A is equal to the Nth element of B.

Procedures:

Get the Nth element of a sequence

Purpose: Produce an object

Inputs: a sequence and an integer (N)

Results: an element of the sequence

Conditions: If N is less than 1 or greater than the length of the sequence, fail.

The sequence is unchanged. We will use the phrases 'the Nth element of S' and 'the element at the Nth position in S' as paraphrases of 'the result of getting the Nth element of S.'

Choose an element from a sequence

Purpose: Produce a member of the sequence

Inputs: a sequence

Results: an element of the sequence

Conditions: If the sequence is empty, fail.

This produces an arbitrarily selected member. It can be used only in nondeterministic schemas. The sequence is unchanged.

Continued in Figure A–19

S E Q U E N C E

Figure A–18. Definition of sequence.

Continued from Figure A–18

Procedures:

Remove the Nth element from a sequence

Purpose: Modify the sequence by deleting an element

Inputs: a sequence and an integer (N)

Results: the element that was removed

Conditions: If N is less than 1 or greater than the length of the sequence, fail.

All elements beyond the Nth decrease their position by one. The length is reduced by one.

Insert an object before (after, in place of) the Nth element of a sequence

Purpose: Modify the sequence

Inputs: an integer (N), an object, and a sequence

Conditions: If N is less than 1 or greater than the length of the sequence, fail.

If the insertion is before a given position, the new element is at that position and all elements at or beyond it increase their position by one. If after a given position, the new element is at that position plus one, and all elements after it increase their position by one. In both cases, the length of the sequence is increased by one. If the insertion is in place of, then the element previously in that place is replaced by the new one and the rest of the sequence (and its length) are unchanged., 'Insert at the front (beginning)' is the same as "before position 1." Insert at the end' is equivalent to 'after the element at the position that is the length of the sequence.'

Copy a sequence

Purpose: Produce a new sequence record

As with a set, this is a top-level copy.

Figure A–19. Definition of sequence (continued).

T A B L E

Describes: a dictionary-like pairing of keys with entries

Prints in columns of keys and entries (see Figure A–6)

Roles:

^c**Keys:** a set of objects; empty if the table is empty

^c**Entries:** a set of objects; empty if the table is empty

These are computable since they cannot be changed separately. They are not necessarily the same size, since the same entry may appear for more than one key We have not defined an equality relationship for tables since it is not used in the book.

Predicates:

a table is empty *Primitive*

Procedures:

Get the entry for a key in a table

Purpose: Produce an object

Inputs: a table and an object

Results: an object

Conditions: Fail if there is no entry for that key.

The table is unchanged.

Put an object into a table with key another object

Purpose: Modify the table

Inputs:

Table: a table

Key: an object

Entry: an object

If there was a previous entry for that key, it is replaced by the new one. Otherwise a new key-entry pair is added.

Remove the entry for a key from a table

Purpose: Modify the table

Inputs: a table and an object

Trying to get an entry for this key will now fail, until a new entry is put into the table for it.

Conditions: Fail if there is no entry for that key.

Figure A–20. Definition of table.

O B J E C T	**Describes:** any object that can be described *Every class is a subclass of this one, although it is not indicated explicitly in the definition.* **Predicates:** An object equals an object *Defined for each class* An object is in a class *Primitive*

T R U T H	**V A L U E**	**Describes:** logical truth or falsity **All Instances:** TRUE, FALSE *Unlike many languages, DL has special objects for truth values, rather than using a zero, empty set, empty list, etc., to stand for false.*

C H A R A C T E R	**Describes:** a character that can be typed on a keyboard, including letters, numbers, and punctuation **Categories:** ^f**Type:** {Letter, Numeral, Punctuation, Math, Spacing} **Instances:** *This class contains a fixed finite set of instances, one for each character on the keyboard. A character is printed in single quotation marks, as in 'x'.*

Figure A–21. Definitions of object, truth value and character.

Standardly defined classes and procedures

The rest of the definitions in this section are not primitive in that they are fully defined in terms of those given previously. They are included here for reference, since we use them in algorithms throughout the book.

C **S** **H** **T** **A** **R** **R** **I** **A** **N** **C** **G** **T** **E** **R**	**Describes:** a sequence of characters *A character string is printed between quotation marks ("...").* **Basic Structure:** a sequence of characters *A character string can include punctuation and spacing as well as literal and numerical characters. Since its basic structure is a sequence, it has the same equality predicate as defined in Figure A–18.*

W **O** **R** **D**	**Describes:** a sequence of letters § **A Kind of:** *Character string* **Basic Structure:** a sequence of characters; each of which is a letter *A character string is a word if it contains only characters that are letters. This does not imply that it is a word of any actual language. In addition to being printable as a character string (using quotation marks), a word can be printed without quotation marks, in italics.*

Figure A–22. Characters strings.

Describes: a sequence of objects used in last-in-first-out order

Basic Structure: a sequence of objects

A stack is printed as the corresponding sequence.

Roles:

^{c}**Top:** the element at position 1 of the sequence

Procedures:

Push an element onto a stack

Purpose: Modify the stack so the object is on top

Inputs:

    Stack: a stack

    Element: an object

Basic Method: Insert the object at the beginning of the stack.

Pop an element from a stack

Purpose: Produce the top element of the stack

Side Effects: Modify the stack by removing its top element

Inputs: a stack

Results: an object

Basic Method: Remove the first element from the stack and return it as the result.

Conditions:

    If the stack is initially empty, then fail.

STACK

Figure A–23. Stack.

Appendix B

An Outline of
English Syntax

Contents of Appendix B

This appendix describes the basic structures of English. It is intended to serve as a reference for the discussions of syntactic and semantic problems throughout the book. The motivation in writing it was to produce a general guide that would be useful to someone concerned with producing a formal system covering a wide range of syntactic phenomena.   This might be someone creating a computer program to parse or understand English inputs, someone developing a new syntactic formalism within the generative paradigm, or a student who wants to master an existing formalism by trying it out on difficult examples. The summary is not uniformly formal and precise, and many phenomena are presented simply as a set of examples. It is certainly not a complete grammar of English, but any grammar or program that could handle the examples given here would have a substantial claim to have covered a significant proportion of the language. A separate index has been included at the end of the appendix containing the formal terms used in it (names of classes, systems, features and functions).

The summary is based on formalisms incorporating some elements of systemic grammar, case grammar, and transformational grammar. Much of the description is based on functional role analysis and the classification of patterns along multiple dimensions, as described in Chapter 6. A reading of the theoretical foundations in that chapter is useful for a full understanding, but most of the material in the appendix can be be read profitably without that background. Its emphasis is on those aspects of syntactic structure that provide a basis for analyzing meaning. There is correspondingly less emphasis on details that determine grammaticality, although many issues relevant to precise rules of grammaticality are discussed.   The outline deals almost exclusively with sentence-level syntax, taking words as the basic units and touching only briefly on morphology.

The appendix is organized around the major units of English syntax: the clause, various groups, and words. The largest part of it deals with the two fundamental building blocks: the *clause* and the *noun group*. The description of each kind of constituent in the grammar consists of several parts: its *functions* within discourse and as a part of other constituents; its prototypical *structure*; the *choice systems* classifying it in terms of features; and the possible *rearrangements* of the structure according to those features. In fitting together the grammar as a whole, these descriptions are intertwined. For example, the functions filled by any one type of constituent make sense only in terms of the structures of the constituents in which it functions. The choice systems are closely related to the structure of a constituent, determining which functions will be filled. One way in which the presentation differs from formal grammars (either systemic or transformational) is that basic structures (e.g., the clause) are described in terms of their most typical arrangement (e.g., SUBJECT – VERB – OBJECT), and other organizations and rearrangements are discussed in a less formal way which uses both the ordering rules of systemic grammar and the transformational idea of rearrangement. In a way, it is closer to Chomsky's (1957) original version of transformational grammar (with its *kernel sentences*) than to more recent generative grammars.

Many of the details in this appendix have been drawn from analyses within the systemic grammar framework and from *A Grammar of Contemporary English* by Quirk et al. (1972). Their extensive analysis of English (over 1100 pages) is in a similar descriptive spirit and provides far more information on the topics covered here. Where appropriate, the description of structures includes a discussion of the transformational approach to the same phenomena based on a variety of sources, as listed in Chapter 4 and Appendix C.

B.1 The clause

School grammars of English generally describe the *sentence* as the unit of communication. Generative grammar has followed this tradition in its emphasis on the sentence as the unit of grammaticality. In grammar book terminology, the sentence *Where is the pencil you had while you were reading?* contains two *subordinate clauses* embedded within it—one corresponding to the sentence *You had the pencil* and the other to *You were reading.* It is called a *complex sentence* because one clause plays a role in another. A sentence consisting of two conjoined clauses, such as *It's heavy and I'm getting tired,* is called a *compound sentence.*

Systemic linguists have generally employed the term 'clause' for both independent and embedded clause structures. Thus a sentence consists of a *major* clause (or several, if they are combined by a conjunction such as *and*), which may in turn contain embedded *minor clauses.* Structures that involve embedding are called *hypotactic,* while those with coordination are *paratactic.*

In order to capture the regularities common to both sentences and embedded clauses, transformational grammarians use a single formal classification for *sentence* (represented by S) which expands into both. In various recent versions, there are a number of structures that cover embedded clauses. There can be an $\bar{S}$ (pronounced 'S-bar'), which contains an S, and an independent $\overline{VP}$ or VP that is not the verb phrase of an S. In this appendix, 'clause' is used for all of these structures, in accordance with the systemic terminology. We refer to 'sentences' when dealing with phenomena that apply only to clauses that are not constituents of other units, such as tag questions like *That's right, isn't it?*

B.1.1 Functions filled by clauses

A clause can function either as an independent constituent of a discourse or as a constituent within another clause or group. From a purely syntactic point of view (ignoring larger discourse structure), there is little to be said about the

---

Statement

> *Snow is white.*
>
> *In this way our idealized model can be useful even if it is wrong.*

Command

> *Call me a taxi.*
>
> *Will you please hold still.*

Exclamation

> *I'll be damned!*
>
> *Isn't that something!*

Question

> *Is the lasagne heated all the way through?*
>
> *Where did you leave the bread knife?*

Figure B–1. Communicative functions of independent clauses.

function of independent clauses. However, we can talk about the communicative roles they serve, as illustrated in Figure B–1.

The functions that clauses fill as constituents of other clauses and groups are illustrated in Figure B–2. These will be defined later, in describing the structure of the units in which the clauses appear. For some functional roles, several examples are given to illustrate the variety of clause forms that can fill the function. In discussing the choice systems for clauses below, the description of each clause type will include a listing of the functions that clauses of that type can fill. Note that clauses of the same form can play quite different functions. For example, *to cause a disturbance* could be a subject (in *To cause a disturbance would be wrong*) or a modifier (*He did it to cause a disturbance*).

B.1.2 Prototypical clause structure

In describing the detailed structure of the clause, it is useful to start with a simplified prototype—one that can later serve as a basis for describing other structures as modifications. Figure B–3 gives the elements of the clause in their most typical sequence. In later sections we will discuss the cases in which some of these elements are prohibited, other markers (such as a relative pronoun) or modifiers (such as certain adverbs) are inserted, and elements are rearranged (as in questions) or omitted (as in relative clauses).

Nominal (noun-like) functions

Subject of clause

What you don't know won't hurt you.

That he did it is forgivable.

To err is human.

His covering it up disturbs me much more.

Direct object of clause

I love *eating Chinese food on the floor.*

Marie told him *that the peasants could eat cake.*

Indirect (first) object of clause

The Newsweek article on recreation gave *visiting the zoo* a high recommendation.

Complement of clause

Her greatest desire is *to be the leader of the band.*

Object of preposition group

by *closing your eyes very tight*

Object of adjunct group

even better than *what you had imagined*

almost as exciting as *really being there*

Appositive

his way, *to believe in the true incarnation,*

Modifier functions

Modifier of clause

I've been to London *to visit the queen.*

Can you do it *standing on your head?*

I'm willing to try *if you are.*

Before you say anything, take off your socks.

Restrictive qualifier of noun group

a man *revered by millions*

the most exciting student *I ever hoped to teach*

the box *containing a home-made jigsaw puzzle*

the only way *to fly*

Nonrestrictive qualifier of noun group

the swami, *who was revered by millions,*

Figure B–2. Functions of clauses in other units.

Modifiers - Subject - Verb-Sequence - 1st-Obj - 2nd-Obj - Modifiers

---

Figure B–3. Sequence of elements in a prototypical clause.

Each of the roles specified in this prototype can be filled by constituents of certain types:

Modifiers. There can be an arbitrarily long sequence of modifiers at the beginning and end of the clause, each of which can be one of several types, as illustrated in Figure B–4. In most of the examples in that figure, a unit of the given type appears both at the beginning and at the end. The particular forms of clause shown there (such as FOR-TO) are defined in the Section B.1.3.

Core clause functions (subject, objects). Each of these constituents is either a noun group, a clause playing a nominal role (see Figure B–2), or an adjunct group. A more detailed specification is given in Section B.1.6 on transitivity.

Adverb

> *Inevitably,* Morris arrives *late.*

Preposition group

> *In reality,* I did it *for the kicks.*

For-To clause

> *To be completely innocent,* you have to do it *for someone else to read.*

Present participle clause

> *Breaking all precedents* he read it *standing on his head.*

Noun group

> *Last year* we finally bought a turkey *the day before Thanksgiving.*

Adjunct group

> *More confident than anyone else,* she ran *as quickly as a speeding bullet.*

Ordinal number

> *First,* we have to establish the rules.

Figure B–4. Units that can function as clause modifiers.

The verb sequence. A clause contains at least one verb and can include a complex *verb sequence* such as *would have been sleeping,* which conveys information about time and modality. The final verb of this sequence is the *main verb* of the clause, and all but the last have the feature AUXILIARY. Each can be preceded by adverbs, at most one can be NEGATIVE (i.e., have a suffix of the form *-n't*). There are precise rules determining which verb forms can follow which auxiliaries, as described in Section B.1.5.

In some systemic analyses, there is an independent unit called a *verb group.* In transformational grammars, there is a *verb phrase* (VP) which encompasses the verb sequence along with the objects and complements. There has been a good deal of debate about whether the VP in English should be considered an independent unit (like S and NP) or should be simply a part of S. In the grammar presented here, the verb sequence is viewed not as an independent entity, but as a substructure of the clause. We will not refer to it as VP since it has quite a different structure from the constituent usually given that label. It contains only the verb and auxiliaries, not the objects following the verb.

B.1.3 The mood system of the clause

The system of *mood* choices applies to every clause, whether it is a sentence or is embedded as a constituent of another clause or group. The choices are realized in the ordering of the basic clause elements (such as subject and verb), in the form of the verb sequence, and in the presence of special markers such as *that, to, what,* and *which.* The term 'mood' (which was initially used by Halliday) is somewhat confusing, since it has nothing to do with the emotional mood of the speaker or hearer. It is more closely related to the use of the term in grammar, as in speaking of 'subjunctive mood,' but even this use is somewhat different. Nevertheless, in keeping with tradition, we will refer to this choice system as 'mood.'

Figure B–5 contains a system network representing the mood choices for English clauses. This classification scheme expresses the choices of *form* for clauses, not of *function.* It is important to remember that formal choices such as DECLARATIVE and IMPERATIVE correspond loosely *but not exactly* to potentials for expressing meaning, such as making a statement or giving a command. Each mood choice plays a role in determining the number, classification, and ordering of the constituents that make up the clause. Some of the phenomena dealt with in transformational accounts (such as the form of imperatives and yes-no questions) are covered in this section, while others (such as unbounded movement, transitivity, and ellipsis) are dealt with in later sections.

The following pages describe the syntactic realizations of the features in the mood system and give examples for each choice. The realization is stated in English rather than in a strict formalism, but the terms used are drawn from this and the other choice systems in the sections that follow. The paragraph

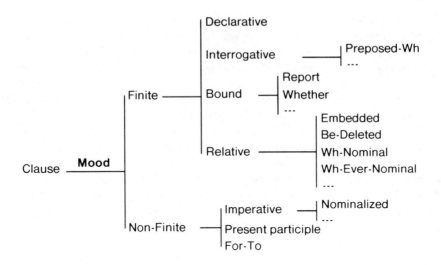

Figure B–5. Mood system for the clause.

introducing each feature begins with its name and a summary (in parentheses) of its entry condition—the other choices that must be made in order for that choice to be relevant. All of the realizations associated with these choices will apply to the constituent, along with the additional realization specific to the choice. In giving examples of features belonging to an embedded clause, the clause, rather than the entire example, appears in italics, and its function is indicated in brackets.

Summary of clause mood features

CLAUSE (—)

    Realization: The mood system applies only to clauses. Every clause includes a VERB-SEQUENCE.

    Examples: *This is a clause. Halt!* [QUALIFIER]:Many clauses have other clauses *that are embedded within them.*

FINITE (CLAUSE)

    Realization: The first verb in the VERB-SEQUENCE is FINITE. A SUBJECT is present. It agrees in NUMBER and PERSON with the first element of the VERB-SEQUENCE.

    Examples: *They are bringing in reinforcements. Which ones did you talk to?* [QUALIFIER]:There are people *who have never tried it.*

DECLARATIVE (FINITE CLAUSE)

Realization: This is the unmarked form of FINITE—only those constraints imposed by that choice apply.

Examples: *This is a simple declarative sentence. You're going to become a what?*

INTERROGATIVE (FINITE CLAUSE)

Realization: Like DECLARATIVE, except that the first member of the VERB-SEQUENCE is before the SUBJECT. If the VERB-SEQUENCE consists of a single main verb, an AUXILIARY *do* is added.

Examples: *Did you see which way they went? Would you have been seeing him?*

PREPOSED-WH (INTERROGATIVE FINITE CLAUSE)

Realization: There is a constituent with feature QUESTION appearing as one of the modifiers at the beginning of the sentence or as a noun group immediately following them. The rest of the sentence has a missing element that corresponds to this QUESTION element, as discussed in detail in Section B.1.4.

Examples: *Who did they choose as president? How many times must a person be told? Which toolbox did the carpenter ask you to tell her assistant to put it in? In which toolbox did he actually put it?*

BOUND (FINITE CLAUSE)

Realization: This has the standard FINITE form, preceded by a single word of class *binder*. The unmarked case of BOUND includes all the binders (including *until, when, because, if, since,...*) except for *whether, if,* and *that.*

Examples: [MODIFIER]:*Before you go,* take out the garbage. [MODIFIER]: I can't, *because I'm already late for the train.*

REPORT (BOUND FINITE CLAUSE)

Realization: A BOUND clause with BINDER *that*. This case is separated because it has functions that are different from other BOUND clauses.

Examples: [SUBJECT]:*That he loved her* was no secret. [QUALIFIER]:His conviction *that things would work out* never flagged. [OBJECT]:They knew *that their love was real.*

WHETHER (BOUND FINITE CLAUSE)

Realization: A BOUND clause with BINDER *whether* or *if,* which can function in nominal functions and as a modifier.

Examples: [OBJECT]:I don't know *whether we can pluck all the chickens in time.* [OBJECT]:I wonder *if we can just leave some of the feathers on.* [SUBJECT]:*Whether it rains* will determine the cost of the picnic. [MODIFIER]:*Whether he comes or not,* we still have to leave room for him.

RELATIVE (FINITE CLAUSE)

Realization: This is basically like a DECLARATIVE, except that it begins with an optional relative marker (such as *which, who,* or *that)* and can have a missing element as described for a PREPOSED-WH. In the unmarked form, the relative marker is a relative pronoun (*which, who, whom* or *that,*) or one of the adverbs *where, when, why,* or *how.* There are a number of detailed restrictions on just which markers can appear in what patterns. The hold mechanisms of an ATN and the unbounded movement rules of transformational grammar deal with the details of this kind of clause, as discussed in Section B.1.4. The unmarked form of RELATIVE clause functions as a QUALIFIER in a noun group.

Examples: an old man *whom I know,* the woman *who lives with him,* the day *that they broke the bank in Peoria,* the day *they broke the bank in Peoria,* the place *where we keep the money,* the reason *why it is impossible,* the woman *whose generosity made all this possible.*

EMBEDDED (RELATIVE FINITE CLAUSE)

Realization: This kind of relative clause begins with a noun group or preposition group that contains embedded within it a noun group consisting of one of the words *which, whom,* or *whose.* The 'hole' in the later part of the clause corresponds to the entire initial element.

Examples: the box *in which we store the elixir,* an experience *the likes of which you have never imagined,* a teacher *whose classes you will never forget,* a report *the height of the lettering on the cover of which was nonstandard.*

BE-DELETED (RELATIVE FINITE CLAUSE)

Realization: This can be thought of as the result of deleting the first two elements from a RELATIVE in which the relativized role is the SUBJECT and the first element of the verb sequence is an AUXILIARY that is a form of *be.* In the examples, the deleted elements are included in brackets. Notice that this structure is more easily described in terms of transformations than by characterizing the form of the result, since many different sequences can follow a *be.* Like other RELATIVE clauses, it functions as a QUALIFIER.

Examples: Goldwater, *[who was]crushed by his defeat in two successive elections,* the team *[that is] expected to be given the go-ahead,* an enchanting island *[that is] waiting to be discovered.*

WH-NOMINAL (RELATIVE FINITE CLAUSE)

Realization: The clause begins with a WH- element, but the subject and verb are not in inverted order.

Examples: [OBJECT of PP]:Everyone was amazed at *which one they chose as president.* [OBJECT]:I couldn't believe *how many people understood the theory.* [SUBJECT]:*What they did next* had everyone rolling in the aisles.

WH-EVER-NOMINAL (RELATIVE FINITE CLAUSE)

Realization: This is like a WH-NOMINAL, but the first word is *whatever, whoever, wherever, whenever,* or *whomever.* It has somewhat different functions from other WH-NOMINALS.

Examples: [SUBJECT]:*Whoever did it* will be sorry. [OBJECT]:I'll buy *whatever you suggest.* [MODIFIER]:*Whoever does it,* I want to be informed of the results. [MODIFIER]:Don't admit anything, *whatever they do to you.* [NONRESTRICTIVE QUALIFIER]:John Dean, *whoever that is,* says he has some tapes you might be interested in.

NON-FINITE (CLAUSE)

Realization: The first verb of the VERB-SEQUENCE is a special form. The exact form is indicated by the next set of choices. There is a wide variety of different non-finite clause forms, each having a specialized set of functions such as the subject or object of selected verbs, or a modifier. Subtle differences in form can have important effects on meaning, as in: *What I want is to sit out there in the sun.* and *What I want is sitting out there in the sun.* In addition, the realization of each choice (in terms of the functions that can appear in the clause) is quite complex. Rather than presenting all the details, the following examples are intended to give some feeling for the differences.

IMPERATIVE (NON-FINITE CLAUSE)

Realization: Like FINITE except that the SUBJECT can be (but need not be) omitted, and the first element of the verb sequence is in the INFINITIVE form.

Examples: *Get your axe in here right now. Be a mensch. Don't look so uppity. If you want him to like you, be impressed by everything he says. You be the doctor, John be the nurse,* and I'll be the patient.

NOMINALIZED (IMPERATIVE NON-FINITE CLAUSE)

Realization: Like IMPERATIVE, except that the SUBJECT cannot be deleted, and the clause may be preceded by *that.* These clauses differ in form from REPORT clauses in that the first verb of the verb sequence is INFINITIVE, not FINITE. There is a corresponding difference of meaning. Notice the contrast between *They insisted that he be demoted to vice-president.* (NOMINALIZED IMPERATIVE) and *They insisted that he was demoted to vice-president.* (REPORT)

Examples: [OBJECT]:They demanded *that he give them bagels and lox.* [OBJECT]:They insisted *he serve it on Wedgwood plates.*

PRESENT PARTICIPLE (NON-FINITE CLAUSE)

Realization: The first element of the verb sequence is a PRESENT PARTICIPLE (a form ending in *-ing*). Traditionally, this kind of clause is called *gerundive* and the present-participle verb is a *gerund.* The SUBJECT need not be present, and if present it is in the POSSESSIVE case.

Examples: [SUBJECT]:*Writing long appendices* is a form of masochism. [OBJECT of PP]: But sometimes you can learn something by *reading them thoroughly.* [OBJECT]:I don't anticipate *everyone's reading all of them.* [MODIFIER]:*Knowing that,* I suppose I should keep them short.

FOR-TO (NON-FINITE CLAUSE)

Realization: The first element of the verb sequence is an INFINITIVE. The SUBJECT need not be present. If it is, it may be preceded by *for* and is in the OBJECTIVE case. As with the other NON-FINITE clauses, the rules for exactly which form can appear in what contexts are complex and have been the subject of much analysis in transformational grammar.

Examples: [SUBJECT]:*For Ann to take the job* would be sheer madness. [OBJECT]:I expect *her to do it anyway.* [OBJECT]:I heard *her reject their offer* several times. [SUBJECT]:*To refuse it* would be a real trauma. [OBJECT]:She needs *to decide immediately.* [QUALIFIER]:I'm not the person *for her to ask about it.*

B.1.4 Long-distance dependencies

The choices described above in the mood system can be thought of as dealing with local structure—with the constituents that make up a clause and the functions a clause can fill. In most (perhaps all) natural languages, there are other phenomena that can only be understood in terms of non-local (sometimes called *long-distance*, or *unbounded*) interdependency. Some element of the structure is constrained by features of another part of the structure that is not its parent or one of its children, but appears at a distant place in the tree. The need to account for this phenomenon is one of the major forces shaping grammar formalisms. It was one of the motivations for the original idea of transformations and in some recent versions of transformational grammar, the only transformations remaining are those needed to handle it. The hold register in ATN grammars, the distant binding arrows of lexical-functional grammar and the derived categories of phrase structure grammar are other examples of special devices that have been added on top of simpler underlying mechanisms in order to handle long-distance dependencies.

The syntactic data are quite complex, and have been a central focus of work in generative grammar. Here we will present the basic issues in a series of steps, each introducing some of the problems. For a more precise characterization of the rules, the reader will need to consult an extensive grammar or look through the transformational grammar literature.

Simple relative clauses. There is an obvious correlation between sentences like *The baby broke the bottle* and noun groups with relative clauses such as *the baby that broke the bottle* and *the bottle that the baby broke.* As a first approximation, we can describe the relative clause as having the same structure as the corresponding simple declarative clause except that:

It is preceded by a relativizer (*that, who, which, when,* or *where*), chosen to agree in semantic category with the head of the noun group.

One of its constituents is missing, and can be thought of as identified with the noun group in which the clause appears.

In transformational grammar, this is dealt with by assuming that in the deep structure the missing constituent is in the place it would be in the corresponding simple sentence, and then it is moved or deleted by a transformation. The missing constituent can be one of the central participants or a modifier, as shown in Figure B–6, in which the potential missing element is indicated with '⌣':

Choice of relativizers. There is a distinction between *restrictive* and *non-restrictive* relative clauses, discussed in Section B.2 on the noun group. This choice is to some extent correlated with the choice of *that* versus *which* as a relativizer. In many books on English style, it is stated that *which* is used only for nonrestrictive clauses, *that* for restrictive, and *who* and *whom* for either. However, in ordinary speaking and writing, many native speakers do not observe this distinction. In the case of place and time modifiers, the choice is not obvious. For some speakers *the place where I saw it* and *the place that I saw it* are equivalent, while for others only the first is acceptable. The relativizer need not be present for most kinds of restrictive clauses. *The thing he wants most* and *the thing that he wants most* are not very different. However, if the missing element is the SUBJECT, then the relativizer must appear, as in *the woman who won.*

Embedding of the missing element. The given description of simple relatives does not account for cases in which the missing constituent is not a child of the relative clause but appears somewhere as a descendant. The examples of Figure B–7 illustrate some of the places it might be missing.

Function	Example
Subject	*the woman who ⌣ broke the bank at Monte Carlo*
Object	*the thing he wants ⌣ most*
First object	*the girl I call ⌣ my own*
Second object	*the turkey that you sold us ⌣*
Complement	*the color Tom painted the fence ⌣*
Time modifier	*the day the world ended ⌣*
Manner modifier	*the way that she combs her hair ⌣*
Place modifier	*the place where everyone has fun ⌣*

Figure B–6. The missing constituent in a relative clause.

Object of modifying preposition group

> *the key he opened it with ⌣*

Object of embedded clause

> *the book they all wanted to write ⌣*

Modifier of embedded clause

> *the day he believed the world would end ⌣*

Modifier of embedded(!) clause

> *the place Sarah said you told John I expected him to leave the car ⌣*

Figure B–7. Embedded missing constituents.

As illustrated by the last example, the embedding can be any number of levels deep. This is the reason that long-distance rules are needed. The interaction between the noun group (*the place...*) and the corresponding missing element (*leave the car⌣*) jumps over all the intermediate structure.

Embedding constraints. The simplest rule to account for embedding would allow any noun group anywhere within the clause to be the missing element. But there are a number of restrictions that apply, as illustrated by the following non-sentences:

> ** the person that I saw Arthur and ⌣*
>
> ** the book that for John to read ⌣ would be difficult*
>
> ** the oysters that for ⌣ you paid fifty dollars*
>
> ** the job that I saw an announcement that ⌣ was available*

Ross (1967) proposed a number of specific rules, or *constraints,* accounting for these problems, with names like the *coordinate structure constraint* and the *sentential subject constraint,* which are discussed in Appendix C. There have been a number of attempts to give more general rules, but it is likely that any satisfactory account will be quite complex.

Nested relatives. A relative clause can contain within it a noun group that includes a relative clause, as in *the trouble that the rumor you started caused.* This kind of *center embedding* makes sentences quite difficult to understand if repeated more than once, but in principle a sentence with several levels is grammatical, as in *the judge that the story that the man that the guard you hired shot told convinced.* The structure must be *well-nested* in that a missing element inside any relative clause can correspond only to the head to which that clause is attached, not to a higher one, as illustrated by:

the book₁ that the man₂ we told the story to ⌣₂ bought ⌣₁

* the man₁ that the book₂ we told the story to ⌣₁ bought ⌣₂

Whiz deletion. It was mentioned above that the relativizer need not appear in most kinds of relative clauses. There is a further reduced form in which both the relativizer and a following verb that is a form of *be* are missing. These clauses (called BE-DELETED in Section B.1.3) could be described without using the concept of deletion, but for most purposes this is the clearest account. The associated transformation is called *whiz deletion* because in the prototypical present tense case it deletes the words *who is, which is,* or *that is*.

> *a fable [that is] told by parents to their children*
>
> *the woman [who is] being nominated for president* (1)

In sentences like (1), the embedded clause has the same structure as a PRESENT PARTICIPLE clause (see Section B.1.3), and could be interpreted as that kind instead. This phenomenon of *structural overlap* is common in grammars. Two different analyses that are separately motivated (PRESENT PARTICIPLE clauses because of their other functions and whiz deletion because of other forms with *be*) could each account for a particular structure.

Embedded relativizers. The noun group **the oysters that for ⌣ you paid fifty dollars* is not grammatical. When the missing element would have appeared in an initial modifying phrase of the embedded clause, the relativizer (which must be *who* or *which*) appears in the place of the missing element, rather than at the front of the relative clause, as in *the oysters <u>for which</u> you paid fifty dollars*. Also, if the missing element is the object of a PP at the end of the clause, its absence would lead to a construct known as a *dangling preposition,* as in *the yoyo you voted for*. This is common in spoken English, but is considered improper by many. In order to avoid a dangling preposition, the entire PP can be moved to the front and the relativizer embedded, as in *the yoyo for whom you voted*. If the PP is in turn embedded in another constituent, that whole constituent can be brought along with it, leading to a phenomenon known as *pied piping:*

> *the report that it is based on* → *the report on which it is based*
>
> *the report he designed the cover of* →
> *the report the cover of which he designed*
>
> *the reports that the government prescribes the height of the lettering on the covers of* →
> *the reports the height of the lettering on the covers of which the government prescribes*

Function	Example
Subject	*How much he knew* was a mystery.
Object	I tried to guess *which sources were reliable.*
Second object	I asked him *what he thought they expected him to hear.*
Object of preposition	We speculated about *how many times he had done it.*
Modifier	*Where they come from,* things like that aren't done.

Figure B–8. Some functions of nominalized relative clauses.

Nominalized relatives. In the description of mood choices in Section B.1.3, we included simple relative clauses and nominalized relative clauses. The latter have a similar structure but function as nominals (e.g., as subjects and objects) and clause modifiers, while ordinary relative clauses function only as qualifiers in noun groups. The syntactic difference is in the relativizing element. While an ordinary relative has *that, which, who, where, when, why,* or *whom* (which may in some cases be omitted), a nominalized relative takes any adverb or noun group with the QUESTION feature, such as *what* and *how many reasons.* Figure B–8 illustrates some functions of nominalized relative clauses. This kind of relative can be combined with other structures, such as pied piping, as in *It has never been clear to me which reports the height of the lettering on the covers of which the government prescribes.*

Questions. Nominalized relatives share an obvious feature with questions in that they begin with a QUESTION element. They differ in that questions also have an inverted SUBJECT-AUXILIARY order as well, except in the case where the SUBJECT is the questioned element. In that case, the question form and nominalized relative are identical, as in *I tried to see who had it.* If there is no auxiliary and one is needed for inversion, the auxiliary *do* is added (as in (2)). This phenomenon is sometimes called *do-support.* It is a common error for people learning English (including children learning it as a native language) to use the question form in place of the nominalized relative (**Tell me where is he*) or the nominalized relative as a question (**Where he is?*). The questions corresponding to the nominalized relative examples of Figure B–8 are:

How much did he know? (2)

Which sources were reliable?

What did he think they expected him to hear?

How many times had he done it?

Where do they come from?

Most of the complexities described above for relative clauses (constraints, recursive embedding, pied piping, etc.) apply to questions, although the exact restrictions aren't always the same. For example, whiz deletion does not apply. The different kinds of clauses can be mixed, as in:

How many bricks did what the man that you hired built require?

For-To qualifiers. When a FOR-TO clause is used in a nominal function (as in *For me to accept would be crazy* or *I want to try it*), the subject may be omitted, but it does not have a missing element of the same sort as a relative clause. However, when it is used as a QUALIFIER in a noun group, it can have a missing element as well, as in:

the man for you to see ⌣
the man to see ⌣
the man to have your friend ask to see ⌣
the first man ⌣ to succeed
the place to do it in ⌣

A similar phenomenon occurs when a FOR-TO clause appears as an object in an adjective group, as in:

Shoshana is easy to please ⌣ .
Ronald is hard to imagine anyone being willing to marry ⌣ .

This applies only to certain adjectives—for example, *Shoshana is eager to please* does not have a parallel structure to *Shoshana is easy to please*. The phenomenon took its name from one of the first adjectives for which it was noted, and is called *tough movement*.

Other long-distance dependencies. In some of the following sections, we will describe other phenomena that can be thought of as involving long-distance dependencies, such as thematic movement and ellipsis. They are not included here because there is a good deal of similarity among all the structures we have been describing which they do not share. For example, the constraints on missing elements apply to all the different structures above—relatives, nominalized relatives, questions, tough movement, etc., but do not apply equally to sentences involving ellipsis. Even though we cannot say *Who did you see and Michael?* or *The girl you saw and Michael* (meaning you saw both), we can answer the question *Did you see Mimi?* with *Yes, and Michael.*

B.1.5 The verb sequence

Section B.1.2 described the clause as containing a *verb sequence* made up of a main verb, auxiliaries, and modifiers. This section deals with the internal structure of the verb sequence and with the effect that additional particles and prepositions have in creating *multi-word verbs*. Modifiers (such as *not* and various adverbs) are discussed in Section B.3.

B.1.5.1 Tense and auxiliaries

The verb sequence carries the marking for tense and aspect in the clause. It is important to distinguish between the system of tense choices for an individual verb and those for the clause as a whole, as determined by the verb sequence. Individual verbs include *modals,* such as *will, can,* and *could* (which have only one form), and ordinary verbs, which have five basic forms: INFINITIVE (*go, be, write*); PRESENT (*goes, is, writes*); PAST (*went, was, wrote*); PRESENT PARTICIPLE (*going, being, writing*); and PAST PARTICIPLE (*gone, been, written*). There is a good deal of irregularity in the details of these forms, as described in Section B.4.2.

The verb sequence can be analyzed as a sequence of verbs and auxiliaries following a set order, as illustrated by the following pattern and examples:

(Modal)	(Have)	(Be$_1$)	(Be$_2$)	Main verb
will	*have*			*gone*
	has	*been*		*writing*
	had	*been*	*being*	*corrected*

The symbols HAVE and BE stand for forms of the verbs *have* and *be*. The parentheses indicate that an element is optional. A clause must have a MAIN VERB and can have any selection of the other elements. Each element determines the form of the one following it according to the rules shown in Figure B–9.

If the sequence contains:	Then the form of following element is:
Modal	Infinitive
Have	Past participle
Be$_1$	Present participle
Be$_2$	Past participle

The first element carries the tense or is modal.
If Be$_2$ is present, the clause is passive.

Figure B–9.   Rules for the form of verbal elements.

In transformational grammar, this agreement is produced by having the base rules introduce markers following the verbs (such as *have -en* and *be -ing*) and then having a transformation called *affix-hopping*, which moves them into the correct position. The sequence *have been being sung* is generated as *have -en − be -ing − be -en − sing*, and is then converted by affix-hopping to *have be -en be -ing sing -en*, which is then transformed through morphological rules into the final form. Tense is also introduced as a marker and handled in a similar way. In a systemic grammar, the different elements are introduced as the result of multiple choices from a tense system (as described below), and the corresponding realization rules produce the detailed structure. In an ATN grammar, a register is kept for the last verbal element found, and the arcs that are taken to parse verbs (auxiliary or main) test that their form agrees properly with the contents of this register according to the rules of Figure B–9.

Given a complete verb sequence, it seems reasonable to ask what the tense of the clause as a whole is. In transformational grammar, since the classificational component of the theory is not highly developed, there is no need to answer the question. There is no such thing as 'the tense of the clause.' There is a sequence of tense markers and auxiliaries, and it is the job of the semantic interpretation rules to treat this as embodying temporal and aspectual relationships.

In traditional grammar, there is a distinction between PAST, PRESENT, and FUTURE, and there are terms *perfective* (for sequences containing HAVE) and *progressive* (those containing BE$_1$) as well as *passive* (those with BE$_2$). FUTURE does not appear in the tables above, since it does not have its own syntactic form but is an interpretation of clauses containing *will* or *shall* as a MODAL. It is important to note that we are dealing here with syntactic rather than semantic distinctions. For example, a wide variety of tense forms can be used in referring to future events, as illustrated by:

I will arrive tomorrow.	*I shall arrive tomorrow.*	*I will be arriving tomorrow.*
I arrive tomorrow.	*I'm arriving tomorrow.*	*I'm going to arrive tomorrow.*
I'm about to arrive.	*I'm to arrive tomorrow.*	*I'm going to be arriving tomorrow.*

In systemic grammar, Halliday proposed a *recursive choice system,* which retains the intuitive past-present-future system, applying it recursively to handle some of the more complex combinations. He also generalizes the range of phenomena, taking sequences like *was going to have finished* as verb sequences. The sequence *be going to* is treated as a single element, with the *be* taking the form required by the previous element as described in Figure B–9, and the following element taking the INFINITIVE form. The tense of a clause is a sequence of features, each member of which is PAST, PRESENT, FUTURE, MODAL, or INFINITIVE. The first element of the tense sequence is the tense of the first element of the verb sequence, unless it is a modal. The rest correspond to the entire auxiliary sequence (all the verbs but the last, which is the main verb), according to the mapping:

Modal	→	Future if the word is *will* or *shall*
	→	Modal otherwise
Have	→	Past
Be₁	→	Present
Be-Going-To	→	Future

For example, the sequence *had taken* has the tense sequence PAST PAST, since its first element is a verb in the past tense form and is a HAVE auxiliary. This corresponds to our intuition that this phrase (as in *Before he got home I had taken the garbage out*) indicates an event that was in the past with respect to some other event, which in turn is now past. Similarly, *will have taken* is FUTURE PAST, as in *By the time he gets home I will have taken the garbage out*. The PRESENT PAST (*have taken*) is more subtle, and has a number of uses in English. For example, we can announce that *Mount St. Helens has erupted,* but cannot say that **Vesuvius has erupted in 250 B.C.* The PRESENT PAST is appropriate only if it the event is recent or if there is a possible repetition, as in *Vesuvius has erupted twice in the modern geological era.* Similarly, *Pablo Picasso has created many famous paintings* is strange if uttered now that he is dead although it would have been perfectly acceptable during his lifetime. A hearer might well respond *Didn't you know he had died?* The PAST PRESENT, as in *Yesterday we were running,* sets up a context in which the past time is 'present' and other events can be described with respect to it. It differs from the simple PAST (*Yesterday we ran*), which simply reports an event.

This compounding of tenses can be carried out more than once, so that *We were going to have finished* is PAST FUTURE PAST. It indicates that at some past time, there was some future time at which finishing would be in the past. The treatment of *be going to* in these terms can be seen as one instance of a more general phenomenon in which multi-word phrases extend the tense system. It is impossible to create PAST FUTURE using the ordinary markers for PAST (past tense verb) and FUTURE (modal *will*). Neither **was will go* nor **will was go* is acceptable. *Was going to go* fills this gap. In a parallel fashion, *have to* and *be able to* make it possible to put the modals *must* and *can* into recursive positions. We can treat *I had to do it* as a PAST MODAL corresponding to the simple MODAL *I must do it*.

In fact, there is a class of *semi-auxiliaries,* such as *be about to, be bound to, be going to, have to, have got to,* and *have better* (as in *I had better go now*). They involve complex rules of combination and have not been treated generally in generative grammars. They are subject to the phonological process of *reduction,* often occurring in speech in forms like *hafta* and *gonna.* Their occurrence can at times be recognized because of this difference in pronunciation. For example, *This is the car you have to fix* allows *have to* to be reduced to *hafta,* but *Give me that wrench you have to fix it* does not.

The examples of Figure B–10 illustrate the basic tense and auxiliary system along with *be going to* and *have to.* The figure is included to indicate the rich-

[Pres] *I fix*$_\text{pres}$ *radios.*

[Past] *I fixed*$_\text{past}$ *one yesterday.*

[Fut] *I will*$_\text{mod}$ *fix another one tomorrow.*

[Mod] *I can*$_\text{mod}$ *fix any kind you have.*

[Past Past] *I had*$_\text{past}$ have *fixed several before you got here.*

[Pres Past] *I have*$_\text{pres}$ have *fixed many a hard one in my day.*

[Fut Past] *By the time I retire I will*$_\text{mod}$ *have*$_\text{have}$ *fixed a lot more.*

[Mod Past] *I might*$_\text{mod}$ *have*$_\text{have}$ *fixed yours at one time or another.*

[Past Pres] *I was*$_\text{past}$ be *fixing one when you came in.*

[Pres Pres] *As a matter of fact, I am*$_\text{pres}$ be *fixing it while we talk.*

[Fut Pres] *I still will*$_\text{mod}$ *be*$_\text{be}$ *fixing it when you leave.*

[Past Fut] *When I was young I (was going to)*$_\text{past}$ go *fix automobiles.*

[Pres Fut] *My son (is going to)*$_\text{pres}$ go *fix computers.*

[Fut Mod] *Soon I will*$_\text{mod}$ *(have to)*$_\text{hafta}$ *fix walky talkies.*

[Mod Mod] *I might*$_\text{mod}$ *(have to)*$_\text{hafta}$ *fix other stuff as well.*

[Past Past Pres] *Before I came here, I had*$_\text{past}$ have *been*$_\text{be}$ *fixing cars for a while.*

[Pres Past Pres] *I have*$_\text{pres}$ have *been*$_\text{be}$ *fixing radios now for a long time.*

[Past Fut Pres] *When I was a boy, I thought I (was going to)*$_\text{past}$ go *be*$_\text{be}$ *fixing cars when I grew up.*

[Past Mod Pres] *When I started, I (had to)*$_\text{past}$ hafta *be*$_\text{be}$ *fixing one a day to survive.*

[Pres Mod Pres] *Now I don't*$_\text{pres}$ *(have to)*$_\text{hafta}$ *be*$_\text{be}$ *fixing that many at once.*

[Past Fut Past] *I once thought I (was going to)*$_\text{past}$ go *have*$_\text{have}$ *fixed every radio in town by the time I was forty.*

[Pres Fut Past] *By the time he's forty, my son (is going to)*$_\text{pres}$ go *have*$_\text{have}$ *fixed every computer in town.*

[Future Mod Past] *Before I go, I will*$_\text{mod}$ *(have to)*$_\text{hafta}$ *have*$_\text{have}$ *fixed this one.*

[Pres Fut Past Pres] *By the time I retire, I (am going to)*$_\text{pres}$ go *have*$_\text{have}$ *been*$_\text{be}$ *fixing radios for a long time.*

[Fut Fut Past Pres] *If the tax laws delay my retirement, I will*$_\text{mod}$ *(be going to)*$_\text{go}$ *have*$_\text{have}$ *been*$_\text{be}$ *fixing them for over forty years.*

[Fut Mod Past Pres] *That's because I will*$_\text{mod}$ *(have to)*$_\text{hafta}$ *have*$_\text{have}$ *been*$_\text{be}$ *paying social security during that many years.*

[Past Fut Mod Past Pres] *Under the new law they almost passed, I (was going to)*$_\text{past}$ go *(have to)*$_\text{hafta}$ *have*$_\text{have}$ *been*$_\text{be}$ *fixing them for a century to get my pension.*

[Pres Fut Mod Past Pres] *Now I think I (am only going to)*$_\text{pres}$ go *(have to)*$_\text{hafta}$ *have*$_\text{have}$ *been*$_\text{be}$ *fixing them for half a century.*

Figure B–10. Examples of tenses in the English clause.

ness of the system and to show how complex combinations can arise naturally in appropriate contexts. For each example there is an indication (in subscripts) of which elements are present from the basic structure, including BE-GOING-TO and HAVE-TO (which can appear following the MODAL). To save space, the presence of the MAIN VERB is not marked, since it is always there. The tense is indicated (in brackets) before the sentence. The figure makes use of the following abbreviations:

Pres = Present   Fut = Future   Mod = Modal
Be = Be_1 Go = Be-Going-To   Hafta = Have-To

There is a spectrum of acceptability. The simple forms are clearly acceptable. As they become more complex, they sound clumsier and it takes more elaborate contexts to make them plausible. However, even quite complicated sequences can and do occur. In order to simplify the system, we have not included any examples of passives or examples of FOR-TO] clauses, as in *To have asked him would have been wrong*. It is an amusing exercise to fill in all of the possibilities for combinations using the elements of Figure B–10 and to see how many of the forms have passive and infinitive correlates.

Additional complications

There are a number of ways in which the discussion of tense above has been simplified.

Ordering and interactions. In giving the sequence of elements, we assumed a fixed order. This is almost right, but there is some variation. For example, *going to* can appear after BE_1, rather than before it, as in *I had been going to fix this one by noon*. In some other cases, *have to* can occur after *going to,* as in *I am going to have to have fixed it by Tuesday*. When the other semi-auxiliaries are taken into account, the rules are quite complex.

The auxiliary *do.* In the analysis above, *do* was treated as a modal, so *did go* was similar to *will go*. But we cannot say **did be going,* and there are rules associated with subject-auxiliary inversion which cause a *do* to be inserted when it otherwise would not appear (as discussed above in Section B.1.3). Similarly, this phenomenon of *do support* appears in the formation of tag questions like *He went, didn't he?,* as discussed in Section B.1.7.

The subjunctive. There are some holdovers in modern English of earlier tense systems, in particular the *subjunctive*. This takes two forms. In one, the verb appears in an INFINITIVE form even though the subject is specified. This happens in clauses like *We asked that he be given a pardon* and *Be that as it may,....* The first of these was described along with imperative clauses in Section B.1.3, and the other is a special form occurring only in idiomatic patterns. The other kind of subjunctive appears in a bound clause with binder *if,* as in *If I were in your position....* It differs from the normal subject-verb agreement in that the plural form, *were,* is used with a singular subject. It is used to indicate a *counterfactual* situation, and appears in the past tense, regardless of the actual time being described, as in *If I went tomorrow, what would you do?*

B.1.5.2 Multi-word verbs

Section B.1.6 describes the relationship between the main verb and the core clause functions such as SUBJECT and OBJECT. In general, we can describe modifiers (such as adverbs and prepositional phrases) as being peripheral to this central core. For example, *He rose up the chimney* involves an action of rising and an additional modifier indicating its location. However, there are many verbs in English that can be combined with modifiers to produce a sentence that is both syntactically and semantically different from what it would be without the combination. Consider:

> *He turned up the street.*
>
> *He turned up suddenly last night.*
>
> *Whenever he played cards he dealt with deft assurance.*
>
> *He dealt with the matter immediately.*

A combination like *turn up* or *deal with* can have a specialized meaning that is not inferrable from the individual words. It can also lead to a different constellation of participants. For example, *give* normally takes at least one and possibly two objects. *Give up* on the other hand can be used with no object.

A native speaker of English knows many hundreds of such combinations. One series on English grammar for foreign students (Collier-Macmillian, 1977) devotes an entire volume (out of ten) to *two-word verbs.* They are especially prevalent in slang, as can be observed in the large number of recognizable combinations produced by choosing one item from each of the two sets:

> {*put, turn, get, get it, go, take, shut, come,...*}
> {*out, on, off, up, down, in, away, around,...*}

Syntactically, we can divide these constructs into three classes:

Verb-particle. In a sentence like *They took over the management of the department,* the word *over* functions as a particle. It can appear immediately after the verb or can follow the object, as in *They took it over yesterday.* If the object is a pronoun, it must precede the particle, as illustrated by the ungrammaticality of **They took over it.*

Verb-preposition. In *They took to him immediately,* the word *to* is a preposition. If it were a particle, we would expect **They took him to* instead. Some words are both particles and prepositions, opening the possibility of ambiguities. For example, *The carriage drew near the village* and *The artist drew near the edge of the canvas* are quite different structures, as are *He drew near it* and *He drew it near.*

Verb-noun. There are a small set of verbs that combine with nouns in an idiomatic way. There are many idioms involving *it* (*Get it?*) and verbs like *take* that are often used as a kind of neutral background for a noun. *They didn't take care to prevent it* and *We took a bath* can both be best dealt with as special combinations rather than ordinary uses of *take.* Forms with particles, prepositions, and nouns can be combined to produce multi-word verbs like *put up with, get on with,* and *get it on with.*

In addition to semantic irregularities, there are also syntactic idiosyncrasies. For example, the passive form *The matter was dealt with by the court* seems perfectly normal, while ?*He was taken to by the children* does not, and **The bus was got off by the passengers* seems totally unacceptable. Except for the basic issues of particle placement, these phenomena have not been fully worked out in generative grammars. In computational systems, the dictionary often contains separate entries for multi-word verbs and the parser has specific rules or special mechanisms to check for them when there is a potential combination.

B.1.6 Transitivity

One of the most difficult aspects of clause structure is transitivity—the presence and ordering of the phrases representing participants in the action or relation described by the verb. As we will see in the volume on meaning, transitivity issues overlap in complex ways with semantic problems. In transformational grammar (except for case grammar), this area has not been as central as others, such as long-distance dependencies. In systemic grammar, there has been more explicit concern with transitivity, and much of our analysis is adapted from systemic accounts.

Transitivity can be described in terms of a mapping between two different sets of functions, the *core clause functions* listed in Figure B–3, and the *case roles* discussed in Section 6.5. Section B.1.6.1 describes the arrangement of core functions in the simple form, and B.1.6.2 deals with a number of additional complexities arising from *implicit fillers.* Section B.1.6.3 describes the basic transitivity choices for English clauses and explains the corresponding case roles. It is not a complete account but is intended to give a general orientation. Finally, Section B.1.6.4 describes the *circumstantial functions*—those indicating time, place, and manner—and the role they play in the case structure.

B.1.6.1 Syntactic participant functions

Most dictionaries distinguish between *transitive* verbs (those that take an object) and *intransitive* verbs (those that do not). Unfortunately, this simple binary distinction is inadequate. A quick glance at a dictionary shows that more words are listed as both transitive and intransitive than as either alone, and that structures like *He broke a dish* and *He suffered a fall* are treated as being the same (both transitive), even though they are intuitively quite different. In fact, almost any verb can be used either transitively or intransitively in an appropriate context. We might consider *hit* and *sleep* as obvious cases of transitive and intransitive respectively, but we can say *When Ali hits, it hurts,* and *We slept three people in the dining room.*

In the simplified grammars used to illustrate syntactic formalisms, we often find the traditional distinction. However, in grammars that attempt to describe the language adequately, there must be more complex features associated with verbs to express the possibilities for the transitivity of clauses containing them.

Figure B–3 listed the functions in the prototypical clause. In addition to the verb sequence and modifiers, there is a SUBJECT and a sequence of zero, one, or two constituents, each of which is an OBJECT or a COMPLEMENT. Figure B–11 demonstrates the different possible combinations of core clause functions. An OBJECT must be a noun group or nominal clause form, while a COMPLEMENT can be one of these or can be an adjunct group as well. This is a quite superficial analysis which will be used as a basis for the deeper case structure analysis later. For example, the sentences containing *feel* describe situations in which the SUBJECT plays quite different roles. These deeper differences do interact in some ways with the arrangement of clause functions, but for a first approximation we can ignore them.

Sequence of participants	Examples
Subject – Object	*She slew the dragon.*
Subject – Object (1st) – Object (2nd)	*She gave her mother the drumstick.* *He knitted her a new hat.*
Subject – Complement	*We must be crazy.* *He seemed a fool.* *He feels soft. He feels sad.*
Subject – Object – Complement	*You drive me completely wild.*

Figure B–11. Patterns of surface participant functions.

B.1.6.2 Implicit participants

All of the examples in Figure B–11 are simple declarative sentences in which all of the participants appear in the standard places. In Section B.1.4, we described how elements can be missing due to being embedded within a relative clause, question, or other such structure. There are several other ways in which the apparent participants can fail to be those we would expect.

B.1.6.2.1 Passive and dative

Sentences like *The wooly bear surprised the hedgehog* and *The hedgehog was surprised by the wooly bear* are closely related. Section 4.3 described how these examples were important in motivating transformational grammar, and Section 5.3 showed how they played a role in motivating the augmentations in augmented transition network grammars. An *active* clause can be converted to a corresponding *passive* by:

1) putting the verb sequence in a PASSIVE form.
2) removing the SUBJECT and optionally including it in a PP with the preposition *by*
3) moving one of the OBJECTS to become the SUBJECT

One of the ways to distinguish an OBJECT from a COMPLEMENT is that only objects can undergo passive movement. We can have *The dragon was slain by her* but not *Very soft was felt by him*. Passivization can go through multiple levels of embedding, as in *John was believed to have been scheduled to be eliminated*. Rather than moving an OBJECT to the SUBJECT, it moves the OBJECT of an embedded clause that itself is an OBJECT.

In a similar way, sentences like *Peel me a grape* and *Peel a grape for me* are related. The form with one object can be converted to the one with two objects by:

1) removing a PP with preposition *to* or *for*
2) inserting its OBJECT in front of the OBJECT of the clause

Some verbs (such as *peel*) have dative forms associated with *for,* while others (such as *bring*) take *to*. In describing these correspondences, we have taken the active and one-object forms as basic and described passive and two-object forms in terms of changes to them. Other descriptions have been proposed, for example describing the active as the result of moving the object of a *by* phrase into the SUBJECT function. This approach was taken in the UCLA grammar (Stockwell, Schachter, and Partee, 1973), as described in Section 6.5. However, it seems unintuitive to think of the passive as closer to the underlying form than the active, and this has generally not been adopted. With dative, although there have been arguments on both sides, the form with one object is generally taken as basic and the two-object form is seen as resulting from a *dative* transformation. However, there are two-object sentences such as *They showed him a good time* that do not have a corresponding one-object form (*They showed a good time to him*).

In all issues of this sort, decisions are made on the basis of their contribution to the overall clarity of the grammar and may interact with other areas of analysis. For example, in some versions of transformational grammar, dative movement is assumed to be a special case of a more general transformation, where its specific form is motivated by the desire to preserve generality. In other versions, passive and dative are not treated as transformations at all, while in still others it is claimed that some passives are transformational and others are not. Since we are not doing a precise transformational analysis, we will not attempt to resolve these kinds of questions, but it is worth noting that even such seemingly simple phenomena are the source of great difficulty and controversy in syntactic theory.

In describing transitivity patterns in Section B.1.6.3 below, we will generally state them for the ACTIVE form, assuming that the PASSIVE can be understood in terms of the above rule. On the other hand, we will explicitly describe both forms in cases of DATIVE to avoid confusion.

B.1.6.2.2 Implicit subjects

Structures involving long-distance dependency allow an element to be missing due to a correlated element somewhere else in the sentence. The rules for what can be missing from where are complex and quite general. There is another class of missing elements that is much less general. In describing the mood choices in Section B.1.3, we listed several kinds of clauses that can occur without a subject—all of those with the feature NON-FINITE. Although the various subclasses are quite different, they all share the properties of having no subject-verb agreement in number and person and having a verb sequence beginning with a fixed form like an infinitive or a participle.

The first subclass, IMPERATIVE, was one of the early targets (along with passives and datives) of transformational analysis. It was argued that although an imperative is usually subjectless (although it need not be, as in *You be home by supper!*), it has an implicit subject of *you*. This explained phenomena like the choice of pronouns in tag questions and the possibility of reflexivization:

> *He will come back, won't he?*   *Come here, won't you?*
> *He stabbed himself.*   *Control yourself!*

In a style similar to the analyses of passive and dative above, an imperative sentence was treated as having undergone an *imperative* transformation in which a deep subject *you* is deleted. In systemic grammar, clauses with the feature IMPERATIVE do not have a role of SUBJECT, and the rules for things like tags need to be stated in terms of the IMPERATIVE feature. In either case, the phenomenon is relatively simple syntactically.

The rest of the NON-FINITE clauses involve more complex possibilities for omitting the subject. There have been many attempts to analyze various aspects of the problem, but no satisfactory comprehensive framework has evolved. For the purpose of this appendix, we present a straightforward descriptive classification, without attempting to organize the examples according to mechanisms that might account for them. There is a good deal of disagreement among schools of grammar, even within fairly closely aligned branches, about just what phenomena are involved and how much should be handled by the syntactic component. There is a current trend away from handling things syntactically towards providing a simple grammar that simply allows the subject to be omitted and having semantic interpretation rules that establish the implied meaning.

There are several possible sources for an implicit SUBJECT, as illustrated in Figure B-12. The clause in italics is the NON-FINITE clause, and the function names refer to the clause in which it is embedded:

Source	Example
Subject	I prefer *sitting near the front.*
Object	The owner told them *to get out immediately.*
Embedded NP	The favorite activity of my uncle's dog is *chasing hedgehogs.*
Generic	*Managing a rock band* is a good way to get ulcers.

Figure B-12. Possible sources for an implicit subject.

The following list is organized by the function that the NON-FINITE clause fills in some other structure, illustrating examples of clauses in that function and stating for each example what the implied SUBJECT of the clause is. In cases where there seems to be a general rule, it is stated informally. It should be taken as a suggestion, not a precise grammatical statement.

Implicit subjects of non-finite clauses in different functions

Subject of clause:

Examples: *To refuse it* would be a real mistake. *To err* is human. *Finishing the book* was his major achievement this year. *Being a father* satisfies me much more. *Using my toothbrush without permission* really annoys me.

Examples like *Being a father...* have at times been treated as a kind of *equi-NP deletion* called *backward equi,* since the missing NP is in a position earlier in the sentence than the one it is implicitly identified with. However, as the other examples illustrate, the implicit subject may be present in an embedded phrase, may be a specific but unmentioned actor (*To refuse it...*) or a generic unspecified 'whoever' (*To err...*).

Object of clause:

> **Examples:** I wanted [agreed, expect, need,...] *to leave*. The man seemed *to disappear*. Students generally prefer *getting them all at once*.

In all of these cases, the implicit subject is the SUBJECT of the surrounding clause. This is one of the simpler kinds of example, and has been treated transformationally with two transformations. *I wanted to leave* is a standard example of equi-NP deletion, in which the subject of *to leave* is deleted because of its identity with the subject of *want*. *The man seemed to disappear* is an example of *raising to subject*. The proposed underlying structure has an S corresponding to *the man disappear* as the subject of *seem*. Through a series of steps, the inner subject *the man* is 'raised' to become the outer subject.

Second object of clause:

> **Examples:** I persuaded Bill *to go*. I promised Bill *to go*. I asked Bill *to be allowed to go*. I believe Carol *to be a genius*.

The implicit subject can be either the SUBJECT or FIRST-OBJECT, depending on the verb. *Promise* and *persuade* are different, while *ask* can be used in either way. Sentences like *I persuaded...* have been treated with equi, while *I believe...* is an example of *raising to object,* in which the SUBJECT of the embedded clause is raised to fill an OBJECT position that was initially filled by the whole clause (as in *I believe that Carol is a genius*).

First-object of clause:

> **Examples:** The Newsweek article on recreation gave *visiting the zoo* a high recommendation.

This is a rare form, since semantic considerations usually require a person as the first object. If we take the analysis of dative sentences given above, it can be treated as a clause serving as the object of a PP that has been moved into FIRST-OBJECT position. This is compatible with the fact that this position shares with the prepositional object position the restriction that a PRESENT PARTICIPLE clause can appear, but not a FOR-TO, as in *They gave to visit the zoo a high recommendation.

Complement of clause:

> **Examples:** His remedy is *to breathe into a paper bag*. The trick he hates most is *putting a tack on his chair*. His favorite stunt is *putting a tack on your chair*.

As with some of the other cases, the source of the implicit SUBJECT is quite open-ended. It can be one of the participants mentioned, or it can be a vague generic.

Initial modifier of clause:

> **Examples:** *To see it* you have to squint. *To be honest,* he hasn't a prayer. *Having been warned,* he kept the door locked. *Throwing caution to the winds,* she jumped out the window.

In general, the implicit subject of the embedded clause is the SUBJECT of the clause it modifies. There are exceptions, like the intrusion of the speaker in meta-comments like *To be honest.* . . .

Final modifier of clause:

> **Examples:** I've been to London *to visit the queen.* I've been taking lessons *to teach me some new tricks.* You can see it better *standing over here.* They seem to be satisfied *living in Miami.* Can you do it *standing on your head?*

In general, the subject is that of the embedding sentence, as with initial modifiers. Sentences like *I've been taking lessons.* . . . violate this but are slightly marginal.

Object of adjunct group:

> **Examples:** John is eager *to please.* The chicken is ready *to eat.*

These sentences are related to those exhibiting *tough movement,* such as *John is easy to please.* There is a significant difference in that tough movement involves long-distance dependency (as in *This sentence is easy to get a systemic grammar to generate*), while non-tough adjectives like *eager* can be followed by a FOR-TO clause, and if it is subjectless, the implied subject is the NP being modified by the adjunct group. Some verbs, like *ready,* allow both forms, and sentences like *The chicken is ready to eat* are therefore ambiguous.

Object of preposition group:

> **Examples:** By *closing your eyes very tight,* you can make it come true. We thanked him for *giving a party.* We pleased him by *giving a party.* We lectured him on *giving a party.* This is a recipe for *baking bread.*

The examples show that there are many possible sources for an implicit SUBJECT, including the generic, as in . . . *baking bread.* As mentioned above, FOR-TO clauses cannot appear in this function.

Qualifier of noun group:

> **Examples:** the man *to buy a used car from,* the only way *to fly* the beaker *sitting next to the kiln.*

In Section B.1.4 on long-distance dependencies, we introduced FOR-TO qualifiers. Like all relative clauses, they are missing an element which is correlated with the noun group in which they appear, as in *the man to show ___ your passport.* However, they can *also* be missing their SUBJECT, as in the above example where both the buyer of the car and the object of *from* are missing. In this case, the missing relativized element corresponds to the head of the noun group in which the clause appears, while the implicit subject is unspecified or generic. We also mentioned the phenomenon of *whiz deletion,* in which a clause such as *sitting next to the kiln* can appear following the head. It was described there as the result of deleting *which is* from an ordinary relative clause. It could also be described as a subjectless PRESENT PARTICIPLE clause, whose implicit SUBJECT is the head of the NP.

This listing has only scratched the surface. There are many complexities that arise in dealing with the interactions between the various kinds of structuring. For example, there are restrictions on the applicability of the passive voice, as illustrated by:

> *They forced Martin to stay away.*   *They wanted Martin to stay away.*
> *Martin was forced to stay away.*   **Martin was wanted to stay away.*

There are also interactions with thematic patterns, as in *It was arranged to have the papers sent directly to Moscow,* and with ellipsis, as in *Seeing is believing.* Any standard textbook on transformational grammar can provide good examples. Akmajian and Heny (1975), for example, devote an entire chapter to the kind of problems raised by *force* and *prefer* in examples like those above.

B.1.6.3 Case roles

Section 6.5 describes the general form of a case analysis and, in particular, the way it has been integrated with systemic grammar. This section does not repeat that discussion but presents an analysis of English case structure adapted from Halliday (forthcoming). In the context of this appendix, it is not possible to go into the many subtle issues raised in Halliday's work and in other writings on case grammar. The framework presented here is intentionally simplified in many ways.

Each clause can be analyzed as expressing a *process* (or *relationship*) with one or more *central participants* and possibly with additional *circumstances.* In general, the verb (or multi-word verb, as discussed in Section B.1.5) specifies the process; the core clause functions specify the central participants; and the circumstances are described in modifiers, including prepositional phrases and (in case-marked languages) noun groups with appropriate cases. This is only a first approximation—at times the central participants are specified in prepositional phrases (as in *It was given to me by him*) and circumstances can appear in core functions (as in *Yesterday was windy*).

Clauses can be classified according to a system of five basic *process types.* Each verb (actually each verb sense) is associated with a process type and a collection of participants and circumstances. This is the *case frame* discussed in Section 6.5. In the case of multi-word verbs, such as *drop out* and *pick up,* the entire combination, rather than the verb alone, serves to identify the case frame. Figure B–13 lists the different process types and the central participant functions associated with it. We will examine each one in turn and specify more carefully the constellation of participants. We will also introduce some combined types like MENTAL-ATTRIBUTIVE, which combine roles from two of the given types. The last entry in the figure lists the circumstantial functions associated with all of the different types of clause, discussed at the end of this section.

Process type	Central participants
Material Process	Agent, Medium, Range, Beneficiary
Mental Process	Cognizant, Phenomenon
Verbal Process	Sayer, Addressee, Verbalization
Attributive	Carrier, Attribute
Equative	Identified, Identifier
Circumstances *(all types)*	Location, Extent, Motion, Cause, Manner, Accompaniment, Purpose, Matter

Figure B–13. Process types for the English clause.

B.1.6.3.1 Material process clauses

The majority of verbs in English have case frames for material process clauses. In most case analyses, pairs such as AGENT/PATIENT or ACTOR/AFFECT-ED characterize the two major participants. Halliday's analysis is based on a more general concept of MEDIUM, which he applies to all of the different process types. In this simplified presentation, we restrict that role to material process clauses, and it is therefore more similar to the AFFECTED, GOAL, and PATIENT roles proposed in other case systems. In some versions of case grammar, there is a distinction between a MEDIUM that exists prior to the process (as in *He read the paper*) and one that comes into being as a result of the process (as in *He wrote a paper*), sometimes called FACTITIVE.

The number of central participants in a material process clause can vary, as illustrated by the following sentences:

The Cheshire cat smiled enigmatically.	(3)
Max always cooks brown rice for dinner.	(4)
The millet gruel in that pot was cooked by Sam.	(5)
Unfortunately, it wasn't cooked quite long enough.	(6)
Millet cooks very slowly.	(7)
Tomorrow night Sam cooks again.	(8)
He'll probably bathe before cooking.	(9)

Example (3) is a simple one-participant clause. Its subject functions as both AGENT and MEDIUM—the cat is the one doing the smiling and the one that the smiling 'happens to.' Example (4) is a prototypical two-participant clause. Its subject is the AGENT who 'does something' and the direct object is the MEDIUM that something 'happens to.' Example (5) is the corresponding passive form, in which the MEDIUM is the subject, and the AGENT appears in a *by* prepositional phrase. Example (6) illustrates the passive form in which the AGENT does not appear. It is understood as implying some AGENT who is not mentioned. The last three examples raise a more subtle issue. Each contains a single participant (the subject) and is not in the passive form. In (7), the subject is the MEDIUM and no AGENT is specified, while in (8), the reverse is true. Example (9) illustrates a further class of verbs that can appear in one-participant active form with the implication that the subject is both the AGENT and the MEDIUM. In some ways, these are similar to simple one-participant verbs like *smile,* but they also allow two participants to be specified separately. If the two are the same and are specified explicitly, a reflexive is used, as in *He bathed himself.* Some verbs (such as *cook*) allow more than one of these forms while other verbs do not, as illustrated by:

Sam cooked the rice.	*Sam cooked.*	*The rice cooked.*
The bull broke the bottle.	* *The bull broke.*	*The bottle broke.*
The lion ate the apple.	*The lion ate.*	* *The apple ate.*

The possible interpretations for one-participant active clauses vary on a verb-by-verb basis, although there are suggestive semantic regularities as to which forms will go with certain kinds of actions. There is a sense in which the participant that is 'most relevantly affected' can appear singly. In eating, the eater is the most relevant; in breaking, it is the thing broken; while in cooking, both are relevant. Such distinctions are quite difficult to make formally, and theories dealing with them are at best provisional.

Concentrating on the two-participant case, we can draw a further distinction between MEDIUM and RANGE. In the sentence *He turned the corner, the corner* is a RANGE not a MEDIUM, as evidenced by the fact that we cannot say * *What he did to the corner was to turn it.* There are many different kinds of ranges, including those traditionally called *cognate objects* (objects implied by the verb), as in *sing a song* and *play a game.* Other examples of RANGE are *the station* in *The train reached the station* and *the wrong course* in *The winner ran the wrong course.*

In addition to normal RANGE participants, there are many sentences in which an *expendable verb* such as *make, take, have, give,* or *do* is used in what is superficially a material process clause with an object, but is interpreted as representing an action described by the NP. Phrases such as *take a walk, have a discussion, make an error, give a hoot,* and *do a favor* share with other ranges the lack of a corresponding sentence like * *What he did to the error was to make it.*

Along with the AGENT and MEDIUM or RANGE, there is the potential of a BENEFICIARY, who is either a RECIPIENT (as in *Give me that envelope*) or a CLIENT (as in *Peel me a grape*). As mentioned above in the discussion of datives, the beneficiary can appear either as a first object or in a prepositional phrase with the preposition *to* (for RECIPIENT) or *for* (for CLIENT). Once again, there is a strong dependence on the particular verb, which can be loosely but not precisely characterized along semantic lines:

Bring me a coke.	*Bring a coke to me.*	*Bring a coke for me.*
Buy me a sandwich.	**Buy a sandwich to me.*	*Buy a sandwich for me.*
Give me a cigarette.	*Give a cigarette to me.*	**Give a cigarette for me.*

Not every clause with a *to* or *for* phrase involves a BENEFICIARY, as described in the explanation of the circumstantial roles below. For example, *We lingered for an hour* involves an EXTENT and *We did it for kicks* involves CAUSE. Similarly, *He kicked the ball to the end of the field* involves a LOCATION and does not have a corresponding two-object form **He kicked the end of the field the ball.* The sentence *Give a cigarette for me,* marked above as unacceptable, can be used in a context where the action is to be done as a surrogate, but does not have the same meaning as *Give me a cigarette.*

Finally, there are some words that appear in what are superficially material process clauses, but with a meaning that does not involve a process. *Dragons don't exist* and *My room adjoined hers* are similar in structure to *Dragons don't fly* and *My dog bit hers,* but it seems a bit odd to think of existing or adjoining as processes. For the purposes of this classification, we will treat them as material process verbs, but in a semantic analysis further distinctions are necessary.

B.1.6.3.2 Mental process clauses

There are three subcategories of mental process verbs, *reaction* (*like, please*), *perception* (*see, hear*), and *cognition* (*think, know*). In all cases, there is a participant that is the COGNIZANT (or 'senser') and another that is the PHE-NOMENON. There are often symmetric pairs allowing either participant to be the subject, as in:

She liked it.	*It pleased her.*
They noticed the difference.	*The difference struck them.*
I forgot his name.	*His name escaped me.*

Unlike material process verbs, mental process verbs take the simple present tense to indicate current time. *I see you* and *Martha knows what's in the locked drawer* indicate a current event or state, while *I eat an apple* is used only in expressing habitual action or in special forms of story telling. A single event or state with a material process must be in the PRESENT PRESENT (*I am eating an apple*) instead. As with a RANGE, the PHENOMENON of a mental process clause cannot be described as having something 'done to it.' The question-answer pair *What did you do to the answer? I knew it* is decidedly aberrant.

There are some mental process verbs that can appear without explicit mention of the PHENOMENON (*I think*) and others that cannot (**I like*). When the PHENOMENON appears, it can be a fact (*I saw that he went*), an action (*I saw him cross the street*), or an object (*I saw Shoshana*). Some verbs allow the PHENOMENON to appear alone as subject or as the object of *it-extraposition,* as in:

The last float finally appeared.

It appeared that he was well. (but **That he was well appeared.*)

*John seemed.

It seemed that he was happy.

That he was happy seemed obvious. (but **That he was happy seemed.*)

B.1.6.3.3 Verbal process clauses

There are many verbs for describing verbal events, such as *say, tell, ask, describe, shout, call,* and *complain.* There is a SAYER, which is normally the subject, a VERBALIZATION, which is an object, and an ADDRESSEE, which appears either as a first-object (as in *Ask me no questions*) or in a prepositional phrase (as in *We told a story to the campers* and *Don't ask any questions of me*).

The form of these clauses is similar to material process clauses with a BENEFICIARY, but there are again some subtle differences:

We gave him a book.	*We gave a book to him.*	** We gave him.*
She told him what happened.	*? She told what happened to him.*	*She told him.*
*She said us that it was over.	*She said that it was over to us.*	** She said.*

The specific grammar of these verbs is complex. They take different kinds of objects, including clauses such as *that it was over* and *whether anything could be done* and noun groups describing linguistic objects, such as *the question* and *the fact that nothing could.* They allow the SAYER and ADDRESSEE to appear in different places in the syntax and with different prepositions. The category is distinguishable from others on grounds of meaning as much as anything else, and its boundaries are not clear.

B.1.6.3.4 Attributive clauses

Attributive clauses specify some attribute that can be ascribed to some object (they have also been called *ascriptive*). In the simplest form, the verb is a *copula* such as *be,* the CARRIER is the subject, and the ATTRIBUTE a complement. In addition to verbs that ascribe an ATTRIBUTE to a CARRIER, there are verbs that indicate a *change* in which the ATTRIBUTE is acquired, and others that indicate its *duration* over time, as illustrated in Figure B–14.

Many verbs combine attribution with some other kind of process, leading to combined types:

Type	Examples
State ('be'):	*The king was in the counting house.*
	This painting is a fake Gauguin.
Change ('become'):	*He turned 17.* (but not *He turned the corner.*)
	They grew serious. (but not *They grew celery.*)
	They got older. (but not *They got the groceries.*)
Duration ('stay'):	*The experts remained in the dark.*
	They kept scratching their heads.

Figure B–14. Attributive clauses.

Material-Attributive. In sentences like *They painted the town red* and *The children ran us ragged,* there is some kind of material process and an additional ATTRIBUTE that holds of the MEDIUM after the process. We can think of the MEDIUM and CARRIER functions as being combined. Often the verb is an expendable verb and the meaning is determined by the attribute, as in *They made me a total wreck, We had it remodeled,* and *He got the clothes washed.*

Mental-Attributive. Many mental process verbs can take a CARRIER and ATTRIBUTE together as the PHENOMENON. In one type of sentence, the CARRIER is the subject, the ATTRIBUTE a complement, and the COGNIZANT appears in a prepositional phrase with *to* if at all:

It looks OK to me. (but **It looks me OK.*)

He didn't even seem grateful.

The soup tasted funny.

Transformational grammarians have proposed a transformation called *psych movement,* which moves the object of an embedded S which is the object of a psychological verb and moves it up into the subject position in the outer S. For example, *the soup tasted funny* is derived from an underlying sentence that includes . . . *taste the soup.*

   Another form of MENTAL-ATTRIBUTIVE clause has the COGNIZANT as the subject, the CARRIER as a first object, and the ATTRIBUTE as a complement, as in *Everyone thought him incompetent.* These have been treated as being transformed from a simpler mental process clause in which an S corresponding to *he is incompetent* is the object of *think.*

Verbal-Attributive. There is a class of verbs known as *performatives,* including words like *proclaim, pronounce, declare,* and *call,* which can be thought of as combining a verbal process with some ATTRIBUTE being associated with a CARRIER as a result of that process or an act expected to result from it, as in *The coroner prounounced him dead, The court ordered it done immediately* and *They call the wind Mariah.*

B.1.6.3.5 Equative clauses

The final clause type is one in which there is an identification being made between an IDENTIFIED object and an IDENTIFIER. The most obvious cases involve *be,* but clauses involving verbs like *equal* and *represent* have been analyzed as equative as well. An equative clause can set up an identity between two objects (*The one on the left is my mother*) or between a word and a definition (*A steeple is a stack containing two green blocks and a pyramid*). It can represent lasting identity, or role playing (as in *Olivier is Hamlet tonight*).

Although it is not obvious at first, there is a phenomenon much like the active-passive distinction observable in equative clauses. The question *Who am I?* implies that I am to be identified by some identifier (perhaps a role). The question *Who is me?* reverses the roles, and could be used only in a context where *me* serves as an identifier (e.g., in discussing the cast for a dramatization of an autobiography).

B.1.6.4 Circumstantial functions

In addition to exhibiting one of the basic process types discussed above, a clause can include a number of *circumstantial functions,* indicating place, time, manner, etc., as listed above in Figure B–13. Although many of these terms

---

Location (spatial, temporal, or conceptual)
  At school we do arithmetic.   *On Thursdays* they wear kilts.
                                           In linguistics we discuss sentences.
Extent (spatial, temporal, or conceptual)
  From Paris to Rome there is no exit.   *From 2 to 4* she is in day care.
                                           He tried everything *from Ripple to LSD.*
Motion (spatial, temporal, or conceptual)
  We walked *uphill.*   They plunged *into the future.*
                                           The class proceeded *towards calculus.*
Cause
  She climbed it *because it was there.*   You will feel better *with a little exercise.*
                                           He surprised me *by going.*
Manner
  They did it *with care.*   They did it *with a planing mill.*
Accompaniment
  They did it *with their friends.*
Purpose
  They destroyed the village *to save it.* He did it *for the money.*
Matter
  We talked *about cabbages and queens.*   I dream *of Jeannie.*

Figure B–15. Circumstantial functions.

imply spatial or temporal properties, they are also used metaphorically in a variety of ways. Figure B–15 illustrates some of them.

The circumstantial functions appear in the form of adverbs, clauses, or prepositional modifiers, either at the beginning or end of the clause. As should be apparent from the table, the classification has syntactic correlates (for example, certain kinds of clauses and prepositions indicate particular roles) but is strongly motivated by semantics. In general, modifiers are simple from a syntactic point of view, although their meaning may interact with the meaning of the verb in complex ways. There are two ways in which the circumstantial functions interact more directly with the case structure: *promotion* to a core clause function and *mandatory presence*.

B.1.6.4.1 Promotion of circumstantial functions

In English, it is common for one of the circumstantial participants to appear in a core function (such as subject) rather than in a modifier. When this happens, the normal filler for that function is displaced and appears in another modifier or not at all. Figure B–16 illustrates this phenomenon for several different circumstantial functions. In each case, a circumstantial participant appears in the subject position.

This phenomenon is related to issues of theme and information structure as described in Section B.1.7. Given a complex scenario in which some action occurs at a particular time, in some manner, with causes, etc., the speaker has a variety of options in deciding what to give the most prominence. Since the SUBJECT is the most prominent clause participant, the ability to put something like the cause or time as subject adds flexibility to the organization of the clause. There is a quite diverse set of possibilities: some have the feel of metaphor; others seem like some kind of deletion; and still others seem best accounted for by extending the basic set of process types to include more specialized ones.

Location (temporal)

    1982 saw more bankruptcies than any year since 1929.

Extent

    Two weeks should handle laying the tile.

Cause

    Watergate sold more newspapers than anything since the Spanish American War.

Manner

    A sharp twist on the knob will open the cabinet.

Figure B–16. Promotion of circumstantial functions to subject.

There is no general treatment of these problems in any of the existing theories, although there are interesting fragments of analysis. Some of the specific issues dealt with in case grammar fall under this heading, such as the generalizations about the circumstances under which promotion occurs. Some of the earlier clause types can also be thought of in this way. *The general dispersed the soldiers* can be seen as a straightforward material process in which *the general* is the AGENT and *the soldiers* is the MEDIUM, or as the promotion of a CAUSE (*the general*) to subject, while the AGENT (*the soldiers*) becomes the object. Similarly, *The provost applauded the decision* can be seen as a promotion of a CAUSE directly to the OBJECT function.

A related phenomenon is the use of verbs like *have, get,* and *make* to represent causation, as in *He had us all run around the gym, He made us do a hundred pushups,* and *He got us to shine his shoes.* In this presentation it is impossible to explore the issues fully, and our goal is simply to point out that complexities like this do occur.

B.1.6.4.2 Mandatory circumstantial modifiers

Some verbs require a modifier of a particular form. Section 6.5 introduced the example of *blame,* with its specific use of *for* and *on.* Section B.1.5.2 (on multi-word verbs) pointed out that combinations of a verb and preposition such as *deal with* have the property that the verb cannot appear without the preposition and carry the same meaning.

As with many transitivity phenomena, this has not been incorporated into a comprehensive syntactic theory. Many computer systems for parsing include special mechanisms allowing a dictionary entry for a verb to include information about the prepositions with which it combines. These are discussed further in Chapter 7.

B.1.7 Theme and information structure

The mood and transitivity structure of a clause play a large role in determining the order of its elements, but there is a good deal of variability both within these systems and in addition to them. This degree of freedom is used in organizing clauses (especially sentences) to indicate theme and information. For example, it is a principle of cognitive psychology that the elements near the beginning and end of any sequence are more salient than those in the middle. The same principles apply to language, and there are many mechanisms that have the function of controlling what appears in the more salient places.

In systemic grammar, there is a distinction between the *theme system,* dealing with placement at the beginning of a clause, and the *information system,* dealing with placement at the end of a tone group. The theme (the initial element) is in some sense what the clause is 'about,' while the elements at the end tend to convey 'new' information. The interactions between these are quite complex, and we will present an analysis that is simpler in two ways. First, it does not attempt to separate the two systems, speaking instead of positions at the two ends. Second, it deals with sentences. Theme and information structures often cut across clause boundaries, and many thematic phenomena that apply to sentences as a whole do not apply to clauses embedded within them. The distinction is not a sharp one, and one can find thematic issues in the structure of every clause.

Sentences with essentially the same ideational content (the same propositions) can appear in very different forms, as illustrated by:

We demand freedom.

Freedom we demand!

Freedom is what we demand.

Freedom is demanded by us.

What we demand is freedom.

It's freedom that we demand.

It's we who demand freedom.

The first obvious issue is the choice of which element will appear first and which will appear last. There are also more subtle issues related to style and intention. Native speakers of a language are quite sensitive to the meaning conveyed by the choices. For example, the passive voice reduces the feeling of involvement of the agent in the action. It is used extensively in scientific writing, which attempts to move the scientist out of the thematic spotlight, but it seems absurd in the context of a placard proclaiming *Freedom is demanded by us.*

There are also issues of coherence. For example, the first pair of sentences below seems much more reasonable than the second:

Yesterday we went to the beach. The waves pounded on the shore.

The beach was where we went yesterday. The shore, the waves pounded.

There are no comprehensive theories of the effects of thematic arrangements. In this appendix, we will just point out the different mechanisms that can be applied, analyzing them in terms of the natural ordering of elements and the possible 'movements' that change the ordering. These movements correspond roughly to some transformations that have been proposed, but are not described here in transformational terms. For a detailed discussion see Halliday and Hasan (1976) and Halliday (forthcoming).

B.1.7.1 Thematic elements

The clause structure described in Section B.1.2 shows that the prototypical sentence (simple declarative) begins with the subject, possibly preceded by one or more modifiers. The subject is the natural (or *unmarked*) theme, but we can look at the modifiers appearing before it as a complex set of thematic elements, some providing textual continuity and others establishing the communicative act of the sentence. Halliday analyzes the following sentence (taken from a recorded text) as containing seven thematic elements of three types: *textual, interpersonal,* and *ideational.*

> *Well, but in that case, Anne, why d'ya think the idea isn't very good?*

The textual elements are labeled *continuative (well), structural (but),* and *cohesive (in that case).* The interpersonal ones are the *vocative (Anne), mood (why),* and *modality (d'ya think).* Finally, there is the ideational theme, *the idea.* We will not go into this analysis in detail, but it illustrates the thematic complexity of conversational English.

Dealing for the moment with the ideational theme, we can see many different resources that the grammar provides for *thematizing* a desired element. We can group these according to whether their main effect is moving things to the front, moving them to the rear, or both.

B.1.7.2 Moving to the front

Core clause function assignment. Many of the mechanisms discussed in the previous sections can be viewed as means of controlling the theme. Passive voice can be thought of as a mechanism to allow one of the objects that would normally appear later to come to the front. This can involve movement out of levels of embedding, as in *The carrots were feared to have been destroyed by the floods* and *This tree has never been slept in before.* The promotion of a circumstantial participant to the subject has the same effect, as in *Advertising sells cigarettes.*

Initial modifiers. The presence of pre-subject modifiers (ideational ones) can also be seen as a thematic choice, as in the difference between *For a while he was king* and *He was king for a while.* There is one peculiar form in which a negative adverb (such as *never* or *seldom*) is thematized and the sentence is put into an inverted form similar to that for a question, as in *Never had I seen such a mess.*

Preposing (topicalization). In addition to the options provided by mood and transitivity, an element can be simply moved to the initial thematic position. This construct is generally avoided in written English but is used extensively in speaking, where intonation patterns help clarify the roles being played by the different elements. It is often used in contrastive patterns, such as *An honest mistake we can ignore, but this kind of consistent mismanagement we just can't allow.* It is related to the phenomena handled by the hold list in ATN grammars, but must be treated somewhat differently. The moved element can be a complement, an NP appearing at any level of embedding, or the main verb:

> *People like that* you don't mess with.
>
> *My nephew* I want you to give all my houseplants.
>
> *Happy* he's never been.
>
> *Dig* we must.

In these examples, the order of the other elements is left unchanged. There are other cases in which subject and verb are reversed, as in *On the roof sat a bunch of tiny reindeer.* For attributive clauses, the complement appears before the verb and the subject after it, as in *Green was my valley* and *A happy people are they who know the Lord.* The verb still agrees with the subject even though their order is reversed, and the construct has a poetic sound.

Clefting. A surprising number of sentences in spoken English have *be* as their main verb and *it* as their subject. They are not just impersonal equatives like *It is nice today,* but include sentences with a complex form in which the complement is followed by a relative clause:

> *It was Kilroy who did it.*
>
> *It's money that I need.*
>
> *It's having been too rough with him that I regret.*

These are known as *cleft sentences* and have been a source of interest (and difficulty) in transformational grammar. Like preposing, they allow an arbitrary element of the clause to be pulled to the front. However, instead of simply appearing at the front, it follows *it* and a form of *be.* In some cases (such as *It was Kilroy who did it*), the resulting form still has the same theme as the prototypical form (*Kilroy did it*), but there is a difference in emphasis that is obvious though hard to characterize formally.

Pseudo-clefting. In the cleft sentences just described, a single element (such as a noun group) is moved into a thematic position. There is a related phenomenon (called *pseudo-clefting*) that allows nearly any combination of the elements of the clause to appear at front or back. The main verb of a pseudo-cleft sentence is *be,* but instead of having *it* as the subject, a nominalized relative clause is created. Dummy verbs like *do* can be used to enable the subject and verb to appear in different halves.

What we need is a good five-cent nickel.

Where we put it was on top of the radio.

Why we did it was to convince them to vote Peace and Freedom.

What he will do to the record is obliterate it.

What he will be after doing it is exhausted.

What we did then was give them back their clothes.

Pseudo-clefting can be done in reverse (with the relative clause as the complement rather than the subject) as in *A big hug is what you need most right now.* Not every sentence with a nominalized relative clause as its subject and *be* as a main verb is an example of clefting or pseudo-clefting. For example, *What we need is obvious to anyone who thinks about it* is a normal attributive clause.

B.1.7.3 Moving to the end

Since any move in one direction causes the remaining elements to shift, every shift can be thought of as a movement in both directions. However, the following phenomena are primarily concerned with what winds up at the end rather than the beginning. Of course, phenomena such as clefting and pseudo-clefting can be thought of in this way too, since in dividing the sentence into two halves they are concerned with both the beginning and the end.

There-subject. The pseudo-subject *there* can be used in a special form that puts the normal subject at the end of the sentence, as in:

Once there lived three bears.

There exists a problem in communication.

There were expected to be a million butterflies in the parade.

Among the daffodils there soared a magenta dragonfly.

There are some reasons to treat *there* as the subject and others not to. For example, it is used where the subject normally would appear in tag questions like *There was a problem, wasn't there?* However, number agreement clearly goes with the displaced phrase (*There was a... There were three...*). There are a number of problems related to this construct that have been treated in the transformational literature.

Relative postposing. A relative clause can be shifted from its place in a noun group to the end of the sentence:

A book was published last year that contained a recipe for bat stew.

We gave somebody a ride who was hitchhiking from here to China.

She had been given a ride in a Buick to Denver the day before that had a chrome plated dashboard.

When the NP losing its relative is deeply embedded, the result is somewhat less acceptable, and sentences with ambiguous postposed relatives such as *A man sold me a car that was smoking a cigar* are often given as examples of sloppy English.

Heavy NP shift. An NP functioning as an object of a clause can be moved to the end of the sentence (past one or more modifiers), but only when it is relatively long and complex:

> *I received a letter last week*
>
> *I received last week a letter from an old girl-friend I hadn't seen for years.*
>
> **I received last week a letter.*

The exact criteria for 'heaviness' are hard to formalize, and sentences that sound completely unacceptable in isolation are often natural when said in context with appropriate intonation and stress.

It-Extraposition. When the subject of a clause is itself a clause (any of the various kinds that can fill the subject function), it can be replaced with *it* and moved to the end. The different types of extraposed clauses are shown in Figure B–17. This kind of extraposition can be applied to relative clauses as well as sentences, as illustrated in the example with *astound*.

As with many of these movements, there are often sentences for which the corresponding 'unmoved' form does not exist:

> *It happens that I will be there myself.*   ** That I will be there myself happens.*
>
> *It would surprise me if he won.*   ** If he won would surprise me.*

In order to account for this formally, it is necessary to postulate a deep structure like the unacceptable sentence and to make the movement obligatory. It can be quite difficult to state regular rules relating the specific constructions and verbs for which such obligatory movements apply. In some cases, there is a superficially corresponding sentence, but with a different meaning, as with the pair *It surprised me when he left* and *When he left surprised me*.

Type	Example
Report	It amazes me *that he gets through the hoop every time.*
Whether	Does it really matter *whether anyone finishes the ostrich?*
Bound	It changes your perspective *when you have a child of your own.*
For-To	It was a bad mistake *for him to send them in.*
Report	The next one was an example it astounded me *he could think up.*

Figure B–17. Extraposed clause types.

Pronoun extraposition. A somewhat more colloquial form of extraposition involves extraposing a subject that is not a clause and leaving behind a personal pronoun agreeing in number, person, and gender. This structure appears much more often in spoken than in written English.

> They behaved themselves last night, *the children.*
> He's a tough cookie, *that John.*
> It was a pleasant experience, *that conference.*

Tag questions. While not really a form of movement, tag questions are similar in that they give emphasis to the polarity of a question by reiterating it at the end, as in:

> You really are going to do it, *aren't you?*
> They believed him, *didn't they?*
> He didn't believe it would work, *did he?*
> There can be more than two, *can't there?*

In various places in the book, the detailed structure of tag questions (for example, the reversal of negative and affirmative and the use of *do*) is used to elucidate details of syntax. Tag questions have played this role in many different grammars, since they are complex enough to provide interesting detail, but the phenomena are rather clean and can be formalized.

B.2 The noun group

The core clause constituents (the subject, objects, and complements) are typically *noun groups.* Just as a clause is built around a main verb, a noun group is built around its *head noun.* In traditional phrase structure and transformational grammars, the term 'noun phrase' (and the corresponding symbol NP, or NP) are used in place of the systemic grammar term 'noun group.' We will retain the familiar symbol NP, but use the systemic grammar term 'group' in discussing these and other groups in this appendix.

Roughly, a noun group can be thought of as referring to or describing an object (or set of objects). It can stand alone as an utterance only in cases of ellipsis (as discussed in Section B.3.4) where the hearer can fill in an appropriate full clause context (e.g., in answer to a question). Its content can be thought of as conveying two different aspects of reference:

Description of the object. The head noun, along with its preceding modifying nouns and adjectives and its following qualifying phrases, describes a thing. Words like *arthropod* and *unpredictable,* phrases like *on the auction block,* and clauses such as *that swallowed the canary* all convey properties of a thing or the relations it has with other things.

Designation of the object. The initial components of a noun group, including the determiner, quantifiers, and numbers, provide a different kind of information. They specify the status of the thing or things being described—whether it is known or unknown, a single item or a set. There are complex interactions between the function of a noun group and the choice of its designating elements. For example, in the question *Did any children survive?* the word *any* indicates that the answer is yes if there is at least one, while in the command *Shoot any intruder!* it indicates that all things fitting the description are to be included in the command.

The noun group is a much simpler syntactic structure than the clause, and has received correspondingly less attention in the generative grammar literature. Its syntactic structure (as distinct from its semantic structure) is rigid and relatively simple, so a straightforward slot-and-filler analysis specifying a precise ordering captures most of the syntactic variability.

B.2.1 Noun group functions

Like clauses, noun groups fill a variety of roles in other structures (including other noun groups), as outlined in Figure B–18.

B.2.2 Prototypical structure for a common noun group

In describing the detailed structure of the noun group, it is useful to start with a description of a simplified prototype, illustrated in Figure B–19. This is the structure of a COMMON noun group. Other kinds of noun groups are discussed in Section B.2.3. Functions with plural names (like DESCRIBERS) can take a

Function	Example
Subject of clause	*Everyone* has a secret desire.
Object of clause	We bemoaned *the fate of humankind.*
Complement of clause	All of us on this bus are *bozos.*
Object of preposition group	In *a very short time* we did it.
Object of adjunct group	Is it fancier than *my file cabinet?*
Modifier of clause	Wiggle it *this way.*
Describer of noun group	He assumed a *man of the world* attitude.
Nonrestrictive qualifier	My wife, *Carol,* is a doctor.
Restrictive qualifier	My brother *Steve* lives in Colorado.
Direct address	You, *my friend,* are in for a long lonely wait.
Possessive determiner	*The former Shah of Iran*'s ceremonial sword

Figure B–18.   Syntactic functions of noun groups.

Segment	Function	Examples
Determiner sequence	Pre-determiner	*half, both, all*
	Determiner	*the, a, this, every*
	Ordinal	*first, second, last*
	Cardinal	*one, two, three*
Modifiers	Describers	*big, purple, enchanted*
	Classifiers	*stone, retaining*
Head	Head	*walls, person, ones*
Qualifiers	Restrictive qualifiers	*in town, that flies*
	Nonrestrictive qualifiers	*John, whom you already know*
—	Possessive marker	*-'s*

Figure B–19. Sequence of elements in a prototypical noun group.

sequence of fillers, while those in the singular (like ORDINAL) take only one or a conjoined structure. Unlike the clause, the ordering of constituents in the noun group is relatively fixed. Most of the choices are realized by including or omitting possible constituents and by features associated with the lexical items themselves. We have grouped the participants into several segments and will discuss these separately below.

B.2.2.1 The determiner sequence

A common noun group begins with a sequence of words chosen from specific closed word classes. There is a limited set of possible words at each position (ignoring the ability to use any integer as a cardinal or ordinal), and there are complex rules governing the possible combinations of choices. The following description gives only the basic restrictions.

Pre-determiner. The pre-determiner must be one of the words *all* or *half,* as in *all the way home* or a phrase consisting of a cardinal or quantifier (or *none*) followed by *of,* as in *three of those red dogs* and *each of the six candidates.* There is an overlap between structures of this kind and *partitive* noun groups, like *a bunch of grapes* and *a group of people,* in which there is a head referring to a collection (*bunch, group,* etc.) followed by a qualifying PP beginning with *of.*

Determiner. The determiner can be an article (*the, a, an*), a demonstrative pronoun (*this, that, these, those*), a quantifier (*each, every, some, most, many, few, no,...*), a question determiner (*which, what, how many*), or another noun group that is *possessive* (as in *all the king's men*). As examples of allowable combinations of pre-determiner, quantifier, cardinal, and number, consider the phrases:

some person	some people	some three people	some of them
each person	*each people	each three people	each of them
every person	*every people	every three people	*every of them
*all person	all people	all three people	all of them
no person	no people	no three people	*no of them
*none person	*none people	*none three people	none of them

The volume on meaning will describe problems of quantification and reference at length, discussing the meanings of noun groups with different combinations of determiners and quantifiers in some detail. It is important to note that the meaning depends both on the specific sequence and on the context in which it appears.

Ordinal. The ordinal is a number such as *first, second,* or *two thousand eight hundred and nineteenth,* or one of a small class of other ordinals such as *last* and *next.* It can appear only in a DEFINITE noun group.

Cardinal. The cardinal is a number such as *one, two,* or *two thousand eight hundred and nineteen.* If it is *one,* the group is SINGULAR; otherwise it is PLURAL.

B.2.2.2 Describers and classifiers

Following the determiner sequence there can be a sequence of modifiers of various sorts. They can be selected from a variety of word classes, as shown in Figure B–20.

There can be a sequence of mixtures of these, but there is a fundamental division into two roles. The *describers* can also be used as the complement of an attributive clause like:

> The flowers were purple.
> The children were laughing.
> The toys were broken.

But the *classifiers* (which must all follow the describers) cannot be transplanted:

Type	Examples
Adjective	the *happy purple* flowers
Present participle	the *laughing dancing* children
Past participle	the *deserted broken* toys
Noun	the *steel kitchen* knife

Figure B–20. Describers and classifiers.

a kitchen knife   * The knife was kitchen.
a fishing trip   * The trip was fishing.
some horse hair   * The hair is horse.

The exact rules for selecting and ordering these elements are very subtle; they have to do with a kind of scale of 'inherentness' on a semantic level, and nobody has really worked out a good formalism for them. Consider the difference between *a beautiful new red wooden wagon* and *?a red wooden new beautiful wagon*.

It is possible for a phrase such as an adjunct group or clause to appear as a DESCRIBER, but only when it is quite short, as in:

a *larger than usual* crowd
a *soon to be released* book
a *tree lined* glen
a *man eating* tiger
a *one eyed one horned* flying purple people eater

We cannot say *a many large oak tree lined glen* or *the papered last year by the wallpaper company room*. Often when written, such phrases are connected with hyphens, as in *man-eating* or *soon-to-be-released*.

When there is more than one CLASSIFIER, the structure relating them is not syntactically marked. For example, *iron soup kettle* and *chicken soup kettle* can both be described as a sequence of two classifiers followed by a head, but their interpretation indicates that they should be grouped differently. Even when grouping is not ambiguous, there are different interpretations that can be marked by stress patterns, as in the difference between a <u>head</u> hunter and the *head <u>hunter</u>* (the one in charge), or between a <u>toy</u> factory and a *toy <u>factory</u>* (for a child to play with). In general, this has not been treated as a syntactic issue but as a semantic interpretation of a syntactic structure which is simply a sequence of classifiers.

Some words can appear as either an ordinal or a classifier, but with different meanings. In the phrase *a first child,* the word *first* is a classifier describing a type of child. It is different from the ordinal *first* in *the first child to get sick,* as indicated by the fact that it can appear in an INDEFINITE noun group.

B.2.2.3 Head

The head of a common noun group is, as one would expect, a common noun. Syntactically, there is not much to say about it except that it is the element that must always appear (except in cases of ellipsis as discussed in Section B.3.4). The number of the noun group as a whole is determined by the number of its head. The main difference among the different kinds of noun groups as listed in Section B.2.3 below is in the word class of the head.

B.2.2.4 Qualifiers

Following the head of a noun group there can be a sequence of *qualifiers,* each of which is either *restrictive* or *nonrestrictive.* A restrictive qualifier serves as part of the identifying description of an object, while a nonrestrictive qualifier provides an additional piece of information about it.

In writing, nonrestrictive qualifiers are set off by commas. In speech, they are each in a separate tone group. The qualifier function can be filled by any of the syntactic structures indicated in Figure B–21. When a noun group appears as a nonrestrictive qualifier, as in *Carol, my wife,* it is called an *appositive.*

In simple syntactic accounts, the qualifiers are not further analyzed, but are simply included as a sequence following the head. However, if we consider

---

Restrictive

Relative clause
> the elephant *that came to brunch*
> the party *they gave*
> the people *setting up camp by the stream*
> the place *to have your back massaged*

Adjunct group
> a heart *as big as all the world*
> a dessert *too sweet to eat all at once*

Preposition group
> an octopus pizza *with all the trimmings*
> a day *in the woods*

Participle
> the time *remaining*
> the fare *specified*

Nonrestrictive

Relative clause
> the elephant, *whom I had met previously,*

Nominal clause
> their idea, *to get it all over with at once,*

Adjunct group
> her answer, *better than all the rest,*

Preposition group
> his solution, *with all of its faults,*

Noun group
> our Toyota, *the car we bought last year,*

Figure B–21.   Structures that function as qualifiers.

noun groups whose heads are nominalized verbs, we see strong parallels between the appearance of qualifiers (as in *the destruction of the temple by heathens*) and the case roles (both central and circumstantial) of the corresponding clause (*the heathens destroyed the temple*). Possessive determiners can also carry roles related to the core clause participants, as in *the heathens' destruction of the temple* and *the temple's destruction by the heathens*.

Much of the analysis of transitivity outlined in Section B.1.6 can be carried over to noun groups. There are different details of correspondence between the superficial syntactic roles (determiner, object of prepositional qualifier, etc.) and the case roles (agent, beneficiary, etc.), and there is specific dependence on the form of the nominalization, as illustrated by:

Beverly bought the car for $15,000	*Beverly's purchase of the car for $15,000*
The car cost Beverly $15,000.	*The car's cost of $15,000 to Beverly*
$15,000 bought Beverly the car	**$15,000's purchase of the car to Beverly*
The car was sold to Beverly for $15,000.	*? the car's sale to Beverly for $15,000*

In a grammar or parsing system that made use of a case analysis for clauses, it would be appropriate to apply it to these kinds of noun groups as well.

B.2.2.5 Possessives

The final element that can appear in a noun group is the possessive marker *'s*. In colloquial English, this can appear at the end of a QUALIFIER, not just at the end of the HEAD, as in *The man that is happy's response*. A noun group that has a possessive element functions as the determiner of another noun group.

B.2.3 Noun group features and systems

The previous section dealt primarily with common noun groups. These are the most elaborate, but there are several other kinds, as shown in Figure B–22. As with the other system networks in this appendix, it is abbreviated and does not directly express all of the dependencies. For example, the full set of choices for PERSON is applicable only to pronoun groups, as discussed below.

Examples of noun group features

all the bright shiny new computer gadgets I know of
> **Features:** Common, Definite, Plural, Third
> **Functions:** [Pre-determiner: *all*] [Determiner: *the*] [Describers: *bright, shiny, new*] [Classifiers: *computer*] [Head: *gadgets*] [Restrictive qualifiers: *I know of*]

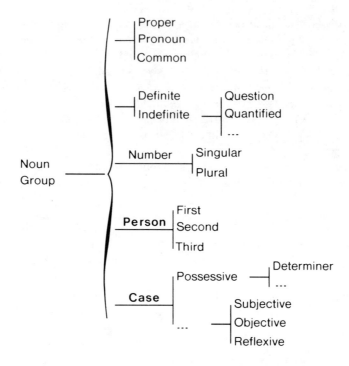

Figure B–22. Choice systems for the noun group.

those first three students in line, whom I have never seen before
   Features: Common, Definite, Plural, Third
   Functions: [Determiner: *those*] [Ordinal: *first*] [Cardinal: *three*] [Head: *students*] [Restrictive qualifiers: *in line*] [Nonrestrictive qualifiers: *whom I have never seen before*]

Alfred Lobachevsky, my uncle
   Features: Proper, Definite, Singular, Third
   Functions: [Head: *Alfred Lobachevsky*] [Nonrestrictive qualifiers: *my uncle*]

anybody living who has any sense
   Features: Pronoun, Indefinite, Singular, Third
   Functions: [Head: *anybody*] [Restrictive qualifiers: *living, who has any sense*]

Mamie was *what famous president's* wife?
   Features: Common, Indefinite, Question, Singular, Third, Possessive, Determiner
   Functions: [Determiner: *what*] [Describers: *famous*] [Head: *president*] [Possessive marker: *'s*]

whom that you know of
   Features: Pronoun, Indefinite, Question, Third, Objective
   Functions: [Head: *whom*] [Restrictive qualifiers: *that you know of*]

he who hesitates
Features: Pronoun, Definite, Singular, Third, Subjective
Functions: [Head: *he*] [Restrictive qualifiers: *who hesitates*]

Summary of noun group features

NOUN-GROUP (—)

Realization: Every noun group includes a HEAD, whose type determines the next level of categorization.

Examples: *a noun group; beans.*

PROPER (NOUN-GROUP)

Realization: The head is a proper noun or a sequence of proper nouns. The exact details of this sequence differ for different kinds of names. There are specialized forms for people, places, publications, etc. In general, proper noun groups do not have constituents other than the head, but there are examples with other constituents.

Examples: *Leland Stanford Jr.; San Francisco; little Timmy; Ivan the Terrible.*

PRONOUN (NOUN-GROUP)

Realization: The head is a pronoun, whose case, person, and number features determine those of the noun group as a whole (see discussion below). Pronoun noun groups normally contain only the head, but there can also be restrictive qualifiers, as in *Everything comes to him who waits*. There are four different kinds of pronouns, each with a slightly different structure: *personal, demonstrative, question,* and *quantified.* Personal pronouns were discussed at length in Section 6.3 on systemic grammar. The others are discussed further in Section B.4.3. A qualifier following a quantified pronoun can be a single adjective or participle, which is not the case for other types of noun group (e.g., we can say *something green,* but not **the lawn green* or **whom green*). The meaning of a noun group headed by a quantified pronoun is closely related to the parallel common noun group containing a separate quantifier and head (e.g., *some green thing*).

Examples: *him; myself; hers; who; what; whom that you know; this; that; these; those in the box; something; nothing you would care about; everywhere in town.*

COMMON (NOUN-GROUP)

Realization: The head is a common noun. This is the most elaborate type of noun group, allowing the filling of all the different possible roles described in Figure B–19. It is possible to delete the head in forms like *one of a kind* and *the first three into the ring.*

Examples: *My oldest brother; a thousand giggling circus clowns; the gentleman I saw you with last night; every chocolate cake in sight.*

DEFINITE (NOUN-GROUP)

Realization: Noun groups can be classified as DEFINITE or INDEFINITE, which affects both their function in other structures and their interpretation. Proper noun groups are DEFINITE. Pronoun groups with a personal or demonstrative pronoun as their head are DEFINITE. For common noun groups, those with a definite article (*the, this, that, those,* or *these*) or a possessive as their determiner are DEFINITE.

Examples: *Salvador Allende; himself; that; the sky; those wonderful ideas.*

INDEFINITE (NOUN-GROUP)

Realization: INDEFINITE noun groups include pronoun noun groups with question or quantified pronouns, since their heads are INDEFINITE, and common noun groups with an indefinite article (*a, an*) as a determiner or with no determiner at all (as in *green eggs* and *three blind mice*).

Examples: *traditional old stories; a stitch in time; four fine feathered friends; anything you can say; which baby; who.*

QUESTION (INDEFINITE NOUN-GROUP)

Realization: A question noun group is a common noun group with a question determiner or a pronoun group with a question pronoun as its head. Question pronouns (*who, whom, what*) are marked for animate versus inanimate, but question determiners (*which, how many, what*) are not.

Examples: *what button; who in this office; how many times.*

QUANTIFIED (INDEFINITE NOUN-GROUP)

Realization: A quantified noun group has a quantifier for a determiner or a quantified pronoun as a head.

Examples: *anything you can say; a few minutes; no idea; every time he does it.*

Number

SINGULAR (NOUN-GROUP)

Realization: The number of a noun group is affected by its head, determiner, and cardinal. When the noun group is the subject of a sentence, it must agree with the verb in number. English, unlike many languages, does not mark describers or qualifiers for number. If the head is a pronoun or proper noun, it has a number feature agreeing with that of the group a whole (see Section B.4.3). If it is a common noun, it may have one or more number features (e.g., *fish*), at least one of which must agree with the noun group as a whole. If the group contains a determiner or cardinal, it must also agree in number.

Examples: *Harold; everyone; the rainbow; a long time; one meatball; each step of the way.*

PLURAL (NOUN-GROUP)

Realization: The number of a noun group is plural if it is not singular. Some noun groups can be both (e.g., *which sheep*).

Examples: *The Smiths; those old melodies; summer evenings; twenty-four bridges; all residents of Metuchen.*

Person

FIRST, SECOND, or THIRD (NOUN-GROUP)

Realization: Noun groups can be classified according to person. Pronoun groups are FIRST, SECOND, or THIRD, depending on the pronoun. All others are THIRD. If a noun group is the subject of a sentence, it must agree in person with the verb. Syntactically, there is no SECOND SINGULAR in English, since *you* always takes a plural verb form (such as *are*), even when it refers to one individual.

Examples: *I; yourself; the other guy.*

Case

POSSESSIVE (NOUN-GROUP)

Realization: A possessive noun group is either a pronoun group whose head is a possessive pronoun or a common or proper noun group that ends with the marker *'s.*

Examples: *her; mine; the committee's; whose; somebody's; which person's; Shoshana's.*

DETERMINER (POSSESSIVE NOUN-GROUP)

Realization: Pronoun groups further distinguish between possessive determiners such as *my, your,* and *their* and other possessives, such as *mine, yours,* and *theirs.* Pronoun groups with the DETERMINER feature can function as the determiner of another noun group, while those without it function as a normal noun group, as in *Mine is bigger than yours.* For all other noun groups, the two forms are identical.

Examples: *my; the antelope's; whose; anyone's.*

SUBJECTIVE, OBJECTIVE, or REFLEXIVE (NOUN-GROUP)

Realization: In addition to possessives, pronoun groups are marked by their head as SUBJECTIVE (*he, she, I*), OBJECTIVE (*him, her, me*) or REFLEXIVE (*himself, herself, myself*). All other noun groups that are not POSSESSIVE are neutral to this distinction. The role a noun group can play in other structures is controlled by its case. For example, the subject of an ordinary clause must be SUBJECTIVE and the object must be OBJECTIVE or REFLEXIVE. REFLEXIVE also occurs in special constructs like *Einstein himself couldn't have done it.*

Examples: *she; her; herself; everyone; the winners.*

B.3 Other groups and specialized structures

This section describes a variety of other structures that must be accounted for in a full syntactic description of English. None of them has the complexity or variety of the clause or noun group, and they exhibit a great deal of idiosyncratic patterning. In transformational grammar, these secondary structures are generally analyzed as the surface remains of clauses that appear in the deep structure. In systemic grammar, some of them (such as adverb groups) are seen as independent units, while others are seen as sub-segments of the constituent structure of the larger units. In this appendix, we will deal with them in a traditional surface-oriented manner, treating them for the most part as though they were independent units. This presentation gives only the basic ideas without much of the finer detail that would be needed in writing a comprehensive grammar.

B.3.1 Preposition groups

The preposition group has a very simple structure and is one of the most commonly appearing constituents of English. It can function as an adjunct to a clause (*On the tenth day, Noah sent out a dove*) or a qualifier of a noun group (*a pizza with anchovies*). It is made up of a *head* consisting of a preposition or multi-word preposition (like *next to* or *in front of*), followed by an OBJECT, which is a noun group or a clause that can serve nominal functions (as in *by following them*).

In forms of grammar other than systemic grammar, this structure is called a *prepositional phrase* and is abbreviated PP. As noted earlier, we have used this abbreviation throughout the book for compatibility, even though it does not match the name 'preposition group.'

Because the last element of a preposition group is usually a noun group, which in turn can end with a preposition group, it is common to have recursively nested structures like *the appearance of the man under the tree with a broken branch near the edge of the road to the town with a market*. One of the common problems for parsers is the high degree of structural ambiguity due to the fact that the structure need not be purely right branching. The sentence *I saw the man on the hill with the telescope* allows five different interpretations. These can be diagrammed as follows, putting parentheses around each complete noun group:

> *(I) saw (the man on (the hill with (the telescope)))*
> *(I) saw (the man on (the hill) with (the telescope))*
> *(I) saw (the man on (the hill)) with (the telescope)*
> *(I) saw (the man) on (the hill with (the telescope))*
> *(I) saw (the man) on (the hill) with (the telescope)*

In some of these, the man has a telescope; in others, I used a telescope; and in others, the telescope sits on the hill. In some, I am on the hill, while in others, the man is. A phrase with one more level of preposition group has 14 possible parsings, and the example in the previous paragraph has 429. In general, the number of possible parsings is the *Catalan number*, which is the number of distinct binary trees of a given size. Many parsers incorporate special mechanisms for dealing with this combinatorial ambiguity, depending on some kind of semantic analysis to determine the scope. In general, most of the combinations will not make sense. For example, *(the appearance of (the man under the tree) with (a broken branch))*... makes sense only if appearances can have branches.

Some preposition groups do not have an ordinary noun group as an OBJECT, but instead have a single noun or noun sequence, as in *on time, at work,* and *by freight train.* These are somewhat idiomatic and can include nouns (such as *train*) which could not normally appear as the head of a singular noun group without a determiner (see the discussion of mass and count nouns in Section B.4.3).

B.3.2 Adjective and adverb groups

There are a number of specialized constructs whose head is an adjective or adverb. We will refer to them generically as *adjunct groups.* They lie somewhere between ordinary syntax (with its general rules for structures) and idioms. They have an idiomatic feel, but are productive in that they allow almost any adjective or adverb as their head. Adjunct groups serve a variety of functions, as illustrated in Figure B–23. Some of the various patterns for adjectives and adverbs are:

old	*soon*
how old	*how soon*
as old as the hills	*as soon as I can*
older than you would think	*sooner than I expected*
too old to behave like that	*too soon to suit me*
old enough to know better	*soon enough to catch him*
so old that it creaks	*so soon that my head spun*
not so old	*not so soon*
ready to wear	*soon to be complete*
yellow with age	*all wrong*
six years old	
six year old	
worth looking at	

Function	Example
Complement of a clause	He is *old enough to know better.*
Modifier of a clause	She ran *more quickly than the wind.*
Describer of a noun group	a *bigger than usual* crowd
Qualifier of a noun group	a crowd *bigger than we had expected*

Figure B–23. Functions of adjective and adverb groups.

In transformational grammar, these are handled by transformations that are specific to each pattern. We have mentioned some of these (such as tough movement) in earlier sections. In other grammars, they are often just included as special cases in the arcs or rules of the grammar. In some cases, these more complex constructs function in the same places as a simpler adjective or adverb, while in others they can take on new functions. For example, in *As happy as he seems to be, I wouldn't want to trade places,* the adjective group serves as an initial clause modifier, while the simpler *happy* would not be allowed. As another example, we have:

He is old	He is ninety years old	*He is ninety year old
*He is an old	*He is a ninety years old	He is a ninety year old
He is an old man	*He is a ninety years old man	He is a ninety year old man

In addition to adjective and adverb groups, there are a number of other specialized constructs that can be thought of as local patterns. In one major ATN grammar of English (Bates, 1978), half of the arcs were included to cover these constructs. Figure B–24 illustrates a few of them. Some of these are rather straightforward, involving a modifier (like *more or less*). Others (such as times and dates) are quite complex.

B.3.3 Conjunction

One of the most prevalent and complex constructions in English (and perhaps in all languages) is *conjunction.* The sentence *They crossed the stream and she tied up her horse and the mules* can be analyzed as containing two conjunction constructs of the form *X and Y.* At the top level, there are two conjoined

Type	Examples
Number	*at least three; exactly two; more than six; about a dozen; ten or more; one thousand four hundred and seventeen*
Quantifier	*not every; more or less all*
Preposition	*right after; just above; sort of inside*
Question pronoun	*What all did he say?; Just who was there?*
Date	*Tuesday; February 24, 1946; March 17th; Tuesday the twelfth; next Monday*
Time	*3 o'clock; half past twelve; 4:23 p.m.; a quarter of noon*
Name	*John Jacob Astor, III; J.L. Austin; King Henry the Eighth*
Address	*2020 21st St., Greeley, Colo.; 1 Preston Park Square*
Money	*$143.17; 3 pounds Sterling; 2 pounds 5*
Institution	*San Francisco General Hospital; Colorado State University*

Figure B–24. Special syntactic constructs.

Conjoined unit	Examples
Sentence	*Stop that or I'll tell Mommy.*
	He said it, didn't he, or did I misunderstand?
Clause	Show me a politician *who listens or who cares.*
	It surprised me *that you went and that he didn't.*
	What I said and what he heard didn't quite agree.
Noun Group	*The owl, the frog, and the pussycat* went to sea.
Preposition Group	Open it *with a key or with a hammer.*
Adjective Group	Is she *faster than a bullet and stronger than a locomotive?*
Adverb Group	I left *as quickly as I could but not as quickly as she wanted.*
Noun	There were some unripe *apples and bananas.*
Adjective	They were covered with *brown and purple* spots.
Verb	They *showered and dressed* in less than five minutes.
	He *may or may not* be there.
Ordinal	The *first and second* items were handled quickly.
Cardinal	Can you send me *three or four* helpers?
Quantifier	We did it *each and every* day.
Adverb	She took care of it *quickly, cleanly, and efficiently.*
Pronoun	*He or she* who hesitates is lost.
Preposition	We need a government *of, for, and by* the people.

Figure B–25. Conjoined structures.

sentences. Internally, there are two conjoined noun groups, serving together as the object of *tied up*. The phenomenon of conjunction cuts across most of the structures described in this appendix. As a first approximation, we can describe it as:

> In place of any unit at any place in the syntax, we can substitute a conjoined structure whose terminal elements are instances of that unit.

There are a number of possible conjoined structures such as *(both) X and Y; (either) X or Y; X but not Y;* and *X, Y, Z,..., and (or) W.* These in turn can be applied recursively to get combinations like *X and either Y or Z.* Figure B–25 illustrates some of the different units that can be conjoined.

Even these simple examples raise problems, and as we explore conjunction further, the data are extremely complex. There has been no satisfactory comprehensive treatment in any grammar, and here we will only point out some of the major issues.

Non-conjoinable structures. There are many places in the grammar where conjunction is not possible. For example, if a noun is used as a classifier we cannot combine it, as in **a kitchen or bread knife.* Particles that occur in combinations sound very strange, as in **I picked it out and up.* Articles resist conjunction (*the or a dog*), as do pre-determiners (*half or all the way*). However, the regularities are not easy to describe, and there are contexts in which some of these are acceptable.

Difference of features. Normally we would expect a conjoined structure to have the features of its elements. For example, *came and went* is in the past tense. For some features, things are more complex. A conjoined noun group is plural if the conjunction is *and* (*the boy and the girl are...*), but with *or* or *but* it picks up the number of one of its constituents. Both *The president or his assistants are responsible* and *The president or his assistants is responsible* sound slightly strange.

Ambiguity. The fact that units at any level can be conjoined leads to a high degree of ambiguity. The sentence *Larry or Curly and Moe will do it* can be interpreted in two ways, depending on whether it is *Larry or (Curly and Moe)* or *(Larry or Curly) and Moe*. As with preposition groups, a string of binary conjunctions will have as many interpretations as there are distinct binary trees of the right size. In other cases, it is not clear what unit is being conjoined. A phrase like *the old men and women* can be interpreted as a conjoined noun *men and women* with a common modifier *old,* or as a conjunction of *old men* and *women,* in which the age of the women is not specified. This becomes more severe when ellipsis is involved, as described below.

Taking a simple view of syntax, ambiguity need not be a concern. As long as the grammar covers all possible combinations, the fact that many sentences have a large number of alternative interpretations is not a problem. From the point of view of building effective systems, however, the choice of the proper alternative is critical and special mechanisms need to be included. These make use of semantic information, so that a sentence like *Willy planned a visit to New Jersey and a vacation* will not be interpreted as conjoining *New Jersey and a vacation.*

Special group interpretation. There are constructs in which the meaning of a phrase with a conjunction is different from the conjunction of the corresponding phrases. *Frankie and Johnny were cowboys* is equivalent to *Frankie was a cowboy and Johnny was a cowboy,* while *Frankie and Johnny were lovers* does not mean *Frankie was a lover and Johnny was a lover.* This can interact with modifiers like *both.* *Liz and Dick are married* is quite different from *Liz and Dick are both married.* As with many of the phenomena of conjunction, one could treat this as lying outside the domain of syntax and handle the complexities in the semantic component. In transformational grammar, there was an earlier attempt to handle them syntactically through transformations, but the more recent trend is to shift the burden to semantics.

The conjunction *but.* The occurrence of *but* involves a contrast of a special sort. We can say *an old but agile gentleman* but ?*a red but wooden wagon* sounds strange, and *Send me two but three helpers* is clearly unacceptable. As a first approximation we can say that when *but* is used, there is a presupposition that the conjunct following *but* is in some sense unexpected given the one preceding it. This explains *she went but she couldn't get in* and *old but agile* and gives some idea of how we could construct a context in which *red but wooden* made sense. However, it does not directly cover the use of explicit negatives, as in *not two but three*.

Parallelism. There is a tendency when conjoining structures to keep them fairly similar. For example, *?I like to dance, to swim, and skiing* is awkward, even though the individual conjuncts could each appear as an object of *I like*. There is no precise definition of what it means for two phrases to be 'parallel,' and in this area, like many, we must deal with a scale of acceptability rather than a simple 'yes-no' notion of grammaticality. Meaning plays a large role in determining parallelism, as in *?The pecan pie and I were baking* and *?I like walking in sandals and in large cities.*

Parallelism is one cue that people use in finding interpretations of potentially ambiguous structures. A sentence like *We vehemently urge that he resign and heartily applaud the efforts of the committee* resists an interpretation in which *resign and heartily applaud the efforts of the committee* is a single conjoined structure, even though on syntactic and semantic grounds it could perfectly well be. Features establishing parallelism can include overall syntactic structure, length of phrases, related vocabulary items, and other such subtle correlations.

Ellipsis. The most intricate aspects of conjunction are those connected with the possibilities for ellipsis in conjuncts after the first. This will be discussed in the next section.

B.3.4 Ellipsis

One of the most pervasive phenomena in conversational English is ellipsis—the omission of elements that would be expected in the full syntactically correct form of an utterance or phrase. Almost any item can be left out, as long as there is an appropriate source in the context from which it could be filled in, as illustrated in Figure B–26.

As with conjunction, the basic phenomenon can be simply described in informal terms. It is as if a sentence initially contained redundant material (material matching something in the previous context), which could therefore be deleted. Also, as with conjunction, there are many complexities.

Restrictions on deletion. Although many different kinds of structures can be *elided* (deleted through ellipsis), not all can. The sentence **We were in the lake and they were the house* cannot result from eliding *in* in the second phrase, and similarly **We were in the lake and they were on raft* could not be the result of deleting *the* from *on the raft*. There have been various attempts to

---

Previous sentence

> *You think he'll be here tomorrow. I predict __ Friday.*

Question-answer

> **Q:** *What kind of ice cream does George like?*
>
> **A:** *Chuck thinks __ vanilla.*

Conjunction

> *You had three pieces with anchovy and I only got two __ pepperoni.*

Adjacent parallel phrases

> *We were searching for many treasures while __ finding few __ .*

Figure B–26. Sources of material for elliptical constructions.

give a precise characterization of what makes a structural element or sequence of elements elidable, but the data are extremely complex.

Gapping. The material that is deleted need not be a single constituent or even a sequence of constituents with the same parent. For example, in *Rachel plans to give them a donation of $10, and Sarah $18,* the deleted material, *plans to give them a donation of,* spans several levels of embedding. Furthermore, it need not be identical in all features to that which preceded it. In the sentence *I plan to give them $36, and Shlomo $54,* the deleted material, *plans to give them,* has a different verb form from the contextual *I plan.*

Substitute nouns and dummy verbs. In many situations where ellipsis seems applicable, it cannot be done directly. We cannot say **Eric got a tricycle with chrome wheels and Melanie is going to get with aluminum.* Instead, we insert a *substitute noun* to get *...and Melanie is going to get one with aluminum ones.* Similarly, we say *You passed the tesi and I did too* instead of ** You passed the test and I too,* using a *dummy verb* to mark the place of ellipsis.

Comparatives. Comparative adjective and adverb groups such as *as fast as...* are a rich source of ellipsis. In place of *I can do it better than you can do it,* we typically say *...better than you* or *...better than you can.* As with all other elliptical structures, the precise rules for what can be left out are difficult to formulate, and there is a potential for ambiguity. *I trust you more than Doug* has two interpretations, depending on whether the phrase before deletion was *I trust Doug* or *Doug trusts you.*

B.3.5 Quotation and address

One of the most fascinating properties of natural language is that in addition to being able to describe everything else in the world, it can be used to describe itself. Linguistic objects such as sentences, utterances, phrases, and words can themselves be the topic of discourse. There are a number of special syntactic mechanisms for indicating that linguistic entities are being talked about. Furthermore, the situation in which language is being used can itself be part of the structure, as when an utterance includes an address to the hearer. We will briefly describe the phenomena of quotation and address.

Direct quotation. Any word, phrase, or longer stretch of text can be used as a noun group by wrapping it in quotation marks:

> *'Chicago' contains seven letters.*
>
> *He said 'I will not resign.'*
>
> *The speech ended with 'Ask not what your country can do for you, but what you can do for your country.'*

The quoted material can be split into pieces, with the rest of the sentence embedded in it, as in *'The only answer,' he exhorted the congregation, 'is to return to the Lord.'* In this special case, the subject of the verbal process can be inverted with the verb, as in *'It is curious,' <u>said Alice</u>, 'that your smile seems not to be acquainted with your face.'*

Indirect quotation. Some clause types, such as REPORT and NOMINALIZED RELATIVE, can be used to indicate the material of a quoted phrase or utterance without literally including it, as in:

> *He said that he would not resign.*
>
> *He was foolish, he admitted, to have given any information at all.*
>
> *The speech ended by asking what we could do for our country.*

In addition to the interposing of sequences like *he said,* the various movement phenomena allow things to escape from the quoted material, as in *With more planning he said he could have succeeded.* The phrase *with more planning* does not modify the saying, as its position would indicate, but is part of the said message.

Intentional expressions. Going one step further, we find verbs like *believe, suppose, hope, want, expect,* and *think,* whose object is *intentional.* The constructs involving these are almost identical to those for explicitly linguistic verbs such as *say, ask, tell,* and *remark* when used to describe rather than quote.

> *He believed that he would not resign.*
>
> *With more planning he believes he could have done it.*

> *He'll be more cautious, I suppose, in the future.*
> *It changes your perspective on a presidential trip, I find, if you are prepar-*
>   *ing for a burglary job when you get home.*   (13)
> *I think he'll be more cautious in the future.*
> *There's a problem, you know, with that solution.*

Attitudinal modifiers. In the previous examples, the sentence as a whole describes a verbal action or intentional state. Even (13) can be analyzed as resulting from some kind of movement from *I find that....* However, there is a class of closely related sentences in which the interposed element is a simple modifier:

> *It will be difficult, unfortunately, to see him.*
> *He certainly will make a try of it.*
> *It's frankly a bunch of bull.*
> *I will hopefully be there on Thursday.*   (14)

These sentences could be analyzed as resulting by movement from structures like:

> *It is unfortunate that it will be difficult to see him.*
> *It is certain that he will make a try of it.*
> *I tell you frankly that it's a bunch of bull.*
> *I am hopeful that I will be there on Thursday.*

This approach was taken in the work on generative semantics (see Section C.1). However, the rules must be more complex and abstract than the kinds of movement described in Section B.1.7, since they involve elements that do not appear in the final structure as well as shifts of word class (e.g., from *certain* to *certainly*).

The exact placement of these modifiers is not completely arbitrary, but it allows a good deal of variation. The modifiers generally must go between top level constituents of the clause. *He will certainly make a try of it* is fine, but **He will make a certainly try of it* is not. However, there are sentences like *It was what they wanted, I guess, to do.* This kind of interpolation is related to issues of focus and theme. The intentional or attitudinal phrase often falls between the *theme* and the rest of the sentence.

Certain attitudinal modifiers (like *hopefully*) are considered substandard, and children are often taught that sentences like (14) are not proper. If there are syntactic or semantic criteria that distinguish it from the other sentences in that set of examples, they are not easy to discern.

Direct address. In addition to interposing intentional and attitudinal comments, one can interpose interpersonal comments aimed at the hearer. Some examples are:

You'll never know, dear, how much I love you.

The flowers are not to be touched, please.

Sam, you made the pants too long.

Amalgams. One last group of sentences involves the use of a phrase which is a part of another utterance in place of one that can be inferred from it, as in *I just saw you'll never guess who, who told me you can't imagine what.* This kind of structure has been called an *amalgam* in transformational grammar.

B.4 Word classes

Throughout this appendix, in describing each syntactic unit we have given a set of functions (such as HEAD and SUBJECT) and described the class of constitutents that can fill each one. At higher levels this is recursive—for example, a preposition group can be a QUALIFIER of a noun group, and in turn have a noun group as its OBJECT. Ultimately, though, the terminal nodes of every syntactic structure are words. This section enumerates the different word classes (or *parts of speech,* as they are traditionally called) of English, describing the features and functions of each. The final subsection (Section B.4.5) goes beyond the level of the word, discussing briefly some issues of *morphology* (word formation).

B.4.1 The classification of words

There are a number of theoretical problems in characterizing the word classes of a language. Although a thorough treatment of them would be far beyond the scope of this appendix, the following paragraphs introduce some of the issues.

Choice of categories. The categorization of words into a small number of classes is primarily based on similarity of the contexts, or *syntactic frames,* in which they can appear, as described in Section 2.2. However, it involves a good deal of arbitrariness. There are many factors determining where particular words can appear, and if we took a strict view that two words are in the same class only if they can occur in exactly the same places, we would end up with hundreds of slightly different word classes. Therefore the linguist makes decisions to ignore certain differences and to group words in a way that provides a relatively small number of classes, each of which has a good deal of internal regularity and a relatively small degree of overlap with other classes. This appendix remains close to the traditional word classes, as described in Quirk et al., (1972). It differs in points of detail in order to fit more coherently with the presentation of the rest of the grammar.

Category hierarchies. The simplest model of word classes would be a partitioning of the vocabulary into mutually disjoint categories. However, this fails to capture a good deal of the generality. We often want to describe two categories as belonging to a larger common category. For example, the verb *do* and the verb *go* belong in different categories, since *do* can occur in constructs like *Does he like it?*, while *go* cannot. However, we would like to consider them both as verbs sharing common properties of all verbs (such as the variation of forms like *doing, going, does, goes,* etc.). We therefore have a hierarchy of classes in which both *do* and *go* are verbs, with *do* belonging to the subclass of *auxiliary verbs.*

Classes and features. As described in the discussion of systemic features in Section 6.3, any classification can be thought of either as a grouping of objects or as a set of features those objects can have. Given the example above, we might well choose to have a single class of verbs and a feature AUXILIARY associated with auxiliary verbs. The choice as to whether to consider a particular distinction as between classes or different features within a class is quite arbitrary. It is generally made in the way that most simplifies the overall statement of the grammar, and this can depend on the details of all the rules. In this appendix we have not tried to be formally precise in making this choice, since the purpose is to give a general understanding of the issues and terminology rather than a formal grammar.

Going one step further, in some current versions of transformational grammar (as described in Section C.3), word classes are treated not as a partition or a hierarchy, but as a collection of features. There is a binary feature pair +NOUN and –NOUN and another +VERB and –VERB. Nouns and verbs each have the appropriate positive feature. The class traditionally called 'adjective' has the features +NOUN and +VERB, while the class of prepositions is –NOUN –VERB. This makes it possible to state certain rules in a very general way that lets them apply, for example, to both verbs and adjectives while not applying to nouns and prepositions. This extreme use of features is controversial, and most grammars use something more like the classification in this section.

Words with special syntactic properties. There is a relatively small group of words (between ten and a hundred) that have special properties not shared by any other word. For example, *to* is used to introduce the infinitive (*to be or not to be*), *by* has a special role in passive voice, *do* is introduced in constructs involving do support (as in *Did you go?*), and *not* occurs in syntactic patterns in a totally idiosyncratic way. In order to account for this, the grammar can either allow specific words to be mentioned in rules or can have special features associated with these words in the dictionary (e.g., a feature TO that is associated only with the word *to*). In the chapters of this book, we have seen both techniques used in different syntactic formalisms. In this section we will continue to use whichever seems to best convey the particular phenomenon.

Naming of categories. Although there are well established names for the major categories, there is a good deal of latitude in the naming of the others, and differences are found between British and American usage, between generative linguists and more traditional grammarians, and even between individuals within a fairly well defined school of linguistics. In the systemic approach, there is an additional problem raised by the desire to distinguish carefully between categories and functions. We want to treat 'noun' as a class of lexical items, while 'head' is the function that a noun fills in a noun group. This has led in the previous sections to the use of strange terms like 'describer,' which is the function filled by members of the 'adjective' class in a noun group.

Unfortunately, there is no a fully developed, commonly accepted terminology. In order to describe the grammar in a style that is understandable and that can be related to different linguistic formalisms, it is often convenient to go along with the accepted usage, in which the distinction between function and feature is not upheld. For example, 'auxiliary' is generally used for both, and it seems very awkward to come up with a name for the role an 'ordinal' plays in a noun group, other than 'ordinal.' Therefore this appendix includes terms that are used both for classes and functions.

Multiple membership. One obvious problem is that many words fall into more than one word class. In fact, a great number of the nouns of English are also verbs, many adjectives are also nouns, etc. Even in the closed classes there are multi-class words. For example, *before* is both a binder and a preposition (as in *before you were in Spain* and *before lunch*), as contrasted with *while,* which is only a binder, and *during,* which is only a preposition. The classification must therefore allow a word to appear in more than one class, with a separate definition (or *word sense*) for each. The same is true of features. If *dog* is described with the feature SINGULAR and *dogs* with PLURAL, then *sheep* must have both. There is also the problem of *homonyms* (words that look alike). For example, *saw* is a singular noun, a present tense verb, and a different past tense verb.

Productivity. Most of the grammars and parsing algorithms described in this book assume that part of the knowledge structure is a *lexicon* or dictionary containing the words of the language. However, new words can be created and understood in the course of conversation. The word *transformational* does not appear in Webster's 7th New Collegiate Dictionary (1972) but was a straightforward compounding of the word *transformation* and the suffix *-al.* A further compounding such as *transformationalize, detransformationalize,* or even *detransformationalization* might well be used in an appropriate context, such as talking about the course of changing allegiances in a linguistics department. Some of the regularities in this process are discussed in Section B.4.5. In addition, completely new terms such as *laser, cellophane, shmoo,* and *zap* are created and come into standard use at a steady pace.

In every language there are two general kinds of word classes: *open classes,* to which new vocabulary items are added frequently, and *closed classes,* which undergo very little change. In English the open classes are the nouns, verbs, adjectives, and some kinds of adverbs. Closed classes include conjunctions, prepositions, and articles. These too can change, as can be confirmed by comparing modern and Shakespearean English, but the changes are slow and are not the result of the intentional coinage of new terms. Open classes, on the other hand, are expanded every day as we encounter new objects, activities, or properties that we want to describe in a single word. Many changes result from cross-linguistic contact, as the words of one language appear as *loan words* in another, gradually losing their foreignness until they merge into the basic vocabulary.

B.4.2 The verb

Just as the clause is the most complex syntactic constituent, its central element (the verb) is a member of the most complex word class. A clause includes a verb sequence such as *would have been sleeping.* The final verb of this sequence, its *main verb,* is a major determinant of both the syntactic structure and semantic function of the clause. Rules concerning the number of other constituents, their order, and the kinds of possible modifiers are all most economically stated by grouping verbs into subclasses, and describing the rules for each subclass. Figure B–27 contains a simplified version of the basic choice systems for verbs.

Auxiliaries. The first choice system distinguishes auxiliary verbs (which can appear at positions other than the main verb) from others. Auxiliaries include the *modals: can, could, may, might, shall, should, will, would,* and *must,* and

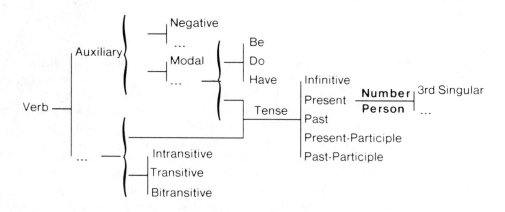

Figure B–27. Choice systems for the verb.

Auxiliary	Non-auxiliary
Are you getting it?	*Are* you happy?
We *don't* agree.	We *do* everything we can.
They *have* been polled.	They *have* bean poles.

Figure B–28. Auxiliary and other uses of *be, do,* and *have.*

the three verbs *be, do,* and *have.* These last three are both auxiliaries and non-auxiliaries, as illustrated in Figure B–28.

The choice network of Figure B–27 includes BE, DO, and HAVE as features, since this makes it easier to state the rules for the special structures each of them enters into.

Negative forms. Auxiliaries have negative forms, such as *can't, won't, wasn't,* and *hasn't.* These can be considered *contractions* of a verb with a following *not,* but it is often useful to consider the entire unit as a single verb with the feature NEGATIVE.

Transitivity. There is a traditional division of verbs other than auxiliaries into *transitive* and *intransitive,* but as pointed out in Section B.1.6, this is too simple a division to serve in a full analysis of clause transitivity. We have added *bitransitive* to indicate a verb taking two objects, as in *Give me a break.* There is no agreed upon set of choices for the more complex phenomena described in Section B.1.6.

Tense. The tense system, as shown in Figure B–29, includes five basic forms for each verb. It applies to all verbs except the modals. As illustrated by these examples, there is a great deal of irregularity in the actual form of the verbs. The abbreviations *-ing, -ed,* and *-en* are commonly used in writing grammars, but should be taken only as abstract abbreviations, since there are few verbs that match them exactly. It is more common for both PAST and PAST PARTICIPLE to end with *-ed* (as with *dropped*) or for one or more of the forms to be irregular (as with *ring, rang, rung* and *break, broke, broken*).

Tense	Examples
Infinitive	*be, drop, ring, break*
Present	*am, are, is, drops, rings, breaks*
Past ('-ed')	*was, were, dropped, rang, broke*
Present participle ('-ing')	*being, dropping, ringing, breaking*
Past participle ('-en')	*been, dropped, rung, broken*

Figure B–29. Tense choices for verbs.

Modals appear in only one form, as they are not marked for tense. There is some correlation between present and past tense and the choice between pairs such as *can* and *could,* but in most analyses this is considered a semantic rather than syntactic correspondence.

Person and Number. Except for the verb *be,* systems of person and number apply only to verbs in the PRESENT tense and are reduced to a system of two choices: a third-person singular (THIRD-SINGULAR) form (*goes, talks*) and a form identical to the INFINITIVE that is used for all other combinations of person and number. The network of Figure B–27 is simplified and does not properly deal with *be,* which has distinct PRESENT forms for each person in the singular (*am, are, is*), using one of these for all numbers in the plural (*are*), and having separate singular and plural PAST forms (*was* and *were*).

In addition to the words normally treated as verbs, there are two classes of verb-like words: *denominal verbs* and *semi-auxiliaries.*

Denominal verbs. In many sentences, a noun appears in the place of a verb. For example, in *I bicycle to work* we could analyze *bicycle* as a verb, but if we do so we must then classify every noun describing a vehicle as a verb, since we could have *Our two-year-old wanted to tricycle to work* or *Once on a vacation we donkey carted from Tlatenco to Mexico City.* Clark and Clark (1979) have pointed out the pervasiveness of this kind of structure in English, and it is in many ways more reasonable to treat it as a special use of nouns.

Semi-auxiliaries. There are many phrases such as *used to, ought to,* and *be bound to* (as in *He's bound to catch on*) which appear at the beginning of a verb sequence much like an auxiliary, but have specialized forms and constraints on occurrence. Section B.1.5.1 treated *be going to* and *have to* as part of the verb sequence that generated the tense of a clause. A more thorough treatment would handle other semi-auxiliaries as well.

B.4.3 The noun

Just as the verb functions as the head of the clause, the noun is the head of the noun group. There are three basic kinds of noun: *common nouns, proper nouns,* and *pronouns.* The further classification of these is shown in the choice network of Figure B–30.

B.4.3.1 Pronouns

A pronoun is the head of a PRONOUN noun group. There are four kinds of pronouns: *personal, demonstrative, question,* and *quantified.* We have not included *relative pronouns* in this list, but discuss them as *connectives* in Section B.4.4.

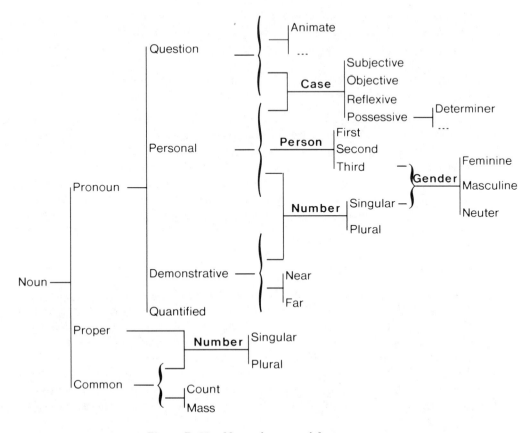

Figure B–30. Noun classes and features.

Personal pronouns. Personal pronouns were discussed at length in Section 6.3 in introducing the idea of choice systems in systemic grammar. There are nearly orthogonal choice systems for number, case, gender, and person, and we will not repeat the analysis here. There are a few additional subtleties not mentioned there or included in the network, such as the impersonal pronoun *one*. In some registers of English (especially British English), the word *one* is used to indicate a person in general. *In this club one does not remove one's jacket* sounds stilted to most Americans, who prefer the generic use of *you*, as in *When you're down and out, you need a friend*. *One* is also used as a *substitute noun* to head a common noun group in a special kind of ellipsis, as mentioned in Section B.3.4.

Demonstrative pronouns. The pronouns *this, that, these,* and *those* can appear as the head of a noun group (as in *That surprises me*) in addition to functioning as determiners (as in *this world*). In addition to a number feature, they have a DISTANCE feature of NEAR (*this, these*) or FAR (*that, those*).

Question pronouns. A noun group whose head is one of the question pronouns *who, whom, whose,* or *what* can appear as the question element in a clause. Usually they appear alone, but they can have a qualifier, as in *who that you know.* Like personal pronouns, they are marked for case (*who, whom, whose*). They are also marked for ANIMACY, with *who* and *whom* referring to people and *what* to other objects.

Quantified pronouns. There is a small set of singular third person pronouns generated by prefixing a quantifier (*any-, some-, every-,* or *no-*) onto a noun (*-thing, -body, -one*) or an adverbial (*-where, -place, -time,* or *-how*). These function more or less like other pronouns, except that they are often the head of a noun group with qualifiers (including one-word qualifiers), as in *nobody I know* and *anything green.* They are not marked for case, person, or number (all are third person singular), and they take the possessive suffix *'s,* as does a common noun.

B.4.3.2 Proper nouns

Proper nouns form a rather special subset of the language. There are a great many of them, and new ones can be created at will simply by naming something or someone. They can be used as single words or combined into complex structures such as *James J. Astor III, San Francisco, South Van Ness Avenue, The Jefferson Airplane,* and *The People's Republic of China.* Many of these include phrases that appear outside of proper names (e.g., *of China*), but the combination has a referent as a whole, rather than by virtue of analyzing its parts. There are standard formats for naming particular kinds of things (people, streets, etc.).

Whether a proper noun is treated as plural or singular in subject-verb agreement depends largely on its referent. We say *The United States of America is...* even though it is superficially plural, and *The Jefferson Airplane are...* even though it appears singular. In the case of proper nouns referring to groups, one has both choices, and there is some difference between British and American English. For example, if a city name is used to refer to an athletic team, an American will say *Boston is playing at New York tonight* while a Briton will say *Oxford are playing at Tottenham.*

Most grammars do not deal with proper nouns except for the simple case in which a single proper noun forms an entire noun group. Some computer grammars have included special sub-grammars for the particular classes of proper nouns (such as human names) encountered in their domain.

B.4.3.3 Common nouns

Common nouns are the heads of common noun groups, whose structure was elaborated in Section B.2. There is a syntactic categorization of these into

PLURAL and SINGULAR, with the number of the noun group as a whole matching the number of its head. Some nouns such as *sheep* and *fish* are both PLURAL and SINGULAR. There is a regular suffix *-s* for plurals, but many words have irregular forms (*goose, geese; alumna, alumnae*), often derived from the languages from which they were borrowed into English. A second distinction is between MASS nouns, such as *water* and *sand,* and COUNT nouns, such as *pretzel* and *atom.* The following examples illustrate the different noun group patterns allowed by the two. Imagine that each noun group is the object of *I bought. . . .*

*pretzel	*pretzels*	*the pretzel*	*a pretzel*	*two pretzels*
sand	**sands*	*the sand*	**a sand*	**two sands*
*a box of pretzel	*a box of pretzels*			
a box of sand	**a box of sands*			

In some cases, a mass noun can be used as a count noun and is then interpreted as referring to a variety, as in *I have tried lots of waters and I like Perrier best.* Although there are semantic correlations in the use of mass nouns for 'indivisible stuff' and count nouns for 'countable objects,' the distinction is not based purely on meaning. *Seeds* and *wheat,* for example, consist of small objects of the same size (in fact, grains of wheat are seeds), but one is a plural count noun, the other a singular mass noun. In some grammars, there is also a feature for a COLLECTIVE noun, such as *committee.* In some dialects of English, collective nouns can be used in their singular form as the head of a plural noun group, as in *The committee have come to a decision.*

As with the denominal verbs discussed above, there is a wide variety of *deverbal nouns.* Verbs such as *desire, doubt, attempt, answer, cover, walk, retreat,* and *love* all correspond to nouns. However, not every verb allows this, as illustrated by **My go to town was fine.*

B.4.4 Other classes

Each specific linguistic analysis makes use of a number of other word classes. In this section we will briefly describe adjectives, adverbs, articles, connectives, interjections, numbers, prepositions, and quantifiers.

B.4.4.1 Adjectives

Adjectives function as describers in noun groups and as the head of adjective groups such as *as big as a breadbox.* They have a normal unmarked form (*old, big, good*), a COMPARATIVE form (*older, bigger, better*), and a SUPERLATIVE form (*oldest, biggest, best*). Any of these forms can be used for a describer (*an old house, an older house, the oldest houses*), although the use of a superlative in an indefinite noun group calls for somewhat special interpretation or context. The phrase *an oldest man* sounds strange in isolation, but it is perfectly normal in *Every village has an oldest man*. Different adjective groups select either the unmarked or comparative form, for example *as (unmarked) as...*, *(comparative) than...*, and *too (unmarked) to....*

B.4.4.2 Adverbs

In traditional grammars of English, the class of adverbs has covered a mixed collection of words. Following usual principles of classification, such as similarity of meaning and similarity of distributional frames, they cannot really be said to constitute a single class. The syntactic determination of just where these words can appear is one of the messiest parts of English. Generative grammars have never treated them thoroughly or systematically, although specific problems (e.g., the placement of *not*) have often served as a productive source of examples for creating and testing hypotheses. The following classification is rough, and is intended only to indicate the variety of these words and some of the problems they raise. Many words appear in more than one of these categories.

Time and place. Adverbs of time and place function as clause modifiers. They include *now, then, soon, immediately, eventually, later, sometime, someday, tomorrow, here, there, yonder, anywhere, nowhere, just* (as in *We just arrived*), and many more. Some (such as *here* and *now*) are *deictic*. Their meaning is relative to the time and place of the utterance in which they appear. Others (*when* and *where*) have a QUESTION feature and can function as the question element of a WH- question. Others (*sometime, anywhere, nowhere,...*) have a structure like the corresponding quantified pronouns discussed above. Some (such as *ago* and *sooner*) cannot appear as simple modifiers but are used in special phrase patterns (like *a year ago* and *No sooner had he said it...*). Place adverbs can also appear as qualifiers in certain noun groups, such as *the way there* and *a trip abroad*.

Manner. The most regular subclass of adverbs is the manner adverbs, such as *quickly, easily, well,* and *happily,* which appear as clause modifiers. They can be formed productively (i.e., new ones can be created) from corresponding adjectives by adding *-ly*. The naive comparison 'Adverbs are to verbs as adjectives are to nouns' applies to this subclass more than to the others. As was mentioned in Section B.3.5 on quotation, a manner adverb like *honestly* can appear in a sentence like *He honestly can't do it* when its meaning is applicable to the manner in which the utterance is made. There are also some special manner adverbs like *somehow* which do not have the regular form.

Intensifiers and hedges. Another fairly regular subclass consists of words such as *very, somewhat, quite, rather, almost,* and *slightly* and phrases such as *sort of* and *just about*. They modify verbs, adjectives, and other adverbs, and some of them can be applied recursively (e.g., *very very*). Some of them can also apply to preposition groups (*rather in a stew*) and nouns (*an almost millionaire*). There are also SUPERLATIVE and COMPARATIVE intensifiers: *most, least, more,* and *less*.

Probability, frequency, evidence, and logical connection. Adverbs such as *usually, sometimes, always, never, probably, certainly, possibly,* and *necessarily* describe the likelihood or frequency of whatever is described in the clause they modify. Others such as *undeniably, evidently, apparently,* and *doubtless* describe the degree of evidence for making the statement. In discourse, the logical connection between sentences or paragraphs is often indicated by including adverbs such as *therefore, however, thus, so,* and *nevertheless*. Others, such as *anyway,* are used to indicate the structure of the overall discourse. All of these words have similar syntactic patterning in that they can appear at the beginning (often set off by commas in writing) or interposed (possibly also set off with commas) in the middle of the clause they modify.

Particles. The discussion of multi-word verbs in Section B.1.5.2 included combinations of a verb with a *particle,* as in *pick up* and *fake out*. The adverbs that can function as particles can also be used with motion verbs to indicate direction, as in *came in, went out,* and *fell down*. There is a special sentence form in which this kind of adverb appears as the theme, with inverted subject and verb, as in *In marched the king*.

Alternatives. Adverbs such as *even, only, too, both, also,* and *just* (as in *Just his parents came*) are used to contrast one event or situation with alternatives from some implicit set. *Only Bertrand understood it* implies that there were others who might be expected to have understood it, but didn't. *Even the skeptics were impressed* implies that there were others who were impressed but the skeptics were the least likely to be impressed. *Plants have feelings too* implies that there are other things having feelings and that plants are to be included. The particular set of alternatives implied is dependent on context in subtle ways, and the placement of the adverb is critical, as illustrated by:

> *Yesterday I hit him on his left arm with my hammer.*
> *Only yesterday I hit him on his left arm with my hammer.*
> *Yesterday only, I hit him on his left arm with my hammer.*
> *Yesterday, only I hit him on his left arm with my hammer.*
> *Yesterday I only hit him on his left arm with my hammer.*
> *Yesterday I hit only him on his left arm with my hammer.*
> *Yesterday I hit him only on his left arm with my hammer.*
> *Yesterday I hit him on only his left arm with my hammer.*
> *Yesterday I hit him on his only left arm with my hammer.*
> *Yesterday I hit him on his left arm only, with my hammer.*

Yesterday I hit him on his left arm, only with my hammer.
Yesterday I hit him on his left arm with only my hammer.
Yesterday I hit him on his left arm with my only hammer.
Yesterday I hit him on his left arm with my hammer only.

Negation. The negation adverb *not* (with the reduced suffix form *-n't*) has complex syntactic properties not shared by other adverbs. It can appear in verb sequences (*did not go*) or as a modifier of adverbs and adjectives (*a not quite real experience*), of preposition groups (*a place not under a tree*), of adjunct groups (*not as big as I thought*), or of quantifiers (*not every*), etc. As mentioned in Section B.4.2, only auxiliaries can take the reduced negative suffix *-n't*. We can say *He isn't here* but not **He livesn't here.* When *do* is used as a non-modal, we say *I didn't do it,* not **I didn't it,* but for some reason, *I haven't a clue* is all right.

Other syntactic phenomena such as as tag formation (see Section B.1.7) and the alternation of the quantifiers *some* and *any* are interwoven with negation. We say *I have some time* and *I don't have any time* but not **I have any time* or **I don't have some time.* Verbs, nouns, and adverbs can carry some kind of negative feature that triggers this same alternation:

*He often has any time.	*He rarely has any time.*
*He expects to take any time.	*He refuses to take any time.*
*his claim that there is any time	*his doubt that there is any time*

B.4.4.3 Articles

Articles function as determiners in noun groups. They are DEFINITE (*the*) or INDEFINITE (*a, an*). Indefinite articles are used only in singular noun groups. As mentioned in Section B.4.3.1, demonstrative pronouns can function as determiners, acting like definite articles.

B.4.4.4 Connectives

There are several different kinds of connectives in English: *conjunctions, relative pronouns,* and *binders.*

Conjunctions. Conjunctions (*and, or,* and *but*) and conjunctive phrases (*X and Y; X, Y, Z, and...; neither X nor Y; both X and Y;* etc.,) were discussed in Section B.3.3. They are used to conjoin syntactic structures of all types. In traditional grammar, these are called *coordinating conjunctions.*

Relative pronouns. The relative pronouns *who, whom, which, where, when, how,* and *that* are used to introduce relative clauses. The *wh-* words are used for nonrestrictive or restrictive and *that* (or nothing) is also used for restrictive, as described in Section B.1.4. A relative pronoun other than *that* must agree in semantic category with the noun phrase it modifies, as in *the man who did it, the time when he didn't do it, the place where he did it,* and *the reason why he did it.*

Binders. A binder such as *because, so, since, until, before,* or *while* introduces a bound clause, which functions as a modifier in another clause. In traditional grammar, these are called *subordinating conjunctions.* Certain other kinds of clauses have specific words that appear initially to indicate the clause type. *That* functions as a complementizer in *That he went surprised us; whether* in *I don't know whether they will succeed; to* in *To give up would be prudent;* and the sequence *for...to* in *For us to do it would take too long.*

B.4.4.5 Interjections

Spoken language is laced with words like *oh, well,* and *yeah* and includes exclamations like *damn, ouch,* and *hell.* These do not appear in a regular way in the syntactic structures we have been examining but are *interjected* into the utterance. They have generally not been of much concern to generative linguists, although they do exhibit some interesting syntactic patterning and there have been some papers on specialized syntactic forms used only in obscenities. The interjections *yes* and *no* appear at the beginning of utterances that are answers to questions, and have been dealt with specially in some computer grammars.

B.4.4.6 Numbers

In describing the structure of a noun group (Section B.2.2), we indicated that it could contain both CARDINAL and ORDINAL numbers. Cardinals (such as *one, ten, two hundred and seventeen*) appear following a definite article or in noun groups with no article. Ordinals (such as *first, tenth, hundred and seventeenth*) appear just before the describers. There are a relatively small number of number words (e.g., *one, two, three,..., ten, eleven, twelve,..., twenty, thirty, forty,..., hundred, thousand, million,...*), which are combined into complex phrases (such as *one thousand eight hundred and seventy three*).

B.4.4.7 Prepositions

A preposition group begins with a preposition, which is either a single word, such as *in, on, at, for,* or *without,* or a multi-word phrase, such as *next to, in spite of,* or *in between.* Prepositions are a closed class, although new multi-word prepositions are occasionally generated. The detailed analysis of the transitivity of clauses (Section B.1.6) depends on the specific prepositions appearing in the preposition groups that modify the clause. In many grammars, features are used to indicate the few prepositions that have special grammatical properties, such as *by* (used in the passive), *to* (used in the dative), and *of* (used in partitive noun groups).

B.4.4.8 Quantifiers

The determiner position in a noun group can be filled by an article, a demonstrative pronoun, or a quantifier. The meaning of sentences can depend on the use of specific quantifiers in subtle ways, and in traditional grammars, they are sometimes grouped according to their meaning. Categories include UNIVERSAL (*all, every, both, each...*), EXISTENTIAL (*some, any, several...*), NEGATIVE (*no*), DEGREE (*many, much, most, few...*), and EVALUATIVE (*enough, too many, too much...*). Some quantifiers (such as *all*) can function as pre-determiners, as in *all the boys*. Others can appear as modifiers before a verb, as in *the people all applauded, the contestants then each told a story,* and *the winners both smiled.* In this case they are interpreted as applying to the subject.

B.4.5 Morphology

The internal structure (or *morphological structure*) of words is complex and has been studied in great detail within the paradigm of structural linguistics. It has been relatively peripheral in more recent work in generative and computational linguistics for several reasons:

Irregularity. Morphological phenomena do not lend themselves well to the methodology of generative grammar because they exhibit a high degree of irregularity and idiosyncrasy, which is frustrating to a linguist trying to find a minimal set of rules. In most generative grammars (including those used on computers), words that do not take the 'standard' form are marked as such and the lexicon includes an entry for the inflected form as it occurs.

Historicity. Any analysis that seeks to find regularities in morphological structure must examine words in terms of their history. Much of the irregularity comes from the fact that lexical items come into a language relatively freely from other languages, and their internal form reflects the morphological structure of the source language as well as the adaptation to the new host. For example, the words *destroy* and *employ* do not have corresponding forms *destruction* and **empluction.* The Latin root of *destroy* has a past participle ending with *-struct,* while the root of *employ* does not. *Indices, schemata, children,* and *cherubim* are all plurals that follow the rules of another language.

Psychological reality. One of the basic assumptions in studying syntax as a cognitive process is that the language user has some psychological structure corresponding to the syntactic rules—that he or she actually uses some form of grammar in production and understanding. It can be argued that to a large degree this is not the case in morphology. The ordinary person does not know the history of words and the complex factors that go into morphological structure, but instead simply knows as individual items all the various forms of words (including those with analyzable internal structure). In this view, the process of language understanding includes morphology as a kind of look-up rather than a rule-based analysis like the rest of syntax.

It is clear that there are some morphological phenomena that are productive and therefore cannot be handled by lookup. For example, if you learn a new verb such as *pronate,* you will understand sentences that involve *pronating* something, *repronating* it, and even ones involving *unpronation.* However, in most computer programs only a few of the obvious morphological phenomena are handled by rules, and everything else must be stored in the dictionary.

B.4.5.1 Types of morphological structure

In structural linguistics, the morphological structure of words has been analyzed using the same formal notions of constituency and choice that are used in the rest of syntax. There are three basic kinds of constituency relationships that occur.

Affixation. Many words can be analyzed as made up of an *affix* together with a root. The affix is either at the beginning (a *prefix*) or the end (a *suffix*). The affix belongs to a class of standard affixes of the language and cannot appear as a word in its own right. Typical affixes are *un-, re-, -ify,* and *-ation.* The set of affixes is relatively stable, but new ones can be invented, as in the case of *-thon,* which was originally one syllable of a Greek place name (*Marathon*) but is now found in words like *telethon* and *walkathon.*

Compounds. Some words are made up of constituents, each of which is a word in its own right. *Blueberry, lighthouse,* and *hummingbird* are all obvious compounds. In general, the word class of the compound is that of its last element. There are cases of apparent compounds that do not have real constituents. For example, *cranberry* appears to be similar to *blueberry,* but **cran* is not a word or prefix in any other compound. This can be the result of phonological change in the language.

Modified forms. Some words exhibit an internal structure that cannot be described in simple constituency terms. For example, there are sets of forms like *take, took; shake, shook* and *goose, geese; tooth, teeth,* in which there are regular alternations of the vowel corresponding to a feature of the word. One of the early appeals of transformational grammar was that it could make use of transformational processes to describe this alternation, whereas the earlier immediate constituent grammars were forced to postulate entities like a *discontinuous constituent, t—k,* which is combined with the appropriate internal constituent for the tense.

B.4.5.2 Functions of morphological structure

There are several ways in which the internal structure of words plays a role in syntax and in producing meanings. These can be classed as *inflections,* which add feature markings, and *derivations,* which generate words with new meanings.

Feature marking. For each of the open word classes (noun, verb, adjective, and adverb) there are choice systems that are correlated with the internal structure of words, as illustrated in Figure B–31 and discussed in the corresponding sections of Section B.4.

There are other feature systems (such as transitivity for verbs and mass versus count for nouns) that are not included here because there are no regular rules correlating them to morphological structure. In many languages, there is a much more elaborate system of markings, such as the *conjugation* of verbs for number, tense, and person, and the *declension* of nouns according to number, person, case, and gender.

Compounding meaning. Many words can be analyzed as a compound formed of two words or of a word and a prefix or suffix that contributes to its meaning, such as *refasten, antimatter,* and *unhappy.* As with other morphological phenomena, the meaning of compounds is idiosyncratic. One could not infer the function of a *lighthouse* or a *greenhouse* from the component words, and although *jailer* and *prisoner* are syntactically similar, their meaning differs by much more than the difference between *jail* and *prison.*

Class	System	Examples
Verb	Tense	*take, took, taking, taken*
	Person/Number	*go, goes*
Noun	Number	*corollary, corollaries*
Adjective	Comparison	*broad, broader, broadest*
Adverb	Comparison	*soon, sooner, soonest*

Figure B–31. Word forms for feature marking.

From	To	Examples
Verb	Noun	*create → creation, creator*
Verb	Adjective	*agree → agreeable*
Noun	Verb	*friend → befriend*
Noun	Adjective	*child → childish, childlike*
Adjective	Verb	*rich → enrich*
Adjective	Noun	*sane → sanity*
Adjective	Adverb	*happy → happily*

Figure B–32. Word class conversion.

Converting word class. Many prefixes and suffixes operate not only to augment meaning of a word, but also to change its word class, as illustrated in
Figure B–32. Often there is more than one form based on the same root. For
example, from *man* we can derive the quite different adjectives *manly* and *man-
nish*. The affixation process can be applied more than once to produce compounds that have gone from one word class to another. For example, the often
quoted word *antidisestablishmentarianism* can be generated by derivations from
verb to noun to adjective and back to noun in the sequence: *establish → establishment → disestablishment → disestablishmentary → disestablishmentarian
→ disestablishmentarianism → antidisestablishmentarianism.*

The wide variety in affixes and their effects on word class and meaning is
illustrated by the following sample, in which each affix is productive (it can be
applied to a variety of words):

> *panic-ky, happi-ness, caus-ation, change-able, en-code, be-head, be-spectacl-ed, trick-
> ster, bake-r, teen-age-r, brother-hood, friend-ship, king-dom, tub-ing, spoon-ful,
> commun-ism, arrange-ment, refus-al, paint-ing, shrink-age, happi-ness, san-ity,
> beauti-fy, symbol-ize, ripe-n, delight-ful, speech-less, man-ly, child-like, meat-y, fool-
> ish, music-al, atom-ic, attract-ive, virtu-ous, . . .*

B.4.5.3 Spelling rules

The previous paragraphs have described several different kinds of irregularity:
the use of different forms for the same syntactic feature (*shake, shaken; make,
made*); arbitrariness as to which morphological combinations can appear (*destruction, *empluction*); the word class of the result; and the meaning it will
have. There is another kind of irregularity that has been handled more systematically in grammars and computer systems—the modification of the form
of an affix depending on the word it is affixed to.

Suffix	Transformation	Examples
-s	C*y-* → C*ie-* C*o-* → C*oe-*	*pansies, dallies* (but *pays, toys*) *potatoes, goes* (but *lotharios, zoos*)
-ed, -en,	*e-* → ∅	*tasted, taken, freest, voter*
-est, -er	C*y-* → C*i-* CV$_u$C- → CV$_u$CC-	*curtsied, driest, curvier* *regretted, drabbest, hotter* (but *lasted, booted, leader, bracketed*)
-ing	C*e-* → C- CV$_u$C- → CV$_u$CC-	*tasting, voting* (but *freeing, hoeing*) *emitting, abhorring, betting* (but *orbiting, laboring, picketing*)
-ly	*y-* → *i-*	*hastily, gaily*

Figure B–33. English spelling rules for suffixes.

We can look at affixing as a process involving two stages. First, there is a choice of the particular affix that has the right syntactic feature or meaning and is the correct one for the root. For example, in order to add the feature PLURAL to a noun, we would chose *-s* for *chair*, but *-i* for *alumnus*. Next, in many cases there are transformations to the pronunciation or spelling of the stem to which it is attached or to the affix itself. In this area there are significant differences between spoken and written form, as any child learning to spell knows all too well. Forms that are regular when spoken may be irregular when spelled (e.g., adding *-ing* to *rot* and *mate*). Others that have a regular spelling involve different phonemes (e.g., the pronunciation of the *-s* in *pubs* and *pups*).

Figure B–33 summarizes the spelling rules for the most common cases. Some of these rules apply to other suffixes as well, but they do not account for all of the phenomena that come up in the sample above. Each line of the table shows a transformation to be applied to the root before the suffix is added, showing the final letters of the root before and after the transformation. The words given as 'but...' in each case have forms that are similar but not identical to the given patterns. This table does not fully give the rules, as there are further interactions between spelling and phonological criteria such as stress and pronunciation. One example that is included is the interaction of stress and consonant doubling. Consonant doubling applies to words ending with CVC (where C and V stand for any consonant and any vowel, respectively), like *regret—regretted,* but not when the final syllable contains a reduced vowel (one pronounced with neutral vowel sound and low stress), as in *bracket—bracketed, exit—exited.* The symbol V$_u$ stands for an unreduced vowel (e.g., the final 'e' in *regret* but not in *bracket*).

The rules of Figure B–33 are stated in terms of production—they tell how to add an ending to a stem in producing a word. In creating a corresponding parser, we need to account for ambiguity, just as with any generative syntactic rules. For example, the forms *pasted* and *pasting* could be formed from either *paste* or *past* according to the rules. This is generally not a problem in parsers that make use of a dictionary, since it is rare for there to be overlapping forms. However, some systems have made use of endings to determine word classes of unknown words, and in this case ambiguity is introduced.

Index of syntactic terms

Appendix C

Current Directions in
Transformational Grammar

Contents of Appendix C

Chapter 4 describes transformational grammar primarily in the form known as the *standard theory,* which was introduced in Chomsky's *Aspects of the Theory of Syntax* in 1965. The standard theory has provided a basic starting point for work in transformational grammar in the subsequent years. In proposing additions and modifications, linguists have been guided by the criteria described in Section 4.5 and have been forced to make choices as to priority. Often these choices have not been conscious, but have resulted from tacit concern for one or another of the criteria. The resulting research has been varied and creative. The original framework has been modified in nearly every way imaginable and arguments have been made for and against every proposal.

It is quite difficult for anyone not an expert in the field to read the literature, since the discussion is usually couched in terms of detailed syntactic arguments, understandable only in the context of all the proposals that went before. We could characterize the contents of a particular paper (or segment of a paper) in terms of a multi-dimensional matrix of theories, authors, papers, phenomena, mechanisms, and criteria. Each element is something like *'Author A_1 in paper P_1 argues that a particular set of data D_1 is handled better by a particular combination of mechanisms M_1 within a theory T_1 than by another set M_2 which was proposed by author A_2 in paper P_2' or 'A collection of mechanisms M_1 is to be preferred on theoretical grounds over other mechanisms M_2 that deal with the same data D_1 on the grounds of some meta-theoretical criterion C_1.'*

In order to have a new coherent theory, one cannot typically make a single small modification to a previous theory. Any one change has consequences for other parts of the system, and anything major can lead to a wholesale revision of a number of assumptions. As a result, any one paper or any one person's position is based on a complex mixture of modifications and assumptions that depend on each other. An argument for a change must be seen in light of the entire system, not just the specific details of the proposal. In addition, different formal devices can have equivalent effects, so it is important to sort out the problems being solved by a given proposal from the formal details of the solution.

It would take a book far longer than this one to explore the different proposals, arguments, and integrated theories in detail. Since much of the work is recent, no such book yet exists. However, it is useful to have an overview that can serve as a basis for further reading. This appendix surveys the basic issues without pursuing the details of all the different positions.

In such a survey, there are several different ways the material could be organized:

Historical. The process of theoretical development is historical and social. There are competing schools of thought, feuds, crucial debates, moments of conversion, and all the other events of human discourse. In transformational linguistics (more perhaps than in older, more established sciences), a familiarity with the anecdotes and personalities is extremely useful in understanding what has been written. Papers have at times been organized not to put forth a particular idea but to attack the complex of beliefs held by some rival. Arguments that appear mixed and chaotic can often be decoded by the realization '*Oh, he's attacking X.*' Students planning to study transformational grammar in depth should learn the history and politics of the field. For the purposes of this appendix, we will describe it only in the barest outline.

Abstract conceptual advances. With the benefit of distance and hindsight, one can describe the development of a field in terms of its major conceptual advances. Things that looked important at the time may turn out to be unimportant variations, while things that slipped in unnoticed may in the long run be seen as the essential ideas. The ideal organization for this section would be an outline that put all of the major ideas into a larger perspective. But it is early and we are still too involved in the details.

Modifications to the model. The third approach, adopted here, is to use the standard model to provide an organizational structure. We will talk about the various proposals in terms of how they modify the components and assumptions of the model. This means that the overall theory of a particular person or group will be scattered into sections for the different modifications they make, rather than being united into a description of the overall approach. It also gives relatively little priority to the debates that led to the various suggestions. However, it provides a framework for understanding the issues in these debates and is therefore perhaps a better introduction.

C.1 Reorganization of the model

Detailed modifications to components of the model fit within a larger framework of organization. Figure C–1 illustrates the model of sentence derivation in the standard theory, as it was described in Section 4.3. It includes a base component that uses a context-free grammar to generate a deep structure. This deep structure is interpreted by semantic interpretation rules (sometimes called *projection rules*) to produce a semantic structure representing the meaning of the sentence. The deep structure is also the input to the transformational component, which produces a surface structure. The surface structure is the input to the phonological rules that produce the phonological structure on which the pronunciation of the sentence is based.

C.1.1 The extended standard theory

By the time the standard theory had been formulated, people were already aware of ways in which it was inadequate. One particular problem was its assumption that deep structure determined meaning. It was pointed out that meaning could be affected by a transformation such as passive, which had been

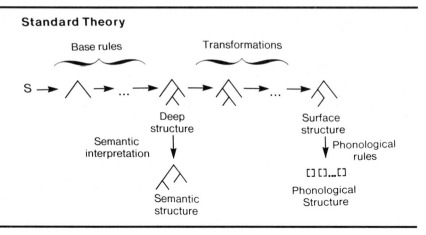

Figure C–1. The standard theory.

considered a typical example of an optional transformation. Examples (1) and (2) differ only in passivization but have different natural interpretations:

Few people read many books. (1)

Many books are read by few people. (2)

The first might be paraphrased *Most people don't read much,* while the second would be *There are lots of unpopular books.* Examples like this led to a revision of the model called the *extended standard theory* (or 'EST'), illustrated in Figure C–2. In the extended standard theory, the semantic interpretation rules operate on the entire set of trees in the derivation rather than on just the deep structure. This change violated one of the most attractive aspects of transformational grammar—the analysis of a sentence as having a surface structure that determined its pronunciation and a deep structure that determined its meaning. However, it was impossible to maintain the cleaner version in the face of the data.

Another change introduced in the extended standard theory dealt with the phenomenon of *nominalization.* Up to about 1967 it was generally assumed that nominalization was a transformational process—that sentences involving words like *criticism* were derived from deep structures containing the corresponding verb *criticize.* In a similar manner, a noun like *eagerness* was derived by transformations from the adjective *eager.* This made it possible to account for the structure of phrases such as *his severe criticism of the press* and *their eagerness to please* as based on the same deep structures as *He criticized the press severely* and *They are eager to please.*

Extended Standard Theory

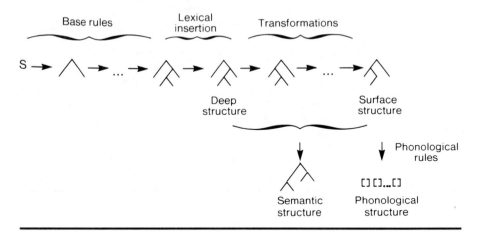

Figure C–2. The extended standard theory.

However, it turned out to be quite difficult to state the relevant rules, and there were many anomalies. For example, the existence of pairs like *impress* and *impression, oppress* and *oppression,* etc., suggest that *aggression* must be drived from a verb **aggress.* But no such verb exists in English. We can describe something as *untouched by human hands,* but *untouched* cannot be derived as a participle from a nonexistent verb **untouch.*

In the extended standard theory, words are no longer derived by transformations. They are inserted before the transformational cycle begins, and pairs like *criticize* and *criticism* are included as separate items in the lexicon, related by lexical redundancy rules (discussed in C.4.2). It was argued that due to the irregularities and the existence of nominal forms lacking corresponding verb forms, this was a necessary complication for the theory and in fact made it possible to capture more generalities. This version is often referred to as adopting the *lexicalist hypothesis.*

As illustrated in Figure C–2, there is a distinct phase of *lexical insertion* in which lexical items are inserted into the base structure before any of the transformations are done. Of course, the semantic interpretation must operate on the result of this component, since it introduces the words on which the meaning is based.

C.1.2 Generative semantics

At more or less the same time the extended standard theory was developed, there appeared a loosely knit group of researchers who worked within a different model called *generative semantics*. Rather than solve the problems posed by sentences like (1) and (2) with minor modifications to the model, they proposed a sweeping change that dealt with this and many other issues, just as Chomsky's introduction of transformations had provided elegant solutions to a whole range of problems that had confronted immediate constituent grammars.

The basic point of the generativists' proposal was that there should not be a separate semantic interpretation component that generated a semantic structure corresponding to some syntactic structure (or set of syntactic structures). Instead, they argued, semantic representations and syntactic phrase markers should be formal objects of the same kind. The derivation of a sentence begins with a *logical form* (sometimes called the *remote structure*) that is directly interpretable in terms of logic. The transformations convert this step by step into the surface form, from which phonological rules can generate an utterance, as illustrated in Figure C–3. There exist no projection rules (rules of semantic interpretation), but only syntactic transformations.

Examples (1) and (2) above are then handled by the fact that the two sentences are not generated from a single underlying deep structure (as they are in the extended standard theory) but from two totally different logical forms, as illustrated in Figure C–4. This change required the base structures to include *logical variables* like X and Y, as discussed in Section C.3.4.

The fact that the base structures are logical rather than syntactic provides a way of dealing with a number of other phenomena as well. One widely debated example was the problem of analyzing adverbial modifiers. Much of the initial interest in transformational grammar came from its ability to characterize the ambiguity of sentences such as *The chickens are ready to eat* as the result of

Generative Semantics

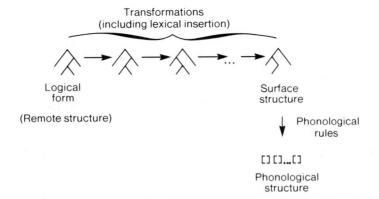

Figure C–3. The generative semantics model.

1)

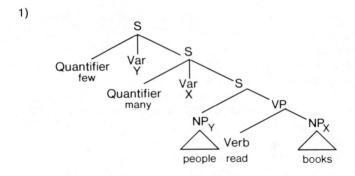

2)

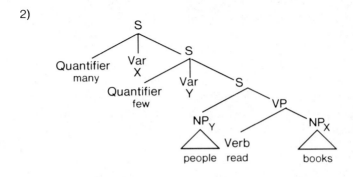

Figure C-4. Logical form of sentences with different quantifier structures.

there being two distinct deep structures from which the same surface structure could be derived. The sentence *They almost killed him* has a similar kind of ambiguity, as illustrated by:

> *They almost killed him, but the doctors did miraculous surgery.*
>
> *They almost killed him, but they decided they couldn't get away with it.*

The generative semanticists argued that there should be two distinct deep structures for *almost kill* and that this could best be done by having a complex structure underlying the word *kill,* corresponding to *cause to die.* The modifier *almost* could then be attached either to *cause* or to *die* in the logical form, accounting for the ambiguity. Transformations could then be applied to convert the complex structure into a single word *kill,* producing the ambiguous surface structure. This was in opposition to the idea that lexical insertion was a separate stage, assuming instead that the substitution of surface lexical items for underlying semantic structures takes place as a part of the transformations.

Much of the debate surrounding generative semantics centered on the question of lexical insertion.

Another debate concerned just what should appear in the logical form. In the standard theory, it was argued that an imperative sentence like *Shut the door* was derived from a deep structure containing an explicit subject *you*, which was deleted by the imperative transformation. This accounted for the appearance of *you* in tag questions like *Shut the door, won't you?*

This kind of reasoning is quite common in transformational grammar and has been the motivation for many of the deep structures. The generative semanticists pushed the argument much further. They argued that a similar extension of logical form is needed to handle sentential modifiers as in:

> *He confidently walked down the garden path.*   (3)
>
> *He apparently walked down the garden path.*   (4)

In (3), the word *confidently* is a direct modifier of the action described in the sentence. In (4), *apparently* does not describe how he walked, but rather says something about the process by which the speaker deduced that he walked. In order to distinguish between these structures, it was proposed that the underlying structure of (4) should explicitly correspond to *It is apparent to me (the speaker) that he walked. . . .* Following this logic further, every sentence was embedded in a variety of *performatives* (structures corresponding to phrases like *I assert, I ask you,* etc.). and *factives* (structures for *it is true that. . .*, *it is apparent that. . .*, etc.).

C.1.3 Montague grammar

During approximately the same period as the development of EST and generative semantics, the logician Richard Montague devised a formalism for treating English as a formal language. He was primarily concerned with problems of semantics and did not deal with the detailed syntactic problems that occupied transformational linguists. However, in the past few years a number of people have extended his theory to make it more comparable with other versions of transformational grammar. The syntactic part is similar to the standard model in overall structure. There is a context-free base (described with a categorial grammar) and a set of transformation rules that operate on a deep structure to derive a surface structure that can be interpreted phonologically.

The difference lies in the way that the syntactic structure and semantic structure are related. Rather than having a set of interpretation rules whose input is a deep structure (as in the standard theory) or a sequence of structures (as in the extended theory), a Montague grammar pairs syntactic and semantic rules. For each syntactic rule there is a corresponding semantic rule. The semantic rule is applied in the derivation of the logical structure whenever the syntactic rule is applied to the syntactic structure. The logical structure is built

Transformational Montague Grammar

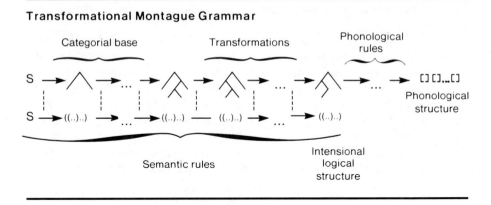

Figure C–5.   Transformational Montague grammar.

up in parallel to the syntactic structure, step by step, as illustrated in Figure C–5.

This one-to-one correspondence of rules makes it possible to shift a good deal of the work into the semantic component. Instead of having constraints on the syntactic rules, there is a general constraint that blocks the application of any syntactic rule if the corresponding semantic rule is not applicable to the logical structure that has been built up. Semantic rules can be used in a systematic way to handle many of the phenomena that call for complex extensions to a transformational grammar, such as the dependence of some transformations on the presence of certain verbs, as in the examples of *force* and *want* discussed in Section 4.4.

In a way, Montague grammar goes against the autonomy of syntax hypothesis, arguing that the rules determining grammaticality are intertwined with semantic rules based on formal logic. It also calls for other extensions (such as the generation of logical variables in the base) discussed below.

C.1.4 Trace theory

A more recent modification of the extended standard theory is of note because it is the theory currently advocated by Chomsky. One problem with the extended standard theory was that although clear in principle, it was hard to flesh out, since the nature of a semantic rule operating on a whole sequence of trees must be complex. In addition, it was noted that the almost universal assumption that the phonological form of a sentence was determined by the surface structure was called into question by phenomena like *contraction*.

This is the oscilloscope Tom used to fix. (5)

This is the oscilloscope Tom used to fix the radio. (6)

Examples (5) and (6) are quite similar in surface structure, although they differ substantially in deep structure. The phrase *used to* in (5) is contracted in normal speech to *useta,* while the same contraction cannot be applied in (6). This implies that phonological processes like contraction are controlled not only by the surface form but by something deeper as well. Rather than suggest that the phonological component operates on the entire derivation, it was proposed that both the phonological and semantic components operate only on the surface structure, but that the surface structure contains *traces* reflecting the relevant information about the deep structure and derivation.

The idea of a trace comes quite naturally from a study of phenomena like those just described. Contraction seems to be blocked precisely in those cases where intuitively we would say 'Something was deleted between the two words we're trying to contract.' In (6), for example, the underlying structure included *Tom used the oscilloscope to fix the radio,* and the phrase *the oscilloscope* was moved out in the formation of a relative clause. If the moved phrase left some kind of trace behind, we could state the contraction rule in a way that blocked contraction across a trace. Once the idea of a trace was established, the same mechanism could be used to convey the necessary semantic information in examples like (1) and (2) above so that both semantic and phonological rules could operate on a surface structure that contains traces, as illustrated in Figure C–6.

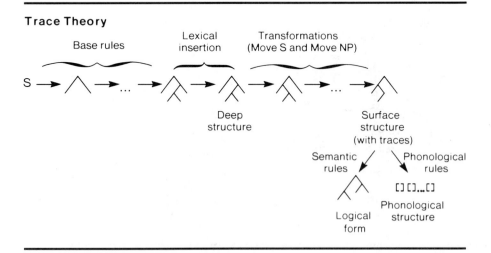

Figure C–6. The trace theory model.

C.1.5 Phrase structure grammars

Perhaps the most radical reorganization of the transformational model is the complete elimination of transformations. Several of the major researchers in the area advocate this step, and even within the main line descending from the standard theory, there is a trend towards reducing the amount of work done by transformations. For example, phenomena like passive and dative are now treated in the base instead of by transformations in most variants of the theory, and Chomsky (1977a) argues that the grammar contains only two transformations: *move S* and *move NP*.

Section 6.7 described an extended version of phrase structure grammar (PSG) which has several additional mechanisms to supplant the use of transformations. We will not repeat the description here, but Figure C–7 fits this theory into the framework presented in this section. In PSG, there is a one-to-one correspondence between syntactic and semantic rules, but this need not be taken into account in the derivation—as it does in Montague grammar (Figure C–5)—since with a context-free grammar the order of derivation is irrelevant. The structure of a sentence is fully determined by the final phrase structure tree (as illustrated in Figure C–7), independently of the order in which the nodes were expanded.

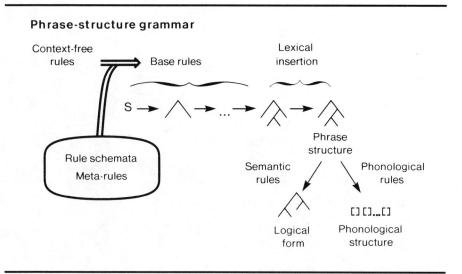

Figure C–7. Phrase structure grammar.

Lexical-functional grammar

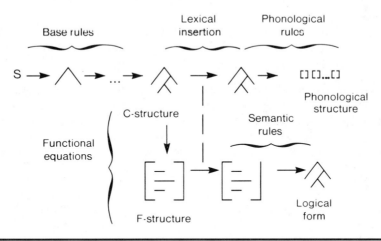

Figure C–8. Lexical-functional grammar.

C.1.6 Lexical-functional grammar

There is a good deal of current interest in one other family of formalisms, the lexical-functional grammars described in Section 6.6 and illustrated in Figure C–8.

The base context-free rules generate a phrase structure tree, to which the corresponding functional equations are applied to generate a functional structure. This in turn is the input to the semantic component. Once again, even though there is a one-to-one correspondence between context-free rules and their associated sets of equations, it is not necessary to carry the derivations forward in parallel, since the rules are not sensitive to the order in which the context-free rules are applied.

In this formalism, as in several of those above, it is possible for the failure to produce an analysis at some later stage (in this case, the building of a consistent functional structure) to block a derivation that succeeded through earlier stages (in this case, the context-free derivation). This *filtering* is a key element of such formalisms.

C.2 Constraints on rule operation

Changes to the overall model are rather large modifications and are proposed infrequently. Much more of the work goes on within one or another of the models, dealing with the formal structures on which the rules operate and with the form of the rules themselves. Changes to structures will be discussed in C.3. Changes to rules can be grouped into two categories:

Adding new kinds of rules. Many of the proposals have presented new kinds of rules that augment the standard set. Often this is necessitated by a shift in the overall model or by the desire to handle a phenomenon previously ignored. We will look at a number of such extensions in Section C.4.

Putting constraints on the form and application of existing rules. At times, the problem with a particular theory is *overgeneration*. If the rules are allowed to operate as stated, they will generate the desired sentences but will also operate in cases where they lead to inappropriate results. One way to deal with this is to keep the basic formulation of the rules and add additional *constraints* to block their application in certain cases.

The word 'constraint' is widely used in transformational linguistics. A grammar can be thought of as a constraint on possible sentences, a grammatical theory can be seen as a constraint on possible mental structuring, etc. At a more precise technical level, there is a body of research on applying constraints to the application of rules. This was motivated by the observation of phenomena like:

Merry wanted to see Barbara.

Merry has a book that pleased Barbara.

Her friend had seen Barbara with Sammy.

Merry finally found Barbara and Sammy.

Who did Merry want to see?	(7)
* *Who does Merry have a book that pleased?*	(8)
Who had her friend seen Barbara with?	(9)
* *Who did Merry finally find Barbara and?*	(10)

In order to generate (7), there is a transformation that moves an embedded NP up to the front of the sentence as a 'wh-' term. This transformation applies to cases in which the NP is an element of an embedded sentence, of a prepositional phrase, and so on, as described in Section B.1.4. However, there are cases like (8) and (10) in which the operation of the rule leads to an ungrammatical sentence. Attempts to rewrite the rule to handle only those cases where it should apply led to too much complexity. It was proposed instead that the rule be left alone and that a *constraint* be added to the grammar explicitly preventing it from operating in certain cases.

Once the idea of constraints began to be widely accepted, a large number of different constraints were proposed. The basic urge was to find the simplest set of constraints that could account for all of the data. As with all of the modifications discussed here, it is difficult to pin down just what simplicity criteria to use. Often the addition of a constraint can simplify the statement of some transformation, at the cost of a more complicated set of constraints. In other cases, changes to transformations or to the base component can eliminate the need for a constraint, but at the cost of other complexities. In some cases, constraints have been justified not only because they have specific consequences for examples but because they fit some other goals. For example, Culicover (1976) argues for a constraint called the *binary principle,* (which is essentially identical to Chomsky's *subjacency condition*) saying *'The binary principle is an essential part of the demonstration that a class of transformational languages is learnable... by a reasonable (formal) language learning procedure.'*

A number of different kinds of constraints have been proposed, some covering the application of specific rules and others applying to derivations in a more general way. The remainder of this section will outline the basic types.

C.2.1 Constraints on individual rules

C.2.1.1 Structures to which rules can apply

The derivation of (8) is blocked by the *A-over-A principle,* one version of which states that an *extraction transformation* (like question formation) can apply only to the highest constituent with a given label. In other words, it cannot pull one NP from inside another NP, although it can pull it out of an S or a PP. This applies to (10) as well, if we assume that a conjunction is analyzed as an NP node dominating two constituent NP nodes. This is an example of a constraint on the structures to which a general rule can be applied. This principle in turn was too general, blocking cases that should not have been blocked. In a number of papers (beginning with Ross, 1967), it has been replaced with more specific constraints. For example, sentences like **Who did you talk to Merry and?* are blocked by the *coordinate structure constraint,* which prevents extraction from a conjoined phrase, while the *sentential subject constraint* prevents the derivation of **Who did that I saw surprise you?* from *That I saw X surprised you* by forbidding a constituent to be moved out of an S that is itself the subject of an S.

C.2.1.2 Structures that a rule can produce

Instead of constraining the form of a structure to which a rule can be applied, a constraint can limit the forms that it can produce. For example, the *attachment constraint* specifies that 'A moved constituent may be attached only to a constituent of the lowest S of which it was originally a constituent, or to the complement of the next higher S if it is moved from a complement itself.' In proposing such a constraint, the linguist is often trying to find a general statement that will cover several things previously dealt with by separate constraints. In addition to specific constraints such as this one, Emonds (1976) has proposed a very general *structure preserving constraint:* 'With the exception of a class of *root transformations* that deal with structures directly dominated by the highest S in a phrase marker..., no transformation may result in a type of structure that is not given in the base rules.' There are some exceptions, such as *stylistic transformations,* but the net effect is to limit strongly the kinds of transformations that can be written and the way they operate. Some researchers see this proposal as a potentially important property of possible human languages and are exploring its consequences for the rest of syntactic theory.

C.2.1.3 Constraints on the form of rules

Section 4.4 mentioned the problems surrounding the use of *essential variables* in rules. They generally appear in rules involving unbounded movement (such as question and relative clause formation) in order to let the extracted phrase come from anywhere within nested structure. Since many of the problems discussed above relate to unbounded movement, it has seemed that they might be solved by limiting the use and nature of variables instead of by imposing explicit constraints. This approach has been explored by Bresnan (1977) and others. Other linguists have dealt with different aspects of transformational form, such as the specification of features and bracketing in the structural description of a transformation and the allowable kinds of structure building in the structural change.

C.2.2 Constraints on derivations

The constraints discussed so far have all dealt with the form or use of an individual rule. It is also possible to specify constraints that apply to the derivation as a whole. This includes the single-rule case, since anything dealing with an individual rule can be thought of as a constraint on the derivation, operating on one particular step. In fact, it has been suggested that transformation rules can be thought of altogether as constraints on legal derivations. There are several ways in which derivations can be constrained:

C.2.2.1 Deep structure constraints

In describing the overall system, one can specify an ordinary context-free base and then add a set of *deep structure constraints* on the structures it can pass along to the transformational component. For example, the *unlike subject constraint* eliminates structures that would produce **I tried for Harry to open the door* and **I screamed for me to open the door* by insisting that the subject of *try* match the subject of an embedded sentence, while the subject of *scream* must not match. These could not be expressed within a context-free base, since they involve identifying parts of two separate constituent structures.

C.2.2.2 Surface structure constraints

At various stages in the history of transformational grammar, people have proposed the use of *surface structure constraints,* at times called *output conditions* or *filters.* The transformation rules work as usual, but at the very end of the derivation, the resulting structure is checked to see if it meets the constraints, and if not, the derivation is rejected. The transformation rules can then be written in a simpler form and allowed to overgenerate, knowing that the bad cases will be filtered out. Culicover (1977, p. 197) says:

> *If the overgenerating grammar that we have established is complex and unrevealing in itself, then there can be little justification for setting up a filter to eliminate the overgeneration. However, if the grammar is elegant and revealing and appears to capture linguistically significant generalizations, then it is worth establishing a filter to eliminate the overgeneration.*

Examples of proposed surface structure constraints are the *internal S constraint* (that putative sentences containing an internal NP that exhaustively dominates S are ungrammatical unless the main verb of that S is a gerund); and Perlmutter's (1971) constraint that any sentence other than an imperative in which there is an S that does not contain a subject in surface structure is ungrammatical. There is another very general use of filters, in which some kind of grammatical marker (often represented as '#') appears in deep structures but is forbidden to appear in a legal surface structure. Any derivation in which such a marker is generated and not deleted gets blocked. Many tricky things can be done with the careful placement and manipulation of such markers.

C.2.2.3 Constraints on rule sequencing

In the standard model, there are a number of conventions for when the rules will be applied. For example, the whole mechanism of the cycle is a kind of 'traffic controller' for the application of the transformation rules. It is possible to think of the transformational component as containing an unordered collection of transformations, and of ordering being the result of constraints on the allowable derivations (e.g., prohibiting those in which a step using transformation A appears following one using transformation B). A number of modifications have been suggested, such as adding pre- and post-cyclic rules, removing the discipline of ordering within the cycle, and letting NP nodes as well as S nodes undergo cycles of transformations. One textbook (Soames and Perlmutter, 1979) discusses a dozen different proposals for cyclicity.

C.2.2.4 Constraining relationships among structures

Each transformation rule specifies a relationship between two tree structures— the one it operates on and the one it produces. It is possible to imagine rules that specify relationships between trees that are not adjacent in the derivation.

Such constraints have been called *derivational constraints*. It has been argued that they are needed in order to get the correct subject agreement in *There {was/were} believed to be {a unicorn/two unicorns} in the garden.* Under some versions of the relevant transformation rules, the verb that at one point of the derivation has *there* as its subject must agree with the NP that was the subject of the relevant embedded sentence at an earlier point of the derivation. It has even been proposed that there are *transderivational constraints,* in which the structures being related are in different derivations. In other words, the applicability of one rule depends on what would have happened if some other rule had been applied. The need for both derivational and transderivational constraints has been a matter of considerable debate.

C.3 New kinds of structures

So far we have been discussing the operation of the rules. It is also possible to make changes to the structures on which the rules operate. We have already seen examples of this, such as the addition of features, in Section 4.4. Often, as in that case, the changes result in something that is formally equivalent but allows generalizations to be stated more directly and easily. In other cases (as in the addition of logical variables), the formal power of the base is altered.

C.3.1 Abstract markers

It was noted in Chapter 4 that the base grammar includes categories for special markers that do not correspond to words of the language. Examples are the 'Q' marker used to trigger question formation and the dummy *pro-form* used for the subject of sentences that will be passivized and have their agent deleted. In the UCLA grammar described in Section 6.5, symbols for case roles (like AGENT) appeared in the base structures. Section C.2.2 mentioned the '#' used to block sentences from passing the output condition, and the traces described in Section C.1.4 are also abstract elements. The status of these elements has often been debated. If used freely, they make it possible to write rules that perform whatever computations could be stated for any computer. If they are not used at all, it is difficult to write a sensible grammar. In general, particular ones have been justified by appeals to universality and constraints on possible human languages.

C.3.2 Syntactic features

As described in Section 4.4, the standard theory assumes that each leaf node in a phrase marker contains a set (unordered) of features. These features play a role in the formalism in three ways: as *inherent features, contextual features,* and *rule features.*

C.3.2.1 Inherent features

Inherent features include *strict subcategorization features* like PLURAL and COUNT, as described in Section 4.4, and *category features,* as described below. This use of features is quite close to that in systemic grammar, as used in Appendix B. Both base and transformation rules can cause features to be associated with nodes, and when lexical insertion takes place, the lexical item must agree with the features for the node into which it is inserted. For example, if the derivation has led to a NOUN node with feature PLURAL, the word *people* can be inserted for the node, but not *person.*

Inherent features have at times been used in ways that are on the borderline between syntax and semantics. For example, the distinction between ABSTRACT and CONCRETE nouns was said to account for the difference in grammaticality between *Sand fell through the cracks* and *Sincerity fell through the cracks,* while the difference between ANIMATE and INANIMATE made *My toothbrush likes tea* ungrammatical. It has been pointed out by many linguists that these features cannot be attached to words on the syntactic level, since there are many examples of contexts (such as fantasy and metaphor) in which sentences apparently violating the restrictions are grammatical. In most recent forms of generative grammar, distinctions like these are treated as semantic.

C.3.2.2 Contextual features

Contextual features, like inherent features, are associated with lexical items, but instead of simply matching the features on a single node, they specify a context surrounding that node. A typical example is their use in dealing with the transitivity of verbs. We want to specify that an intransitive verb like *sleep* can appear in *They are sleeping* but not in *They slept him,* while the transitive verb *hit* appears in *She hit the ball* but not in *She hit,* and *eat* appears in both forms. There can be more precise restrictions, for example stating that the verb *lie* (for the sense of the word indicating physical position, not falsehood) must appear before a PP or an adverb, as in *Lie down* or *You can lie on the couch,* but not *We will just lie.* We can associate one or more contexts with a lexical item, as shown in Figure C–9.

The underline indicates the context in which the word appears—a notation similar to that for context-sensitive grammars, as described in Section 4.2. The

sleep	Verb, [___]		*lie*	Verb, [___ PP]
hit	Verb, [___ NP]		*lie*	Verb, [___ Adverb]
eat	Verb, [___ NP]		*rely*	Verb, [___ [PP *on* NP]]
eat	Verb, [___]			

Figure C–9. Contextual features associated with lexical items.

entry for *hit* indicates that it must appear before an NP, while the one for *lie* indicates that it must appear before some PP or adverb. The entry for *rely* is even more specific, indicating that it must precede a PP whose preposition is *on*. This is too simplistic a view of the linguistic data to be a full analysis of transitivity, as we do get sentences like *This room sleeps ten* and *She hits like a Mack truck*. However, these are treated as involving other aspects of the grammar.

Contextual features are also used to formalize the kind of restrictions mentioned for features like ANIMATE above. Verbs are given contextual features (called *selection restrictions*) specifying inherent features of other nodes in the context in which they appear. For example, *admire* has the contextual feature [+ANIMATE ___], indicating that it must be preceded by an animate subject, thus ruling out *Sincerity admires John*.

C.3.2.3 Rule features

Rule features are associated with words in order to indicate the applicability of particular rules to structures containing those words. As a simple example, the *equi* transformation introduced in Chapter 4 allows us to derive *Wendy wanted to dance* from a deep structure in which *Wendy* is the subject of *dance*. But we cannot derive *Wendy forced to dance,* which needs an explicit pronoun, as in *Wendy forced herself to dance*. We can indicate this by associating different rule features with the verbs *want* and *force*. The detailed formulation of these features and the rules for their application is a matter of debate and we will not pursue it further.

C.3.3 Categories

C.3.3.1 Category features

It is now standard in many forms of transformational grammar to consider lexical categories (such as VERB and NOUN) as just one kind of feature. Since the mechanisms needed for feature categorization can do all of the work needed to deal with lexical categories, the general consideration of parsimony has led to treating them together. In the simplest form, there is a feature associated with each syntactic category, such as +VERB, +NOUN, and +ADJECTIVE. However, once categories were treated as features, it was noted that certain generalizations could be captured by breaking lexical categorization into orthogonal components.

Certain general rules apply to verbs and adjectives but not nouns, while others apply to nouns and adjectives but not verbs. To express this in the most parsimonious way, it was suggested that in place of the traditional categories there be two independent feature dimensions, ±NOUN and ±VERB. A verb is +VERB -NOUN, a noun is -VERB +NOUN, an adjective is +VERB +NOUN and a preposition -VERB -NOUN. Rules can then be stated as operating on anything with a given feature (for example, +VERB), thereby covering more than one category. Other analyses have suggested different factorizations, for example proposing that both nouns and verbs are +SUBJECT while nouns and adjectives are +OBJECT. The details of this analysis are controversial, but many different current versions of transformational grammar replace at least some traditional lexical categories with sets of features.

C.3.3.2 The X-bar convention

There is another kind of generality that has led to similar extensions, dealing with the rules relating a lexical category to the composite syntactic category of which it is the head. It was motivated by the problems of nominalization raised by the generative semanticists. If (as in the extended standard theory) the words *destroy* and *destruction* are not related by transformations, there needs to be another way to capture the generalizations that cover both NPs (*the destruction by the heathens*) and VPs (*was destroyed by the heathens*). There is a systematic way in which the category NP is related to NOUN that is similar to the relationship between VP and VERB and the one between PP and PREPOSITION. In order state this regularity systematically, rules can be formulated in terms of the relationship between any category (X) and the category of which it is the head, labeled '$\overline{X}$' or 'X'.' Thus, for example, NP becomes $\overline{N}$, since its head is a noun. This *X-bar convention* can be compounded, leading to categories such as $\overline{\overline{V}}$, a category whose head is a $\overline{V}$. There have been proposals that every symbol (terminal and nonterminal) of the grammar must be either a specific lexical item or a *grammatical formative* made up of combinations of features with some number of bars. Other researchers argue that there are constraints on the form of rules, such as one that a rule for a category $\overline{X}$ must contain a constituent of type X and cannot contain another $\overline{X}$. Some of these, such as the one called the *uniform three-level hypothesis,* place very complex constraints on the way that barred components can be combined into rules, arguing that they reflect universals of the human language faculty.

C.3.3.3 Semantic categories

In developing semantic interpretation rules for grammars, it has always been assumed that they will be organized in some way around the different categories—that an NP will correspond to one kind of semantic structure, a VP to a different one, a NOUN to yet another and so forth. In Montague grammar, this correspondence is the basis for determining the syntactic categories. As a result, the grammar includes a large number of syntactic categories corresponding to all of the possible semantic classes. Since the semantic classes are developed compositionally out of simpler classes, it is convenient to use *categorial grammar* for the syntactic component. The category of each node is not a single symbol but a formula constructed of basic symbols, as described in Section 3.5.

C.3.3.4 Squishes

One final variation on categories is different in a unique way, in that it denies the basic possibility of assigning items to a finite number of categories and stating rules in terms of membership in them. It grew out of the observation by Ross (1967) that there were structures that could generally be used in place of an NP, but with different degrees of acceptability. A phrase such as *his going* can be used in many of the same positions as a normal noun phrase, as in the sentences:

> *I regretted his going.*
> *His going surprised me.*
> *?After his going we hired an athlete.*
> *??His going's main effect was to end the feud.*

These sentences differ in their acceptability to many speakers. According to Ross's proposal, properties like *nouniness* were assigned along a scale called a *squish*. He then attempted to formulate rules relating these squishes to degrees of acceptability. This did not lead to a clear formalism, and although phenomena like this have been noted by many linguists, current formalisms do not attempt to deal with them.

C.3.4 Logical variables

Even though transformational grammar moved beyond context-free grammars in its notion of derivation, the structures it works with in the standard theory are still context-free—each node has a complex of features and a sequence of children. For many purposes, however, it is necessary to have some kind of interdependence between nodes that are not adjacent in the tree. As an obvious example, in order to state the reflexive transformation, we need to be able to state that the two noun phrases are *co-referential*. The sentence *He bit him* must be transformed into *He bit himself* if the subject and object refer to the same person, and must not otherwise.

The most obvious notation here is to use some kind of variable (like those of formal logic or algebra) which has an identity and can appear more than once. Thus reflexive is applicable to *He$_x$ bit him$_x$*, but not to *He$_x$ bit him$_y$* with x and y not equal. In this case, the variables are associated with the action of the transformation. They indicate identity between two pieces of the phrase structure, and they are often called *indices,* since they index this structure.

However, there are other phenomena for which the most direct formalization calls for having variables appear in the structures themselves, not just in the structural description or structural change of transformation rules. The phenomenon of *pronominalization* has been a continuing area of research. Given a sentence like *Caesar got what he wanted,* we can posit a deep structure in which the subject of *want* is an NP matching the one that is the subject of *get*—that it is essentially *Caesar got what Caesar wanted.* A transformation can substitute a pronoun for an NP when it is identical to one in an earlier position. In fact, this rule is slightly more complex, as indicated by the sentences:

> *Alice was confused when she woke up.*
> *When she woke up, Alice was confused.*
> * *She was confused when Alice woke up.*
> *Realizing that he was unpopular didn't disturb Oscar.*
> * *Realizing that Oscar was unpopular didn't disturb him.*

In these examples, the starred sentences are grammatical but can not be given the *coreferent* reading, in which the name and pronoun refer to the same person. Lees and Klima (1963) gave transformation rules to explain just when pronominalization could take place, and developed a concept of *command* to describe the relationship of the pronominalized phrase to its *antecedent*.

However, this kind of analysis ran into problems with many sentences, such as:

> *Everyone loves his wife.* (11)
> *Goldwater didn't win, although it had been predicted.* (12)
> *The man who shows he wants it will get the prize he deserves.* (13)

In (11), the rule given above would require that the deep structure correspond to *Everyone loves everyone's wife,* which of course has a quite different meaning. In (12), the antecedent of *it* would have to correspond in meaning to *Goldwater won,* but in the way that negation was treated in the rest of the theory, there was no constituent having this meaning without the negation (in fact, this was one of the examples used by the generative semanticists in arguing that there is a logical structure instead of a deep structure). Finally, (13) leads to an infinite regress, since the antecedent of the second *he* is *the man who shows he wants it,* which contains the pronoun *it,* which is a substitute for *the prize he deserves,* which in turn contains *he.*

Examples like these led to the postulation of more abstract deep structures in which the phrases underlying pronouns contain logical variables rather than copies of their antecedents. There are many problems in dealing with the meaning of such variables and the ways that they combine syntactic and semantic considerations. They play a significant role in some of the newer forms of transformational grammar, especially those that eliminate some or all transformations. Many of the interdependencies that were captured by having transformations move things from one place to another can be stated instead by having multiple occurrences of a variable. Often this goes along with the shifting of work from the syntactic component (which has traditionally not made use of variables) to the semantic component (which is usually based on a formalism such as the lambda calculus, which deals with variables as one of its central points). As described in Chapter 6, variables play a major role in lexical-functional grammar and generalized phrase structure grammar.

C.3.5 Derived categories

In order to eliminate transformations, one must find other means of handling phenomena such as unbounded movement. In the newer versions of phrase structure grammar, this is done by introducing a new kind of category called a *derived category*. Each derived category represents a constituent of some ordinary category that has a 'hole' where some other category is missing. The details and application of these categories were described in Section 6.7.

C.4 New kinds of rules

Many of the proposals mentioned above call for adding some new kind of rule to the basic transformational and context-free derivation rules. Some of them call for relatively minor changes, while others are radically different. As with the other modifications, it is important to understand the way that a new kind of rule fits into an overall framework. It may add new complexities but at the same time allow simplifications elsewhere in the formalism.

C.4.1 Transformations using relational structure

One of the proposed changes has been the use of relational structure in the formulation of transformations. In the standard theory, relations like 'subject' and 'indirect object' play no formal role. We can choose to call the NP that is the first constituent of an S its subject, but in doing so we are only providing a name for discussion—the rules deal only with the structure of the tree. In formalisms other than transformational grammar, such as systemic grammar and case grammar (as described in Chapter 6), the identification of functional relations between structures plays a much larger role.

Some linguists working within the transformational model have proposed that transformations be stated in terms of relations instead of in terms of specific tree structures, thus achieving greater generality, including the ability to capture generalizations that cut across languages. As discussed in Section 4.5, the desire to find linguistic universals has been an important motivation in the development of formalisms. More thoroughly developed theories of this kind, such as *relational grammar* (Johnson, 1977), posit the existence of a universal *relation hierarchy,* and rules related to it, as described in Section 6.2. Some other formalisms, such as *cognitive grammar* (Lakoff and Thompson, 1975) and *arc-pair grammar* (Johnson and Postal, 1980), have adopted a similar relational approach, and there are many connections to case grammar, as described in Chapter 6.

C.4.2 Lexical redundancy rules

Several earlier sections have mentioned the application of *redundancy rules* that relate one lexical entry to another. These rules are often used to capture generalizations that would otherwise require some kind of transformation. Several different kinds have been proposed.

C.4.2.1 Feature redundancy rules

In discussing the use of features in Section C.3.2, we pointed out that features are often organized into hierarchies. For example, if there are features HUMAN, ANIMATE, and ABSTRACT used in selection restrictions, it will always be the case that the presence of +HUMAN implies +ANIMATE and –ANIMATE implies –HUMAN. Similarly, –ABSTRACT is implied by +ANIMATE. If the formalism simply associates an arbitrary set of features with a lexical item, this generalization is not part of the analysis—there is no systematic rule preventing combinations like +HUMAN –ANIMATE, even though they never appear.

Redundancy rules are a means of stating such relationships. They specify that an item having a particular combination of features must (or conversely must not) have certain other features. Thus, for example, the grammar writer need only specify that *person* has the feature +HUMAN and the presence of +ANIMATE and –ABSTRACT will follow. Similarly, if features are used for lexical categories, we would have rules indicating that the feature +PRONOUN implies +NOUN and –COMMON, +TRANSITIVE implies +VERB, etc.

C.4.2.2 Related verb forms

Once the general idea of redundancy rules was accepted, it was noticed that it could be used to describe other syntactic phenomena that had been problematic. It had long been noted that there was a systematic relationship between pairs of sentences such as *Ray broke the glass* and *The glass broke*. These were not as systematic as the passive voice (*The glass was broken by Ray*), since many verbs could take both forms independently. For example, *Tom ate the apple* does not correspond to *The apple ate*. Jackendoff (1975) suggested that there was a redundancy rule relating two different lexical items associated with the word *break*. We can represent them as shown in Figure C–10.

/broke/ *(phonological)*	/broke/ *(phonological)*
+Verb	+Verb
+Past	+Past
+[NP$_1$ ___]	+[NP$_1$ ___ NP$_2$]
Break(NP$_1$) *(semantic)*	Cause(NP$_1$, Break(NP$_2$)) *(semantic)*

Figure C–10. Related lexical entries.

A general redundancy rule can be formulated that operates on the contextual and semantic features:

$$\{+\text{Verb}, +[\text{NP}_1 \underline{\quad}], X(\text{NP}_1)\} \rightarrow$$
$$\{+\text{Verb}, +[\text{NP}_1 \underline{\quad} \text{NP}_2], \text{Cause}(\text{NP}_1, X(\text{NP}_2))\}$$

This rule applies to any lexical item having the features specified on its left-hand side, producing a new item in which they are replaced by the ones on the right, unless the item is marked as not being appropriate for this rule.

The same idea has been applied to things that had been traditionally handled by transformations, such as some instances of the passive. The sentence *the glass was broken by Ray* is generated using a lexical item of the form:

/broken/ *(phonological)*
+Verb
+Past Participle
$+[\text{NP}_1 \ be \ \underline{\quad} \ [_{\text{PP}} \ by \ \text{NP}_2]]$
$\text{Cause}(\text{NP}_2, \text{Break}(\text{NP}_1))$ *(semantic)*

This item could be created by a redundancy rule:

$$\{+\text{Verb}, +[\text{NP}_1 \underline{\quad}], X(\text{NP}_1)\} \rightarrow$$
$$\{+\text{Verb}, +[\text{NP}_1 \ be \ \underline{\quad} \ [_{\text{PP}} \ by \ \text{NP}_2]], \text{Cause}(\text{NP}_2, X(\text{NP}_1))\}$$

Many of the details have been simplified or ignored here, but a more elaborate version of such rules can be used to account for a wide variety of sentences that previously called for transformations.

It has been argued that such lexical rules are more 'local' and that it is easier to allow unsystematic exceptions to them than to the more general transformation rules. In theories using redundancy rules, numerous idiosyncratic exceptions to a relationship are taken as evidence for handling it in the lexicon. Even a fairly regular relationship like the passive has exceptions, as indicated by:

The committee arrived at a conclusion.

The committee arrived at the stadium.

A conclusion was arrived at by the committee.

* The stadium was arrived at by the committee.

In advocating the use of contextual features (as described in Section C.3.2), Bresnan (1978) argues that a formalism that puts more of the regularities into the lexicon is more 'realistic' from a psychological point of view, since it is computationally easier for a person to look something up than to compute it each time it is needed. Clearly, the human lexical capacity must be large, just to hold the tens of thousands of distinct vocabulary items. It is not unreasonable to think that it is several times larger in order to contain grammatical features as well.

C.4.3 Meta-rules

Section 6.7 described the use of *meta-rules* whose outputs were rules, rather than phrase structures. These rules provide elegant solutions to a number of syntactic problems, and are described further in that section.

C.4.4 Semantic rules

Throughout this appendix, there have been a number of discussions of the use of semantic rules in conjunction with syntactic rules. The trend towards linking the two components more closely is visible in almost every variation of transformational theory, and the most active new theories place a heavy emphasis on the use of formal semantics. Most of the semantic formalisms are based on some form of the *lambda calculus*. In some theories (such as Montague grammar and phrase structure grammars), there is a pairing of semantic rules with individual syntactic rules. In others (such as trace theory), the correspondence is not as tight, and the semantic rules (which may include more than one kind) operate on some output of the syntactic component. We will not go into the details in this volume, but they are discussed at length in the volume on meaning. In this section, we will list some of the major ways in which things formerly done with syntactic rules (usually transformations) have been shifted to the semantic component.

Capturing structural generalities. We noted above that there is a good deal of similarity between the structure of a sentence and of the corresponding nominalized NP, such as *the severe criticism of the press by the President*. In the original theory, both were generated as Ss in the deep structure and the NP form was produced by transformations. In the newer theories, the two are produced independently. The rules for expanding NP and those for expanding S have all of the relevant components on their own. The commonality is captured by having them interpreted by semantic rules that produce similar semantic structures.

Movement and deletion. Many structures have generally been characterized as involving movement (as in *Which eggplant did you tell him to cook?*) and deletion (as in *Omar wanted to go*). However, they can be formalized instead as exhibiting semantic dependencies between separate parts of the phrase structure. Instead of treating *which eggplant* as having been moved out of a position as the object of *cook*, we can say that it was generated at the top and that a 'hole' was generated as the object. The fact that it is the eggplant that gets cooked is accounted for by semantic interpretation rules dealing with structures containing wh- phrases and holes. Similarly, the fact that Omar is the one who would do the going as well as the wanting is seen as a relation between a higher NP and a null subject, rather than the result of deleting an NP containing *Omar* from the embedded S. In a similar way, the relationship between *Mary* *gives Fido to John* and *Mary gives John Fido* can be captured by the lexical redundancy rules and by the semantic rules, not by the syntax.

Pronouns and quantification. As discussed above in Section C.3.4, pronouns and quantifiers have always been difficult to handle syntactically. Their proper treatment has been a major area of debate between exponents of the standard theory and those favoring generative semantics and Montague grammar. By allowing logical variables to be generated in the base and by interpreting them through the use of *semantic construal rules,* it is possible to treat them in a more regular way.

Selectivity. Many of the newer theories allow the grammar to overgenerate on the assumption that the semantic component will eliminate the undesired outputs. For example, the difference between transitive and intransitive verbs can be ignored in writing the phrase structure rules and can be represented instead in the semantic formulas associated with the lexical items. The verb *arrive* has a semantic form that calls for only one argument, while the rule 'VP → VERB NP' calls for the insertion of the semantic interpretation of its object NP as the second argument of the semantic representation for the verb. *They arrived him* is ruled out because of a mismatch of semantic types. This kind of semantic filtering is used extensively in the phrase structure theories and functional grammars discussed in Chapter 6.

Ambiguity. In many theories that reduce the role of transformations, the base structures are closer to the surface form than in the original version. For example, the sentences *Warren is eager to please* and *Warren is easy to please* are generated with identical base rules. It is therefore necessary to have a mechanism to account for their different interpretations and for the ambiguity of *The chicken is ready to eat.* By allowing identical syntactic rules to have different associated semantic rules, it is possible to induce different semantic representations for these, without assigning distinct syntactic structures.

It should be apparent from this list that there is a tremendous potential for dealing with phenomena in the semantic rules. This wealth of possibilities goes hand in hand with the problem of formulating the rules so that they account for the data without being *ad hoc.* Just as the development of transformational grammar in its first decade was devoted to exploring the form and power of transformations, the theme for the coming years will be the exploration of semantic formalisms and their integration into the grammar.

Further Reading for Appendix C

The general readings for this appendix are the ones listed for Chapter 4. More specific details are contained in the papers referenced explicitly in the appendix.

Appendix D

An ATN Grammar
for English

Contents of Appendix D

This appendix contains a summary of the augmented transition network formalism and grammar developed in Chapter 5. It is intended as a reference and depends for understanding on the presentation in that chapter. Section D.1 contains the DL definitions for the structures and procedures discussed in Chapter 5. It does not include the additions needed for proper treatment of the hold register, and does not give a detailed account of the operation of conditions and actions. Section D.2 summarizes the English grammar developed in Chapter 5. This grammar covers many of the major structures of English but is by no means complete. In particular, many of the parsing constructs with semantic content, such as conjunction, ellipsis, and noun modifier or prepositional phrase attachment, are not included. Also omitted are some things that were left as exercises, such as the proper sequence of auxiliaries and relative clauses with an embedded relative pronoun. However, the grammar given here should provide a useful reference for following the examples of Chapter 5 and for anyone trying to implement an English natural language system.

D.1 Formal definitions for ATN structures and processes

A T N
G R A M M A R
	Describes: a formal structure defining a language
	Roles:
	  Networks: a set of *augmented transition networks,* each with a different label
	  Distinguished network: one of the networks, usually with label 'S'
		D–2

Figure D–1. Augmented transition network grammar.

Describes: a pattern for the constituent structure of a composite category

Roles:

Label: a *composite syntactic category*	3–8
States: a set of *states*	§
Arcs: a set of *arcs*	§
Initial state: a state of the network	
There is only one initial state and no terminal states (see the text).	
Feature dimensions: a set of *feature dimensions*	5–10
Role names: a set of *role names*	§

Classes:

AUGMENTED TRANSITION NETWORK

ARC

Describes: a transition in the network

Kinds of Arc: *Category, Seek, Jump, Send*   D–7 D–8 D–9 D–10

Roles:

Label: – *depends on the kind of arc*
Starting state: a state of the network
Ending state: a state of the network
Initializations: a set of *initializations*; possibly empty   5–9
Conditions: a set of *conditions*; possibly empty   5–9
Actions: a sequence of *actions*; possibly empty   5–9

STATE

Describes: a state in the network

Roles:

Label: a sequence of characters
No two states in a grammar can have the same label.

^c**Outgoing arcs:** the set of arcs in the network with this state as their starting state
^c**Incoming arcs:** the set of arcs in the network with this state as their ending state

ROLE NAME

Describes: a name for a role register

Basic Structure: a sequence of characters

A role name has no relevant internal structure. All that matters is that it be distinct from other role names and the names of feature dimensions associated with the same network.

Figure D–2. Augmented transition network.

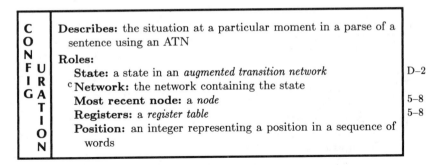

Figure D–3. A configuration representing the state of an ATN parse.

Parse a sequence of words with an ATN grammar (nondeterministic)

Purpose: Produce a structure representing a parsing of a sequence of words as a sentence in the language defined by the grammar

This definition together with the following ones include the basic ATN operations. Some additional mechanisms (such as hold registers) are not included but are described in the text of Chapter 5.

Background: an *ATN grammar*   D–1

Inputs: a sequence of words

Results: a *register-structure node*   5–8

This node represents the sentence as a whole. Its registers will contain nodes for its constituents, as illustrated in Figure 5–7.

Basic Method:
- *Create a register table* for the distinguished network of the grammar with no initializations and a null configuration.   D–5
- *Match* the distinguished network against the sequence of words, beginning at position 1, starting in its initial state, with the register table.   D–6
- If the match succeeds and the position returned is one greater than the length of the word sequence, return the node resulting from the match. Otherwise fail.

Figure D–4. Top-down parsing with an ATN grammar.

Create a register table for a network with a set of initializations using a configuration

Purpose: Create a table with registers set to initial values

Inputs:

    Network: an *ATN*   D–2

    Initializations: a set of *initializations*   5–9

    Configuration: a *configuration*   D–3

    This configuration is used to determine the values to be used in initializing the new node. There will be no configuration given for the top-level instance of the distinguished network, which has no initializations.

Results: a *register table*   5–8

Working Structures: a register table; initially empty

Basic Method:

■ For each *feature dimension* of the network do: 5–10

    Add an entry to the table whose key is the name of the dimension and whose entry is the default for the dimension.

■ For each of the initializations do:

    ■Find the *value* in the configuration.

    ■Add the result to the register table under the *key*.   5–9

■ Return the register table.

Figure D–5. Procedure to create register tables.

Match an ATN against a sequence of words beginning at a position, starting in a state with a register table (nondeterministic)

Purpose: Test whether there is a match

Inputs:

    Network: an *augmented transition network*   D–2

    Words: a sequence of words

    State: a state in the network

    Position: an integer representing a position in the word sequence

    Registers: a register table

Results: a node and an integer representing a position in the words

This position is the word following the constituent parsed. It will be one greater than the length of the sequence if the constituent completes the sequence.

Working Structures:

    Configuration: a configuration; initially a new configuration with: D–3

        ▪state = the state

        ▪position = the position

        ▪most recent node = empty

        ▪registers = the registers

Basic Method: Keep repeating:

■ Choose one of the outgoing arcs of the state of the configuration.

■ *Match the arc* against the words, using the configuration.   §

■ If the match succeeds, then assign its result as the configuration. Otherwise fail.

■ If the chosen arc was a *send arc*, then: D–10

    ▪Create a new node with:

        ▪label = the label of the network

        ▪registers = the registers of the configuration

    ▪Return this node and the position of the configuration.

Procedures:

Match an arc against a sequence of words, using a configuration (nondeterministic)

Inputs: an arc, a sequence of words, and a configuration

Results: a configuration

The procedure for matching is different for each of the four kinds of arc, as defined in D–7, D–8, D–9, and D–10.

Figure D–6. Match an ATN.

	Describes: a transition by matching a single word	
C A T E G O R Y	**A Kind of:** *Arc*	D–2
	Background: an *ATN* and a *dictionary*	D–2 D–11
	Roles:	
	Label: the name of a *lexical category*	D–11
	Starting state: a state of the ATN	
	Ending state: a state of the ATN	
	Conditions: a set of *conditions*	5–9
	Actions: a set of *actions*	5–9
	Procedures:	

A R C

> Match a category arc against a sequence of words, using a configuration (nondeterministic)

Purpose: Produce a new configuration

Inputs: a category arc, a sequence of words, and a *configuration*   D–3

Results: a configuration

Working Structures:
   Word sense: a *word sense*   D–11
   Category: the lexical category that is the label of the arc

Basic Method:
- If the position from the configuration is greater than the length of the sequence of words, then fail.
- Choose a word sense in the dictionary entry for the word at the position and assign it as the word sense.
- If the category of the word sense is not the category, fail.
- Create a new node with:
  - label = the category
  - registers = an empty table
- For each feature dimension of the category, put an entry into the registers of the new node with:
  - key = the name of the dimension
  - entry =
    - if there is an entry for the dimension in the word sense, then that entry
    - otherwise, the default for the dimension.
- Create a new configuration, copying the old one but with:
  - most recent node = the new node
  - state = the ending state of the arc
  - position = one plus the position from the old configuration.
- *Test the conditions* of the arc on the new configuration. If they fail, then fail.   5–9
- *Carry out the actions* of the arc on the new configuration   5–9
- Return the new configuration.

Figure D–7. Category arc.

Describes: a transition by recursively matching a network

A Kind of: *Arc* D–2

Background: an *ATN grammar* and a particular network in which D–1
the arc appears

S E E K

A R C

Roles:

> **Label:** a symbol that is the label of a network of the grammar
> or a state in one of the networks
> **Starting state:** a state of the network in which the arc appears
> **Ending state:** a state of the network in which the arc appears
> **Initializations:** a set of *initializations* 5–9
> **Conditions:** a set of *conditions* 5–9
> **Actions:** a set of *actions* 5–9

Procedures:

Match a seek arc against a sequence of words, using a configuration

Purpose: Produce a new configuration

Inputs: a seek arc, a sequence of words, and a *configuration* D–3

Results: a configuration

Working Structures:

> **Network:** a network; if the label of the arc is:
> > ■the label of a network, then that network.
> > ■the label of a state, then the network containing that
> > state.
>
> **State:** a state; if the label of the arc is:
> > ■the label of a state, then that state.
> > ■the label of a network, then the initial state of the
> > network.
>
> **Position:** an integer that is the position from the configuration
> **Registers:** a register table that is the result of *creating registers* D–5
> for the network with the initializations of the arc using the
> configuration

Basic Method:

- ■ *Match the network* against the input sequence beginning at the D–6
  position, starting in the state, with the registers.
- ■ Create a new configuration that is a copy of the old configuration except with:
  - ■most recent node = the node returned by the match
  - ■state = the ending state of the arc
  - ■position = the position returned by the match.
- ■ *Test the conditions* of the arc on the new configuration. If they 5–9
  fail, the match fails.
- ■ *Carry out the actions* of the arc on the new configuration. 5–9
- ■ Return the new configuration.

Figure D–8. Seek arc.

J
U
M
P

A
R
C

Describes: a transition that uses no words from the sequence

A Kind of: *Arc*   D–2

Background: an *ATN*   D–2

Roles:
    Label: the symbol 'JUMP'
    Starting state: a state of the ATN
    Ending state: a state of the ATN
    Conditions: a set of *conditions*   5–9
    Actions: a set of *actions*   5–9

Procedures:

Match a jump arc against a sequence of words,
using a configuration

Purpose: Produce a new configuration

Inputs: a jump arc and a *configuration*   D–3

Results: a configuration

Basic Method:
- Create a new configuration that is a copy of the old configuration except with:
  - state = the ending state of the arc.
- *Test the conditions* of the arc on the new configuration. If they fail, the match fails.   5–9
- *Carry out the actions* of the arc on the new configuration.   5–9
- Return the new configuration.

Figure D–9.   Jump arc.

S E N D **A R C**	**Describes:** a transition that terminates a network

Describes: a transition that terminates a network

A Kind of: *Arc* D–2

Background: an *ATN* D–2

Roles:
  Label: the symbol 'SEND'
  Starting state: a state of the ATN
  Conditions: a set of *conditions* 5–9
  Actions: a set of *actions* 5–9

  A send arc has no ending state or initializations.

Procedures:

Match a jump arc against a sequence of words,
using a configuration

Purpose: Produce a configuration

Inputs: a send arc, a sequence of words and a *configuration* D–3

Results: a configuration

Basic Method:
- *Test the conditions* of the arc on the configuration. If they fail, 5–9
  the match fails.
- *Carry out the actions* of the arc on the configuration. 5–9
- Return the configuration.

Figure D–10. Send arc.

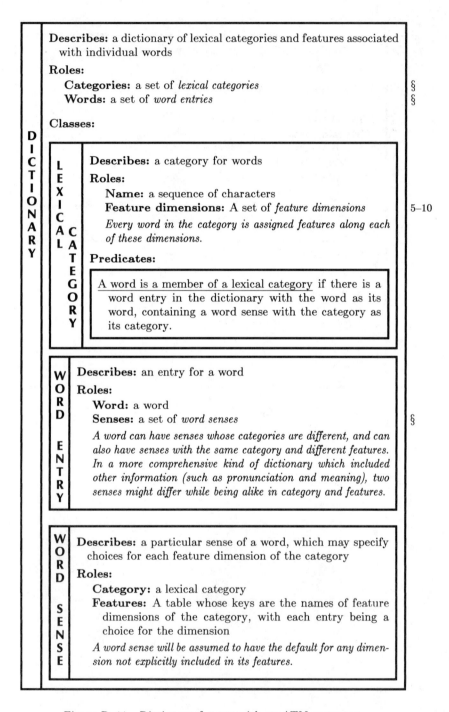

Describes: a dictionary of lexical categories and features associated with individual words

Roles:

    Categories: a set of *lexical categories*   §

    Words: a set of *word entries*   §

Classes:

D I C T I O N A R Y

L E X I C A L   C A T E G O R Y

Describes: a category for words

Roles:

    Name: a sequence of characters

    Feature dimensions: A set of *feature dimensions*   5–10

    Every word in the category is assigned features along each of these dimensions.

Predicates:

A word is a member of a lexical category if there is a word entry in the dictionary with the word as its word, containing a word sense with the category as its category.

W O R D   E N T R Y

Describes: an entry for a word

Roles:

    Word: a word

    Senses: a set of *word senses*   §

    A word can have senses whose categories are different, and can also have senses with the same category and different features. In a more comprehensive kind of dictionary which included other information (such as pronunciation and meaning), two senses might differ while being alike in category and features.

W O R D   S E N S E

Describes: a particular sense of a word, which may specify choices for each feature dimension of the category

Roles:

    Category: a lexical category

    Features: A table whose keys are the names of feature dimensions of the category, with each entry being a choice for the dimension

    A word sense will be assumed to have the default for any dimension not explicitly included in its features.

Figure D–11. Dictionary for use with an ATN grammar.

D.2 An ATN grammar

For the sake of compactness, this section uses a number of abbreviations, as shown in Figure D–12. Abbreviations for the register and feature names are given with the individual networks. The network drawings have also been simplified by combining all arcs with the same starting and ending states into a single arc, labeling it with all of the arc identifiers.

Abbreviation	Notation used in Chapter 5
Referencing:	
C.R	The R of C
R.last	The last member of R
COPY	a copy based on ↑
dummy X(xxx)	a dummy X with word $= xxx$
Initializations:	
R1←↑.R2	Initialize R1 to the R2 of ↑
Actions:	
R1 ← R2	Set R1 to R2
R1 ⇐ R2	Append R2 to R1
Conditions:	
C.R=X	The R of C is X
C.R $\neq$ X	The R of C is not X
R $= \emptyset$	R is empty
R $\neq \emptyset$	R is not empty
R $\equiv xxx$	The word in R is xxx
(R1+R2) $\in$ dictionary	R1 and R2 have a combined dictionary entry

R stands for a register (possibly *); C for a constituent; X for a feature or constituent.

Figure D–12. Abbreviations used in the networks.

The S network

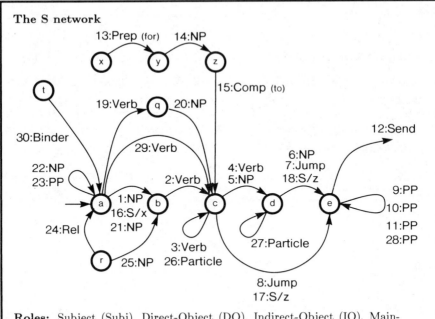

Roles: Subject (Subj), Direct-Object (DO), Indirect-Object (IO), Main-Verb (MV), Binder, Auxiliaries (Auxs), Modifiers (Mods), Question-Element (QE)

Feature Dimensions: Voice: Active Passive; *default,* Active.
Mood: Decl Int Imper Bound Rel WhRel; *default,* Decl.

The hold register is not part of any network, but is handled by a special mechanism.

Initializations, Conditions, and Actions:

a1b.   **C:** [*.Ques=No *.Case=Subj; Mood≠Int]   **A:** [Subj←*]

b2c.   **C:** [**Subject-verb agreement** (*As below, with * replacing* MV)]
       A: [MV←*]

c3c.   **C:** [**Verb sequence conditions** (*See below*)]
       A: [Auxs⇐MV; MV←*]

c4d.   **C:** [*.Form=Past-Part; MV.Type=Be]   **A:** [Voice←Passive;
       Auxs⇐MV; MV←*; DO←Subj; Subj←dummy NP]

c5d.   **C:** [*.Case=Obj]   **A:** [DO←*]

d6e.   **C:** [*.Case=Obj]   **A:** [IO←DO; DO←*]

d7e.   and c8e.   *No initializations, conditions, or actions*

e9e.   **A:** [Mods⇐*]

Figure D–13. The S network.

e10e. **C:** [*.Prep≡*by*; Voice=Passive; Subj=dummy NP]
      A: [Subj←*.Prepobj]

e11e. **C:** [*.Prep≡*(to or for)*; IO=∅] **A:** [IO←*.Prepobj]

e12. **C:** [If Mood=Int or Mood=WhRel then Hold=∅; **Transitivity conditions** (*See below*)]

x13y. **C:** [*≡*for*]

y14z. **C:** [*.Case=Obj] **A:** [Subj←*]

z15c. **C:** [*≡*to*] **A:** [MV←dummy Verb with Type=Modal]

a16b. **A:** [Subj←*]

c17e. **I:** [Subj←↑.Subj] **A:** [DO←*]

d18e. **I:** [Subj←↑.DO] **A:** [IO←DO; DO←*]

a19q. **C:** [*.Type≠Non-Aux; Mood=Decl or Int] **A:** [MV←*; Mood←Int]

q20c. **C:** [*.Ques=No *.Case=Subj; **Subject-verb agreement** (*As below with * replacing* Subj)] **A:** [Subj←*]

a21b. **C:** [*.Ques=Yes *.Case=Subj; Mood=Decl] **A:** [Subj←*; QE←*; Mood←Int]

a22a. **C:** [*.Ques=Yes Mood=Decl] **A:** [QE←*; Hold←*; Mood←Int]

a23a. **C:** [*.Ques.Prepobj=Yes; Mood=Decl]
      A: [QE←*.Prepobj; Hold←*; Mood←Int]

r24a. *No initializations, conditions, or actions*

r25b. **A:** [Subj←*]

c26c. **C:** [(MV+*) ∈ dictionary] **A:** [MV←dictionary entry]

d27d. **C:** [(MV+*) ∈ dictionary] **A:** [MV←dictionary entry]

e28e. **C:** [(MV+*.Prep) ∈ dictionary; DO=∅] **A:** [MV←dictionary entry; DO←*.Prepobj]

a29c. **C:** [*.Form=Infinitive; Mood=Decl]
      A: [Subj←dummy NP with Head=*you*; MV←*; Mood←Imper]

t30a. **A:** [Binder←*; Mood←Bound]

Subject-verb agreement conditions:

    Either: MV.Type=Modal or MV.Form=Past
    or MV.Form=3rd-Sing and Subj.Num=Sing and Subj.Person=3rd
    or MV.Form=Inf and either Subj.Num=Plural or Subj.Pers ≠ 3rd

Verb sequence conditions:

    If MV.Type=Modal or Do then *.Form=Infinitive
    If MV.Type=Be then *.Form=Pres-Part
    If MV.Type=Have then *.Form=Past-Part
    If MV.Type=Non-Aux then fail

Transitivity conditions:

    If IO ≠ ∅ then MV.Transitivity=Bitransitive
    If IO = ∅ and DO ≠ ∅ then MV.Transitivity=Transitive
    If DO= ∅ and IO = ∅ then MV.Transitivity=Intransitive

Figure D–13. The S network (continued).

The NP network

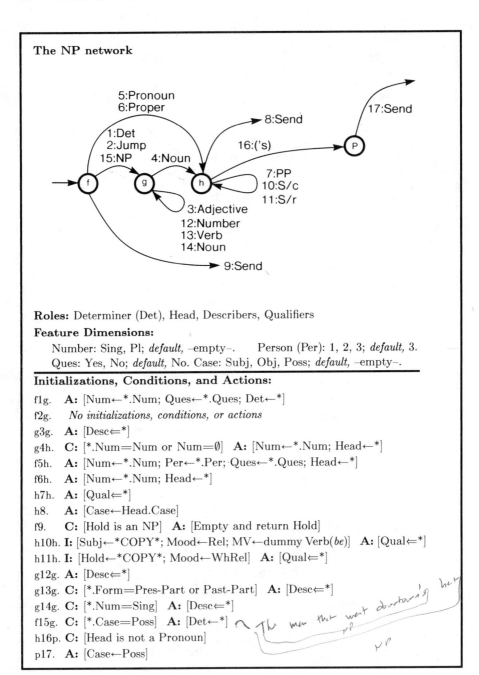

Roles: Determiner (Det), Head, Describers, Qualifiers

Feature Dimensions:

Number: Sing, Pl; *default*, –empty–.   Person (Per): 1, 2, 3; *default*, 3.
Ques: Yes, No; *default*, No. Case: Subj, Obj, Poss; *default*, –empty–.

Initializations, Conditions, and Actions:

f1g.   **A:** [Num←*.Num; Ques←*.Ques; Det←*]

f2g.   *No initializations, conditions, or actions*

g3g.   **A:** [Desc⇐*]

g4h.   **C:** [*.Num=Num or Num=∅]   **A:** [Num←*.Num; Head←*]

f5h.   **A:** [Num←*.Num; Per←*.Per; Ques←*.Ques; Head←*]

f6h.   **A:** [Num←*.Num; Head←*]

h7h.   **A:** [Qual⇐*]

h8.   **A:** [Case←Head.Case]

f9.   **C:** [Hold is an NP]   **A:** [Empty and return Hold]

h10h. **I:** [Subj←*COPY*; Mood←Rel; MV←dummy Verb(*be*)]   **A:** [Qual⇐*]

h11h. **I:** [Hold←*COPY*; Mood←WhRel]   **A:** [Qual⇐*]

g12g. **A:** [Desc⇐*]

g13g. **C:** [*.Form=Pres-Part or Past-Part]   **A:** [Desc⇐*]

g14g. **C:** [*.Num=Sing]   **A:** [Desc⇐*]

f15g. **C:** [*.Case=Poss]   **A:** [Det←*]

h16p. **C:** [Head is not a Pronoun]

p17.   **A:** [Case←Poss]

Figure D–14. The NP network.

The PP network

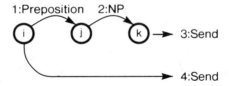

Roles: Prepostion (Prep), Prepobj

Initializations, Conditions, and Actions:

i1j. **A:** [Prep←*]
j2k. **C:** [*.Case=Obj] **A:** [PrepObj←*]
k3.   *No initializations, conditions, or actions*
i4.   **C:** [Hold is PP] **A:** [Empty and return Hold]

Figure D–15. The PP network.

Bibliography

In the following entries, abbreviations are used for the major journals and conferences in the areas related to artificial intelligence and natural language. The Association for Computing Machinery (ACM) publishes a journal (JACM) and a communications (CACM). In addition there are newsletters of its special interest groups in artificial intelligence (SIGART) and programming languages (SIGPLAN). There are two major artificial intelligence conferences, the biennial International Joint Conference on Artificial Intelligence (IJCAI) and the annual meeting of the American Association for Artificial Intelligence (AAAI). The Association for Computational Linguistics (ACL) has an annual meeting and publishes the American Journal of Computational Linguistics (AJCL). There is also an annual International Conference on Computational Linguistics (COLING).

Adjukiewicz, Kazimierz. Die syntaktische Konnexitaet. (1935) Translated as Syntactic connection. In *Polish Logic*. Edited by Storrs McCall, 207-231. Oxford: Oxford Univ. Press, 1967.

Aho, Albert.V., and Jeffery D. Ullman. *The Theory of Parsing, Translation, and Compiling, vol. 1*. Englewood Cliffs, N.J.: Prentice-Hall, 1972.

Akmajian, Adrian, and Frank Heny. *An Introduction to the Principles of Transformational Syntax*. Cambridge, Mass.: MIT Press, 1975.

Anderson, John R. Induction of augmented transition networks. *Cognitive Science* 1(1977), 125-157.

———. A theory of language acquisition based on general learning principles. *7th IJCAI* (1981), 97-103.

Anderson, Stephen R., and Paul Kiparsky, eds. *A Festschrift for Morris Halle*. New York: Holt, Rinehart and Winston, 1973.

Bach, Emmon. *Syntactic Theory*. New York: Holt, Rinehart and Winston, 1974.

Baker, Carl L. *Introduction to Generative-transformational Syntax*. Englewood Cliffs, N.J.: Prentice-Hall, 1978.

Barr, Avron, and Edward A. Feigenbaum, eds. *The Handbook of Artificial Intelligence*. Los Altos, Cal.: William Kaufmann, 1981.

Bates, Madeleine. The theory and practice of augmented transition network grammars. In *Natural Language Communication with Computers*. Edited by Leonard Bolc, 191-260. New York: Springer, 1978.

Bates, Madeleine, and Robert Ingria. Controlled transformational sentence generation. *Proc. 19th Ann. ACL* (1981), 153-158.

Berry, Margaret. *Introduction to Systemic Linguistcs 1: Structures and Systems*. New York: Saint Martin's Press, 1975.

——. *Introduction to Systemic Linguistcs 2: Levels and Links*. London: Batsford, 1977.

Bierwisch, Manfred. *Modern Linguistics, its Development, Methods and Problems*. Janua Linguarum Series Minor, no. 110. The Hague: Mouton, 1971.

Birnbaum, Lawrence, and Mallory Selfridge. Conceptual analysis of natural language. In *Inside Computer Understanding*. Edited by Roger C. Schank and Christopher K. Riesbeck, 318-353. Hillsdale, N.J.: Erlbaum, 1981.

Bloomfield, Leonard. *Language*. New York: Holt, Rinehart and Winston, 1933.

Bobrow, Daniel G. Natural language input for a computer problem solving system. In *Semantic Information Processing*. Edited by Marvin Minsky, 133-215. Cambridge, Mass.: MIT Press, 1967a.

——. Syntactic theory in computer implementations. In *Automated Language Processing: The State of the Art*. Edited by Harold Borko, 217-251. New York: Wiley and Sons, 1967b.

Bobrow, Daniel G., and Allen M. Collins, eds. *Representation and Understanding: Studies in Cognitive Science*. New York: Academic Press, 1975.

Bobrow, Daniel G., and J. Bruce Fraser. An augmented state transition network analysis procedure. *1st. IJCAI* (1969), 557-567.

Bobrow, Daniel G., and the PARC understander group. GUS-1, a frame driven dialog system. *Artificial Intelligence* 8:2(April 1977), 155-173.

Bobrow, Daniel G., and Bertram Raphael. New programming languages for artificial intelligence research. *Computing Surveys* 6:3(1974), 153-174.

Bobrow, Robert J., and Bonnie L. Webber. Knowledge representation for syntactic/semantic processing. *1st AAAI* (1980), 316-323.

Boden, Margaret A. *Artificial Intelligence and Natural Man*. New York: Basic Books, 1977.

Borko, Harold, ed. *Automated Language Processing: The State of the Art*. Huntington, N.Y.: Wiley and Sons, 1967.

Bresnan, Joan W. Variables in transformations. In *Formal Syntax*. Edited by Peter W. Culicover, Thomas Wasow, and Adrian Akmajian, 157-196. New York: Academic Press, 1977.

——. A realistic transformational grammar. In *Linguistic Theory and Psychological Reality*. Edited by Morris Halle, Joan W. Bresnan, and George A. Miller, 1-59. Cambridge, Mass.: MIT Press, 1978.

Bresnan, Joan W., and Ronald M. Kaplan. Lexical-functional grammar; a formal system for grammatical representation. In *The Mental Representation of Grammatical Relations*. Edited by Joan W. Bresnan. Cambridge, Mass.: MIT Press, forthcoming.

Brown, Roger. *A First Language: The Early Stages*. Cambridge, Mass.: Harvard Univ. Press, 1977.

Bruce, Bertram. Case systems for natural language. *Artificial Intelligence* 6:4(Winter 1975), 327-360.

Burton, Richard R., and John Seely Brown. Toward a natural-language capability for computer-assisted instruction. In *Procedures for Instructional Systems Development*. Edited by H. O'Neill, 273-313. New York: Academic Press, 1979.

Carbonell, Jaime G., and Philip J. Hayes. Dynamic strategy selection in flexible parsing. *Proc. 19th Ann. ACL* (1981), 143-147.

Chafe, Wallace L. *Meaning and Structure of Language*. Chicago: Univ. of Chicago Press, 1970.

Charniak, Eugene, Christopher K. Riesbeck, and Drew V. McDermott. *Artificial Intelligence Programming*. Hillsdale, N.J.: Erlbaum, 1979.

Charniak, Eugene, and Yorick Wilks, eds. *Computational Semantics: An Introduction to Artificial Intelligence and Natural Language Comprehension*. Amsterdam: North Holland, 1976.

Cherry, Lorinda. Computer aids for writers. *SIGPLAN Notices* 16:6(June 1981), 61-67.

Chomsky, Noam. *Syntactic Structures*. s'Gravenhage: Mouton, 1957.

——. A review of *Verbal Behavior* by B.F. Skinner. *Language* 35(1959), 26-58.

——. *Aspects of the Theory of Syntax*. Cambridge, Mass.: MIT Press, 1965.

——. *Language and Mind*. New York: Harcourt Brace Jovanovich, 1968.

——. Some empirical issues in the theory of transformational grammar. In *Goals of Linguistic Theory*. Edited by Stanley Peters, 63-130. Englewood Cliffs, N.J.: Prentice-Hall, 1972.

——. *Reflections on Language*. New York: Pantheon, 1975.

——. On wh- movement. In *Formal Syntax*. Edited by Peter W. Culicover, Thomas Wasow, and Adrian Akmajian, 71-132. New York: Academic Press, 1977a.

——. *Language and Responsibility*. New York: Pantheon, 1977b.

Clark, Herbert H., and Eve V. Clark. *Psychology of Language: An Introduction to Psycholinguistics.* New York: Harcourt Brace Jovanovich, 1977.

——. When nouns surface as verbs. *Language* 55(1979), 767-811.

Cleaveland, J. Craig, and Robert C. Uzgalis. *Grammars for Programming Languages.* New York: Elsevier, 1977.

Closs (Traugott), Elizabeth. Diachronic syntax and generative grammar. *Language* 41(1965), 402-415.

Colby, Kenneth M. *Artificial Paranoia: A Computer Simulation of Paranoid Processes.* Elmsford, N.Y.: Pergamon, 1976.

Colby, Kenneth M., Roger C. Parkison, and William S. Faught. Pattern-matching rules for the recognition of natural language dialogue expressions. *AJCL* (September 1974), 5-70.

Cole, Peter, and Jerrold M. Sadock, eds. *Syntax and Semantics 8: Grammatical Relations.* New York: Academic Press, 1977.

Colmerauer, Alain. *Metamorphosis Grammar. Natural Language Communication with Computers.* Lecture Notes in Computer Science, vol. 63. Edited by Leonard Bolc. Berlin: Springer, May 1978.

Crystal, David. *Linguistics.* Gretna, La.: Pelican, 1971.

Culicover, Peter W. *Syntax.* New York: Academic Press, 1976.

Culicover, Peter W., Thomas Wasow, and Adrian Akmajian, eds. *Formal Syntax.* New York: Academic Press, 1977.

Damerau, Fred J. The derivation of answers from logical forms in a question answering system. *AJCL* Microfiche 75(1978), 3-42.

DeJong, Gerald. Prediction and substantiation: a new approach to natural language processing. *Cognitive Science* 3(September 1979), 251-273.

Dertouzos, Michael L., and Joel Moses. *The Computer Age: A Twenty Year View.* Cambridge, Mass.: MIT Press, 1979.

deSaussure, Ferdinand. *A Course in General Linguistics.* New York: McGraw-Hill, 1966.

Dik, Simon C. *Functional Grammar.* Amsterdam: North Holland, 1978.

Dresher, B. Elan, and Norbert Hornstein. On some supposed contributions of artificial intelligence to the scientific study of language. *Cognition* 4(1976), 321-398.

——. Response to Schank and Wilensky. *Cognition* 5(1977a), 147-150.

——. Reply to Winograd. *Cognition* 5(1977b), 377-392.

Dreyfus, Hubert L. *What Computers Can't Do: A Critique of Artificial Reason.* 2nd edition. New York: Harper and Row, 1979.

Dyer, Michael G. Integration, unification, reconstruction, modification: an eternal parsing braid. *7th IJCAI* (1981), 37-42.

Earley, Jay. An efficient context-free parsing algorithm. *CACM* 6:8(1970), 451-455.

Eisenstadt, Marc. Alternative parsers for conceptual dependency: Getting there is half the fun. *6th IJCAI* (1979), 238-240.

Emonds, Joseph E. *A Transformational Approach to English Syntax: Root, Structure-preserving, and Local Transformations*. New York: Academic Press, 1976.

Feigenbaum, Edward A., and Julian Feldman, eds. *Computers and Thought*. New York: McGraw-Hill, 1963.

Feldman, Jerry, and David Gries. Translator writing systems. *CACM* 11:2(1968), 77-113.

Fillmore, Charles. The case for case. In *Universals in Linguistic Theory*. Edited by Emmon Bach and Robert T. Harms, 1-90. Chicago: Holt, Rinehart and Winston, 1968.

Finin, Tim, Bradley Goodman, and Harry Tennant. JETS: Achieving completeness through coverage and closure. *6th IJCAI* (1979), 275-281.

Firth, J.R. *Papers in Linguistics*. London: Oxford Univ. Press, 1957.

Flores, Fernando C., and Terry Winograd. *Understanding Computers and Cognition*, forthcoming.

Floyd, Robert A. Bounded context syntactic analysis. *CACM* 7:2(1964), 62-67.

Fodor, Jerry T., Thomas Bever, and Merrill Garret. *The Psychology of Language*. New York: McGraw-Hill, 1974.

Friedman, Joyce. Directed random generation of sentences. *CACM* 12(1969), 40-46.

——. *A Computer Model of Transformational Grammar*. New York: Elsevier, 1971.

Gazdar, Gerald. Phrase structure grammar. To appear in *The Nature of Syntactic Representation*. Edited by Pauline Jacobson and Geoffrey K. Pullum. Dordrecht: Reidel, forthcoming.

——. Unbounded dependencies and coordinate structure. *Linguistic Inquiry* 12:2(Spring 1981), 155-184.

Gazdar, Gerald, Geoffrey K. Pullum, and Ivan A. Sag. A phrase structure grammar of the English auxiliary system. To appear in *The Nature of Syntactic Representation*. Edited by Pauline Jacobson and Geoffrey K. Pullum. Dordrecht: Reidel, forthcoming.

Gleason, Henry Allen, Jr. *Linguistics and English Grammar*. New York: Holt, Rinehart and Winston, 1965.

Goldman, Neil M. Conceptual generation. In *Conceptual Information Processing*. Edited by Roger C. Schank, 289-371. Amsterdam: North Holland, 1975.

Golomb, Solomon W., and Leonard D. Baumert. Backtrack programming. *JACM* 12:4(1965), 516-524.

Green, Bertram, A.K. Wolf, C. Chomsky, and K. Laughery. BASEBALL: An automatic question answerer. In *Computers and Thought*. Edited by Edward A. Feigenbaum and Julian Feldman, 207-216. New York: McGraw-Hill, 1963.

Grimes, Joseph. *The Thread of Discourse*. The Hague: Mouton, 1975.

Grishman, Ralph. A survey of syntactic analysis procedures for natural language. *AJCL* Microfiche 47(1976), 2-96.

Haas, Norman, and Gary Hendrix. An approach to acquiring and applying knowledge. *AAAI* (1980), 235-239.

Hahn, W.v., Anthony Jameson, Wolfgang Hoeppner, and Wolfgang Wahlster. The anatomy of the natural language dialogue system HAM-RPM. In *Natural Language Based Computer Systems*. Edited by Leonard Bolc, 119-253. Munich: Hanser/Macmillan, 1980.

Halle, Morris. *The Sound Pattern of Russian: A Linguistic and Acoustical Investigation*. Description and Analysis of Contemporary Standard Russian Series, no. 1. New York: Humanities Press, 1959.

Halle, Morris, Joan W. Bresnan, and George A. Miller, eds. *Linguistic Theory and Psychological Reality*. Cambridge, Mass.: MIT Press, 1978.

Halliday, M.A.K. Categories of the theory of grammar. *Word* 17(1961), 241-292.

——. Notes on transitivity and theme in English. *Journal of Linguistics* 3,4(1967), 199-244, 179-215.

——. *Explorations in the Functions of Language*. London: Arnold, 1973.

——. *Language as a Social Semiotic*. Baltimore, Md.: University Park Press, 1978.

——. *A Short Introduction to Functional Grammar*. London: Arnold, forthcoming.

——, ed. *Readings in Systemic Linguistics*. London: Batsford, forthcoming.

Halliday, M.A.K., and Robin Fawcett, eds. *New Developments in Systemic Linguistics*. London: Batsford, forthcoming.

Halliday, M.A.K., and Ruqaiya Hasan. *Cohesion In English*. New York: Longman, 1976.

Harris, Larry R. User-oriented data base query with the Robot natural language query system. *International Journal of Man-Machine Studies* 9(1977), 697-713.

Haugeland, John. *Mind Design*. Montgomery, Vt.: Bradford Books, 1981.

Hayakawa, S.I. *Language in Thought and Action*. 4th edition. New York: Harcourt Brace Jovanovich, 1978.

Hayes, John R., and Herbert A. Simon. Understanding written problem instructions. In *Knowledge and Cognition*. Edited by L. W. Gregg, 167-200. Potomac, Md.: Erlbaum, 1975.

Hayes, Philip J. A construction-specific approach to focused interaction in flexible parsing. *Proc. 19th Ann. ACL* (1981), 149-152.

Hayes, Philip J., and George Mouradian. Flexible parsing. *Proc. 18th Ann. ACL* (1980), 97-103.

Hays, David G. Dependency theory: a formalism and some observations. *Language* 40:4(1964), 511-524.

——. *Introduction to Computational Linguistics.* New York: Elsevier, 1967.

Heidorn, George E. Automatic programming through natural language dialogue: a survey. *IBM J. Res. Dev.* 20:4(July 1976), 302-313.

Hendrix, Gary G. LIFER: A natural language interface facility. *SIGART Newseletter* 61(February 1977), 25-26.

Hendrix, Gary G., Earl D. Sacerdoti, Daniel Sagalowicz, and Jonathan Slocum. Developing a natural language interface to complex data. ACM *Transactions on Database Systems* 3:2(June 1978), 105-147.

Hopcroft, John E., and Jeffrey D. Ullman. *Formal Languages and their Relation to Automata.* Reading, Mass.: Addison-Wesley, 1969.

Hudson, Richard A. *English Complex Sentences: An Introduction to Systemic Grammar.* Amsterdam: North Holland, 1971.

——. *Arguments for a Non-transformational Grammar.* Chicago: Univ. of Chicago Press, 1976.

Jackendoff, Ray. A system of semantic primitives. In *Theoretical Issues in Natural Language Processing.* Edited by Bonnie L. Nash-Webber and Roger C. Schank, 24-29. Cambridge, Mass.: MIT, 1975.

Jacobs, Roderick A., and Peter S. Rosenbaum. *Readings in English Transformational Grammar.* Waltham, Mass.: Ginn, 1970.

Jacobson, Bent. *Transformational-generative Grammar.* Amsterdam: North Holland, 1978.

Jacobson, Pauline, and Geoffrey Pullum, eds. *The Nature of Syntactic Respresentation.* Dordrecht: Reidel, forthcoming.

Johnson, David E. On relational constraints on grammars. In *Syntax and Semantics 8: Grammatical Relations.* Edited by Peter Cole and Jerrold M. Sadock, 151-178. New York: Academic Press, 1977.

Joshi, Aravind, Bonnie L. Webber, and Ivan Sag. *Elements of Discourse Understanding.* Cambridge: Cambridge Univ. Press, 1981.

Kaplan, Ronald M. Augmented transition networks as psychological models of sentence comprehension. *Artificial Intelligence* 3(1972), 77-100.

——. A general syntactic processor. In *Natural Language Processing.* Edited by Randall Rustin, 193-241. New York: Algorithmics Press, 1973a.

——. A multi-processing approach to natural language. In *Proc. of the 1973 National Computer Conference,* 435-440. Montvale, N.J.: AFIPS Press, 1973b.

———. On process models for sentence analysis. In *Explorations in Cognition*. Edited by Donald A. Norman, David E. Rumelhart, and the LNR Research Group, 117-135. San Francisco: Freeman, 1975.

Katz, Jerrold J., and Paul M. Postal. *An Integrated Theory of Linguistic Descriptions*. Cambridge, Mass.: MIT Press, 1964.

Kay, Martin. Experiments with a powerful parser. *Proc. 2nd Int. COLING* (August 1967), #10.

———. The MIND system. In *Natural Language Processing*. Edited by Randall Rustin, 155-188. New York: Algorithmics Press, 1973.

———. Functional grammar. *Proc. 5th Ann. Meeting of the Berkeley Ling. Soc.* (1979), 142-158.

Keenan, Edward L., ed. *Formal Semantics of Natural Language*. Cambridge: Cambridge Univ. Press, 1975.

King, Margaret. Design characteristics of a machine translation system. *7th IJCAI* (1981), 43-46.

Knuth, Donald E. Semantics of context-free languages. Mathematical Systems Theory 2(1968a), 127-145. Errata, *Mathematical Systems Theory* 5(1971), 95-96.

———. *The Art of Computer Programming* (7 projected volumes). Reading, Mass.: Addison-Wesley, 1968b, 1971,...

Korzybski, Alfred. *Science and Sanity: An Introduction to Non-Aristotelian Systems and General Semantics*. 4th ed. Lakeville, Conn.: Institute for General Semantics, 1958.

Kowalski, Robert. Predicate logic as a programming language. *Proc. IFIP* 74(1974), 569-574.

Kress, Gunther, ed. *Halliday: System and Function in Language*. London: Oxford Univ. Press, 1976.

Kuhn, Thomas. *The Structure of Scientific Revolutions*. Chicago: Univ. of Chicago Press, 1962. 2nd edition, 1970.

Kuno, Susumo. The predictive analyzer and a path elimination technique. *CACM* 8(1965), 453.

Kuno, Susumo, and Anthony G. Oettinger. Multiple-path syntactic analyzer. *Information Processing* 62(1962), 306-311.

Kwasny, Stan C., and Norman K. Sondhemier. Relaxation techniques for parsing ill-formed inputs. *JACL* 7:2(April-June 1981), 99-108.

Lakatos, Imre, and Alan Musgrave, eds. *Criticism and the Growth of Knowledge*. Cambridge: Cambridge Univ. Press, 1970.

Lakoff, George, and Henry Thompson. Introducing cognitive grammar. *Proc. 1st Ann. Meeting of the Berkeley Ling. Soc.* (1975), 295-313.

Lamb, Sydney. *An Outline of Stratificational Grammar*. Washington, D.C.: Georgetown Univ. Press, 1966.

Landsbergen, S.P.J. Syntax and formal semantics of English in PHLIQA1. In *Advances in Natural Language Processing*. Edited by L. Steels. Antwerp: Univ. of Antwerp, 1976.

Langendoen, D. Terence, and Thomas G. Bever. Can a not unhappy person be called a not sad one? In *A Festschrift for Morris Halle*. Edited by Stephen R. Anderson and Paul Kiparsky, 392-409. New York: Holt, Rinehart and Winston, 1973.

Lees, Robert B., and Edward S. Klima. Rules for English pronominalization. *Language* 39(1963), 17-28.

Lehmann, Winfred P. Interpretation of natural language in an information system. *IBM J. Res. Dev.* 22:5(September 1978), 560-571.

Lesser, V.R., R.D. Fennel, L.D. Erman, and D. Raj Reddy. Organization of the Hearsay II speech understanding system. *IEEE Trans. ASSP* 23(1977), 11-23.

Levine, Arvin, and William R. Saunders. The MISS speech synthesis system. *Proc. IEEE* (March 1979), 899-902.

Lewis, David. General semantics. In *Semantics of Natural Language*. Edited by Donald Davidson and Gilbert Harman, 169-218. Dordrecht: Reidel, 1972.

Lindsay, Peter, and Donald A. Norman. *Human Information Processing*. New York: Academic Press, 1972.

Lindsay, Robert. In defense of ad hoc systems. In *Computer Models of Thought and Language*. Edited by Roger C. Schank and Kenneth M. Colby, 372-395. San Francisco: Freeman, 1973.

Lockwood, David G. *Introduction to Stratificational Linguistics*. New York: Harcourt Brace Jovanovich, 1972.

Lyons, John. *Introduction to Theoretical Linguistics*. Cambridge: Cambridge Univ. Press, 1968.

——, ed. *New Horizons in Linguistics*. Harmondsworth: Penguin Books, 1970.

——. *Language and Linguistics: An Introduction*. Cambridge: Cambridge Univ. Press, 1981.

Lytle, Eldon G. Junction grammar: theory and application. *5th LACUS FORUM* (1979). Columbia, S.C.: Hornbeam Press, 1980.

MacLellan, Esther, and Catherine Schroll. The clock's secret. In *One Hundred Plays for Children*. Edited by A. S. Burack, 164-171. Boston: Plays Inc., 1949.

Marcus, Mitchell P. *Theory of Syntactic Recognition for Natural Language*. Cambridge, Mass.: MIT Press, 1980.

Mathesius, Vilém. *A Functional Analysis of Present Day English on a General Linguistic Basis*. Janua Linguarum Series Practica, no. 208. Edited by Josef Vachek. The Hague: Mouton, 1961. Translated by Libuse Duskova, 1975.

Matthews, G.H. Analysis by synthesis of natural languages. *Proc. 1961 Int. Conf. on Machine Translation and Applied Language Analysis.* London: Her Majesty's Stationery Office, 1962.

McCord, Michael. Slot grammars. *AJCL* 6:1(Jan-March 1980), 31-43.

McDonald, David D. Natural language generation as a computational problem: an introduction. To appear in *Computational Theories of Discourse.* Edited by Michael Brady. Cambridge, Mass.: MIT Press, 1982.

Meehan, James. TALE-SPIN. In *Inside Computer Understanding.* Edited by Roger C. Schank and Christopher K. Riesbeck, 197-226. Hillsdale, N.J.: Erlbaum, 1981.

Michie, Donald, ed. *Machine Intelligence.* New York: Halsted Press, 1971-.

Miller, Lance A., George E. Heidorn, and Karen Jensen. Text-critiquing with the EPISTLE system: an author's aid to better syntax. In *Proc. of the National Computer Conference 50,* 649-655. Arlington, VA: AFIPS Press, 1981.

Minsky, Marvin. *Computation: Finite and Infinite Machines.* Englewood Cliffs, N.J.: Prentice-Hall, 1967.

——, ed. *Semantic Information Processing.* Cambridge, Mass.: MIT Press, 1967.

Mylopoulos, John, Alex Borgida, Philip Cohen, Nicholas Roussopoulos, John Tsotos, and Harry Wong. A natural language understanding system for data management. *4th IJCAI* (1975), 414-421.

Newell, Allen. A tutorial on speech understanding systems. In *Speech Recognition.* Edited by D. Raj Reddy, 3-54. New York: Academic Press, 1975.

Newell, Allen, and Herbert A. Simon. *Human Problem Solving.* Englewood Cliffs, N.J.: Prentice-Hall, 1972.

Newman, Edwin. *Strictly Speaking: Will America be the Death of English?* Indianapolis: Bobbs Merril, 1974.

Newmeyer, Frederick J. *Linguistic Theory in America.* New York: Academic Press, 1980.

Nilsson, Nils J. *Principles of Artificial Intelligence.* Palo Alto, Cal.: Tioga Press, 1981.

Norman, Donald A., and David E. Rumelhart. *Explorations in Cognition.* San Francisco: Freeman, 1975.

——. Reference and comprehension. In *Explorations in Cognition.* Edited by Donald A. Norman and David E. Rumelhart, 65-87. San Francisco: Freeman, 1975.

Norman, Donald A., David E. Rumelhart, and the LNR Research Group. *Explorations in Cognition.* San Francisco: Freeman, 1975.

Parkison, Roger C., Kenneth M. Colby, and Wiliam S. Faught. Conversational language comprehension using integrated pattern-matching and parsing. *Artificial Intelligence* 9(1977), 111-134.

Partee, Barbara H., ed. *Montague Grammars.* New York: Academic Press, 1976.

Paxton, William H. The language definition system. In *Understanding Spoken Language*. Edited by Donald E. Walker, 17-40. New York: Elsevier-North Holland, 1978.

Percival, W. Keith. The applicability of Kuhn's paradigms to the history of linguistics. *Language* 52:2(June 1976), 285-294.

Pereira, Fernando C. N., and David H. D. Warren. Definite clause grammars for language analysis—a survey of the formalism and a comparison with augmented transition networks. *Artificial Intelligence* 13:3(1980), 231-278.

Perlmutter, David. *Deep Structure and Surface Constraints in Syntax*. New York: Holt, Rinehart and Winston, 1971.

Peters, Stanley, ed. *Goals of Linguistic Theory*. Englewood Cliffs, N.J.: Prentice-Hall, 1972.

Petrick, Stanley. Transformational analysis. In *Natural Language Processing*. Edited by Randall Rustin, 27-41. New York: Algorithmics Press, 1973.

――. Field-testing the transformational question answering (TQA) system. *Proc. 19th Ann. ACL* (1981), 35-36.

Pierce, J. R. *Symbols, Signals and Noise: The Nature and Process of Communication*. New York: Harper and Row, 1961.

Pinker, Steven. Formal models of language learning. *Cognition* 7:3(September 1979), 217-284.

Pirsig, Robert M. *Zen and the Art of Motorcycle Maintenance*. New York: Morrow, 1974.

Plath, Warren. REQUEST: A natural language question-answering system. *IBM J. Res. Dev.* 20:4(July 1976), 326-335.

Postal, Paul M. The best theory. In *Goals of Linguistic Theory*. Edited by Stanley Peters, 131-170. Englewood Cliffs, N.J.: Prentice-Hall, 1972.

Postman, Neil, and Charles Weingartner. *Linguistics, a Revolution in Teaching*. New York: Dell, 1966.

Pratt, Vaughan R. Lingol, a progress report. *4th IJCAI* (1975), 422-428.

Quirk, Randolph, Sidney Greenbaum, Geoffrey Leech, and Jan Svartvik. *A Grammar of Contemporary English*. New York: Seminar Press, 1972.

Rahmstorf, G. and M. Ferguson, eds. Proceedings of a workshop on natural language for interaction with data bases. *Int. Institute for Applied Sys. Analysis* (1978).

Raphael, Bertram. SIR, a computer program for semantic information retrieval. In *Semantic Information Processing*. Edited by Marvin Minsky, 33-145. Cambridge, Mass.: MIT Press, 1967.

Reddy, D. Raj. *Speech Recognition*. New York: Academic Press, 1975.

Reibel, David A., and Sanford A. Schane. *Modern Studies in English: Readings in Transformational Grammar*. Englewood Cliffs, N.J.: Prentice-Hall, 1969.

Rieger, Charles, and Steven Small. Word expert parsing. *6th IJCAI* (1979), 723-728.

Riesbeck, Christopher K. Conceptual analysis. In *Conceptual Information Processing*. Edited by Roger C. Schank, 83-156. Amsterdam: North Holland, 1975.

——. An expectation-driven production system for natural language understanding. In *Pattern-directed Inference Systems*. Edited by Donald A. Waterman and Rick Hayes-Roth, 399-414. New York: Academic Press, 1978.

Robinson, Jane J. DIAGRAM: A grammar for dialogues. *CACM* 25:1(January 1982), 27-47.

Ross, John R. *Constraints on Variables in Syntax*. Ph.D. dissertation, MIT, 1967.

Rustin, Randall, ed. *Natural Language Processing*. New York: Algorithmics Press, 1973.

Sager, Naomi. *Natural Language Information Processing*. Reading, Mass.: Addison-Wesley, 1981.

Salton, Gerald. *Dynamic Information and Library Processing*. Englewood-Cliffs, N.J.: Prentice-Hall, 1975.

Scha, Remko. A formal language for semantic representation. In *Advances in Natural Language Processing*. Edited by L. Steels. Antwerp: University of Antwerp, 1976.

Schank, Roger C., ed. *Conceptual Information Processing*. Amsterdam: North Holland, 1975.

Schank, Roger C., and Robert P. Abelson. *Scripts, Plans, Goals and Understanding*. Hillsdale, N.J.: Erlbaum, 1977.

Schank, Roger C., and Kenneth M. Colby, eds. *Computer Models of Thought and Language*. San Francisco: Freeman, 1973.

Schank, Roger C., and Christopher K. Riesbeck. *Inside Computer Understanding: Five Programs plus Miniatures*. Hillsdale, N.J.: Erlbaum, 1981.

Schank, Roger C., and Robert Wilensky. Response to Dresher and Hornstein. *Cognition* 5(1977), 133-146.

Sgall, Petr, Eva Hajičová, and Eva Benešová. *Topic, Focus and General Semantics: A Functional Approach to Syntax*. Mathematical Linguistics and Automatic Language Processing, no. 7. New York: Elsevier, 1969.

Shannon, Claude E., and Warren Weaver. *The Mathematical Theory of Communication*. Champaign, Ill.: Univ. of Illinois Press, 1949.

Sheil, Beau. Observations on context free parsing. *Statistical Methods in Linguistics* (1976), 71-109.

Simmons, Robert F. Semantic networks: their computation and use for understanding English sentences. In *Computer Models of Thought and Language*. Edited by Roger C. Schank and Kenneth M. Colby, 63-113. San Francisco: Freeman, 1973.

——. Answering English questions by computer. In *Automated Language Processing: The State of the Art*. Edited by Harold Borko, 253-289. New York: Wiley and Sons, 1967. Also appears in *CACM* 13(1970), 15-30.

Simmons, Robert F., Sheldon Klein, and Karen McConlogue. Indexing and dependency logic for answering English questions. *American Documentation* 15(1964), 196-204.

Simmons, Robert F., and Jonathan Slocum. Generating English discourse from semantic networks. *CACM* 15(1972), 891-905.

Skinner, B. F. *Verbal Behavior.* New York: Appleton-Century-Crofts, 1957.

Slocum Jonathan. A practical comparison of parsing strategies. *Proc. 19th Ann. ACL* (1981), 1-6.

Small, Steven. Viewing word expert parsing as a linguistic theory. *7th IJCAI* (1981), 70-76.

Snell, Barbara M., ed. *Translating and the Computer.* Amsterdam: North Holland, 1979.

Soames, Scott, and David M. Perlmutter. *Syntactic Argumentation and the Structure of English.* Berkeley: Univ. of Cal. Press, 1979.

Sparck-Jones, Karen, and Martin Kay. *Linguistics and Information Science.* New York: Academic Press, 1974.

Spiro, Rand, Bertram Bruce, and William Brewer, eds. *Theoretical Issues in Reading Comprehension.* Hillsdale, N.J.: Erlbaum, 1980.

Steinberg, Daniel, and Leon Jakobovits. *Semantics.* Cambridge: Cambridge Univ. Press, 1971.

Stockwell, Robert P. *Foundations of Syntactic Theory.* Englewood Cliffs, N.J.: Prentice-Hall, 1977.

Stockwell, Robert P., Paul Schachter, and Barbara H. Partee. *The Major Syntactic Structures of English.* New York: Holt, Rinehart and Winston, 1973.

Teitelman, Warren. *INTERLISP Reference Manual.* Palo Alto, Ca.: Xerox PARC, December, 1978.

Tennant, Harry. *Natural Language Processing.* Princeton, N.J.: Petrocelli, 1980.

The Key to English: Two-Word Verbs. New York: Collier-MacMillan, 1977.

Thompson, Frederick B., P.C. Lockemann, and Bozena Henisz Dostert. REL: a rapidly extensible language system. *Proc. of the 24th National Conference of the ACM* (1969), 399.

Thompson, Henry. Chart parsing and rule schemata in PSG. *19th Ann. ACL* (1981), 167-172.

Thorne, James, P. Bratley, and Hamish Dewar. The syntactic analysis of English by machine. *Machine Intelligence 3.* New York: Elsevier, 1968.

Toma, Peter. SYSTRAN as a multi-lingual machine translation system. In *Commission of the European Communities; Overcoming the Language Barrier,* 569-581. Munich: Verlag Dokumentation, 1977.

Turing, Alan M. Computing machinery and intelligence. *Mind: A Quarterly Review of Psychology and Philosophy* 59(1950), 433-460. Reprinted in *Minds and Machines.* Edited by Alan Ross Anderson, 11. Englewood Cliffs, N.J.: Prentice-Hall, 1964.

Van Wijngaarden, A. Orthogonal design and description of a formal language. Technical Report MR 76. Amsterdam: Mathematisch Centrum, 1965.

Walker, Donald E. *Understanding Spoken Language.* New York: Elsevier-North Holland, 1978.

Waltz, David L. An English language question-answering system for a large relational data base. *CACM* 21(July 1978), 526-539.

Wanner, Eric, and Michael Maratsos. An ATN approach to comprehension. In *Linguistic Theory and Psychological Reality.* Edited by Morris Halle, Joan W. Bresnan, and George A. Miller, 119-161. Cambridge, Mass.: MIT Press, 1978.

Warren, David H. D., and Luis M. Pereira. Prolog—the language and its implementation compared with Lisp. *Proc. ACM Symposium on AI and Prog. Lang. SIGPLAN-/SIGART Newsletter* (August 1977), 109-115.

Weaver, Warren. (1949) Translation. In *Machine Translation of Languages.* Edited by W.N. Locke and A.D. Booth, 15-23. New York: Technology Press of MIT and Wiley and Sons, 1955.

Webber, Bonnie L., and Nils J. Nilsson. *Readings in Artificial Intelligence.* Palo Alto, Cal.: Tioga, 1982.

Webster's 7th New Collegiate Dictionary. Springfield, Mass.: C. & G. Merriam, 1972.

Weizenbaum, Joseph. ELIZA. *CACM* 9(1966), 36-45.

——. *Computer Power and Human Reason: From Judgment to Calculation.* San Francisco: Freeman, 1976.

Wexler, Kenneth, and Peter Culicover. *Formal Principles of Language Acquisition.* Cambridge, Mass.: MIT Press, 1980.

Whorf, Benjamin. *Language, Thought, and Reality.* Cambridge, Mass.: MIT Press, 1956.

Wilks, Yorick. An artificial intelligence approach to machine translation. In *Computer Models of Thought and Language.* Edited by Roger C. Schank and Kenneth M. Colby, 114-151. San Francisco: Freeman, 1973.

——. An intelligent analyzer and understander of English. *CACM* 18(1975a), 264-274.

——. Preference semantics. In *The Formal Semantics of Natural Language.* Edited by Edward L. Keenan, 329-350. Cambridge: Cambridge Univ. Press, 1975b.

Winograd, Terry. *Understanding Natural Language.* New York: Academic Press, 1972.

——. On some contested suppositions of generative linguistics about the scientific study of language. *Cognition* 5(1977), 151-179.

——. Towards convivial computing. In *Future Impact of Computers: The Next Twenty Years*. Edited by Michael Dertouzos and Joel Moses, 56-72. Cambridge, Mass.: MIT Press, 1979.

Winston, Patrick H. *Artificial Intelligence*. Reading, Mass.: Addison-Wesley, 1977.

Winston, Patrick H., and Richard H. Brown, eds. *Artificial Intelligence: An MIT Perspective* (2 volumes). Cambridge, Mass.: MIT Press, 1979.

Woods, William A. Transition network grammars for natural language analysis. *CACM* 13:10(1970), 591-606.

——. An experimental parsing system for transition network grammars. In *Natural Language Processing*. Edited by Randall Rustin, 111-154. New York: Algorithmics Press, 1973(a).

——. Progress in natural language understanding: An application to lunar geology. *AFIPS Conference Proceedings* 42 (1973b), 441-450.

Zampolli, Antonio., ed. *Linguistic Structures Processing: Studies in Linguistics, Computational Linguistics and Artificial Intelligence*. New York: Elsevier-North Holland, 1977.

Zwicky, Arnold, Joyce Friedman, Barbara Hall, and Donald Walker. The MITRE syntactic analysis procedure for transformational grammars. *IFIPS Proc. Fall Joint Comp. Conf. 1965*, 317-326. Washington, D.C: Spartan Books, 1965.

Author index

Topic index

*, in ATN, 216
    in generative linguistics, 165
    in PROGRAMMAR, 393
    in regular expression, 54
    in slot analysis, 79
    see also Most recent node (in ATN)
+, in regular expression, 69
    in transformation, 160
=, in DL, 431
<, in transformation, 160
>, in transformation, 161
#, in transformation, 161
    in transformational grammar, 571, 572
↑, in ATN initialization, 228

A-over-A principle, 569
AAAI, 410
Abstract noun, 573
Acceptability, versus grammaticality, 186
Accessible value, in ATN condition, 229
Accompaniment; *see* Cases
Accusative; *see* Cases
ACL, 410
Acquisition, of knowledge; *see* Knowledge of language, 19, 175, 178
Action, of ATN, 204, 208, 229, 586
Activation, in situation-action parser, 406
Active chart, **119**, 120–26, 203, 267
Active edge, **119**, 120
Active node stack, in PARSIFAL, 404
Active voice; *see* Passive

Additive description, 334
Address, direct, 530
    structure of, 524
Addressee; *see* Cases
Adjective, **53**, **539**, 575
Adjective group, 483, **523**
Adjunct group, 472, **523**
Adjunction, 160
    Chomsky; *see* Chomsky adjunction
    sibling; *see* Sibling adjunction
Adjunction transformation, 159
Adverb, **53**, 166, 247, 472, **540–42**
    conjunctive; *see* Conjunctive adverb
Adverb group, 247, **523**
Adverbial modifier, 561
Affix, affixation, 545
Affix-hopping; *see* Transformations
Agenda, 127
    in GSP, 262
Agent; *see* Cases
Agent deletion; *see* Transformations
Agentive; *see* Cases
Agglutinating language, 48
Agreement, 162, 167, 210, 245, 252, 344
Agreement rule, 75, 304; *see also* Subject-verb agreement
AI; *see* Artificial intelligence
Algorithm; *see* Fully defined algorithm
Alternation, 331
Alternative, adverb, 541
Amalgam, 531
Ambiguity, 91–93, 368, 409, 582

621